PENGUIN BOOKS
FANIE DE VILLIERS

Born and educated in New Zealand, Trevor
cricket writer and journalist with more than f
He has covered four World Cups and worked as senior cricket writer
for the then Argus Group (now Independent Group) of newspapers
in South Africa for more than twenty-five years. He continues to
contribute to the *Indian Express* and his web site TheWicket.com
and covered the International Cricket Council Champions Trophy
tournament in Colombo in September 2002 for these two organizations.
He has worked in New Zealand, England, Australia, South Africa, Sri
Lanka and Zimbabwe and has travelled extensively in Africa and South
Asia. Since May 2000 he has been managing editor of the cricket web
site magazine, TheWicket.com which is based in Colombo, Sri Lanka.
He is one of a group of cricket specialists who own the site and is
also a senior director. A former first-class umpire and umpire
administrator, he has stood in provincial and first-class games in New
Zealand and South Africa. Since the late 1970s he has been involved in
the upliftment of the game among the disadvantaged in South Africa.
    This is his third book on cricket.

Chesterfield is a veteran
than forty-six years experience.

FANIE DE VILLIERS

'Never Say Die'

Vinniger as ooit

Trevor Chesterfield

PENGUIN BOOKS

PENGUIN BOOKS

Published by the Penguin Group

Penguin Books India Pvt Ltd, 11 Community Centre, Panchsheel Park, New Delhi 110 017, India

Penguin Group (USA) Inc., 375 Hudson Street, New York, New York 10014, USA

Penguin Group (Canada), 90 Eglinton Avenue East, Suite 700, Toronto, Ontario, M4P 2Y3, Canada (a division of Pearson Penguin Canada Inc.)

Penguin Books Ltd, 80 Strand, London WC2R 0RL, England

Penguin Ireland, 25 St Stephen's Green, Dublin 2, Ireland (a division of Penguin Books Ltd)

Penguin Group (Australia), 250 Camberwell Road, Camberwell, Victoria 3124, Australia (a division of Pearson Australia Group Pty Ltd)

Penguin Group (NZ), cnr Airborne and Rosedale Roads, Albany, Auckland 1310, New Zealand (a division of Pearson New Zealand Ltd)

Penguin Group (South Africa) (Pty) Ltd, 24 Sturdee Avenue, Rosebank, Johannesburg 2196, South Africa

Penguin Books Ltd, Registered Offices: 80 Strand, London WC2R 0RL, England

First published by Penguin Books India 2003
Revised edition 2005

Copyright © Trevor Chesterfield 2003
Photographs © Annie Laing 2003

Typeset in Gatineau by S.R. Enterprises, New Delhi
Printed at Chaman Offset Printers, New Delhi

For all marginalized young cricketers who have had to look at the sport's culture from the outside—from one who overcame untold handicaps to shatter the barriers

'Believe in yourself. I was born poor, black and disenfranchised, which I did not merit or create. These were the obstacles I needed to overcome and learn the meaning of brotherhood among all and also discover within, my own identity. It taught me how, through cricket, dreams have a meaning and that what we can achieve is not beyond all boundaries.'
—Sir Conrad Hunte, West Indies opening batsman (1932–99), at the opening ceremony of the Africa Zone VII tournament in Pretoria, September 1996.

Contents

Foreword

Every now and then a captain finds a player who is a real pleasure to have in the team. For me it was someone whom I could rely on to give one hundred per cent all the time regardless of the magnitude of the task. Fanie de Villiers, a swing bowler of immense ability, was such a player.

What made him so valuable was the fact that he was prepared to fight the battle under all circumstances. He was of course lethal when conditions suited him, but even under adverse conditions he taught himself how to be effective and do a good job for his team. You could throw the ball to him at any time in the knowledge that more often than not he would fulfil the task you had in mind. He was always fiercely independent, but at the same time a fantastic team man.

Respect was central to Fanie's way of thinking: once he respected you, and knew that the feeling was mutual, he would walk through the valley of death for the cause.

It is well documented that we are friends and although he was quite a handful at times, I always enjoyed being with Fanie as a friend and as a teammate. We spent many hours in the various gyms on tours discussing all sorts of things while training. You tend to get to know people pretty well under the circumstances that prevail on cricket tours. If South African cricket had eleven men like Fanie de Villiers in the team they would win every World Cup.

There are times these days when it may seem that he dwells more on controversial matters than is required. I feel this shows just how much he cares for the cause and the intensity of his desire to see South Africa win with pride and professionalism. It is something we all want and in this he has the support of all the former players.

This biography by Trevor Chesterfield, a personal friend of Fanie's for many years and a journalist whom I respect and trust, is written in his usual thought-provoking style. It will make for terrific reading and I hope it is hugely successful because this is a story which needs to be told.

Port Elizabeth
October 2002

Kepler Wessels
Captain of the South African
cricket team, 1992-1994

Foreword

Initially this book was to have been published in late 1998 but, as is explained later, a variety of reasons delayed its publication until now. From my own viewpoint there was that incredible whitewash of the West Indies in South Africa in 1998-99; the Makhaya Ntini of the rape case; the World Cup of 1999; the stark events of Cronjegate, first unmasked in April 2000, followed by the accident which led to the tragic death of Hansie Cronje, the King Commission and successive reports highlighting the match-fixing story; the successful tour to the West Indies in early 2001 with its related dagga (hashish) smoking incident and the transformation issues. There was also the serious illness in 2001, which affected the health of the author, Trevor Chesterfield, and then the traumatic and most interesting incident: the scrapping of the quota system and after that the so-called enforced targets in the team. All these factors had to be brought into my life's story and the background scenes of the events portrayed here.

Much has happened in the years since I retired in March 1998; there have been some dramatic changes. One is the United Cricket Board's decision in late June 2002 to end the quota system at the senior provisional level. What, however, worries me is whether South Africa's cricketing image has reached a point where the team might not be looked on as a top-rated side: not so much on the field as off it.

There are those who have for long pointed fingers at Pakistan, Sri Lanka and even India about how badly the game is run in those countries. Has South Africa been that much better? None of this sits well if the team and the administration are judged on their more recent records. What we need to consider is how many of the scandals worldwide within the sport since 1999 were nearly all South Africa-related. From Ntini's court cases to Cronje and match-fixing, dagga smoking in the West Indies to the disruptive selection policy and coaching fiasco concerning both Australian tours in the summer of 2002—these are just some of the incidents. There was also the issue of the United Cricket Board placing the Eastern Province Cricket Board under judicial management in June 2002 to clear up administrative and financial mismanagement. This is important if the game is to achieve the transparency needed to satisfy all of us that it has indeed rid itself of the critical illness that has damaged its image.

What also seriously concerned me these last eight years is: what has happened to the rock solid support base that the side had during the 1990s? It was a highly successful team and also highly rated worldwide; you felt this strong support coming from all quarters. Everyone wanted to be identified with the side; there was a vibrant and developing cricket culture. Where are all those small boys and girls, their fathers and grandfathers and every old *Tannie* (auntie) who wanted to be a South African cricket player, whether young or old? Where has that support gone? Shaun Pollock asked this question in 2000-01 during the New Zealand and Sri Lanka tours and also in 2002 when the Indians and Australians played in South Africa.

There are some who feel that people have been losing interest in the game in South Africa because of the scandals and poor performances. I was disappointed to read not long ago the following comment on an Indian website: 'While the nation was stunned yet rallied behind the team in the Cronje aftermath, there is now a bemused "who cares?" public response about the side as it is ripped apart by political machinations and internal uncertainty.' This is not what we should be reading.

Another worrying concern is: where are the replacements for the tough players, the gentlemen and the entertainers of the 1990s, when we first made our comeback? It was a time when we still played the game to entertain the masses on and off the field and there was pride and honour in doing so. Most of us started playing at the age of 27-28 because of the pre-92 era and the difference was that we all had a 'University of Life Degree'. I am sure our older boys handled the fame better. We now lack the toughness of players such as Brian McMillan, Kepler Wessels and Peter Kirsten; gentlemen such as Dave Richardson, Jimmy Cook and Clive Rice; and the 'naughty' guys such as Pat Symcox, Adrian Kuiper and myself who with a touch of humour lightened a grey afternoon.

There are many I know who will strongly disagree with me when I say that the difference between those of us who started out in those first years of post-isolation and today's players is that we were the pathfinders of that era: from fitness and playing skills to details such as negotiating salaries and organizing clothing, to touring and playing in countries not open before to ordinary South Africans. We led the way even when it came to image building. It was not easy playing against some of the most mentally tough and streetwise Test players of that time, and I would go so far as to say that if you had not played the game during those late pre-isolation and early post-isolation years of the late 1980s and early 1990s, with all the political changes and turmoil, then you really have no idea of the struggle to get where we are; it is something which affected everybody across all demographic and socio-economic lines. It was also a time that created a special type of player. We played in an era where change was taking place, and we helped to structure that change and are proud of our efforts.

In the last five years Pat Symcox, Kepler Wessels and myself have been criticized for what we have been saying; we are considered negative, jealous and miserable because we are no longer playing. This is not true at all. We believe that in highlighting the errors and mistakes, we have in some way helped create the platform to improve the system. None of us enjoyed seeing our team beaten as badly as it was by Australia in 2002; it hurt us all deeply. It is hard, however, for those who have not been in our position to understand how we feel and why we feel that way.

For me it has always been the honour of being part of what was a brilliant team of competitors, where pride ran deep, and glory was always a matter of victory and how it was achieved. It is disappointing to see those who played major roles within the team and the system at that time disappear: Paddy Upton, one of the finest biokeneticists with whom I have had the pleasure of working, was one. Bob Woolmer was another. He was someone who pulled the team together and made most players all-rounders in their batting and bowling skills; he worked hard to make South Africa the best.

It is, however, not easy for me to talk about my former teammate and captain Hansie Cronje. It is a pity to have to admit how Hansie worked to sideline those who opposed his ideas, even if his ideas were wrong. I believe South African cricket has paid the price for allowing Hansie too much power. For example, I believe that easing out Paddy Upton has affected team fitness. Unfortunately, all our bowlers have lost pace, most are permanently injured and Corrie van Zyl was denied the opportunity of working with a right-hand man for his bowlers. If Paddy had been there in recent years, I know we would have had the fittest team to take on the Australians. And believe me, the side would not have indulged themselves in touch rugby for fitness exercises. Hansie also undermined Bob's ideas when he started influencing his choices and decisions; later he intimidated the younger players. This was hard for me to accept.

What has been harder to accept is how the team has slipped below the high standards needed to compete in international cricket. In March and April 2001 we beat the West Indies 2-1 in the Caribbean and then won the limited-overs series. Yet all the success against teams such as West Indies, India, New Zealand and Sri Lanka has not seen us go forward the way it was expected.

It has been equally hard to accept coaches who have not had test experience. Some come from an era unknown to the players, who are thus unable to relate to them. What has also bothered me is how little the coaches are paid. In South Africa coaches are not paid enough money for someone in charge of an international squad. A coach possibly gets a package of approximately R35,000 a month, while coaches in other countries are paid as much as R150,000–R250,000 a month. What this means is that the South African board thinks that coaches, and consequently the players and the game, are not worth much. And it doesn't surprise me that with such low salaries on offer, former Test players are not interested in being involved.

It is my firm belief that any modern system requires strong coaching and support groups if it is to maintain quality levels of excellence from club through Test levels. From my years of experience I have come to understand that there are two different types of coaches—those with Test-playing experience and those without. In our system we have had coaches who did not have any Test experience. Yet it seems to me you need to have Test experience to realize just how little you know the game. You also need to use experienced players in specialized fields to help and advise. The game has changed dramatically through the late 1990s and there is a need to move forward with improved skills and innovations. It is imperative to include former Test players as coaches and advisors, no matter the cost involved. For South Africa to do well in the future, we need a strong coach with Test-playing experience along with a strong support group of staff and advisors.

* * * *

I wanted my biography to be far more than the story of my life as a player. That is why I needed someone to help write the story of South African cricket during its most turbulent fifteen years of modern history, from isolation through to the rebel era to unification and international reacceptance, providing insights from his knowledge of the game and of what went on behind the scenes. I happened to be a player in an era that experienced far more than just cricket. I wanted this book to also be about those who were involved in this process and about those who made it possible for me to have earned a living from it.

There were many who could have written this story and wanted to. I entrusted this task to my long-time friend Trevor Chesterfield, who has an unbelievable passion for the game and a love of its history. He also had the ability to read a cricket match and write about it in such a way that while many may not agree with his views, they enjoy his frank and critical, if not lively, analytical style.

From those early years at college in Pretoria when I first met him as a naughty Afrikaans lad working my way through what was really a tough era, Trevor has been a mentor. He taught me about the game and its similarity to life; about the heroes of the past and its history; of how cricket started and grew; and how it could be fun and yet influence a way of thinking to help you take up challenges and work for a better life for all.

World Cup 2003 was more than the bringing together of a nation or the gathering of countless visitors who came to watch, cheer, groan or cry. It was supposed to be a celebration of a dream—a dream to forge a new identity and to move forward. Now we know it wasn't the case. It was without a doubt the most embarrassing tournament in our short World Cup history. I really hoped that our country could have benefited from it, for the sake of all our children.

The big question is: should we have anticipated this World Cup disaster? Are we capable of anticipating other problem areas or are we just going to accept and manage wrongdoings again? We are not proactive anymore!

Centurion   **Fanie de Villiers**
January 2003

Preface

Years before Fanie de Villiers became a folk hero in South African sport he would arrive at the sports office of the *Pretoria News* looking for pictures of any athlete to adorn the bare walls of his cramped residence room at Tugela *koshuis* (hostel) on the old Pretoria Onderwyskollege campus in Sunnyside. Here was a highly likeable young man who, while anxious to make a good impression, was not that shy to ask if he could look through the pile of discarded pictures before they were eventually thrown out.

There was, at first, the mistaken impression that he really wanted to play rugby for the Northern Transvaal Blou Bulle (Blue Bulls) or become a good javelin thrower. After all, his mother, Hanna, had been a javelin thrower in her school and tertiary years, and had even represented Free State. Yet his perspective remained the broader sports canvas which included cricket and grew until cricket, at which he had shown considerable talent in his pre-high school years, attracted as well as demanded more of his attention.

It was on a warm afternoon towards the end of October 1983 when the late Doupie Calitz, then senior coach of the senior side at the Pretoria Onderwyskollege, telephoned and suggested a visit to the nets to look at a young fast bowler who was 'simply scaring the daylights' out of the batsmen in the nets. 'If you can't manage to get to the nets, what about coming to see the match we're playing this Saturday?' was another eager suggestion.

Such was his keenness for me to be at the game that Calitz sent a memo to the *Pretoria News* on Friday: the message was well understood. Along with Sid Dugmore, one of the provincial selectors, I arrived at the ground at around 11.30 a.m. on a bright, cheery morning to take a look at the new pace 'wunderkind'. But the students were batting and we contemplated coming back later in the day. However, an inspection of the scorebook explained it all: de Villiers had 'blasted the opposition' (Calitz's cheery comment); figures of 7 for 37 told the story of an accomplished performance. We did see him bowl after tea: two short bursts of about 6 overs each. As wickets tumbled and while a couple of catches were put down, there was no mistaking the raw talent or the burning ambition in those thoughtful blue eyes. With the right handling, this young man could go places, I thought.

At that time, South African cricket was struggling in a quagmire known as international isolation caused by the apartheid government's racial policies. But the rebel era was in full swing with the second West Indies tour. Also, the South African Cricket Union had put together annual training camps to nurture new talent and by the latter half of the 1980s, Fanie de Villiers had attended successive Plascon Academy sessions in Pretoria after missing the initial one in Bloemfontein in 1986. It was at the L.C. de Villiers Oval venue in Pretoria where Neil Adcock, the former Springbok fast bowler and one of the coaches, enthused at the overt eagerness of the young Afrikaner. 'He reminded me so much of what it was like in my day. He just didn't run up and go through the motions as most others seemed to do; he was really keen, and I admired that,' Adcock admitted months after the 1987 academy had ended. Words of comfort and deep insight long before Fanie himself thought that one day he would be bowling for South Africa at cricket's hallowed and most popular venues such as Lord's, the Sydney Cricket Ground or even Eden Gardens.

Fanie de Villiers' story is not a simple one; it is the study of a young man who, as he grew to maturity and adulthood, overcame trials and tribulations as well as language and pain barriers to develop into one of the finest bowlers of his generation; he became a hero for the young and old, a humorist, a leather hat collector, and a raconteur. Above all, to overcome handicaps, confronted with which most others would have given up even before beginning, he had what Sir Conrad Hunte, that fine West Indian batsman of the late 1950s and early 1960s, admired so much: determination, a belief in his ability and the urge to dream and stretch that dream far beyond its boundaries.

There is little doubt that Fanie was at the forefront of the first wave of the new generation of Afrikaans-speaking cricketers; a pathfinder whose gentle way with children of all ages, whether signing autographs at the boundary or coaching them, became a revelation. His unsung work in the townships in the late 1980s and mid- to late 1990s is just a part of the many facets of a young man who became an outspoken proponent for a better deal for South Africa's top players for the right reasons. In retirement, he has been used as a TV commentator and runs an Afrikaans TV programme, speaking his mind when needed and treading on a few toes which officialdom in all its guises does not enjoy.

If South Africa brought some dishonour to the game through the ensuing row after white politicians banned Basil D'Oliveira in 1968 and the dishonesty uncovered in 2000 through Cronjegate and Hansie Cronje's misdemeanours, it has also given the sport Fanie de Villiers. This book is a testimony to the courage and determination of that young man who overcame several barriers to become one of South Africa's finest cricketers and sportsmen.

Author's Notes

It was during the 1992 World Cup in New Zealand and Australia that the seeds for this book were first sown, when in numerous long discussions with Donald Woods (the former banned editor of the *Daily Dispatch* in East London), I mentioned that but for a broken toe my young friend Fanie de Villiers would have made that particular South African side. It was a name with which Woods was not familiar, so I gave him a brief biography of the Northerns fast bowler. At the time the intention was to write a series of essays on twelve Afrikaans-speaking players who had made their name in a sport which a Nationalist Party MP in the late 1960s had called 'that foreign summer game which has no relevance in our modern (Afrikaner) society'. I was, however, engaged, working on another project with my dear friend, Jackie McGlew, writing what eventually became *South Africa's Cricket Captains*. Woods agreed that the cricket world needed exposure to such Afrikaans players as Fanie de Villiers, but such stories, he felt, needed time to mature and gain more substance which would come at a later date.

Work on the manuscript started in late 1994, and several attempts have been made over the years to publish this book. The first was in late 1998 which ran into a series of problems when a lightning strike in April of that year caused a hard drive failure and most of the manuscript was lost through a corruption of computer files as well as the back-up discs. A lengthy recovery of the files and rewriting of some of the earlier manuscript from scratch while travelling in countries as diverse as England and Sri

Lanka, meant that plans to have it ready for publication to celebrate the millennium summer of 1999–2000 also had to be shelved. Further, the Hansie Cronje scandal and his untimely death meant a number of serious revisions. Other reasons for the delay have been explained elsewhere.

Some interviews with Fanie's contemporaries began in the late 1980s as part of general updating of newspaper profile material; other interviews began in September 1994 when he asked me to write this biography and continued over the next seven years. It is because of these people—unfortunately some of whom have since passed on—who gave of their time, patience and in some cases photographs, that this story has been made possible.

My deep appreciation must first go to the ever-delightful de Villiers clan—Braam senior and Hanna, his parents, the effervescent Judith, Fanie's wife, and Neels, his older brother. They always found time to answer a list of endless questions and occasionally check the accuracy of dates found in less reliable sources. Kepler Wessels was always a source of help and refreshed the memory when needed; many others helped with comments and hints. Heinrich Schulze, who translated some important Afrikaans material and explained the value of some cultural activities, also added his thoughts and advice. Former colleagues Michael Doman and Brendan Nel read the manuscript and offered suggestions. My thanks too to Kathryn—her ever-cheerful encouragement through those 'winter days' of illness in 2001 are not forgotten.

In is natural that after almost half a lifetime of living in South Africa, I look on the country as 'home'. Yet, since July 1998, travels have taken me far and wide and the manuscript went with me. There has been the discovery of a new, and in many ways happy, rewarding life among dear South Asian friends and colleagues in Sri Lanka; in particular Sutami Ratnavale, of Horton Gardens, Colombo, whose friendship I treasure. She helped the healing process in 2001 and added her encouragement to the pages of this book. There was also a visit to Zimbabwe and, of course, the tours within South Africa for the website TheWicket.com which is based in Colombo and of which I am a part owner and director.

V.K. Karthika, of Penguin India, with her gentle patience and guidance eased the way in understanding the intricacies of the world of publishing. From the first eccentric enquiry from a weird New Zealand cricket nut transplanted in South Africa, she has displayed that South Asian calm and charm and played with a straight bat every verbal 'googly' I have bowled with a metaphorical beguiling smile.

No story of this scope or depth is possible without help from countless others. My grateful thanks to: Neil Adcock, Qamar Ahmed, Eileen Ambler-Smith, Hoosain Ayob Mohammed Azharuddin, Dr Ali Bacher, Jack Bannister, Lee Barnard, Dr Willie Basson, Bob Blair, Allan Border, Tertius Bosch, Jackie Botten, Jane Bramley, Colin Bryden, Matthys (Doupie) Calitz, Sylvester Clarke, Vernon Cresswell, Russell Cobb, Jimmy Cook, Ewie Cronje, Hansie Cronje, Daryll Cullinan, Mike Coward, Geoff Darkin, Mark Davis, Noel Day, Gerald de Kock, Aravinda de Silva, Peter de Vaal, Mike de Villiers, Chris Day, Gerrie Dippenaar, Allan Donald, Sid Dugmore, Vernon du Preez, Etienne (Tubby) du Preez, Steve Elworthy, Anton (Yogi) Ferreira, Naas Ferreira, Ranjit Fernando, Brandon Foot, Bokkie Gerber, Anton Geringer, Tony Grieg, Gerbrand Grobler, Asanka Gurusinha, Ranjit Fernando, Graham Ford, Guy Hawthorne, Avril Harrison, Richard Harrison, Ian Hawkey, Mike Haysman, Omar Henry, Jackson Hlongwane, Merv Hughes, Sir Conrad Hunte, Ray Illingworth, Robin Jackman, Sanath Jayasuriya, Ray Jennings, Alan Jordaan, Pierre Joubert, Peter Kirsten, Adrian Kuiper, Brian Lara, Kenneth Lebethe, Denis Lindsay, Pradeep Magazine, Monica Magodielo, Khaya Majola, Neil Manthrop, Roger Mann, Fred Marner, Malcolm Marshall, Barrie Meyer, Cyril Mitchely (senior), Cyril Mitchley (junior), Jackie McGlew, Kevin McKenzie, Keith Medlycott, Niels Momberg, Andre Odendaal, Chris Old, Rodney Ontong, Pieter Oosthuizen, Roy Pienaar, Jim Pressdee, Mike Procter, Brett Proctor, Shaun Pollock, Peter Pollock, Arjuna Ranatunga, Krish Reddy, S.K. Reddy, Jonty Rhodes, Clive Rice, John Reid, Dave Richardson, Mike Rindel, Peter Roebuck, Peter Robinson, Johan Rudolph, Kevin Rule, Andrew Samson, Coraline Samson (neé Van der Stoep), Cliff Sekowe, Ravi Shastri, David Shepherd, Craig Smith, Greg Smith, Joubert Strydom, Pat Symcox, Sachin Tendulkar, Steve Waugh, Craig Tibshraeny, Chaminda Vaas, Peter van der Merwe, Chris van Noordwyk, Bennie Venter, Shane Warne, Willie Watson, Grant

Weber, Mark Weber, Paul Weaver, Sidath Wettimuny, Ray Williams, Kepler Wessels and Bob Woolmer.

Finally, a brief explanation on usage. To avoid the tiresome repetitive use of the egotistical personal pronoun, the term Chesters (by which I have long been known to friends, players, colleagues and administrators in South Africa, Sri Lanka, India, Australia and the UK) has been used where necessary when referring to the author. For corporate reasons Centurion Park was changed first to SuperSport Centurion in 1998 and then SuperSport Park in 1999. The venue has been referred to variously in the book, although it was known through most of Fanie de Villiers' career as Centurion Park.

Limited-Overs Gladiator

Fanie de Villiers Oval is not quite where you would expect it to be. Locating it requires a voyage of discovery through the predominantly black dormitory town of Soshanguve, about thirty minutes north of (SuperSport) Centurion Park, where development and transformation programmes have become part of everyday life. This is where such venues belong in the South Africa of today, more so perhaps than say Fonteinê Primary, in Sasolburg, or Hoër Volkskool Heidelberg, where Fanie left indelible imprints. The cricket ground at Soshanguve is, however, no lush green tribute to one of South Africa's finest swing bowlers of the early post-isolation years; not that the bareness of the patch of open ground outside the cricket school has ever made Fanie hesitant to escort visitors there.

Kashane, one of several schools within half an hour's drive of Centurion, was established by Northerns Cricket Union with support from Transnet to improve skills and excellence in the 'Reach for the Star' project. Unfortunately the area has since been rendered useless as unthinking municipal authorities, without consultation, put in a culvert to handle stormwater drainage alongside the concrete pitch.

The daily routine of a black suburb such as Soshanguve can be a harsh experience for those who are plucked from a comfortable environment and suddenly subjected to it. It is about survival and bread and butter issues as well as helping motivate people to overcome the problems left by the apartheid era. To survive this pot-holed, mine-laden path requires more than determination, belief and courage: it requires what Sir Conrad Hunte, the great West Indian opening batsman of the 1950-60s, called a dream.

The image of the rainbow nation has been tarnished by those who blame apartheid for all ills. There are those who are willing to work and make a better life for themselves; there are also those who also have strong feelings about where their fellow man is going and worry about the nation's future. As Jackson Hlongwane, an economics student at the University of South Africa explains, the apartheid past is dead; it is time to stop blaming something that ended a decade ago for modern ills. Jackson feels that there are too many lazybones riding the trains, wasting time gambling on street corners or thinking up schemes to rob those who have worked hard for a better life. This is an ugly festering pimple on the modern mosaic of society.

Things have changed from the apartheid days; the young and disadvantaged now get chances to win scholarships (or bursaries, as they are known) to high school: better education opportunities are available for the disadvantaged through cricket. This is all part of the long-term, modern, quixotic dream of an emerging nation, which is struggling to map comprehensible new identities and boundaries in the changing world of southern Africa.

On a typical afternoon, Fanie steps out of the car, smiles at the eager group of youngsters, signs several autographs and is soon immersed in a coaching session as part of the larger clinic. Almost a hundred youngsters, aged between nine and twelve, mill around before being divided into groups of ten as other coaches from Northerns development supervise the eager but serious youngsters. As he looks at the youngsters in the nets, a touch of envy forces a momentary frown. There was nothing like this in Deneysville where he started out bowling in 1972, or later in Sasolburg. Why, these youngsters have more facilities than he did at Fakkel Hoër in south Johannesburg.

'I wish I had something like this when I was their age,' says Fanie. 'This is more organized than the farm cricket we had.' He frowns as he looks over at a couple of youngsters bowling open-chested in the nets. 'Not quite MCC coaching manual perfect, but we can get them right. And I didn't have the perfect action, did I . . .?' Grinning happily at what he is doing, he signs more autographs.

'Makes you think though. When I was their age and wanted an autograph it was different. You would say "sir" to Clive Rice, Vince van der Bijl, Garth le Roux or Jimmy Cook when you went to get an autograph. That's how it was . . . we were farm kids. If we didn't show respect we got nothing—apart, perhaps, from a hiding.'

At that time, those from the privileged white or Asian backgrounds demanded autographs while those from less affluent economic groups asked more politely and shyly because they were overawed at the sight of their heroes. Other things have changed too. There are now many role models: Jonty Rhodes, Allan Donald, Lance Klusener, Paul Adams, Makhaya Ntini, even Mfuneko Ngam when he's fit; kids can name their own favourites, there are plenty of good guys around. Fanie had no heroes. No role model. It was not important then. Not the way it is now. Who did de Villiers himself want to be? le Roux? van der Bijl? Rice? What was wrong with being '*Vinnige* (fast) Fanie'? Or even Faantjie, 'little Fanie', as he was known through most of his school days.

Most children know who Fanie is, but autographs pushed into pockets mean little to ten-year-olds; the scraps of paper are soon lost in the dusty surrounds as they hear about the importance of rhythm and swing and approach and delivery stride. At Kashane they show the same sort of respect you find on the streets of South Asia; the only difference is that on the subcontinent you are quickly mobbed, while in Sosh they merely grin and watch closely as they go through the first steps in bowling. The instructions are repetitive: rhythm, it is all to do with rhythm, getting the run-up right. The more you practice the better you get: the all-important basics. Fitness too, he emphasizes, is equally important. It was far simpler in the late 1700s, days of Hambledon and the Nyrens (Richard and John) when they delivered underarm grubbers: overarm bowling was still a century in the future and the game had little of the sideways movement that is now taught in the schools or club nets, or even in the backyards.

'It's mainly a sideways game so you have to bowl this way,' he smiles at the attentive group. 'If you look at the coaching videos of all the top bowlers, you always see how important the basics are, such as the sideways movement and the rhythm and swing.'

He laments how the classic bowling actions of fast bowlers, Sir Richard Hadlee, van der Bijl and Rice are not on any coaching video he has seen. The spinners need to study the actions of Shane

Warne, Anil Kumble, John Emburey and Pat Symcox as well as your typical left-arm roller. Yet it still comes down to the correct methods: if they do not get the basics right at an early age it is hard to correct faults and at a later stage to prevent possible injury on growing bodies.

* * * *

One of the joys of travelling through Sosh on any given weekend is counting the number of games children play and noticing a larger involvement in street cricket than in other sport. Boys, girls, even young adults join in. Every patch of ground has its own special identity. At Kashane they had him put his hands on a wet slab of cement: a genuine Fanie de Villiers imprint for aspiring kids.

Everywhere youngsters are playing the game: inspiration has created dreams of being an Adams, Makhaya Ntini or a Gary Kirsten; even that left-handed mover and shaker Mike Rindel, who opened the batting for Northern Transvaal and South Africa, has his admirers. And while soccer was the sport for the blacks and rugby belonged mainly to the whites, cricket would in time be the sport of the unified nation with its strong demographic links.

Even during the troubled times in Vryburg in 1998-99, a conservative Afrikaner town in North West Province riven by racial conflict, Dutch foreign correspondent Ernest Landheer discovered an impromptu game in the street. A tall township youngster used his pencil case as a bat and what passed for a ball was a small pencil eraser, bowled at the schoolbag which was used as 'stumps'. Cricket was at that time already ceasing to be the game of the privileged class, even among whites; the elite image it once had, has long since disappeared in the dust of the Fanie de Villiers Oval at Kashane, and similar grounds at Vryburg, Mamelodi, Atteridgeville and Tembisa.

A few minutes drive away from Kashane is the Soshanguve Oval with a pavilion and spacious dressing rooms; net facilities and two concrete strips and a small stand are all part of the scene. The ground is the envy of many and part of the development project. It is a place of fun and laughter. A new generation is learning that there is more to the game than batting, bowling and fielding skills; there is a culture of discipline.

Development, however, is not just about Herschelle Gibbs,

Adams, Ntini, Victor Mpitsang or Justin Ontong. Its scope is far broader, encompassing as it does the old and the new with its growing socio-economic demographical image. While the old Cape regions have a carefully developed cricket culture dating back more than 110 years, political partition created a bitter climate of mistrust for more than a century, and consquently prevented the interactive growth of the game. Structures were erected that for generations denied the game a chance to establish an identity that is truly South African—a rich, spicy character that is unique to the country, and which can only be achieved through the assimilation of the distinctive cultures of the coloureds, blacks, Asians and Cape Malays. Hopefully future generations will learn more tolerance and understanding than is common today, which will be necessary in the development of a burgeoning identity.

In the old Afrikaner-dominated Transvaal and Free State provinces the game prospered only among the English developing Afrikaans roots. The melting pot has barely started to bubble in terms of identifying areas of excellence in the game. Learning about equal opportunity weighs heavily on the shoulders of the modern generation. Unlike the West Indies and the United States, South Africa did not get a sniff of equal opportunities until the mid-1980s when the education system changed. After that, if parents had the money they were able to send their children to fancy schools under what was called the Model C programme. Rather than the educated, comparatively affluent and privileged urbanized African, the government wants to help those locked into a system which still carries the apartheid image in a political system that benefits only a few. It will take a generation, or even longer, to achieve the aims and ideals of the equal opportunities programme and the United Cricket Board's development schemes.

Given that the game was introduced to black areas in the old Transvaal and Free State around 1983 (when apartheid still ruled) through mini-cricket schemes, how long would it take to develop a player of say Ntini's ability? Ntini himself of course hails from an area where the game has had deep roots for more than 120 years.

In the Transvaal and Free State regions the game is going to take its own time to evolve in the diverse communities where there are new converts. Although exposure has helped heal some lacerations, the scabs of generations who have suffered from cruel deprivation are still visible among the adults. It is little wonder that there was a time when baffled parents asked, in all seriousness, why their sons, dressed in smart whites, stood in the same place under a hot sun, and only now and then chased a ball hit by a club-wielding youngster. Their puzzlement could be likened to that of Groucho Marx, the American comedian who, when attending a match at Lord's in the 1930s asked in all sincerity, 'Say, when does the action start?' after he had been watching for half an hour.

But with careful nurturing and demographic awareness, cricket has the chance to become the sport of the South African masses. In the high density suburbs overflowing with good humour, young exuberant neophytes now brandish bats in dusty streets indulging in games of tip and run. It is neither Brian Lara nor Sachin Tendulkar who inspires their probing imaginations when they play their street games. Their heroes are homegrown: a Jonty Rhodes . . . or an Ntini—players who excite them and represent national values.

* * * *

Even at the rebirth of his career, Fanie de Villiers felt as frustrated as any modern teacher or administrator dissatisfied with the lack of progress in the process of transformation. On a November afternoon at Centurion Park in 1992 he complained about feeling rebuffed to Chesters: 'I'll never play for South Africa. The selectors are just not interested.'

It was a bald statement and the disappointment showed as he grabbed his sweater from the kit bag and pulled it on while a chilly wind swirled around the nets. 'Look, I'm bowling better than I can remember and they still ignore me. It really does show that they are not interested in how many wickets I take, or how I get them.' He shrugged.

It was hard to argue with the fast bowler when he was in such a mood; always known for his forthright views and positive thinking he has usually let those around him know if he feels that something is wrong. Being overlooked for the second Test against India at the Wanderers (Johannesburg) was, he felt, a major selectorial blunder. He had already taken 20 wickets in three Castle Cup matches that season at an impressive average of 18.57, which placed him at top of the national first-class bowling averages. But the declaration of the South African team that was to play Mohammad Azharuddin's Indians at the Wanderers five days later, supported earlier inside information that Fanie was not in the Test squad.

Selectors are rarely in the habit of explaining reasons for their decisions. And Peter Pollock's panel was not about to change course and select the Northern Transvaal outswing bowler on the strength of the 20 wickets he had taken so far that summer. In their wisdom, they preferred the Western Province captain Craig Matthews as the replacement for the injured Brett Schultz, the young, blond pace bombshell who had pulled a muscle during the first Test in Durban.

In his own mind Fanie felt robbed. He had experienced similar injustices before in his bowling career. It was a new era in South African sport and he desperately wanted to be part of it; not because he headed the bowling averages at that stage of the 1992-93 Castle Cup season, but because he felt he deserved to be in the South African bowling attack.

What he did not realize at the time was that the selectors needed confirmation of his fitness after the tribulations of the previous November when he had experienced a crippling toe injury—they needed to know if his fitness rehabilitation was complete. To his way of thinking, his performances as a swing bowler against Mike Gatting's rebels two summers before made him an obvious choice for the 1992 World Cup in Australia and the tour of the West Indies.

Long before the Indians arrived, Fanie had trained hard—in England and at Centurion Park on his return—with the idea of earning that Test cap and a permanent place in the side led by Kepler Wessels. He had spent the 1992 northern summer in one of the minor southern leagues in Torquay (Devonshire) contemplating his future with the quiet determination which has been the hallmark of his career.

He used the time in England to work on his fitness after the toe injury had almost ended his career. The full toss from Ezra Moseley which hit Fanie on the foot at a net practice on 29 October had wrecked what promised to be another good season for the aspiring Test bowler, and with it, a possible place in the 1992 World Cup squad.

It was an unthinking act by the Bajan against a teammate who was often his new-ball partner in the first weeks of that summer. On his return to South Africa after an absence of several seasons Moseley developed the nasty habit of bowling yorkers to perfect his length during practice sessions. One side of the ball had a rich glossy red shine while the other was scuffed with deep scratch marks obtained by rubbing the ball against the wire mesh at the nets. The idea was to achieve an accentuated reverse swing, which he claimed was good practice for the batsmen.

On that particular warm afternoon the practice run-ups and part of the pitches were still damp from a heavy early morning shower. This meant that instead of bowling over the wicket, Moseley went around the wicket: so wide in fact that he was almost bowling from the practice pitch alongside. It resulted in Fanie being forced to open his stance to the extent that he would be facing mid-on if he hoped to hit the ball. With the ball coming at the batsmen from almost nowhere, they were often late in picking up its flight and sharp reverse lateral movement, delivered often at 140 kmph. Fanie was not the only one concerned about being hit on the toe. Mike Haysman and Mandy Yachad felt that the full-pitched yorkers (almost full tosses) were lethal, and Yachad, captain of Northern Transvaal that season, had asked Moseley not to bowl them to anyone who batted below seven in the order. The Bajan, however, ignored the request.

As soon as he was hit, Fanie knew that the big toe on his left foot was broken. The sight of the pink and blue swelling was confirmation. Only later did he feel the pain.[1]

Perhaps it was a cruel act of fate; just the sort that had dogged Fanie de Villiers through much of his sporting career. And it was something about which, privately among close friends, he would really gripe. In public, however, he cloaked his disappointment

---

[1] At the time the Centurion Park practice nets were among the best in South Africa, but far from the world-class facilities they have become since the Indians captained by Mohammad Azharuddin arrived in October 1992, and have impressed every touring side since. Little wonder that the Australian and England sides regarded them the best in the world. New Zealand were more than happy to have them as part of their training base before the 2003 World Cup.

with the open sanguine bonhomie for which he is known. South Africa was at a new dawn, sports horizons were finally opening, and the Northern Transvaal fast bowler's participation in it all had been waylaid. Ag, man! What a thing to happen. A special gift for those born on Friday the thirteenth. It meant that when his chance came, he would need to do some catching up to play alongside Allan Donald and the others lucky enough to be in the Test or one-day squads.

This was the man who fourteen months later, in the early hours of a South African morning, turned a groggy nation on its head through 112 minutes of absorbing bowling at Sydney. The practical joker with the beguiling smile, the inveterate tourist, whose charismatic image earned him an ever-growing list of sobriquets, became the genie who rubbed his own lamp and helped pull off the impossible. Defeat? What's that . . .?

* * * *

No job has ever been too big or too small for Fanie—climbing a seventy metre light tower to raise funds for the deaf or skydiving into the Wanderers during the dinner break of a day-night international slog with Radio 702 personality John Robbie. Then there was the 'Tour de Fanie': the cycle ride that earned hundreds of thousands of rand for the same cause. It was a journey which began in the mist atop Table Mountain and finished in Pretoria some 2,600 kilometres later after a lengthy spell of visiting schools along the coast. And what about the 'Fanie Buggie'? Remember how he used it to collect donations for the Sydney bushfire relief during the 1993-94 tour of Australia? Thousands, still overcome with grief and desperately wanting to forget the flames that engulfed their lives, found comfort in the spirited generosity of a warm-hearted Afrikaner whom they came to admire for his spontaneous action. The toy truck, driven inside the boundary while the game was on, was used to collect cash donations from the spectators as part of the South African team's contribution to a worthy cause. What a pity he did not patent the idea! Rugby and other sports, as usual, gatecrashed the party and tried to market it as their invention. Fortunately the image of the toy truck will always be linked to Fanie de Villiers.

Although born on Friday, 13 October 1964, Fanie is far from superstitious about the date. He has had to overcome too many pressing dramas and traumas during his years of growing up on a Free State farm and his school years in Sasolburg and beyond, to pay attention to such phobias. After all, life is short enough. At primary school he was small for his age and the continual battle to keep one step ahead of the snapping pack was challenge enough. A tough life in an environment that was often hostile gave him an insight into the thinking of a young, uncertain and occasionally confused mind. Yet he was different: thoughtful, gentle and caring, although with odd touches of boisterous schoolboy humour.

Now, as a father there are family matters that need careful attention; and his special relationship with his daughter, Suné, was a bond developed long before the discovery that she was deaf. Her deafness created, early on, an awareness that there were other children who were also affected, as had been his eldest brother, Braam junior, as well as the special sign language they developed as a way of communication. It also triggered the realization that there were parents who could not afford medical treatment for their children. Hence the setting up of the fund for the deaf, which has gone some way to alleviate a distressing problem.

There is also the fisherman in him, as well as a little of the rebel. It once landed him in trouble with John Reid when the former New Zealand captain was coaching Northerns in the late 1980s. On the day of an important session at Centurion Park, Fanie had spent several hours in the hot sun at Hartbeespoort Dam, catching carp. Then he arrived late at the nets trailing the rod over his shoulder and wearing his battered *visvanghoed* (fishing hat) at a jaunty angle. With old socks around his ankles, and his bandy legs poking from his shorts, he gave a cheerful grin. Lee Barnard, then the Northerns captain, looked sideways at the fast bowler as Reid shook his head.

'You're late,' grumbled Reid. 'We have a big match this weekend.'

'Ag . . . sorry, boss,' replied de Villiers.

'And look how you're dressed!'

'I've been fishing.'

'I can smell that.'

'Got a nice carp for you,' grinned the fast bowler.

'That's all I need.'

At that moment the versatile all-round sportsman and fellow fast bowler, Gerbrand Grobler, arrived wearing rugby shorts and a T-shirt that belonged to an opposing sponsor, his boots slung over his shoulders.

'You two, go and get changed,' the coach told them. 'You look indecent the way you are now.'

'But boss, we have our clothes on,' smiled Fanie.

Reid sighed, exasperated. Afrikaners! What in hell did they know about cricket? He failed to see that Fanie and Grobler were taking the mickey out of him in a big way.

Yet another time Fanie took on the establishment with a similar sense of mischief was in Nairobi during the four nations tournament in September 1996. He had the number of the Johannesburg-based radio station, 702, cut into what remained of his hair after taking a razor to the rest as 'payment' for a lost bet that South Africa would beat Sri Lanka. Only the innocent or Fanie de Villiers would accept such a madcap wager and he almost got away with it. While the radio station promoted his deaf fund campaign, Judith, his wife and greatest supporter, chided him about his 'disrespect for the team'.

Broad-shouldered in build when he matured in his final high school year, Fanie de Villiers was always going to be a fast bowler. He fitted comfortably into Trevor Bailey's view that bowlers are born, not made. Fanie possessed a natural ability, and in his distinctive way, he has created his own image as a fast bowler and a team man. He has this way of bowling at batsmen; it is his way.

As Allan Donald explained in Port Elizabeth during the Test series against Australia in March 1997, Fanie did not need anyone to tell him how to do it; he did it the way he had always done. There was this unshakeable belief that the way he did it would succeed. Or, as Chesters wrote for an Australian magazine: 'He's a bit of a legend really. We know what a character he is. Even those South Africans who have no interest in the game will give you their opinion on Fanie de Villiers. He is popular because he will do things other players shy away from, like signing loads of autographs or travelling. He will even miss a team meeting to buy one or two shirts in some market after haggling over the price! Then, at the next team fines meeting, he cheerfully accepts punishment.'

Those who know him well enough love him for his sincerity and honesty. It is easy to identify with a man of character and firm beliefs. In an era of troubled uncertainty caused by on-going brutal taxi warfare, rampant car hijacking, senseless housebreaking, murder and rape, South Africa needs people like Fanie de Villiers, whose values give hope to a distressed and mentally bruised nation in desperate need of succour and comfort.

* * * *

Fanie, sitting with Chesters, and enjoying a light lunch shortly after his return from England in September 1992, exuberantly outlined his plans for the summer: they were clearly defined and ambitious. He displayed the sort of confidence which suggested that before the India tour had ended, he would have earned that Test cap. While his early season form was more than promising, he was overlooked for the President's XI that played the tourists in a four-day match at Centurion Park: the selectors felt the need to give other candidates a chance. It was a decision he shrugged off with stoic calm. There were going to be more chances, more games to prove his ability as a swing bowler. It was amazing how the selectors could ignore him and the results. He is the sort of bowler who has always fought the harder battle; who always felt that he had the ability to knock over the top three.

Yet there was some hope of playing in the first Test. His 5 wickets for 49 runs against Transvaal in the opening Castle Cup game did elicit the glimmer of a query about his form. But Pollock and company were more interested in Fanie's genial Northern Transvaal teammate Tertius Bosch along with Brett Schultz, the left-arm quick from Port Elizabeth. Bosch had been Allan Donald's new-ball partner in the Bridgetown Test against the West Indies team that announced their comeback into test cricket. There he had, admittedly, bowled without luck. The needs of selection etiquette had to be served: they could not simply discard a man in possession without giving him a trial. In this respect Pollock and his co-selectors needed to be given credit for thinking ahead. First they wanted to have a good look at Bosch.[2] What South Africa needed in that first Test was a pace blitz to rip through the tourists, and if Bosch, a little overweight and unfit, failed, they had Schultz as the main alternative. He was fast; a left-arm bowler with awkward bounce and hostility: a made-to-order weapon of destruction who would instil fear in the Indians.

Nor was there place for Fanie in the Invitation XI which played the Indians at Springbok Park in Bloemfontein: a line-up that also consisted of several Test aspirants, Craig Matthews among them. The selectors had, it seemed, misplaced Fanie de Villiers' call up papers in a pigeonhole they could no longer find.

Shortly before the United Cricket Board President's XI was selected there had been the theory, advanced in private by Peter Pollock, of selecting the young Eastern Province bowler, Schultz, to test the Indian batting against his aggressive left-arm pace. Pollock had not long been appointed convener of the selection panel after the retirement of Peter van der Merwe, and, as a former Test fast bowler, was well aware of what was required to beat Test match opponents. The Indians had been in trouble against the lanky west Australian, Bruce Reid, in the Adelaide Oval Test the previous season, and the selectors were thus more interested in Schultz's tactics as the side for the first Test in Durban began to take shape.

In damp, overcast conditions at Centurion Park, with the ball tracking around off the seam and swinging through the air, the big, blond twenty-two-year-old from Port Elizabeth, whom Kepler Wessels and van der Merwe had predicted would earn a Test place if he could sort out his action, had the top Indian batsmen in the sort of trouble which mentally haunted them for the rest of the tour. His 5 wickets for 35 in 17 overs in their first innings led to the jittery tourists abdicating a first innings lead by the substantial margin of 104 runs. When it came to discussing teams it is known that Fanie's

---

[2] Tertius Bosch, who played in the one-off Test against the West Indies, died under what are said to be suspicious circumstances a month before his thirty-fourth birthday in a clinic near Durban on 13 February 2000.

name did crop up, although to be fair, the selectors were looking at what genuine strike forces were available. The Northern Transvaal bowler didn't quite fit into the permutations sought by the Test selectors for Kingsmead (Durban) and the Wanderers.

Normally, when selectors go into a meeting, each has a list of players whom they feel should be considered: two spinners for Newlands was one of the requirements in the pre-United Cricket Board era, while a strike-force of three or four for the Wanderers, with the bouncy pitch, was equally important. And while this may seem contradictory in the light of what eventually took place, Fanie, it seems, was rarely far from their deliberations when it came to selecting the sides for the first three Tests that 1992-93 season.

For Fanie though, it was a frustrating period. On paper, the Northerns' bowling attack was among the best in the country, but in reality it was flawed, lacking consistency as well as form. The former insurance broker had bowled with the late away swing which troubled the best batsmen in the country. The end came the day after Northerns lost their Castle Cup match against Border.

Wispy clouds streaked with light orange and with yellow gilt edges hung around Centurion Park on that November afternoon, but the mood was far from golden as Fanie undid his boots and packed them with the rest of his kit. The wind had an irritating cool edge as he closed the lid of the long case that players call a 'coffin', and his brow furrowed in disappointment as he stood up.

What now? Because of the touring Indians Northerns did not have any more games for a month. It wasn't going to help his cause to play Premier League matches for his club Oostelike: national selectors wanted something more than club bowling figures to guide their deliberations. There was little doubt that Fanie had the credentials. After all, he had earned colours in the rebel era against the Mike Gatting Englishmen; an interesting bunch of Poms caught in the political crossfire of South Africa in a volatile mood in those turbulent, early months of 1990. And five years earlier he had experienced the anguish of his talents being ignored by his first provincial captain, Lee Barnard. He was given a couple of consolation overs in a Currie Cup game, an action for which Barnard was strongly censured by the newspapers. Fanie had earned his place in the side the hard way.

This was more serious. In November 1992 he was no longer 'Vinnige' Fanie de Villiers, the tearaway fast bowler in the nets at Onderwyskollege across the road from Berea Park. Those days were far behind him. What he wanted as he walked out of Centurion Park on 24 November 1992, was some explanation from the selectors—*what was he doing wrong, or wasn't getting right?*

As he packed away his 'coffin' in the boot of the car, he chatted for a couple of minutes with Chesters. They had shared many confidences in the past. Mike Haysman, the former South Australian who had been a member of the Kim Hughes rebel side in the mid-1980s and was the Northern Transvaal captain for 1992-93, had said there would be no more net sessions that week and the last thing Fanie wanted to do was to train with his club. Not after all the hard work he had put in to get fit for the Indians. The way things were, he was not going to get a chance to bowl at the Indians. Under the circumstances, it is hard to be totally positive that something would come along and turn it around. Lurking in the selectors' thoughts, however, was the theory that Fanie de Villiers was a proven one-day player. They had figures from the Gatting tour to prove it; four limited-overs matches with a runs-per-over ratio of 3.97. Only at the Wanderers, on a pitch designed for run-scoring thrills, did his figures suffer—75 runs in 10 overs. Allan Donald was similarly treated: giving away 22 runs off 2 overs which forced the captain, Jimmy Cook, to remove the Free State fast bowler from the attack before they could do more damage to his figures.

In the first three limited-overs games against the Gatting rebels Fanie had been spectacularly economical with a runs-per-over rate of 2.75. There was an impressive spell at Kingsmead in Durban where he ended with 2 for 33, doing much to end the rebels' surge for victory against what was in fact a moderate bowling attack. Donald was well known for his fiery pace and had already been capped by Warwickshire, Clive Rice was still a fierce competitor, while Richard Snell, though a new name at this level was one whose reputation as an inswing bowler was being developed. Fanie owed his selection for the rebel one-dayers in February and March 1990 to a combination of factors, but Peter van der Merwe, then convener of selectors, admitted that his (then)

Currie Cup form and a particularly fine spell of outswing bowling against Free State at Centurion Park earlier in the season had much to do with it. This was allied to the 43 wickets in 1988-89 which turned the young *boereseun* (farmer's son) into a swing bowler who definitely had a future in the game at a higher echelon.

So, while the second Test against India was played at the Wanderers, the critics lined up their one-day teams. Fanie's name popped up regularly as one of the candidates for a series of seven matches from 7 to 19 December, or a game every second day. Being labelled as a limited-overs bowler was a disturbing trend which dogged him that first year of his international career. But his name was only mentioned (reluctantly by the Johannesburg press) because of Meyrick Pringle's injury and doubts about Schultz's ability as a limited-overs bowler. The great guessing game had begun.

What added to the selection mystery for the one-day internationals against India was a matter of fourteen names on a slip of paper. It had been left next to Chesters' telephone in the press box at Centurion Park while he was off interviewing Peter Kirsten in the dressing room after he had led Border to a convincing win over Northern Transvaal. Chesters had no idea who the list belonged to and no one came to claim it. Fanie's name was on it, but there was a line through it and Richard Snell's was placed along side; also included were those of Dave Callaghan and Schultz. There had been two selectors present that last afternoon of the Border game, Pollock and S. K. Reddy.

The squad for the first four matches of the one-day series against the Indians was to be announced the day after the second Test at the Wanderers. Speculation whether Snell would make it, along with Stephen Jack, the explosive Transvaal fast bowler, was the main concern of the Johannesburg press; others who had a more global view were inclined to include the players with proven one-day records, with the bowling line-up based on containment as well as penetration.

To be fair to the national selection panel, they had, since the historic tour of India, carefully examined all their options. The common denominator here was the cheery Pringle, a bowler similar to Fanie in his ability to swing the ball away late from the batsman. Pringle eventually bowled himself into the 1992 World Cup squad through several impressive Castle Cup performances, especially in December and early January. What had initially ruled him out was a back injury which was only discovered on the eve of the Western Province pre-season excursion to Northern Transvaal. It didn't look good at all at the time as there was a feeling that Pringle had failed to disclose the problem to the Province selectors. There was also the controversial view, through never substantiated, that he was a better bowler in coastal conditions than inland.[3] Memories of Pringle's afternoon of destruction at Lancaster Park (Christchurch, New Zealand) during the 1991-92 World Cup group games linger among South Africans. On a hard and grassy pitch he dismembered the West Indies top-order in a fine demonstration of late outswing bowling. In only 11 balls Pringle terminated the innings of Brian Lara, Richie Richardson, Carl Hooper and Keith Arthurton. There were only four scoring shots from his bowling (his final figures were 4 for 11) and he ended with a man of the match award. It was a game that South Africa needed to win to stay in the race for the semi-finals. With this in mind the selectors felt that as Pringle had not let them down he deserved a chance in the Test series against the Indians ahead of Bosch. But the squad for the limited-overs matches against India was a more complex matter.

1 December 1992, a Tuesday, was another blistering highveld day with barely a breeze. The team was due to be announced mid-afternoon, with the names listed alphabetically after that of the captain and vice-captain. Fanie de Villiers was fifth on the list, and after comparing the mystery list to that read out, the only change was that 'Vinnige Fanie' was in and Snell was out.

But the de Villiers family was not in town.

On the Sunday after Northerns had lost to Border, Fanie and his wife Judy joined other members of the family on a game farm on the outskirts of the water spa resort of Warmbaths about an hour's

---

[3] Initially Pringle's exclusion by the national selectors from the provisional World Cup list of twenty, announced on 29 December 1991, was all but overlooked because of the controversy surrounding the omissions of Clive Rice, Jimmy Cook and Peter Kirsten. Those who didn't harbour personal animosity towards the selection panel suggested that Pringle, like Peter Kirsten, had a chance to fight his way into the final squad before it was named twenty days later.

drive north of Centurion. It had been a relaxing day. Forgetting the disappointment of missing selection for the second Test, swimming and doing a bit of game spotting on the back of a large buggy. Late in the afternoon, Fanie, his brother Neels and father Braam lit a fire for the *vleisbraai* (barbeque) and prepared the meat for the evening meal. Inside the cottage Judy sat watching the 6 p.m. television news and when the South African team was announced and the names printed out on the screen, she called out excitedly, her voice heavy with emotion.

'Fanie . . . Fanie . . . you're in . . . you're going to play the Indians!'

By the time they got inside the cottage, the names had disappeared from the screen, but hey, at last there was something to celebrate.

A Star is Born

There is a misconception that South Africa's re-entry to test cricket at home after twenty-two years of isolation was a bit of a flop. The Durban Test against India which drew pathetically small crowds triggered off a lot of talk. Adding his own comments was Naas Botha. A former leading South African rugby player who has become a popular TV critic of that particular sport, he struck a minor sour note with comments about how full Ellis Park and Newlands had been during the matches involving the rugby 'Springboks' against New Zealand and Australia in the winter of 1992. The historic Test at Kingsmead, Durban, drew an attendance of 30,000 over the four days when play occurred. The scheduled play on day four was washed out, condemning the match to a draw. No one, Naas Botha said, was interested in cricket Tests against India. It was an interesting observation; a little like the catch Steve Waugh offered and Herschelle Gibbs dropped at Leeds in the 1999 World Cup.[1] The reported Waugh remark (though what he really said was not quite accurately recorded) made for a good story at the time.

What many South Africans and the United Cricket Board did not realize was that barely twelve months before there had been no cricket contact between South Africa and India. It was a matter

---

[1] In the 1999 World Cup Super Six League match, Australia vs. South Africa, Steve Waugh was dropped by Gibbs off Klusener while batting on 56. At that time, Australia was chasing 272, and desperately needed a tie to qualify, while the South Africans were already through to the semis. The apocryphal story is that Waugh said, 'Son, you just dropped the World Cup'. Waugh then went onto score an unbeaten 120 and Australia won the match by 5 wickets with 2 balls to spare.

of discovering new territory. Had the UCB involved themselves in a serious market research exercise, they would have understood the pertinent fact that you cannot just stage a Test and expect people to arrive in thousands simply because it is a Test. After all, who were the Indians? At that stage most of the Indian players were shadowy figures to the South African public. It requires time to develop an understanding and an acceptance of a new culture with its new identity.

It was forgotten that in South Africa, the Indians had for generations been largely disenfranchised, despite the sham of the House of Delegates, the apartheid government's bastard offspring. This had been designed to give them a form of facile autonomy which failed to work as it was a limited franchise. Also, knowledge about the Indian subcontinent was flimsy; much of it was based on ignorance and judging people by skin pigmentation. The India that white South Africa knew came from school textbook imagery. It was a superficial view. It was quite forgotten that India was part of the nuclear club and South Africa was not. Also, despite being part of Africa, the South African republic was outwardly more European in orientation; the old colonial masters, Holland and England, and the mix which made up the Afrikaner nation attracted more public focus than the Africa north of the Limpopo. India was a whole continent away. Little wonder that Botha and his rugby brethren and thousands of other South Africans were missing the point. In fact South Africa's return was greeted with more enthusiasm on 10 November 1991 than Botha and the rugby hierarchy would have thought possible of their home-based efforts some eight months later. On that day, one stadium in far-off South Asia had held more spectators than Ellis Park and Newlands combined.

This unlikely venue was Eden Gardens, located on the banks of the Hooghly River in Calcutta (now Kolkata), a venue which had hosted the 1987 World Cup final, the riot-riddled semi-final of the 1996 World Cup and the Asian Test Championship match against Pakistan in 2000. It was India who had proposed South Africa's readmission to the International Cricket Council (ICC) in July 1991, so India were given the honour of the first tour: to go elsewhere would have been an insult to their administrators.

A surge of emotion ran through the air-conditioned media box as Jimmy Cook and Andrew Hudson walked out to bat at Eden Gardens. This was not Lord's or Sydney, not Newlands or Auckland, or Melbourne or the Wanderers: the old traditions had gone. These were the first steps taken by the new South Africa with its new horizons and a more global view of international affairs than those held by the racist regime which had ruled for decades. Eden Gardens, with its passionate audience, was an implausible setting because a tour of India under an apartheid government would have, politically, been out of the question. Also, it must not be forgotten that it was the African National Congress who made the Indian adventure (and the tour to the West Indies the following April to play the first comeback Test) possible after Pakistan pulled out of a tour of India barely days before its scheduled start.

Pakistan withdrew because they felt their tour of India would fuel further sectarian animosity with the threat of anti-Muslim action coming from the militant Hindu leader, Bal Thackeray, of the Shiv Sena party. There were repeated threats by Thackeray, who has been reported to openly support many of the principles of Adolf Hitler, to disrupt the Pakistan tour, although the planned disorder had been widely condemned within India. In January 1999, on the eve of Pakistan's long-awaited tour which was to feature two Tests and several limited-overs internationals, Thackeray's right-wing followers drew further condemnation from the Indian premier, Atal Behari Vajpayee after the playing surface at the Ferozshah Kotla (New Delhi) stadium was vandalized by Shiv Sena activists.[2] Yet another reason advanced for Pakistan's decision to renege on the 1991 tour was the biting criticism by the Indian media of the Sharjah tournament that had been played a couple of months before. It was alleged that the final played between India and Pakistan was 'rigged to give Pakistan a favourable result'. These charges at the time drew vehement denials from the then Board

---

[2] Thackeray and his fanatical followers have done much to heighten political tensions between the neighbouring nations. In 1993 the Shiv Sena dug up the pitch at Wankhede Stadium, Mumbai (Bombay), to stop a game between the two countries. Until the World Cup match in Bangalore in March 1996, Pakistan had not played in India since 1987.

of Control for Cricket in Pakistan which was later replaced by a reconstituted body called the Pakistan Cricket Board.[3]

The Indians were furious at the cancellation and, in late October 1991, sought approval from the UCB delegation, then on a goodwill visit to India, to accept an invitation for what became a historic three-match limited-overs series.[4] Although it was organized at the same frenetic pace as the first three rebel tours in the early 1980s, it involved some strange, if interesting, bedfellows: one being the Marxist government of West Bengal.

In any event, by nine in the morning on 10 November 1991, Eden Gardens was packed with about 92,000 spectators (official figures were unreliable: 90,450 and then 91,800), an unofficial world record for limited-overs internationals. Outside was another estimated 60,000 setting off crackers and thunder flashes as scores were relayed to them. That tells us there were about 150,000 inside and outside the ground. An impressive figure all right. And what about the Indian television audience? On that most significant day in South African sports history, it was estimated that between 430 and 450 million Indians, from Nagercoil in the south to Jammu in the north, were said to be watching. There were a further estimated 60 million viewers in Pakistan, Sri Lanka and Bangladesh: incredible if true.

---

[3] Since then a number of charges have been made that linked past and present Pakistan players to the bribing of opponents to throw Tests and one-day internationals. While the claims first surfaced in England midway through the 1992 Pakistani tour, they had become rife two years later. In March 1995 investigations by the newly constituted Pakistan Cricket Board led to the initial suspension of Salim Malik, captain of the Pakistan side. He was later cleared and then banned again. At the King Commission in Cape Town in June 2000, Hansie Cronje, who had been accused by the New Delhi police of match-fixing, named Malik as the man who first approached him to throw a game.

[4] At the time the board's trip to the subcontinent was more of a diplomatic mission than anything else: showing appreciation for the support India had given South Africa during their successful application for membership of the ICC at Lord's five months earlier. It was coincidental that the visit was to include watching a couple of the India-Pakistan matches.

As they were declared with such ease, it was initially felt that the figures were perhaps a figment of some eager official's fertile imagination. When approached at the time, Jagmohan Dalmiya, a former secretary of the Board of Control for Cricket in India (BCCI), then president of the Cricket Association of Bengal (CAB) and later chairman of the ICC and BCCI, insisted that the figures were 'more or less correct'. Dalmiya contends that the sport has, in South Asia, as wide a support as the TV figures indicated. The question asked then was whether there were 400 million television sets in India, a country with large pockets of poverty. What was worrying for the South Africans was that the figures were neither official nor accredited to any government agency.[5]

In the end, Neel Patri, who was the New Delhi correspondent for the South African Argus Group at the time, was contacted to find out whether someone in the Indian government could give accurate viewing figures. Between Patri and Sandeep Nakai, then a correspondent of the *Hindustan Times*, whose help was also enlisted, there was corroboration: an estimated 420 million had watched the match at Eden Gardens. As Patri pointed out, there were (then) close to 900 million people in India and it was estimated that possibly a third had access to TV sets while more than half the population owned radios.

Nakai also forwarded evidence that in terms of officials, players, spectators and mass support, the sport had, in November 1991, a following in excess of 600 million: or a little less than two-thirds of the population. Which meant that between TV and radio, about 420 million people in India definitely watched or listened to the game at Eden Gardens. What later added credibility to the Eden Gardens '420 million viewers' story was a comment from a telegraphist in the parliamentary press gallery telex office the day the South Africans arrived in New Delhi for the third game. He explained that there were thousands of communities where there were two or three television sets (some had just one) set up in

---

[5] At that time, India had no cable TV and the government channel Doordarshan was the sole broadcaster. But in the context of a poor nation like India, far more important than the number of TV sets is the number of viewers who have access to each of those sets. This number was far larger than the myopic South Africans suspected.

popular meeting points and which drew large, very patient audiences. Qamar Ahmed, the London-based Pakistan cricket writer, later confirmed this when a more independent view was sought and he was quizzed about such an enormous following.[6]

When it is considered that even in the 1960s a municipal area in India with a population of 100,000 was regarded little more than an average-sized town, figures of more than 600 million supporters are far easier to accommodate. The population, said Indian officials, needs to reach 500,000 before a dot on the map assumes the mantle of a city. And as the population exploded, so did TV viewership support for the sport. This has been confirmed in recent years during Chesters' travels to and his growing enchantment with the region and its diverse population and cultures.

Unfortunately, the story of the size of the television audience was not published in South Africa as it was assumed that the figures were distorted while the copy from Patri's home in New Delhi was being telexed to *The Star*'s head office in Johannesburg. Three other stories sent through the same fax medium: interviews with the Indian captain Mohammad Azharuddin, a preview of the New Delhi day-night match, and the problems facing South Africa as they emerged after twenty-one years of isolation were, it was learned later, 'mislaid'.

Clive Rice and later Kepler Wessels led the country out of years of sports isolation (with the support of the ANC). This was the sport which John Vorster, then prime minister, and his henchmen tried to bury in the late 1960s and early 1970s through the ban of Basil D'Oliveira.[7] No one could blame Krish Mackerdhuj, Geoff

---

[6] After multi-channel cable TV arrived in India in 1994, the market has grown rapidly. According to credible industry estimates including estimates by MNC rating agencies like A.C. Nielsen, there are an estimated 130 million cable connections (circa 2002) with perhaps another 200 million sets being linked only to terrestrial broadcasts.

[7] England's tour of South Africa in 1968-69 was banned by the apartheid government of John Vorster in September 1968. This was after seam bowler Tom Cartwright failed a fitness test and the MCC selectors, led by Doug Insole, included South Africa-born Basil D'Oliveira as the replacement. The banning and subsequent cancellations of the South African tours of England in 1970 and Australia 1971-72 led to the country's international isolation.

Dakin and Dr Ali Bacher for those early days of jubilation: first at Lord's, then in Sharjah and later in India.

Since a majority of first-class games in India are played in the winter months, taking daylight factors into account, the games start around nine in the morning. Fanie de Villiers was one of those who rose early that Sunday of 10 November to watch South Africa's first official game in twenty-one summers on the national channel (SABC). Judy, his wife of a few months, set up the TV set as he was still nursing the broken toe.

It was painful to watch Allan Donald, his new-ball partner in the limited-overs matches during the Mike Gatting rebel tour of South Africa twenty months earlier, mark out his run-up. Fanie felt that had it not been for the injury he would have been a member of that historic touring party led by Clive Rice—possibly opening the bowling instead of Richard Snell, or at least taking first change. What he had to work on now was earning a place in the side for the World Cup four months away. That is, if the injury healed in time.

* * * *

From his earliest days Fanie de Villiers was always a competitor. If you look at the 1.90 metre tall, broad-shouldered fast bowler who took the new ball for South Africa from Christmas 1993 until March 1998, it is hard to imagine him as a small, scrawny lad. In fact, all through his childhood, until he went to Onderwyskollege in Pretoria, he was universally known as Faantjie or 'little Fanie'. Not that it made him shy of taking on anyone several years his senior and twice his size. While cricket didn't occupy a lot of his sporting attention in his early youth, he displayed a natural talent for bowling quite early in his primary and high school years.

Unlike Naas Botha, de Villiers came from a disadvantaged background; disadvantaged in that, during the years of isolation, in country areas, the summer game lacked the patronage it deserved. He was locked into an education system that was decidedly rugby and athletics oriented, and when he did get the opportunity to get into the trials, the city youngsters in Bloemfontein (and Welkom for that matter) adopted an elitist attitude about their gawky country cousins.

Many of them had come from schools in which funds were scarce, and there were no concrete nets with all-weather (metal) stumps. Often such youngsters had to make do with whatever was at hand: in some cases branches cut from a nearby tree were punched into the ground and a dusty, bumpy practice surface on which to bat and bowl was marked out. This sort of endemically hostile environment did not stimulate interest in the game. And to survive such physical barriers and the mocking antagonism of their city-reared peers, most youngsters from country schools needed to be either extroverts or shrug it off as part of the growing up process.

His first school was a good example of the typical country environment. Deneysville Primary, on the banks of Vaal Dam, had a rugby field and little else to foster interest in other sports. The athletics track consisted of a stretch of dirt road leading to the school from the main road. There were sixty-five children and they all competed in various track events. Before their weekly athletics meeting, the children had to clear the dirt road of stones so as not to injure their feet. The lanes were then marked with a type of white chalk dust which the children scattered with their hands. As for cricket, it was a backyard event as the school in Deneysville had no pitch and no practice facilities.

When the family moved to Sasolburg, Faantjie was fortunate in one sense. His father Braam, a teacher at Fonteinê Primary, a dual-medium language school, was a dedicated coach in most sports. There was, however, an immediate problem at his new school: there were no pitch or practice facilities. It meant spending the best part of several afternoons laying in both amenities for the school. Braam would drive an old battered tractor and trailer in from the farm close to the town, and with the help of a couple of labourers gave Fonteinê Primary the best facilities for the summer sport in that part of the Free State. As the school's coach he taught the youngsters the all-important basics as well as a fondness for a game that was not particularly high on the list of sporting priorities among the country schools; it was a tolerated stepchild with a season which lasted no longer than five or six weeks. Yet during those forty or so days there was a thriving league in Sasolburg in which the talents of the young 'Vinnige Fanie' were nourished.

While in South African terms that particular school league would have at the time been dismissed as a backwater event, it had a right to exist, just as much as do the bigger leagues in Centurion, Bloemfontein, East London, Cape Town, Pretoria, Johannesburg, Soweto, Alice, Mamelodi and elsewhere where the game is played. It was from his father that Faantjie learnt the rudiments of fast bowling—why a bowler must develop rhythm; how to hold a ball; how to get the arm up high enough to look over the left shoulder and down the pitch at the batsman as you go into your delivery stride, all the essentials that mould a youngster's action. In those days all he wanted to do was run up and bowl, and bowl fast, which is a natural instinct for a young athlete.

What counted in those years when it came to the trials, no matter how good you were, was having the right credentials. It did not help the youngsters that then and even today, the selectors usually spent about thirty minutes at the nets looking at the talent and placing either a tick or a cross next to the name of potential trialists. It was a nefarious system designed to cull the less-talented. Not all those weeded out lacked genuine talent; a large number did have talent, and the ability—not obvious at the under-13 level— often emerged at high school or later.

Faantjie was far from being a late developer. He had, even at an early age, the mental strength and character to overcome the unthinking jeers aimed at country school players. Short and thin as he was, he had the heart of a competitor who, seventeen years later, would win a Test for South Africa in Sydney.

Another handicap this largely pre-pubescent group faced was a genuine lack of coaching expertise in country schools; as far as technique was concerned which doesn't mean that those dedicated coaches lacked knowledge and the skills to correct errors in a player's mental make up. The problem was that flaws, so obvious to the trained eye, were later exposed at higher levels of competition. The so-called experts instead of helping, carelessly rejected many talented youngsters.[8] Anyway, Faantjie must have made quite an impression. In 1977 the Free State junior school selectors were impressed enough with Faantjie to include him in the Free State side for the PermLazer under-13 week in Pretoria.

---

[8] It was the same view which for years bedevilled black and white relations and efforts to coach township youngsters. Many lost interest because of the lack of communication and the ignorance caused by the laws of the apartheid system.

It is interesting how Tobie van Rooyen (the team's assistant manager and coach), from Welkom Primary, could not recall whether the future South African outswing bowler had any special talent other than being particularly fast for a boy his size. It should not come as a surprise, either, that Fanie and others remember van Rooyen's abrasive attitude. Most felt threatened by the burly school teacher, who always seemed to be shouting and was quick to fault his young charges. Most of the time Faantjie felt that he was the focus of van Rooyen's critical assessment, because of his country school background.

One theory advanced then for van Rooyen's attitude was that Faantjie, being a fast bowler, was in direct competition with his son, Riaan. Yet the fear of criticism also had its effect on the Sasolburg youngster. Nervousness and a bumpy outfield resulted in him fumbling the ball in the second game of the 1977 Perm Lazer Week at the massive Pretoria University sports complex. When he looked up, Faantjie saw van Rooyen walking towards him. He felt panicky and decided to move in from the boundary as far as possible to escape yet another reprimand. Then he returned to his mark backwards to avoid facing him.

'Apart from his son, I think we were all scared of him,' said Craig Tibshraeny, the team's vice-captain. 'He would come down on us quite hard at times.' His usual habit during the games was to walk around the boundary. On one occasion he went to where Faantjie was fielding and shouted at him saying, 'This is not farm cricket.' The youngster later developed one of the best arms in the game when it came to returning a ball from the outfield.

What appeared to upset van Rooyen was how Faantjie, instead of walking towards the boundary after each ball was bowled, moved backwards to see where the rest of the fielders were. The burly assistant manager also ignored that he was the best boundary fielder in the side. Long, hot afternoons often spent throwing stones at tins placed fifty metres or more away had been a regular part of his regimen of physical exercises. It taught him the importance of accuracy: picking up the ball and getting it back to the wicketkeeper in the three quick movements needed to be effective, is far from easy. Later, throwing the javelin further developed his arm. The javelin throwing improved the speed at which he returned the ball to the wicket: the accuracy had already been acquired.

This was noticeable not only in those early club games in Sasolburg, but also when he turned out for Onderwyskollege. Steve Vercueil, the Northern Transvaal B wicketkeeper, quickly discovered the power of his arm when Fanie made his provincial debut at Berea Park on 25 October 1985, fifteen days after his twenty-first birthday.

'I was used to guys hurling them in,' said Vercueil. 'Most were accurate, but now and then they'd be wild and woolly and you'd be diving to save an overthrow instead of trying to run-out a batsman. This rocket (Fanie's first return from the boundary) was into the gloves from backward square, on the fence . . . and it stung. I had a good look to see who it was and made a mental note to relax the hands when he next threw one to me.'

Sid Dugmore, one of the Northern Transvaal selectors, spent most of the first day at that game and made some notes of his own. 'For someone playing in his first big game, it was impressive. He knew just where to throw the ball, and to do it so accurately meant hours of training. I know that a couple of the Natal B batsmen also noticed the fast returns and decided not to get too ambitious by gambling for a third run when they knew two would be safe enough,' he said as his eyes twinkled and his round features creased with a broad grin.

Sasolburg, an industrial town on the old Free State and Transvaal borders where the country's oil-from-coal programme is run, was a geographic conundrum in terms of its sporting identity. Although it belonged in part to a country area known as the Vaal Triangle, Sasolburg was, in primary school terms, also part of the Free State Goldfields, and largely ignored as a source of talent. Which meant that only those with exceptional ability outside the Welkom, Kroonstad and Virginia conclave of the Northern Free State were able to join that select group. No wonder there was the mistaken impression among the Bloemfontein boys that Faantjie came from Kroonstad. Even the 1977 Perm Week programme clearly demarcates the Goldfields schools from those of Bloemfontein. It is strange, therefore, that Faantjie's school, Fonteinê, did not carry such an identity tag. Recent investigation suggests that it was an administrative-political decision: some egos were too embarrassed at the time to admit that Faantjie was neither a product of the Bloemfontein nor the Goldfields system. Although time, like the wheels of the ox-wagon, is often slow in recognizing achievements, there have been, since the mid-1980s, several Sasolburg youngsters who have earned their Free State under-13 colours with the town getting rightful acknowledgement.

Having made it through one trial and survived, the young 'Vinnige Fanie' was included in the Goldfields side to play Bloemfontein in the final Free State under-13 trials. Usually selectors indulge in a good deal of horse-trading when it comes to selecting such sides. But Faantjie was exceptionally talented. So when Allan Donald was only in standard four at Grey College primary and Hansie Cronje, his future national captain, was in grade two (also at Grey primary), Faantjie was already making a name for himself in another part of the province.

In early November 1977 Faantjie was chosen for Free State Primary Schools to play Griqualand West. Later that month he received a letter confirming his selection for the Free State Perm Week side. The country lad was about to have his first taste of life in Pretoria as the under-13 week was held in the Jacaranda City that December.

An obvious question is, who else took part in that tournament held at the L. C. de Villiers sports complex in Pretoria University? Well, two future South African teammates were all-rounder Dave Callaghan (Border, and later Eastern Province captain) and medium-fast seamer Craig Matthews (Western Province); Steve Elworthy, who at times shared the new ball with Fanie when playing for Northern Transvaal, and was a member of the Rhodesian (Zimbabwe) squad. Others from the junior class of 1977 were Mark Rushmere (Eastern Province, and for a time Transvaal) and Graeme Hick (Rhodesia, who earned Test caps for England).

In fact it was on Thursday, 20 December 1977, when Faantjie first met Craig Matthews; although when you ask either whether they remember much about that day you'll end up with puzzled frowns. Pressed for an answer, botn of them still got it wrong, citing 1986. On that particular hot December day both took 2 wickets, although Faantjie was a fraction more economical: 28 runs from 9 overs to Craig's 37 runs from 11 overs.

Yet Faantjie was extraordinarily sharp for one so young. And that indefatigable spirit, which often carried South Africa's bowling attacks through 14 Tests from Melbourne over Christmas 1993 to Auckland in early March 1995, had already manifested itself.

In the 1977 Perm Week he was expected to bowl as many as 15 overs an inning. The first six would be with another seamer, usually Riaan van Rooyen, the team's captain, while the remainder were bowled in tandem with left-arm spinner Renier Weideman. There was one match against Natal, when he bowled almost through the innings. Nothing really changed.

It often surprised many who faced him, from those Under-13 Week days until he injured his knee at Newlands early in the 1989-90 season, that he was as fast in the tenth or fifteenth over as he was at the start of the innings, always hitting the bat hard. It came from an inherent desire to tackle a batsman head on. Don't let it worry you if you get hit; sooner or later you'll get his wicket. And at the under-13 level he was more successful than most.

What is interesting is that until December 1996 so few knew of his under-13 exploits: this was a part of South African sports history that escaped the notice of many. For Faantjie it was just another chapter in his career. In the light of what happened after that, it was an important stage in his development. There is still a certain pride, too, in that he was the first primary schoolboy from the Sasolburg area to be selected for the Free State Perm Week side.

Renamed the Standard Bank Week the five-day festival has been, since its inception in 1968, an important cog in the game's education and development wheel, especially during the isolation years. It fostered interest at the under-13 level as the noose of international banishment tightened.

While the role played by this Week is becoming increasingly important, 1977 was a year of particular note. The South African Cricket Union (SACU) had just been formed with Rashid Varachia, an industrious Lenasia businessman with a keen feel for the sport, as the first president. Enshrined in the SACU constitution was the right of all players (of all races) 'to know and feel that every honour his province or country can bestow upon him, is open to him'. Considering the repressive, demeaning *baasskap* (white supremacist) system in existence then, that phrase has, for many, smacked of misguided piety.

Yet, for the first time, players of all races were able to mix freely. It was quite an eye-opener for the Free State youngster, as was the bustling city of Pretoria to curious, youthful eyes. It was an experience that implanted the seeds of equality in his inquisitive mind. Dining together, going to the same church service, playing against each other, rubbing shoulders with that ever-so-slowly burgeoning part of South African history was effective. Little was he to know that ten years later he would be coaching in Mamelodi and Atteridgeville.[9]

In 1977, however, Faantjie was one of the fortunate youngsters. While the historical complexity of South African society created its own problems, cricket was always quick to demolish the artificial racial barriers deliberately fostered for generations by successive governments to protect white minorities. This in turn encouraged the egregious sense of superiority so abhorred by the Breyten Breytenbach's of this world: true Afrikaners who have a love of their race, of all colours, language and culture. In recognizing the rights of all to be equal, Breytenbach and others were forced to fight the system from outside the borders and were disgracefully shunned by their kin.

Imagine the embarrassment the young players faced when Tobie van Rooyen, their assistant manager/coach, decided to press himself into service when one of the umpires failed to arrive for the game with Western Province. With his son, Riaan, as captain, van Rooyen senior proceeded to direct Free State's on-the-field operations in violation of the laws of the game. It created an unpleasant atmosphere with objections from the Western Province management.

While the national under-13 Week will continue to serve its purpose in identifying young players, the number that filters through

---

[9] His cheerful honesty and charismatic image, then as it is now, turned the young fast bowler with a growing reputation into an instant success in the townships around Pretoria. In 1987, like most young students, he was looking for ways to earn a little extra cash: so why not put his expertise as a provincial player to use? The suggestion to Dr Ali Bacher that he should take over the role came from Russell Cobb, the Leicestershire county player, who at the time was the coach at Onderwyskollege and found coaching in the townships a more than worthwhile exercise in bridge-building.

to high school (Nuffield and now Coca-Cola) level remains alarmingly low. From 1977, fifteen players went on to play for provincial teams, but only eight of those, including Hick, were still involved at this level twenty-three summers later. And from statistics of other weeks, the numbers vary: ten made it to provincial level from the 1980 week in East London, including Test caps for Gary Kirsten and Rudolf Steyn; but only six emerged at provincial level from the 1979 week, among them Meyrick Pringle; and five players from 1981.

Major concerns, however, still exist. Internal school politics aside, there is a strong accusation of bias in team selection policy. Since unity, the parity between establishment and development players widened in the mid-1990s with the distinct impression that there were those who wanted to keep it a 'whites only' week with a few token development numbers.

Little wonder then, that a few within the United Cricket Board (UCB) were disenchanted with the selection system and the choice of managers. Lack of exposure was harming the game at such an intricate level of development: the privilege system was still entrenched eight years after unity. The only way it could be dismantled was through the radical manoeuvre of taking the game out of the school system and placing it in the hands of a central committee and a sub-committee appointed by the UCB. The other alternative was the introduction of a quota system to rid the game, at this level, of its inherent racism: not a step which young disadvantaged blacks accept as readily as politicians; their preference is merit selection.

Hopefully the UCB's Transformation Charter with its monitoring committee led by Professor Andre Odendaal can eliminate the racial stigma through sections one, two, three, four, six, seven and ten of the charter. Unveiled as it was amid controversy on the second day of the fourth Test against the West Indies at Newlands in January 1999, it is at least an honest attempt, whatever some media and politicians with their own agendas may suggest, to introduce stricter accountability rules to a sport designed for all.

Young Faantjie had such pace in those primary school days that the inability of the school's wicketkeeper to stop the ball led to more games being lost than won. Bowling fast and straight had its problems. Mr Extras was often top score with as many as 24 byes being let through. While this led to an old-fashioned long stop being employed in a bid to cut down the number of byes, there were occasions when even this ended in failure, much to the chagrin of Faantjie's father, Braam. It was all very much part of what has become known as that cliché, the learning curve. But there was no mistaking his talent. It led to his selection for the Sasolburg Town third side in 1978 (at fourteen years of age) with matches in the Vaal Triangle league involving clubs from Vereeniging, Meyerton, Vanderbijlpark and Sasolburg.

There is a photograph of the Sasolburg Hoër side of 1978 which has his brother Neels, in his matric year, seated in the middle of the front row as captain of the side, while a short, thin tow-headed Faantjie sat in front at his feet. This is not as surprising as it may seem as Faantjie has always looked up to his older, school-teacher brother.

Yet when they played in the same school side, and for the Sasolburg Town third team in 1978, it was the only time the older and younger de Villiers brothers played in the same school team. There was a lot of pride in playing for the same side, and it indicates the close relationship of the de Villiers family, who have always put a strong emphasis on doing things together. While Faantjie's early high school years were productive, there were times when his size went against him and his bowling would be tested when he faced better than average batsmen. Yet he was an energetic player for Sasolburg Town, often bowling second or third change in the Vaal Triangle league.

The side was formed to give young talent in the town a chance, with Neels as captain, Faantjie and another fast bowler, Okkie Kotze, also from the same school, in the side. In the club nets, Faantjie gave as good as he received from the other members, and in matches it was nothing for him to pick up a couple of early wickets when he came on to bowl.[10]

---

[10] Playing at club level outside the school system has its benefits and in the long term has launched any number of first-class careers. Northern Transvaal schoolboys Jacques Rudolph, Pierre Joubert and David Townsend are recent examples. They have learnt more from senior club players, including those in the provincial squads, than they would from their peers at school, and for that matter the coaches.

There were those, however, who were in their late twenties or early thirties, and like van Rooyen, the Welkom schoolmaster, who felt the young *witkop* (blond) teenager wore bowling boots which were three or four times the size of his actual potential. Another case where confidence and competence were mistaken for cockiness. After all, he may have revelled in bowling fast because he enjoyed the challenge of trying to take wickets, but the sneering references about size and 'beginners luck' among the more senior club batsmen in the Meyerton, Vereeniging and Vanderbijlpark teams displayed a lack of appreciation as well as maturity in sizing up a gifted player.

Beginner's luck? Not a damn. He may have been scrawny and in the first phase of a three-stage apprenticeship which led eventually to his first-class debut at Berea Park almost eight years later, but the competitiveness was noticeable as he moved up the ranks from Fonteinê Primary to Sasolburg Hoër. It may have been because of the hat-trick he took against Vaal High of Vereeniging, the first of his career and which earned him a trophy that even now, for sentimental reasons, he is not shy about displaying. It indicates that he is proud of his roots as a budding fast bowler.

Not that cricket occupied most of Faantjie's sporting attention in those active early years. His general skills as an all-round athlete, even for one so small, were impressive. It could be that he developed it during his pre-school years when his mother, Hanna,

---

Joubert and Townsend, fast bowlers playing for Northern Transvaal B, are following the same path that Fanie trod ten seasons before. In fact Northern Transvaal was the only province in South Africa, up until 1995-96, that had not selected a schoolboy at senior provincial level. Yet Joubert did not emerge because of a void in the system. Like Fanie he too played in the national under-13 week (for Northern Transvaal in 1991) and was seen to have ability. But the high school he attended, Eldoraigne, was not recognized for producing cricket talent. That he prospered was due to his association with Harlequins, a leading Northern Transvaal Premier League side. In December 1993 he was included in the South African Schools B team to play Zimbabwe, and went on to earn his national school colours in 1995. Rudolph, however, developed through the school system to earn a place in the South African side in Australia in 2001-02 and the World Cup squad for 2003.

would drive along a dusty road to a farm cafe, about three kilometres from the farm school where his father was teaching. He would then run back to the house while his mother took time over her purchases of milk, bread, eggs or whatever was needed. It gave him a good start and enabled him to be almost two-thirds of the way home before she passed him.

If Faantjie enjoyed such contests at that early stage of his life no one should be surprised at the outcome of one particular school outing. As a nine-year-old he attended a sports meeting at Taaibos, a school some ten kilometres from Sasolburg close to the coal mines and won a race meant for older boys. It was a family day fête with a variety of food and clothing stalls and to end the athletics meeting there was a 3,000 metres race which was for all those boys, twelve or older, who wanted to enter.

He lined up with the tall, the tubbies, the short and the thin ones, such as himself. For most of the event he hung in towards the back of the field; lap after lap on the bruised kikuyu grass surface, closely watching those in front so that there was not too much distance between them. With two laps to go, his father Braam told him it was time to make his move. His family knew his capabilities as a runner over all distances, and recalled his pre-school years when he would run home from the cafe. Slowly disengaging from the bunch, he moved to the outside and began to haul them all in: the fatties at the back, the short ones who were now out of breath, and the taller, stronger ones who had no stamina to last three kilometres.

Coming straight out of the back the little boy with pure white hair overtook the leaders on the top bend. They were all strung out behind him: bits of struggling driftwood unable to summon a last challenging burst. As he moved with a final surge away from the fifty or so boys aged between fifteen and twelve, he crossed the line well ahead of the competition. His triumph drew warm acclaim from the adults who admired his spirit. The young champion was an instant hero but he did not dwell on the flattery that victory created; it is not the way of Fanie de Villiers, and although he did not realize it then, the 'Vinnige Fanie' legend had been born.

On a train ride from Colombo to Mount Lavinia during South Africa's tour of Sri Lanka in August and September 1993, and his first overseas with the national squad, Fanie bought a third-class ticket and joined the cheerful throng entering a carriage. Taking off his leather hat he announced himself to his awed audience and warmly shook hands with them. Everybody knew him well enough, but Sri Lanka is that sort of country; a nation obsessed by a game inherited from the British Raj. They could not believe how such a famous personality would want to share their ramshackle travelling accommodation. It is rare for even a top Sri Lankan sports personality to undertake a train journey, let alone mingle with the ordinary public in a third-class compartment on a train.

'Hello, my friends,' he said with breezy cheerfulness. 'My name is Fanie de Villiers, from South Africa. May I join you?'

The station at which he bought his ticket is in a rundown area known as Slave Island, about a twenty-minute walk from the team's hotel on the beachfront in Galle Face Road. In Colombo, as in most of the Indian subcontinent, it is common for luxury and poverty to rub shoulders. The differences between Slave Island and Galle Face Road are no exception. Yet the open friendliness belies the state in which most live. As he sat down and happily signed autographs, Fanie's main interest was in the people: why were they on the train and were they also going, to Mount Lavinia or further south? Kalutara? Bentota? Hikkaduwa? Galle? perhaps or Unuwatuna or even Matara? He had been given a day off from the tour and decided to do a little exploring. Mount Lavinia was about as far as he was going on that particular day.

As his fellow passengers discovered, part of the Fanie de Villiers charisma is that he will always make time to greet anyone he has not met before, anyone who wants to shake hands with him or thrust a grubby piece of paper at him with a badly chewed ballpoint pen. Signing autographs for youngsters while fielding on the boundary and talking to them is not just for display. In Durban during a Castle Cup match one season, he signed a sheet of paper in five designated areas and thought nothing of it. The next day he was handed another sheet by the same youngster and on enquiry was told they were for school chums too shy to ask. Fanie made a point of it that they should come and get their own. For the remaining three days he had his own Kingsmead fan club. As a public relations exercise it is good for the game to have a Fanie de Villiers to whom youngsters can relate.

Several years ago a large group of schoolboys at Dale College in East London wanted to hold a white ball, stained with grass, that Fanie had signed and given to umpire Robbie Noble after playing in a domestic day-night series match at an up-country venue. To them it held a special magic. As with the train ride to Mount Lavinia, or when signing autographs for the youngsters on the boundary, he knows all too well how important it is to be modest in nature. After all, it has long been a de Villiers family trait to be generous and giving. He is also prepared to stand up for his principles and say what he thinks when he knows something is not right.[11]

In June of 1979 Braam de Villiers was told of his appointment as vice-principal to a school in the southern suburbs of Johannesburg. It was just the sort of position he wanted and in December that year, the family, now consisting of Braam, Hanna and Faantjie were on the move again; it was farewell to Sasolburg and the end of the family's stay in the Free State.

Neels was already at the teachers' training college in Potchefstroom: the second of four children to follow the well-trodden path established years before by their father. Braam, promoted to deputy head at Francis Vorwerg, a junior school for children with cerebral palsy, had enrolled Faantjie as a standard eight pupil at Fakkel Hoër. As it was across the road from the house in the Francis Vorwerg grounds in Rifle Range Road, Faantjie was no more than five minutes from the practice nets or the sports fields where the rugby field doubled as a cricket ground with an athletics track ringing the arena.

And while at the time it did not seem important, the move to Johannesburg was the first of several factors that influenced the future of the young teenager who has since become a national hero.

---

[11] It is a characteristic that has not always been appreciated or met with general approval in the dressing rooms of either Northern Transvaal or South Africa. It has also earned him disapprobation from officials at Pretoria Onderwyskollege, and at times from the UCB. Even Sports Minister Ngconde Balfour did not understand the principled views of someone who took ability and not race into account when criticizing his selection.

Pride and Prejudice

It was about two-thirty on a blustery, early August afternoon when a neatly dressed young teenager, whistling cheerfully, walked casually towards the unkempt nets at Fakkel Hoër. School had been over for almost an hour. For Fanie de Villiers it had been an unusually long hour, and he was anxious not to be late for that first practice session. As usual, his ridgeback puppy, Petrus, ran in front, sniffing clumps of grass thick with dust from the dry winter months. Above, a few puffballs of white clouds tinged with grey whipped around the sky.

A brisk wind with a chilly edge greeted him as he made his way across the deserted rugby field to the nets, situated between two unpretentious single-storey brick and stucco classrooms. The gusts kicked up discarded sweet wrappers near a large rusting rubbish bin close to the open stand, as well as dust from the bare patches of red earth on the rugby field. But Faantjie did not feel the wind; his spare frame had long been conditioned to weather changes from years of growing up in the Free State. Why, it had been snowing (in October if you please!) when his father and mother drove home from the nursing home in Vereeniging five days after he was born.

On that particular August afternoon in 1980, he was, not surprisingly, the first to arrive at the nets, giving him time to reflect about the short season ahead. Six or seven games would be played over the next five weeks, from mid-August until the end of September; barely enough to whet the appetite of any keen youngster earnest about improving his game. And Faantjie was keen. Although small for his age, he found fast bowling one way of proving himself.

The masters at Fakkel Hoër treated cricket in much the same way as other Afrikaans schools in the Free State and what was then Transvaal: it was a filler between the more seriously-regarded rugby and athletic seasons; a stopgap exercise before the most significant part of school life—exams. The site on which the nets were built gave the impression that the facility was a hurriedly erected afterthought. Even tennis was given preference over cricket at Fakkel.[1]

A further complication arose because the extra-curricular activities during the third term included two thinly-disguised cultural pursuits: cadet drill and *Voortrekker* (Boy Scouts and Girl Guides) activities, which were then all part of the process of political indoctrination. Nothing was allowed to shake the baasskap domination ingrained in most students from an early age.

While some cricket coaches were serious about improving standards and stimulating interest in what meagre talent there was, a large number, such as those at Fakkel Hoër, simply paid lip service to the training guidelines designed to help the schools. Yet when time allowed, Faantjie often practised bowling alone in the nets at Fakkel. Usually after school when no one was around, he would climb through a gap in the fence carrying a bag that contained five old balls. The impoverished state of the run-ups made it difficult for bowlers to generate the rhythm which is as essential to a fast bowler as it is to a spinner or medium-paced trundler. During those afternoons when he practised on his own, Petrus would always be close by.

---

[1] What needs to be remembered is that the Free State and Transvaal (now Gauteng) provincial cricket bodies did little during the years of isolation to encourage the development of the sport among the Afrikaans schools. They had enough problems of their own, but at that time in Transvaal, with English-speaking schools playing a dominant role, only the especially talented Afrikaans youngsters progressed beyond the trials. That cricket survived at some Afrikaans schools was largely due to it being a part of the education curriculum and the dream of winning what was then the Administrator's Trophy.

Fakkel Hoër's reputation as a rugby school was well known. Yet in the past even Fakkel had managed occasional success during the brief Administrator's Trophy, the big sports prize among Afrikaans high schools. There were four major Administrator's trophies: with rugby at the top of the ladder followed by athletics and then tennis; cricket was at the bottom. In the early 1990s the term Administrator was replaced by the name Director but it no longer had the prestige it had enjoyed in the era between the 1950s and the late 1980s.

At Fakkel, net sessions were essential, but far from compulsory, during the first week of the fourth term. If, by some miracle, the school reached the zone play-offs, the season would be stretched to perhaps nine matches. It had happened before—not often of course—but you needed players with the sort of flair to make the Transvaal Nuffield Week trials for the Afrikaans teams. Of course such players were not to be compared to those who played in the Craven Week rugby trials: at schools such as Fakkel Hoër the rugby players were the real heroes, idolized by teachers, parents, brothers and girlfriends.[2]

It was not easy, however, for Afrikaans-speaking youngsters to make an impression in cricket. Just as the school rugby hierarchy in some provinces of the old South Africa largely overlooked English-speaking youngsters, cricket was often seen as the preserve of the fashionable school system: a playground for an elite few in the years of mistrust and discord. From the 1950s through to the early 1980s, so few Afrikaans youngsters filtered through the Transvaal system that there was genuine cause for concern.[3]

---

[2] It has long been forgotten that during the era when government tactical support made rugby the flagship sport of the whites, Craven Week (and other sports weeks) was actually an idea borrowed from cricket's Nuffield Week (now Khaya Majola/Coca-Cola week). The Nuffield Week was an under-18 festival which had led to the discovery of any number of test players since its inception in 1940.

[3] This was despite the intense interest created among a large section of Afrikaners after the success of Peter van der Merwe's team over Bobby Simpson's Australians in 1966-67. The exciting Pollock brothers, Peter and Graeme, the explosive Mike Procter, the gentlemanly Trevor Goddard and the spectacular batting of Denis

Although there was growth in the Cape, Natal and Northern Transvaal, there was little in the rugby-oriented schools of Transvaal and Free State (and Pretoria, for that matter). A number were wooed to the game by the success of the 'Springboks' under Peter van der Merwe. But embracing a sport seen in the majority of Transvaal and Free State areas as part of the English-speaking culture created a few problems.

The physical and mental discipline and skills of cricket were foreign, especially to those less-appreciative of how the same discipline should be part of growing up. In recent years a number of famous black soccer players, Jomo Sono among them, have preferred the disciplines of the summer game to the aggressive, physical approach of their own sport.

In the mid- to late 1960s and early 1970s, Francois le Roux, Johann van Rensburg, Marinus van Wyk and Mike de Villiers were four Afrikaners who achieved a level of provincial success. But there were no heroes in the Kepler Wessels mould. By the time the 1980s dawned, Wessels, the most famous of the modern Afrikaans pathfinders, had moved to Australia to carve out his niche.

Wessels, like Hansie Cronje, Joubert Strydom and Allan Donald, was part of a Free State education system blessed with men of foresight such as Johan Volsteedt and Cronje's father, Ewie, to smooth the rocky road. Had Fanie de Villiers been fortunate enough to attend Grey College in Bloemfontein there is no doubt he would have emerged as a name for the future. Instead, falling by chance into the Northern Transvaal system the way he did, he was regarded as an entry through the unfashionable back door.

At least Wessels and, to an extent the young de Villiers, escaped the trauma suffered by Arend du Preez, a promising wicketkeeper who at one stage kept to Pat Symcox when he played for Adelaar, a club in the northern suburbs of Pretoria known as 'The Moot'. Du Preez went to an Afrikaans high school, which at the time did not have a cricket team. That was not young Arend's fault, just a question of being in the wrong school zone. But when the annual

---

Lindsay created an aura of invincibility. But it was van der Merwe, captain of the successful South African team that toured England in 1965, who moulded them together.

Northern Transvaal Afrikaans Schools' trials came along, the best wicketkeeper was overlooked because his school did not have a cricket team. This was a crucial selection because it was here that a combined Afrikaans side was selected for Mitchell Week (the Northern Transvaal Nuffield Week trials). When questions were asked of the Afrikaans selectors, they merely shrugged. The policy was that he had to play for a school; it was not their fault if he did not. For some strange reason they did not view it as a form of discrimination. 'Anyway,' came the comment from Ernie Winter, then in charge of this particular nefarious system, 'he is coached outside the schools system and plays for a senior club in the leagues. It should be reward enough.'

This unhappy episode is one of many that show how the system worked against itself, and failed. The politics of selection not only affected players and the schools they attended, but it also created the mistaken impression that the schools' team was made up of the best players. A recent Test player (not Fanie) was also a victim of the old boys selection club policy in his province. He did not go to a fashionable school, but because the traditional schools did not have their quota of eleven players, out went a future Test star and in came a nobody whose name has been quickly forgotten. Since South Africa's re-emergence this overlooked player has built an enviable reputation.

In 1979 Fakkel Hoër had four teams: A and B, an under-15 and an under-14 team. Occasionally the under-15 XI was split into two sides if there were more players than usual. Normally the season began with a couple of friendlies followed by the zonal games for the Administrator's Trophy. While four teams for a school the size of Fakkel may seem a lot for an Afrikaans school of that era, sport participation was encouraged because of the competitive spirit it generated. Not at all a bad idea.

Faantjie, who was regarded as a fair scrum half when he was at Hoërskool Sasolburg, filled the same role for the Fakkel under-15 B rugby side. But the team's coach, Jappie Visbeck, had no idea how multi-talented this particular youngster was; nor, if one goes by the impression years later, did he really care: not at least until he realized that the South African fast bowler he was looking at on television during the many replays of the famous caught and bowled dismissal of Glen McGrath at Sydney, had been in one of the under-15 teams he coached at Fakkel Hoër.

As always, the late highveld winter sun was bright. While rugby practice for the first and second teams would be held later in the day, the pretence of the first net session had to be held. At the time Fakkel Hoër was involved in the build-up for what was then the region's rugby Administrator's Trophy finals, and these were paramount in the thoughts of most boys (and girls) at the school. So it was quite understandable that after the July holidays that year no more than a handful of players turned out at the first net session.

For young Faantjie the chance to test his bowling skills against senior boys from schools other than those at Sasolburg excited him. He had, with some success, bowled to men when playing for the Sasolburg Town team and had played for the Vaal Triangle under-15 side the previous year, but this, he felt, was different. He wanted to impress the cricket master and his peers and earn a place in the first team for the opening friendly match two weeks away. Which should have been easy enough judging the talent at the school.

But the expectancy proved to be a big disappointment. Not only was he surprised by the poor organization, but the turn out was also well below his expectations. This after all was Johannesburg, and a sport like cricket at such a large school should be run more professionally. He knew that with his brother Neels in charge, the nets at Sasolburg Hoër would have had enough players to fill four or five teams; eventually about nine boys, in a variety of gear that would double for cricket and rugby practices, turned up.

Then he became the victim of a tactless teacher, for after bowling about 10 balls he was told not to bowl so fast. He would, came the complaint, injure one of the batsmen. Part of the problem was that the concrete base over which the matting was placed contained several barely discernible ridges. They only became noticeable when the odd fast ball started shooting around at pace.

It was not surprising that he was told to put a brake on his pace, since a couple of those who turned up at the nets were also valued members of the first rugby team. Both were in their matriculation year. It was the first time in their lives that they had faced anything as fast, especially from one so small, and only in standard eight. One of them, the fullback of the rugby side that was fancied to win the knockout stages of the Administrator's Trophy play offs, was a key component in the back line for the first game being held at the school the following Saturday. It was claimed that this particular fullback would unflinchingly stand his ground taking the high balls while about to be tackled by several flying forwards. But facing young Faantjie that afternoon, the fullback found it more prudent to back off towards square leg, his back foot moving outside leg stump and the front foot far from the line of the ball and inching between middle and leg.

This was the first sign that Faantjie's pace was too hot for the other schoolboys. His off stump channel was also too accurate. He had the ability to dip the ball in to the batsmen, followed by some away swing, which led to a tentatively angled bat that was well away from the body. While this came from a natural body movement, he preferred bowling fast. 'Knock 'em over, and knock 'em over quick' is the universal motto of teenage tearaways. In the one (friendly) match he did play for Fakkel not only was Faantjie highly successful, but the team won their first match in three years.

On that particular afternoon, however, they found it hard to believe that anyone so small could generate such pace. There were grumblings that his accuracy was too good. Understandably Faantjie was upset at being unable to bowl at full pace. If the batsmen found it difficult to handle his pace, how would they manage in a match situation when faced with fast bowlers in the opposition's team? He was also concerned that the deep furrows in the run-ups had not been filled. They were, he felt, a recipe for a serious mishap: an injured ankle or damaged knee. As it is it resulted in bowlers falling away, and Fakkel did not have a coach astute enough to spot such a basic flaw, which didn't help their game at all. Little wonder that young Faantjie was far from impressed and full of complaints when he got home later in the day.

Years before, at a primary school in Deneysville, a recreational township on the banks of the Vaal River, Braam de Villiers had taught a cheerful group of youngsters. He had umpired a practice match between the under-12 and 13s. They were eager youngsters, for the teacher had the knack of turning practice sessions into fun. It was his belief that in a serious world youngsters should be taught that sport could be enjoyed. Although the sports field was regularly watered, it was still dusty, because it needed rain to give the grass body. One of the problems of living in a summer rainfall area such as the Free State or Transvaal was that the real rains only began in October. On that particular sunny afternoon, however, Braam de Villiers had looked around the dusty field that Bennie Venter had set for the right-arm in-swing bowler, and made a couple of suggestions he remembered from a coaching manual. 'You need to have a couple of fielders behind square-leg. They will stop the batsmen scoring runs in that area,' he had said. Later he exhorted, 'Come on, Bennie. You need to bowl straighter. I know you can do it. I have seen you do it.'

So it was in August 1980 that Braam de Villiers, after listening to the grievances from his son, contacted Bennie Venter, now a teacher at Volks Hoërskool Heidelberg to make arrangements for Faantjie's entry to the boarding school that is about fifty kilometres southeast of Johannesburg. There had been suggestions at the beginning of the year that Faantjie would go to Volkies, but his father felt it would be better if they stayed together as a family. To send him to Heidelberg after the initial decision was hard on the parents, more so on Braam than Hanna, but their youngest son welcomed the move. It was in his long-term interest and had a direct influence on his future. It came as a relief to leave Fakkel Hoër behind; he had made few friends in what was a cold and discordant environment.

Faantjie had already displayed remarkable ability for one so small and he sustained his enthusiasm for bowling fast: it was what he was best at, and although during his days at Volkies he was considered a javelin thrower of promise, the subsequent back injury forced him to review his options about the sporting career that he would follow.

There was glamour in athletics, and hard work too if you wanted to progress, which he did at provincial and national junior levels for Eastern Transvaal and later Northern Transvaal where he earned a competition medal. It should not come as a surprise that he

established javelin-throwing records. While his m[...]
Tollie Burger, were 'in their day' Free State javel[...]
record-holders (in the early 1950s Tollie was t[...]
champion), Faantjie's athletic abilities came[...]
competitiveness as well as talent in abundance.

At the 1983 South African under-21 athletics cha[...]
Germiston he not only came second in his age gr[...]
briefly held the Northern Transvaal record. It was n[...]
however, without pain and aggravation to the spine i[...] he had
picked up when at Heidelberg Volkshoër. He was already taking
Voltaran (an anti-inflammatory medication athletes use for injuries).
But the fascination of fast bowling with its twin accomplishments
of swing and seam continually captivated his attention; although
to be fair, Faantjie was more interested in bowling fast than studying
the fascinating subjects of seam and swing. That only came much
later, when he attended the fast bowler's course at the national
Plascon Academy at Pretoria University.

In the lazy, quiet days before the gold rush, a German, H.J.
Uekermann, who had been educated at Heidelberg University,
built a trading station below the rocky ridge known as Suikerbosrand.
Its location, at the junction of the wagon trails linking the Free
State and Natal to Transvaal made it an ideal stopover, and by
1865, three years after establishing the station, Uekermann laid
out a town around his store, naming it Heidelberg. Not surprisingly
it became a favourite watering hole during the gold rush on the
Witwatersrand when there were as many as eighteen hotels in the
growing boomtown. With the Blesbok River, a tributary of the Vaal,
close by, it has become a busy modern town with a school that
although not as famous as some, has educated a large number of
academics and the occasional top sportsman since it was founded
in 1915.

Not surprisingly, Faantjie's late admission to Volkies created a
fair amount of interest and speculation among the cricketers after
Bennie Venter made the announcement at the nets two days before
he arrived. Even if he had come in at the start of the second term
it would have been understood. But here it was two weeks into
the fourth term. Anyway, just who the hell is this kid who thinks
he's such a big cricket star?

his size that caught them by surprise. Instead of a ...pping six-footer here was a standard eight pipsqueak who ...eeded to be taught a lesson or two. He can't just walk in and expect a place in the first team. After all, there were procedures that had to be followed. The other masters had to see him before teams for the next matches were announced. Some thought it was quite a cheek that anyone so small could be regarded as an automatic choice for the first team.

During his first night in residence at Concordia House he was knocked unconscious, in his sleep if you please, by another youngster wearing a plaster cast. The next morning he woke up with a blinding headache and a blackened right eye. He knew it was not going to be easy, but he did not expect such aggravation— not so soon after his arrival.

Faantjie, though, was made of tough material and had no fear, nor did he back down when faced with a challenge. Before he knew it, he was forced into a fight with the resident bully. What got up the bully's 'nose' it seemed, was the smart checked shirt and well-pressed longs, the first Faantjie had worn. By the third night after his arrival the heavier, taller and sneeringly confident ruffian and his friends had summoned the towheaded youngster to meet them in the ablution block. Beating up kids half his size was easy enough, so this wouldn't take too long: perhaps five minutes. Little did he know what awaited him.

While at home in Sasolburg, Faantjie and Neels often donned gloves and sparred a few rounds, regarding it as good exercise for body coordination, mental discipline and stamina. It didn't take more than thirty seconds for the 'tough guy' to realize that he had mistaken this adversary. The white-tiled room was packed with standard eight and nine hostel boys who were equally surprised.

As the bully began to lash out with his feet, Faantjie backed off and quietly suggested, '*Komaan, man, hou dit skoon!* (Come on, man, keep it clean)'. The bigger boy tried for a minute to box properly, but he knew he was beaten and had started to fight dirty again when the budding fast bowler gave him a bloodied nose. It brought an abrupt end to the fight and there was a brief handshake with a new respect for Faantjie and embarrassment for the vanquished.

It was a tough if unpleasant initiation, but his fearlessness also established him as someone who, despite his size, was not going to be pushed around. Bennie Venter knew he had someone special when he watched Faantjie in the nets. Unlike those at Fakkel, the Volkies nets received care and attention. Already, along with his pace, Fanie had developed a hint of outswing: not as cunningly disguised as it became in later years, yet good enough to impress the Volkies selectors; it was more than enough to silence his detractors.

Remarkably (or is it?) before the end of the brief season he had earned half colours. His ability to bowl fast, and mostly straight, gave the side extra penetration when they played in the Vaal Triangle zone of the Administrator's Cup, where they reached the quarter-finals. Three years before Fanie's arrival Venter had been successful in coaching the Volkies team that won the Transvaal (cricket) Administrator's Cup and the girls' hockey prize as well. He had similar joint successes when he joined Bergsig in Rustenburg but was unable to win the cricket trophy. Yet, just as it would have been at Fakkel Hoër, the cricket season had barely begun before it was over. Later on, there was the selection for the Vaal Triangle under-15 side and Fanie played in two trial matches.

Yet his talent was not just confined to the sport of flannelled fools. He had developed, for his size and age, into a capable tennis player, which earned him a place in the school's B team as a singles and doubles player and he was then included in the A team.

If 1980 had seen his introduction to Volkies, 1981 was a year of physical and mental development. During this time he often sought advice and motivation from Bennie Venter. His abilities as a fast bowler, first noted at under-13 level, had progressed to the extent that he helped Volkies win the Vaal Triangle high schools competition. He was also awarded with his full colours for consistency and earned a place in the South-Eastern Transvaal side for the first time. While it would not make quite the impact it would have if he had played for one of the bigger schools where competition was far stronger, it helped earn Faantjie further recognition as a gifted teenager with more than one string to his sporting bow. There were no record-breaking performances in his two and a half years at Heidelberg Volkshoër, no startling figures to indicate that here was a budding Test player: just steady progress that went hand in hand with his sense of fun.

His abilities as a tennis player did not surprise the de Villiers clan. It was one of the first sports he remembered playing as his father moved up the education ladder from primary school teacher to vice-principal. Tennis was more than just a sport that involved all members of the family: it was linked to the enjoyment of being out in the open, building eye and muscle coordination as well as developing the body. One of the requirements during the years the de Villiers children were growing up was that the annual summer holiday was at a place where there were tennis courts and a golf course, enabling Fanie to develop his skills in a sports-oriented environment. (Not surprisingly, his golf handicap before the South African selectors called him up was around eleven.)

At Volkies, while there was always an opportunity to play tennis, develop his javelin expertise and improve his skills as a rugby scrum half and centre, he could also work on his bowling technique. He knew he was far from being an expert—his line and direction were at times wayward—yet terrifying to opposition batsmen facing him for the first time. Bennie Venter did what he could to channel young Faantjie's energies along more productive lines. There was little wrong with his outfielding but now for the first time his batting showed improvement. It was always a joke that he would one day score a century or two, even perhaps score several half centuries at first-class level.

By the start of the fourth term in 1981, with full colours beckoning, Bennie Venter and his now sixteen-year-old pupil ironed out a few kinks in his follow-through. It was not a classical run-up and it had its flaws. But the charge to the bowling crease was easy and free-flowing. This may surprise those who have only followed his career since he earned his limited-overs international (half) cap. But early in his provincial career his follow-through was stylish and smooth; really a matter of getting the rhythm and balance right. It was only after he injured his right knee in the late 1980s that his action gradually changed to what it later became, although the balance and rhythm remained.

Those fortunate enough to have seen him bowl over a period of thirteen summers will easily recall the subtle changes in his action. From the time he takes the ball to walk back to his mark, he does it all wrong. It would have the coaching perfectionists shaking their heads and wondering if he was a freak. Instead of turning in from the right, he turns from the left. He also bowls wide out, which is the normal action of an inswing bowler. This is why his late outswing and off-cutters come as a surprise to most batsmen. As for his yorkers, they are part of the craft he has worked on and perfected over the years.

While playing for Sasolburg Town and Sasolburg Hoër had helped bridge the gap between school and club teams, his years at Volkies made him appreciate the advantages of competition with an older peer group. It also enabled him to confidently branch out in other fields to the extent that his athletics career, limping along since his primary school days, blossomed. He achieved a place in the senior squad at the local inter-high meetings and full colours in his last year, along with establishing his reputation by breaking the Eastern Transvaal under-18 javelin record; full colours in what was for a time his second sport, followed.

Bennie Venter, also in his last year at Volkies, Faantjie and the first team's captain Francois van der Merwe, felt they had a good chance of winning the Administrator's Cup that year. It would, the three of them felt, be their own gift to the school. 'We had done particularly well in reaching the semi-finals,' Venter recalled. 'We had beaten a couple of the more fancied teams and Faantjie was bowling particularly well.' But it didn't quite go according to plan. Gymnastics, although not compulsory, was another sport Faantjie enjoyed and during the vault discipline, he came down on his left ankle, spraining it so badly at first that they thought it was broken. He had it strapped tight to allow him to play, but he was restricted in his movements, bowling off only five paces. With their star fast bowler hobbled by the injury, Volkshoër were eliminated to the disappointment of more than just the trio.

Well before his final year ended with him walking away quite easily as Volkshoër sportsman for 1982, he had attracted attention from such top teacher training institutions as Potchefstroom, Goudstad and Pretoria Normaal. Each showed a special interest in him and his talents as an all-round sportsman.

Faantjie had already made his name in Schools' country district cricket tournaments, playing for Vaal Triangle in the annual Triomf Week in 1982 along with Hermanus Viljoen and Francois van der Merwe. It should not come as too much of a surprise that at his third Triomf Week he played against Louis Vorster, who was to later become a teammate at Northern Transvaal. Piet Botha (Transvaal and Border) and Pierre Tullis (Northern Transvaal B and Eastern Province B) played in opposite sides. There was a chance of making the South African Country Districts side for the 1982 Nuffield Week, but the combination of the ankle injury and back problems suffered earlier in the year, when throwing the javelin at a meeting in Meyerton, had curbed his pace and forced him to concentrate more on his batting technique.[4]

From around the middle of 1981 Fanie started to grow: the scrawny Faantjie his family had known for so long became Fanie the all-round sportsman with broader shoulders and longer torso and legs. Four times during the next eighteen months his parents had to outfit him in new clothes. But as the body developed, so did the growing pains, as the extra effort he placed in throwing the javelin increased the strain on the soft tissue of the lower spinal vertebrae. A growing body can only take so much pressure, and in Fanie's case he had pushed it further than he realized.

There was the temptation to do his military service first but he would have been declared medically unfit because of his spinal problem. Getting some form of qualification through a teachers' training college therefore had more appeal.

Why Pretoria? It was a simple case of the financial and sporting benefits at Normaalkollege Pretoria (NKP) being more attractive than those at either Potchefstroom (Neels' seat of tertiary learning), or Goudstad in Johannesburg.

Had he gone to the Western Transvaal town of Potchefstroom there is a chance he would have eventually filtered through the

---

[4] Such back injuries to the lower regions of the spine are not new. A former Free State all-rounder Bradley Player and his provincial fast-bowling colleague Nico Pretorius—both javelin throwers in their schooldays—have had similar injuries, with Player needing a major back operation early in his provincial career.

system. But you can forget provincial honours. Transvaal had their all-conquering 'mean machine' led by Clive Rice and Bacher's Babes (Transvaal B) and, well . . . he would have been just another country lad lost in the 'mighty' Gauteng (then Transvaal) system.

At Goudstad he may have attracted some attention, but again it would have been a forlorn long shot. An annual appearance at the teachers' college week with some success, perhaps followed by an occasional invitation to play in some Transvaal Board XI would have been about as far as he could expect to go. These were token gestures rather than a genuine attempt to select players with a future. Although Louis Vorster and the lanky Piet Botha did get some recognition, this did not necessarily mean that the future Test bowler would have earned similar acknowledgement.

It was not that he was unknown in Johannesburg cricket circles. In the summer holidays Fanie and Neels played a number of games for the Wanderers lower leagues; teams arranged by their ever-thoughtful father to give them extra games in December. It was an experience which in later years could have led Fanie to playing for the famous Johannesburg club. Loyalty has, however, no price tag when it comes to the Fanie de Villiers' of this world.

What finally persuaded Fanie to go to the Jacaranda City was Professor Hennie Maree, the NKP rector, addressing the pupils at Volkies one night. A conservative, austere man by nature, Professor Maree also had some past links with the de Villiers family, which in turn helped smooth the way. But ultimately it was Fanie's exuberant sports talent which was the attraction. It was a move that in the long term he has never regretted. And while phase two of his apprenticeship as a fast bowler had come to an end at Volkshoër, the first part of phase three was not too far off.

On 5 December 1982 he left Volkies and parted company with Bennie Venter, his coach of the past three-and-a-half years. As Venter headed for Bergsig in Rustenburg, Fanie, after Christmas and New Year, prepared for the most important move of his young life. One decision, which had to be made soon, was consulting with an orthopaedic surgeon about the growing back spasms that often made him as stiff as a board. He was even unable to sit too long and watch much of the Currie Cup games on television.

Little did he realize that within ten years not only would he be taking part in those matches, he would also be playing for his country.

A New Image

West of Walker Street, Sunnyside, Pretoria, lies a sports complex that was, for over forty years, the focus of recreational activity at the old Normaalkollege Pretoria. Bordered by Van Boeschoten Avenue to the west and Piet Uys Avenue to the south, this part of the Jacaranda City is steeped in history. A century ago, Sir Henry Rider Haggard, a public servant during the first British occupation of the Transvaal, strolled along well-worn paths in the veld. This is where he developed the plots and characters of colourful adventure stories like *She, Jess, King Solomon's Mines* and *Allan Quartermain*.[1]

On the other side of Van Boeschoten Avenue is Berea Park in a decaying colonial suburb. Once a famous landmark and cricket venue, it is now a dowdy relic that has seen better days, the victim of progress and a long-projected road expansion programme. In Haggard's time, Berea Park was known as the Widow Hoffman's ground, and it was used well before the turn of the nineteenth century for major sports and recreation events.

The fate that has overtaken Berea Park has also left an ugly scar on the NKP sports field: these were two venues where Fanie de Villiers forged his bowling skills during those first few summers in Pretoria. The nets on the eastern side of the NKP ground, where the 'Vinnige Fanie' legend was born, have long been removed.[2]

---

[1] Rider Haggard Street, in close proximity to Berea Park, was named after the author who lived on the street and whose house is now a national monument.

[2] Johan Volschenk, sports editor of a now long-defunct morning paper known as *Oggenblad* ('Morning News') one day needed a catchy

Yet, if you stand and listen long enough, the summer breeze rustling through the heavy foliage stirs the ghosts of conversations from another era. You can almost see Albert Myburgh, who was in charge of NKP cricket, talking to Fred Marner as they welcome new members to the nets.

It is 26 January 1983 and there is a buzz around the place. Lawrence Rowe's rebel West Indians have already been in the country for thirteen days. They have lost to South Africa at Newlands in the first of the four-day pirate tests and there is criticism of Peter Kirsten's captaincy in the Johannesburg papers. Which is nothing new. The argument is that Barry Richards, in the absence of the injured Clive Rice, should take over for the second match to be played at the Wanderers. Far removed from that cauldron of off-the-field intrigue, a young Fanie de Villiers is padding up; his bowling days have, for the moment, been partly curtailed by the back injury received the year before while at Heidelberg Volkshoër.

Across the road at Berea Park, Alan Jordaan is leading the Northern Transvaal B squad in a practice session as they prepare for a Castle Bowl match against Eastern Province B later in the week. Some interesting names in the two sides have been announced earlier in the day: Brett Proctor and Craig Stirk for Northern Transvaal B (now radio and television commentators); in the Eastern Province B ranks were Dave Emslie (now their chief executive officer), Tim Shaw and the Howell twins, Ian (now a first-class umpire) and Dave.

Fanie is unaware of the Berea Park practice session. All he is interested in is the severity of the pain in the lower back when he does get to bowl a few balls and he hopes that Voltaran will take away the persistent pain.

And so to the first game. The students are playing Harlequins B in a Reserve League match, and although Fanie's back pain barely allowed him a handful of overs, he wrecks their first innings. The following Tuesday the *Pretoria News* carried a brief mention of his handiwork: 'New Onderwyskollege fast bowler Fanie de Villiers

---

headline for a story written by a Tubby du Preez and came up with 'Vinnige Fanie' ('Fast Fanie') and the label stuck, adding to the identity of the then twenty-one-year-old NKP fast bowler.

took four wickets in fifteen balls to help the students record a fine win over Harlequins B at NKP.' Just three lines in a weekly column devoted to junior matches, but it is a start. Yet, if he was to progress, Onderwyskollege needed promotion to the Premier League, and at the time, that seemed as far removed as South Africa's hopes of playing official Tests. Not in a month of Sundays would they earn that sort of status.

There were some caustic comments flying around the senior clubs in those days; the East Rand were ever mindful of their shaky position within the Northern Transvaal Cricket Union. You couldn't blame them. It had been some years since they had lost much of their provincial identity, with Pretoria lawyer Werner Barnard hellbent on forming a united body under one banner. It had always been politics: Pretoria against the East Rand with Pretoria dominant; the two had rarely struck an accord on anything. The dissension went so deep that, in the 1950s, catches would be dropped in Currie Cup matches when the bowlers hailed from Springs, Benoni or Boksburg and the fieldsmen from Pretoria. Not until Alan Jordaan was reinstated as captain in the mid-1970s was there genuine accord among players.

If institutions such as NKP, or for that matter Technikon and Police, were to climb out of the trough of the Reserve League and attract a better class of player, they needed to be given a rope to do their climbing.

Unknown to Fanie of course, the Northern Transvaal Cricket Union were investigating a format designed to restructure the senior league system in the province. This would not only overcome the fears and objections of the East Rand clubs, it would give players such as the talented bowler a chance to establish a reputation in a two-tiered system, and give him an opening to a higher level of competition.

Fanie's back problems were becoming a decided burden. And there was an extra challenge—he became involved in NKP athletics, and without so much as a serious practice run, earned a place in the Northern Transvaal team for the under-21 national championships in Germiston.

He was so stressed all the time that he was forced to bowl in shorter spells. To further ease the distress, Fred Marner, the captain, gave him 4-over bursts that often proved to be too much for the opposing teams whose batting capitulated against the raw pace that they rarely encountered at such level. What aggravated the injury was that he was still growing and his bones were still soft. It is a lesson that he has always remembered: in your teenage years you should always pay more attention to your physical strengths and weaknesses.

When in early March Fanie was forced to stop playing and missed the last two games of the 1982-83 season, he reflected on where his career was going. There was the matter of the under-19 javelin event in Germiston. But it didn't require too much detective work to realize that if he was to bowl again without discomfort, or for that matter play any form of sport—competitive or social—he would need a major back operation.

In the waiting room of a medical clinic in the centre of Pretoria Fanie barely glanced at the pile of *Readers' Digests* on the stand. For possibly the only time in his life as he looked at the stark pictures on the wall, he wondered what lay ahead. The old theory that life is a question mark crossed his thoughts more than once that afternoon. He picked up *Huisgenoot* and skipped through the Afrikaans women's magazine, but nothing registered. His mind was on more important matters.

In another room the orthopaedic surgeon, Mornay du Plessis, examined the series of X-rays of Braam de Villiers' youngest son and came to the conclusion that if the talented young sportsman was to have a meaningful sporting career, his three lower vertebrae needed to be fused. It would mean that whatever plans he had to further his athletics career or play a little rugby would be brought to an abrupt end. And while he could play tennis and golf, his chances of playing cricket again would be reduced to learning more about batting techniques than applying his developing bowling skills.

The news was not good. While it was a bad injury, the specialist was confident that since the young man in his consulting room had a strong upper body, he would, in time play sport again. Just how long that would take was up to Fanie de Villiers and his determination. There was no timetable, just a set of exercises once the operation was over. The rest was up to the healing capabilities of the youngster now barely a few weeks out of high school.

A few days after a highly successful javelin event in mid-April, Fanie had the operation. It was calm and warm, a beautiful middelveld autumn day and some of the trees around the campus were already starting to shed their yellowing leaves. When a groggy Fanie awakened a few minutes after being wheeled into the ward, a heavy smell of disinfectant hit his nose.

There is little comfort during the first few days after an orthopaedic operation; those who have hip replacements wonder whether the arthritic pain was preferable to that experienced during those first few days after the operation. These days they have a fine range of drugs that swiftly cure such old curses as osteomyelitis or Perthes' disease; pain is minimal, but there is little you can do about the pain of a back operation. With three vertebrae being fused there was always going to be discomfort. What is surprising is how months later you forget the agony of those few days after the operation. It is better to remember the success than to dwell on the pain as you read a the pile of get-well cards. And Fanie did have quite a few of those to chuckle over.

For the first few weeks after the operation the eighteen-year-old sportsman had to lie on his back in his parents' flat in Gerhard Moerdyk Street, Sunnyside. He would, of course, have preferred to be training in the nets, throwing the javelin, or even playing rugby for his Tugela koshuis. But for the time being, life indoors was bearable. It was a five-minute walk from the college. And his brother Neels was a regular visitor along with a couple of new friends at NKP.

Braam de Villiers had at the beginning of the year been promoted to inspector of schools for handicapped children and was now based in Pretoria. Which was handy as it gave Fanie's mother, Hanna, a chance to keep an eye on her energetic son during those crucial early days after the operation. For a young man like Fanie, who in past years had always been active, the weeks of inactivity became a mental and physical burden and it led a the loss of ten kilograms. This meant that by the time he returned to lectures he was badly in need of a lengthy period of gym work to get fit again. And he knew that was not going to be easy. Sure, the specialist was happy with the success of the operation and his positive attitude, but the next step in his rehabilitation programme needed careful planning. He had to find a gym within walking distance and develop a fitness programme that would not only help him regain the lost kilos but redevelop his muscles.

He found a gym not far from his parents' Sunnyside flat and divided time between his studies and rebuilding his body. It was a solid, steady routine that lasted more than six months. For several hours each day, as had Dennis Lillee, the great, hardbitten Australian fast bowler of another era, he dedicated himself to the programme. Ten years before, Lillee had followed a tough fitness course to overcome the problems of a spinal stress fracture. Fanie de Villiers showed a similar stubborn streak: there was good reason to get fit for next summer. Quiet whispering in the corridors of Northerns cricket suggested to Albert Myburgh that NKP would, along with several other sides, earn senior league status in a twin-tiered system. It was the challenge Fanie and the other students needed.

Some readers will recall Fanie's famous comment after the New Year Sydney Test of 1994, when the South Africans won by a mere five runs. 'You know South Africans, we never give up . . .' he told a media conference at the Sydney Cricket Ground, a venue that has had more than its share of famous victories. In early May 1983, the same indomitable spirit and confidence that had helped him overcome older, stronger children in that 3,000 metres race at Taaibos school all those years before, surfaced again. Not only was he going to get fit and build his strength, but he was also going to become an example others should follow. It would be hard work, but he had never been one to shirk hard physical work.

* * * *

Russell Cobb, a twenty-two-year-old right-hand batsman from Leicestershire, sat in a sleek jetliner that was about to land at Jan Smuts Airport, Pretoria. He had filled out the forms for passport and emigration control as well as customs officials. Looking out of the window to his right he saw a clump of low squat buildings: grey and brooding on a sunny, late-September morning. He was in a strange country, knew no one and wondered what in hell he had let himself in for, so far from the comfort and safety of Leicester.

It might have been better to take a winter job at home instead of coaching perhaps little more than the basics to a bunch of high-spirited

Afrikaans college lads. Negotiations between the college, through the NTCU, and Leicestershire for Cobb's services had been hastily, if amicably arranged. They had come about after the union's decision, announced only weeks before by Professor Willie Basson, the Northern Transvaal president, of the acceptance of the two-tiered league format to be run on parallel lines.

Some sceptics, mainly at the club level, had their doubts whether including such institutions, as NKP and Police, in the system would succeed. It was the view that they were after all essentially Afrikaans-speaking and lacked the sort of cricket culture that Cobb took for granted. It was a decidedly patronizing and racist opinion and carried a stigma, which was later applied to clubs such as Mamelodi and Atteridgeville. So how were they going to learn? There had been few efforts over the years to help bridge the gap and create an awareness about cricket, which is why young Russell Cobb's arrival was eagerly awaited.

As he pushed his luggage trolley through the sliding doors into the international arrivals hall Fred Marner, Marius Delport, Dewald Kruger, Johan Rudolph and Fanie, along with Albert Myburgh, recognized Cobb from conversations with a Leicestershire county official. There were handshakes and smiles and a beaming Fanie took over the luggage trolley.

'Hello, I'm Fanie . . . Ah . . . *baie welkom* to South Africa . . .!'

Fred Marner and the others smiled at the English-Afrikaans mix. Yet they could do little else but follow as Fanie led the way. Marner, Rudolph, Kruger and Delport flanked Myburgh and the slimly built Leicestershire batsman as they walked towards the entrance. If the idea was to make him feel at home they had done a good job.

The image of the serious teenager of the Heidelberg Volkshoër days had been replaced by a more outward-looking personality. It should not surprise anyone that the cheerful mood of the Afrikaans students eliminated whatever apprehensions had bothered Cobb as the jetliner landed. It seemed to the Englishman that he was being welcomed back among old friends, not meeting new ones in a country whose details he barely remembered from his history and geography classes.

It was just what he needed to make him feel at ease on a campus where Afrikaans was the lingua franca. Sure English was occasionally spoken but Fanie and Fred were usually on hand to translate, if and when they were needed, as he settled into hostel life in central Pretoria.

A few hours after Russell Cobb's arrival, another newcomer to the city was attending his first net practice at the Adelaar Club in a north Pretoria suburb. A year older than Cobb, Pat Symcox was taking over from Chris Old as the club's professional. Symcox knew it was not going to be easy. Old, a former Yorkshire captain and England all-rounder, had spent two summers at Adelaar, but the season before had been shabbily treated by Northern Transvaal, playing a handful of one-day games and only two Currie Cup matches. Although at the time the SACU allowed for the use of two overseas professionals, Northerns selectors had preferred his county colleague Phil Carrick as their main overseas professional. Before the summer of 1982-83, the debate among the Northern Transvaal selectors headed by Rodney Falkson was that as there were more than enough fast-medium pace bowlers, Carrick's left-arm spin would be a handy variation. Also for some reason, they ignored the credentials of Willie Morris, the lanky left-arm spinner and handy lower-order batsman, which Carrick was not. But an injury in early December 1982 had forced Morris to miss the second half of the summer. The 1983-84 season was, however, meant to be the start of a new era for Northerns, and among several wide-ranging decisions, apart from the restructured senior league, was one to dispense with the services of a professional player. It was a bold, imaginative step that surprised the more fashionable provinces who during the 1970s and early 1980s dominated the Currie Cup.

Transvaal, for example, had West Indians Sylvester Clarke and Alvin Kallicharran; Eastern Province retained the use of former England XI rebels Wayne Larkins and Peter Willey; Natal had Les Taylor, apart from an ageing Mike Procter and an emerging Robin Smith; and Western Province had Graham Gooch and John Emburey in their ranks. A highly useful group of hired hands: it was the rebel era, and having illustrious names on the books was good for business and brought sponsors. So, what were Northern Transvaal playing at? No professionals! How the others laughed.

Unlike the big four of those years, Northerns were considered the gauche Cinderellas of the A Section and lacked a major sponsor.

So, to boost their playing strength they relied on the pickings available from the South African Defence Force (SADF). With compulsory national service training then requiring trainees to spend a two-year stint in the services, it created a steady supply of sporting talent for the province. The use of SADF players had been one of the cornerstones in the province's motivation in 1979 to earn A Section status after years of languishing in the B Section.

It was into these uncertain waters in 1983-84 that Symcox (then recognized more as a batsman rather than a useful off-spinner) plunged, to swim and survive. He had calculated that his move to Pretoria from the backwater of Griqualand West would help him learn the A Section ropes. It was, he felt, a good career move. But, it was hardly as simple as that. Apart from the selectors he also had to impress John Reid and the provincial captain Lee Barnard. Reid, a highly successful former New Zealand captain, had been appointed in 1982-83 as Northerns' coach and manager for a three-season stint. Barnard, who had regularly led Transvaal B in the past, had been made captain several weeks before Reid's position was confirmed.

Later, when the Currie Cup results were not upto expectations and the Nissan Shield limited-overs series failed to go according to plans, some Northern Transvaal executive members privately expressed concern whether they had made the right choices. It was the old Northern Transvaal mentality among the clubs (and the public). They expected immediate results without consulting their own long-term planning manifesto.

As Symcox was to discover later in his first season, the Northerns side was starting to split into two camps which lasted for eight seasons: one was known as the Wanderers Club with Barnard, Noel Day and Gordon McMillan as founder members; the other was the Local Connection made up of Willie Morris, Anton Ferreira, Paul Robinson, Vernon du Preez, Eugene Klopper and later Fanie, Gerbrand Grobler, Symcox and Anton Geringer. In later years, players like Mandy Yachad, Steve Elworthy and Kevin Rule were seen as part of the Local Connection. Membership always varied, but largely it was an 'us' and 'them' situation. In those first three years, John Reid was a fringe member of both groups, with leanings toward the Wanderers Club. Batsman Kevin Verdoorn sat on the cross benches.

While selection policy of the A Section side now rested with Alan Jordaan (the new convener) and the four other members of the panel, there were other considerations. Reid's views, because of his international background, were respected. While he had a vote, Barnard, the captain, was an ad-hoc non-voting member— the sixth voice on the panel. It was a fact of life involving in-house politics, as Fanie discovered in the first months of his provincial career.

No wonder Symcox, a hard-hitting batsman who scored more than 500 runs in club matches in the first half of that 1983-84 season was puzzled by selection policy tactics, especially in the day-night series matches. In those early years of limited-overs games, the plan was to accelerate the scoring rate after the first twenty overs, while remaining mindful, of course that the run rate should not, if possible, fall below three an over in the earlier stages.

In his own way Symcox was a pioneer of fast scoring rates. He gave any number of exhibitions of how to accelerate the run rate during limited-overs league matches run by the province in that season. To Symcox the answer was a matter of hitting the ball over the top of the inner ring. For those who query the tactics when Symcox went in at three for South Africa in the Pepsi Cup tournament in Sharjah in 1994 and months later in the Titan Cup in India, look where he batted for Northern Transvaal B that first summer. He opened the innings in three games, and was often the highest-scorer but was ignored by the selectors when it came to the senior squad.

As Pat Symcox and Russell Cobb settled into their new environments, Reid, Barnard and other senior members of the Northern Transvaal senior squad were deep in discussion and looking over the programme for the new season. Barnard, in his second summer as captain, was quick to pick up on how, because of the second rebel tour by Lawrence Rowe's West Indians, there were fewer first-class matches than usual.

It was then Reid's turn to express his views. Rarely one to waste time on words in his playing days, Reid, as the team's manager/coach spelt out the harsh realities of the months ahead. As New Zealand's captain, he had often needed to rescue the side from lost causes at Test level. And he was not prepared to spend time nursing another team through a wasted summer. Looking around the changing room that Tuesday afternoon at the impressive and expansive sports facilities at Pretoria University, the message he conveyed to Barnard and the rest of the squad was effective. Northerns, he advised them, were in the second phase of a team rebuilding programme. This meant there would be no overseas professional. And as there were only four Currie Cup games, along with the usual limited-overs fare, it would require more than just hard work and the slices of luck needed to reach the semi-finals in any of the three competitions. 'It is going to be a tougher summer than you think. But that is the way it is going to be if you want to become winners,' he told the players.

Barnard was heavily involved in rugby commitments and did not attend too many of the pre-season practice sessions, but he had long been made aware of the set up. Also, there were a number of exciting new players in the defence force. Mandy Yachad was still in his first year while Francois Weideman and Dave Richardson had arrived mid-term, along with Eugene Klopper, a local product who had gone to Stellenbosch University. Klopper, like Weideman, was Afrikaans-speaking, and soon to be joined by Gerbrand Grobler, yet another exciting Afrikaans talent. If with this one included Corrie van Zyl, who along with Grobler and Kepler Wessels studied at that top Free State school, Grey College, it became evident that the modern Afrikaans pathfinders of cricket were emerging.

Reid, however, was at that early stage more interested in closely examining his bowling options than the question of language. That would come later. But as the manager and coach he used his knowledge and knowhow of South African conditions to his team's advantage. On occasions when he was overruled on selection policy, he might have privately grumbled; and was often proved right. As the first-class programme in 1983-84 would run to no more than seven matches, if they reached the Currie Cup final, it made sense to build bowling success around a pace and seam attack. Reid, a willing party to the plan to ditch the role of the overseas professional and replace him with the 'local is *lekker*' ('local is nicer') policy, felt that Northerns had the bowlers to do the job he wanted.

Anton Ferreira, another local product, who had been an all-rounder on the staff of English county Warwickshire since 1978, was the solid foundation stone to this plan. Part of the scheme would be to alter the character of the pitches at Berea Park. It was a narrow table, carrying no more than three or four pitches and a change of top-dressing pre-season was needed to successfully accomplish such a revolutionary step. But, with the changes at club level, the more pronounced phases of the team rebuilding plans were slowly taking place. Later it was seen that the Berea Park pitch experiment did not always work in Northerns' favour. For one thing, the bounce was often irregular and led to complaints by the batsmen.

As for spinners, there was Willie Morris and little else in the cupboard. Barnard had always fancied himself as more than a mere spare-parts off-spinner. Thus, there would be no place for Symcox in the senior squad. By the time Symcox established his credentials, the first-class season was almost over. To be fair to Barnard, the Northerns captain did not bowl a lot that summer. But neither did the selectors appear interested in Symcox as a future prospect.

It was a less complicated issue for Fanie de Villiers. All he wanted to do was to get fit and bowl, terrify the others in the nets with his pace and show the rest of the Northern Transvaal senior cricket world what bowling fast was all about.

He did have a reputation to protect, even if it was one gained only at high school level. Several years before, during the brief October holiday break a group of schoolboys from Western Transvaal were in Nelspruit in what was the Eastern Transvaal lowveld. They had a day off from an Administrator's Cup regional tournament and were holding a vleisbraai on a riverbank. Louis Vorster, a talented left-hand batsman, and other members of the team spotted a much younger boy fishing. Next to him were a bat and a ball. It would be easier, they decided, to borrow his gear than spend half an hour going to get their own.

'Not a problem at all,' said the youngster when asked if they could use his playing gear.

'Just tell us when you need it again,' Vorster told him.

The youngster carried on fishing, but without luck. He was patient. Flicking the line into the water and sitting quite alone on the riverbank. When it was time to go, he packed away his rod, collected his bat and ball from the other boys and headed for Nelspruit.

Four days later the cocky Western Transvaal guys, having won the toss, decided to bat first on a pitch that looked to be flat. After all, they were a particularly strong batting side. And there marking out his run to bowl the first over was the young fisherman. Their first mistake was to look on him as a primary school boy. Their second was, because of his size, to underrate his pace. The fisherman who had been generous earlier in the week was not so generous now. Many were ruefully rubbing their bruised ribs that night, too embarrassed to show their team members.

It was a late mid-week afternoon when Cobb was introduced to the local media. After all, a young Englishman coaching a group of mainly Afrikaans-speaking students in Pretoria, was not your everyday occurance. No doubt that was the reason for two news reporters from the Afrikaans afternoon paper, *Transvaler*, treating it like a sideshow. But if they thought they were going to get a good laugh by soliciting a clumsy phrase or two from the young batsman they were in for a nasty surprise. Cobb was far too polite to embarrass his hosts by showing up the ill-mannered Afrikaans reporters. When they left, they were highly peeved about how their scheme had backfired.

It had come to their attention that only a couple of days earlier Russell Cobb had addressed the college assembly in Afrikaans, an action applauded by many. Yet it had really been a simple matter. The night before, in Fanie's hostel room, they had sat down and carefully gone over what Cobb wanted to say. He selected four sentences and wrote them down phonetically as Fanie slowly went over the words in Afrikaans.

The young Pommie was an instant hit with the Pretoria Onderwyskollege students. It was a sign of respect for their language, and they genuinely appreciated that he had at least made the effort. For a majority of students the only English they usually heard would be either on television or at the cinema, which meant that they were often too shy to grapple with its semantics. Cobb's show of respect for the Afrikaans language brought him any number of friends among the small cricket family at the college.

Yet his real work was still ahead of him.

Fanie saw nothing wrong in developing a close working relationship with the coach. While he was not yet ready to bowl, and missed the first couple of matches in the bottom-tiered Epsilon League because he still needed to build his upper body, he trained in the nets. And when he did play, he was quickly among the runs, batting at five, and occasionally six, in the order. Not surprisingly Cobb scored 508 runs at an impressive average of 127.00 that first season. He was far too experienced for the bowling in the league, and along with Symcox, cornered a few headlines. Fanie's own progress was, at the start, static. He introduced the young coach to his training programme and together they worked hard at developing Fanie's back and shoulder muscles.

Fanie knew he was a good enough middle-order batsman to keep his place, and he had always fancied himself as a batsman. He even felt he had enough talent to qualify for the Sir Richard Hadlee school of all-rounders. Unfortunately he was rarely given a chance to put this theory on trial outside his NKP days when, with Cobb's help along with that of Fred Marner and Johan Rudolph, he was allowed to indulge in his batting fantasy. He could give the ball a good thump too, when it was needed; he enjoyed doing that.

* * * *

It was stifling. Not even a light breeze to stir the leaves, or hurry along a few wispy clouds. It was the second week of December 1983, not too long before Christmas, and Fanie had a few days with Mom, Dad and Neels. Perhaps they would go fishing. Perhaps a game or two of golf. Even tennis, as the back fully recovered.

Dr Mornay du Plessis, pleased with Fanie's progress had okayed a full return to fast bowling in the nets; or to throwing the javelin if he wished. But Fanie's success as a batsman in the Epsilon League also meant that Marner and Cobb would allow him to keep his number five spot in the NKP side at the South African College Week. Fanie of course would tell anyone within hearing distance that he 'really felt most comfortable batting at five'. He wasn't going to change. Something to tell the family about. Batting at five. And at the famous Wanderers.

It is not the first time he has played at the Wanderers, but it is the first time he has had time to look around the grounds. After all, he was only a schoolboy when he played for the club while home for weekends from Heidelberg Volkshoër.

Fanie is enjoying the walk around the boundary at Oval 2 where NKP are playing Potchefstroom. At Oval 3, Johannesburg College of Education are ladling out the punishment to the side from Durban. No wonder. Brian McMillan and Mike Rindel are putting the bowling attack through the mincer. Rindel, the busy left-hander with a style and run-making magic of his own, has already attracted the Transvaal selectors' attention. McMillan will have to wait another twelve months. But his name has also been noted.

There's quite a commotion at Oval 3. The Rindel-McMillan partnership is nearing 100 which is good for that level of competition. Yet how often do you get future provincial players, let alone international caps, in action at the SA College Week? Precious few. Fanie, leaning over the fence looking at the batsmen scampering up and down, sees what appears to be a white cottage above Oval 3.

Fred Marner tells Fanie 'That is Charles Fortune's office', when he asks about the building.

'The radio commentator?' is the surprised query.

'He is also secretary of the SACU. Only he's not there today.'

But that is not a problem for Fanie. He walks over to the building, a quarter of the size the UCB offices are today, knocks on the door and is met by Eileen Ambler-Smith.

'Hello, Tannie, I'm Fanie . . . Fanie de Villiers and we're playing down the road. I just wanted to have a look at the place.'

'Come in then, Fanie. Anything special you want to see?'

He looks around, confronted by photographs of old South African teams, some dating back to the previous century, adorning the white walls. So this is it, the core of South African cricket. Not the Wanderers Stadium, or Newlands, or even down-at-heel Berea Park. *This is the place!*

Fanie shakes his head. 'No thanks, Tannie. This is fine. I'll just have a look at these photos.'

Mrs Ambler-Smith, an indispensable private secretary to a succession of SACA, SACU and UCB administrative secretaries and managing directors for more than forty years, has seen young players come and go. But rarely one who spoke Afrikaans. She watches young Fanie: a nineteen-year-old stripling, eager to see the photos of past national teams, his questioning blue eyes noticing the changes and style in dress. Outside, Rindel and McMillan have lost their wickets during the final overs of the innings when that last turbo surge for runs becomes all-important.

Inside the white building, it is like a sanctuary, something special.

As he turns to go Fanie gives a big smile. '*Baie dankie*, Tannie.'

Two days later he is in the building again, this time talking to Charles Fortune. Speaking his best English he finds himself discussing the importance of the Week and how teachers can play a long-term role by producing new players. Before he leaves, Fortune goes into a storeroom and returns with two ties, giving both to Fanie. The first is an original Datsun Shield tie; the second is the one to celebrate the seventy-fifth anniversary of the SACA. It is green with narrow yellow stripes and the seventy-five is in roman numerals.

Little did he know then that in the not-too-distant future Fanie de Villiers would not only get to know Mrs Ambler-Smith better, but also play a small role in the fledgling development programme.

5

Fanie Who . . .?

On a sun-baked mid-November afternoon Fanie de Villiers is doing his best to convince two very important people that he really *can* bowl fast. He has been at it for more than half-an-hour as John Reid and Lee Barnard take a close look at the sweating twenty-year-old college student, straining to get extra pace out of the sluggish pitch and force the batsman into making a few mistakes. Which is not easy on a surface where the ball is doing nothing. But facing him during this trying spell have been both opening batsmen: first Vernon du Preez and now Roy Pienaar, Northern Transvaal's latest recruit. Stylish and fluent in his strokeplay, Pienaar enjoyed hitting on the up. On this pitch he was quick to pick up the line and was rarely harried by the pace.

Of course Reid and Barnard had heard of Fanie de Villiers. Five wickets for Northern Transvaal B against Natal B in a Castle Bowl match. That was two weeks ago, on his debut. One newspaper report proclaimed it was a belated twenty-first birthday present. Another boldly suggested, 'Fanie de Villiers is another Afrikaans fast-bowling hero . . .' Yet another, the *Pretoria News,* suggested that Northerns had unearthed a new star: 'Just how they missed debutant Fanie de Villiers' sharper pace in the first innings became all too evident yesterday. With his right ankle strapped, the powerful youngster bounced back to take 5 for 33 in a 17-over spell. We saw Natal B sliding from 106 for 2 to 144 for 7 . . . There is no mistaking the quality of his performance, or the feeling [that] we have found a special new fast bowler. Perhaps not one of our own, but one we should encourage to think this way.'

It was described as typical sensational reporting.

Reid, the coach, and Barnard, the captain, were unconvinced that 'Vinnige Fanie' as he had been labelled in the Pretoria Afrikaans press, could help solve the lack of penetration in the Northerns bowling attack that 1985-86 season.

This was the first time they had *really* noticed (as opposed to seeing) him up close. And while they could not but help see he was fast, he was to them, well . . . all tearaway action. Nothing special at all. Just the impatience of youth out to impress his elders. He still had to qualify for his L plates as a bowler.

Certainly *no* replacement for Eric Simons. But was not this the real issue? Finding someone to replace Eric Simons? The fast-bowling hero of the previous season? The national serviceman from Cape Town who, at the same age as Fanie de Villiers, did much to bowl Northerns into two finals the summer before?

In three hours' time Alan Jordaan, a former provincial captain and NTCU board vice-president, would convene a meeting of the provincial selectors at Memorial Park (CBC Old Boys). It was a meeting where Jordaan had earlier told Reid and Barnard the name of Fanie de Villiers would, among other matters, come up for discussion. As it is, Jordaan had only twenty-four hours earlier sat in the Northerns dressing room at Berea Park with Reid and Barnard during a team discussion of the unpleasant debris of the Currie Cup defeat against Border. He had said little as the coach and captain listed as one of their main problems the lack of a bowler to take over from Simons, who was now back with Western Province. The irony of the meeting at Memorial Park was that it was about selecting the team to play a Western Province side that now included Simons.

Jordaan and the rest of the selectors, which also included Reid, knew Northern Transvaal's problem areas all too well. Two of the players around whom most of the success of the 1984-85 season revolved had returned home. Simons with an impressive strike rate of a wicket every 5.3 overs, had taken a record Currie Cup haul of 51 wickets (at 14.25) by a Northerns bowler in the A Section. Mandy Yachad, opening the batting, had matured as a batsman: he scored a record 751 runs in 20 innings, breaking Jimmy Pickerill's thirty-three-year-old record of scoring the most runs in a season.

Northerns had played in two finals against Transvaal and lost both but the team had a season that shocked other provinces; without an overseas professional, they were initially, not taken seriously but they had found the hunger to win games. What they lacked was the experience of playing finals.

To a large extent Pienaar's arrival, as a prelude to a two-year national service spell, had offset the loss of Yachad. But Cyril Mitchley junior, although a willing new-ball bowler, did not have the ability to swing the ball quite as much as Simons.

There were also other areas of concern. A series of serious injuries caused a major run on the team's fast-bowling resources: Gerbrand Grobler's foot injury had not, as Reid had expected, healed. The colourful left-arm fast bowler with the Grey College and South African Schools backgrounds felt he was partly to blame for the defeat against Border by 2 wickets. It was a harsh assumption by the young man but he was trying to be honest with himself and his teammates. Two weeks before the Border game, Grobler had bowled with impressive hostility against Natal at Kingsmead before limping off after 14 overs in the first innings of the drawn match.

Mainly to blame for the unfortunate injury was the quality of the boots Grobler used that season. After about the twelfth over, one of the studs in the right boot had been pushed through the thin sole of the boot with the force of his delivery stride pounding the foot hard on the surface. Two overs later the left-arm bowler quit in agony. Francois Weideman replaced him for the first-leg semi-final Nissan Shield match against Transvaal at Berea Park. There was another five days rest before the Border match. But Reid needed an answer about his fitness—whether to keep Weideman on standby, just in case. After a tough fitness test, Grobler declared he was ready to play the Currie Cup game against the newly promoted Border.

For Grobler there was the added challenge later in the month of playing against Kim Hughes' Australian team in the limited-overs day-night match. It was known that a couple of the national selectors would be present, but more as a reconnoitring mission of the rebel tourists than to check out any of the Northerns players. But Grobler felt that the gamble of playing in the Border match at Berea Park was worth the risks involved.

When Lee Barnard declared Northerns' second innings closed at 219 for 5 he had allowed his bowlers six hours, or about 90 overs, to dismiss the former B Section team. As they needed to score a record fourth innings Currie Cup total of 310 runs for victory, at almost 3.5 runs an over, it was acknowledged to be a stiff target. At 220 for 7 with overs in hand Border were still 90 runs short of causing an upset. Mike Clare and Cyril Mitchley junior were expected to wrap up the bottom end of the innings; only that old batting war horse, Lorrie Wilmot, coerced out of retirement for that summer to lend experience to the Border batting, proved to be the rock on which Northerns' hopes agonizingly foundered.

Earlier in the afternoon Wilmot had retired hurt, his face a bloodied mess. The forty-two-year-old veteran miscued a pull off a lifting ball from Clare into his face, splitting open the left side from the eyebrow to below the cheekbone. Rushed to the emergency section of a nearby medical clinic he was not expected to bat again. His departure saw Greg Hayes and Tommy Ballentyne put together a partnership of some substance while Barnard gambled with an attacking field: the plan being for both batsmen to give the slips a little catching practice. And all the time he was unable to call on Grobler. The well-muscled left-arm fast-bowling weapon was off the field nursing the recurring foot injury. Although his 10 overs were expensive, so was the missed catch off his bowling when Ian Howell was dropped in the gully before putting a run on the board.

Eventually, when Ballentyne lost his wicket, the seventh to fall, caught by Barnard off Rodney Ontong, a brave Wilmot reappeared. Apart from the twenty-three stitches needed to bind the wound, his face was heavily bandaged and he could only see out of his right eye. It was a time when the penetration Simons had added to the Northerns bowling the previous summer was sorely needed; only, the bowler who Reid and Barnard expected to do the job, Grobler, had damaged the bruised left foot again and sat frustrated watching Hayes move towards an effective century.

Then midway into the last 20 overs Ontong, bowling off-spin from the Fountains end, induced the Border batsman to give Noel Day a catch 8 runs short of the three-figure mark. It swung the game again on its tight axis. With 20 runs required, Tommy Ball joined Wilmot on the crease.

Usually, whenever Ball went out to bat in East London it was a signal to the groundstaff to start up the roller and wait for the inevitable end of the innings.

Yet, with careful manipulation of the strike, Wilmot won the match; the miracle had been achieved. For after Ball only an injured James Carse, waiting to bat with a runner, remained. So near yet so far: both Wilmot and Ball gave catches which were dropped. Ball, with 11 runs remaining, and Wilmot off what was the last ball of the match when third slip grassed a sharp chance off Mitchley junior that raced through for the winning boundary.

Grobler, who was to have taken over Simons' role as the destroyer of partnerships, limped into the dressing room with the other shell-shocked members of the side; inside, the atmosphere was oppressive as the door closed on the rowdy celebrations in the Border changing room next door.

A game Northerns should have won had been lost and the embarrassing post mortems began. Forget the four dropped catches in the final two sessions (Ballentyne was missed twice in successive overs off Anton Ferreira's bowling). It was all part of the agony, and the expectations at tea, of an extra 10 points.

Against this background Jordaan and other selectors, Mike de Villiers, Sid Dugmore and Reid, felt added pressure to find a permanent answer, if possible, to the gap left by Simons. But it was just not on. Reid admitted as much in confidence a week later, minutes after the Western Province match ended in a draw. Also, the former New Zealand captain felt let down by Grobler. He had expected so much from the ever-willing bowler. And the defeat by Border, with two lesser West Indians in their ranks and a bowling attack of little account, rankled. Not for the first time did he wonder whether the Afrikaans psyche had any understanding of such a technique-orientated game.

There are those who would view such a comment as a sign of unaccountable arrogance that does not belong in the game: not with players such as Kepler Wessels and Corrie van Zyl, who through their performances were ideal role models for future Afrikaans-speaking generations re-learning the game's attraction. Yet, to be fair to Reid, it was a careless comment, born out of frustration and without any racial undertones. It should be remembered that he viewed the game from the lofty heights of a world-class Test all-rounder, who set such high levels that few could match them.

Fanie de Villiers was yet another Afrikaner: a raw, young fast bowler trying to impress an old professional like Reid. It was not going to be easy. And Fanie also had to get past Lee Barnard, the captain. Was an hour's bowling spell in the nets at L.C. de Villiers Oval enough to earn him a place in the final twelve? Already the *Pretoria News* and *Beeld* had commented that 'Fanie de Villiers has done enough to warrant serious consideration by Alan Jordaan's selection panel for inclusion' in the team to play Western Province at Berea Park. But Reid was having none of it. For only the second time in their long association did the two New Zealanders have a disagreement.

'You're becoming too pushy with this new superstar of yours,' he growled when Chesters turned up at the nets with a photographer. 'I've been reading the headlines . . . But I haven't even seen him play. Neither has Lee. You're putting unfair pressure on us.'

'But his record . . .'

'I'm the manager and the coach, and don't you forget it, my friend. And tell that to others [press] as well.'

He wagged a schoolmaster's finger.

Something had upset him and it was not the story. But there was no use arguing. John 'Bogo' Reid was not only a shrewd coach. He was quick to spot a flaw in a player's technique; he was also quick to snuff out trouble in the camp. In his first season as manager/coach of Northerns in 1982-83, he won a serious joust in matter of team discipline with former England one-day cap Graham Stevenson, who was known to be a loud mouth. The Yorkshire all-rounder was then playing for Oostelike (Easterns), one of the leading clubs in the Northern Transvaal leagues, and had been selected against Reid's better judgement for a day-night match early that season. Apart from a series of financial demands he was generally disruptive along with threatening a player walkout if demands were not met.

'Well, you can pack your kit and go,' Reid told him.

'Like 'ell. You're not 't selection convener or 't bloody chairman . . .,' Stevenson snarled in broad Yorkshire vernacular. 'I'll be doin' nowt.'

'We'll see about that . . . I'm the boss in this dressing room and in the nets. So, if you don't pack and go, I'll do it for you. I'm not going to have you in my team. And that's *final.*'

It was an incident that those who were present have not forgotten. What Stevenson and the rest of the squad did not know was that Reid had the support of the Northern Transvaal executive when it came to team discipline and rooting out troublemakers.

Oh yes. John Reid could be tough when he wanted. He could also be sympathetic and understanding. Earn his confidence and keep his trust and he was a good friend, even if you crossed verbal swords on rare occasions. At the nets at L.C. de Villiers Oval that afternoon he was, however, in no mood to hear another point of view.

The CBC Old Boys Club at Memorial Park in Groenkloof had for some time been the meeting place of the Northern Transvaal senior selection panel. On the night of 12 November 1985, Chesters sat in the bar with three members of the senior provincial side— Noel Day, Kevin Verdoorn and Cyril Mitchley—along with Lance Coetzee, the B team captain, Pat Symcox and young Fanie. Outside lurked a woman photographer from *Beeld*, who had come to take a picture of Fanie if he made the side.

Day and Verdoorn soon departed. They knew their places were safe. After all, they were members of the Wanderers Club and had only called in at Memorial Park after the provincial nets to talk briefly with a club member about a weekend fixture matter.

Off to the right, in a far corner of the lounge, Alan Jordaan sat with the rest of the selection panel and Lee Barnard, who was still an ad-hoc member. Usually the selectors gave Reid and Barnard the sides they wanted, but asked questions when it was needed. Occasionally there were discussions about the form of promising B team players or those in the Omicron League (the Premier League) and on the fringes of both sides. It was shortly after 7 p.m. when Reid confirmed Jordaan's comment that the news on the injury front was not good. Francois Weideman's elbow had not responded to treatment; Grobler, despite the Border game fiasco, would probably be fit to play against Western Province; Eugene Klopper had picked up a shoulder injury apart from a major business commitment, and Mike Clare's form was a worrying factor.

As the B team were not playing, Gerald Ackermann and Jan van Duyker (or Jack Daniels as he was also known) could be considered. The doubts were only about Ackermann. He was injured for the B team game in which Fanie made his debut, and despite exposure over the last two seasons, he had failed to establish himself. There were also serious doubts about van Duyker's action. South African umpires were, for some reason, reluctant to call a bowler. It could be that they couldn't pick the dubious delivery, which was usually the faster ball.

Now Fanie de Villiers' name emerged as Mike de Villiers, supported by Dugmore and Jordaan, offered him as a strong contender for a place in the side. Apart from that afternoon's spell in the nets neither Reid nor Barnard had seen him in action. After all, he played for NKP who were in the Epsilon League, the lower tier of the senior league structure. So it was a bit unfair to expect them to make a snap decision on the evidence of a sixty-minute workout. What was he like under pressure? Could be bowl a long spell? How was his accuracy and his economy rate?

They had spoken to Vernon du Preez and Roy Pienaar and their reactions had been mixed. Yes, he was fast all right, but that was not the issue. It was a question of experience. And Western Province had a strong side: Peter Kirsten, Kenny McEwan, wonder boy Daryll Cullinan, Adrian Kuiper. Now Northerns was expected to field a 'new wonder boy'. The idea was to win matches to reach the Castle Currie Cup semi-finals, not to lose them.

They admitted that 5 wickets against Natal B in a Castle Bowl game were fair credentials.

But were they enough? And who of note was in that Natal B side? Andrew Hudson, Mike Mellor, Kevin Dawson, Claude Lister-James, Kenny Cooper. Not much class batting there; perhaps Mellor and Dawson, but forget the rest. (It had been Hudson's first-class debut.)

Lance Coetzee was called in for his views. He was asked a few questions by Reid and Barnard, and left after five minutes. 'Fanie? Yes, he's a good bowler. A bit rough about the edges, perhaps, but the talent is there. With the right approach he'll go a long way. Yes, I like him. He's a hard worker and makes honest efforts. He also has a refreshing attitude.'

There had been long-term plans for Coetzee to become captain of the Currie Cup side, but as he was more interested in qualifying as a medical specialist, the captaincy plan was quietly shelved.

Now he had been appointed as the B team captain for this one season and was doing a solid job.

The selectors continued their discussions. A side that should have taken thirty minutes at most to finalize was still under review.

* * * *

One of the flaws in the twin-tiered senior league system had been exposed. Because of the demands of the provincial side Reid and Barnard had been away almost seventy per cent of the season, and because there was a rebel tour, the programme was off to an early start. The first round Nissan Shield game against Free State, who like Border were also promoted from the B Section, was to be played in the third week of October. The Currie Cup season was to open against Natal at Kingsmead. There was barely enough time to sort out any new talent from the leagues. What was being seen would be noted and passed on by Jordaan, Mike de Villiers or Dugmore. Yet it surprised Jordaan and the other selectors as they sat around the low table in the corner of the lounge that Reid and Barnard could not recall too much about Fanie from the previous season's discussions on promising young players.

Apart from causing a stir by taking 27 wickets in his last five club matches Fanie was, in mid-February 1984, rewarded for his efforts with the twelfth man berth for the B side. As it turned out, the appointment was mere crumbs from the table. Yet, in what had been a mediocre season for the B team, it was surprising that the selectors, for the final Castle Bowl game of 1984-85, did not feel that Fanie should be making his debut.

The match was against Western Province B at Berea Park. The general idea was to give him a taste of what to expect the next summer. Pat Symcox was the other Epsilon League player in the B side, but he had a proven first-class record when he arrived in Northerns. Better to stick to the tried and trusted routine. Likeable Gerald Ackermann took 12 wickets in the game, which the selectors felt, proved their point. And as Eugene Klopper and Jan van Duyker were available there was no need for a fourth new-ball bowler in the side. Next season perhaps.

Northerns B had squeezed out a victory by 8 runs, with Ackermann taking 7 wickets for 69 during a protracted spell in the

Western Province B second innings. Symcox, after some disappointment as a batsman that summer, had scores of 63 and 43 and the selectors all made a careful note of that performance. More interesting perhaps is that Craig Matthews was the Western Province B twelfth man at Berea Park, also along for the experience.

While Reid and Barnard had become aware of Fanie in August and September during the 1985-86 pre-season training programme at L. C. de Villiers Oval, their limited knowledge of his bowling ability came from information filtered through by Sid Dugmore and Mike de Villiers; and all of it from the summer before. The two selectors had kept an eye on, and presented a low profile, at a few Epsilon League games in 1984-85. Fanie's bowling success in February and March 1984 were also noted in the *Pretoria News* and *Beeld:* 11 wickets for 190 runs at 17.27 were solid enough in terms of a comeback effort. But as Russell Cobb pointed out, the economy rate of 2.28 an over was impressive, considering the young man had only been bowling in the nets a few weeks before the South African College Week at the Wanderers.

When Fanie had started bowling again in the nets, Cobb took a long look at the whipcord action and noticed the position from where he bowled. The idea then occurred to the young Englishman, who now carried the nickname *Soutie,* that to be more effective Fanie should bowl closer to the stumps.[1] They had spent time discussing the problem on fishing trips to Hartbeespoort Dam, half-an-hour's drive from the college. And while it was all very well discussing the theory of the problem, in practice it was not so simple. He wasn't going to change his action for anyone. Not now.

If he had known it then, Fanie would have pointed to the action of the great West Indian, Malcolm Marshall.

'What about that, then?' he might have asked, his sharp blue eyes as penetrative as a yorker.

Marshall, a tough competitor, a quality player and a thoughtfully pleasant Bajan, had an action that defied all the coaching theories.

---

[1] 'Soutie' is an Afrikaans term for British or English-speaking people, said to have come from the use of salted beef by the British troops during the first Anglo-Boer War and normally refers to anything of a British nature.

Yet he swung the ball sharply, and at the sort of velocity Mike Procter generated. The mention of Procter also invokes memories of an action that defied those who believed that pure-bred fast bowlers must always be side on.[2] Forgetting, of course, how stress on the weaker parts of the back, knees or ankles can create added problems.

There are also those who mistakenly looked on Fanie as a product of a Northern Transvaal club system that merged the open clubs as well as the tertiary and services institutions, such as the old SADF, and the Police and Correctional Services, into a strong league. While that may be true of some players, Fanie de Villiers was different. He was special. A young man with a genuine mission.

Politically, Willie Basson's NTCU executive needed someone to come out of the Epsilon League to prove, mainly to the doubting East Rand clubs, that the twin-tiered system would be a success. There was just one flaw in the system: there was only one Fanie de Villiers. Janie Groenewald and Morné Ferreira, also at NKP, were only identified after 'Vinnige Fanie' had blazed his own pioneering path.

When the two-tiered plan was first advocated and sold to institutions such as NKP, the rector, Professor Hennie Maree, felt it would help attract promising Afrikaans-speaking cricketers to the college, and give it a new image in a sport that for years had received little encouragement. For this reason money was made available, with some help from the NTCU, to bring out an English coach, who would also play for the side. All part of the cricket culture plan among Afrikaners.

Yet, other hidden factors hindered the development of the available talent in the Afrikaans institutions of what was then Transvaal, from the early 1950s until the 1980s. One of the problems faced by sports administrators at an institution such as NKP Pretoria was the way politics was used to work out budget requirements. Sports bursaries were readily available for athletics and rugby, and money was lavished on these facilities. It was a well-catered gravy train that squeezed the budget orange until there was little juice left for anyone else. There were certainly no

---

[2] An all-rounder with a world-class reputation, Mike Procter played for and captained Gloucestershire in a long county career from 1968 until 1984.

fancy bursaries for other sports. If cricket desired one, they could organize it themselves. Even rugby, to an extent, took a backseat as the sports bureau cultivated the image of being a recruiting body for top athletes. And Henry and Bessie Windell earned the institution an enviable reputation, from the 1970s through to the early 1990s, of being a leader in South African athletics. It was the sort of fame that the rector, Professor Hennie Maree, jealously guarded. Along with the Windells, of course. Naturally, the bigger the athletics budget, the more record holders and national champions there would be to show off. It was an iniquitous system favouring a pampered, privileged group, who regarded themselves an elite class enjoying the privileges of the Pretoria NKP athletics section.

It is easy to understand, then, the frustrations of Fanie and other members of the NKP cricket side regarding the overbearing attitude of sports bureau officials in the late 1980s. A request for R200 to buy a set of T-shirts for the team to wear at the annual South African College Week was laughed off as other bureau staff sniggered behind a set of bulging files marked 'tracksuit sizes for athletes'. All that the players wanted was some informal identity as a team. To show that they were proud of their institution. Fanie, Johan Rudolph and the cricket organizer, Doupie Calitz, among others, were forced to arrange their own sponsorship for the T-shirts. It was early December. Christmas was not too far off. They did get some sponsorship and their T-shirts with 'NKP Pretoria' splashed across the back and front. Better than nothing. But the way they were forced to get the funds left a bitter aftertaste.

For Fanie it was another of the tribulations he had to endure. Such as John Reid and Lee Barnard being of the view that he still had to qualify for his place in the team.

Yet he felt strong enough in 1984 to play some rugby for his house, Tugela, before Russell Cobb returned for another season and watched a stronger, fitter and much faster Fanie de Villiers in the nets. He started knocking over the wickets right from the first game that 1984-85 season. As an encore the following weekend he wrecked Adelaar, including Pat Symcox, to give the students an impressive victory.

Little wonder that an excited Doupie Calitz, the new NKP cricket organizer, phoned Chesters at his office after the Adelaar game, suggesting a visit to the nets and to bring along a photographer, a selector, anyone who mattered. Failing that, they had to be present for the next match. Calitz, an energetic sort, had taken over from Albert Myburgh before the start of the new season. The new organizer was not exactly a stranger to Chesters; they had met during the Northern Transvaal Nuffield Week trials in Benoni, in December 1983; also, there was no doubting Calitz's sincerity. The call came as a surprise as he had promised to stay in touch, having arrived at NKP the previous January.

Chesters was however a small step ahead of Calitz. Russell Cobb and Fanie had called in at the *Pretoria News* with a couple of Tugela hostel friends, Dewald Kruger and Marius Delport, looking for old sports photographs to plaster around the walls of their rooms. Fanie, a big grin spread across his face, looked at the massive pile of discarded photos, most of them wired from various overseas agencies. He sat down, with Cobb, Delport and Kruger, and the four of them systematically went through 200 or so sports photographs that ranged from athletics to yachting, with a fair amount of cricket in between, including a quality action shot of Richard Hadlee that had become fuzzy in transmission. Although his English was rough and ready, he attempted polite conversation until he was more certain of his ground. He also promised to return to get more pictures, which he often did.

It was also easy for Chesters to accede to Calitz's request since October was relatively free and as the senior side were in Kimberley that weekend for a first round Nissan Shield game against Griqualand West, there was a chance to concentrate on lesser league matters. He also wanted to have a look at the NKP side. Having met Fanie and listened to his enthusiastic babble, the inducement to see him bowl in a game was very much there. He certainly looked strong enough to be the fast bowler Russell Cobb claimed he was. The English professional had worked hard on the side since his return, but admitted that the lack of batting depth was their downfall. That would, hopefully, change in the second half of the season with one or two recruits.

On a Saturday morning in October, the town was busy with shoppers and the traffic congestion building up, even this far from the main Sunnyside business area. The arrangement between

82

Chesters and Sid Dugmore was to meet at the ground in Walker Street. As Berea Park were playing Pretoria University they would perhaps get a chance to watch both games before lunch.

Dugmore was in his third season as a provincial selector and their routine start to the season in those years was to sit on the embankment next to the sight screen, to the right of the superb net facilities at L. C. de Villiers Oval, and talk about the new playing talent seen at the pre-season nets. With a quick wit and a good eye for spotting technical flaws in a player's make up, Dugmore was not shy to advance a comment about a player's ability, or lack of it. Early in the season he usually carried a blue hardcovered notebook in which he wrote down the names of promising players. 'You basically know the make up of your Currie Cup squad from last season. But there are a few new players who have arrived and you need to look at them,' he explained, forgetting it was the same opening gambit he had used the season before. What worried them both at the time was the lack of local talent that had failed to come through the system. They were looking for reasons why local talent had disappeared.

On 20 October 1984 it was no different. In Kimberley, Northerns were battling to get a partnership going to build a total.

'Know anything about this kid?' he asked Chesters.

'Only that he's quite fast. Pat Symcox speaks highly of his ability. Can score runs as well, I gather.'

But this scrap of information was not enough for the pragmatic Dugmore. 'We'll see.'

A rugby field, with a pitch in the middle is not ideal for playing cricket, especially not in South Africa where the thick, durable kikuyu grass had become even thicker after the first spring rains. Which means that trying to score a boundary requires extra effort from the batsman. The students were batting while Police were sulking in the field after being routed. Checking in the scorebook, Dugmore and Chesters noticed that the visiting team had been dismissed for 107. 'Vinnige Fanie' had lived up to his name if not to his growing reputation: figures of 7 for 42 runs told its own story. What a pity. Police had decided to bat first because they had scored in excess of 200 runs in similar circumstances at NKP the previous season.

Now, what was it Sir Donald Bradman had said about pitches changing biorhythmic character between seasons? Or was it a bowler who made the comment? Sir Richard Hadlee or perhaps Alec Bedser?

Young Fanie casually walked around the ground to greet Chesters, chatting away in his best English. He spoke a little about fishing, and how the photographs from the office had brightened up his room. Trying to get Fanie to talk about his bowling spell earlier in the day draws a blank. After Fanie walks off, Russell Cobb gives Dugmore the information he needs.

When they eventually leave, Dugmore suggests to Chesters they meet back at the NKP ground after three. That is when they will get a chance to have a good look at the young fast bowler who had just turned twenty. He was hostile, keeping the ball up to the batsman, although inclined to drift down leg on occasions as he bowled wide of the stumps. Dugmore admits there was talent. For this level of the game Fanie was still a little raw, but better than any player, other than Cobb of course, in either team. While Symcox mentioned his bowling and batting, he failed to mention what a class outfielder he was. Anything from the boundary was over the stumps to the wicketkeeper. There was something else that Dugmore noticed: the late outswing.

There were other club games to see, players' forms to check on, but enough had been seen to know that Fanie de Villiers would go into Dugmore's notebook.

It was around this time that the term 'Project Red' first surfaced during a discussion Chesters had with Willie Basson at a Northern Transvaal practice session at L. C. de Villiers. Also a member of the South African Cricket Union's board, Basson, a former Pretoria University scientist, had for some time been looking at venues other than Berea Park, where the NTCU had their provincial headquarters and a permanent office for a growing staff at that time. But harsh economic realities had to be faced. Basson told his executive in April 1984 that Berea Park would, eventually, lose its status as a venue for the rebel one-day international matches, and more rebel tours were being planned. Eleven months later, on the eve of the Castle Cup final, in which Northerns met Transvaal, Basson called a media briefing and spelt out the union's long-term future.

'To keep pace with the game's growth in this area Northern Transvaal needs to function on a more professional level,' he said. 'We have one season left here before we move to a new ground. To put it bluntly, this venue has become too small.'

Berea Park's image as a dowdy sports venue had been growing since the late 1970s when its owners, South African Railways, declined to spend money to upgrade the facility. At most it could hold 5,000 to 6,000 spectators. But when Rowe's rebels played the South Africa XI in a one-day game, almost 8,000 crammed every known area of space to see them play; it was far too crowded with mischiefmakers, making crowd control difficult. There was a similar scenario at any number of venues during the 1999 World Cup in England where field invasions made it dangerous for players and umpires.

In his search for a new ground, and discussions with a number of people, Basson became disillusioned with the apartheid-steeped Pretoria City Council. They had Loftus Versfeld (rugby) and were planning to upgrade Pilditch Stadium (athletics and cycling). So why really bother about cricket? There was nothing in it for the council and if Northern Transvaal wanted to move from Berea Park, well it was their problem and they could go and find their own patch of turf. But this was the 1980s and since the rebel era began, the summer sport had partly come out of the mothballs of isolation and was showing signs of growth.

When news that the Centurion (old Verwoerdburg) Town Council had made land available and joined the NTCU in the venture, the fossils that inhabited Munitora (the council chambers) did not realize that they had lost a chance to give their city another significant international sports venue.[3]

While the 'Project Red' factfile and the reasons for a new venue moved slowly through the negotiation phases, Fanie's fast-bowling talents, having been noted by Dugmore, were examined more closely again in January. This time, however, with fellow selector

---

[3] In South Africa's restructuring of municipal boundaries in late 2000, Centurion was hijacked into a greater metropolitan region known as Tshwane (a Sotho word meaning 'togetherness') along with Pretoria and Akasia municipalities.

Mike de Villiers as a partner. They saw enough to suggest to Alan Jordaan that the young student be invited to the B team nets. Forget that the opposition was not particularly strong, or that he had taken few wickets the previous November and December. He had, after all, earned a place in the 1984 South African Colleges' team. What did a lot to clinch the invitation was the publication in early January in the *Pretoria News* of the updated combined senior club averages. Fanie occupied fifth place among the bowlers: 23 wickets at 14.12, and an economy rate still less than 3 an over.

This was about the time Naas Ferreira, chairman of Oostelike, had his first contact with Fanie. Ferreira, known to have a soft spot for struggling Afrikaans-speaking cricketers, used any number of students from the University and NKP in a Ferreira XI that played matches against various Pretoria Afrikaans schools. Ferreira even had a team tie designed, and handed it out to provincial players who turned out for the side. About twelve months after he started bowling again, the twenty-year-old student found himself moving up the rungs in the Northerns recognition ladder: invitations to play for the Ferreira XI and attend the B team nets, and now, a high placing in the senior club averages that combined both Omicron and Epsilon Leagues. Willie Basson's experiment was slowly showing success.

Northerns were in the process of slipping to an innings defeat at Newlands as de Villiers attended his first B team nets at Berea Park on 21 January wearing a copper T-shirt, discoloured white shorts and plastic tennis shoes. As it is, the B side had the better of a drawn game against Boland in Pietersburg with Paul Robinson, certainly the tallest fast bowler to represent the province, and Francois Weideman taking nine of the wickets between them on an interesting pitch. Selection for the next game was unlikely. The shifting demands of the senior side, however, saw Weideman win his A Section cap. In those days Northerns had incredible depth in the seam and pace bowling departments.

Three weeks later, at Berea Park, Fanie was in the squad as twelfth man. He had since moved to the top of the senior club bowling averages and become the second bowler to take 50 wickets that season. But he needed to do more than that to win his first B team cap.

This had nothing to do with the Wanderers Club establishment. It was a question of whether the selectors wanted to play him, as the extra fast bowler, ahead of Martin van der Merwe who, in any event, managed only one more game for the B side, or use the occasion to give him an idea what the game at provincial level was all about. In fact, they did not even consider such options. He was to be the team's 'skivvy' for three days. Here was a young man who didn't know where three rand for the next hamburger was coming from, wore plastic *takkies* (tennis shoes), had to catch a bus to and from the senior team net practice at L. C. de Villiers Oval and knew nothing about the duties of a twelfth man.

* * * *

Nine months later, at the CBC Old Boys Club, in Groenkloof, the woman photographer from *Beeld* had long packed her camera bag and gone. Pat Symcox finished a last drink with Fanie and promised to drop him off at the hostel. In the corner of the lounge the selectors were still talking and it was close to 10 p.m. Time for Chesters to go. It was about then that the meeting suddenly ended. Alan Jordaan walked into the bar with John Reid and Sid Dugmore but the others had slipped out through a side door.

Jordaan handed Chesters a slip of paper on which fifteen names were written, and mentioned that Gerald Ackermann, Francois Weideman and Grobler would need fitness tests. At the bottom of the list he had written the name of Fanie de Villiers. Then it was John Reid's turn, with the permission of the selection panel convener, to explain that the fitness tests would be held on the Thursday. He was hopeful Grobler's foot injury, after treatment, would have healed.

'It has been diagnosed as a bruised bone. Nasty, but he's strong,' Reid confided.

'If he fails who of the others will come in?' asked Chesters.

'We'll have to see. Perhaps Ackermann . . .,' Reid looked at Jordaan for confirmation.

'No. It'll be your pal de Villiers,' Jordaan half smiled. 'If Grobler fails the fitness test, the young teacher will play against Western Province. It should make you happy. The twelfth man will only be known after Grobler's fitness test tomorrow.'

It was a good story. From B team twelfth man to Currie Cup bowler in nine months and only a Castle Bowl match against Natal B in between as experience. What had helped him at the time were the extra bowling lessons with Charles Anderson, a coach at St. Alban's and for a time a Northerns Nuffield team selector. Anderson also had a hand in coaching Eric Simon in Cape Town some years before. And whenever top Transvaal batsmen Kevin McKenzie or Henry Fotheringham had developed a fault, they would motor down the highway from the Wanderers to have it corrected. But this was different. Fanie de Villiers, unknown to the general public, was about to make a little history. Not that the public gave a tinker's cuss. Fanie who . . .?

It was an honest query left unanswered.

6

Sweat, Trial and Error

Lance Coetzee took less time to decide he would accept the offer of the captaincy of the provincial B team than it takes to check the heartbeat of a patient. It would, he knew, be his final season. He was twenty-five with a promising medical career ahead, and leading Northern Transvaal B in the summer of 1985-86 would not interrupt his studies. The decision, once made, brought in a new urgency about the game he played for enjoyment and comradeship. Play it hard, but play it fair and play it for fun.

Tall, with a spare frame, he was regarded as a good slip fielder and a solid top-order batsman and was respected for his leadership skills: always inventive and with a shrewd eye for detail. The way Alan Jordaan put it to him, Northerns were in a fix and the selectors saw him as the obvious replacement for Steve Vercuiel, who had led the B team in the previous two seasons.

Vercueil had moved to a new job and it was not possible to play in all the games that 1985-86 season. It would, he suggested, be far better to hand over to someone who was available for all the games and not have to worry about dividing leadership between two players. Jordaan, as convener of the selectors, also saw it that way. Few sides function successfully when they have two or more captains in a season.

As Jordaan, who had managed the B side the previous two seasons was not available for a third term, Coetzee, as captain of the B team, would at least retain some continuity. He was also part of the pre-season squad, allowing him to get to know the B team players, and the new talent. Among the more regular members of the squad, the slim figure of Fanie de Villiers was, at first, a mystery. During those first practice sessions Fanie, who hardly knew anyone, spoke mainly to Pat Symcox and Anton Geringer, whom he had met when playing for the Naas Ferreira XI.

But for Coetzee the NKP student did not remain a mystery for too long. He found his effervescent personality the opposite to what he had expected. When it came to bowling he was sharp and lively in the nets. Sure he was inexperienced, but he did get some movement off the pitch and through the air as well. What the new B team captain found intriguing was the away swing Fanie managed when bowling wide of the crease. It was confusing. You shaped up to play the ball moving in only to find, too late, that it was dipping away to the slips. The batsmen had got it wrong and were playing him as an inswing bowler. No wonder he had taken more than 50 wickets in the previous club season.

What was also important to note, from the scorecards, was that a large proportion of the wickets which young Fanie de Villiers took were predominantly those in the top order. There were also the usual rabbits and ferrets who inhabited the lower echelon of the innings. It meant he had the ability to knock over the tail as well as the top five. And Coetzee agreed that while some of the Epsilon League batting were a little better than reserve league standards, 55 wickets for a club in any season was a fair haul. No wonder Jordaan was impressed and had wanted him in the select pre-season training squad. Coetzee was also impressed. Pity Fanie wasn't a local. After he had qualified and done his two years national service he would be off somewhere else.

Jordaan, at the urging of fellow selectors Sid Dugmore and Mike de Villiers, and with further input from Doupie Calitz, the NKP cricket organizer, had invited Fanie to a B team middle net at Berea Park. There was no harm in looking at the youngster. Epsilon League or not, he had earned impressive press coverage. Standing as an umpire at the Fountains End of Berea Park Jordaan had a good look at the bowler. He was fast and he bowled straight and even swung the ball at times. Not much, but there was swing.

Oh yes, he was going to be good all right, thought Jordaan. He's raw and needs more coaching, but this definitely was a top fast bowler in the making.

When the first selection meeting came around, Coetzee, already aware that there were work and fitness problems among some of the players, was presented with a suggested squad list. Pat Symcox, now in his third season with the B side, would be his senior lieutenant. Symmo should have been playing for the senior side, but there was Rodney Ontong and Willie Morris. And Lee Barnard, the skipper, still fancied himself as a spinner for the one-day games. Yet Symcox did not have a memorable 1984-85 season by his own standards. Perhaps this summer would see the breakthrough.

Patience can only last for so long.

The Northerns selectors had already made decisions about the long-term advantages of several players for the early games. It was a mix and match set up. As usual the early limited-overs fare was given priority: a first round Nissan Shield game (Northerns were drawn away to Free State), and the opening B&H match against Western Province at home. Then came the opening Castle Currie Cup match: away to Natal at Kingsmead. Cyril Mitchley junior was the replacement for Eric Simons, which sorted out one problem, but there were more. Willie Kirsh, into his second year of national service and who had a good run in a vintage summer, was now batting without Mandy Yachad at the other end. Ontong had returned to add further experience and batting depth to the middle-order and bolster the spin department, and Anton Geringer, a young talented all-rounder, replaced Lourens de Lange, giving the side a more balanced look.

Yet the bowling focus was on the left-handed Gerbrand Grobler. John Reid, over a pre-season lunch, confided to Chesters that he felt the former South African Schools' fast bowler would play for South Africa against Kim Hughes' Australian rebels that season. If he fulfilled the role mapped out for him, the gap left by Simons' return to Cape Town would also be well plugged. A return of 1 for 27 in 9 overs against Free State at the Ramblers confirmed Reid's early viewpoint. But four days later, at Pretoria Technikon Oval (Northern Transvaal's first home venue for floodlit matches) Grobler dispatched so many short-pitched deliveries that he travelled far too often for Reid's comfort. There were too many four balls. Reid argued that limited-overs games are the same for all bowlers: flat pitches, leg-side restriction and other factors contributed to them receiving a lot of rough treatment. But there is no excuse for bowling balls that are more often in the bowler's half of the pitch; it gave the batsmen plenty of opportunities to practice improving their hook and pull repertoire.

Coetzee was told to concentrate on the players he felt would make the B team for the first game of the Castle Bowl season at Berea Park. Among those on the list of fifteen that Jordaan gave him were Willie Kirsh and Lourens de Lange who had played for the Currie Cup squad and might do so again. There were eight bowlers; three of them were all-rounders and one name that he did not recognize—Clive Eksteen.

'A left-arm spinner doing his national service,' Symcox informed him. 'Played for South African Schools a couple of years ago. Very useful.'

This puzzled the new B team captain as Eksteen had not been in the pre-season squad. Not to worry, the pace and seam attack was highly promising: Gerald Ackermann, Eugene Klopper, Jan van Duyker, Francois Weideman and Fanie de Villiers. Then Ackermann strained his left calf in a club match and the selectors, undecided whether Fanie should play this early, met on the Monday at CBC Old Boys to confirm the two squads.

Before the meeting Jordaan was asked by Doupie Calitz whether Fanie had a chance of playing ('We have a tough club game on Saturday'). It was a polite hint that NKP could make more use of his services than the B side if the plan was to have him do only twelfth man duties.

Selecting the senior side took less than ten minutes as Reid and Barnard confirmed their satisfaction with the performances so far, and with Kirsh being moved to the B team. At this stage they excused themselves and Coetzee, who had been listening quietly, was now brought into the discussions. The meeting lasted far longer than Jordaan had planned. Did the side really need two spinners (Symcox and Eksteen) at Berea Park? And places had to be found for de Lange and Mike Rindel. In fact Rindel could be the fourth seamer if needed. He had a useful record playing for Harlequins in early league games.

'What about the new ball attack?' Coetzee asked.

'Van Duyker, Klopper and . . . de Villiers,' Jordaan nodded as the other selectors confirmed. 'Ackermann is still injured and there's doubt if he can get Monday off.'

So there it was: Symcox was out, de Villiers was in.

Celebrations started at Tugela hostel a couple of hours later. After all, when did an NKP student last play cricket for Northern Transvaal? No one knew. In fact at that moment no one cared. One of the guys in the hostel knew where they could get some beer after hours. So these rands saved up for hamburgers and cokes, and stashed in a variety of hiding places came in handy.

Russell Cobb and Doupie Calitz contacted Professor Hennie Mare, the NKP rector, with the news as he attended a cocktail party in Johannesburg. The educationalist drank a small toast to the twin success of Fanie's selection and the vision of the NTCU executive who, against opposition from the East Rand, had launched the twin-tiered league system. It had its flaws, but it also had a number of good points. Fanie de Villiers was one of them.

There was excitement at home as well. Fanie had contacted his father, Braam, now back at Francis Worwerg as the school's principal, with the tidings. The *klein witkop* (small blond), who during his primary and high-school years had broken a variety of athletic records and was regarded as a future South African javelin champion, had overcome trials, tribulations and prejudices to win a place in the Northern Transvaal B side. He had every right to feel very proud as any boereseun would.

It was well after 11 p.m. when an excited Fanie de Villiers finally got to bed. Beer had rarely tasted better; the hamburgers had gone down well. Now they were all broke. So what was new? They were students; they were always broke.

Four days later the same students who celebrated with him and a few who did not arrived at Berea Park to give Fanie solid support on the opening day of the Castle Bowl match against Natal B. They put up a few large sun umbrellas to the left of the ancient scoreboard and sat back to watch the young man mark out his run from the Union Buildings end of the ground. Sitting among the students were Doupie Calitz, Russell Cobb and Braam de Villiers.

The *Pretoria News* and *Beeld* had mentioned that Fanie was making his debut in the match. 'A natural athlete who has had to overcome a back operation to fulfil a life's ambition of playing in a provincial match . . . and deserves a chance to prove himself,' had been the *Pretoria News* comment the day before.

To the right Muckleneuk Hill was covered in a pastel purple carpet from the jacaranda trees now in full bloom. While it was not blazing hot, the late October sun would quickly tire the bowlers if they had to bowl long spells. No wonder there were groans when Lance Coetzee lost the toss, condemning his side to a long, hot day in the field. Not that Fanie really cared at first. Hey, he was playing; that was the main thing.

Facing Fanie's first ball in a provincial game was the Natal B captain, Mike Mellor. At the other end stood a quiet, shy twenty-year-old Andrew Hudson. Hudson had made his debut twelve months ago, against Griqualand West in Kimberley. Nothing startling that first season: 258 runs in 12 innings for an average of 21.50; just an appetizer. At Berea Park that weekend Hudson, known affectionately to his friends as Hudders, left few in doubt of his class: innings of 62 and 71 did much to ensure Natal B a comfortable victory by 138 runs.

But that first morning, shortly after the end of his seventh over, Fanie, at deep mid-on to Jan van Duyker's bowling, twisted an ankle and limped off. Coetzee was not the only one to get that sinking feeling as the NKP student disappeared behind the old railway stand at the ground. His one penetrative bowler was unlikely to bowl again that day: perhaps in the match. Unlucky Fanie. Unlucky Northerns B. The pitch was flattening out and Eugene Klopper and van Duyker found it hard, thirsty work. Between them they bowled 66.1 overs, a further 34 came from a third future Test cap, Eksteen, and the all-rounder Rindel, with his useful left-arm swing.

As a match, the contest was over on the first day. Natal B were 300 for 7 at the close: five dropped catches and a missed stumping added to the hard labour the bowlers had to endure in the highveld heat. Hudson enjoyed an early life; Coetzee, at first slip put down a sharp chance off van Duyker.

You cannot drop such a modern aristocrat of batting and expect no retribution. Two quality half-centuries were his answer to the carelessness of the Northerns B fieldsmen. How they suffered: it was grim, it was tiring, and everyone was footsore. All Klopper and van Duyker wanted to do was put their feet up. There was no fun bowling in such heat: not with so many chances spilled. The promise shown by Fanie in those first overs bowled on that Friday meant the difference between a Northerns B success and failure. He had been getting swing and had fooled the batsmen into thinking he was an inswinger.

Not even a century by de Lange on the second day could bring much relief to the hard-pressed Northerns B management and captain. Fanie, his right ankle strapped, was undefeated on 3 in a last wicket partnership of 4. On Monday, however, he showed his teammates what the attack missed in the Natal B first innings. It was all get up and go, the tireless energy of a fresh-faced youth as he bowled an unbroken spell of 15 overs from the Union Buildings end. Yet what rewards on an unresponsive Berea Park pitch: 5 wickets for 33 runs during two hours of concentrated fast bowling. Coetzee used four bowlers: van Duyker, Klopper and Eksteen playing supporting roles. When Mellor declared the Natal B innings at 165 for 8, Coetzee knew that the 268 runs victory target, on a pitch that few batsmen at this level could handle with confidence, was not a realistic prospect. Yet the fighting qualities that have become synonymous with Fanie de Villiers surfaced again. Of the 13 runs in a desperate ninth wicket partnership, the young student collected 12.

'*Oom*, I hate losing,' he told Chesters after the match. 'It's like drinking poison. I'll feel a lot better tomorrow, but not now.'

Coetzee, who had nursed the youngster during his nervous early overs of the match, knew he could lose the one bowler who was a match-winner, and to win games you needed to bowl a side out twice. He recognized that Fanie had that ability.

If the third year NKP student felt that his performance would make it easier to win a place in the senior squad, he soon discovered the unpleasant truth that captains, like selectors, have their favourites. Fanie firmly believed that to overcome a problem you first look at the global picture, discard the negative and take a closer view of the positive factors and turn those to your advantage. To get past the closed inner circle you have to prove yourself. And the only way to do that is to go one better than the player likely to keep you out of the side. A simple philosophy, but one that Fanie, in those days, trusted.

The first he knew there was a chance to earn a place in the senior squad if the injury crisis was not solved came when the

Pretoria newspapers, quoting Alan Jordaan, indicated he could play in the game against Western Province. Not long after lunch, while practising with Cobb at the NKP nets, Calitz walked down from his office with the news that the selectors wanted him to attend the senior practice at L. C. de Villiers Oval. He was to be there at four. Calitz drove him to the Pretoria University sports facility, but Fanie would have to find his way back to the hostel. And here he was at the venue where years before he had started his climb up the tricky slope in the national Under-13 Week.

After the Currie Cup defeat by Border, Northerns also lost successive limited-overs matches to Transvaal: the Nissan Shield first-leg semi-final at Berea Park and the B&H game at the Wanderers. Both were convincing defeats against their powerful neighbours with Weideman playing in both games as Grobler was rested to give the heel injury more time to recover.

But what a bowling line up Transvaal had that season: Sylvester Clarke, Neal Radford, Alan Kourie, Hugh Page and Clive Rice. By any standards it was a Test attack: well, the nearest to one you would experience in South Africa in those days, headed by the feared West Indian Clarke and well-directed by Rice, the captain.

From the first match he played for Transvaal, Clarke (or Sylvers if you prefer) demanded respect. He may have thrown the quicker one; only which was his quicker ball?

Cyril Mitchley senior, later a top ICC Test umpire and known to his associates as 'Squire', once smilingly tackled the strapping, barrel-chested Bajan by posing a rhetorical, 'I know you throw, but which one is it?' Sylvers grinned back. 'That's for you to find out, Mr Umpire . . .'

What was interesting about his action, for an inswing bowler, was how high the arm came through, showing the batsman the chest instead of the left shoulder as he went into his delivery stride.

Fanie watched him closely from the discomfort of the rickety stand at Berea Park on 3 November, the day Northerns played that first-leg Nissan Shield match. A massive hailstorm turned the summer countryside into a winter landscape in less than an hour; the damage, running into several millions of rands, causing general havoc. Although the match was delayed by twenty-four hours, Clarke posed the biggest danger to the Northerns batsmen, the sort of danger Fanie wanted to create with his pace. Only a week before he had been bowling to the Natal B batsmen, taking his first 5-wicket haul. The exhilaration generated by that experience was still very real and embedded in his thoughts. Nine days later he was training with the boys he had watched at Berea Park. Life was starting to move fast. Perhaps too fast for the normally cheerful student whose only dream now was to be faster than Sylvester Clarke and show Lee Barnard and John Reid that he could repeat the 5-wicket haul taken against Natal B.

In the wake of the two limited-overs defeats by Transvaal and the continuing injury crisis, Jordaan, in consultation with Reid and Barnard, had examined the options available and asked Gerald Ackermann and Fanie to join the senior squad. It was a Tuesday and the third Currie Cup game of the season against Western Province was due to start at Berea Park on Friday: four days in which to come up with an answer.

After sweating in the late afternoon sun for almost two hours, for one of which he was carefully scrutinized by Reid and Barnard, Fanie was sure he would not be invited back. Neither the coach nor the captain said much to him, although Barnard, looking at his T-shirt and takkies suggested that Fanie go and collect some training kit.

'But there's none left,' Fanie reminded him.

Which was true. The training kit had long been handed out to all senior squad members. A few of the B team were given T-shirts, but nothing else. They had to arrange for their own gear. In today's world of high profile sponsorships the system in the mid-1980s may seem like the dark ages. You were lucky to get anything. By comparison, the 1950s and 1960s, in terms of sponsored gear were part of the prehistoric age: bats, equipment, some clothing perhaps, but only for the top Test players.

'You'll have to do better than come to practice in plastic takkies,' was Barnard's critical assessment of Fanie's footwear. 'You have to practice bowling in boots. We can't afford another injury.' It was a fair comment but the brusque manner in which it was said, hurt.

As a student, Fanie had no allowance other than what he earned from a few odd jobs: most of it was from welding repairs and small construction work. It became useful when he needed the money, but most of it went towards paying fuel costs to get to practices at

L. C. de Villiers Oval. From the time Fanie left school he had made a deal with his father that he would buy his own clothes. It became a matter of pride for the young man. In his often cash-strapped state he could not afford boots. When the players, as part of the pre-practice warm up did a three-kilometre run around the obstacle course of the trim park, Barnard noticed the takkies and Fanie felt embarrassed if not shamed by the cheapness of the footwear.

Later in the season, at the Wanderers, it was Anton Ferreira who came to his rescue. The burly all-rounder provided leather pads and gloves to replace the inferior plastic pads and cotton batting gloves with their outdated spiky rubber finger guards. Ferreira took one look at Fanie's gear and wanted to know, in that typical teasing yet caring way he has, what sports museum he had visited before the game.

Apart from Symcox and Ackermann none of the regular B team guys were at the nets. But he did not know Ackermann. Symcox said little at the time as he was waging his own battle to be noticed. So there was no one to talk to about getting boots for training. He could have spoken to Doupie. In fact, the only person who talked to him at length was Chesters, and he was jovially chatting with Reid, Jordaan or the other players. He passed on to Fanie the message that he was to return to the nets the next day. It would not be the last time he would pass on a message to Fanie, or offer advice and encouragement.

Chesters had, it seemed, adopted the determined, yet cheerful student. For one thing, Fanie was not pretentious; his brother, Neels, had knocked that out of him years before and his parents would not tolerate insincerity, arrogance or conceit. The journalist appreciated Fanie's openness and the fellowship he created. It led to a relationship which developed, over the years, into a strong bond.

It was only when Fanie read the early edition of the *Pretoria News* the next day that he understood the importance of being invited back to the nets. He had been drafted in the senior squad of fifteen and realized, for the first time, that he had a genuine chance of playing in a Currie Cup match. Yet he still wondered. Ackermann was more experienced and in with the CBC Old Boys camp. Francois Weideman had an elbow injury and was doubtful. Grobler, he gathered, had such a serious foot injury that it was uncertain when he would be fit again that season; it was news that infuriated Reid.

Although Barnard spoke to him at the net practice session that Wednesday afternoon, nothing was said to Fanie indicating the way the selectors were thinking. The impression was that Ackermann or Weideman would be preferred. Only when Chesters winked at him did he know he was perhaps closer to the team than the other two bowlers. For a second his serious features creased into a grin. Although the *Pretoria News* article that day has indicated that the possibility of playing Fanie was a risk and that he needed more experience in the B side to develop, the article also noted that as he had no fitness problems he would most likely earn selection. But Fanie still had his doubts.

Barely twenty-four hours later, the wait was over. Grobler spent only ten minutes in the nets and all the time Reid could see how he was struggling. The New Zealander went across to Barnard and the two men disappeared into the small office in the pavilion to call Jordaan. The word came back.

'Tell de Villiers he is playing,' Jordaan told Reid, who passed on the message.

Barnard, delaying the inevitable for as long as possible finally went over to Fanie and smiled at the student, unsure of what to say until he saw the woman photographer from *Beeld* aiming a camera at them. 'Smile for the camera. You are playing in the side tomorrow,' the Northerns captain said to the team's latest recruit.

For Fanie it was a special moment. He was going to play for Northerns in a Currie Cup match against Western Province at Berea Park the next day. He could not believe his luck. A boereseun playing for Northern Transvaal. He felt very proud as Chesters shook his hand. '*Baie geluk* (Good luck),' he commented, and for someone whose entire Afrikaans vocabulary consisted of about twenty words, it was quite a mouthful.

Another night of celebrations with his hostel buddies, along with Calitz and Russell Cobb. So much had happened in a matter of eighteen days that he wondered if it was not part of a dream depicting a giant hoax. Not once in his young life, starting with primary school in Deneysville on the Vaal Dam to Sasolburg and when he earned his Free State under-13 cap, had he expected to get so far. He had excelled at athletics to the extent that he had won a pile of certificates for every event he entered. Now it was cricket. A real souties game. A sport where he could really go places, even play a role where he could help win a game or two.

He did not know it then, but for the next six weeks he was to become part of a developing controversy that almost cost Barnard the Northern Transvaal captaincy.

* * * *

The dawn of 15 November 1985 was bright and cheerful and by the time Fanie arrived at Berea Park students and teammates from NKP had already set up their umbrellas, along with Fanie's father, at the end of the ground. For Fanie, however, the game became a passing parade of stars, facing Garth le Roux, the often erratic left-arm genius, Stephen Jefferies, Eric Simons and even Adrian Kuiper.

Now Fanie found he had a problem with Eric Simons. From the moment he had been selected he kept hearing stories about Simons, of how good he was and how many wickets he had taken the previous season. He disliked being told stories about the now Western Province fast seam and swing bowler. He even admitted, privately, to hating the name. Later, when he got to know the ever-friendly Simons he readily admitted to being wrong. He also felt the all-rounder was a special type of player: a clever bowler and a determined one.

Instead of a solid contribution when making his A Section debut that mild early summer day, Fanie was all but ignored as a bowler. He had not expected to share the new ball, but he had expected to be asked to put in a solid spell. His outfielding, as always, was spectacular and made Peter Kirsten think twice about looking for a second run on a couple of occasions. The tall, sparely built youngster deep backward of square, in what they now call the sweeper position, had the ball back to Noel Day so quickly there could be a risk in taking a second; so forget trying for a third to this chap. He rarely threw the ball wide.

It was well into the first session of the second morning when Barnard finally threw the ball to Fanie. Allan Elgar and Kirsten had taken Western Province's first innings' total just past the 90 mark and Anton Ferreira, the beefy Northerns all-rounder, was bowling from the Union Buildings end. To Fanie the ball reminded him of a tightly rolled red rag with one side partly shiny and the other with a series of loose scabs. Nothing at all like the ball he used in the second innings against Natal B the month before.

'See what you can do,' Barnard said without a word of advice or a query about his field.

The Northern Transvaal captain had his own idea about the field Fanie should have. It is called experience. He seemed to know who should be in what position without needing to ask. There were no specific instructions: just run up and bowl a line. Any fool with a couple of summers of practice could do that. But he was more nervous than he had been before the Natal B game. This was different. It was against Western Province. And facing him was Peter Kirsten, not just any old Piet Koekemoer from Klipkosspruit.

Fanie first bowled to Elgar and then to Kirsten. He must keep the ball up. Not give them any half volleys to drive. In his third over Kirsten moved inside to drive only to give the wicketkeeper, Noel Day, a catch to his right. Glory! Kirsten his first Currie Cup wicket! The Saturday morning crowd enjoyed the success, too. It had been a good ball, moving away and catching Kirsten by surprise with the pace off the pitch as well as through the air. But that was all. Barnard took him off at the end of the over and brought on Rodney Ontong.

The press box, side on at Berea Park, buzzed over Barnard's decision. Ontong went on to bowl an unbroken spell, apart from the lunch and tea breaks, of 30 overs. Roy Pienaar was given a spell of 14 overs; Barnard tried himself for 2 overs and gave the fast bowlers Mike Clare and Cyril Mitchley junior the occasional short bursts. Shortly before tea, with the Western Province first innings drawing to a close, Barnard gave Fanie what seemed to be two consolation overs for his fielding performance. Yet he wondered whether he should not have had Elgar's wicket as well. There was a definite nick but Day did not appeal; in fact, Fanie got the impression that the alert wicketkeeper did not pick up the sound.

In the second innings, late on Monday, after having ignored Fanie for 32 overs while the visitors cautiously batted for a draw, Barnard threw him the ball for what was to be the final over of the match. He bowled a maiden after which everyone shook hands and trooped off. Barely a word was said to Fanie in the dressing room afterwards. He may have made his A Section debut, but ask him about it and there was the distinct impression that he was there merely to make up the numbers. His first Currie Cup match would be better remembered for his fielding than his bowling.

Barnard had his reasons. After the defeat by Border he was not prepared to risk another defeat. Sacrifices had to be made: was Fanie bowling only 6 overs in the match one of those sacrifices? Why not go for extra batting depth and play Rindel? He could have bowled 6 overs just as economically and scored a few runs as well.

Minutes after the drawn game Jordaan arrived with Mike de Villiers and Sid Dugmore to select the side for the day-night series match against the Impalas, a side drawn from the Border, Boland, Free State and Griqualand West teams. Although Border and Free State were playing A Section, they were still on probation and only earned their day-night status later.

In the 1980s the *Protea Annual* could be relied on to make so many errors, it should not surprise anyone to discover that in the Northerns match against the Impalas at Technikon Oval on 20 November, two players who did not play were listed in the scorecard. In any event Fanie was selected to make yet another debut, this one was for his day-night career, and he ended up with the fielding prize. Barnard turned a blind eye to the young man alertly patrolling either third man or deep backward square on the fence and putting together another outstanding fielding performance.

Barnard may have felt he had enough bowlers to do the job, and well, Fanie de Villiers was not Gerbrand Grobler, who would not have tolerated such shabby treatment. Jordaan and other selectors were not impressed with Barnard's handling of young Fanie and planned to discuss it with the captain and the manager/coach, John Reid. True, Barnard had not faced Fanie in a league match, but he trusted his own judgement. A couple of seasons later, also in a day-night game at Centurion Park, Barnard pulled the same stunt on Willie Morris, the tall left-arm spinner who had a good limited-overs record.

There were, however, more problems ahead for Barnard. The Afrikaans press became highly critical of the way he handled Fanie and posed the same question the *Pretoria News* had done: 'If the bowler was either Gerbrand Grobler or Francois Weideman, it is doubtful whether Barnard would have employed such tactics. After all, the Impalas posed no genuine threat to Northerns' record total and a few overs from the youngster would have given the spectators something extra to cheer about. Instead they roared their approval of an excellent fielding performance. No doubt the money for his fielding award went into the team pool.'

Both *Die Transvaler* and *Rapport* were more critical than the *News*, with the suggestion that Barnard's tactics and the respect he had earned as a provincial captain were now being seriously questioned. Jordaan was also quoted in *Die Transvaler* where he was critical of Barnard's leadership over this one issue: 'If Gerbrand Grobler played, and was only half fit, I am sure he would have bowled. It is distressing for us to pick someone and not see him utilized for the job for which he was selected . . . How, as selectors, can we judge him, and his ability to cope, if he is not given an opportunity? It makes our job that much harder to judge how he would fare against a team such as Transvaal.'

Two days after the Impalas fiasco Fanie was selected for the one-day game against Kim Hughes' Australian rebels at Technikon Oval in a day-night match. After that selection meeting Barnard and Reid were summoned to meet Willie Basson, the strong man in the NTCU executive ranks, and as president of the union, the man with the most influence. With Basson was his new vice-president, Ian Buchanan, who asked Barnard whether he had a problem with the selection of Fanie de Villiers, and how he justified his decision not to bowl the young student.

Basson's message was all too clear. He told Barnard that as the Northern Transvaal captain, and Reid, as oach and manager, it was their job to utilize the talents of those players selected for a specific role. Young de Villiers had been selected to perform a task in the side. The NKP student was seen as part of Northern Transvaal's long-term strategy. 'He's not just another student who is here today and gone tomorrow. We are looking at him becoming an important cog in our bowling attack for the next decade,' Basson told Barnard and Reid. 'In this respect, guys, we will not tolerate interference. If either of you are unhappy with this policy then I think we need to review your positions.'

There it was; Barnard suddenly found his job on the line.

To his credit, when he voiced his concerns, Barnard had an unshakeable belief in his role as a captain. He had to be responsible for running a team where stability and performances were important to the players and the team as a unit. If that meant under-utilizing players of obvious talent it was not so much a criticism of the selectors or the player, or of the players selected, as it was of the role intended. Sometimes situations arose where an untried bowler did not fit in with a developing game plan. There would be other matches.

But Barnard also saw Basson's point of view. As it was, Northerns were in their third season without an overseas professional. It was hard work playing against teams which had them. By now Western Province and Eastern Province had followed their example and were encouraging local talent. The wheel, which had taken so long to turn, was slowly moving in the opposite direction. As Peter Kirsten once suggested, you always need to strike the right balance.

Other factors were also starting to appear. One was that Northern Transvaal would soon have to start preparing for the post-John Reid era. While the former New Zealand captain's coaching job was never at risk, Barnard was all too aware that he might have to start playing nursemaid to some of the younger players. In early August 1985, on his return from a trip to New Zealand to see his aged parents living in Taupo, Reid invited Chesters to lunch at their regular meeting place, La Madeleine, an upmarket restaurant then in Sunnyside. About half an hour into the meal 'Bogo' Reid sat back and, calmly sipping a glass of Cape chardonnay, commented that he was 'returning home early in the New Year'. The journalist, also a Kiwi, sat stunned.

'Look. I haven't yet told Willie or Lee. I'm doing that this weekend when we meet to go over the plans for the season. So don't even whisper this, Chesters. To no one.'

'When will it be made public?'

'Later in the season. I don't want them to press too many panic buttons.'

'And who is going to take over then?'

'Good question, Chesters. I have someone in mind. But I need to talk to him first.'

It was 27 November and still no announcement had been made about Reid's departure at the end of January. Technikon Oval was packed for the mid-week game between Northerns and the Hughes rebels who, after four preliminary warm up matches and a game against Free State, in which the matric student Allan Donald had made his debut, the tourists arrived in the Jacaranda City.

They were also embroiled in an all-too-familiar umpiring row that simmered all season. And one scorer became so confused she did not know how the new system worked: whether to count the wides and no-balls as part of the extras or add them to the bowlers' analysis. She did both. It was chaos. The board had Northerns 215, one official scorer 209 and another 212. They had all got it wrong. And the balls did not add up either. One of the umpires, Pierre de Klerk, turned down an lbw decision that Rod McCurdy felt was so plumb he could not believe that Noel Day had survived. Later McCurdy bowled Fanie for a duck.

That night Technikon Oval overflowed with a record crowd of 6,000. If Fanie felt that his debut in the Currie Cup game had been interesting, he was in for a surprise. The evening, complete with singing, Mexican waves and vleisbraais, was an entertaining one. Signing autographs for young hopefuls, dads and moms was becoming a cheerful routine at day-night games. In the Impalas match, he once joked, he signed more autographs than he bowled balls. In between overs a well-wisher fed him chunks of a rather juicy piece of *wors* (spiced sausage) at fine leg while Cyril Mitchley junior bowled an inspired spell. Fanie was busy chewing a last mouthful when Barnard called him up and tossed him the ball.

'Okay, Fanie, show me what you can do,' the captain said. 'You've got 5 overs.'

Under the bright lights Fanie marked out his run. He had, of course, bowled in a couple of day-night games at the same ground in the Northerns domestic day-night league. But this was different. He was bowling to Kim Hughes, a former Australian captain. In front of the press tent the scorers' box was in confusion, the young woman who scored with coloured pencils suddenly realized she didn't have a colour for Fanie de Villiers and panicked. He was not supposed to bowl. Was he?

To the chants of 'Fah-nie, Fah-nie, Fah-nie . . .' for the only time in an international match in Pretoria, the fast bowler charged in only to be met by an attacking Kim Hughes. Fanie had already caused a couple of near run-out problems and now here he was bowling. He gave away 22 runs in his first 3 overs by bowling wide when Rodney Ontong casually sauntered over.

'You have to bowl straight, Fanie. Put it into the block hole. Don't give them room to hit you.'

'Block hole? What's a block hole?' He was puzzled. It was the first time he had heard the expression.

Ontong, with a wealth of English county experience as a Glamorgan all-rounder and captain, was offering him the first genuine advice of how to bowl in a limited-overs situation. Keep it up and keep it straight. Okay. So, why had no one explained this tactic to him before? He wondered why John Reid and Barnard had left him to his own devices? He may have been just too happy to be playing but he also needed help. In the end Fanie went for 38 in 8 overs. Brought back for a second spell he trapped John Maguire lbw for 28, just as the lower-order batsman was creating problems for Northerns in their bid to cause an upset. Forget that it was another instance of poor umpiring: a wicket is a wicket. And that was not too bad for the young bowler. But these were early days and Ontong's advice helped immensely.

A really good guy, Ontong. It was as though he had read Fanie's mind and stepped forward when the student needed help the most. It made Ontong a special teammate.

Two days later, he was playing at the Wanderers in his second Castle Cup match. There, although used sparingly by Barnard, he showed signs of coming to terms with the high level of competition and challenge offered by teams such as Transvaal. Barnard, taking a catch to get rid of the beefy all-rounder Alan Kourie, gave Fanie his second Currie Cup wicket. It was a game where he managed to get a closer look at Sylvester Clarke than he had almost a month before. Only 10 overs: was Barnard already backtracking on his commitment to give the youngster more work to do? And on a pitch, and in conditions, favouring seamers? Fanie still fired off bazooka shots; blast them out if all else fails. It really required a touch of subtle seam and swing, and he was learning. He was swinging the ball. So much to learn.

What did bother him was being brought into the attack with a big score already on the board and batsmen settled in a run-scoring mood. In later years he acquired the knowledge how to handle such situations and captains who expected him to produce wicket-taking deliveries or containing overs. In those early days it upset him and would have discouraged those with less heart and nerve. There were, of course, other factors: from watching one Nissan semi-final leg to playing in the next. And this time in the Wanderers' bullring. At least he managed to pick up Jimmy Cook's wicket.

There was also more advice from Ontong who knew what the young fast bowler was going through. He was raw and inexperienced and doing his best to make sure he was being noticed. For Fanie, it was another chance to see Clarke in action.

Further reward came after the match when Cyril Mitchley junior invited Fanie out and he found himself seated next to the burly Bajan in a Corlett Drive restaurant. The journey he had made from seeking Clarke's autograph a month before to sharing a meal and talking about bowling with him made him realize that there were those who had accepted him. It was a good, expansive feeling.

The next time they were to meet would be in Virginia with Fanie bowling to the big West Indian in a game he helped Northerns win to put them in their first Nissan Shield final.

Shortly before Christmas the curtain abruptly fell on his Currie Cup season when playing Eastern Province. He went for plenty off 2 overs in their first innings and was not called on again. More frustration as he grappled with the realization that he was being kept out of the firing line to regroup his thoughts. In the second innings he was given 10 overs, after putting together a tidy undefeated innings of 23. In those 10 overs he picked up yet another wicket. This one was of Dave Richardson who had assumed the Eastern Province captaincy and combined it with his wicketkeeping duties that season.

On the second day of the game John Reid pulled Chesters aside and told him that the announcement of his return to New Zealand was being made the next day. Belonging to the age before such fancy electronic equipment as laptops and instant communication through modems and mobile telephones had become necessities, he hammered out the story for the group Saturday afternoon editions in Johannesburg and Cape Town and the *Sunday Tribune* in Durban and then had to dictate his story over the pay phone.

Not long after the morning drinks session on the last day did Northerns finally announce that 'John Reid was returning to New

Zealand' story and the union's PR officer approached the media table on the second level at Berea Park with a handout. So far so good. At least the group had the story first. Then the *Sunday Tribune* blew the cover off Chesters' inside knowledge. While sitting downstairs with David Trist, the then Eastern Province coach, the amiable Joel Merwis, a veteran sports hack for the *Sunday Express* picked up the *Pretoria News* telephone when it rang, and the sports desk in Durban thinking it was Chesters asked the obvious question: who would be taking over from John Reid?

Reid's replacement was the quietly spoken, urbane Willie Watson, a former England Test cap, who had also played soccer for his country. He had agreed to act as caretaker coach for the remainder of the summer, the idea being he would accept the job the following summer. He may not have been John Reid, but then, there are not too many Reids in this world. Watson, however, was just as shrewd: he could also spot a flaw in a player's technical make up and, with a few quiet words, help sort out a problem.

Mitchley junior had badly injured his ankle in one game and when he came back, had a run-up problem, falling away badly with the ball straying down leg. Spindly with a high action he should have taken more than 25 wickets that Currie Cup season. The canny Watson whispered some advice and Mitchley was bowling with a technically correct action again.

As for Fanie, he did not have the benefit of being able to learn from Watson's sophisticated wisdom. The Yorkshireman, who for years had batted in the shadow of that master of the crease, Sir Leonard Hutton, was in his own quiet way controversial. He had also played with, and against, a generation of England fast bowlers, starting with Alec Bedser, who make the current crop, with perhaps the exception of Darren Gough and Andy Caddick, appear like peashooters in a coconut gallery.

If you examine Fanie's bowling figures that first Currie Cup season—28-2-88-3—and compare them with his Castle Bowl return of 88-14-211-16, it is easy to understand the reluctance of Barnard to give the young student more overs. The difference between Barnard and Coetzee was that the medical student appreciated Fanie's developing style and skill and gave him a chance to experiment. In the tougher Currie Cup arena there was little time to learn; also the margin of error was much smaller. Moreover, in those days, there was the impression that you had to know it all before being selected and that was the tough part.

Coetzee also consulted with the young bowler about his field placing and encouraged him to think out his own plan of action. It was a good combination. Had Coetzee found the time to captain the side the following season, Fanie would not have found the transition to the Currie Cup scene difficult.

It was enough for him to head the Northerns B Castle Bowl averages that first season (13.18) well ahead of the more experienced Gerald Ackermann and Jan van Duyker, who had taken the bulk of the wickets between them. Economically, however, Fanie was superior; compensation perhaps for his hard work. Also his overall first-class season's figures of 19 wickets at 15.73 was a record which could not be ignored.

While it was left to the left-arm spinner, Omar Henry, to bowl the last ball in a first-class match at Berea Park in eight years as Boland beat Northerns B (and Pat Symcox took the last wicket for a Northerns B side), Fanie's 6 wickets in the match represented his best return that season. There were hopes that the next summer would see the young fast bowler develop even further.

These were increased when in a day-night match between the A and B teams in late September, Fanie, who bowled the second over in a match at Centurion Park to Roy Pienaar, collected 4 wickets. His efforts, which helped the B side win the match, went unreported, however. For some particular reason, the scorecards or the result, were never published. Willie Basson felt that as it was 'a friendly' the result and performances should be ignored. However, the season which began with so much promise, soon lost its momentum with the selectors failing to define a role for the college fast bowler.

As the country waited for the return of Kim Hughes' Aussie rebels, Willie Watson quietly bowed out of the coaching scene and Doug Neilson took over John Reid's portfolio of manager/coach for 1986-87. Although he could be controversial, Neilson was disturbed at how powerful and influential the Wanderers Club clique had become in the last two seasons of the first Reid era. He saw it playing a detrimental role to the advancement of some players. A former Transvaal new-ball bowler who had joined the Pretoria Club Oostelike in the early 1980s, Neilson was all too aware of the divisions within the side and the unhappiness of some players.

His idea was to neutralize, as far as possible, the ruptures which existed. It was obviously not going to be easy. Although he tried to carry out a few ideas of his own, he was often given a rough ride. Mike Rindel earned his belated A Section spurs during Neilson's season and the talented Vernon Cresswell was preferred to Noel Day as wicketkeeper. There was always an uneasy truce when it came to team selection, and later in the dressing room. It was not Neilson's fault that the provincial programme got off to a wet, shaky start in the Wanderers bullring.

On a showery mid-October evening the spectators and media were treated to a scene which smacked of pure burlesque. After the third stoppage of the evening, the umpires, Ted Wood and Jimmy Peacock, had to recalculate, on the field, a readjusted victory target and the number of overs to be bowled. How different in later years when first there was the Clarke-Samson system followed by the Duckworth-Lewis method, the latter often seemingly incongruous to the actual needs of the slogs.

Neilson, bemused by the antics the new day-night series rain-affected clauses caused, was equally unimpressed with the way the former Transvaal players behaved throughout the season and launched a scathing attack in the *Sunday Times* on their unprofessional attitude. Reid was not there to provide the comfort zone into which the Johannesburg players had been cocooned from early 1984 and the unhappy friction between players and their manager/coach continued to spill over in public. What also added to the problems that wet summer was that the net facilities were rarely dry. Another factor was that Neilson's tougher attitude was neither popular with the senior players nor did he have their respect.

Conversely he did not respect them. All of which created an unhappy cul-de-sac.

How much Fanie suffered from this unhealthy atmosphere has, down the years, been the subject of conjecture. Apart from Yogi Ferreira and Cresswell there were few who seemed to be anxious to advance the cause of the NKP student. Neilson, though, saw the potential which was developing. And Pat Symcox, one of his closest confidants among the players, was still trying to crack the Currie Cup side. But Fanie was a good listener. He was also facing a series of decisions about his long-term future. Like Symcox he also needed to know where he stood. Mike de Villiers, always sympathetic to Fanie's cause, did his best, and although the young man was taking wickets, no one seemed to care. Little wonder that he felt mentally harassed over the selectors' dalliance.

Just what was going wrong? It was, after all, the summer he was to have achieved a permanent breakthrough into the senior ranks. Symcox felt similar frustrations after several successful performances. Yet with Ontong around he knew there was little chance outside the occasional limited-overs matches.

During their selection for the South African Test and limited-overs teams, one query which has often hovered in the thoughts of some is whether Symcox and Clive Eksteen have ever bowled successfully in tandem to win a match. At Oude Libertas, Stellenbosch, in 1986-87 they took 4 apiece for Northerns B on a dusting pitch: Symcox 4 for 61 and Eksteen 4 for 40, and in 20 overs; in fact Eksteen shared the new ball with Francois Weideman in that match against Boland.

In his weekly 'Spinner's Tales' column in the *Pretoria News*, around mid-December, Chesters suggested that the selectors had lost touch with some long-term objectives. One of their problems was ignoring talent such as Fanie de Villiers. He was taking wickets but either Barnard or Neilson, or both, preferred not to think of him at all or that he should be playing for the B team now led by Lee Selsick. The Spinner's Tales comment did not go down too well, but Chesters stuck to his opinion, especially after Fanie's 9 wickets in the Castle Bowl match against Transvaal B at the Wanderers.

Selsick and Cresswell were highly impressed. Only Barnard was not interested. He did not want to hear the opinions of either the B team wicketkeeper or captain. He would, as he had explained to Willie Basson the season before, make up his own mind when the time was right to play Fanie in the A side. From what he could see there was still some way to go before that would happen. There was no rush was there? Perhaps another season?

Fanie, after long hours in the nets, had with help from Russell Cobb and others learnt to swing the ball more, and the 9 wickets in the bullring had caught Barnard and Neilson by surprise. Divided into 3 for 39 off 20 overs in the first innings and 6 for 57 in 22 overs in the second, it demanded their attention.

'Northerns selectors need to take a hard look in the mirror tonight before they select the squad for the festive season's coastal tour,' Chesters had written in the *Pretoria News*. 'They need to check to see whether they are still seeing straight after Fanie de Villiers reminded them that he is ready for an A Section recall after his 9 wickets against Transvaal B. Rumours are that Gordon McMillan, the Transvaal B captain, was so impressed with de Villiers' ability to deliver the cunning outswing from wide of the crease that he contacted Lee Barnard and advised him to give de Villiers a chance.'

It came as no surprise when Neilson telephoned Chesters and said the story had sown such dissension in the ranks of the side that it was advisable if he did not turn up at the nets that afternoon or for the rest of the season. He was not even to call Neilson regarding team selection but to go through Willie Basson, the Northerns president. This would apply to all *Pretoria News* queries for the rest of the season. The watchdog had, it seemed, barked too loudly. Told of Neilson's attitude, Dr Basson put a swift end to the coach's suggestions; it was his job to deal with the media and he would have to accommodate all press and radio enquires whether or not he approved or disapproved of the person with whom he was dealing.

In any event, Fanie earned belated recognition by being included in what was his first coastal tour. Although he had been twelfth man for the match against Free State at Centurion Park, where Free State had given Northerns a thorough mauling, he replaced an injured Mike Clare in the squad for the Port Elizabeth and Durban games.

Eastern Province have had their reasons, down the years, for producing the type of pitches at St. George's Park that often do little to make for an attractive game. At that point of time, only a rare genius could score runs because the cabbage patch had become the abode of green mambas. It must be remembered that Currie Cup matches, in those years of isolation, were played over three days and each province played to its strengths.

Barnard and Neilson were well aware of the then-recent St. George's Park history. It was claimed that before the start of one particular season, sand had been spread over the surface to help the spinners. Whatever the truth of that particular story, the oldest Test venue in South Africa had become a graveyard for anyone of pace. Whatever success there had been for quick bowlers was largely the result of hard work and luring the batsmen into committing errors they would be ashamed to admit they had made.

The de Villiers family, always a close-knit unit, cut short their 1986 Christmas Day festivities and drove through the night to surprise Fanie at St. George's Park the next day. But he was left out, although Barnard had initially pencilled him in for the game. One look at the pitch the next morning led to an immediate decision: Northerns could not afford to be minus a batsman (Mark Venter), so who should lose out? Why, Fanie, of course. After lunch on the first day the disappointed de Villiers family adjourned to the beach at Summerstrand and left the next day.

Fanie did get to play in Durban, with Andrew Hudson now in his first A Section season, in the Natal side. Barnard came in for more criticism for his negative tactics in a game doomed to a draw when the Northerns captain elected to bat on after lunch. In reality he could have declared earlier, but it would have set up a limited-overs scenario, and he lacked the faith in his bowling attack to win the match in two-and-a-bit sessions. On his arrival back in Pretoria on 4 January 1987 Fanie immediately contacted Chesters.

'I really don't know what I should do. Barnard has no faith in me.'

'Why do you say that? You did well in Durban.'

'Not really. It would have been better if I had been given the field I wanted when they batted.'

It sounded like an excuse.

'Next time I play, I'm going to show him I'm the fastest bowler in South Africa.'

'Is that necessary? We both know you are as good as any of the top bowlers in the country. Be patient, my friend.'

'You don't win that way. Next chance I get, I'm going to blast out the batsmen.'

He was frustrated. He was upset. He also saw himself going nowhere.

'Be yourself, Fanie. Keep on bowling the way you have. You'll convince them.'

'What books do you have on fast bowling that I can borrow?'

Chesters thought for a moment. 'There's one by John Snow which may be of use. And another by Garry Sobers. Come over for supper tonight and we can have a look.'

Fanie did just that.

Two days later at a net session, Chesters confirmed with two of the players who had played in Durban Fanie's view about the field placings at Kingsmead. But Fanie did not miss another game for the seniors that season. He played in the game against Kim Hughes' rebels and then took 4 wickets in the first innings rout of Border in the last Currie Cup game of the season. It was his first big A Section haul and his overall tally of 17 wickets for 415 runs were a fair return at 24.41. Although his economy rate went to 3.07 an over, it was a steady improvement. He even improved his day-night series record, taking 3 wickets in the semi-final against Transvaal. Two of them came from sharp outswingers, a delivery he had been working on with Russell Cobb.

While all this was going on, Fanie's replacement in the B side was judged as the 'fastest white bowler I've faced in two years' by then Warwickshire opening batsman, Andy Moles, who was playing for Griqualand West. Years later when he became the Free State coach, Moles had much to say about someone faster than Allan Donald. In three matches the new recruit earned 16 wickets at 16.87, took 5 wickets twice in an innings and, but for an umpiring error by Teddy Carter (Vlam Michau was given not-out at 2 and he had edged the ball low to Noel Day), may have created a record for a bowler making his first-class debut in South Africa.

Tertius Bosch had arrived!

7

A Long Way from Sasolburg

In keeping with the region and its history, Todmorden is not a pretentious place. Neither are its inhabitants. The town knows where it belongs and anything which has its roots in the eighteenth-century industrial revolution will always have a touch of soot and cotton mill about it. Yet, like Fanie's old hometown of Sasolburg, the thriving borough of Todmorden is within easy reach of several bigger Yorkshire and Lancashire cities. And like Sasolburg, Todmorden's location has led to an occasional identity crisis down the years. Even the club's badge, an entwined white and red rose, has a quixotic flavour: it would horrify ardent supporters of both Yorkshire and Lancashire.

The town is normally part of the Lancashire league, yet it has also been known, in the past, to be associated with one of the Yorkshire leagues. That is what comes from being at the crossroads of the two fiercely rival counties on either side of the Pennines.

Although close to the centre of the town, the ground is mainly surrounded by those redbrick mid-Victorian structures known as terrace houses. There are a few trees for shade and ample public seating near the whitewash and green pavilion, which also carries an air of late Victorian vintage.

It is unlikely that before 15 April 1987 anyone in England, let alone Todmorden, had heard of Fanie de Villiers. But by the end of that summer, the humble, cheerful Afrikaans youngster had not only developed an impressive reputation based on his 120 per cent exploits on the field, but he had also left a legacy of hard work and determination that turned him into a legendary figure in that thrifty, canny part of the British Isles.

This of course may, or may not, surprise those who care to examine a list of a few former players who have, for fifty years or more, brought success and fame to the thirty clubs which make up the Lancashire and Central Lancashire leagues. Sir Frank Worrell, Vinoo Mankad, Cecil Pepper, Colin McCool, Sir Clyde Walcott, Sir Everton Weekes, Ray Lindwall, John Reid, Bob Blair, Fazal Mahmood, Johnny Wardle, Tony Lock, Sir Vivian Richards, Neal Radford, Gus Logie and Michael Bevan are a small cross-section of former or current Test players contracted as professionals to teams such as Ramsbottom, Nelson, Rochdale and Todmorden.

Fanie de Villiers' personality is such that it should not surprise anyone that the people of Todmorden and the Lancashire league remember him with deep fondness. He may have been known as 'Vinnige' Fanie on the field, off it he was 'Friendly' Fanie. While other professionals rarely spoke to the spectators, Fanie's approach was refreshingly disarming and he had soon elbowed the previous images of impervious professionals out of the pavilion window.

He enjoyed sitting with spectators and would willingly sign autographs for their children. When Todmorden were batting, and club officials wanted to find Fanie, all they needed to do was look for a group of youngsters. It quickly became his trademark. It was also a time when he realized the depth of the game's culture and how it affected his thinking; for the first time he discovered there was much more to cricket than bowling, fielding and batting. He discovered that the sport was also an art form and what traditions meant and how important they were . . . and not merely in this part of England.

As he soaked up the atmosphere for the first time, he also began to understand the moods and attitudes of the crowds. How else was he able to win over to his side a particularly aggressive, noisy section of the Headingley crowd in 1994? Yorkshire crowds can be rough. They are also noted for their merciless attitude towards anyone not playing for the White Rose County. Remember the scene during South Africa's second Test of the 1994 series in England? The notorious Western Terrace was heckling Fanie after some exuberant appeals for hoped-for lbw and caught-behind decisions. Like the old Sydney Hill, or Bay 13 at the Melbourne Cricket Ground, the Western Terrace has, over the years, earned its own infamous reputation. That Sunday afternoon Fanie gave the occupants a casual dismissive wave that riled them even more. But he knew the north of England psyche well enough. As their derision of his actions reached new decibel levels, a big grin spread across his features as he plucked a red card from umpire David Shepherd's top pocket to show them they had been censured for their actions. How they loved him. It was the kind of action they understood. At the end of the over, those in the vicinity of third man applauded him loudly when he returned to his position. Soon they were talking rugby and soccer and swapping jokes.

It was his refreshing approach to the sport which gave the game's image of cold, stoic professionalism a more human face. They will tell you in Colombo, Sri Lanka, how he calmed a vociferous section of the Premadasa Stadium crowd during the second limited-overs international by teaching them the intricate rudiments of the Mexican wave during a particularly tense moment of the game. He was as highly popular on that lovely pearl of the Indian Ocean, as in Sydney, Leeds, or at snobbish Lord's. Although how the thought of bowling an apple in the 1994 Test would have gone down is debatable; his wife Judy was not impressed at all by the suggestion.

As the Northern Transvaal season of 1986-87 ground to another disappointing close, Fanie was sitting for his finals. They had been delayed because of his hectic summer schedule. Not that it was perceived as a problem, but the future had now become a question mark. Then, one late March morning, Doupie Calitz called him to his office, casually explaining that he had an interesting offer. To Calitz, it was an answer to a problem that had been worrying him for weeks: Fanie's plans for the winter.

'How would you like to spend six months in England playing cricket?'

'Is that a possibility?'

'Yes. The union have asked me to see if you are interested in playing for Todmorden in the Lancashire league,' Calitz said. 'They need the answer this afternoon.'

Fanie's eyes grew wide with surprise and Calitz understood the sudden bewilderment.

Hey, there—not so fast! This was something he needed to discuss with Braam; seek some parental guidance. A season in

England? It sounded like a good idea. It would mean leaving all his friends: his room-mate Dewald Kruger, Johan Rudolph, Morné Ferreira and Jannie Groenewald. It had been Kruger who had gone with Fanie to the *Pretoria News* during those early years of college life and helped select the photos in the sports office. Kruger, Rudolph and Ferreira, the young talented left-handed bat, had often shielded Fanie from the blame when their student pranks went awry. Now he would be on his own.

Calitz, always the quiet gentleman, understood Fanie's hesitancy. A boereseun spending six months playing in a famous English competition, going where no NKP student had gone before. At least it would put an end to his playing rugby and the worry of a serious injury. The previous August, Calitz had had a difference of opinion with the fast bowler when he injured his right thumb and index finger during a koshuis league match. Fanie's argument was that as Gerbrand Grobler also played rugby, and at a far higher level, without a serious injury, the NKP cricket director should not worry.

Naturally Calitz was upset by Fanie's stubbornness.

'One day you are going to bowl for South Africa,' he said angrily. 'Grobler will never do that. He's had his chances.'

Play for South Africa? Against some rebel side? Fanie guessed it was possible, if the rebel tours continued. Kim Hughes' Aussies had come and gone, and from the whispers around the pavilions, no more tours were planned. Certainly not next summer. What was it Clive Rice had said? Prime your bowling tactics for the season after next. That is when the next bunch of rebels will arrive. Perhaps Doupie is right. Perhaps he should stop playing rugby. Chesters had told him often enough during the summer. He, too, said he would play for South Africa one day. Forget what Barnard had told him in Durban about him having a short career as a fast bowler; a throwaway comment . . . or was it?

He contacted his father and asked his opinion.

'You go. It will be good experience.'

Fanie's next call was to the *Pretoria News* where he spoke to Chesters who had lived in England for five years. What did he think? His answer was the same as Braam's. The decision, it seemed, had been made for him. He would take up the offer. But Doupie Calitz had already given a positive response to the Todmorden request. When the exams were over, Fanie was able to concentrate more on the Todmorden proposition and spent extra time in the nets at Centurion Park, bowling to Anton Ferreira, who had stopped playing for Warwickshire. Fanie also sought Ferreira's advice about the trip to England.

'I wish I was your age again. It is going to be the experience of a lifetime,' was Ferreira's frank assessment. 'You'll also learn a lot . . . And come back a better bowler.'

He could have also added that it would shut up those doubting his ability as his apprenticeship as a fast bowler continued. Ferreira was also of the view that Fanie would eventually succeed. If all went according to long-term planning, not one but two Afrikaans-speaking players would open the bowling for Northern Transvaal in 1987-88.

The other would be Tertius Bosch. Ferreira, who had with Chesters discovered Bosch bowling in the nets at L. C. de Villiers Oval one afternoon was in no doubt: Northerns had two potential Test new-ball bowlers in the side. Exciting times were ahead. There were also problems. Mike Clare and Francois Weideman's national service days were at an end; Clive Eksteen's hopes for a bursary at Pretoria University had been snubbed; Jan van Duyker's career as a fast bowler was about to come skidding to a halt because of illness and Northerns would be looking for a new captain for the B team as Lee Selsick was going back to Johannesburg. Even Pat Symcox seriously wondered about his future in the province.

By September 1987 almost eighty per cent of the B team's attack that Fanie had been a part of, including another future Test player, did not fit in with the long-term planning or so the befuddled thinking went. During the winter of 1987 Symcox often debated with Vernon Cresswell and Vernon du Preez whether he should not take up another offer. As for Eksteen, Transvaal were not exactly falling over themselves to welcome him back. He felt he had a chance with Northerns if he could get into the university. All around there was the feeling that uncertainty and apprehension stalked the corridors of executive power at Northerns.

When Russell Cobb called in at Todmorden one day that first summer Fanie spent in England, he found the enthusiastic NKP student offering advice to several senior players. And not one to shirk responsibilities he also welcomed the mid-week games, so often a chore for some club professionals. Todmorden was a long way from Sasolburg, a long way from that unhappy interlude at Fakkel Hoër in southern Johannesburg. It was also a major step from the new traditions being established at Centurion Park. But it was an important part of Fanie's education.

Not surprisingly, as they patrolled the boundary later in the day, watching the game and chatting about NKP and next summer, a relaxed Fanie turned to Cobb.

'Soutie, this is what I want to do.' It was the statement of confident youth.

'How do you mean?'

'I want to become a full-time professional. Make the game my living.'

Cobb was surprised. He looked at the young man next to him, chewing a piece of grass and wearing that old, battered hat he used when he went fishing. A twenty-two-year-old Afrikaner planning to dedicate his life to the sport which had created new friendships and opened many doors in the heart of the north of England. Fanie's only problem was playing sport on a Sunday. It sorely pricked his conscience as it prevented him from going to church. It may be different in England, but in South Africa there were certain priorities and church on a Sunday was one of them. Although he came to terms with the need to play on a Sunday, it did not alter his deep, spiritual feelings.

* * * *

There is no real mystery about the development of cricket among Afrikaners. Yet it is a story which for decades was steeped in Boer-Brit antagonism and was harboured by an education system which had divided language groups. It needs to be remembered, however, that the early Afrikaans pioneers spoke Dutch, and did so until the 1920s. This initially encouraged sectarian mistrust and led to a general feeling of unfortunate superiority (the master-servant syndrome). How often have we come across that boorish remark: 'Afrikaners have no cricket culture'? But how were they expected to develop the culture of a sport they were not encouraged, because of their language (as opposed to colour), to embrace?

The Afrikaners' growth in cricket had two distinct roots: one as strong as English oak (the Cape influence), the other withered and deformed because of a state of mental solitary confinement. The latter was the result of the colonial masters excluding the Boer from what they mistakenly considered an elitist sport. Fortunately this attitude underwent a slow, if at times tortuous, metamorphosis, from the late 1950s.

Throughout the country, especially among the private schools, with their privileged English backgrounds, the sport prospered from the 1870s. This narcissistic attitude was further encouraged with the establishment of other private and English-speaking semi-government schools from around the turn of 1900. It was similar to the regulations that the (British) colonial establishment applied in the West Indies.

There were, of course, some high schools and places of higher learning (mainly Grey College in Bloemfontein and the Afrikaans universities) where because of their links with the colonial past, cricket was played among a large section of Afrikaners. Sadly, because of its English stigma and class rule, Afrikaans schools (notably in the Free State and the old Transvaal), from as early as the pre-World War II years, preferred athletics as their summer sport.

They had also taken to rugby, from as early as the late 1870s (in the Cape). Although what argument could be used to advance rugby as a true sport for Afrikaners has not been satisfactorily explained; an intellectual Afrikaans friend, who had at school and university played both sports, once jokingly suggested to Chesters that it was because the rough and tumble boisterous nature when playing rugby showed that they were all really big boys at heart.

Yet if rugby was so dominant among the Afrikaners when the first shots of the Anglo-Boer War were fired, why was it that those Boer prisoners, incarcerated in Sri Lanka, preferred to play an English sport instead of rugby? The explanation is to be found in Colombo, at the venue where the game was played, and Diyatalawa, their camp. The Nondescripts Club, latterly famous as the Sri Lanka base of Aravinda de Silva, Russel Arnold and Kumar Sangakkara, was the venue for the match, and in an old book the names of several players reveal they have close ties with teams representing Free State and Transvaal. However, it was P.H. de Villiers, the Dutch-speaking first secretary of the Western Province Cricket Union (1890) who had the organizational skills to set up the game. Widely known and respected in South Africa, he also played matches against the first touring teams from England in 1888-89, 1891-92 and 1895-96 (Lord Hawke's team). Although wounded twice, he impressed his captors with his accounts of playing against those pioneering tourists in Cape Town.

For P.H. de Villiers, however, cricket was not just a game for the elite (private schools), or the racially inclined colonial establishment rulers. To him, it was a sport for everyone. It was designed to build bridges and foster harmony among all people: without language or colour bias. Through his energetic enthusiasm not only was he able to establish a thriving club of seventy players from among the Boer prisoners (who all spoke Dutch), but he also had them play regular games at Diyatalawa. It is a touch of irony that P.H. de Villiers and the rest of the Boer group spent the night after the match at Mount Lavinia. Here is a hotel which is not only rich in colonial past but also one where Fanie made such an impression during the 1993 tour that he was still remembered in 2001. 'Ah . . . Fah-nie,' headwaiter Jayasumara enthused, pointing to the closed off swimming pool. 'He sat in that chair and signed so many autographs for the children . . . and the not so young children.' The Fanie de Villiers legend is strong in Sri Lanka too.

As for the other de Villiers, P.H., he returned to Cape Town and continued to play and use his influence among Dutch (later Afrikaans) schools to nurture the game.

Yet from where, and from whom, did the former POW and others among the Western Cape Dutch community acquire affection for the sport and skills to play it? The same can be asked of those in the Eastern Cape, where the colonial establishment while not so demeaning, was still often overbearing.

In this sporting melting pot in the 1850s we meet a certain Christoffel Albertyn. The son of an itinerant Dutch schoolmaster from the Swellendam district, Albertyn first watched cricket played among members of the local British garrison. He was so intrigued that he was soon practising with the soldiers, learning to master the intricacies of a totally foreign exercise. Although not the first of Afrikaner stock to get involved, he soon established a side at one of his father's schools. Around 1860 he was sent to England to further his education and, as part of the exercise, played for clubs in and around London. It was only several years after he returned to Cape Town, possibly in 1863, that Albertyn set up a type of coaching clinic. It was from such small branches that the game spread its roots among the Afrikaners. What Albertyn did learn in England, however, was tolerance, which was noticeably absent among the colonial masters in the Cape.

In fact the Cape influence among the Afrikaans-speaking cricket pioneers (whites and coloureds) has always been strong, and the education system was, until 1948, more tolerant than those of the Free State and the old Transvaal. It is claimed that Nicholaas Theunissen, whose only Test was against Major Wharton's 1888-89 side at Newlands, was a pupil of Albertyn. But the story does not end there. It is merely a beginning.

For years *Wisden* and early historians claimed that J.J. 'Kodjee' Kotze was the fastest bowler in the world (shades of South Africa's second 'White Lightning'—Allan Donald). He also began a highly unusual odyssey in 1901 when he walked through his own Boer lines from his Karoo farm to join the South African side to tour England that year. Kotze toured England three times—1901, 1904 and 1907—yet only played in three tests. In the 1920s he was the Newlands groundsman and was responsible for the transition to a turf pitch.

Another fast bowler with an Afrikaans background is Peter Heine, son of a Natal farmer, who with Neil Adcock provided South Africa with a formidable pace attack in the mid- to late 1950s. A man of good humour, who toured England in 1955 and became a tougher, competitive bowler when facing the Australians in 1957-58, Heine lacked the success he deserved.

There was a mischievous claim that Buster Nupen, who destroyed touring batsmen's reputations on matting, but was neutralized by the turf pitches in England, was an Afrikaner as well. On the Saturday of the Test against Mike Smith's team in early 1964, Louis Duffus, the long-time and venerated cricket writer for *The Star,* sat in the old Wanderers press box. With him was a tall, strongly built man and shortly before the day's play started Duffus turned to several South African sports writers and said: 'I want you to meet the only Norwegian to play Test cricket.' All the time Duffus had an amused look while Nupen, too, enjoyed the 'Afrikaans' joke.

Izak Buys was also of Afrikaans parentage. Born in Somerset West, this slow, medium-pace inswing bowler quietly disappeared shortly after World War II started and is one of two Test players whose date of death and where it took place is still a mystery. But there was nothing mysterious about the quiet, urbane 'JP' Duminey, who like Albertyn, upheld all the good qualities that stem from the summer sport, especially tolerance. Born in Belville he played for Western Province and Oxford University before he ended his career in Transvaal. A Rhodes Scholar in 1921, the all-rounder enjoyed the challenge offered by the game and did much to foster it among Afrikaans students in the Western Cape schools.

In 1929 he was on holiday in Switzerland when South Africa's captain Nummy Deane sent him an urgent message to aid an injury-plagued side for the Headingley Test. A soft-spoken, distinguished and respected academic among Afrikaans and English peers, Duminey became vice-chancellor of Cape Town University in 1959. A progressive thinker, he was known for his development work at non-racial level long before it became the fashionable 'good deed for the day' among many whites; government policies, however, did much to thwart his efforts. A strong critic of the nationalist government Duminey more than once in the late 1950s and early 1960s told the then foreign affairs minister Eric Louw how the government would 'in time, come to seriously regret the ethnic and sectarian policies and separation of the schooling system' along dual medium lines which he saw as an unnecessary polarization of the language groups.

While Afrikaans developed as a language there were any number of Afrikaners who benefited the game by passing on their knowledge. André Bruyns, from the Natal midlands is one. He went to Stellenbosch University and opened the batting for Western Province and carried for years the Afrikaans mantle for a sport that had developed a decided identity crisis, especially among country schools in the (then) Transvaal and Free State provinces.

While the success of South African teams in the 1960s did much to resuscitate interest in the game, it was left to players such as Bruyns and the incorrigible fast bowler Houtie Niewoudt, and among others Marinus van Wyk, Francois le Roux, Mike de Villiers and Johann van Rensburg and the famed Joubert family from the Free State, to keep the Afrikaner attention focussed on the game.

Problems, however, remained. Isolation meant that a major infusion was needed to recapture public awareness and sweep away the decaying fusty image the sport had gained. Studies of social patterns of the decade show that to a large extent the game had, by 1978, become the playground of bilingual male yuppie elitism in the major cities and towns. Sure the unhealthy rebel tour era did much to reawaken some of the heady enthusiasm of twenty years before but what really caught public interest was the saturated attention which day-night games received through heavy media hype, especially on national television.

Administrators were quick to recognize that here was a readymade marketing tool to sell their product as entertainment. With glossy and catchy TV advertising came the creation of a new image. The floodlit arena, with its own brand of razzmatazz, fashioned a new type of spectator within a couple of years: a spectator who went to be seen not to watch. This was especially noticeable among the fast-growing affluent female audience who, through their loquacious and disportive nature, sought to draw and create maximum attention.

Or, as a provincial administrative officer once explained in the late 1980s, 'You know it is not all about putting bums in seats to help pay our wages or keep the sponsor happy. It's entertainment. It's about the excitement of how young athletes perform on a warm night and how that creates the sort of frenetic physical atmosphere for young women to show themselves off.' How right he was.

The return from Australia in the mid-1980s of Kepler Wessels gave the Afrikaans cause fresh drive. It created a new awareness in what was already a decade of polemic change within the country. Not all whites, though, agreed that rebel tours were necessary to keep alive public interest as the SACU embarked, with tacit government approval, on playing the mercenary game. What it did do was highlight the new generation, which was earning provincial recognition and to an extent was led by Fanie, Louis Vorster, Piet Botha, Stefan Jacobs, Francois Weideman, Anton Geringer and Eugene Klopper along with Gerbrand Grobler and Tertius Bosch.

What also helped was the role Wessels played in the early years after isolation: the Wessels era was noticeable for its discipline, respect and passion for the game; the Hansie Cronje era followed the years of integrity displayed by those who began their Test and limited-overs international careers under Wessels' leadership. By the end of the 1996 World Cup, while discipline was a major feature, Fanie noticed that the respect he had received on the tours of Sri Lanka, Australia and England was already showing signs of erosion.

As isolation had taken its toll in the 1970s and early 1980s through a shrinking public interest, only schoolmasters such as Bennie Venter, (Piet) Vorster in Potchefstroom, and Johan Volsteedt, of Grey College, Bloemfontein, managed to cut through the grey curtains of uncertainty that created its own polemic issues: the advancement of colour, race and creed—areas that other Afrikaner establishment sports had ignored.

In this respect, the three masters were among the growing band of new disciples—restoring prestige to a game that was creating a new, improved image, while rugby, for a change, felt the chilling winds of isolation. These bit even deeper after the fiasco of the efforts to hold a rebel rugby tour in 1986. Kepler Wessels, a young man with burning ambition to become a Test batsman, and Corrie van Zyl, another Grey College success, and later Joubert Strydom, became icons among a now-growing Afrikaans following.

A school better known for providing South African rugby players with household names, Grey College had suddenly created a new, more exciting, talent outlet. There were also Allan Donald and the talented Louis Wilkinson. Almost ninety minutes away in Kimberley, Diamantveld Hoër had produced Rudolf Steyn and Gerhardus (Gerry) Liebenberg, and as more names began to emerge, the talent provided by the growing band of new missionaries proved to be better, in quality and in quantity, than the majority that emerged in the 1970s.

Since 1991 that roll-call has shown remarkable growth: Hansie Cronje, Donald, de Villiers, Bosch, Steyn, Liebenberg, Nicky Boje. There is also the next generation: André Seymore, Pierre Joubert, Malan Morkel, Dewald Pretorius, Dirkie de Vos, Martin van Jaarsveld, Johann Myburgh, Jacques Rudolph and Andre Nel; each year the list grows. It has become the sport of the 1990s and the next millennium as new pathfinders emerge. The vision Stoffel Albertyn once had for the game has not come full circle, but it is getting there and a new exciting and talented generation has emerged.

* * * *

For no particular reason, mainly as a result of plain carelessness, some past editors of the South African Cricket Annual made a regular habit of causing any number of inexcusable gaffes. Fortunately the editorial board under Colin Bryden did a remarkable job in a relatively short time to correct the errors that others regurgitated. The 1991 edition showed this incompetency when it ran a fine action picture of Peter Rawson, the former Zimbabwe and Natal all-rounder, and captioned it 'Tertius Bosch'.

What an embarrassment.

In years to come, anyone looking through that annual will, when they come to page 46 and casually glance at the picture on the opposite page, assume that it is a picture of the late fast bowler. Not until they reach page 282 will they come face to face with the genuine article. Although the tall, athletic Northern Transvaal fast bowler had in 1990-91 taken 42 wickets, setting himself up for an eventual national call up, when the 1987-88 season dawned, he was still a skittery colt: lean, with a whipcord action and a penchant for foot-faulting.

A chilly, damp September night at Centurion Park in 1987 did not seem to be the right setting to launch a career. However, there has to be a starting point where recognition becomes more than just a name on the scoreboard. Since so few were around to see his debut performance of 5 for 58 against Eastern Province B, those who saw him take 3 for 26 in a day-night benefit match for Anton Yogi Ferreira will regard that spell of hostile bowling as his genuine introduction to the big arena. He bowled fast and straight and openers Henry Fotheringham and Mandy Yachad battled.

Yet behind the glitz and glamour of that floodlit spectacle lay one of the lesser-known talent-spotting stories in South African sport during the mid-1980s. Whereas Fanie de Villiers battled for more than two seasons for acceptance by Lee Barnard and the Wanderers Club, Bosch, with only three Castle Bowl matches to his credit, earned admission to the senior ranks without having to prove too much.

During a visit to see Ferreira in late February 1986, Chesters found himself idly watching a group of energetic koshuis league players anxious for some net practice before a league final. A gangly, wiry youth with a mop of curly black hair was generating pace that was too much for most batsmen, finding them hastily backing off towards leg. Here was raw, untapped talent and given the chance could develop into a quality fast bowler. Pretoria University could certainly use one. But here he was, a second year dental student, as fast and as fiery as anything Ferreira or the journalist had seen in years. Fanie was fast, but had the advantage of outswing. This youngster fired off his rockets in a way that reminded Chesters of Brett Matthews (the older brother of Craig Matthews), who in his early years was a left arm quickie with the lethal accuracy of a Sidewinder missile.

Bosch had agreed to make up one of the numbers in the side when someone in the koshuis discovered he had played at school and bowled in the Southern Transvaal League playing for Vereeniging. Well, here was a link with Fanie; he was born in Vereeniging as well.

One of the batsmen complained about the pace, asking Bosch to cut it down.

'Apart from "Rocket", has this guy got a name?' the journalist asks Ferreira.

'Tertius Bosch. Played for SA Country Districts Schools and toured England with their under-16s in 1983.' Ferreira looked thoughtful. 'What do you think?'

'He's fast all right. Is there time to give him a league game before the season ends?'

'The Fezelas still have a couple of games. I'll suggest we pick him for the game against Technikon. It's an Epsilon League game, but it will give us an idea.'[1]

'I wonder if Transvaal know what they have allowed to slip away,' the journalist remarked with a wry grin.

'Rand Afrikaans don't have a dentistry school,' Ferreira smiled. It was not their precious rugby so why should they care?

---

[1] Fezela (named after a type of bushveld antelope) was the second side of the Pretoria University side which was playing in the second tier of the Northern Transvaal Premier League.

If young Bosch eventually joined Fanie de Villiers as a new-ball bowler, the long-term policy adopted five years before would start producing genuine results. Chesters asked the gangling student a couple of questions in order to put the puzzle together, only to find the lad from Vereeniging shy and lacking confidence about his bowling talents; shades of Fanie that first meeting.

'It is a big university, and I really didn't think I was good enough at this level,' he admitted.

Two days later he fired off more than enough rockets. With thunder and lightning rumbling away it was as though Thor had decided to drop in on the koshuis final at L.C. de Villiers Oval. The calling card Bosch left that afternoon was 6 for 18 as Taaibos beat Sonop in the hostel league final. The following Saturday, for Fezelas against Technikon, he picked up 6 for 41. And he did not even bowl fast. 'Did not want to hit anyone,' he mumbled shyly.

Shortly after Fanie's mother and father joined him in Todmorden in early August 1987, Dr Ali Bacher, managing director of the SACU, contacted the young fast bowler about being selected as a member of the second intake in an academy course for promising South African talent. The course, he was told, would be held at Pretoria University with Plascon overseeing the financial costs. Although the official announcement was not being made until early September, Dr Bacher was of the opinion that the second academy intake would answer one of the more pressing problems facing the game: creating a larger pool of young talent and developing the skills to improved levels. It was worrying that outside the majority of the first group of twenty-four, there was little that had emerged to eventually replace the fading, older forces.

It is interesting now to check the names on the list of the first and second academies. When South Africa did make their eventual return to the international arena, the list of academy players those first two seasons came from that four-day exercise in Bloemfontein. There were Daryll Cullinan, Andrew Hudson, Brian McMillan, Mark Rushmere, Eric Simons and Fanie; of the others only Mike Rindel was given a belated opportunity.

* * * *

It is a warm spring afternoon, 5 September 1987, and Dr Ali Bacher is looking over a list of names he is to hand to the press at a media conference to launch the second Plascon Academy in Pretoria. Outside, the winter debris is being removed from Oval 3, the hockey goalposts are being taken down. In a few minutes his office will be crammed with journalists and reporters from newspapers, radio and television and he will tell them about the event he feels will herald the second phase of a new era in South African sport. Several have arrived and are talking to his secretary, Di Sime. Ali smiles when he sees Chesters; he has a special angle for him about the academy.

The meeting has gone well. There are few questions. One comment from a radioman catches attention: Kim Hughes may be coming back to South Africa to play for a province. That is not only news to Ali, it is also news to Hughes when contacted a couple of hours later. It is not an April Fool joke, either: just look at the date. Anyway why bother with denial stories; rather make it a bold dot at the end of the big story that has leaked out: Allan Lamb and Sylvester Clarke have agreed to play for Free State. And that has caused a stir.

Slowly the meeting is breaking up; a few linger over coffee and biscuits, catching up on what has gone on since the end of last season. Ali asks Chesters if he has a moment and gives a short interview. The next day the afternoon newspaper carries a story that has a hint of prophecy: Pretoria student-teacher Fanie de Villiers, spending a useful summer in England learning the skills of fast bowling, could become one of the most feared bowlers of the 1990s.

The story went on to quote the good doctor: 'We (the SACU) are hoping the academy will play a vital role in honing the considerable talents of players like Daryll Cullinan and Brett Matthews. To put it bluntly, we want to turn batsmen capable of scoring attractive fifties into the sort of players who can frequently score 150; and turn fast bowlers capable of taking the odd key wicket into destroyers like Sylvester Clarke.'

Then came that special sliver of information: 'The talent of the Northerns' bowler (de Villiers) is already there. All that needs to be done is point him and the others in the right direction. A direction that will see a more professional group of players emerge.'

After just two seasons, Ali Bacher, a former South African captain, had earmarked Fanie as a potential world-class fast bowler after watching him in action only occasionally. And what was the comment of Jackie McGlew, a Test captain of an earlier vintage, at the Wanderers in March of that year? 'This boy of yours has real class.' A pertinent thought, that one. So why were Barnard and others so slow in recognizing the talent so obvious to former Test players? Perhaps success at the academy would be the final bridge to cross for a permanent place in the Currie Cup side.

In England, the young, popular Afrikaans fast bowler is preparing for the weekend and playing against a side led by Viv Richards. It is a surprise for the twenty-two-year-old South African to suddenly meet the tall West Indian batsman; a man revered from his home island of Antigua to Taunton, from Glamorgan to the Lancashire leagues and just about anywhere else. It is claimed that not since the retirements of Sir Donald Bradman and Sir Garfield Sobers has a single player exerted such influence on the game.

Many consider him arrogant: as a batsman and as a person. But such comments camouflage the truth, for the tall Antiguan is all too aware of his role in a complex society and the race he represents; someone to make them proud, but with a touch of humility of that gifted West Indian writer, C. L. R. James. Bowling to a man of his calibre requires the sort of skills Fanie has learnt in the months he has been playing for Todmorden.

It has been a wet year and most run-ups at Lancashire league grounds have been affected. They are heavy and he is worried that he has lost the ability to swing the ball late towards the slips cordon.

Yet what an honour it is, bowling to a genius. Something for the guys in Northerns and the guys selected for the academy in Bloemfontein to think about. It is starting to come together: all the loose jigsaw puzzle bits are starting to take shape. There is a big crowd to see the West Indian captain, but there is no indication that he is aware of the spectators ringing the ground, nor does he acknowledge the bowler. He asks the umpire for guard, holding up two fingers to show he wants middle and leg. Taking guard, he looks down the pitch at Fanie's new-ball partner. The reputation of driving mercilessly off the front foot is not a myth. He drives hard, into the gap. Do not make the error of dropping it short, either. It is hooked with the same artistry. Smash and grab tactics. Run-scoring for fun. Give the crowd something to remember for the rest of the season.

Three overs have been bowled and now it is Fanie's turn to bowl to the big West Indian. Remember this moment, Fanie. You are no longer the scrawny kid being moaned at by Tobie van Rooyen in the Under-13 Week, or the lad bowling for Sasolburg Town, or battling with the net conditions at Fakkel Hoër. This is Viv Richards, the world's number one batsman.

Fanie runs in, looking at Richards' stance, aiming to move the ball to the slips. He digs it in and Richards pulls it down for a single. Richards' partner slaps Fanie's next delivery for a single. Now it is Fanie against the West Indies' captain again. He dips it towards slip and the batsman allows it to go through. More spectators are walking through the gate on this bright sunny afternoon to watch the great man bat. They have been talking about this all week. Watch that drive off the front foot. Do not present him with a half-volley.

Richards shapes to work the ball through the leg-side only to be surprised by the movement of the delivery and his off-stump is knocked back. He shakes his head at the way he misread the ball, and smiles down the pitch at the young bowler. The score is in the book: I. V. A. Richards b de Villiers 37. Bowled by the first Afrikaner he has faced; the Todmorden crowd is upset. They had come to see one of their batting heroes score runs, not their own professional, Fanie, take wickets.

* * * *

Todmorden was a fast receding memory when he arrived home on 19 September 1987, meeting the other academy squad members at the university. And because of his late arrival in the country, Mike Rindel, who had also spent a summer in the leagues in England, had news for him. John Reid was back as manager/coach. It was Northern Transvaal's Golden Jubilee and the hard word was, they were out to win a trophy. Nothing new in that.

As Fanie digested the news of John Reid's return as Northerns coach, his immediate rhetorical query was, would the Wanderers Club members reassert their influence? If so, what would be his future in the province?

He was not present when Yogi Ferreira went up to the wicketkeeper, Vernon Cresswell, and opening batsman Vernon du Preez. But it should be easy to visualize the scene. Yogi would have commiserated with both players. In Neilson's season, Cresswell had done a good job with Noel Day being dropped to the B side and du Preez knew from experience what to expect. Yet he prospered, meeting the challenge with any number of quality performances still remembered. Had he been given more exposure and support by all the selectors there is little doubt that du Preez too would have been in with a chance of playing for South Africa. Whether this would have been in the latter days of the rebel era, or the early days of the normalization, is open to conjecture. Like Fanie, he was one of the few strongly loyal players for the province.

From experience it was well known that Reid would prefer Day, no matter how well the classy Cresswell performed. A top hockey player who once earned international colours, Day had, when he first joined Northerns, been a leading run-scorer. But 1986-87 is not a summer he will look back on with any comfort. After two A Section matches, he lost his place to Cresswell and ended with, for a man of his talent, a B Section average of 14.16 in six innings. Yet he did play a number of match-winning innings, including two classic limited-overs performances, in the season of Reid's return.

However, the question whether Barnard would be replaced as captain was raised in the Pretoria papers well before Reid's came back. Frankly he continued in this role because, at the time, there was no one else. But a large question mark hovered against his name when it came to his batting abilities. Apart from the 1989-90 season, when he finished third in the Northerns averages with 32.09, the little left-hander usually occupied the middle to lower regions of the province's Currie Cup averages.

It was a continual source of aggravation among the Northerns bowlers (and supporters) how their top batsmen regularly failed. After nine seasons Barnard's Currie Cup career average for Northerns was a low 23.92 and only in four summers did he crack an average of 25 plus. While his limited-overs record was little better, he at least played several match-winning innings. What the bowlers such as Fanie, Tertius Bosch and Willie Morris needed down the years was support from their top batsmen. So few have consistently managed an average of 35 or more a season that it became a continual source of embarrassment for the bowlers. They would set the side up to win a match only to see them lose it. During a period of sixteen seasons, only four batsmen regularly reached an average of 40 a season: Mandy Yachad, Mike Rindel, Mike Haysman and Clayton Lambert. With more opportunities, Vernon du Preez's name would also be on that list.

But Fanie found, when he was at L.C. de Villiers, that the four days at the academy became an extension of what he had learnt at Todmorden. The experiences gained from listening to former Test bowlers like Neil Adcock and Frank Tyson helped increase his knowledge. It also gave Adcock an opportunity to study the developing talent emerging from the young Northerns bowler. During his career as a fast bowler, Adcock destroyed any number of innings at Test and Currie Cup levels and had become a strategist on fast bowling techniques. He was also disenchanted with what he called the 'modern professional outlook'. Yet he found Fanie's fresh eagerness a source of encouragement and reported as much to Dr Bacher.

Having agreed, before he returned to South Africa, to play for Anton Ferreira's XI in the benefit match, Fanie found, after his arrival from Bloemfontein, that his new-ball partner for the game would be Tertius Bosch. Between the two of them, on that damp spring evening, they cruelly dismembered the lower order of Graeme Pollock's All Stars. In a dramatic slump, which started when Fanie got rid of Pollock, 5 wickets fell in a matter of 14 balls, sending the innings cartwheeling from 217 for 6 wickets to 220 all out.

Not only was a stirring new fast-bowling partnership born, it was delivered before almost 10,000 excited spectators. Conceived during the winter months in the mind of Yogi Ferreira, it was the new-ball attack Northerns had sought since Eric Simons' departure for Cape Town four seasons before. And although Simons played in the benefit match, it is doubtful whether he, or many officials present, realized the significace of the de Villiers-Bosch association on 29 September 1987. Cyril Mitchley junior certainly did. The spindly fast bowler went for 54 in 9 overs and realized that Lee Barnard had witnessed the impressive performance by the new pair.

Before the end of October Mitchley had, in a fit of pique, departed for Transvaal after being dropped in favour of Bosch. It was a sad annulment of his Northerns connection and he blamed the *Pretoria News* for his non-selection after two flat performances in the day-night domestic series. Had Mitchley listened to Reid, he might have been spared such an ignominious exit. 'Go and find your form at club level' was his advice.

Fanie was the first to admit, however, that he had learnt several tactical ploys from the beanpole quickie during the few matches they had played together. For one thing, there was no profit at all in bowling short of a length. If you want to put pressure on the batsman, the best plan is to bowl fuller: force him into the error of thinking that he can drive. Allied to this plan is bowling a half-volley wide of the off stump and give the batsman a chance to hit a four-ball. It was a clever tactic. Mitchley's theory was to give the batsman a two, or a single, or even a boundary if it meant you would get his wicket. There was no advantage in becoming an economical bowler declining to attack if you did not work to a plan.

Also, there is no advantage in keeping it tight by bowling outside the off stump to a five/four or six/three field if it means that the batsman will wait for the loose ball. The more you attack, the more the batsman will play his shots and the better chance you have of earning his wicket. It was a tactic Fanie had used with success in Todmorden and it earned Adcock's approval. Whereas Mitchley was slow enough to earn successful rewards, Fanie's pace was still sharp. Yet, he also benefited when he made use of the tactic. Especially if there were reliable slips and gully fieldsmen in the teams.

There is no doubt that as a result of his Todmorden and Plascon Academy experiences Fanie matured as a new-ball bowler. He was sharp, he was attacking; he had a Currie Cup return of 25 wickets at 23.76. And even if Bosch was not the initial success Northerns had hoped, his potential was too obvious to ignore. What was disturbing was that he was given such few overs.

Gerbrand Grobler, playing his best in three seasons, deserved a better return than 15 wickets at 34.93. Yet Fanie's season can be summed up in three overs: two in Virginia and one at Centurion Park. Forced into a third leg Nissan Shield semi-final against a Free State side that contained Alvin Kallicharran, Allan Lamb and Sylvester Clarke, Northerns managed to defend a total of 170 in a game where unusually heavy, unseasonal rains forced it to be played in the Goldfields. Then umpires Lou Rautenbach and Karl Liebenberg, reduced the match to thirty overs a side, after heavy overnight rain.

The two overs in Virginia were a masterpiece of tight, yet fast, bowling.

At the start of the twenty-fourth over, Lamb and Robbie East had Free State on target, the asking rate then was 6.83. It was getting tougher, and there was some superb fielding, geed up by the astute Barnard; Fanie's bullet returns to Day, cutting twos to singles along with similar exploits by Vernon du Preez, Pat Symcox and Roy Pienaar checked the run rate. It was Ferreira who broke through, enticing Lamb to go for the big hit. The result was a catch to Vernon du Preez. Sylvester Clarke then joined East, pushed up the order to increase the run-rate. Then disaster struck. East was run-out in a desperate bid to turn a single into two runs. What folly. The Free State crowd had worked itself into a frenzy in a bid to upset Northerns' concentration, but they failed. Just as East had done in trying to beat Symcox's accurate return to Day's end.

At 154 for 8 Fanie was brought back with 4 overs remaining: the equation was 19 runs off 24 balls and bowling to Clarke was never easy in a tight situation. Grobler and Morris had bowled the 6 overs allowed and Symcox had gone for 19 in 4. Anything wayward would create a problem. Clarke smashed a six off Fanie over long on: 13 wanted off 13 balls. The crowd was chanting: 'Six . . . six . . . six . . .!'

The decision to allow Fanie to bowl had been a calculated risk and was made only after consulting Pienaar, Yogi Ferreira and Day. In fact Barnard momentarily thought about bringing himself, or Symcox, on for the twenty-sixth over of the innings. But that six was so expensive. Ferreira gave away 2 off his next over. Now 11 runs were required off 12 balls. The odds were still on Free State. Barnard backed Fanie again; it was his first genuine test as a limited-overs bowler: Bowl full and bowl tight. Remember . . . do not give them anything to hit!

The result was Clarke's wicket for 13, well yorked. And only 7 runs off the last 12 balls Fanie had bowled, including that six. He had fired them in hard and fast while the raucous Free State crowd had tried hard to unsettle Fanie's rhythm with crude remarks. They failed yet again.

At the start of the last over Free State needed 10 runs. They managed to scramble only a single, with Bradley Player the third run-out victim of the innings. Barnard talked about the fielding under pressure and Ferreira's bowling. He also talked about team character.

'And Fanie?'

'What can you say? That Dutchman can really bowl. Two superb overs, Chesters.'

They were far more than that. Following his quality spell of 7-3-7-1 on the Saturday in a match Free State had won, any fears there had been about Fanie's temperament under pressure had quickly been dismissed. It was an open admission from Barnard that Fanie was a better bowler than he had grudgingly acknowledged for so long. If Grobler and Bosch had been so easily accepted as team members why did recognition take so long for Fanie? It was not, as the Afrikaans press had so often erroneously made out, a Boer-Brit issue; it is a question which has still not been adequately answered.

In Johannesburg, Dr Bacher could afford to smile. It may have been the first time in his career that Fanie was one of the main components in assuring that Northerns reach a final, but it was not going to be the last. He repeated the Virginia performance several times before his retirement, but the most remarkable was at the Wanderers six years later against Allan Border's Australians. In the penultimate over of the innings he bowled those six amazing yorkers in a row, to the Australian captain, and gave way just a single in the process. It not only helped South Africa win the opening one-day limited-overs match on 19 February 1994 by 5 runs, it proved that he had not lost that magic touch: control, accuracy and an ability to bother the batsmen. Remember Sydney. Remember the Wanderers. Remember the Harmony Sports Club in Virginia. It was a venue where Fanie de Villiers built a reputation for being one of the world's finest limited-over bowlers of his generation.

That other over came in the Nissan Shield final when he bowled to a rampant Kenny McEwan as Eastern Province won by 7 wickets. He gave McEwan a four-ball and had him driving hard, and then catching the edge in three successive balls. Two flew low and wide, eluding Willie Morris in the gully. The last went to first slip, the ball falling centimetres short of out-stretched hands.

For Fanie, the season was over. For Pat Symcox it was the end of his career with the province. Although he took a record 30 wickets for the B team at 23.43, no one bothered to return his calls made one afternoon to two selectors to tell them he had a job offer in Kimberley. Chesters made a call to Willie Basson, but he was overseas, and Ian Buchanan, the vice-president, was busy in a meeting. Northerns had their long-term plans and they did not include Symcox. Not with Barnard in the role as the extra off-spinner. Having lost one future Test slow bowler in Eksteen they were about to sacrifice a second. A bowler who, by his own admission, Fanie regarded as his chief foil when bowling in tandem in limited-overs internationals.

8

Development Plans

For Russell Cobb, it was the end of an era. And as he reviewed it on his way to the Wanderers that March afternoon ir 988 there were no regrets: just a touch of sadness that it was over. Helping introduce a group of Afrikaans students to a game as complex as cricket was always going to provide a trunkful of memories: most of them happy, many of them special. After all, yo ' do not spend five summers doing the same coaching job if tnere is nothing to lure you back the next summer. In that span of time he had seen Onderwyskollege become a proud force at club level in Northern Transvaal, and had witnessed the emergence of Fanie de Villiers. When he drove up Corlett Drive to the SACU offices to take his leave of Dr Ali Bacher, he had a plan in mind which he knew would be a success.

During the past two seasons Cobb had been coaching in the townships around Pretoria: Atteridgeville, Mamelodi and Shoshanguve, as well as Tembisa. In the summer of 1987-88 he had used Fanie to help spread the gospel of the game among a group of underprivileged kids. Some would turn up in T-shirts that proclaimed they had played in Baker's mini cricket matches; others wore a variety of ragged tops and torn shorts. Most were without footwear. Those who did have plastic takkies soon discarded the torn and broken relics of an older brother's football excursion of a couple of years before. It reminded Fanie of when he had arrived that first time at the Northerns B squad nets wearing a copper-coloured golf shirt.

The one worry Dr Bacher had when he knew Cobb was not returning for a sixth season at Onderwyskollege was finding a reliable replacement. Cobb had, without hesitation, recommended Fanie. Not only did he have an exceptional manner with youngsters, but he would get involved at other levels as well. For one thing there was a need for practice facilities and Fanie was quite prepared to build concrete nets at various schools. It was the sort of information Dr Bacher needed. He would see that money was available to buy the necessary material to help the young fast bowler.

While Fanie had entertained the idea of returning to play in one of the English leagues, he knew it would mean another delay in his national service call up. He had also developed a relationship with Judith Odendaal and did not want too many distractions that winter, especially as she had become an important part of his life.

A hurdler, with a lithe well-balanced, graceful style, she had just registered for her second year when he spotted her that mid-morning of 18 January 1988.

'Hey, what a beautiful girl.' There was no hiding his admiration: the future South African fast bowler was floored.

'That's Judy Odendaal,' Dewald Kruger told him.

'She has to be the most beautiful girl on the campus.'

'Go and talk to her,' suggested Jannie Groenwald.

'No. I can't do that.' He shook his head. 'I can't just go up to any girl and start talking to her, not without being introduced.'

With typical brash student bravado his teammates were not prepared to let it rest and invented a plan. They wanted him to take bets within their group about her accepting his invitation to the weekly Wednesday night disco at the Pretoria Club, a fifteen-minute walk from the campus. Fanie looked at his friends, his confidence growing. He knew this was not going to be easy.

'Look, I'll tell you what. If you guys put on enough beer I'll invite her out, and within two weeks she'll be my girlfriend.'

They agreed instantly, and as Kruger, Morné Ferreira and other NKP campus friends at Pioneer hostel looked on, Fanie, with a rare show of arrogance, called her name, watched her turn, look at him and walk on. It was as if she had not seen him. For Fanie it was not the beer, or the bet, which had inspired him but her looks. He was totally captivated by her smile. He ran up to her and started talking without introducing himself and quickly got to the point before his courage failed him. Judy stopped while her friends walked on slowly and gave him a warning look.

'Your name is Judy Odendaal?'

'Yes,' She eyed him, uncertain of what he wanted.

'Well, I think you look fantastic.' He was smiling at her. 'Won't you come and have a milkshake with me?'

She looked at him, totally bemused by his enthusiasm. Just who was this guy? She had heard her name being called, turned and seen at a tall, cheerful, athletically built student whom she did not recognize. She had walked on, ignoring his call until she realized he was running after her.

Judy shook her head, exasperated, wanting to join her friends, Karen Zietsman, Tania du Toit and Estee Windell. She was neither impressed by the invitation nor his attitude. 'No thank you.'

Judy preferred dark haired guys. Anyway, she did not have much of an opinion of anyone wearing a tracksuit unless it was on the sports field; she was not snobbish, it was more about the way she had been brought up.

But Fanie refused to be put off by such a rebuff. 'I'll come and collect you tomorrow and take you out.'

'No. I am really studying for some rewrites and I just don't have the time,' she explained.

His blue eyes lit up.

'There are some great places where we can go,' he persisted. 'One is the Students' Den.'

She shook her head, irritated by his casual yet determined manner.

'You can relax for one night.'

Judy was unimpressed. As she said to her friends later, 'I don't like guys who think a lot of themselves.' Then, as an afterthought, she queried 'Does anyone know who he is?' There were a lot of blank stares among her friends.

'He didn't even have the courtesy to introduce himself.'

She dismissed him with a shake of her head. He was rude.

Such was Fanie's interest, however, that he discovered who her lecturers were. His next step was to find out when she had to do her rewrites and he visited the lecturer to see when she was free. That afternoon, still wearing his blue tracksuit, he turned up again; this time, riding a bicycle, he confronted her with the knowledge that she was doing only one rewrite, on Wednesday.

As it was only Monday Judy felt trapped, but still fobbed off his attentions.

'Look, I'm not sure when I'll be free.' He knew well enough it was the 'Don't call me, I'll call you' routine.

Some weeks earlier he had broken up with his first serious girlfriend and had, at the time, made up his mind that he would pursue a relationship only if he met someone he thought he could really care about. He also needed a little luck to get a positive response. When he turned up the next afternoon he learnt from Karen Zietsman that Judy was training for an athletics meeting.

Perhaps it was the gap he needed? As it was, Ms Zietsman was impressed by Fanie's efforts to date her friend. She found him sincere and although she knew that Judy was far from keen on the idea of a date with him, she decided to do a little matchmaking of her own. She told Fanie that Judy would go to the Students' Den the following night and suggested he arrive at around 7:30. On cue, he turned up at the girls' hostel and called her down on the intercom.

'Karen, do you know anything about this?'

'Know about what?'

'This guy downstairs wanting to take me to the Students' Den?'

Karen Zietsman shook her head, trying to keep a straight face.

'Do you know his name?'

'No. Don't you?'

'You really have put me in a very awkward position. How can I go out with someone I don't know?'

'Why not try it this once? Give it a chance. He seems to be a nice guy, Judy.'

As Fanie waited, another suitor turned up asking to see Judy.

'Why are you calling her?'

'She's a friend.'

'That's not possible.' Fanie shook his head. 'Are you a student?'

'No.'

'I didn't think so.'

Fanie looked at him seriously.

'On this campus there are two hostels, Pioneer and Natalie. What is happening is that the guys in Pioneer are dating all the girls in Natalie—this hostel. So, I suggest that unless you want a fight, you had better leave.'

For a moment the other man eyed Fanie, wondering whether to call his bluff, when three other students walked in to the foyer. As they stood there talking, they looked an imposing quartet and, not wanting to get involved in a fight, he decided to leave quietly. That was the easy part. Getting her down to the foyer was going to be a lot harder. And Fanie knew he had to turn on the charm. The brash image of two days earlier had been brushed off, replaced by the friendly person everyone knew.

Eventually, she agreed to go on the date. And when she caught sight of his battered red Alfa her heart immediately softened. But on opening the passenger's door Judy, so used to polite, wellmannered people and tidiness, was met by a sight which could have permanently terminated any form of relationship. During the months he owned the car, Fanie had turned the passenger seat area into a personal rubbish bin. Judy suddenly found herself trying to sit in a seat surrounded by empty cold drink cans and bottles, crumpled hamburger and hot dog packets, drinking straws, half-empty packets of crisps, sweet wrappers and newspapers. Clothes, mostly tattered T-shirts, lay everywhere.

Little wonder that her eyes opened even wider. She shook her head and started laughing.

'I love this car,' she said earnestly. 'It really has got a certain character.'

His whole approach and casual explanation about how no one messed with his 'rubbish bin' struck a sympathetic chord. Although for weeks he assumed she loved the car more than him and for that reason made no effort to clean it: inside or out.

Another surprise greeted her at the disco where all the students seemed to know him. Some called him 'Vinnige' or 'Stephanus'; others referred to him as Faantjie and still others knew him as either 'Fanna' or plain Fanie. Before the night was over she was totally confused.

It was now the middle of January and his friends had not seen him since he had earned a few headlines during the holidays. Judy found herself at a disadvantage, especially when girls came up and started talking to him about cricket and asking him how he was enjoying the season since he had come back from England. It was a new environment for the nineteen-year-old girl who had been a top hurdler at Höerskool Waterkloof two years before. But she enjoyed herself thoroughly.

The next afternoon Fanie sent a first year student, Henk, across to Natalie with a bunch of roses for Judy: twenty red and one white. She looked at the bouquet and knew who it was from.

'What is this guy's name?'

'Oh . . . It's Fanie . . . Fanie de Villiers. He plays cricket for Northern Transvaal.'

Judy Odendaal looked at the flowers and shook her head. So, the lean, athletic 'big mouth' was a provincial cricket player. Coming from a family which had only followed rugby, her knowledge of cricket was limited to having heard only of Graeme Pollock, Clive Rice and Jimmy Cook. She was also intrigued about Fanie's background and his immense popularity. If she planned to go out with him again, which she had decided was not such a bad idea, Judy had to know more about him. All she knew now was that he was a provincial player and thus must be a top sportsman. The rest was a mystery.

It was not, however, to remain that way for long as Northerns were playing the Impalas at Centurion Park in a mid-week day-night game. Fanie made Judy sit in the aisle leading to the players' dressing room. During the last 2 overs of the match, Fanie scored 17 runs in a desperate effort as Northerns sought to win a semi-final spot. When Tertius Bosch joined him, 21 runs were needed off 14 balls. Fanie hit a big six off Kenny Watson, and Bosch ran a risky single to give the fast bowler a chance to score the 8 runs wanted off the last 3 balls. Judy watched, enthralled.

Everyone around the ground was in an uproar, shouting: '*Slaan die ball* (hit the ball), Vinnige . . .! Slaan die ball, Vinnige . . .!' He did his best to oblige with a six and a four. At the time, however, he lacked the experience of someone like Anton Ferreira to win a match in such a situation. It was a brave effort by the youngster to take up the role of a senior player. Five years later he had a similar experience and added 51 with Richard Snell, saving South Africa from total embarrassment in the third one-day international against Sri Lanka at Premadasa Stadium in Khettarama, Colombo.

At Centurion Park on 17 February 1988, Judith could barely breathe as the frenetic pace and excitement grew around her. It was all so new to the young woman. Two runs were needed off the last ball and poor Bosch failed to read Fanie's 'run like hell' intentions as he faced the last ball. The roar of the spectators close to Judy approached hysteria: the way it could be at schools' athletics meetings or rugby matches. Then there were groans. The scores were tied and the PA system blurted out something in English, then Afrikaans, getting the result of the match wrong as Fanie and Tertius walked off and up the steps. Fanie stopped in front of Judy and putting an arm around her shoulders kissed her for the first time. Some spectators whistled, others laughed, some told Fanie he should have hit another six.

Minutes later there was disappointment and added commotion over the result when it became known that the Impalas had won by losing fewer wickets. There was, however, still some confusion in the press box where the *Pretoria News* and *Beeld* had the scores at 209 and extras at 26, not 25. But the scorers insisted they were correct. Weeks later, the NTCU statistician, having collected the scorebook from John Reid to work out the final averages, discovered a major discrepancy in the Northerns innings of the Impalas game. Working out the scoring rates for each batsman he counted that 274 balls had been faced during the Northerns innings. Counting the three wide balls, it should have been 273 balls. Checking back, the statistician saw that in Simon Base's seventh over a wide had been recorded, but had not been reflected in the sundries column. While the discovery supported the *Pretoria News* and *Beeld* scores it was, as John Reid said, far too late to raise the issue. He agreed it should have been spotted on the night of the game, or on the next day.

Eleven days after the Impalas match Judy attended a celebratory dinner at a steakhouse in Welkom along with most of the Northern Transvaal team after beating Free State in the third leg of that Nissan Shield semi-final. Although still shy, her knowledge of cricketers' names had grown to include many of the who's who.

She was also soon known as 'Fanie's girl', which had a nice ring. He also did not waste time in getting a picture of her to put on the board in his room. It was one of Judy clearing the last hurdle in a race, culled from a pile of discarded athletic photos from the *Pretoria News* files.

Less than a year later, Judy Odendaal was crowned the Pretoria Onderwyskollege Campus Queen, 1989.

Once the season was over and his relationship with Judy had settled down, Fanie took over the development coaching role organized by Cobb and was soon hard at work building eight concrete nets in Mamelodi. For that particular job, he enlisted the help of his brother Neels and they were proud of their construction labours. Eight nets are not a lot when that, at the time, the Pretoria University's L.C. de Villiers sports complex in Hatfield had five artificial and ten turf nets. But at least Mamelodi had double the number of nets in Soweto. By 1998 the L.C. de Villiers quota of nets had grown to eight artificial and twelve turf, with each turf net having three pitches. Coaching was hard work and Fanie recruited a couple of volunteers from the ranks of the NKP team to lighten the load. At least they knew where the money for their hamburgers and soft drinks was coming from.

In the years since the Soweto uprising changed the face of apartheid, most of South Africa's thriving townships had undergone a major metamorphosis. Mamelodi is one of them. Under the banner of South African cricket's first, but doomed, unity in 1976-77 a burly sports administrator from the Department of Education and Training DET addressed a group of township teachers in a hall in Laudium. Two minutes after he stood up to sell the concept of a cricket coaching programme, the hall was all but empty; all it took were two chilling sentences. 'Today we have brought you here to tell you about a new cricket coaching programme for your schools. My name is Mr Nel. You will call me *baas!*' When the story was used in the *Pretoria News* two days later, the DET responded by claiming it was said as a joke, not to be taken seriously. If that is the case, why say it at all?

The idea was to encourage the teachers, not cower them with a verbal baton. The result of that sneering racist remark was that the teachers bussed in from Atteridgeville and Mamelodi, walked out, leaving a few Indians to hear what the 'baas' had to say. His next remark suggested that if the teachers were not interested in cricket, they would not be allowed to learn the game. Instead, the status quo would remain. They would continue to play their soccer.

'It is cheaper and easier to run,' Nel told two uncomfortable black officials on the stage.

For a moment it seemed that the ugly truth of DET sports policy had unthinkingly, in a careless comment, been unmasked. Soccer: cheap to run, easy to organize, no maintenance, little coaching. Just put up two goalposts and let them play. The apartheid sport.

The same ingrained racial attitude was used by a gateman at the Wanderers on 13 February 1993 to block Krish Mackerdhuj, president of the UCB, from entering the ground. Sir Clyde Walcott, then president of the ICC, and their wives were with him. They were on their way to attend the historic West Indies-Pakistan one-day game in the Total Triangular series. Ahead of them was a car driven by two white officials. Although they went through unimpeded, the gateman held up a hand as soon as he saw the faces in the car. Mackerdhuj showed the security official the relevant parking ticket, but he was unimpressed. A major row was averted when a Transvaal Cricket Board official hastily intervened.

Conversely, it was not easy for whites to go into a place such as Mamelodi or Atteridgeville in the late 1970s. Kenneth Lebethe, a *Pretoria News* sports staffer and a member of the Pan-African Congress (PAC), knew he could get into 'political' as well as official trouble when, in 1977, he introduced Chesters, his cricket writing colleague, to the youngsters in Atteridgeville, west of Pretoria. They went to a school and met Charles Kekana and, for more than an hour, talked earnestly about starting a cricket programme with his help. It did not come as a surprise that the plan did not materialize because of lack of funds and interest from provincial resources.[1]

Ten years later in Mamelodi, Lebethe and his colleague went to see another group of schoolteachers. Among them was Monica Magodielo, from Mmangolwane Primary School, who was then studying for a cricket coaching certificate through the SACU plan engineered by Dr Ali Bacher. Hard working and inspirational, her

---

[1] In 1977 Lebethe and Chesters had organized equipment to take to Atteridgeville and Mamelodi as part of a coaching programme, only to have it confiscated by the South African police, saying that it was an unauthorized intrusion since permission and permits were needed. As neither had been obtained the DET said they would run their own programme. As far as the author is aware, no cricket coaching took place until the SACU launched their coaching plan in 1983.

affection for the game spread in Mamelodi and the suburb has since produced a wave of young quality players. Several have won scholarships to different Pretoria high schools and earned places in the Nuffield (Coca-cola) Week teams. Ms Magodielo, now a grandmother, allowed others to take over while she concentrated on environment studies. Yet, from small beginnings in 1985, the development scheme is growing. By early 2000 her interest had been renewed through the formation of the Mamelodi Cricket Club at the inauguration of the Mamelodi Oval.

In early October 1988 Fanie called Chesters and took him and the *Pretoria News* photographer, Walter Pitso, to Mamelodi for a picture shoot of the eight nets he had produced to serve thirty-seven primary schools. He was proud of the work he had done to help in the upliftment of youngsters. Eight years later, when he drove into a school ground anywhere in Mamelodi, he would be mobbed and have scraps of paper thrust at him to be signed. At the time, Dr Bacher felt Fanie's work had a special magic which drew children of all ages.

'I must say we were impressed at the way Fanie spoke to the Mamelodi coaches the first time he met them,' Dr Bacher, then chief executive of the South African Cricket Union, said in late 1988 when talking about the SACU project said. 'It was little more than a ten minute motivational speech but so positive in ideas. They were soon listening with equal enthusiasm. Coaching a bunch of development players is not easy. But he turned it into a fun thing. He revolutionized the way the game is taught to these youngsters.'

The youngsters at Mmagolwane learnt that while cricket is essentially a sideways game with puzzling semantics, it had its own form of the three Rs, the DAC: dedication, application and concentration. You can also add a fourth: discipline. Soweto has long had its own stadium, Atteridgeville, an oval opened by Jonty Rhodes. Mamelodi? Well, Mamelodi's facility was opened during the 1999-2000 England tour. As for Soshanguve, their oval was opened in early October 1996: Conrad Hunte and Denis Lindsay played in a celebrities XI. Built at a cost of R400,000, Dr Bacher brought a smile to the serious young faces when he asked what they wanted most. After a couple of haphazard guesses, the UCB managing director told them that a private benefactor had given him R250,000 to build a clubhouse.

It is a pity Dr Bacher departed for Johannesburg before the speeches were finished, as he would have received a message from the young players.

'Man, we are tired of hearing about Soweto,' said Tebogo Sikho, the least shy of the players. 'All we hear is Soweto this and Soweto that and how great Soweto is. Well, I have a message. This is Soshanguve, not Soweto and one day the people are going to hear how great Soshanguve is.'

Although developing a culture takes time, a future Test player, who once played barefoot at school in Deneysville and Sasolburg and coached in Mamelodi, knows all too well the pot-holed road which has to be travelled. In 1988, as a twenty-three-year-old student-teacher at Pretoria NKP, Fanie de Villiers was not too proud to deny the youngsters their chance and was prepared to pass on the knowledge he had acquired in the recent seasons in the Northern Transvaal side.

As a preface to the 1988-89 South African centenary season, Mamelodi was as good a place as any to start a training programme. Apart from the gym work, the building of the concrete pitches helped strengthen his back. Yet he did not expect that as he worked towards the start of his fourth provincial season, his career was bubbling merrily below the surface and would soon erupt. During his third Plascon Academy session at Pretoria University, he expressed an interest in learning more about Test and international stars to his journalist friend. With his days as an understudy over, he needed more responsibility as a new-ball bowler. Already there was a hint that Northerns were aiming to sign Sylvester Clarke. Natal were also after the big Bajan, with Mike Procter claiming he would play for Natal.

After the fiasco of the previous summer when Clarke turned out for Free State having broken a 'gentleman's agreement' involving the former Test player and Northerns, Dr Willie Basson was not taking any chances of being robbed this time. Apart from Clarke, Mandy Yachad had returned after several unproductive summers at the Wanderers, and Mike Haysman, a member of Kim Hughes' Australian rebels, had also signed on. An impressive trio of experience to boost Northerns' trophy plans. Sylvester Clarke was the name Fanie really cared about. There was the wrench of losing Pat Symcox, his friend from his B team days, while watching Jannie Groenewld and Morné Ferreira progress to the provincial B team level was satisfying.

Sitting in the foyer of the Burgers Park Hotel, he asked Chesters for some advice.

'I know that Sylvester Clarke comes from Barbados and has played in Tests. But I need to know a lot more about him. I need to know a lot more about other players. I want you to help me.'

'That's easy, Fanie. There's a book called *The Complete Who's Who of Test Cricketers*. You can borrow that.' Then, as an afterthought, 'Tell you what, Fanie. If you take thirty wickets this season, I'll give it to you.'

'A deal,' grinned Fanie.

Anton Ferreira also promised him a Warwickshire jersey if he took more than thirty-six wickets.

Earlier rumours of another rebel tour, this one said to involve New Zealand, had long been discounted. But the international scenario was still cloudy and would continue to be for some time for South Africa, now into a centenary summer. In fact, the 1988-89 season was to be the last of the old order as forces inside and outside the game were to change it for the better, for good.

Rodney Ontong's injury, the result of a nasty car accident in England, had ruled him out for the season, and although Willie Morris was to play in all the Currie Cup matches that season, Fanie had a sneaking suspicion the Wanderers Club connection would still have squeezed out Symcox as they had done others. Already a critical Gerbrand Grobler had voiced his opinion wondering 'if the day will not come when our practice sessions and team talks will be held at the Wanderers nets and not Centurion Park'. It was a comment which did not go down well with either Reid or Barnard. Willie Basson, in his last season as Northerns president, was not overly impressed with Grobler's concern. Yet the way the left-arm fast bowler now saw it, Yachad and Haysman joining the side meant that seven members of the senior squad were residents of Johannesburg. Where did it leave those who were not?

Fanie, however, was doing his best to stay out of the team's political machinations. Apart from being an unpleasant intrusion in his preparation for the season, he found the clique mentality affecting his relationship with some team members. He worked in the nets with Tertius Bosch and Grobler; when Clarke finally arrived, he enjoyed the quip made by his captain Barnard. 'Finally we have the good news,' Barnard grinned. 'Welcome to Centurion Park, Sylvers. Your arrival is the best news I've had this season.'

In those days Northerns did not play many pre-season friendlies of note. This time, however, there were a couple of matches against Natal sides in Pietermaritzburg and Durban, with Fanie bowling in both with moderate success. Although some of the more senior players were involved in occasional benefit matches, Fanie was not yet a name and few were after his services. It gave him time to work in the nets, which is what he wanted, perfecting his outswing and the theory he had developed that there was no harm in the half volley that moved towards the slips. Give the batsman something to drive and catches are bound to follow. He could argue that with almost fifty per cent of the catches being pocketed by either the slips or gully, it was a success.

However, there were frustrations too. That opening game of the day-night series season against Natal at Centurion Park on 28 October was such an illustration. Making his debut was a fresh-faced Jonty Rhodes. With Brian Whitfield and Andrew Hudson both failing to score, it is easy to sympathize with the then nineteen-year-old walking in to bat with the scoreboard reading 4 for 4. The top-order, apart from the captain, Rob Bentley, was mystified at the amount of swing Fanie generated that afternoon. It was a little overcast, but the cloud cover was not heavy. Again, there was not a lot of wind, not enough to help generate the sort of swing that had batsmen driving wildly off the front foot at half-volleys. Poor Rhodes. He did not stand a chance, becoming Bosch's second victim of the innings, picked up by the ever-alert Haysman in the slips. Fanie, using what help there was in the conditions, and slanting the ball sharply away at times, had figures of 4-2-4-3.

Yet Natal were allowed to escape. They had slipped to 44 for 7 and should have been shut out of the game. But, badly directed leg-side bowling, with Anton Ferreira coping a fair amount of stick, saw the advantage that the two fast bowlers had won fritter away. England's Dominic Cork enjoyed firing them down the leg-side during England's first tour of South Africa after isolation, and in the

1996 World Cup. It is a nasty habit. But Ferreira's leg-side tactic enabled Neville Daniels, a solidly built all-rounder, to thrive with what became a match-winning innings. Barnard should have given himself a couple of overs to restrict Daniels' batting strategy.

Fanie watched the carve up from third man, distressed by the too-casual approach of some teammates as victory was allowed to slip away. It was not going to be the only time that season, or in summers to follow, that he would become aggravated at the careless culpability of most Northerns batsmen in limited-overs matches. One victory in eight limited-overs games that summer was not a record to be remembered with any sort of pride.

At least he was taking wickets, and economically. His two 4-wicket hauls in the shorter games were still part of an adjustment from the eager tearaway who bowled in a defensive role to that of an attacking bowler. It was another part of his education that season. Remarkably, his economy rate showed a gradual rather than a marked improvement. For a large percentage of the season, he bowled without Clarke as his partner. Yet it became the largest factor to the youngster relying on swing and pace as his twin weapons of destruction. He found that with Clarke and Bosch at the other end there was plenty of pace, and that by turning more to swing he was picking up more wickets.

Clarke's enforced absence for six weeks due to a knee operation and Bosch's heel injury in the South African Universities tournament forced a serious selection rethink in the middle of the opening match of the Currie Cup season. This was against Transvaal at the Wanderers, one of the two South African grounds where Fanie has enjoyed a large measure of success. He has always found the challenge of the bullring and the spectators rewarding.

However, after a steady, though unimpressive performance in the opening Currie Cup match, the big West Indian's right knee was still causing problems. If he broke down again he could be out for the rest of the season. There were six games in as many weeks and it was a tough programme. So no one could blame Barnard for asking Fanie, Gerbrand Grobler or Anton Ferreira to shoulder the attack as Transvaal decided to chase a victory target of 171 in a matter of forty minutes and 20 overs. In limited-overs terms it was a mere gallop.

Recognized throughout his first four seasons as little more than a fast bowler with a hint of occasional outswing guile, Fanie switched his style in the second innings. The pace was there but he had slowed down, allowing himself to generate the same amount of swing, which had Natal in trouble in the day-night series game.

As he prepared to bowl to Jimmy Cook and Henry Fotheringham, who were then South Africa's premier first-wicket pairing, the NKP student knew he was facing a serious challenge to his new bowling image. He need not have worried. In his own mind he knew what he must do—force the batsmen to attack. Give them the four-ball if necessary, but make them reach for it; not at all an easy task against such an accomplished duo.

No one knew it then, but in a matter of forty-eight balls Fanie de Villiers changed from the bowler with the tearaway run-up to a young man who realized the benefits of swing and seam. Of course, the transition would take longer than a mere eight overs at the Wanderers. But it was the beginning. And what a wreckage he caused that late Johannesburg afternoon! Transvaal's top three batsmen were regarded among the best in South Africa: Cook and Fotheringham were then considered among the top six opening batsmen in the world. They were effective and efficient, cunning and calculating. Such was their menace that bowling to them was often a nightmare. They were run-making experts who easily picked the holes in the field and knew the art of sending the ball into the gaps for those irritating singles and twos. The four-balls were extras, often in plentiful supply during a long partnership.

So here was this student bowling to the masters, and successfully rewriting the script. In a matter of 15 overs Transvaal stumbled to 49 for 4: Fanie took the wickets of Cook (11), Fotheringham (3), Roy Pienaar (28) and Louis Vorster (3). Patching the innings together after that collapse were Bruce Roberts and Clive Rice. Little wonder that Vaal were happy enough when umpires Barry Lambson and Rudi Koertzen called off the game with 6 overs remaining.

From the Wanderers Fanie found himself at Newlands, possibly his second favourite South African venue, and quickly among the wickets. Grant Symmonds, a more than useful raw-boned seamer, was a late replacement for Clarke, but Fanie's new-ball partner for the match was his old sparring friend, the left-handed Grobler. While he was earning respect for himself, Fanie had great respect and admiration for Garth le Roux, the old Province warhorse. In his first two seasons as a provincial bowler the NKP student was of the opinion that if he wanted to continually bowl fast he needed a physique similar to that of le Roux's. He later realized that it was not the broad shoulders and strong legs that counted in bowling fast. It had more to do with making the most of your physical attributes.

Bowling as he did at the Wanderers that second Transvaal innings, Fanie went on to clean up the Province innings in what was then his career best Currie Cup figures of 6 for 47. The wickets of Peter Kirsten (bowled for 66) and Gary Kirsten (26) were among the haul. Yet, what counted most were the catches in the slips-wicketkeeper area with batsmen committing themselves to the front foot against the swinging ball. It had always been Clarke's view (some would suggest arrogance) that he knew exactly where to bowl to all the top South African batsmen. It came from his ability to study their front- and backfoot techniques, and know where to pitch the ball to get the best effect. At best it is a risky supposition, based more on theory than fact. It can work if the batsmen are given the opportunity to attack. What made it easier for the bowler was the type of pitches they prepared in those days of isolation: usually fast with bounce and a tinge of green. It made for an interesting three-day game.

No wonder the flat seam and shaved pitches in England in 1990 were such a culture shock for Fanie. He had to relearn the fast bowling trade. But this was where he started working a lot more on his off-cutter—that second weapon of success and the delivery that destroyed Australia in Sydney six years later.

At Newlands, however, Fanie almost ended Northern Transvaal's long history of defeats or being on the losing end of a draw at this particular venue. He had scored an undefeated 24 as they needed 3 runs off the last 2 balls to win, for the first time in a Currie Cup game in the lengthening shadows of Table Mountain. Grobler's madcap charge resulted in a run-out, leaving Fanie to score 3 off the last ball. Again Northerns had made an awful hash of winning a match. Mike Rindel had scored a masterful maiden Currie Cup century to set it up; in the end lack of experience counted against Northerns.

His 8 wickets at the Wanderers and 8 at Newlands came from spells of quality bowling. 'The Dutchman who couldn't bowl' was becoming a star performer. Although the one wicket at St. George's Park was a setback, it was not a serious one. Yet he did get a good view of Willie Morris' amazing hat-trick which won a game that had, at tea on the last day, all but been lost. 'If we want to win this match, you and I will have to bowl them out,' was Barnard's advice to Morris at tea. Victory was even more enjoyable when he managed to pull Reid, the manager/coach, into the shower after the match.

For Fanie, however, wickets continued to clatter into his basket. Each venue, apart from St. George's Park, brought a smile. Even in Pietermaritzburg, in a match against Natal, there was success as his swing bowling skills matured. There were three man of the match awards, too, but he was more interested in victories. He also managed to take more wickets away from Centurion Park (24) than he did at home (19). And while he prospered, so did Rindel. Two heroes. Growing household names. They were at it together as spectators, even from the West Rand, packed their picnic hampers, braai equipment, sun umbrellas and deckchairs and headed for the largest open air steakhouse in southern Africa. Centurion Park also became a favourite haunt for those living in the Midrand and the plush northern suburbs of Johannesburg. The Wanderers? Well, it has its place.

On a Saturday or Sunday, all roads led to Centurion Park and a vleisbraai. 'Hey, this cricket is real lekker, Ou Boet,' were the comments. 'Almost as good as the smell of sizzling wors.'

Into the twelfth over of Transvaal's second innings in the return match, Fanie had Roy Pienaar caught by Noel Day with a good ball that drifted across and lured the batsman to his downfall with clever swing. Just as he turned to wring a successful decision from Natal umpire, Karl Liebenberg, Fanie felt the pain in his lower back. It was as if he had been pinched; a sharp reminder that it was there.

Rindel, Vernon du Preez, Willie Morris, Mandy Yachad' Mike Haysman, Anton Ferreira and Barries (Barnard) congratulated him on his first wicket of the innings. But Fanie was worried about the pain. As he collected the ball and started to walk back, he felt an ache in his right hamstring. He needed a Voltaran tablet. Like he did all those years ago when he first hurt his back and was throwing the javelin . His right knee also started to give trouble, forcing him to limp.

He looked at Barnard. The skipper had his own problems. He was not scoring runs and the press were howling for his head. As it is Barnard had to write off Clarke for the season. 'He says it is up to us,' was the wry comment from Grobler after the news broke about the Bajan.

Bosch and Grobler filled in the fast bowler's slot with all they had: Bosch all pace and Grobler all guts. Fanie grinned as he walked back to the bowling mark. Louis Vorster, the new batsman, was talking to Henry Fotheringham. Vorster was a left-hander, a useful batsman. Fanie remembered bowling to him once in Nelspruit.

Fanie stretched the leg. Oh, hell. What now, *Ou Maat*? This pain is new. Not at all good. Finish this over and go off for a painkiller. Could it be an injury?

By the time the game was called off, Fanie had bowled a further fourteen overs for Bruce Roberts' wicket, while Fotheringham executed another quality century. Only what with the rain wiping more than a session out of the match, it was always going to be a stalemate: unless, of course, Transvaal collapsed. Which could never happen with that batting line-up.

Going into their last Currie Cup game of the season, Northerns needed six or seven batting points against Free State, and a victory, if they were to squeeze out Transvaal from the Currie Cup final. 'One last effort, my friend,' Fanie had told Chesters at the previous night's net session.

'And at the Hennops River end we have the team's workhorse, "Vinnige" Fanie de Villiers.' Gerald de Kock does not need binoculars to spell out the names of the slips fielders. 'There is Mike Haysman, Gerbrand Grobler . . . Noel Day behind the stumps, of course.' More overs for Fanie to bowl: the genuine workhorse of the season. No one mentions his tired legs, or the growing hamstring injury, quite deep-seated now. It is a worry.

The Wanderers Club members had to admit how Fanie turned out a lot better than they expected. Also good for a laugh the way he mixed his English tenses, or did not quite get the syntax right in a colloquialism. However, beneath a smiling facade, was another pain. Only that this one could not be seen.

From the Free State match there was a third 5-wicket haul and a man of the match award. However, the pain was growing; uncomfortably so. Fanie helped Northerns to a third victory of the season; yet, they were still two points shy of elbowing Transvaal off the top of the log in their section.

When it was over, it was time to relax; he would put his feet up and get away for a break with Judy.

Fanie won his copy of the *The Complete Who's Who of Test Cricket* that season, and Anton Ferreira willingly handed over the promised Warwickshire jersey.

Tony Lewis, the former England captain-turned-journalist and radio and television commentator, paid Fanie his finest tribute that season. 'His enthusiasm is a beacon for other young players. His adaptability was a factor which made him a dangerous bowler. And it would be fair to suggest he is certainly a star of the future . . . whatever future there is for South Africa. What a pity the best bowler in the country is not playing in the centenary final.'

These comments were made on the South African Broadcasting Corporation (SABC) and Lewis discovered, as did Dr Bacher, that Fanie was not the average budding provincial star hidebound by theories or browbeaten by statistical data. He was all too aware of his humble beginnings and had never forgotten them. If a tour was in the offing in the next season, Fanie would be the first to be selected. A pity that it was not going to be that easy.

There was further speculation in the Afrikaans press suggesting that Barnard should do the honourable thing and hand over to Yachad, but there was not much chance of that happening unless the executive made the decision.

When the official part of the season was over, there was another trip to Newlands for Fanie. This one was for Omar Henry's benefit match with the young Northern Transvaal fast bowler earning an invitation on the strength of his bowling that summer. After all, it was going to be hard to ignore his 56 wickets in the three official competitions. Now he found himself in a side with Clive Rice, Kenny McEwan and Jimmy Cook. His family also decided to make the trip to the fairest Cape to support him in his first major match. Unfortunately,

Henry's side turned their innings into an exercise too embarrassing to remember and ended with 134 runs: not nearly enough.

As Adrian Kuiper opened the innings with Lawrence Seeff, Fanie turned to McEwan. 'What's going on here, Kenny? Kuiper doesn't normally open the innings.' McEwan shrugged. 'Don't worry, Fanie. It is just a benefit match. A friendly . . . sometimes things are done a little differently.'

But when Fanie bowled the first ball, Kuiper's intentions became clear. It was a good ball, well pitched up. Taking one step down the pitch Kuiper dispatched Fanie into the Oaks for a massive six. While a bemused Fanie was wondering what was going on, McEwan was laughing, congratulating Kuiper, patting him on the back and shaking his hand.

It transpired that McEwan, a cattle farmer, had bet Kuiper before the innings that if he hit a six off the first ball he would present him with a cow. A smiling, determined Kuiper hit the second ball for six as well. A towering straight drive, this time from an attempted yorker. Newlands erupted. Kuiper was in form. Anyway . . . who was this Fanie guy? The third ball was bowled fuller and Kuiper edged it through the slips. 16 off 3 balls. And Kuiper was just warming up! A third six followed. 22 runs off 4 balls.

'Fanie, what's wrong? We have to keep this guy quiet.' Omar Henry had walked over to Fanie. 'I mean the idea is to keep the people here as long as possible. Do you want fielders on the fence in the next over?'

'No. No, Omar, it'll be all right.'

A scrambled single followed another four. 27 runs off the first over.

Kuiper the destroyer was far from finished. There were 30 runs off Fanie's next over—three sixes and three fours. This frenetic pace could not continue. But no one wanted to bowl. Not even Clive Rice, not before a baying Newlands crowd with Kuiper in full flow. All that was missing was the full moon. Who can blame him?

A leg-bye off the first ball of Fanie's next over was further punishment. He managed to score 15 runs off the over. Still, no one wanted to take over from Fanie. Being a youngster, it was left to him. His third over was another disaster. The top Currie Cup bowler, with 11 day-night series wickets, was being put through the thresher. 10 runs came off the third over. That meant 52 runs off 3 overs. Then there was a miracle: Fanie delivered a solitary maiden. In the end, he gave away 65 runs in 5 overs. And the match was over in 11 overs.

* * * *

Rumours of a rebel tour for the 1989-90 season were well advanced when Dr Bacher, managing director, and Joe Pamensky, president of the SACU, flew to London in January 1989 to argue the union's case with the then ICC. It was a traumatic meeting, eventually leading to the recruitment of an England rebel side, captained by Mike Gatting. This came the after ICC's decision to ban, in future, anyone with contracted links with tours organized by the SACU. While it was a harsh decision and most South African whites may have felt it was a form of betrayal, the political facts and realities were far harsher.

Betrayal? What a quaint assumption. And how erroneous. How often since the formation of the UCB have people swept horrendous acts from the past under a convenient carpet called unity? It is forgotten how people were jailed for their opposition to the oppression caused by apartheid laws. The ICC's view (and quite rightly) was that, until the whites-only elected government revoked all apartheid legislation and released their political foes, South Africa would receive no succour or comfort from legitimate agencies. It was not just sport that was involved here, disenfranchised millions were affected.

While it is easy to admire the stance that Pamensky and Dr Bacher took on behalf of the sport they administered, it is just as easy to sympathize with where they stood: squarely opposed to government policy. Yet because of the rebel tours they had to seek government support. Strange companions indeed.

While political rumblings were taking place, Fanie, starting his two-year national service, also had the problem of a troubled knee to take his mind off the omnipresent back and hamstring problems. If there was to be a rebel tour he wanted to be fit to bowl against whoever came.

9

A Question of Loyalty

No one said that fast bowling was going to be easy. But neither did anyone explain just how hard it was going to be; that it was full of confrontation; or that pain would become a persistent, unwelcome companion. No one even mentioned that losing a big toe nail would become a twice-in-a-season ritual. That blood would regularly ooze through the socks; blood from toes battered to a near pulp after the consistent thumping of the right foot onto the sun-baked surface. Certainly there had been no suggestion of almost being unable to walk because of blisters, some of them ugly blood blisters the size of an old R1 coin. And no one hinted that on some mornings doing a simple everyday thing like getting out of bed would become a serious negotiation between the mind and the body.

Become a fast bowler. Become a national hero. What a glamorous occupation. Let people look in admiration and cheer. And look at those headlines. Look at those batsmen retiring hurt. Give the ball to the fast bowler. Let him become the strike force, the tough storm trooper in the trenches of Test or international combat. Always creating controversy. Just what is needed to bring in the crowds.

A new type of street-fighter that Harold Larwood developed in the 1930s, Ray Lindwall perfected, and Dennis Lillee and Jeff Thomson, and the West Indian batteries of the 1970s and 1980s put into operation with frightening purpose, has been more than sixty years in the making.

As a schoolboy it is a matter of running up and letting the ball fly. The spirit of adventure, the spirit of winning the battle over the common enemy—the batsman. But the older you get, the more you want to pin the batsman. Draw a little blood. Instil in him a sense of fear. Stare into the whites of his eyes and read the anxiety.

Oh no. No one said it was going to be easy; even becoming a swing bowler with added cunning and guile had its moments when the body complained about the rigours of practising and learning to get the ball in the right place.

Fanie had hobbled out of the 1988-89 season and admitted over a morning coffee chat one late autumn morning that he was battling with a serious knee injury and would need an operation. He also hinted that Transvaal had made an approach. Nothing serious just yet, but it was worth thinking about, especially if the rumours of a rebel tour were true. It would give him added exposure than he would get by playing for Northerns.

'Why Transvaal? Why not Western Province or Natal?'

'They are too far away. Anyway, Pretoria is my home. But, if Barries and Day and the others from Jo'burg can play at Centurion Park, what's to stop me from playing at the Wanderers for Transvaal?' He had a point.

Clive Rice, it appeared, was impressed by the progress Fanie had made in twelve months and unimpressed with the poor financial return the fast bowler received from Northern Transvaal. Rice had suggested that Transvaal could offer him a better deal. For one thing, it would mean more money to buy a car to replace the heap he felt too embarrassed to drive now. In late March 1989 he had had to ask some of the Transvaal players, after a couple of end-of-season day-night benefit matches at the Wanderers, to push-start the battered vehicle.

There was a distinct impression, however, that it was neither money nor the offer of a new car that mattered. It was all about appreciation for his efforts. You do not throw away years of service like that; he wanted to remain loyal.

Sure, the Northerns public may have applauded his performances. But the financial rewards were those of a pauper compared to a newcomer like Richard Snell, who had played only half a season for Transvaal, or Brian McMillan. Why, Allan Donald, was earning almost three times the amount. And Natal were not shy at all about paying Trevor Packer or Rowan Lyle double Fanie's earnings.

Northerns, it seemed, expected more than a pound of flesh for loyalty. So it came as no surprise when one player managed to clear only R17 that 1988-89 season. Most, however, did much better than that, but their earnings were still well below those paid to the top players in other provinces. One interesting fact that emerges is that Fanie, in 1993-94, earned more in a month from his first UCB contract than he did in six months for Northerns in 1988-89. Fanie's R10,500 was well below Donald's R40,000, Rice's R50,000 plus, or Packer's R25,000 minus other benefits and endorsements.

As Donald was also playing for Warwickshire, his Free State earnings were a handsome extra bonus. For Fanie, his stipend was poor reward indeed for loyal service, not to mention his three man of the match awards. Mike Rindel earned even less. No wonder Transvaal's offer of R40,000 seemed so attractive.

The view among the mandarins at Centurion Park in 1988-89 was that because he was doing his national service they could hold on to him. Later in the year, when Dr Willie Basson and all but one of the executives retired they may have left a legacy of solid financial management, but the team was unhappy about the meagre monetary rewards. Chesters was criticized by two board members when he wrote that the payment rewards for Northern Transvaal players failed to match those of other provinces and quoted figures of Bradley Player and Corrie van Zyl of Free State, and Trevor Packer from Natal. All three were fast bowlers.

There were diverse views as well. Signing Sylvester Clarke had cost the province more than they realized. His salary bill alone cost more than what five players earned in a season. Or, as Johan Hartman, the Northern Transvaal financial administrator said, 'Fanie is not such a big star to demand that sort of figure.' It was unclear whether this was his opinion or that of the executives. 'When he becomes as good as van Zyl or Eric Simons or Packer even, we'll look at what he is worth,' said Hartman weeks after the 1988-89 season ended. The question of payment had, it seemed, become a political issue. Was it a subtle way of showing Fanie the door, as they had Pat Symcox? 'Not at all,' says Dr Basson several years after retiring from the board. 'From what I remember, we felt it was a simple matter of value in the marketplace. It has to be remembered it was still the years of isolation and must be viewed as such.'

In the latter years of his presidency of Northern Transvaal, Dr Basson was a firm believer in the open market system; he had long held a view that if players wanted to accept a better deal elsewhere, they could do so. To deny them this right was restraint of trade. So if Fanie wanted to take up the Transvaal offer why stop him?

When Alan Jordaan took over as the Northern Transvaal Cricket Union president, he was faced with several early dilemmas; the senior side had under-achieved the previous three seasons and the results graph since 1984-85 had been erratic. The B team was stagnating, there was no vigorous youth programme policy through the schools and development in black areas was not moving forward the way it should have. Whichever way Jordaan looked at it, the modern buzz phrase 'serious restructuring' was needed at provincial player level. Certain deadwood would have to go and new ideas were required.

For a start, there was a need for a new manager or a coach as strong substantiated rumours showed that John Reid had lost touch with the trends in the modern game. In his first season in 1982-83, his ideas were firm and strong and based on sound practical expertise and principles. The advent of the rebel era slowly changed all that; new ideas and innovations, especially from the two Kim Hughes tours and from those of the overseas professionals had seriously altered the way the game was played, and the pace at which it was played.

In one of his first moves, Jordaan declined to re-engage Reid and brought in Doupie Calitz, a member of the new executive, and one of Fanie's close NKP associates. For a time Jordaan was happy with Barnard remaining captain. But when he was confronted with Fanie's predicament, he was seriously worried. As Rice and Transvaal were pressing Fanie for an answer, the fast bowler knew the time had come to take a decision.

'You are close to Fanie,' Jordaan said to Chesters one September morning. 'Why would he want to see me urgently?'

'You had better see him and hear what he has to say,' Chesters advised. 'But it is important that you do see him as soon as you can.'

Chesters knew it would get him in trouble at his office if the news leaked. However, in this case confidences, friendship and trust went a lot further than breaking a story that Fanie de Villiers had been made an offer by Clive Rice. It had never been his style. Years ago he had sat on a story that if the sponsors could be found, Northerns would sign Barry Richards.

Jordaan and Fanie met at the nets at Centurion Park on a warm early September afternoon and Fanie, still recovering from the knee operation, did not waste time over pleasantries. He wanted to know from the man who had been the selection panel convener in 1985-86 when he was first selected where he stood with the team and the new executive.

'I have always been a loyal Northern Transvaal player and have never asked for money,' de Villiers told Jordaan.

'Fanie, I have been out of it for a while, so you had better fill me in,' suggested Jordaan.

'Well, sir, I received ten and a half thousand last season and would like to know what I am going to be offered this season. Will there be any change from the last season?'

'I am not sure whether all the financial details have been worked out at this stage. But how can we help?'

'It is like this: why is it that other provinces come to me with these big offers? It is three times more than I earn as a Northerns player.'

Jordaan could not believe what he had been hearing. Northerns could ill-afford to lose their top bowler of the past season. One already earmarked, from what he had been told, as a certainty for the Tests and limited-overs games against Mike Gatting's rebels. As it is there were still doubts about Sylvester Clarke's fitness. But losing Fanie . . . The new president shook his head as he listened.

'Sir, I don't really want to go and play for Transvaal. I prefer it here. But the offer of forty thousand is just too good.'

Jordaan was stunned by the figure in the Transvaal offer.

'Well, Fanie, what I can promise is that we will give you fifteen thousand for a start. As for the rest . . . we will get a sponsor, or sponsors, to make up the difference.' Jordaan was hopeful it could be done.

'In that case, sir, you have a deal,' Fanie said.

Of course, it was not quite that simple. A couple more meetings were held before the final agreement was drawn up, and the young lieutenant was happy to play for Northerns. But as he explained to his friend, Gerrie Dippenaar, his family and Chesters, it was not a case of threatening to leave, it was a matter of getting a better deal, being paid what he was worth.

While the financial side of Fanie's life for that season was being sorted out, there was still a serious concern about his right knee. The operation earlier that year had not been successful and he had spent hours in the gym with Neels Liebel, a defence force biokineticist, to sort out the problem. There was also concern about his general fitness progress. Even the work in the gym with Liebel and his wife, Marina, had marginal effect. Although he attended the first pre-season training sessions in early August with the others, Fanie knew he might not be ready when they were to move into the nets in the first week of September.

He was then faced with two problems. Because of the rebel tour the Currie Cup programme was starting earlier than normal. In mid-October, Northerns had matches against Free State, at Centurion Park, and Western Province, at Newlands. The second worry was whether the knee would withstand such tough punishment so early. Especially as the Nissan Shield series was being played over six weeks. Dr Ali Bacher had, in late August, told the media that the 1989-90 season's programme had been designed to allow the players to concentrate on their Currie Cup commitments during December and January. It was also felt that spreading the day-night matches would help prepare the players before the Gatting rebels arrived towards the end of January.

Although he knew it was going to be a risk, Fanie felt he owed it to himself and Northerns, apart from his growing band of supporters, to play in the Currie Cup games. It would be a tough trial but would help him get fit for the Nissan Shield and floodlit series. He needed, he knew, several good performances to convince the national selectors, led by Peter van der Merwe, that he was ready to take on Gatting's Gang when they arrived. In fact, he had already been told that given an injury-free season, there was no reason why he should not play in the two 'Tests' and six limited-overs games. Northerns were also keen to have a local 'Test' player in their ranks again. A fit, happy Fanie would make a difference.

When the 1989-90 season ended, Barnard admitted that had Fanie been fit for all the games, there was no reason why they should not have beaten Eastern Province in the Nissan Shield final. Although Northerns had the services of an impressive trio of pace and seam bowlers in Tertius Bosch, Sylvester Clarke and Gerbrand Grobler, de Villiers was the one bowler they needed most. For one thing, his phenomenal ability to swing the ball late had become an imposing feature of his armoury. Mike Haysman, standing in the slips in the opening Currie Cup match against Free State, was amazed at the amount of swing Fanie generated in both innings. He took 9 wickets that game: 4 in the first innings and 5 in the second.

The one-time South Australian, who had had a disappointing first season with Northerns in 1988-89 (and was not afraid to admit it), was a regular slip fielder during his five summers at Centurion Park. With the reputation for having a quick eye and a classic pair of hands, he caught numerous batsmen in the slips. Not surprisingly, 'caught Haysman bowled de Villiers' was a regular feature in the scorebook those five seasons. Also a solid batsman who later took over the captaincy of Northerns, he had a lot of pride in his ability and, like Mandy Yachad, was not a genuine member of the Wanderers Club. He had a lot of pride for what he called 'wearing the (Barberton) daisy', the Northerns' motif.

Yet Fanie's second and third wickets in Free State's first innings were lbw decisions executed by Barry Lambson. The first was Glen Hughes, younger brother of Kim (then captaining Natal), the second, two balls later, was Gavin Victor.

His ability to straighten up the ball, or pull it back from wide out to earn lbw decisions caused much debate in South Africa. Robin Jackman, a former England Test bowler, went on record before South Africa's 1994 tour of England to suggest that county umpires would not be as lenient as those in South Africa.

'He bowls from too far out,' was Jackman's learned opinion when he spoke to the South African Cricket Society at a monthly meeting in Johannesburg in the winter of 1994. 'He won't get as many lbw decisions as say Craig Matthews, who bowls much closer to the stumps.'

Fanie ended the England tour with eight lbw decisions, four of them in Tests: Allan Donald, Matthews and Brian McMillan earned four apiece, while Pat Symcox had three, and Richard Snell two. Which proved that such assumptions about Fanie's lbw decisions could not be based on off-the-field theory. The first negotiating point between the bowler and the umpire under Law 35 is 'did the ball pitch in line between wicket and wicket?'. But the Northern Transvaal bowler had faith in the English umpires. Four seasons earlier, when playing for Kent, he had earned nine lbw decisions.

In fact, standing in his first club match of the 1995-96 season, as Fanie made his long awaited comeback to win his place in the World Cup squad, was his journalist friend. It gave Chesters, a former first-class umpire, a close view of the bowler and his craft in action. Standing in because he was the only qualified umpire available, the journalist gave him one lbw decision out of numerous appeals. But there were many marginal calls as well: mostly for hitting the batsmen too high and not because the ball pitched outside the stumps. More importantly, his wicket-to-wicket direction was as tight as it looked from the media area.

Being a club match and his first serious outing since the two unsuccessful day-night 'trials' at Newlands and in Paarl, Fanie used the match as a serious middle net. He had opted out of the four-day A Section new year game against Natal at Kingsmead, citing fitness problems. In his own mind, and that of Anton Ferreira, the coach that 1995-96 season, there was still doubt whether he would last four days. The club match, however, was different. He needed the practice, with no disrespect to the batsmen. If he was to earn a place in the South African side for the seven limited-overs internationals against England and qualify for a place in the World Cup squad, he had to prove his fitness.

While most had written an epitaph for his career as an international player (indeed a few were busy composing obituaries after he had opted out of the four-day game), Fanie's determination and skill earned him a well-deserved reprieve. It also soon had the South African media scurrying for his cell number and an 'exclusive' interview.

How Fanie chuckled. It was not the first time he had proved them wrong.

In early October 1989, however, there was one spell in the game against Free State when he and Tertius Bosch had the visitors grasping for a respirator. They were 45 for 5; de Villiers 3 for 15; the ball a lethal weapon as he swung it about and catches flew off the edge to Anton Ferreira, Noel Day and Haysman. In three overs Joubert Strydom, the Free State captain, played and missed often because he had difficulty in reading the line of the ball. It was bowling of the highest quality and drew such acknowledgement from him.

When Strydom became Fanie's third victim and the fifth wicket to fall, it was left to Johan van Heerden and Omar Henry to form a rescue phalanx to save the innings from sinking without trace. In fact, but for a couple of dropped catches, Northerns would have won inside two days. Henry was dropped by a battling Sylvester Clarke when offering a catch off a top edge. Had the big Bajan, lumbering to mid-wicket, held the catch, Fanie would have recorded his first 10-wicket haul. This is one of the more interesting trivial pursuit questions: what has Fanie de Villiers achieved for South Africa that he has not for Northerns? 10 wickets in a first-class match, of course. That was until late November 1997 when, after being a controversial omission from the South African side to tour Australia that summer, he took 10 wickets for the euphemistically named Northerns President XI against the West Indies A side during their 1997-98 tour of South Africa.

Seven days later at Newlands his 1989-90 season was brought to an abrupt hiatus, until mid-January at least. Fanie is the sort of person who will tackle Mount Everest alone on a crutch and expect to conquer the world's highest peak. All he will have to prop him up is his unshakeable confidence and faith in his ability. As for motivation, try an inbuilt will to win. It is an endearingly stubborn streak. But it can also end up causing hours of agony and heartache when the body has been pushed too far, once too often.

On a wet, bitingly cold October afternoon, a disconsolate Fanie sat in the Northerns dressing room at Newlands. When Chesters arrived, he was examining the extent of the bruise on the big toe of his right foot. A doctor, the bowler admitted, had told him that his knee was in a bad way. Glumly they shared an orange juice and digested the news. As Northerns had already lost the match when he limped off, there was not much use prolonging the agony. Anyway, few players in their right mind would seek to hide their disappointment in dressing rooms as bleak as those at Newlands in 1989. Fanie did. His gamble had failed. It had been a miserable weekend. There were few happy memories other than visiting the barrackers in the Willows. Sign a few autographs, chat with the children. No wonder there was empathy among the crowd in the Willows when Fanie limped off. It was an area where there was much humour and character. Like District Six, however, the Willows has gone forever and no one these days mourns the loss of that part of history. It is as though those in charge of Western Province cricket after unity wanted to wipe out an unkempt, if charismatic, image and replace it with unbecoming snobbishness.

In the same match, Tertius Bosch, who was being tipped as a candidate for the 'Test' series against Gatting's rebels along with Fanie, was bowling to a Western Province batsman in the teeth of a none-too-pleasant Cape 'breeze'. Bosch grunted loudly when he delivered the ball and after about three overs from the lanky dental student one wag in the Willows shouted: 'Hey, Bosch. Is you in labour?' Lee Barnard, fielding at point and teeth gleaming on a grey, blustery day, started laughing, causing the wag to yell, quick as a flash: 'Hey, Tande, *versigtig wees of djy's sy eerste pasient* ('Hey you with the toothy grin, if you are not careful you'll end up his first patient!') Such colour has been lost to Newlands.

On 12 April 1989, the summer a fast fading memory, Chesters got a telephone call around midday from Ian Todd of *The Sun* in London. The night before Dr Ali Bacher, managing director of the SACU had given an impressionable, impassioned address as guest speaker at the annual Wisden dinner to launch the 1989 edition of world cricket's bible. As usual, Fleet Street tabloids were looking for something extra to spice their follow-up stories. Already Ted Dexter, chairman of England's selectors was, jittery about SACU's plan to organize another rebel tour the next southern summer. It had become common knowledge that a tour was likely.

Todd's query was a simple, 'Do you think Clive Rice will be fit enough to lead South Africa against the next group of rebel tourists?'

'Interesting question, Toddy. If a tour takes place, it's a long time off.'

'The side is being signed up right now,' Todd assured Chesters. As it later transpired, that information was wrong. Then came an interesting snippet. 'Ted Dexter is trying to find out what players are being fingered by your chaps.'

'Are you sure it is England? I have been told it may not be England.'

'No, it's definitely an England side.'

'I imagine, if there is a rebel tour next season, that Ricey will be among the leading candidates to captain the side. He looked very fit when he played in the Currie Cup final. And as far as I know he has not hinted at retirement,' Chesters replied.

'You may want to use this, then. Dexter is holding a meeting with the top eighteen players today and tomorrow,' Todd said. 'I suspect he and the TCCB are looking at loyalty clauses in the long-term contracts.'

'Thanks for that, Toddy.'

'Could be an interesting weekend. Watch the wires. Will call you in a week or two or earlier, if something interesting develops.'

Of course there was going to be a rebel tour. A reliable coastal source within the SACU had told Chesters during the day-night series final at Newlands some three weeks before that plans for the tour were well advanced. There was some opposition in the ranks but it was not too serious. When a speculative piece was written, the Argus Group of newspapers treated the item with caution; as usual *The Star* played it low-key—it was not written by one of their staff members, so Julian Kearns the sports editor had it stripped to four paragraphs. This was despite comment from Dr Bacher that further rebel tours were inevitable.

'We shall be looking closely at the options that we (the SACU) have been left by the ICC. But yes, a tour is most likely next (southern) summer,' Chesters quoted Dr Bacher from comments he had made to him during a call to London, hours before the dinner.

In London Dr Bacher also told dinner guests that players going to South Africa, whether as teams or individuals, would be obliged, by contract, to help the SACU's development programme. A significant portion of gate monies from matches involving international teams would be used to fund coaching and buying equipment, and helping with developing facilities. Along with private enterprise and sponsors, he expected that R3 million annually 'will be ploughed into developing black cricket'. Improving old facilities and creating new ones was one of the plans the SACU were investigating.

'It is a terrible fact of life, then, that the ICC's decision hits the development programme hard in two ways. It makes us pay more for fund-raising tours, which means less for the development coffers, and acts as a deterrent to coaches coming to South Africa to help in the townships.'

He ended what was acknowledged as an outstanding address by saying, 'I would like (tonight) to bring a message to you from those involved in cricket in South Africa. Out of Africa will come something new. It will be dazzling, it will be strong and it will be good. Thank you for letting me tell you about its birth.'

If anyone doubted his sincerity all they had to do was read the South African papers of 12 April, which carried his address of the previous evening. The question remained: was another rebel tour worth the acrimony it would cause? Although Dr Bacher opened a development facility in Atteridgeville in August a few days after the announcement of the names of Mike Gatting's team, early doubts about the tour were surfacing. The pirate ventures by Lawrence Rowe's West Indians and Kim Hughes' Australians had been, more than anything else, exercises in rebuilding public interest. As with the Graham Gooch SAB 'dirty dozen', Gatting's Gang was going to receive a mixed reception just how mixed it would be was something that the SACU and South Africa would, in time, find out.

* * * *

Days before the Gatting crew arrived in South Africa and ran into a variety of welcoming committees, Fanie de Villiers had started training seriously again. He had undergone another knee operation, but the scraping of the right patella had not solved the problem. Bowling in the nets still caused him excess pain and in desperation he went, with Neels Liebel, to see a doctor in Pretoria for injections. Mentally he was strong. The way he bowled in the nets was impressive for one who had been out of action for almost three months. He moved the ball away sharply, and the outswing was working well. It did not take Barnard and his vice-captain Mandy Yachad too long to decide that if Fanie agreed, he could return to Currie Cup action.

South Africa's selectors were also anxious to discover the fitness of the Northerns swing bowler and Peter van der Merwe had already made discreet enquiries outside team sources. The word was that if he could play one game and prove his fitness, there was a good chance he would play for South Africa. It was this message, through an independent source, which was filtered to Fanie one afternoon while he was at the Defence Sports Office at Voortrekkeerhoogte. A chance to play for South Africa! Was it possible? After all the problems since Newlands? It seemed too good to be true. Now he had to prove he could do it.

Northerns was playing the return match against Free State in the last Currie Cup game of the season. They had done well enough to reach a stage where a victory over Free State at Springbok Park would get them in to the final against Western Province; a juicy carrot if they were up to it. They selected seven batsmen who had scored centuries and four fast bowlers, including Fanie.

Almost two and a half hours after the game began, an even bigger event was taking place about 500 kilometres north of the Free State capital: amid tight security, a tired Mike Gatting and the rest of the troupe had arrived at Jan Smuts airport.

From the outset, there was something about that last rebel tour which had 'the end of an era' stamped heavily across it. There was an uncomfortable feeling when the announcement was made in early August 1989 that the SACU had embarked on the foolhardy exercise. It seemed they wanted to prove a point to the ICC at Lord's; a 'them' versus 'us' fight, with the SACU taking on the international establishment after the total banning of any player(s) who coached or played in the racist country. While some apartheid laws had been removed and others revised, the whites-only stigma remained. No leopard changes its spots that quickly: not after the minority white government had spent forty-two years in power. Change was taking place though, and the Gatting tour was merely a part of the metamorphosis that South African society had begun to undergo, for some an uncertain journey.

Part of the ugly face of confrontation involving the law and demonstrators was evident on the way to Jan Smuts international airport on 19 January 1990. Thirteen days remained before F. W. de Klerk's famous speech in Cape Town which heralded the end of one era and the dawn of a new one.

Some British journalists sent out to cover the tour, wrote their own colourful arrival stories. Paul Weaver, of the British tabloid *Today*, penned his version under the heading: 'Demo Bloodshed That Tarnishes Every Tour Rebel'.

The blood was still damp at Jan Smuts airport when Mike Gatting and his rebel cricketers arrived in Johannesburg, three hours after the terrible violence that left me feeling weak and nauseous.

It left 300 peaceful demonstrators feeling decidedly worse; their flesh torn by the police dogs, their bones broken by the batons wielded with such vicious relish by the outrageous South African police, their eyes streaming from the tear gas canisters which in this wretched corner of the world are as common as bathroom aerosols.

You don't need tear gas to tweak the nostrils in South Africa—the stench of evil is everywhere if you inhale properly . . .

Three hours later, Gatting arrived, his Henry VIII features creased in a broad grin. All sixteen cricketers were smiling. They are a motley collection of the greedy, the stupid, the disillusioned and the unthinking. And I feel sorry for them.

Harsh, damning words all right. Weaver later admitted that although he was at the airport at the time of the violent clash between the demonstrators and police, he did not see the events and based his report on accurate eyewitness accounts. His version of events has never been questioned. Anyway, Gatting and Co. were far from smiling as they entered a large upstairs VIP lounge; they were pensive, a bit apprehensive and anything but jolly. Their arrival met with heated polemic discussion.

How ironic that sixteen months later Sir Garfield Sobers, the great West Indian all-rounder, held a press conference in the same room as the first VIP attending the inauguration of the United Cricket Board of South Africa. More ironic than this was that only thirty-six months after the arrival of Gatting's Gang the same room was used to welcome the West Indies and Pakistan sides to play in the Total International triangular series.

By then, many who had been cast as political opposites for generations, were part of the greater brotherhood of the game as well as a new nation in the making. There are those who felt the Gatting tour had created a climate for change; only, that is an oversimplification of the wider issues that simmered below the surface in the fermenting cauldron of a people in waiting. In late January 1990 you could feel it when you drove through Soweto and talked to the kids at Elkah Stadium in Rocklands and in other areas of the sprawling south-western townships on the edge of Johannesburg.

Weaver's own view of South Africa then and now has not changed: disgust for the iron-fisted policies of the horrendous minority apartheid regime, reserved admiration of the more open honesty of the new South Africa. Nothing, as he pointed out at St. George's Park during Fanie's last Test, is perfect. He has also developed an admiration for the changes which have taken place since Gatting's Gang departed. But he remains strongly of the opinion that the tour was wrong. 'I think that all the rebel tours were morally wrong; Gatting and the English players knew it. Ali Bacher and everyone else went into this final voyage with the wrong motives. Besides, momentous change in South Africa was already on the way,' he said.

There are many among the millions who voted for the Mandela image in the 1994 elections who have become critical of the African National Congress (ANC) government and the wheels within wheels power struggles which drive the machine. The same illness of corruption, which bled the taxpayers under the old National Party system, has merely been transferred to the new.

Weaver felt that what he wrote at the time was a fair commentary of events seen against a background of change with the apartheid regime struggling and kicking to hold on to its power with whatever means available. A dying system unable to accept the inevitable. While the Nationalist Party's mandarins still had a fortnight before the gathering in Cape Town heard de Klerk deliver his magnum opus against growing international pressures, the dissonant events at Jan Smuts airport allowed an eerie gloom to settle over the rest of the afternoon.

The rumour machine was working overtime. There were rumours that de Klerk had cancelled the tour; another suggested that Gatting and Co. were under siege in their hotel; a third claimed that a dozen had died from a car bomb at Sandton City and that there was tight security everywhere; yet another story claimed that the tour would affect the Commonwealth Games.

On the Monday, at the first practice session at the Wanderers, John Emburey, the vice-captain and a member of the Gooch 'Dirty Dozen' rebels of 1992, was asked a few questions about how he saw his future and that of the other players. As the reconstituted ICC had now banned them, how did Emburey or Gatting or the other players in the rebel squad view the ban? Did they feel that at some stage the bans might be lifted? 'Yes, I see that as a distinct possibility. I feel that in three or four years time we'll be free to play for England again,' said Emburey, confidently fronting up to the barbed questions from the British tabloid writers. 'You should know how Gatt (Gatting) and I have discussed this and you may recall what we said last August, when the tour squad and other arrangements were made. We said then and I'm repeating it now, in time the bans will go and we'll play for England.'

Emburey was asked how confident he was. 'I'm most confident of such a possibility.'

David Graveney, the team's player/manager, offered similar sentiments. Yet *The Star's* news desk and sports office fused their wires when they read news agency reports of how the British tabloids in far off South Africa were beating the drums of what was an old story. 'We'll beat the ban' says rebel tourist.

'It's been said and written before,' said Chesters. 'Anyway, I sent it out last night.'

The Star sports editor Julian Kearns claimed he had not seen the item as the wire lines were down.

A telephone rang in the hotel room occupied by Chesters. It was late Sunday afternoon: day three of the rebel tour.

'What do you think of Jimmy Cook as captain of the Test side?' The voice was muffled but familiar.

'Are you being serious?'

'Certainly. There could be a couple of other surprises, too.'

'Fanie de Villiers?'

'We'll have to wait and see on that score. But I gather he bowled well against Free State today.'

'What with all the tour drama I haven't had a chance to check today's scores.'

'He got an early wicket. But I see he swung the ball nicely.'

'Jimmy Cook, eh?' queries Chesters. 'He hasn't had too many opportunities to lead a team.'

'Remember what we discussed in August? Think about it. I know the selectors are.'

On the day Dr Bacher was entertaining Gatting's side and the travelling media (who included a couple of the usual gatecrashers) at his house in Sandton, Northerns had been left a target of 269 runs in about 64 overs. They failed, of course. But Fanie impressed as a batsman, scoring an undefeated 32. He showed more than a spark of the old spirit, and his bowling, considering the long lay-off, was not too bad. Three wickets in the first innings. It was unknown to everyone that Neels Liebel was giving him injections in his right knee. It was the only way he was going to get through the game.

Anybody who ever claimed fast bowling was easy needs their head examined.

The next day *The Star*'s backpage lead story was a thumbsuck based on a comment from David Graveney, the rebels' manager/ player: Rice had to captain the South Africans in the two 'Tests' or South Africa would fail. The story about Jimmy Cook as a possible captain was squeezed on to the end of this item. Graveney was upset by the story. Sure he had said Rice was an important member of the side but there had been no discussion about the captaincy issue. 'It didn't arise at all,' complained an annoyed Graveney when he cornered Chesters at the first net session at the Wanderers. 'In fact I didn't even know there was anyone from *The Star* in the group where I was sitting. It's just like our tabloid mob, making up a story based on something else. Several of us were having a discussion about who might or might not be in the South African side and someone asked what role I thought Rice would play. I said it would be foolish for the South African selectors to ignore him.'

For weeks there had been speculation whether Rice would lead the side for the rebel series. Rice had admitted that there had been no contact between him and the selectors for an exchange of views on the form or fitness of the players likely to be considered by the panel headed by Peter van der Merwe. This it appears had been the normal practice but uncertainty surrounding the captaincy had lingered since before Christmas. Chesters' own contacts were saying little and the only lead had been the call the previous Sunday.

Pinning down the 'Cook as captain' angle was not going to be a simple matter. For one thing, van der Merwe, a former South

African captain, had been surprisingly guarded in his comments about the team and selection policy. Then it came, about an hour after Gatting's Gang and the media party arrived in Kimberley. It was unofficial confirmation that Cook would captain South Africa in the two 'Tests' and six limited-overs games. The captaincy announcement would come on the Saturday, the second day of the game in Kimberley. Chesters was told that a speculation story about Cook being placed in charge would not be very wrong. The story was reissued with a new angle and comments from van der Merwe about 'possible surprise team selections'.

For some reason known only to Kearns and the night sports sub, Mark Colley, *The Star* continued to ignore the Cook captaincy story but other papers in the group did not. When it broke on the Saturday around 2.30 p.m., Rodney Hartman, the sports editor of the *Sunday Star*, was quick with his congratulations and knowing *The Star* set up admitted he was not 'too surprised' as they had peddled their own theory all week. The South African selectors, however, were not going to be dictated to by a Johannesburg newspaper's views of what their selection policy should be. The two colleagues had a quiet chuckle.

In Kimberley, however, real trouble was gathering pace. Gatting had already defused a potential problem when he went to talk to about eight hundred or so anti-tour demonstrators opposite the team's hotel in Kimberley. The former mining city, famous for its big hole and the historic founding of the SACU almost a hundred years before, was alive with rumour and suspicion. The large contingent of British media, especially those from the tabloids, was enjoying itself. They were more interested in the demonstrators opposed to the tour than the games. No one can blame them. They were there to do a job and wanted to get the best inside story they could. One was of Gatting being refused service at a local steakhouse by black staff.

If the British tabloid media felt that Gatting and the rest of the side were only interested in the so-called 'blood money' to be earned from the tour, then that was the way the stories would be presented. It is a pity, however, that some of the more serious journalists twisted facts to suit their purposes. It is easy to forget that South Africa is a complicated country with complex issues and politicians had cleverly brainwashed two-thirds of the white population with the iniquitous *Swart gevaar* (beware of the blacks) image. Some of the more conservative members of the local press felt that the visiting media were dressing up thumbsucked copy: yellow journalism was presenting a decidedly jaundiced view.

Yet examine the facts: the SACU was seen as part of the white establishment; no matter how the privileged conscious members of the union voted at general election time, they would always be linked to the establishment body. Trying to draw parallels and argue, as some South African journalists did, that the Marylebone Cricket Club (MCC) and Test and County Cricket Board (TCCB) also tried to dictate government policy, is a sad, fallacious comment.[1] So many South Africans forgot at the time that the anti-tour protesters were a small section of the disenfranchised majority. In England, unless you are a foreigner, there is no voteless majority (or minority).

One argument raged: what about the House of Delegates, or House of Representatives?

These two impious bodies, one representing the Indians and the second the coloureds, were a sham. The whites' house, or the mandarins of power, still had the final say. No wonder there were hundreds of thousands who declined to soil their hands by refusing to vote. The partial autonomy they were allowed to exercise was as dishonest as the system which allowed it to exist and sow seeds of corruption.

Later in the tour there was also a view, quickly disposed of, that had there been a Democratic Party in power, would they have faced reality as F. W. de Klerk did, and start the process that led to South Africa's long-awaited *Uhuru* (freedom)? What would they have done indeed? Firebrand anti-government rhetoric is fine, even from the white opposition benches. Put them in power and most would need to watch where they tread.

It is so easy to talk and write from the outside looking in. There was no glamour living in your average (former) township home.

---

[1] The MCC (Marylebone Cricket Club) in 1968 was the game's governing body in England. Their duties as rulers were ceded, in 1971, to the Test and County Cricket Board (TCCB) reconstituted in 1997 as the England and Wales Cricket Board.

Yet it was certainly worth the experience of spending time there—a night, a day or a week—to get the feeling of what it was like to be part of the disenfranchised millions and encounter the burden of bringing up a family of four or five on subsistence wages and battling to put a meal on the table.

* * * *

Police are everywhere on the way to the De Beers Country Club on 26 January 1990. They check the press credentials of the *Argus* and *Times Media Limited* men and wave them on. There are rolls of razor wire and a couple of barricades. The two journalists wonder if they have entered a war zone instead of journeying to a match cricket. Far away they hear the noise of the demonstrators. The police will not budge. The demonstrators are restless. It is a stalemate: a Mexican stand-off without the Mexicans. Yet the demonstrators are unsure why they are there; they had held their demonstration the previous day. But if it means another chance to protest against the apartheid regime, 'lets go then brothers'.

As several hundred, mostly-white spectators settled down to watch the opening salvoes, with Border's Kenny Watson bowling to Chris Broad, the impatient demonstrators were barred by the police from marching closer to the ground. Enter Krish Naidoo, a razor-sharp lawyer and then senior official of the National Sports Congress, a recently delivered offspring which had close ties with the ANC. The body had grown out of frustration with the archaic views of COSAS (Council on Sport in South Africa), which was then seen to be slowly aligning itself to the Pan African Congress. As Broad hit Watson for the first runs of the match, Naidoo was also becoming increasingly frustrated.

For one thing, the jittery police were confronted with a situation they did not quite know how to handle and worried about it running out of control. Should they call in the army? Or should they sort it out themselves? Quiet diplomacy or the iron fist approach? A nice set of options to consider at such a volatile time. Who the hell had allowed this cricket match to take place?

Naidoo had fought for the tour's abandonment and hinted at the time that if the SACU were to throw in their lot with the ANC, South Africa would be playing without the trappings of isolation and have an ICC-sanctioned tour within a year. The meeting was held in the plush surrounds of Sun City and the offer was tempting. Perhaps the rationale behind the refusal was that after the John Vorster betrayal in Bloemfontein on a hot September night in 1968, Geoff Dakin, Joe Pamensky, Dr Bacher and other SACU members were wary of linking themselves to a political party. It was all too combustible.

Naturally there were some media sources that scoffed at Naidoo's promise when it was leaked. Others who had followed the SACB's viewpoint of what a non-racial cricket board could do were curious. Were they serious? Oh yes. Wait and see. It could be done; they talked, rather than boasted, of friends in far higher places than the SACU could dream possible. It was ironic that the four limited-overs matches allowed to take place when the tour was curtailed were sanctioned by the ANC. Another irony was that Gooch, the 1982 rebel leader, was now captain of the official England side in the Caribbean.

By the time Dr Bacher and Naidoo managed to get the protest legalized, Gatting was batting with cool, calm assurance. He was by far the most experienced of the batsmen and his display was an example of his professional creed. He had faced, and had his nose smashed, by the West Indian pace battery; he had also tackled Shakoor Rana, a Pakistan Test umpire whose questionable decisions were symptomatic of the later-dissolved sycophantic Board of Control for Cricket in Pakistan (BCCP). Through all this he had observed countries with shaky political infrastructures as well as the people who lived in them. He had seen and experienced the good, the bad and the ugly in each one. But he admitted that South Africa, those five weeks in January and February 1990, was far different from anything he had seen or experienced. The country was in political turmoil, and not just because of the tour.

The stirrings of *Ubantu* (freedom) were being felt even in quiet Kimberley; it was a surreal scenario as the dream of freedom started becoming a reality. A true African dawn was slowly awakening. The apartheid era was being consigned to an ugly file, which would still take a generation or longer to close. Africanization with the West Indian model had not yet started to take shape; the revolution had yet to hear the first bugle call. In the midst of such embers of freedom was a tour only some wanted; the real story was the political crystallization taking shape around the tour.

Not surprisingly, considering the strength of the Combined Bowl XI opposition, the tourists won easily by 254 runs shortly before tea on the final day. Their first innings score of 305 was the highest they were to make in a first-class match during the tour; the tall, likeable David Graveney took 10 wickets and John Emburey 8. This was the only time their bowlers were able to win a match.

When the 'Gatting road show' reached Bloemfontein for the mid-week game against South African Universities, speculation about what de Klerk would say in his address the following Friday was on in full swing. Three British journalists were off to Cape Town to cover the event and fly out to England the following day.

Those left behind watched the students, led by Hansie Cronje, take command of the match on the first day. Cronje could not help but smile at his performance. There was nothing showy about the way he batted at Springbok Park, but anyone scoring a maiden first-class century would feel proud of the achievement. Among the students were four other future Test caps: Rudolf Steyn, Andrew Hudson, Clive Eksteen and Tertius Bosch. The bowling glory, however, went to Stefan Jacobs with 5 for 29.

Close by were the demonstrators: chanting, taunting, and commenting. Inside the ground were youngsters from the local township development programme who, like the players, were caught in the political minefield of uncertain yet exciting times. It was bizarre and quixotic. All the while, the need for dialogue between the SACU and the SACB leadership was growing.

Around 10.30 p.m. the telephone rings.

'There will be no match in Maritzburg, my friend. You can publish that in *The Star* tomorrow.'

The voice is well disguised, but unmistakably Asian.

'How do you plan to have it called off?'

'You will have to wait and see, my friend.'

The phone goes dead and Chesters looks at the receiver. Must be one of the students playing a prank. If not, then who? It is the second such call since the tour had started. The first call suggested the Kimberley game would not take place.

Friday, 2 February, dawns. On the way back from a midnight trip with several of the Universities players and two media men to the Taba'Nchu Sun casino back there is more discussion of what de

Klerk is going to say to the nation in a few hours. Views range from the radical ('release Mandela') to take the heat off politicians, to the pessimistically conservative martial law option. No one wants it; yet there is the awful feeling that this is what is going to happen. World opinion? What is that? International pressure with financial embargoes, a banning of the Rand from overseas markets, gold supplies cut off.

De Klerk, it is felt, is not pragmatic enough to go the martial law route. Apprehension hangs heavy as the media party is split between accommodation in Durban and Pietermaritzburg.

Gatting's Gang have already left by bus for Umhalanga Rocks outside Durban in a bid to shake off the increasing press posse. When Colin Bryden and Chesters arrive at Louis Botha airport in Durban, de Klerk's historic address is long over and the two men run into Mike Procter, then a national selector, in the car park.

'What did you think of de Klerk's speech?' is his first remark.

'You'd better tell us, Mike. We haven't heard a thing,' said Bryden. 'We were flying from Bloemfontein.'

'I can't believe it,' he said. 'He's done it all. Unbanned everyone and everything. Mandela's to be released soon. He didn't say when, but very soon. It's great news for the country. In a year or two we'll have a genuine tour.'[2]

Relief. It is oppressively hot but that is no longer a worry. In Mamelodi they will be celebrating . . . in Atteridgeville and Soshanguve, too . . . Chesters' friend Kenneth Lebethe is no longer alive to share the excitement, but his ghost will be dancing. And Monica Magodielo and her family can look the world in the face—Ubantu is coming.

* * * *

Jan Smuts Stadium in Pietermaritzburg is an attractive enough ground with little atmosphere. Paid-up members of the flat earth society seem to have prepared the pitch for the game between the South African XI and Gatting's tourists.

---

[2] Almost twenty-two months later Mike Procter became the coach of the first official South African team in twenty-one years when the whistle-stop tour of India was held in November 1991.

Fanie de Villiers took one look at it and shook his head.

'They expect me to bowl on this?'

With the help of Neels Liebel's injections, Fanie had survived the rigours of the Currie Cup match against Free State. Now he faced the prospect of a three-day battle on a pitch that would offer no assistance. The ball, he suggested, would quickly become a tattered relic from the era of timeless Tests.

'It is on days like these that I hate being a bowler,' he told Chesters. 'How am I expected to take wickets?'

He pulled hard on the brim of the old visvanghoed he usually wore in those days and started chatting with youngsters and signing autographs. In the same side was a very young Jonty Rhodes. More importantly, however, Fanie got a chance with bowl with Meyrick Pringle and Craig Matthews. Omar Henry was given plenty of overs, and collected a lot of stick. It is still a sore point with Fanie that he did not take any wickets, but his second innings return of 11-3-12-0 did more than anything to impress Hylton Ackerman and Procter, two of the national selectors at the game.

It was after lunch on the first day when a chanting horde of protestors, estimated at between eight and ten thousand, lined up outside the ground venting their displeasure: more at the immoral apartheid system and its downfall than the tour. It was the first protest since de Klerk's speech twenty-four hours earlier. During the tea break Dr Bacher, Gatting and other tour officials went to meet them and were immediately engulfed, but they were not in any danger. There was a violent anti-(apartheid)tour address to the sweating, cheering, demonstrating mass and there was a demand that Gatting, standing on the back of a truck, accept a petition. As in Kimberley and Bloemfontein, there was anger, frustration and bitterness. And no one could blame them. Yet few marchers had grasped the significance of de Klerk's speech of the previous day. Words and promises. Who could trust the whites after generations of denial?

Dr Bacher had long known that the second tour, planned for 1990-91, could not take place, and this one, hijacked by the National Sports Congress (NSC) as a vehicle for protest, was listing heavily. Also, his own views had undergone rapid change. Tragically the development programme, the core of his policy to uplift, was being rejected. Parents of the children involved did not want them to be associated with the white establishment (SACU). All the work that Fanie had done in 1988 and 1989 was being destroyed. The 'exciting birth' Dr Bacher had spoken about at the *Wisden* dinner almost ten months earlier was in danger of being stillborn.

Inside Jan Smuts Stadium, Mark Rushmere was on his way to the first of two centuries as the South African XI scored 305 for 2 and declared. While Daryll Cullinan batted with the same fluent perfection displayed by Roy Pienaar as they scored half-centuries, Rhodes and Dave Callaghan did not get a chance to display their gifted talents even in the second innings.

After the game ended in a draw, David Graveney, the team's player/manager and at the time secretary of the (England) Cricket Players' Association, became the first member of the Jonty Rhodes 'class fielding act' fan club. Tall, angular and a talented slow left-arm floater more than a spinner, the ever-diplomatic Graveney conducted most post-match conferences taking the pressure off Gatting, especially after the Kimberley fiasco, where he was deliberately misquoted by the British tabloids who had blown up the story to highlight the underlying political nature of the tour. For those who have followed the Rhodes 'school of fielding expertise' Graveney's full quote is worth a mention. Especially as it was a little more than two years before that spectacular run-out of Inzamam-ul-Haq at the Gabba, Brisbane, in the 1992 World Cup. 'I must say that if I was a captain I would welcome a player of Jonty Rhodes' ability in my side. He must have saved 40 runs out there today. His anticipation was magic. It forces the batsman to think twice about the extra run. The last time I saw such an outstanding performance by a fielder was Clive Lloyd, before he became the West Indies' captain. Before that? I'm not sure. I didn't see Colin Bland. He was before my time, but certainly there is no one in England of this class. I feel he has a bright future.' Told that Rhodes had played for South African Schools, and captained the South African Universities to a 7-wicket victory over Transvaal at the Wanderers in December, Graveney said he was not surprised. It was forgotten that Hansie Cronje was only made captain of the Universities side to play the rebels because of Rhodes' absence.

As the tour struggled back to Johannesburg for the first 'Test', the political battle entered a final, crucial phase. Sifting conjecture from rumour was hazardous and the heavy, grey rain clouds that hung about added further gloom. Even a trip into Soweto with Chesters did not help Imtiaz Patel, then the SACU development officer, to cheer up. His mood matched the weather as he saw the carefully structured programme slowly tearing apart. Little wonder he was so despondent as he drove to Elkah Stadium.

'Where do you think we are going to from here?' he asked Chesters, who was next to him. 'It will take years to rebuild this programme.'

'Come on, it's not that bad. Politically things are going to improve.'

'Can you see a positive side to all this?' He looked at the journalist.

'Oh yes. I can see there will be no rebel tour next season. And that will help. But talks between SACU and SACB must come soon. De Klerk's speech has made anything possible.'

'No, no. Mackerdhuj and the rest, Krish Naidoo, the NSC. They won't meet with Dr Bacher or the SACU. Not until after general elections. That could take years.'

'I hear there has been contact already,' said Chesters.

'You know something?' Patel asked.

'Not much. Meetings. Telephone calls. That sort of thing.'

There were a few youngsters in the nets at the stadium and Patel talked to them. 'They want to watch the cricket on Saturday,' he smiled. 'But that's not possible. They have games here. At least I hope they still have games on Saturday.'

The match was played against the eerie surrealistic background of unseasonably cold weather, Mandela's impending release, the Wanderers bristling with imposing tight security, and a pitch which was later condemned by Dr Bacher 'as not being fit for even a three-day game'. South Africa, led by Cook, beat Gatting's side all too easily by 7 wickets late on the third afternoon of what was meant to be the first of two five-day rebel 'Tests'.

Fanie de Villiers, watching part of the match on television, was far from impressed. Allan Donald and Richard Snell bowled too loosely, giving the batsmen plenty of four-balls. Fortunately they got away with bowling too short and their bad line: a mixture of poor stroke selection, solid ground fielding, and the realization that it was a five-day game, all contributed to a lacklustre opening day. Although Donald fired in a succession of bouncers, he was not impressive.

On the Friday, amid growing rumours of the tour being aborted, Kepler Wessels, so cheerful three days before, looked tired and upset. It had not been too bad a season for him, and playing for his country had long been a dream; a view expressed during the summer of 1977-78 when he played for Northern Transvaal in the then Castle Bowl. It had been the left-handed Wessels, steering the ball past gully for a 2 off Robbie Muzzell, who had earned Northerns a 7-wicket victory over Transvaal B in the final. He wanted to stay on and do some coaching as well as study, but Northerns had gone to sleep on that one as well.

By mid-morning on Sunday, the Gatting Rebel tour script had developed so many sub-plots it was impossible to keep track of the main story. The majority of the British press, or the 'Rat Pack', had flown to Cape Town to cover Mandela's long-awaited release from prison in Paarl, Wessels had packed his bags and checked out when no one was around, and amid all this Graveney and Gatting declined to be interviewed until they arrived in Cape Town.

'That is if we get to Cape Town,' Graveney parried.

'What does that mean?'

'Nothing at all now. I'll talk to you on the plane.'

The impression was that the tourists were still in shock, and not only because of the heavy defeat. A couple of umpiring decisions on the Saturday had not gone their way either. Correct decisions would have prolonged the match into the Monday. Peter van der Merwe was not available to discuss what the selectors' thinking was for the Newlands 'Test' or the one-day side. Dr Bacher was also not available. Geoff Dakin, the SACU president, was not available, and neither was Colin Bryden, the press liaison man.

What was that Graveney had said? *If we get to Cape Town.*

Something highly suspicious was up. But what?

Outside, the sky had become an ominous, chilling metal grey. More like an afternoon in Derby, the English midlands city, which has the most windswept venue of any British cricket ground, and is famous for biting cold mid-summer afternoons when thermal underwear becomes more than an optional extra.

A quick call to Fanie. On the Saturday he had bowled Defence to victory over Harlequins, taking 6 wickets for 50-odd; yes, a solid performance, and he is happy. The knee is still sore, and although disappointed at not making the 'Test' side, he partly accepts the selectors' decision to go for Richard Snell, the inswing bowler.

'They don't want to risk me in the five-day game yet. Next season . . .'

'What about the limited-overs games?'

'What about them? You think I have a chance?' There is hope in his voice.

'As good as any. That final spell in Maritzburg should have convinced them.'

'We'll see, my old friend.'

After lunch, Chesters is putting together a rehash of the first 'Test' debacle for the morning editions in the group. The telephone rings and the voice, which had made prophecies about the matches not taking place in Kimberley and Pietermaritzburg, makes a new claim.

'A decision is being made, right now, to cancel the tour.'

'Your previous information has not been entirely accurate.'

'Believe me.' He is very persistent.

'I need more proof than just your word.'

'Call Dr Ali Bacher after five. Or Krish Naidoo.'

'Who is this?'

The line goes dead. Strange. Very strange. Rumour or not, it has to be followed. But the secret talks between the ANC and the SACU are still in progress. No Newlands 'Test'. No six limited-overs games. The matches in the Cape are abandoned. Okay, four then. Settle for four. Better than nothing. New tour arrangements have to be made. And the last rites have been read over the second tour. Time to switch on the television. Mandela is being released. South Africans, after thirty-four years, finally come face to face, on the TV screen, with the man incarcerated for his opposition to the laws which deprived millions of more than their dignity.

There's another telephone call. This time it is Peter van der Merwe, convener of the national selectors, returning the earlier call, as always polite and chatty.

'Kepler Wessels has made himself unavailable for the rest of the matches against Mike Gatting's team,' van der Merwe comments.

'Any reason?' Chesters is feeling regret. He has a soft spot for Wessels.

'It is all in an embargoed press release that Colin Bryden should have soon.'

'Thanks, Peter. Anything yet on the likely line-up of the limited-overs squad?'

'Call me tomorrow on that one. I'll give you Kepler's replacement for Newlands at the same time.'

'Is it Cullinan?'

'Call me again. Tomorrow morning.'

The Wessels story is written and sent to the group's morning papers. Being the era before mobile phones, tracking down certain information was not easy but Wessels had confirmed the decision. Off the record, he was upset at comments made about his Australian connection.

It is just after 5.30 a.m. on Monday, 12 February 1990 when there are two telephone calls. The first says the tour has been cancelled, although there is a rearranged limited-overs itinerary. The second confirms it. Amid all this rush, the call to Peter van der Merwe to confirm the side is forgotten. In a matter of fourteen hours the journalists are pushed out of one hotel and into another and the limited-overs side for the series is announced, along with a hectic media conference.

The limited-overs squad contains an interesting mix. Added to the 'Test' squad, minus Wessels, are Daryll Cullinan, Mark Rushmere, Clive Rice, Tim Shaw and Fanie de Villiers. The young man, denied a chance to bowl in a day-night match five years before because his captain, Lee Barnard, declined to take a risk, has won a limited-overs cap against Mike Gatting's rebels.

Yet, if the second rebel tour has already been terminated—initially angrily denied by Dakin—why the selection of a number of promising players?

'We have our long-term plans,' hints Peter van der Merwe. 'There is a lot of experience in the squad and we feel the youngsters can learn from the older players.'

Long-term plans for what? Sixteen players for four games.

'It's a big squad for what you need.'

'But it is a competitive one. And they will all get a game,' van der Merwe confirms.

Fanie de Villiers

Almost twenty-two months later, eight of the sixteen were selected for the historic shuttle tour of India: Rice replaced Jimmy Cook as captain while Peter Kirsten, Adrian Kuiper, Richard Snell, Allan Donald, Brian McMillan and Shaw make that tour. For India, the selectors also included Mandy Yachad, Kepler Wessels, Craig Matthews, Andrew Hudson, Clive Eksteen and Dave Richardson.

Fanie is sitting in the Northern Transvaal Command sports office in Voortrekkerhoogte when his telephone rings. It is just after 11.30 a.m. and a newspaper reporter is calling, wanting to come and take a photograph.

'Why do you want a picture of me now?'

'Haven't you heard? You are in the Bok squad for the one-day series against Mike Gatting's team.'

'Well. That's nice. Thanks for telling me.'

'Haven't you heard? Been told?'

'Not a word from anyone.'

And that is true. The normally efficient SACU machine was tied up with other matters. A critical media conference was looming. Anyway, the media had the team. Letters to the players would go out later. So much to do. Then the phone rings, confirming his selection.

In the office with Fanie are Mark Davis and Mark and Grant Weber.

'What was that about?' Davis asks. The Weber brothers look up enquiringly.

'I am told that I've been picked for the Boks!'

His colleagues are more excited than he is, shaking his hand and telling everyone who comes into the office. The scene reminds Fanie of the day four seasons ago, when Roy Pienaar was congratulated by Noel Day at Berea Park. The tall, elegant batsman, then playing for Northerns, had just been selected for the one-day series against Kim Hughes' Australians. There was no emotion: just cool, calm acceptance of being selected for a 'national' side. Fanie had felt that it was out of place. Now, had it been him, he would have wanted to show people how proud he was being selected for the Boks. Yet that morning in the sports office at Voortrekkeerhoogte he feels the same way Pienaar had that lunchtime at Berea Park. It is a rebel series . . . nothing genuine at all.

There is a quiet celebration with Judy, his mom and dad. However, checking into the hotel, being congratulated by Rice, Pienaar and Cook, and collecting his team kit for the first time: that's when the excitement and the emotion first sweeps through him. Fanie, the tearaway kid from NKP, now an SADF lieutenant, goes into the first team meeting in the manager's hotel room. Cook, named as captain for the series, is sitting, relaxed, talking to Rice and Peter Kirstsen. When the meeting is called to order and tactics and planning are being discussed, Cook looks over at Rice and grins. 'Okay, skipper, what do you think? I think you are the best person to tell us what to do.'

Other members of the team seem to agree. Rice is the team's unofficial captain; there is no question about that. The youngsters sit and listen, awed. They have a lot of respect for the Transvaal skipper: they look up to him after all the years he has been in England leading Nottinghamshire. Having played against each member of Gatting's tourists, Rice is wise to their tactical shortcomings. For Cook and the rest of the team, taking orders from Rice is a logical starting point. On the field Cook may direct the operations, but Rice, often fielding like a twenty-year-old on the boundary, is the real general in charge.

It is a madcap chase around the country. Centurion Park to Durban; tight security at Jan Smuts Airport demands all bags be unpacked, all electronic gear be checked; off to Bloemfontein and back to Johannesburg. Fanie wears his blue blazer with the Springbok head with pride, but admits it is not the real thing. 'When I play in a Test, my friend. That is when I know they are genuine colours.'

Fanie, swinging the ball appreciably, takes the wicket of Chris Cowdrey, a former England captain, when the tourists bat first in the opening day-night game at Centurion Park. And throughout his 11 overs he is economical, giving away 29 runs as the top five batsmen have difficulty with his ability to move the ball both ways. Nothing fancy, just relying on his expertise to swing the ball. At Kingsmead in Durban two days later, his bowling is equally tight, although the figures do not reflect his accuracy. Bowling Kim Barnett for 76 helps South Africa to win the second game. This time there is better support from Allan Donald.

On to Springbok Park in Bloemfontein. Adrian Kuiper's match: he scores 117 off 52 balls (the century off 49 balls); Fanie bowls

Chris Broad for a single in his first over as the rebels innings swiftly slides into decline. They are 23 for 4: Donald has 3 wickets and Fanie one in just half an hour. Then the left South floodlit pylon trips a switch and the umpires after consultation allow play to continue.

Of course there was much more to Kuiper's all-round talents than the one-man limited-overs road show which hit South Africa in the late 1980s. For example, in March 1989, he hit 23 sixes in 5 innings. In the following October, there was that impressive 161 in the Currie Cup game against Natal at Kingsmead. It was an example of how desperately he wanted to show the national selectors that he could play a big first-class innings.

So, while the 117 at Springbok Park was, sentimentally for Kuiper, his 'best limited-overs innings because it was for South Africa', there was a much earlier day-night innings that season, which was far superior technically. At Centurion Park, in the Nashua Challenge north-south benefit match he shared with Lee Barnard, Kuiper hit 124. Nine sixes and eight fours off a bowling attack equal to that mounted by Gatting's tourists: Donald, Corrie van Zyl, Steve Elworthy, Rice, Willie Morris and Anton Ferreira. In one incredible over bowled by van Zyl he scored four sixes: off the second, third, fifth and sixth balls. From 17 for 0 in 5 overs (respectable enough figures), van Zyl watched in horror as the next 12 balls he bowled went for 36, or 3 runs a ball. It was a merciless flogging. Little wonder he threw the ball to Barnard and suggested that it was his turn to bowl to 'that bloody butcher'.

Rice's comment was, 'When it's like this, you hope you bowl straight and he mishits a single so you can safely have a go at the other batsman.'

If the innings in September was one of grace and poise, a juxtaposition of coordination, technique and skill in ball placement, the innings at Springbok Park was a marvellous piece of bludgeoning: a swashbuckling riposte to a certain group of spectators on the old left embankment, whose knowledge of the most basic rudiments of batting skills are usually found through the bottom end of a brown bottle.

At Springbok Park, Peter Kirsten's role was reduced to that of a stage prop waiting for something to happen and scoring 3 while

Kuiper hit 48. As it is, his arrival was a planned push up the order should the innings get off to a good start. He sauntered in at 128 for 2 in the thirty-third over. When he was dismissed, 66 balls later, he had 117 to his credit: a scoring rate of 10.66 runs an over. Not surprisingly, most shots were played outside the conventional V, with only four of the sixteen boundaries between mid-off and mid-on, one being the second six off John Emburey.

South Africa's original 'pinch-hitter' has, save for the innings against India in New Delhi on the historic tour in November 1991, rarely performed with such perfected aggression since.

Throughout the rebel limited-overs series Chris Cowdrey, captain of Kent, was looking for a bowler to prop up his often-sorry, county bowling attack. He asked a number of questions of a number of people and the answer each time was, 'try Fanie de Villiers'. There was also Clive Rice's personal stamp of approval. 'You won't go wrong with Fanie,' said Rice with an enigmatic grin. 'He's a good team man, will give you more than a hundred per cent and can be quite a card when he wants to be.'

It was Gatting who wrapped up the tour with an impressive bowling performance at the Wanderers to give his side a face-saving victory. In England he was regularly called 'Fat Gat' or 'Cap'n Cock-Up', the latter after his well publicized run-in with Shakoor Rana.

Mud clings. Even today there are those who, with no intimate knowledge of the events in Kimberley in January 1990, serve up their inaccurate version to a forgetful public of how 'Gatting—never a man famed for his diplomatic subtlety—began to get his foot wedged in his mouth with increasing frequency'. How easy it is to ignore the facts for the sake of some naïve embellished jingoist thought based on hearsay. But then South African sports magazines are famous for their inaccuracies.

On the hot, sunny afternoon of Sunday, 28 January, Gatting sat in the grandstand above the changing rooms, cheerful enough after the victory by 254 runs. John Emburey and David Graveney had shared the spoils in the second innings: Graveney's skills as a left-arm spinner netting him 10 for 65. For about fifteen to twenty minutes, the questions delved into tour strategy, batting and bowling tactics, the form and fitness of players and the strength of the opposition along with pitch conditions. There were also some thoughts expressed about a possible side for the match against South African Universities in Bloemfontein, starting two days later. Throughout, watchful security officers sat below.

The Rat Pack representing the British tabloids on the tour were not interested in the game at all. They wanted a juicy comment or two: something to twist into a story that would make their editors happy. But then most of the English press on this particular tour were only interested in the sort of mischief-making that would perpetuate the 'Cap'n Cock-Up' image.

Amid all this came the question: 'Gatt, have you any view on the distractions, which you know about, which happened off the field?'

He walked into their carefully baited trap. Had he said 'no comment', he would have been pilloried in the tabloids for not preparing to discuss the protest. He wanted to be open, so he felt an honest reply was the best course to follow: 'As far as I'm concerned, there were a few people singing and dancing and that was it. I didn't know of anything else happening. We were more concerned with playing cricket and that was it.'

While the grammar was far from perfect, it was a captain's reaction regarding the demonstration during the game. The rat pack, sniffing success, gathered below the grandstand, discussing for several minutes how they would handle the story. Agreement reached, they filed their copy and were merciless in their reports of Gatting's 'insulting dismissive remarks of tour protestors as a few people singing and dancing'.

What was conveniently forgotten was the erstwhile England captain's open support for those who wanted to protest against the tour. Days before the side left an ice-bound England, Gatting had told various media sources of his backing for those groups who objected to the tour, and that he was happy to meet them.

On the last night of the tour at the Wanderers, his 6 for 26 were remarkable figures for a medium-paced trundler. But the tourists had built a solid platform—294 for 8 off 50 overs was always going to be a mountain to climb for South Africa.

Kim Barnett began the carnage when he put together a dazzling century, taking 15 runs off Fanie's first over: a memory the South African still carries. There were three successive fours. It hurt. It injured his pride as well.

Fifteen hours later at the Sandton Holiday Inn, Fanie packed his kit and headed for Voortrekkerhoogte. His discussion with Cowdrey had been successful. Now he was going to see his unit commander, Koos van Vuuren. All he needed to get was his approval to sign a season's contract with Kent.

Inside the hotel his journalist friend was at a media conference. They would talk later about the experiences over the past hectic eleven days.

David Graveney, sharing a last cup of coffee with a couple of South African cricket writers, took them into his confidence.

'You should know by now we won't be back next season,' he said. 'A word of advice, though. Keep your ears very close to the ground. It is going to be an exciting twelve months for South African cricket. And the country.'

An hour later, about the time the main party of Gatting's rebels headed for a game park near Warmbaths, north of Pretoria, Mike Atherton, a promising opening batsman, had scored 91 for England A at Mutare in Zimbabwe, and another tour was off to a successful start with an easy victory over a Young Zimbabwe XI.

* * * *

It is almost two years later.

In a plush upstairs hotel lounge in Harare, Graveney spots one of the two cricket writers he last saw in Sandton. Chesters is travelling with the South African side on their way to Australia and the World Cup and Graveney is now captain of the newly promoted county side Durham, leading the team on a pre-season tour of Zimbabwe. He waves to the journalist and offers to buy a 'cold Castle for old times' and to share a couple of memories and thoughts.

'Remember what I told you in Johannesburg? That exciting times were ahead?'

'Oh yes. I wrote about it, too. Later in the year.'

'We had a good touring team. But for the lack of preparation and the politics overrunning it, we would have played better cricket. I am happy, though, the way it has ended. I have a soft spot for South Africa.'

'Any regrets?'

'None at all. Look what has come out of it. Anyway, enjoy your World Cup.'

10

More than an Explosion

A few lazy clouds float in the bright blue October sky as Lieutenant Fanie de Villiers goes about organizing several of the ground staff at the sports club in Voortrekkerhoogte into a detail for a special job. The young commissioned officer has not long returned from Pretoria where he had gone to a morning show at a cinema with his long-time friends, Gerrie Dippenaar and Chris van Noordwyk. It was an unexpected visit and they are now in the sort of trouble schoolboys face when caught bunking class.

The working party was supposed to be mixing lime to draw lines on the parade field but the call of the cinema had been stronger. Chastised by Commandant Koos van Vuuren, the officer in charge of the Northern Transvaal Command sports office, Fanie checks the bags of lime and the location of the water tap. The idea is to make the job easier for the khaki-overalled labourers, who roll out an old battered drum from a clump of trees next to the bags of lime. There is a farewell parade the next day for the retiring SADF Sergeant Major John Holliday and van Vuuren wants arrangements to go without a hitch. In another part of the field, Commandant Wolf Steinbach, manager of the rugby club, is looking at a plan showing the line demarcations along with Johnnie, one of the ground staff.

As the ground staff mixes the water and lime, Fanie starts walking back to the sports office. It is about 12.15 p.m. on 29 October 1990 and unpleasantly humid. A thunderstorm is likely to occur later; it could possibly interfere with what would be a voluntary provincial practice. Since it is a Monday, there is no major rush. Northerns does not have another Nissan Shield game for three weeks and the day-night series was just starting. Optional practice or not, he does not need a rained off net at this stage of the season.

Damn. I do need a long bowl in the nets.

No one is aware that the drum, standing under the trees for a number of months, has not been rinsed out since it was last used to mix lime to mark lines. Not that it usually matters. This time, however, the delivery is of unbleached lime, instead of ordinary lime, and no one has checked the bags. But lime is lime. Or is it? Hours later, Fanie remembers how, when he was young, he saw unbleached lime mixed with pig fat to make a type of soap used on the farms; the chemical reaction when mixed with water was different: highly dangerous and combustible.

On their way to play fifteen minutes or so of touch rugby before lunch are troopies van Noordwyk, Mark Davis and the brothers Mark and Grant Weber, who are among the national servicemen seconded to the NTC sports office. They are laughing at a joke Davis has just made as they pass the ground staff mixing the lime and water.

'Say, don't we need lime to mark the pitch for our next club game?' van Noordwyk asks.

'We do, Pinkie, but it can wait. It's only Monday,' Davis tells him.

The ground staff open another old bag of unbleached lime, empty it in the drum and add more water, turning the mixture into thick bubbling porridge. One of the overalled staff is far from happy at the way the mixture is behaving as he checks its level. He frowns and calls to another workmate. Something is not quite right.

'Hey, why is it bubbling like this?'

'*Ek weet nie, jong* ('I don't know, friend'). I think we'd better call the lieutenant.'

Now the bubbling mixture is similar to a thermal mud pool: the smell is just as foul. The more it loses steam, the harder the top layers get encrusted, and the broomstick the staff are using becomes embedded in the mess.

Steinbach and Johnnie, walking back from looking at the plans, feel they can finish the job after lunch. Fanie is summoned by Johnnie, and walks towards the group around the drum. Juxtaposed in his mind are thoughts of the provincial nets and whether the staff created a problem as an easy way to take an early lunch break.

Fanie de Villiers

Puzzled, he looks at the now-steaming mixture and at a glance sees how a hard, thick white crust has formed. He also sees the sides of the drum expanding. Unbelievable!

Turning away, he moves to talk to Steinbach, standing some fifteen to twenty metres from the drum, to express concern about what appears to be a chemical reaction between the water and the lime. It might be an idea to let this lot cool down, scrape out the mess and start again after lunch. He turns to walk back to the drum with Steinbach who stops to talk to a member of the ground staff.

'Commandant, I think we'll have to...'

Bhhaammmm! Whooossshhh!!

The noise of the explosion and the accompanying hissing sound hits them at the same time that parts of the thick, flying, lime-porridge slap their faces. Fanie and Steinbach reel back, eyes and skin on fire as the lime splashes over their faces, arms and uniforms. The force of the eruption spews the lime compound geyser-fashion in all directions; Johnnie also gets a load in the face. The others are more fortunate than Fanie, whose face is covered by the thick, foul-smelling muck.

There is yelling and screaming and it is raining lime: the smelly flying mess splashes Davis, van Noordwyk and the Weber brothers, some on the face, some on bare shoulders. It is burning, eating at the flesh. Fanie is trying to wipe it off his face and out of his eyes. He attempts to open his eyelids and scrape out the lime, feeling his eyeballs move as his index fingers scrape across the surface. He is worried when he cannot get the muck out of his eyes; worried by the chemical reaction as the unbleached lime begins to slowly chew at the upper cell layers of his eye balls.

An elderly maid from the kitchen staff runs to help Fanie as he tries to get up. He cannot see and knows he must get to the water tap to clean the muck out of his eyes.

'Please help me . . . please help me to the tap,' he tells her.

The pain is unbelievable—a burning sensation. Fanie finds the water burning his skin where the lime has splashed. There is a searing pain around his mouth and inside and outside his nose. But worst of all his eyes! He can't open them!

'Quick!' He is gasping and shouting from the pain. 'Please get someone, help us.'

All he can see is a blurred whiteness. And it is scary. Very scary.

Hardly has she moved when others are running from the direction of the hall and the sports office. There are loud voices, then a series of urgent, thick, guttural commands.

'Quick! Someone! We need an ambulance. Urgently. Fanie looks as though he has been blinded.' And Commandant Steinbach. 'Quickly! Quickly! An ambulance!'

Any military hospital, because of the nature of the work involved, is equipped to handle most serious eventualities. 1 Military Hospital in Voortrekkerhoogte is better than most. Within fifteen minutes of the explosion, Fanie and Commandant Steinbach are in the ER and the doctor in charge is immediately aware of the urgency to arrest the looming danger.

'It is unbleached lime and unless we clean all that stuff out of his eyes this guy is going to lose his eyesight,' he tells the nursing staff to emphasize the danger. 'I have seen this type of thing before, so we are going to have to work very quickly on this one.'

The nurses have rigged up a shower arrangement to wash the lime porridge off the skin and out of the eyes.

Fanie's eyes are still burning like hot coals. He is strapped to a type of bed arrangement, facing downwards as his eyelids are forced open by paper clips. He hears soft voices asking questions and making the sort of comments he does not want to hear.

'This guy is too old,' is one response. 'He is going to lose his eyesight.'

'You think it's that bad?'

'It depends how many layers it has burnt through. He's twenty-seven. We had a woman in here the other day, who lost her eyesight after falling into some unbleached lime while jogging. She was in her thirties. It's really dangerous stuff to have lying around.'

There is a silence. Two doctors are whispering.

'You don't know who this guy is?'

'No.'

'It's Fanie de Villiers, the cricket player.'

'Oh, hell. The fast bowler. We have to do something.'

The doctors have a look at the shower arrangement and are unhappy with the results. It is not working the way they had hoped. The longer they delay, the harder it is going to be to save his eyesight. If there is still any left to save.

'We will have to set up water drips to clean out the stuff. I hope it works.'

The drips to wash out the eyeballs are erected, the eyelids kept open by the paper clips. It is an agonizing operation, causing mental torment: a torture he did not expect, playing tricks on his mind.

Drip! Drip! Drip!

Whatever they want to know I'll tell them. Secrets. . . anything. They've just got to stop this. Please!

Then the doctor is back looking at the effects of the drip. He is not satisfied.

'No,' he says. 'There's a lot of muck in there. We'll have to continue for some time. I'll come and check later.'

The torture continues; the pain is cruel and excruciating, forced on him by some unseen captors.

Lord, just what am I thinking?

He knows his mind is playing tricks with this water torture, this drip, drip, drip. How long is it going to last? And this terrible pain. When is it going to end?

For three hours the treatment continues. The doctor checks the progress every half hour, peering into each eye with a small flash, but is not happy with the results. He knows they will have to clean the rest of the particles out with small needles, and that is dangerous.

At last the drips come down and the eyes are covered with cotton wool eye patches. But he knows the treatment is far from over. And there is this gritty feeling under his eyelids.

The doctor returns with an optometrist. They remove the eye patches, open his eyelids again and start poking the eyeballs.

'Keep your head very still,' says the specialist. 'If you move so much as a fraction of a centimetre this needle will go into your eyeball.'

Fanie knows. It is enough to stop him moving his head as they take out the remains of the microscopic lime particles, which can seriously damage the cell layers covering the eyeballs. The blurry white sensation has gone but he cannot focus, which as the optometrist explains, is a normal phenomenon. What is important now is to see whether the cells start growing again.

Much later, after supper, he calls Judy.

'Listen, skat. There was a small accident today and I'm in 1 Mil, but don't worry. There was an explosion and I guess I am lucky. I'm really okay.'

Eternal optimist. He is not going to tell her about the possibility that he might have been blinded.

'Would you come and visit me, please?'

Although he sounds calm and reassuring, he is also desperately worried. The news from the specialists is not good. He could lose sight in both eyes: the right one especially. There is better news for Steinbach and Johnnie. Davis, van Noordwyk and Mark Weber suffered minor skin burns and had been discharged. Really. What a bloody mess. What in hell was wrong with that lime?

Judy does not hesitate. The man she loves is in trouble and needs her. She is soon sitting next to him in the hospital distressed at what she sees and further disturbed as the events of the afternoon are revealed. Almost numb with deep inner apprehensions about her fiancé's future, she calls Braam de Villiers when she gets home with the news. Minutes after the call, Fanie's equally alarmed father drives to the hospital to find out for himself the extent of the damage.

When the telephone rings after 10.30 p.m. at night, it is either a wrong number or bad news. In this case it was bad news, not the sort Chesters wanted to hear. Braam de Villiers was on the line, chatting calmly as he passed on the important message about Fanie being in hospital after being hit in the face by exploding lime. 'It may not turn out to be as serious as it sounds.' He seemed to be trying to convince them both that Fanie was not really in danger.

One of the problems a fast bowler faces in any county season is not so much staying fit, but finding the time to work on a fitness plan. Following a simple daily routine has its problems. Consequently, remaining fit is hard work. It had not been long since Fanie had returned from a hard season with Kent and an English summer he would prefer to forget. Especially as it had made serious inroads into his fitness and physical condition. Neels Liebel, his physio, had worked out a gym programme, designed to rebuild his stressed and overworked limbs and get him into shape for the coming season in South Africa. Fanie's net sessions at Centurion Park became a battle as he strapped on leg supports to help him in his run-ups.

It was also a time of important changes in the Northern Transvaal camp. While Fanie was playing for Kent, Mandy Yachad had taken over as captain from Lee Barnard, Rodney Ontong now assumed the role of manager/coach, Ray Jennings had quit Transvaal to join the 'enemy' north of the Jukskei River, and a decision was made not to employ an overseas professional. The argument was that there was no need for a professional player: not with players such as Tertius Bosch, Fanie de Villiers, Mike Haysman and now Jennings in the ranks.

'We are professional enough,' was Ontong's view.

Fanie was now a respected senior player and had been asked to give coaching help and advice. Occasionally wide-eyed schoolboys would hang back after their under-13 or under-15 net sessions to catch a glimpse of their hero. He always had a cheerful word for them and spent a few minutes signing autographs. There had been one other change that Fanie did not like. Shortly before his return, Gerbrand Grobler had decided to turn rugby into a career and had gone to Italy. Grobler no longer had the stomach to play in a setup so predominantly Johannesburg-oriented that it had been suggested, tongue-in-cheek, that some practices be held at the Wanderers.

Yet, what was worrying was that outside the under-13 and under-15 teams, the pool of talent was drying up in the province. This was not the case only with the pool of Afrikaans talent. English schools were also being overlooked by a selection system which was as selective as it was discriminatory. There were only one or two genuine local heroes the youngsters could identify with. Fanie de Villiers was one of them.

As he lay in hospital that first night, Fanie remained confident. The eye specialist admitted, when pushed for an answer, that it was far too soon to tell. What if the eyesight had been impaired enough to stop him from playing? He had heard when he was in England how a couple of Test batsmen had managed to cope by playing again after losing an eye: Ollie Milburn and Tiger Pataudi. But he was a bowler. You need both eyes for that, don't you? At that stage he had not heard about Eiulf Nupen, also known as Buster, who had lost an eye in a freak accident. Tall and broad-shouldered, Nupen was an aggressive bowler, brilliant with his off-cutters in the days when South Africa played on matting surfaces.

Better look on the bright side, though. And hey, how long would it take to learn something like braille?

* * * *

Braam and Hanna de Villiers were not going to take any chances with their soon-to-be-born fifth child. About five days before the event, they moved in with relatives in Vereeniging to be near the nursing home. The weather that October in 1964 was not good. In fact, it was as though winter had not been swept away by the brisk winds. On Thursday, 12 October, they had gone to the local drive-in, relaxed and cheerful. It was on their way back home that Hanna felt the all-too-familiar labour pains. A few hours later, on Friday, 13 October, a day not exactly noted for its good luck charms, a lusty Petrus Stephanus de Villiers was born.

Named after his paternal grandfather, he was wrapped up warmly the day Braam and Hanna drove home with their youngest son. Snow had been predicted and there was a bitter wind blowing as they made their way from Vereeniging to Deneysville. As they crossed in to the Free State, it began to snow. What a welcome into the world! And some of his more superstitious relatives were worried about him being born on 'Friday the thirteenth'. Not that his proud mother and father were disturbed by such superstitious nonsense.

The de Villiers lineage is fascinating for those who have some curiosity about family trees. A little myth clutters a lot of generally accurate genealogical reasoning in the history of the family. The foundations are firmly rooted in staunch Huguenot stock.

The association with South Africa began with the docking of the Zion (Sion) in Table Bay in May 1689. On board were the de Villiers brothers, Pierre, Abraham and Jacob. Victims of the conflicts and persecutions of a Europe seriously divided along religious lines, they left France, the country of their birth, to seek shelter in the convenient arms of the Protestant-dominated Cape.

From the moment Louis XIV revoked the Edict of Nantes in 1685, the Huguenots knew that all they owned as well as their religious and civil autonomy was at risk. The restricted universal independence granted to them by the edict, issued in 1598 by Henry IV (Henri of Navarre) had allowed Catholics and Protestants to coexist for almost a century. But his grandson, the 'Sun King' Louis XIV, wanted to 'cleanse the country of our religious parasites'.

As with the majority of French Protestants at the time, the de Villiers brothers first went to Holland and then, ironically, through the port of La Rochelle in Burgundy to the Cape. Little wonder perhaps that the ancestors of Fanie de Villiers were wine makers. And, with a name such as Braam, the elder statesman in this de Villiers family can trace his origins to the hardy and intuitive Abraham de Villiers. The way Fanie's father explained it, there has always been an Abraham de Villiers in their particular branch of the tree: from the early 1700s to modern times, a proud tradition spanning more than 250 years.

It should be expected, given the upheavals in Europe after the Nantes Edict was torn up and the massive destruction of church records in France (Catholics suffered as much of an identity problem through similar vandalism of parish records), that there is conflicting evidence about the origins of the de Villiers name. One thing is certain, the coat of arms comes from around the late twelfth century, granted to a de Villiers (or Villiers) knight who rendered exceptional service to the French royal family during one of the Crusades.

In the first years of his life, Fanie would sit with Oupa Burger, his mother's father, and watch him make and mend things on the farm. He would trail after him and shoulder his own fishing rod when they went fishing. Those were the happy days of growing up on a farm. There are family album snaps with him in athletics kit at Deneysville; in later years, scrapbooks carefully put together by his mother and father display a variety of athletics diplomas and certificates from his first primary school in Deneysville to Fonteinê in Sasolburg, Northern Free State Amateur Athletics Association and Eastern Transvaal schools. First place in the javelin, second for the long jump, second in the 800 metres, or first in the relay, third in the high jump. Gold, silver and bronze, the cards depict a testimony of triumph and determination. In 1976 he earned a special certificate from the Sport Foundation of Southern Africa for winning the javelin event in a prestige meeting. The next year he won two more awards from the foundation: for third place in the long jump and first place in the pole vault. He is proud of clearing 2.43 metres that stifling February day to beat the other under-13s. They even created a special trophy for him at Fonteinê Primary that year for his outstanding athletics efforts. He played in the side that went on to win the Far Northern Free State primary schools league. They now have a special showcase of Fanie's memorabilia at Fonteinê.

There is a picture of him playing rugby: about to unload the ball from his scrum half position in a game against Fakkel, the other Sasolburg primary school. And a clipping from *Volksblad*, the Bloemfontein Afrikaans daily newspaper with the names of the Free State under-13 side for the 1977 Perm Week in Pretoria. There is even a picture of the Sasolburg School choir in which Fanie sang.

What a multi-talented lad: cricket, athletics, rugby, fishing and singing. In later years he would also go hunting on the farm, often alone. By then the family had long conditioned themselves to his mealtime absences. They knew that at some stage he would turn up. It was not that he was a loner: there were times when he preferred his own company. It gave him a chance to test his mental and physical skills. And he was always prepared to try something new. The fishing and hunting were part of growing up.

In his sleep that first night after the explosion he was restless as his mind grappled with past events.

So, Fanie, why cricket? A real Souties game, eh?

Why put yourself and your body through all this agony? Remember 1988-89 when you found yourself, with Mike Rindel and Tertius Bosch, on Clive Rice's list of 'Bok' candidates for the next rebel tour 'Tests'? Other provinces eyeing your fine talent. What about Dr Willie Basson, the Northerns president saying that the free-market enterprise system would allow you to take a better offer, if you wanted it? Did you?

Transvaal came up with a good offer, didn't they?

There was the time you bowled to your brother Neels down in Potchefstroom and he *klapped* (hit) you for four the first delivery: *boet* to *boet* (brother to brother). Made Neels smile. Got a few runs that day, did Neels. Usually he looked out for you, especially during the camping holidays. Remember, Fanie? As the tent pegs were being anchored, your eyes could begin searching, looking to see if there was anyone of your age with whom to play or to go fishing. *Ja, ou Neels.*

Now this season with Kent. 1990. It was a tough one, eh? It was tough, ou boet. They changed the ball and the conditions. Fanie the Lion Heart, the Crusader. Man, what a joke.

Among the more accepted myths in the cricket universe are wet English summers and soft, slow pitches, hot Australian and South African seasons and hard pitches, ditto the West Indies, where it is also humid, the same with Sri Lanka and India. Pakistan is a bit like New Zealand: chilly in some places, warm or muggy in others; different pitches though. The bounce is often low and variable in the Shaky Isles Down Under, the pitches slow; in Pakistan, surfaces can be much truer, although bounce can be a problem. The one factor which links them all is that the swing bowler can usually move the ball around in all conditions; the good leg-spinner can be effective, too.

Sifting through the instant mental replay system takes Chesters to Lancaster Park in Christchurch. An hour or so of watching a much younger Sir Richard Hadlee on 12 March 1974 proved the point. Another tear away, like Fanie in his early years, Hadlee liked to bang them in. Get the surface of the pitch to do a little work as well.

Poor Fanie, though. The England summer of 1990 is hot. The pitches are flat. The seams are flat, and day after day the ground staff shave the grass off the pitch until they are down to the roots. 'How in hell are we expected to bowl on a heap like this?' Fanie asks Chris Cowdrey when he sees what they have done to the pitch at Folkestone. He had been bowling in the makeshift nets, preparing for his first four-day county game for Kent, when the ground staff checked the pitch, lowered the blades on the hand mower and cut the grass again. The mandarins of the TCCB had, in their wisdom, decided that if they were to rebuild England's batting to the levels last attained in the 1970s, conditions would have to be made easier for the batsmen.

Graeme Wright, an erstwhile articulate editor of *Wisden*, had much to say in the 1990 edition of the game's famous 'bible' on the subject of the parlous state of the county game. What he found disturbing was how dependent counties had become on limited-overs matches and how these had led to a serious decline in standards of most areas other than fielding. Added to that depressing state was the way the Reader ball had been changed to allow the seamer, as opposed to the swing bowler and the spinner, more room for success. He also raised the hairy subject of the TCCB cutting back on the number of first-class games instead of the one-day variety. At least the recently formed United Cricket Board had the good sense to realize at the end of the 1991-92 season that the Nissan Shield/Total Power series had outlived its usefulness.

But when Fanie took one look at the ball he was to bowl with in England and the pitches on which he had to bowl, he mused about his decision to play a county season. Especially since it was not just a dry summer, it rained only on about two days in five months. An exaggeration of course, but that is how it seemed. It was a different story from the summer he spent with Todmorden when it had rained for days on end. Richard Ellison, a member of Gatting's rebels in South Africa the previous southern summer and now one of Fanie's Kent teammates, was a quality swing bowler. During the South African tour he had found he was able to swing the ball away again. And how that had pleased Gatting. 'I haven't seen him swing a ball like that in perhaps four seasons,' Gatting admitted after the Wanderers fiasco. 'It is so good to see.' In 1990 he too battled to get his swing going.

Then there was the batsman's view of England, circa 1990. Jimmy Cook, so used to South African conditions, enjoyed the challenge offered by the variety of pitches he came across in England during his three summers with Somerset. The first few games were a disaster. Then the change: the seam bowling did not worry him as much as it did most others. There were other factors in his favour as well: for one thing, he played the ball late, making him well-equipped to handle the conditions. Also, he enjoyed the game. There was fun in batting. Work out the pitch and the bowlers and you were away. Little wonder that he was a success.

Fanie, however, just shook his head. This would never do. A flatter seam was supposed to mean more skill. Of course, grassless pitches did not help. Added to these problems was the recurring hamstring trouble. No wonder that the good folk in Torquay asked his English mentor Roger Mann in April 1992, just who was Fanie de Villiers? 'He made so little impact on the county scene in 1990 that people simply missed him altogether,' he recalled with a chuckle. 'It's understandable.'

Initially Fanie had different views of English county pitches. He bowled a few overs in the nets at Canterbury, shortly after his arrival with his fiancée, Judy, and felt a county season was going to be a great success story. The way he moved the ball made him think that a minimum of 125 wickets would show the Poms how a strapping boereseun was better than anything they had seen in years. His total haul of 25 wickets at 39.68 was, however, a big let down. It taught him a lesson of how not to be so boastful.

Saw his ass, he would sometimes cheerfully admit. The way he had that night at Newlands when Kuiper had gotten hold of him in Omar Henry's benefit.

For one thing, the flatter seam with the lower join partly negated the bowler's skill. Yet it was not very different to the ball he had used in South Africa. The difference here was the make. South Africa provincial matches are played with a four-piece ball made in Australia, which has a flat seam and a lower join. At least he could swing that ball. In English conditions with an English ball there was little in the way of swing. When he did get the ball to swing, it would move the way *it* wanted to, almost akin to reverse swing without even trying. Such a frustrating exercise. To bowl 280 overs in twelve games and take only 25 wickets did little justice, he felt, to his bowling ability. It forced him, more often than not, to utilize and perfect his use of the off-cutter. And, to an extent, he became bored when bowling in such conditions. The bowler, ran his argument, should get some help. A no-contest pitch makes for bored players and a boring game for the spectators.

Four summers later, it was a different story. He was a much wiser bowler. The long, hard road of apprenticeship had been served and he had qualified for his papers when selected to play against the Indians in 1992-93. Yet the off-cutter was the ball on which he based his attack and what he had predominantly bowled in that Sydney New Year Test to help South Africa win the match by seven runs.

Like Sir Richard Hadlee, he had learnt the genuine art of swing bowling in any number of unforgiving conditions, and cleverly applied what he learnt. His season with Kent gave him another opportunity to extend his desire to become a batsman in the Hadlee mould. Well, almost. Fanie had long harboured ambitions of batting higher in the order at provincial level. It went hand in hand with his positive attitude towards the game. And as his summer with Kent enabled him to score 264 runs at an average of 22.00, he felt that the new team management at Northerns should take more note of his batting talents.

Throughout that summer, however, the worry of the hamstring problems nipped at his subconscious. He regularly took painkillers that enabled him to bowl in the four-day games. Although it was often an ordeal, it was nothing compared to his later experiences.

But oh yes! England in 1990 was no ordinary season for 'Vinnige' Fanie. Through the tiredness, frustration and pain, there also emerged the development of another world-class bowler. Stronger in mind and with a new, stubborn will.

What he did not need right now was that explosion of lime in his face. For Judy it was just as traumatic, seeing him in 1 Military Hospital, his eyes covered by thick cotton wool protection shades. The swaggering braggart of more than two years before, when he had picked her out from a group of friends, was now her fiancé. Since she had known him, he had gone through two knee operations, had earned selection for South Africa in the last of the rebel tours and had, because of the pain, almost crawled off some of the fields in England when playing for Kent. Painkillers did not always do the job as he stretched himself to achieve that extra effort. Now this. And the fear of him not seeing again.

It left her with an uncomfortably deep bruised feeling and it refused to go away. Amid all this came unwanted attention: smile for this press photographer, Judy. Smile for the other press photographer. Smile, Judy! Her thoughts in a turmoil, all she wanted to do was cry. 'Don't worry, skat,' he told her cheerfully. 'I'm going to be all right, you'll see. BP. Be positive.' Gerrie Dippenaar was positive, Pa and Ma were positive, Chesters was positive. Neels was positive. 'We are going to pull through this,' he repeated.

The burning sensation was still there and the worry about the lime deposits in his eyes was of some concern. There were visible signs as well of the lime burns about the face and uncomfortable skin chafing. Not as severe as it had been over the first forty-eight hours. There was a 'get well' message from Dr Ali Bacher and the guys from the Defence sports office—Van Noordwyk, the Weber brothers and Mark Davis—visited him. Anton Ferreira and Chesters too. They told him about the draw against Free State in the Nissan Shield.

'I'm going to play in that game,' he told Judy.

She was not surprised at this declaration: his confidence was as strong as ever, an inner strength developed from a simple belief in his own ability. It was a good sign.

A chemistry boffin at Pretoria University, Professor Sarel Lotz, at first indicated it was difficult to establish what caused the chemical reaction as the contents of the drum before the lime and water were thrown together were not known. The acid, it was said, would cause the mixture to bubble and explode. It was the acid which caused the burning, not the lime. It was a theory debunked by the doctor attending Fanie. He had seen enough accidents involving lime, especially unbleached lime, to know its dangers. They did not, he argued, understand its dangers.

It was on the fourth morning after the 'exploding drum' incident that the specialists were prepared to admit cautious confidence. For three days they had checked and there had been nothing: now there were signs the cells were growing again.

By 2.00 p.m. the next day, after a thorough examination, they were satisfied that there would be no complications. Naturally there was still concern and there were no plans to release him immediately. Another forty-eight hours, perhaps. There were times, however, when the pain was so severe, it forced him to ask the nurse for extra eye drops to take away the burning agony. He felt like a tight throbbing band of hot steel had been wrapped around his head, growing tighter and tighter. How much longer could this last? All the time the nurse was worried that the drops would not help regenerate the growth of the eyeball tissue. She had been warned, so had Fanie.

It was now a critical period.

'Please, nurse, more drops. This pain's killing me.'

'Lieutenant, you know what the specialist said.'

'Damn the specialist, nurse. Please. This pain . . .'

Another twenty-four hours passed and those irritating cinders continued to smart behind his eyelids.

The knee ops, the worry with the hamstring and the growing back problem . . . they were minor aggravations compared to this continuous torture. His face is flushed, his head aches. His mouth is dry and he wants water. Or a beer. A nice cold beer. Now that would be lekker!

It was the fifth day and the specialists stood around, hopeful. A few more tests perhaps, to make sure he would regain his full eyesight.

'Okay. Blink. Can you see this finger?' Fanie nodded. He closed the left eye. He closed the right eye. What a relief! The real danger was almost over. Although they had removed most of the remaining lime granules from his lower eyelids, there was still some discomfort. That was where most of the damage had occurred, not so much to the eyes, as the skin inside the eyelids. Also, there was some injury to the first protective layer—enough to worry the specialists. It was this area, they later acknowledged, that had caused them most concern. The use of the eye drops did not, as expected, retard the recovery process.

'Okay then, doc. When can I go home?'

'Why the rush?'

'I have to start training again,' he grinned. 'It's most important. Northerns have a game in a couple of weeks and I want to be ready to bowl. Perhaps hit the winning runs.'

There was a cautionary note from one of the specialists who was worried about the right eye. 'It might,' he explained, 'give you a few problems. So, don't put too much strain on it.'

Before the accident Fanie had played in two Castle Cup games, against Transvaal at the Wanderers and against Eastern Province at Centurion Park. He had not been happy with his performances. The niggling back problem was bothering him again and he carried on taking pain pills and injections.

Most of 13 November, two days before the day-night game against Impalas, was spent relaxing and fishing at Hartbeespoort Dam. It allowed him to talk with his father and think about whether or not he should play. The fishing exercise had given him time to focus his right eye on small items and partly helped him make up his mind to play.

When he returned to the nets at Centurion Park there was a warm welcome from his team members. The agreement had been that he would begin with a light work out. Not to rush it. Give him time to adjust. Mandy Yachad, the captain, and Rodney Ontong, the new manager/coach, felt it would be wiser if he used that Wednesday's practice session as a final trial. As it is, they were only too happy to have him back. It was good for team morale.

Not surprisingly, with all the publicity, there was a large curious spectator gallery at Centurion Park when he turned up at the nets the next afternoon, the day before the Impalas game. It had only been fifteen days since he had been 'blinded' and here he was, as the *Pretoria News* so quaintly expressed it, ready for an 'eyeball to eyeball confrontation'.

National Television cameras turned up to record the event and a couple of radio stations as well as newspapers, which did not normally visit the nets. The practice had almost degenerated into a sideshow when Ontong and Yachad had enough of the interference and asked the electronic media to wait until the session was over. After half an hour's bowling, he passed himself as fit. There was no urging from either Yachad or Ontong. Of course, they closely watched the proceedings. The miracle man was bowling with a relaxed style, although he had strapped his left knee to help ease the back pain as he did not pivot his body in such a way that it would jar the lower part of his back.

The Impalas game was not entirely unsuccessful. There was warm applause when he bowled his first ball and he soon picked up the valuable wicket of Louis Koen. He only travelled for 23 runs in 9 overs, not too bad considering the ordeal. As usual, that season he shared the new ball with Tertius Bosch, now showing the promise of developing into a leading bowler. In this game Bosch bagged 3 for 31, and rocked the Impalas by getting rid of both openers in rapid succession.

As for Fanie, it was steady progress: nothing spectacular as he was troubled by the hamstring problem, with Neels Liebel working hard to correct the niggling injury making him train, doing his leg exercises, and ensuring a largely successful pain-free period. Yet there were times when he was forced to sleep with a pillow between his legs. It is a process advocated by orthopædic surgeons after hip-replacement operations as it eases pressure off the lower back nerves as well as relaxes the legs.

Not surprisingly, Fanie's bowling in the two Nissan Shield matches against Free State were tight and impressive, although at times he battled to reach the bowling crease. The two games were played over successive Saturdays at Centurion Park and in Bloemfontein. Only the batsmen, who were doing so well in the Currie Cup, badly let them down at crucial stages in the limited-overs matches. Anyway, it was not his fault when in the second leg quarterfinal he was pushed up the order to four in order to pick up the scoring tempo and was promptly run-out for a duck. It was comical, yet tragic, with Mike Haysman failing to respond.

'Yes' . . . . 'No' . . . 'Okay' . . . 'Oops!'

'Jammer (sorry), *ou Vinnige,'* Corrie van Zyl grinned.

'Have a good shower!' chortled Allan Donald on what was a scorcher of a day.

Such incidents made him wonder. Perhaps he should have taken up that Transvaal offer the season before. At least he would have been playing in a side that could win matches. And a trophy occasionally, even when they did not have the best of sides. That motto, 'BP', comes in handy, whether it is being positive, being prepared or even being competitive. With a quality player like Clive Rice around, the 'BP' sign can always be attached to any of the three. Fanie learnt a lot from Rice in those few days than in previous season when he had played in the four limited-overs matches against Gatting's Poms. Fight fair, but fight hard.

In that season of 1990-91 the SACU introduced the disastrous thirteen-man squad experiment, an almost slapstick gimmick that backfired. With declining public interest because of the day-night game, the Nissan Shield programme had been tinkered with so often in the SACU 'workshop' that, from the mid-1980s, each new summer saw a new model; each one failed. The competition was foundering, no longer attracting the crowds of the 1970s and early 1980s, and the 'spare-parts factory' was running out of ideas. The decline was noticed from around 1985-86 as fewer spectators attended the early round matches, which that had once drawn spectacular crowds. The semi-finals and final alone attracted attention and the end of an era was unfolding.

Whether the squad experiment hastened its demise, or whether it was the coming thrust of the international arena, is a matter for conjecture. But the substitution clause, and the umpires signalling the changes to the strains of 'Heat is On' blaring over the PA system, was an intrusion. In some sections of the media, even umpire Barry Lambson's hip-wiggle became a laborious point of discussion.

The basis of laws one and two were torn up for this incongruous exercise although some were amused by it. For others, there was confusion: Derek Amore, from *The Citizen*, not surprisingly asked

Dr Ali Bacher to run through the law changes a second time after they had been carefully explained, 'as I have lost the thread'. The eye of the needle in this case was that some of *The Citizen* sports staff, along with those of *The Star* at that time, were rarely noted for their grasp of anything out of the ordinary. Even the comment about the format in the 1991 *SA Annual* was one of those hindsight thumbsuck efforts and equally absurd.

Not surprisingly, serious statisticians recoiled at the plethora of data that was churned out match after match. Every player who was on the field for only fifteen minutes was deemed to have played in the match. Of course, Kepler Wessels and Rice manipulated the system to suit their sides. Sanity prevailed, and thankfully the bizarre format was scrapped. Yet, at the time, Peter Pollock, the venerated convener of selectors from August 1992 until the 1999 World Cup, commented, in all apparent seriousness (although one suspects tongue-in-cheek), how great this particular innovation was.

So, the country, which propagated and fostered rebel tours, was seen to be introducing another scheme to raise the blood pressure in some fusty boardrooms across the globe, while others regarded it as a typical response to an era of isolation. It was as if the South African organizers were, if need be, prepared to sell the summer game to the United States: a sad indictment of an era, which happily, was slipping away. Born as the Gillette Cup, it was at first, a rebel event held outside the confines of the then SA Cricket Association. Eric Rowan, a modern renegade, saw it as an opportunity to make some cash, when the first games in late March 1970 drew curious spectators.

Apart from the remodelled Nissan Shield, the last under this particular sponsorship, 1990 was becoming a watershed year. Thirty years after Harold Macmillan had warned of the 'winds of change blowing through Africa', President F. W. de Klerk released a heady breeze of political change and expectation through transformation. Ironically, both speeches were delivered in the same house of parliament in Cape Town. On 3 February 1960, Macmillan had spoken of the pending decolonization of Africa. De Klerk's message on 2 February 1990 was equally forceful and highlighted a change, which geared South Africa's future towards a long-term, internationally recognized survival.

In the autumn, winter and spring of 1990, meetings were held to bring the SACB and SACU together to form a single body.

Although Dr Bacher had seen his township scheme being temporarily destroyed, it was patched together by a number of people, including Mthobi Tyamzashe, later director general of the department of sport and recreation. New friendships were forged as the 1990-91 season became the last example of the old racial divisions. In April 1990, Dr Bacher even hinted about the shape of a new order; the game was on the move again and Chesters felt an urgent vibe in the SACU offices at the Wanderers. David Graveney's parting comment made weeks before, as Gatting's troupe departed for a game reserve before heading home, had borne some fruit after all.

In those days, early mornings in the editorial offices at the *Pretoria News* (as with most afternoon papers) was usually a time when there were tight deadlines and a demand for tight, accurate news, especially in exciting times such as 1990. Sometimes you could get a good whiff of the adrenaline pumping. A normal morning routine in chasing up a story in those early, often-stimulating, expectant, summer months of 1990-91, often consisted of calls to contacts who may have some item of value. Some would call back, others not. At about 8.00 a.m. on 12 December 1990, Chesters got an unexpected call.

Geoff Dakin, the president of the SACU, was on the line.

'Are you coming to the Nissan final at St. George's Park on Saturday?'

'Not at this stage, Geoff.'

'I think you should tell your editor that it would be worth your while. We're having a big meeting with the SACB and a high-ranking ANC member. I can tell you now, my friend, history is going to be made.'

'I'll try, Geoff. But I don't know whether...'

'Tell him that South Africa could be involved in an official tour within twelve months. It might make him his change his mind.'

'Who else knows?'

'From the media? No one other than you.'

Chesters knew several administrators in the SACB camp but two better than most: Dr Goolam Karim and Rushdi Magiet. He made contact with Dr Karim to find out how close the talks were to agreement. There was also Krish Naidoo, but he was overseas, and Krish Mackerdhuj. However, he was in a quandary; having only briefly met the SACB president, he doubted whether he would comment. Or, if he did, he would not give away too much. Not to a white, perceived-establishment journalist he barely knew. And that was fair. There had already been problems with a Durban-based writer who made up his own quotes and Mackerdhuj was, understandably, wary. In the end Chesters contacted Dr Karim, a GP who had a practice in Seccunda in then Eastern Transvaal (now Mpumalanga).

A quietly spoken intellectual who was forced to study medicine at Trinity College, Dublin, because of the apartheid system, Dr Karim was a man of principle. Although not on the SACB executive, he knew what was going on within their inner ranks. He was also the chairman of the Cricket Association of Transvaal (CAT), which replaced the discredited Transvaal Cricket Board. Also important were his close ties with Dr Ali Bacher, the SACU managing director. Both men had, from the first days of negotiation, built a sound relationship based on mutual regard and respect and a committed drive to unify the sport. In the first months of unity, Dr Karim offered calm, wise counsel to cool the fires of those who failed to see the more global picture. His advice, as with his judgement, was deeply respected.

'Goolam, do you think much will come out of Sunday's meeting?'

'Yes. From what I have been told it could be historic, if they manage to control the hot heads. You know how it is. Steve Tshwete, someone you'll get to know, is brokering it. He's a big name in the ANC ranks.'

The *News'* editor, Mostert van Schoor, when told of the background and the possible implications had no trouble in sanctioning the trip to Port Elizabeth. What with the serious illness of Chesters' wife, van Schoor also knew of the inner conflict the journalist had of being away from home for lengthy spells. The story had got to be worth it.

Four days later, on Sunday, 16 December, history was made around 5.00 p.m. Dr Ali Bacher sent off a series of faxes to various media agencies alerting their attention that the most important story in South African cricket in more than 100 years was about to break. On the Day of the Vow (it was also referred to by some as

Dingaan's Day), the first steps of unity were forged in the Elizabeth Room in the old Elizabeth Sun on the Summerstrand beachfront. It was a matter of irony that such an accord, a long-fostered dream for many, took place on the holiest day of the Afrikaner calendar. Two hours later, Chesters filed the following story for the Argus Group of newspapers.

> South African cricket is now firmly on the road to forming a single body as the unity talks here yesterday cleared all remaining obstacles during a five-hour meeting that ended with a historic accord.
>
> Although this does not signify an end to the long winter of 'international isolation' it is at least a hesitant step forward.
>
> Smiling members of the rival bodies, the South African Cricket Board and the South African Cricket Union, and the meeting's chairman, Steve Tshwete, an executive member of the ANC, emerged from talks at a beachfront hotel 'totally committed to being united under one body'. From the ashes of the traumatic Gatting rebel tour earlier in the year comes a clear message of 'peace and goodwill' which has little to do with Christmas but creating a climate in the summer sport that will send an important signal to the International Cricket Council, soon to meet in Australia.
>
> One of the more important steps is that the SACB and SACU are to write to the secretary of the ICC as well as member ICC countries informing them of that 'unity' and that 'one voice in South African cricket is underway'.
>
> It is expected that the ICC will be asked to make South Africa an agenda item in terms of involvement in world cricket in the not-too-distant future.
>
> A nine-point statement of intent was read to the media at a conference after what Mr Tshwete described as a watershed meeting. It was Mr Tshwete who first broke the news that unity was not far off when he said, 'Having a regard for the future of South Africa, the SACB and the SACU declare it is their intention to:
>
> • Form one non-racial democratic controlling body under a single constitution. The vision of non-racialism in a

What a legend ... Tendulkar!

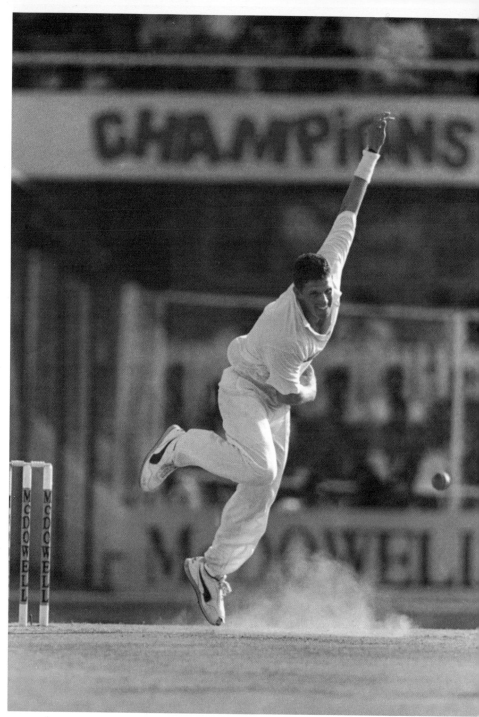

Dusty and flat pitches of foreign countries
always made touring difficult.

You can rely on Defy.

The boys always bounced me!

Celebrations with Paddy Upton our Biokenetist.
I'm pouring beer on him. He kept me on the field.

1998 St Georges Park; Port Elizabeth My last test.
"Emotional times for the two room mates of eight years.

Jonty, Clive Eksteen and Brian McMillan behind me.

Ford**Direct**

u and Gogga having fun.

HIRSCH'S

Glen McGrath... My last wicket in that historical test match in Sydney, 19
Caught and bowled.
The best 10 wickets of
my career.

ansie carrying me off the field after that historical Test Match in Sydney.

The sky is the limit!

LEAD THE WAY **TOYOT**

Makaya Ntini in South Africa.

LAZARUS
MOTOR COMPANY

Always a great experience to beat the Poms on home soil.

sed this hat for about seven years

Carrying Allan Donald back to his bowling mark.
We were a great team.

Waqar Younis, myself , Allan Donald and Sshaun Pollock

Jonty's favourite shot - the sweep slog.

lan Donald with Herchelle Gibbs

My last Test... My last wicket, Shoaib Akhtar, the last ball of the game and the last ball in my career. 1998 St. Georges Park, Port Elizabeth P.S. "You are only as good as your last ball."

Bowled Pakistan out to win the series. Took most of the twenty wickets between us.

MUTUAL&FEDERAL

Who would be your opening bowlers?

NASHUA TITANS

My older brother Neels, who was instrumental in igniting the cricketing light in me, also enjoys passing it on to our enthusiastic youth

SEE THE WORLD IN A NEW LIGHT **OSRAM**

SHARP

This man saved me a 'helluva' lot of runs!

We were opening partners in all my Test Matches.

SHODEN
DATA SYSTEMS

1992/1993 Season. Early days!

The Godfather of cricket umpires. Had to 'red card' Uncle Dave for a bad decision.

Good old days!

SAHARA

THE ULTIMATE IN PC'S

Wetting the ball under my armpits, creating
reverse swing.

legend dismissing a legend.

Inzamam Ul Haq... if this wasn't LBW,
we would've run him out later!

MACSTEEL

If ever there was a player with flair, he tipifies it.

Tournament in India. Any wicket for a fast bowler
in India is a bonus.

OMEGA
Financial Solutions

You won't believe it, but I loved batting more than bowling

Raising you bat as a fast bowler was memorable. Reverse sweeping
Mullick was even better.

future South Africa shall include equality irrespective of race, colour, creed, sex and religion and shall mean equality in every sphere of life.

- Develop, administer and make available opportunities for all those who wish to play cricket at all levels as soon as possible.
- Both bodies acknowledge the existence of imbalances in regard to separate educational systems, sponsorships and facilities. (To immediately form a committee of members of the SACB and SACU and the business community that would formulate strategies to urgently address these imbalances.)
- Contribute through cricket the creation of a just society in South Africa where everybody democratically has a common say and a common destiny.
- Respect the sports moratorium against tours to and from South Africa. To respect existing individual contracts of overseas professional cricketers in South Africa at present. (It will be the responsibility of the newly formed national body to determine the desirability of overseas professionals playing in South Africa.)
- Have respect for and obtain recognition from, and membership of, the ICC.
- Establish a working relationship with Sanroc and the Supreme Council of Sport in Africa.
- Administer and share, with immediate effect, the resources within the development field.
- Undertake to inform their respective constituencies of the spirit and letter of this document with immediate effect.

It is understood that Mr Tshwete, a former Robben Island prisoner, played a major role in the talks as a facilitator and was invaluable in advising both sides and helping to get rid of any remaining suspicions and hidden agendas.

Krish Mackerdhuj, the SACB president, felt the nine-point document of intent was only part of the success of the negotiations. 'We went into these talks uncertain of the future but emerged triumphant in the cause of South African cricket and the role it has to play in shaping the future of our country,' Mackerdhuj said.

It was agreed that Dr Ali Bacher, managing director of the SACU, will continue to act in the same administrative capacity in the as yet unnamed unified body on an ongoing basis until the official formation. This is likely to take place after April when a final meeting is to be held. The meeting will panel beat the finer administrative points into shape, and will include the size of the board, a new executive and the financial implications.

Dr Bacher agreed with Mackerdhuj when he said it was, significantly, the most important day in South African cricket, whether you are affiliated to the SACB or the SACU, during the last 100 years. 'From now on we are looking forward and will do it together. Total unity will not be far away.'

For some reason known only to those in charge of their sports pages, the afternoon editions of *The Star* on 17 December carried a concocted story bearing little resemblance to the version sent out from Port Elizabeth the night before. The treatment saw a rephrasing of certain key sections of the accord and placed an erroneous slant on the story, claiming an official Test series would be played in South Africa the following Christmas. It was hinted that the tourists would be either England or Australia, forgetting both were already committed: England in New Zealand and Australia hosting India. Also conveniently ignored was that as Australia were hosting the fifth World Cup in the latter half of the season, their schedule left no space for agreement to tour anywhere until April. Besides, South Africa had not formed a united body and was not a member of the ICC.

There was immediate stinging criticism from the SACB president. Mackerdhuj felt that his sense of fairplay, and that of his executive, had been violated by a story that lacked credibility and substance. 'This is not what we agreed to and what appeared in other papers. It is misleading the public,' complained Mackerdhuj, first to Chesters and then to the South African Press Association sports editor, Bill McLean.

Dakin also had a problem with the concocted story in *The Star* when a copy was faxed to him later in the day and Dave Richards, then chief executive of the Australian Cricket Board (who later held the same post with the ICC), was quite aggressive in his denunciation of *The Star's* 'tour hosting' claims when Chesters asked for his comment on the success of the unity talks. 'These people need to be careful about making such claims without checking their facts,' he said. 'I'm barely aware of the (unity) details and am awaiting a comprehensive report from Dr Bacher and those who brokered the meeting, the African National Congress representatives. What I have read (about the unity talks) so far is most encouraging.'

Others saw *The Star* report as a minor hiccup and not at all serious: a couple of would-be mandarins of the establishment press who missed the original story making little more than misguided, pretentious noises about an exciting issue. Only Mackerdhuj felt compromised: it went against the new-found friendships and bridge-building of the previous twenty-four hours. The article was also faxed to the ICC secretariat for comment and this had Sir Colin Cowdrey, then the ICC chairman, asking what was more important: a return to Test matches or the formation of a united board?

'South Africa need to first form a united body and then think about what might follow,' he said. 'It should be remembered that the countries mentioned in this story are already committed and there is a World Cup in Australia. This is the worst kind of tabloid writing.'

Cowdrey seemed to forget that *The Star* was meant to be, at international level, a respected broadsheet; to be called a tabloid showed the depths to which it had slipped in the eyes of the last English president of the ICC. Naturally they used none of the comments from Richards or Cowdrey and glossed over Mackerdhuj's biting remarks. What was used was a story from their writer Simon Hoff, in East London for a day-night game, about the possibility that professional players with rebel links might be barred.

The unity story was a happy ending for one veteran South African administrator. Harry Stavridis, then the long-serving president of the national badminton body, which had been unified since the late 1970s, had often expressed doubts whether South Africa would again host genuine international sports events.

Seventeen years before, on a mid-winter evening he attended a dinner given by the Department of Sport and Recreation where a large number of the establishment sports administrative panjandrums had gathered. Held in a Pretoria hotel, the then prime minister, John Vorster, delivered, in several, carefully selected phrases, a chilling message in a beautiful, air-conditioned room. For Stavridis, the last nails in the coffin known as isolation, were being knocked in with callous indifference. Vorster, his cheeks flushed after a heavy intake of brandy, told the administrators in July 1974, that he admired their hard work to keep their international links open. 'While I congratulate you on your achievements, I must also warn you not to seek our help when overseas sports bodies ban you from their organizations,' Vorster said in typical defiance.

Then, stabbing a finger at them he reaffirmed nothing had changed. For some administrators the ghost of the Basil D'Oliveira row of September 1968 began chanting the last rites of South African sport. The exception of course was rugby. Vorster's iron-fisted handling of the D'Oliveira affair has always been a touchy subject. Yet Donald Woods, the once-banned editor of the East London newspaper *Daily Dispatch*, painted a different picture of the episode when he and Chesters discussed the D'Oliveira case in Sydney during the 1992 World Cup. 'Something that was quite serious must have forced him (Vorster) to change his mind,' Woods said. 'I gained the impression a week or two before he went to Bloemfontein that he had it in mind to allow the tour to take place if D'Oliveira was selected. Vorster's view was if sport became isolated, sanctions against the economy would not be too far behind.'

Vorster liked his cricket. He regularly attended Currie Cup matches at St. George's Park over the Christmas-New Year holidays. At the time of the brewing D'Oliveira row, he also felt that the top players of that era—the Pollock brothers, Eddie Barlow, Trevor Goddard, Barry Richards and Ali Bacher—needed to say they had no objection to playing against D'Oliveira. It seems, however, that the players did not want to get involved. Not then. They did not want to be seen taking a political stance in public. Yet in discussions with some of those mentioned, Chesters also discovered that it was a message, which the SA Cricket Association had not accurately conveyed to the players.

There is also a story, which some say is apocryphal, but Ben Schoeman, a former senior cabinet minister in charge of transport, claims is authentic. In 1965, when South Africa were touring England, and there was a debate on the budget, Vorster would have a parliamentary messenger bring him the Test scores. On the day South Africa won at Trent Bridge, the messenger approached the then minister of law and order with the news 'the English have won by 94 runs'. With a puzzled frown, Vorster turned to the messenger and whispered, 'Oh . . . our English or their English?' Another version of the same story says it was during Peter May's MCC tour of South Africa in 1956-57 after the second Wanderers Test where South Africa won by 17 runs.

At least he was not as confused as the then prime minister D. F. Malan who smiled expansively when meeting Dudley Nourse at a parliamentary reception for the South African side to tour England in 1951. 'I wish you and your team an enjoyable tour of South Africa.'

South African politicians of most persuasions, colour and creed have not, down the years, been known for their understanding of what ought be a diaphanous issue. It displays typical ignorance and poor advisement by those who should know better. Woods and Stavridis agreed with this opinion.

Six-and-a-half years after D'Oliveira was banned, the hardening of political views gave Stavridis (and Woods) the impression of a white minority manacled to a cruel ideology as it was the manifestation of a mindset based on racial superiority. It should not come as a surprise that at the 1974 Pretoria dinner, Vorster said rugby would always be the exception because of its influence in Afrikaner society. 'There is little doubt that rugby was near and dear to the government because they were brought up within its culture at their schools. Although they conceded, amid much laughter, to allow the English to play it,' Stavridis said.

Vorster's message that chilly July evening was a simple reminder of government, or the National Party's, dogma; or what it presumed was the overriding panacea for the country's traditional ills.

Do not think for one moment that we will waver from our path of separate development. And do not think for one moment that we will give up our birthright in order to allow you to invite teams or sportsmen or sportswomen who are not of our thinking or our persuasion.

This is our country. We will not change for the sake of a few overseas sports teams. We will tell you who can come and who cannot . . . This is our policy. It is the wish of the volk.

Stavridis admitted there was a time during the evening when he felt he was in a time warp and attending a Nazi-style rally. It was frightening.

If you examine the events leading to the D'Oliveira fiasco, both the National Party and to an extent the SACA, were culpable. Later information, gleaned through the Truth and Reconciliation Commission probes into the apartheid era, indicates that Woods' information was not so unreliable; it was being presented to him with typical political ambivalence designed to draw a red herring across a government double-cross.

As Schoeman admitted many years later, the decision had already been made by the Cabinet's inner circle. It was not so much D'Oliveira being the issue but the Cape coloureds' possible reaction to his inclusion. As Stavridis pointed out, there was no place for genuine non-racial sport when it could create a climate for unrest. Vorster was the hangman who pulled the lever on the tour, abetted by SACA and MCC stumbling, for the sake of what they felt was face-saving expediency. In some circles it was felt that the red herring tactic started on 10 April 1967 when Vorster announced a new government stratagem that South African sportsmen and women could, in future, play against non-whites overseas; neither would there be a ban on non-whites being included in teams visiting South Africa. How history has laughed and thumbed its nose at the efforts of those South African administrators who believed in such a switch of policy.

Australian journalist Dick Whitington, who for a time lived in Johannesburg, and wrote several books in collaboration with the great Australian all-rounder Keith Miller, believed in such a simplistic dogma. In a book about the 1966-67 Bobby Simpson tour of South Africa, the writer takes a smug, whites-privileged view of Vorster's statement and has dressed it up in a chapter titled 'Hello Dolly and Goodbye Apartheid in International Sport.'

The policy was going to allow for a continuance of future rugby tours (especially with New Zealand). Whitington, for some reason, felt the 10 April edict would also remove whatever problems were likely to arise regarding the 1968-69 MCC tour of South Africa should D'Oliveira be included in the team. All would be well in South African (white) sport. Wow! Well, that is how Whitington saw it. To suggest that Vorster's quiet and well-reasoned diplomacy and negotiation should be regarded as a 'triumph', as it led to ending a looming international sports impasse was equally naïve.

Showing equal naïvety recently is writer Leo McDuling who, in a newspaper article titled 'Our Glorious Heritage: A Tribute To South Africans who Made their Mark' in the *Pretoria News*, attempts to link D'Oliveira and the Vorster banning to modern sports racial quota problems. For some unexplained reason, McDuling viewed the problem of Justin Ontong's initial non-selection in the South African Test side for the game against Australia in Sydney in 2002 as being embedded in the Vorster-run regime's banning of D'Oliveira on 17 September 1968.

To blandly suggest that shameful incidents in South African history led to the modern row over racial quotas is also a simplistic way of skimming over the facts of something which has bedevilled South African sport for more than a century. In Ontong's case, the national selectors were wrong by not playing him in the Test series against Zimbabwe the previous September. What this has now led to is a ruling that a minimum of three players from disadvantaged communities have to be selected either for Test or limited-overs international teams.

On 16 December 1990, however, the gloom had lifted. For the first time in the country's demographic history, there was no longer just a pinpoint of light at the end of a tunnel. It had disappeared: replaced by a new dawn, burnished with a rising sun.

In the aftermath of the unity talks in Port Elizabeth, Fanie de Villiers was wondering where his career was going. Against Western Province at Newlands in the Christmas match he had picked up 6 wickets, including an impressive 4 for 44, while Gary Kirsten had posted his seventh century with a solid 113. Then another injury caught up with Fanie and he did not play against Eastern Province in Port Elizabeth. Perhaps it was just as well. Kepler Wessels, dropped twice before reaching fifty and again in the seventies, scored an impressive 197 in a drawn match on another lifeless St. George's Park pitch. This was followed by one of the most remarkable first-class performances in South African history in the return game against Western Province at Centurion Park. It came after Craig Matthews' only first-class century saw Province set up an imposing victory target of 270 in 110 minutes and 20 overs, or a run rate in excess of 4.5 runs an over. The partnership of Yachad (115) and Mike Rindel (promoted to number three and scoring an undefeated 115), broke a long-standing record of 215 by Ray Currer and Bobby Hicks. It was scintillating stuff that kept people talking well into the winter. It was Northerns' miracle batting performance of the decade, led by the positive Yachad. It again proved how the first-class game is so often more exciting than the limited-overs variety.

Consider, however, the game against Transvaal at the same venue the following weekend. Fanie's first innings figures of 30-8-56-3 in a total of 400 for 8 declared, was an example of his improvement as an accurate swing bowler. Yachad agreed, with reservations, with the views expressed by Chesters and Henk Steenkamp (a Pretoria-based sports writer for *Beeld)* that he was approaching the form exhibited the previous summer. They had tackled the captain after the day's play and a match report was not enough for the sports pages the next day where sudden extra space meant that a good local story was needed.

Because of a migraine that was to do with a minor complication associated with the 'lime explosion', Fanie was forced to sit out the remainder of the game. A disgruntled public also suffered a post-lunch third day headache: they were treated to another Rice-motivated draw. It was suggested then by Yachad and the team's coach/manager, Rodney Ontong, that perhaps the absence of Fanie's swing bowling had caused the problem and the ensuing row through the media, which followed the stalemate draw.

Anyone knowing Rice's psyche should have known at once that he was not about to allow Northerns a second opportunity within a week to turn up the run-making turbo; once was quite enough. Transvaal wanted to qualify for the final later in the season and a successful Northerns assault on their bowling would impair their points tally and boost Northerns' log position. Interestingly, the story in *The Star* the next day carried someone else's byline credit.

The next weekend in Bloemfontein while 'Desert Storm', with 'Stormin' Norman' in charge was in progress in the Arabian Gulf, Fanie put together another superb display of swing and seam bowling. Why he saved some of his best performances for matches against Free State is one of those remarkable coincidences. Three wickets in the first 8 overs reduced Hansie Cronje's side to 57 for 5 and later 69 for 6. But Free State recovered to draw what turned into an exciting game.

Was he satisfied with eventual first innings figures of 22.1-7-51-6? It is hard to say. Certainly Yachad was. Fanie later rated it better than the 21-3-70-6 for Kent against Middlesex at Canterbury during the 1990 English season. That was his best haul on the county circuit and cost Middlesex their eighth victory and several places gained on the county championship table. Against Middlesex, Fanie bowled straight with a certain amount of swing in humid, overcast conditions. At Springbok Park he bowled with equal fire, but his swing was more pronounced. Fanie was again showing the form which earned him his one-day rebel series cap against Gatting's team the season before and Yachad had no more reservations.

His second 5-wicket haul, this one against Natal at Centurion Park, set up what should have been a Northerns victory on the third day. And this followed what had been an amazing first innings capitulation. Sent in on a pitch which contained some juice, Northerns were dismissed for 89. However, in a match of contrasts, Natal went on to force an unlikely draw after Yachad scored an impressive 179. It was then the turn of Willie Morris to turn the screws. So often a victim of selection policy, the left-arm spinner collected 6 for 78 on a surface, which turned enough to give him a chance to take wickets.

Although Tertius Bosch earned most wickets with 42 at 26.40 for Northerns that season, and that giant in terms of height (and ability), the left-arm slow bowler Willie Morris picked up 24 wickets at a fractionally lower 26.37, Fanie's 33 wickets at 20.30 defied all medical opinions. Five months after the 'lime explosion' and a medical report that hinted worse problems in the way of his growing neuro-muscular back injury, he was fourth in the national bowling averages. Bosch's 7 for 75 against Free State in their first innings in the Centurion Park game was equally impressive in pace and delivery. Every time Free State had attempted to stage a recovery, Bosch whipped out another couple of batsmen. Yet his 42 wickets that season could easily have been 54 if the number of spilled chances is taken into consideration. Surprisingly, the Northerns slips fielders, who clung to almost everything that came their way in 1989-90, dropped seventeen catches off his bowling in the arc between gully and wicketkeeper Ray Jennings.

* * * *

For some, 4 November 1991 was not an average relaxed suburban Sunday. The United Cricket Board (UCB) was to discuss, at a hotel near Jan Smuts airport, an invitation by India for a three-match tour. Although not entirely unanimous, it was accepted. It was a moment full of irony as, nineteen years before, on a bitter mid-winter morning, Hassan Howa, another intractable foe of apartheid with a smile as inscrutable as you will ever find, had put an end to unity talks. In the wake of the abandoned 1971-72 tour of Australia, the two sides had been drawn together to seek an accommodation. Boon Wallace of Cape Town and Western Province chaired the meeting and imagine his surprise at what happened minutes after the meeting was opened. 'I am not in agreement with these documents,' he said. 'They do not tackle the issue of why we are here, the government's policy which separates us. I am prepared to sit back with folded arms for twenty, even twenty-five years, and wait for the day when those in power have come to their senses. Cricket will live as it has for the last hundred years—we will all see to that—but we cannot do it together until the laws are changed; it's as simple as that.' Some nineteen years and six months later, Dr Ali Bacher, then managing director of the UCB, invited the media to his new home to hear the announcement of the names of the fourteen players for India.

It had already been a year of exhilarating experiences for South Africa's long embattled cricket administration. No longer did the mandarins in Cape Town control sport: it was Steve Tshwete and the NSC. The eras of Vorster and P. W. Botha had disappeared, as if vaporized by the 16 December 1990 accord.[1] From that sprang the agreement, on 20 April to form the UCB. This was done at the Wanderers on 29 June followed in the evening by a banquet.

Movement on the international front had been generated at such a pace that at times there was difficulty in keeping up with events. From the day the UCB was accepted as a member of the International Cricket Council at Lord's, doors opened and long-term plans were made.

Through this, Fanie and Judy waited until 21 August before they were married in Centurion in a mid-winter ceremony attended by those members of the Northern Transvaal side still in South Africa and a number of personal friends, with the soon-to-retire Anton Ferreira as MC.

In late October, some startling information emerged from New Delhi. Sandeep Nakai, of *The Hindu* contacted Chesters about the possibility of a tour. South Africa's mission on a goodwill visit of South Asia, he said, had provisionally accepted an invitation for a three-match tour following the cancellation of Pakistan's visit. It would, he said, need ratification by the UCB board when the mission returned to South Africa. The India tour announcement had come within days of the ICC agreement in Sharjah that South Africa be invited to play in the 1992 World Cup in Australia and New Zealand.

When the team of fourteen for India was announced, the convener of selectors, Peter van der Merwe said they had been swayed to consider the form of the side from the previous season. No one could argue with that. But players such as Clive Rice, who failed to finish the summer because of a recurring back injury, Peter Kirsten, Jimmy Cook and Kepler Wessels, were certain of selection because of their experience.

There were, however, a few queries, if form in the 1990-91 season was a guide. Ray Jennings had an exceptional season as a wicketkeeper-batsman, yet he was thirty-seven, perhaps two years too old, although still a quality gloveman. Mike Rindel, sixth in the batting averages after scoring 612 runs at 43.71 and a natural

---

[1] Tshwete died late on the night of 26 April 2002 in 1 Military Hospital, Pretoria (Tshwane) from kidney failure. At the time he was the Minister of Safety and Security. A day later Dr Ali Bacher, holding the position of executive director of the 2003 World Cup, paid a tribute to the former Robben Island inmate for his role in the 1990–91 unification process.

limited-overs games player, was passed over for Adrian Kuiper, who at thirty-two, had displayed shaky form for most of 1990-91. Gary Kirsten, Peter's younger brother had often batted with more conviction. Roy Pienaar was also missing, so were Daryll Cullinan and Mark Rushmere. It was also hard to find an argument supporting Clive Eksteen, whose 15 Currie Cup wickets had come at a pricey average of plus 41.00.

It seemed that both Tim Shaw and Eksteen, essentially defensive slow left-arm bowlers, were chosen because they were left-arm bowlers and the attack needed variety with the ball moving away from the bat. That being the case, Omar Henry would have been a wiser choice.

No Bosch? No Steven Jack? Two of the leading wicket-takers of the previous season had been overlooked. As they had Allan Donald, it seemed to be enough. And Richard Snell? It was presumed he earned his place because Fanie was sidelined with a broken big toe on his left foot. Not, however, according to the selectors. Snell, it seems, was in on merit. And had Fanie not been injured? His record would have been examined along with the rest of those considered. Which meant that like Bosch and Rindel, he too would have been excluded. Tough about the broken toe, though!

There could be no argument over Mandy Yachad's selection. He was the leading run-scorer in 1990-91 with 994 runs, four centuries and five fifties. For some particular reason, Yachad and Rice were given this one chance. Whatever the polemic issues surrounding Rice's exclusion from the World Cup side were, Yachad deserved better treatment from the selectors during 1992-93 when Mohammad Azharuddin's Indian side were on tour.

Fanie was hobbling around the Northern Transvaal Command sports office at Voortrekkerhoogte when he heard the news late on the Friday that South Africa's delegation to India were heading home to talk about the tour invitation. He knew he would miss that. But damn it, the World Cup . . . surely a chance? If he became fit in time he could make the side. It was an outside chance. The reality was much harsher: his body was tired, and his legs and his back hurt.

The road to recovery was neither smooth nor easy. On 25 October he played in a day-night match against Free State and bowled only one over when the lighting system failed and rain added a damp end to a thoroughly miserable outing. After that a gaping silence. How soon people forget; the mood of a fickle South African public. Out of sight, out of mind. There was the World Cup. New faces, new players: a curious new public taking an interest in 'our boys'. Say, Fanie who? Oh, yeah . . . that guy . . . Yeah . . . Hey, what *did* happen to him?

The hero of 1988-89, who came back from a knee operation the following summer to earn a place in the South Africa squad for the rebel limited-overs series, had disappeared. No one questioned his absence. When squads for the World Cup were being drawn up, there was no mention. Only Chesters talked to him, and even then not regularly. It was a heavy season with the World Cup looming. Exciting days ahead. All the time Fanie was working on his fitness, strengthening his back and legs. Time to do some long-term planning.

'I saw Fanie de Villiers in the nets the other day. Is he ever going to play again?'

The query came from Jackie McGlew, a former South African captain and selector. He was sitting next to Chesters, watching Ezra Moseley and Tertius Bosch demolish the Natal innings in the second leg of the Nissan Shield quarterfinal at Centurion Park.

'Oh, yes. He'll play again. He'll be back I should think; in January or February.'

McGlew, a shrewd judge of a player's ability, was not convinced.

'Bosch looks good. They'd be crazy not to pick him for the World Cup. But I'm sorry about your friend Fanie.'

'He's been training quietly for a couple of weeks. You do know Moseley broke the big toe on his left foot?'

McGlew nodded. 'I remember reading about it. Something you wrote . . . Pity . . .'

'Well, Jackie you should know how long it takes a fast bowler to come back from such an injury. I would say that but for that injury he would be in my World Cup squad.'

'Yes, they need swing bowlers over there, cobber. It's your part of the world . . .'

To the right of where they sat, Fanie de Villiers was training in the nets. He had a fitness agenda of his own that included playing for Northerns in January. He also had a plan that would take him back to England the next year. A Northerns teammate, Blaise Sommerville, had played for a club in Torquay two years before. Now Fanie was thinking seriously about another league summer, and, from what Alan Jordaan, the Northerns president, had said, Torquay were looking for a professional for 1992.

* * * *

To prepare South Africa for the arduous Test scene and the series against India the next summer, the UCB had decided that A Section matches in 1991-92 would be played over four days. Bonus points were also scrapped and first innings victories were reintroduced after twenty years. Fanie remembered the agony of playing four-day games for Kent in 1990. But when he proved to himself that he was fit enough to play for the provincial side again, he approached the selectors and suggested playing in for Northerns B against Free State B in Bloemfontein. But these (President's Competition) matches were over three days, which helped. A hard four-day game could retard his fitness progress.

At the same time, there were two semi-final legs of the Nissan Shield series to be played against Eastern Province. The first leg, on 12 January would be the day after the President's Competition match ended and would be played at Centurion Park. What with the final selection of the World Cup squad looming in a week's time, Fanie's comeback performance received little coverage. After all, it was only a B team match. But no one can sneer at figures of 22-5-46-2.

'How did it feel?' Chesters asked him when they went up to his flat in Arcadia.

'It went well. Although I would have liked to play in Saturday's Nissan Shield match.'

'You are playing in Port Elizabeth next Saturday.'

'I know. But it's too late. The selectors have already made up their minds.'

Which was true. Chesters' coastal confidant had already indicated they were only uncertain about a couple of players and Meyrick Pringle's name was high on the list of candidates.

The day before the World Cup side was to be announced, shortly after noon at St. George's Park, Fanie put together an impressive display of swing bowling. Bosch got rid of Kepler Wessels and Mark Rushmere in the opening over. What prize wickets! But he went for 56 in his 11 overs, Moseley also went for 50 and so did Steve Elworthy; bowling can be an expensive exercise if line and length are not perfect. Yet Fanie displayed all the cunning of the past three seasons. He swung the ball, used the off-cutter and troubled the batsmen. To his annoyance he also delivered the occasional half-volley getting rid of Martin Venter, driving too soon and edging the catch to Ray Jennings.

Mandy Yachad's team were already back at Jan Smuts airport, heading home when Geoff Dakin read out the names of the fourteen World Cup squad members. Not surprisingly Fanie closely followed the fortunes of the team, always wondering what might have been but for the broken toe. He looked closely at the way Pringle bowled, and Richard Snell and Craig Matthews. Good bowlers all. If he was to make any impact he needed to be in top physical shape. The rest, he knew, would automatically follow.

On 6 February 1992, the day before South Africa arrived in Perth for the opening pre-World Cup warm-up matches phase, Fanie was commandeering the car of the surprised *Beeld* writer Henk Steenkamp, in Bloemfontein. Judy, expecting their first child, had been at a stork party for Sandy Ferreira (Yogi Ferreira's wife) in Pretoria when around 9 p.m. her water burst and she was rushed to the nursing home. When he was contacted two hours later Fanie tried to hire a car, but all the agencies were closed.

Well, it is Bloemfontein. And 11 p.m. So what else do you expect?

He then quickly discovered who had transport. Not long after midnight he knocked at Steenkamp's door.

'Henk, I need your car urgently,' he said with that charming grin he offers. 'Judy is in the nursing home expecting our first child and I want to be there when it is born. You can get a lift back with one of the team.'

Fanie, in Bloemfontein for a Northerns Currie Cup game against Free State, had already spoken to Yachad about the problem and the Northerns skipper agreed to let him go, putting in a call to get Gerbrand Grobler down as a replacement. Under the circumstances, it is hard to refuse any proud dad the chance to be with his wife when she is about to give birth for the first time. Within minutes he was packed and on his way to Pretoria. He had planned to be in the city before the baby was born. Talk about life in the fast lane! He arrived around 5 a.m.

To allow Fanie time to reach the hospital her gynaecologist placed Judy on a drip. Around 8.45 a.m. on 7 February, Suné de Villiers was born. For Fanie, looking at a tired Judy cuddling the bundle was an event he would not have missed. Now, had he been selected for the World Cup, he would have had to forfeit playing in Harare, Perth and Adelaide if he was to be present at her birth. He still smiles at the memory. For the pleasure of attending as special an event as his daughter's birth, he would have even forgone playing in those pre-World Cup games.

11

Fanie's Corner

There are other pretenders to the title but, for all too obvious reasons, Torquay is in the middle of what some might call the Riviera of England. There is more of the Continental air about this attractive Devonshire town than places such as Hastings, Eastbourne, Brighton or Bournemouth. The Torquay area is known for its gentle, dry climate, azure sea and near sub-tropical vegetation (well, for England!). There is also a row of handsome, if expensive, hotels near the harbour. Famous for its picturesque setting on the wooded hills above Torquay, the region is full of ancient footprints: ice age inhabitants once roamed the coastline, and sabre-toothed tigers and bears are preserved in large limestone deposits.

In the 1950s, they even held festival matches in the town: North versus South and England XI versus Commonwealth XI. These were usually played early to mid-September. And as expected, those teams attracted a fair number of the top names of that era: Sir Frank Worrell, the great George Headley (or the black Bradman), Frank Tyson, Don Kenyon, Tony Lock, George Tribe, Fred Titmus, and even Jack Bannister and Ray Illingworth. Sadly, a series of wet Septembers and other circumstances saw the matches transferred to other holiday places such as Blackpool and Hastings. Perhaps because they were an anachronism of a more relaxed age, there was no place for them in the frenetic world from the mid-1970s. England's cluttered county programme, with a surfeit of one-day games was another reason why the festival games were squeezed out of the system. Anyway, it was felt that with Torquay being too far west and not serving a major county area, such games were no longer important.

In mid-April 1992 Fanie de Villiers arrived in Torquay with Judy and Suné: a young Afrikaans family experiencing their first months together in a relaxed environment and far from home. Such was his determination to play for South Africa against India that Judy knew Fanie had not come on a fool's errand. He knew that to win the confidence of Peter Pollock's national selection panel, he had to rid himself of the injury jinx which had, for the past three years, harassed his career. What he needed was a total makeover and that would, as he admitted to Chesters before he left, take time, patience and support. Torquay, he was convinced, would provide what he needed.

A successful bowler does not rely only on his know-how or skill to win matches. There has to be a certain amount of heart involved as well. Fast bowling also makes heavy demands on the body and mind to overcome the physical stress of bowling hour after hour in trying conditions. Above all, mental strength must match the physical fitness.

The need for mental strength and physical fitness had entered Fanie's thoughts at Centurion Park four months earlier. Northerns were playing Natal in what was his first Castle (Currie) Cup game of the season and while he preferred the new ball, it was far from easy with bowlers such as Ezra Moseley and Tertius Bosch in the side. Who was he to argue with Mandy Yachad's views on the matter? Especially after the Northerns selectors had debated at length whether Fanie's fitness would last four days.

It was Bosch's last game for Northerns that summer as he prepared for the World Cup. For Fanie it was a different story. He had known for weeks that his career as a future Test bowler was going nowhere, that he was being left behind. After weeks of training hard, the edge he needed as well as the hunger for success was missing.

It had nothing at all to do with the way he was easing himself into an insurance broker's job and looking after his cheerful, pregnant wife. His Northerns new-ball partner Tertius Bosch would shortly head for the World Cup, and no doubt the tour of the West Indies and a Test cap. The temperamental Bajan, Moseley, did not want to renew his contract; even Gerbrand Grobler's future was doubtful after general criticism of the Northerns' team in a telephone hotline column. Talk of splitting practices between the Wanderers and Centurion arose yet again and Grobler had grown tired of the hypocrisy about the 'us' and 'them' (Wanderers Club and Centurion Park camps). All that was left was Steve Elworthy and Chris van Noordwyk and little else was coming through.

As the World Cup, 1992 version, had passed him by, it was time for a serious rethink. Even after impressive figures of 19-10-21-4 in the Natal first innings, Fanie knew there was a question mark about his future. He had swung the ball nicely and set up a couple of catches: Peter Rawson's wicket for a duck came from a straightforward gully catch snared by Louis Vorster. Yet those four wickets in the first innings should have been six. The normally reliable Ray Jennings and Mike Haysman had put down catches, Jonty Rhodes was dropped at 7 and Arthur Wormington before he had scored. At times Fanie laboured during his run-up; the rhythm was missing and Jackie McGlew went to Chesters to ask what Fanie's problem was. He noticed how the bowler battled to reach the wicket. What also concerned Fanie were occasional spasms of neuro-muscular pain. It was all going wrong.

As McGlew gave his journalist friend a bon voyage card for the World Cup trip, he wondered aloud if they were seeing the last of someone who had been developing into a fine swing bowler. At that stage the 195 first-class wickets at 23.88 was a fair return. McGlew sat and watched his old province go on to win the match. No one can really grumble though about taking 5 wickets in a match. Although, as Rhodes later admitted, Fanie did not at the time have the pace to really trouble the top batsmen. His late outswinger was occasionally hard to play; as for the rest he looked as he bowled—tired and laboured. That old zip was missing. Perhaps it was time to go back to England. Pick up the pieces of a decaying career. Better still, find a cure to rebuild a meaningful future as a player.

When Fanie first enquired about a third season in England he was looking back on 1991-92 with regret and frustration. A feeling that he was not meant to play for South Africa had cropped up often enough and niggled at his subconscious. Fitness was the key word. Peter van der Merwe, then the selection panel convener, had spelt it out when he announced some of the requirements for inclusion in the World Cup squad: no player carrying an injury or illness would be selected. Meyrick Pringle had overcome his. It was all part of the harsh reality of South Africa's international re-entry.

It was with this in mind that Fanie examined his season, thinking about the future and what he had achieved. It was then that he realized that to play for South Africa again he would need a hard training programme. He could either do it at Centurion Park or in England. He also looked at his priorities and ticked them off.

One goal at a time.

Confidence: he had plenty of that. Okay, what about an inventory of the rest?

Aims: train hard to achieve physical fitness; remain competitive.

Plan: find the right place to achieve the above.

Ambition: that was easy—to play for South Africa.

Motto: always be a winner.

It was time to make positive plans as well as move on. Fanie went to see his controller, André Brand, at the insurance company and as usual, spoke his mind.

'If I hope to play for South Africa, I need to go to England and play cricket somewhere.' Brand nodded. He knew Fanie's reputation as a fast bowler. But his injuries . . . Better talk him out of it. From what he had been told, Fanie no longer had a future as a provincial or international player. It was time to wise up to this simple fact.

'Think, Fanie. You are young. Your wife has just had a baby and here you want to go to England. You're chasing a dream. Anyway, you can't make a living out of the game in this country.'

'I've done it before.' Fanie was stubborn.

'How old are you now? Twenty-seven? And you're just starting out. Think of the long-term, Fanie, think of your future, your family. There's no money in cricket. Not enough to make a living. Anyway, it's not a professional sport in this country. There are also the injuries. You have had a lot of those. I really don't think it is wise.'

It was a strong persuasive argument. But Fanie was also running out of time. He needed those six months in England; he owed it to himself.

Blaise Sommerville, his Northerns' teammate had, two years before, played for a side in Torquay whose main benefactor was Roger Mann. He recommended that Fanie consider this as an option. Especially as the weather would be right for what he had in mind. Fanie thought about it for less than a minute. He went back to the flat and sat down and had a serious talk with Judy. For months, while carrying Suné, she had watched her frustrated husband battle with a succession of injuries without complaint, watched him struggle to overcome the depressing pain and injuries to bowl again.

'There are a few weeks to go before the England season starts, why don't I contact someone and see if there is an opening?'

'If you think that will be the right thing, let's go. It'll be fun. Six months on our own in England,' she agreed.

Being an airhostess she knew all about long absences from home, she knew the value of time together in another country. She also knew that Fanie made friends easier than most people and that made it so much easier.

'Thanks, skat. I knew you were the right girl for me that first day I saw you at college.'

They laughed, but behind the smiles he knew her support was crucial. After all, he was giving up security to chase a dream. And little Suné? She was barely a month old. Only, if he were to have a chance, they would do it together. The three of them. If England was going to be the place to get his career going again, what could be better?

Eight weeks later, with the South African team in the West Indies, Fanie and Judy packed their bags, dressed up their tiny daughter and headed for Torquay. It was his third trip to England and he knew it was the most important trip of his career. Fanie had sat with Neels Liebel, the Northerns physio and a friend, and planned out what he had to do to keep in top physical shape and win a Test cap. He had long passed the apprentice stage. But he felt he had not earned his papers either, and had now given himself ten months to earn them. Like Kepler Wessels before him, Fanie de Villiers admitted that he also had a burning ambition.

Roger Mann, owner of one of the largest collections of cricket memorabilia in the world, held several telephone discussions with Fanie before deciding to offer him the post as professional for the Torquay Cricket Club for 1992. Although the club had been in the habit of employing several amateurs since 1982, it was the first in five seasons that they had employed a professional. He met Fanie and Judy at a motorway service station near Torquay and took them to his home for high tea.

Some minutes after arriving at the house, Mann called up a young Australian, Mike Gerits, to come and meet the club professional. But the young Aussie was a shy lad. Gerits stood at the doorway in embarrassed silence, not really wanting to meet anyone so soon after having arrived. Fanie was quick to pick up the situation

'Hi, Mike. I'm Fanie de Villiers.' He extended his hand towards the shy Australian. 'What do you do, Mike?' Fanie did his best to put the youngster at ease.

'Well, I'm a batsman.'

'That's great. I'm a bowler and my batting is bloody awful. But, I tell you what, Mike. If you teach me a bit about batting, I'll help you with bowling. How does that strike you?'

Gerits, as shy as he was, developed an instant rapport with the South African fast bowler. They often spent time training together, either on a fitness machine outside the Aussie's flat or in the nets. It was hard preparation, but worth the hours they spent working at their game or the fitness course Fanie had set for himself. Such a friendship developed that on the day Fanie bowled South Africa to victory against Australia in the Test at the Sydney Cricket Ground he went over to the boundary fence and looked into the crowd. He spotted Mike and waved. Then, taking off his sweat-soaked shirt, he threw it to his old Torquay teammate. What a memento to throw away. Then again, friendships forged from happy hours spent together playing for the same team have special bonds and lingering memories.

Yet there was a noticeable atmosphere those first couple of weeks in the Torquay team's dressing room. Some of the quieter players felt a little put out at the display of robust confidence which oozed from Fanie. Here was someone different. Always seeking answers to questions. A few players found this a little disturbing until they realized that it was also for their benefit. He also wrote with a felt pen above a peg in the corner of the dressing room, 'Fanie's corner'. His sensitivity towards their feelings and his quick support for their causes is fondly remembered in that special corner of Devon.

* * * *

Down the years Fanie has had many brushes with players who have brashly crossed his path, swaggering in their arrogance rather than offering the off-the-field camaraderie often enjoyed by players over a beer or two. Corrie van Zyl's first brush with Fanie at Centurion Park in the 1986-87 season was one example of how the more senior player went out of his way to 'soften up' the cocky pup. There was some needle between the two on the field when van Zyl fired in a few extra fast deliveries and followed them up with Aussie-style sledging. Not one to back off, Fanie confronted the Free State player as he walked up the steps to the dressing rooms.

'Hey, what's your problem?'

Van Zyl ignored the question and was about to brush past the Northerns bowler when Fanie lent across and took hold of him by the front of his shirt.

'I asked, what's your problem? You want to play hard? We'll do that—on the field. But cut out the remarks.'

For a moment van Zyl was taken by surprise. He stood up, placed a hand on Fanie's shoulder and smiled. He had not expected the youngster to tackle him and admired his courage. Especially as he had seen older players who had more experience sulking in some changing room corner after an encounter with the Free State all-rounder.

Conversely, Fanie's relationship with the late Gerbrand Grobler was much closer and of a vastly different nature. 'Over the years we became sports friends more than house friends. I guess it developed that way because we opened the bowling for the same club (Oostelike) and on occasion for Northern Transvaal,' he said. 'It would be strange if we did not become friends. But he was different. Also, we needed each other's support during our early days in the side. Two Dutchmen against the Souties. I don't think they realized what they were trying to do in taking us on.' He grinned at the memory of sharing the same room on away matches.

Known for his boisterous behaviour, the rugged left-arm fast bowler, Grobler, needed careful handling. He would often perform like a student on his first field trip. Wanting to watch a film on cable TV at two in the morning was a way of relaxing. But to watch a film, he felt, also required company. Fanie would suddenly find himself lying on the floor among his clothes and the bedding, looking up at the beaming face of the swarthy Grobler.

'Come on, ou pal. A lekker movie has started. Watch it with me.'

When Fanie would go to a school to give a talk, and instead of talking about himself or his match-winning performances, he would tell the awed youngsters about the other members of the side. 'Who do you want to hear about? Hansie or Jonty?' he once asked the children at Capital Park Primary School in Pretoria. When the chorus shouted 'Hansie', he soon captivated the youngsters with pleasing stories about a player with whom he had a shaky relationship during his playing days.

Yet as always, there was a tough, inquisitive streak in the young man. He would not take the easy way out: not accept that there is only black and white in the world when he knew that there were other hues. His curiosity often creates the impression that he is argumentative: yet as in his early years as a schoolboy bowling to adults, it was a question of self-confidence.

While in Torquay, the South African also broke any number of fusty business rules when working for Roger Mann's fruit and vegetable wholesale business. He would make the deliver to a variety of business houses before 6.30 a.m. on most mornings, often coming back late for the next delivery. As Mann discovered, Fanie, having delivered to one hotel, would go into the hotel next door and suggest they buy 'the best fruit and vegetables in town'. 'Of course people in England are not used to such an approach and were flabbergasted. Yet it was successful,' Mann smiled.

It was in Torquay that the handyman expertise Fanie is noted for was put to the test with impressive results. During a period when there were no games, Fanie asked if there was any job he could do to earn extra money. At the time Mann was taking quotes for a large sign to be put up at the back of his warehouse—about twenty-five metres long and five metres deep—and Fanie, after some discussion, put in his quote. Understandably Mann was sceptical that the young insurance broker could do a better job than the professionals, especially as the sign had to be lit at night. After all, what would the comments from the shareholders be if the signs that went up were of an inferior quality?

As if shrugging off the indignity of being hit for 30 runs in 2 overs, Fanie put his skills to work and the sign was ready. But before he completed the job, he asked his boss to look over the lettering. 'That looks great, Fanie. There is only one problem, lad: we don't spell wholesale "holesale".' They both laughed. The signs were completed and put up, including the flashing lights, with the spelling error. Such was the professionalism of the job it was left unchanged: a permanent reminder of Fanie de Villiers. The lights were still in perfect condition more than two years later when the South African team toured England and played Minor Counties in Torquay. And they were still working in 1999.

Another antiquated custom he swiftly consigned to that cobwebbed pigeonhole of 'dos and don'ts' was the habit of the club professional ignoring the spectators, especially the older members. As in Todmorden five years before, he made it a ritual, whether waiting to bat or during a lengthy break in play, to walk around the ground and have a casual chat with the spectators. At first they were surprised by his general bonhomie. In the north it is readily accepted. In the south, where stuffy traditions die hard, the spectators were unused to the club pro doing the rounds as if dispensing tea and cucumber sandwiches.

'This South African fellow . . . Fanie, er . . . Yes, Fanie. Well, it's quite unbelievable for a club pro. Chatting away as if he was the next door neighbour.'

Of course it did not take too long before they began to welcome his cheerfulness. 'Hello, Sir. I'm Fanie de Villiers. How are you? Are you enjoying the game?'

Established in 1851, Torquay Cricket Club was 141 years old when Fanie joined them. Their home venue, the Recreation Ground, overlooked the English Channel, but the pitches were hard and flat and good for batting. During South Africa's tour in 1994, in Kepler Wessels' opinion, the surface was the best they had played on during the tour. A little better than the Lord's pitch. And that was a tribute to the ground staff.

Little wonder that on such benign surfaces Fanie discovered that the only way he was going to be successful was to bowl yorkers or off-cutters. For those who remember that remarkable penultimate over against the Australians in the limited-overs international at the Wanderers during the 1993-94 tour when he bowled those six consecutive yorkers, one of which removed Allan Border, the Torquay season was just as valuable for this side of its education as had been the seasons with Todmorden and Kent. And was it not the reason he had decided to spend a season here?

One of the weekday trips deep into the county took Roger Mann and Fanie to a village where, by chance, they met a few of the local players in the pub. They spent a pleasant couple of hours over lunch and Fanie promised to return the next Sunday. Naturally they thought that he was not sincere in his offer. Of course they would not see him again. Typical of those visiting chaps. Making all sorts of promises, taking telephone numbers. 'Will phone you Friday.' That is the usual story.

But this was Fanie de Villiers. He did phone on the Friday and confirmed he was going to play. On the Sunday, he turned up with Judy and Suné in the car, and they spent a great day enjoying themselves. And how the village players valued his input!

It was during the 1992 season in the Devon League, which is little more than a 46-over Saturday slog that Fanie admitted, not only to himself but also to Roger Mann, that there were faults in his bowling make up. Which is not as surprising as it seems. Since the second knee operation in October 1989, he had faced a succession of physical hindrances.

These in turn had affected not only his fitness, but also retarded his growth as a bowler. Agreed, he had lost his pace, but not his ability to swing the ball, especially in South African conditions. However, by the time he arrived in Torquay in April 1992 it was his Northern Transvaal teammate Tertius Bosch who looked to be the future Test partner for Allan Donald. He had been moderately successful in the one-off Test against the West Indies and had impressed Jackie McGlew, co-manager of the South African youth side with Khaya Majola and led by Dale Benkenstein.

But Bosch had other priorities. For one thing, the life of a professional sportsman did not attract him as much as the life of a professional businessman. Although he liked the idea of being a Test bowler and winning limited-overs international caps, driving each day between his Vereeniging dental practice and Centurion Park to practice was demotivating. Also, no one really sat with the tall, likeable Bosch and listened to his problems. Too many people were worried about their own problems to really care about what was bothering Bosch, why he was distracted. The Northerns coaching and selection set up in 1992-93 and 1993-94 also bothered him. Instead of progressing he complained to Chesters in November 1993 that his bowling was sliding backwards.

In April 1992, however, Fanie's life as a player seemed less promising than it was at the start of the 1990-91 season: a summer which saw him fighting a continuous battle to overcome the restrictions imposed by the neuro-muscular problem, simplified in layman's terms as an extended hamstring injury. He may have collected 33 Currie Cup wickets in 1990-91 but he only survived the season because of a daily dose of pain killers.

It would have been hard to convince anyone, other than Fanie and Judy when they arrived in England, that the best years of his career were ahead of him. Chesters, not long back from the World Cup, also wrote an encouraging piece the day before Fanie left for England:

> After another frustrating summer Fanie de Villiers heads for England tomorrow, seeking to rediscover the bowling skills and stamina which should, next season, earn him the attention of the national selectors' when the Indians make their historic tour.
>
> Sources have suggested that as Peter van der Merwe is about to vacate the post as convener of the South African selectors in favour of Peter Pollock, there will be an increased emphasis on looking past the World Cup and West Indies' touring squads to build a longer-term dual-purpose pace attack.
>
> Although van der Merwe looked on with much sympathy as de Villiers tried to prove himself too late for inclusion in the World Cup squad, Pollock, if he gets the convener's job, will as a former fast bowler hopefully view de Villiers as more than a one-day bowler. All it needs is for de Villiers to have a good season in England and to emerge with growing confidence next South African summer for the selectors to take serious note of him. He knows all

too well that to achieve this he needs to perform, and perform well.

His career has been blighted since the explosion that almost blinded him in October 1990. Hopefully the glowering clouds which have occluded his passage as a fast bowler will be swept away by the brisk winds of the determination that those close to him know so well.

Fanie knew all too well what he needed to do. While the Devon League consists of twelve teams, competitive levels are not particularly high. Yet, as Fanie discovered, the bowlers needed to work hard on the unsympathetic pitches. As in his 1990 summer with Kent, he knew that on the flat surfaces in England he needed to bowl straight. He learnt all too quickly that unless he fired in a series of yorkers and produced clever variation and changes of pace, there was little chance of success. And being the club pro, he was expected to take wickets, score a few runs and field with superb aplomb to win matches. In the end, he managed to equal the league record of 93 wickets, with 9 in his last two matches.

The Sunday games were of agreed overs duration. The first team would perhaps bat for as many as 60 overs leaving the second side say 45 overs to rattle off the runs. He took precautions designed to improve his bowling skills to win matches, especially as he was often unable to obtain as much swing as he wanted. As the overall level in both leagues is not particularly high, the demand is for the overseas players to lift the standards.

Anyone who examines Fanie's South African team career will discover just how important the Torquay experience was. Not only was it the final fingerpost pointing the way forward, it convinced him that he had made the right choice. Gradually he exorcised from his system the frustrations of the 1991-92 South African summer and rebuilt his bowling make up. The weeks he spent in the seaside town enhanced his cricketing knowledge. There was an increase in the use of the yorker in his repertoire; he also made careful studies of the techniques of a variety of batsmen to earn their wickets. There were those with the 'two-eyed' or square on stance, batsmen who were strong off the front foot or those who were anchored to the crease. He was also mindful to bowl tighter and not give away wides or no-balls. At all times he worked on his physical well-being as well as his fitness and stamina.

There are any number of Test and first-class bowlers who are prepared to claim they have the ability to win matches. But try to find one ready to admit his mistakes, and there are not too many. While in Torquay, Fanie was prepared to acknowledge his faults and work on correcting them. It gave him added incentive to tune his skills and bowl with even tighter discipline. Through it all he was aware of a niggling back pain; not that it was as serious as it had been.

By mid-September when the young de Villiers family returned to South Africa, his campaign to convince the national selectors that he was a reborn bowler was carefully plotted and launched. What he did see himself as was a candidate for the Test, not for the limited-overs, team. All that was needed was for Neels Liebel to help him in the nets. Their strategy was simple. Plenty of hard gym work, a lot of bowling in the nets and the use of the video camera to further improve his variation and action. It would, they knew, need a lot of hard work and sweat.

What pleased Fanie was the significant improvement in his energy levels from the training in England. It had seen him perfect his control of the outswinger, helped expand his use of the off-cutter and develope the yorker until he used it as either an attacking or a defensive weapon. His economy rate in limited-overs games had also improved to less than 3.50 an over and such bowlers were what a captain needed in either Test or limited-overs matches.

It had the promise of being an exciting season. He could almost smell it as he worked, often alone, in the nets at Centurion Park. Four Tests against India, a series of seven limited-overs internationals and the Total Trophy series. That part involved Pakistan, the West Indies and South Africa. Later in 1993 would be the tour of Sri Lanka, home for a short break, then off to India for a one-day series followed by a tour of Australia. Those were the goals.

The first aim was to become a permanent member of the Test team; not easy with some players already established from the World Cup and West Indies tour, and this despite Peter Pollock's claims that the selectors wanted to add to the pool of international players. Hard work, he knew, would be the recipe for success.

Yet the summer in Torquay had been as much a holiday as it had been a finishing school. And spending hours among the books in Roger Mann's considerable cricket library taught him of a past rich in character: of a history whose door he slowly unlocked and began to look inside. It helped him develop a new understanding of the game and of those who had been responsible for its growth in the past 250 years and before.

* * * *

For some peculiar reason there is this quaint myth that before W. G. Grace the game was little more than a rural pastime, presided over by indulgent landed aristocracy who ran it as their private domain. Just how far the game predates the Hundred Years War (1336 to 1431) between England and France requires more than fancy detective guesswork. Its roots go far deeper than such a superficial opinion would suggest.

As it is, there are two important factors surrounding its growth, which are firmly linked to cricket's prehistory: these are the number of players in a team and what evolved into the laws. Also involving prehistory is a measuring or numbering system, either based on or borrowed from the figure eleven or multiples of eleven (that is, the make up of the team and the length of the pitch in yards). There is little doubt that, as with the laws, these came from local playing customs (or conditions), and most descended from the villages which dotted the wealds of Kent, Sussex, Surrey and Hampshire. It was here that the priests (or monks) from latter centuries of the first millennium enjoyed being involved in a pastime that demanded the defending of the stump of a tree against a round object delivered underarm.

As for the numbering system, which had eleven as its quotient, it was used extensively in northern France. Curiously, research shows that it went beyond anything that was in use in England at the time and predates 1066 and the Norman invasion. As the elevens numerical system in England was only peculiar to the southeastern regions, it is assumed the teachers were monks of French origin who taught it to the locals.

Anyone who has a serious interest in the history of the game and its growth would quickly dismantle some of the more fanciful theories about the Hambledon Club. Strangely, there are still some adherents to the romantic belief of Hambledon being the game's cradle and first nursery and that the evolution of the laws were formed under their patronage. History proves otherwise. It was not a parent, midwife or a wet-nurse.

Hambledon's position during what can be termed cricket's 'development stages' was that of one of the game's most important rustic staging-posts. What it did become for a time, however, was the most important classroom for forty years. Hambledon was formed around 1750, about six years after the original 1744 code of laws for cricket were agreed on. As the game was widely played throughout Kent, Surrey, Sussex and Hampshire in the 1670s, it is hard to accept those who lay claim to this Hampshire village's influence in cricket lawmaking. What is important is that during its sphere of influence, from about 1756 until 1789, the game, through Hambledon's fame did reach a wider audience; quality technical skills were also needed as the levels improved through the famous player and coach Richard Nyren. Years later, his son John produced a famed coaching manual, *The Young Cricketers' Tutor*, after the club passed into the pages of history. It has, however, been proved that Nyren's work is cribbed, with some variations of his own, from a guide for coaching young players published under the name of William Lambert. Lambert, a Surrey-based all-rounder and the first player to score two centuries in what was then termed a 'big match', could neither read nor write; what appears to have happened is that a publisher, John Baxter, ghosted *Instructions and Rules of the Noble Game of Cricket* some fifteen years before Nyren 'borrowed the manuscript' for his own ends.

Of course the pitches of those years were far from the pampered, manicured, watered and rolled surfaces of today. There were fast bowlers such as Edward 'Lumpy' Stevens and David Harris, who made the most of the rough surfaces on which they played. Also, it was an era when players such as Stevens and later Harris, with their underarm deliveries, were often given the option of selecting their own pitches, and heaven help the poor batsman: it was the age of the shooter, skinned knuckles and one of the laws which allowed a batsman to charge down the fieldsman if he was trying to take a catch. Gentleman's game indeed!

For those of a more curious nature, the third stump was first added in 1775 and involved Stevens who had a particularly cunning delivery which was twisted and bowled (underarm, of course) at such pace that the batsmen were unable to master the ball. Stevens became alarmed at how the ball passed between the two stumps (allowed by the laws of the time). There is some dispute where the event took place. Some report it at the Artillery Ground in London; others suggest Sevenoaks, Kent. As with most additions to the laws in those years, the addition of the third stump took a matter of some five years before it was acknowledged in the laws.

****

One of the more serious problems facing South Africa's re-entry on 10 November 1991 was that the selectors, given an urgent mandate by the UCB to select a side did so without the usual fear or favour that often accompanied the teams of the rebel era. While some UCB members were opposed to the goodwill tour of India, the selectors were suddenly under pressure. There was the worry that the eventual fourteen chosen should not be seen as being part of a side that was slapped together 'at a moment's notice'.

There were two other concerns: the first being form; the second, the composition of the squad. Was it possible for a collection of individuals who suddenly found themselves packing for Calcutta instead of concentrating on the first round of A Section games to be moulded into a competitive unit? They were being asked to play three limited-overs internationals in five days and the experience of Clive Rice, Jimmy Cook and Kepler Wessels was required.

India. Had anyone been to the subcontinent before? Yes. Wessels, for Australia.

What a quandary for van der Merwe's panel. By ironic coincidence the restructured national selection panel, with three members from the SACU and two from the SACB, were in Johannesburg on 4 November holding their first World Cup strategy meeting.

In the end they came up with what they thought was the right mix. And all those who were chosen wanted to do well. Who would not, under those circumstances?

Yet Andrew Hudson, as an example, carried the scar of his failure at Eden Gardens around with him for most of the 1991-92 season. He was even referred to by Barry Glasspool as 'that young failure' in an article in *The Star* the day after the preliminary list of twenty for the World Cup squad was announced. This was because the selectors had overlooked Jimmy Cook (Transvaal) as opposed to Hudson (Natal). It was a polemic parochial view and created a problem when it came to team building. Anyway Glasspool's opinion did not count at all with Kepler Wessels and Mike Procter. However, Wessels, and to a lesser extent Alan Jordaan and Procter, have not earned the credit they deserve for easing South Africa out of the international wilderness and laying the solid foundation for what has since followed. For ten weeks they acted as nursemaids and midwives as the side toured Australia in a hectic three-week build up, followed by the World Cup and then the Caribbean venture.

For a start, the years of isolation and a fierce provincial rivalry between sides allowed for only rare off-the-field communication among some of the top players. Naturally there was respect for Rice, Peter Kirsten, Cook, Ray Jennings and Garth le Roux, while the aura of the Transvaal 'mean machine' of the 1980s gave the impression of an unsinkable ship. This had long disappeared by 1991. The message was clear enough: we may not be part of the world but we will do our best to beat whoever wants to play with us.

And some of the hired hands that made up rebel teams in the 1980s added to the problem. They were mostly seen as mercenaries with little to be sanguine about. While this was blamed on the pressure created by their banning, their general contribution was, outside the team for which they played, a muted one. Those who played in the eras leading up to the 1980s would make time after matches to sit together in changing rooms. Over a beer or two, they would exchange thoughts on how to improve their game, either at a personal or at the team level. As Jackie McGlew, a past South Africa captain, and Bob Blair, the former New Zealand fast bowler, were to confirm, it was a tough school of learning. But it was worthwhile and resulted in life-long friendships.

The Packer era, accompanied by the gloomy quagmire of isolation, changed all that. By the early 1980s the after-match dressing room spirit had been replaced with an unpleasant stench of paranoia. Sadly, its odours infected the state of mind of most of the players and team management. Commercial interests and in-house political dealings became of primary concern. Even former school- or teammates in opposing sides barely greeted each other. Friendship was paying a heavy price. This was most noticeable during the two pirate tours under Kim Hughes when the South African provincial players were at first suspicious of the Aussies' dressing room fraternization policy.

It was mostly after a match, occasionally at the end of a day's play. Yet they would share a few stories and share a drink or two. Their open friendliness was an antithesis of the prevailing cold shoulder atmosphere that was found in the changing rooms from Centurion Park to Newlands.

Alan Jordaan took over as Northern Transvaal president in 1989 to fill the gap left by Dr Willie Basson, and he was also a member of the UCB. Jordaan was handed the job of managing the World Cup side after the flying India visit. Along with Wessels and Procter, he was given the task of moulding a side out of fourteen players who, for years, had barely talked to each other, let alone played together.

The relationship between Jordaan and Wessels had always been close, beginning almost eighteen years before at Berea Park in Pretoria. The left-handed standard nine batsman from Grey College was stunned when the names of the players for the 1974 South African Schools side were read out. He could not believe he had been dropped. Sitting with his Free State Nuffield teammates he did not know which way to look, or how to hide his disappointment as he sat at the dinner table. Jordaan, who years before had been baffled by his failure to make the Northerns Schools' side, consoled the younger Wessels. He put an arm around his shoulder and told him not to worry.

'It's not the end of the world. Just the part of accepting your good fortune and your bad luck,' Jordaan told the future South African captain.

'I thought the selectors would understand.' he replied. 'They knew my (Free State) side was weak in batting. There were times I had to bat that way to save us.'

In that 1974 Nuffield Schools side was Peter Kirsten, with Lee Barnard as the captain. Others were provincial players Robbie Armitage, Ivor Foulkes, Neville Daniels and Gary Bicknell; as for the rest, they soon retreated from the competitive stage, their school's colours a lasting souvenir. Bicknell, a promising left-arm spinner, was killed in a train accident while on his way to a border posting in Namibia when doing his national service—another tragic victim of the callous apartheid era.

Four years later, Wessels, then a national serviceman and more mature as a player and a person, played under Jordaan, a Pretoria advocate, in the Northerns side. In court, Jordaan was known for his clever turn of phrase and often transferred his oratory skills to the dressing room when he captained Northerns. There were also times he could be blunt, and he once chastised Trevor Quirk, the Northerns wicketkeeper of that era, for being late for a practice that Quirk had asked to be arranged. As for Wessels, he felt the 1977-78 season under Jordaan was more than a worthwhile sojourn and respected him for his leadership and frankness. Did he learn from that experience? Oh, yes. It became part of his all-important education as a player. Although their paths parted for fourteen seasons, their mutual respect remained.

They met again in 1989-90, the season Jordaan took over as Northerns president. It was more to reopen communication links. But it laid the groundwork for what happened later as they talked about past and present. They met in India during the brief tour and enjoyed each other's company. Shortly after Jordaan was named team manager for the World Cup and the tour of the West Indies, they met again. Although they had discussed the problems of what was expected of the players at the international level, they were not entirely comfortable with what they knew from the provincial set up. From his playing days, Jordaan had dealings with Cook, Rice, Dave Richardson, Wessels and Adrian Kuiper and knew Mandy Yachad and Clive Eksteen through their Northern Transvaal connection. As for the remaining seven, they were new faces. It was an exciting, new adventure. For other players: Jonty Rhodes and Hansie Cronje, and Brian McMillan and Meyrick Pringle, their only off-the-field association came from playing in the same sides. Not an easy foundation on which to build a competitive, match-winning team.

On 7 February 1992, the South African team was about fifteen minutes out from Perth when Jordaan looked across at Procter and asked the coach what it feels like.

'What do you mean, Jordi?'

'Being part of a touring team, Proccie?'

'You mean now?'

'No. When you've travelled before.'

'I haven't, you know. Apart from India, this is my first. Like you.'

As the two men looked at each other they suddenly realized that the only person in the team with any overseas touring experience was the captain. There were some survivors from the trip to India, but that was not really a tour in the true sense. Sure, Allan Donald was with Warwickshire and Procter was coaching in England, but that is a different scenario, as had been the Packer Circus.

Within half an hour of landing, the three faced a media grilling. Although Jordaan, Procter and Wessels each had their own roles to play at the conference, it was basically a new experience for them. Chesters also felt a certain pride as the side emerged from the international section to the main concourse: headed by Wessels and Procter.

Welcome to the real world you guys. It is tough out there too.

The tour of India was such a high-pressure event at the social level that the players did not have much opportunity to settle down. Or, for that matter, get to know one another. Travelling from South Africa to Calcutta, Agra, Gwalior and New Delhi and back to Jan Smuts in a matter of nine days gave little time for general team unity to form.

It was for this reason that plans were formulated to deal with on-the-field and off-the-field disciplines before the World Cup. Jordaan and Wessels, with inputs from Procter, met and discussed the levels of priority. For one thing, they introduced a policy that had the players from different provinces sharing rooms for the first month. The idea was to break down the provincial barriers and develop team spirit. To an extent it worked, and throughout the World Cup the players' relationships were one of mutual respect and understanding. Admittedly, some of the problem was that apart from Wessels and Donald it was all very new. The magic image of playing for South Africa in a tournament that was not even a pipe dream twelve months before had the adrenalin pumping faster than normal.

Even those with limited county and English leagues experience, like the all-rounder Brian McMillan and Omar Henry, were drawn into the World Cup excitement: of being the new players in the limited-overs circus as it moved from Sydney to Auckland and other cities where they played their matches. Wessels apart, the side, in terms of global experience, were 'babes in the wood' and acknowledged as such by Procter and Jordaan.

As always, Wessels was totally disciplined and, most of all, professional. He shrugged off such thoughtless comments as 'The public of South Africa demand a victory' in *The Star*. He was not interested in the over-heated rhetoric of a few South African writers, especially those not linked closely to the team but on a fly-by-night freebie. For most, it was the first great adventure by a South African sports team in twenty-one years, and there were those who failed to understand that there was a work ethic involved.

Wessels' plan with Jordaan and Procter was to mould the players into a competitive unit, while not losing sight of the small things that counted. He worked the players hard, and there were times when some thought it was too hard. Also, he would not allow the side to be split along provincial lines. And no player was bigger than the team. That was made all too clear from the start. Slowly, that view began to filter through. Harmony, fun, playing the game for enjoyment is rarely easy if you keep on losing. Wessels knew this, Jordaan preached it and Procter was a strong advocate of togetherness.

Although there were setbacks against New Zealand and then Sri Lanka, after coming off that euphoric cloud from the Sydney triumph over Australia, the Jordaan, Wessels and Procter triumvirate worked together to produce harmony within the squad.

With Wessels there is only one dividing line: you accept him or you do not. All too many of the South African media, from writers to radio and television journalists and broadcasters, found him tough and uncompromising, which is not true. He did not suffer fools gladly, and during the World Cup, there were a few South African journalists who did not have a clue just how fierce a competition it can be. There were also those who often took his tight-lipped moodiness as a sign of being a switched-off robot. However, he had much on his mind. What did the tiresome media know about planning strategies to win matches? Not a thing. It was his job to get the other players to think along the same lines. Peter Kirsten understood, so did Kuiper and Omar Henry. Best of all, in Sydney, Clive Rice added his support. Yet, as Wessels readily admitted to Jordaan before the World Cup venture began, he hardly knew the players, apart from Mark Rushmere and 'Swinger' Dave Richardson, his two Eastern Province teammates. But he quickly worked at building a relationship with each member of the squad.

With high expectations of success at home he was, not surprisingly, under pressure. It was always there, peeping over his shoulder and it is not easy to shrug off a load that heavy. But then, he had been under pressure most of his playing career. He smiled wryly when asked if it would not have been easier to allow Jordaan or Procter to handle the media conferences. No. It was his job to do that.

'In Australia we all had a role to play,' he said in Port Elizabeth, the weekend he announced his international retirement on 17 December 1994. 'And we saw it for what it was—a team effort. We were in it for each other. And it showed. We came so close... People are inclined to forget just how close we came to playing Pakistan in that final.'

How true. All that the public want to remember are the 22 runs needed off one ball equation; not how they reached that position.

It was team effort. And their captain knew just how that hard work had achieved a miracle in Sydney that damp March evening. Does it still haunt him? There is the scrap of a rueful smile in his probing eyes. You have to accept such cruel twists of fate. In limited-overs matches, even those not shortened by rain, the margin for error is so small. A fine catch, a startling yorker, a marginalized run-out, or a six: any one of these can and has changed the direction and the result. It is all part of the character of the game. Wessels would agree with this assumption. Just as he would with mental discipline being as important as the physical preparedness needed to win matches.

Jordaan, Procter and even Wessels have admitted that the levels of fitness of the South African squad between three World Cups have shown 100 per cent improvement. In 1992 they were impressive. By the time the 1996 side under Bob Woolmer gathered for the Indian subcontinent, the change was equally phenomenal; by 1999 and England it was exceptional and focussed. Against the Australians in 2001-02 it had slipped alarmingly and Wessels expressed concern during the limited-overs series in South Africa.

What Wessels had on his side in 1992, and the others did not, was the background and experience of playing for Australia. He learnt the tough, hard-line commitment the street-wise Aussies took for granted, when playing either Test or limited-overs games. Even when there is nothing left in the game. That is when the ruthlessness becomes more omnipresent. It is what the South African captain tried to instil in his players.

During a 1992 pre-World Cup warm up match training session in Adelaide, Wessels looked at the lean Hansie Cronje and surprisingly found some flab around the waist; he took it between his thumb and forefinger and smiled grimly at the younger man. 'If you want to be a Test player you'll have to get rid of this.' It was more than just a message for the man who eventually took over the captaincy: he was giving notice to the rest of the squad. Wessels, true to his professional code, was a perfectionist and rightly demanded the same obedience from the others.

'You want to win, you have to go about it with ruthless efficiency,' he once said of a Nissan Shield final victory against Northern Transvaal at Centurion Park. 'Keep on knocking them down . . . hard!'

After India, the spectators, who had kept the game alive during the dark ages, were almost engulfed by a new public awareness. They followed the televised matches demanding to know more. The pity is that some of their knowledge was fed by shaky media reports—any number written by those wanting a freebie hitchhiker ride to the 1992 World Cup. It is a pity that after India, the masses who now followed the sport were not given a simple potted history guide to explain from where South Africa cricket had come since Trevor Goddard's side toured Australia in 1963-64.

Thus, thousands were ignorant that the team for the World Cup campaign of 1992 was the first official South African team to go on a tour since 1965. For some it was a long time, for others a lifetime. Most of the players in the squad had not even been born in 1965, let alone know about the exciting victory over England at Trent Bridge that enabled Peter van der Merwe's side to win the series 1-0.

By the time the side gathered for the historic tour of the West Indies, it was noticeable that all the hard work during the World Cup to instil a feeling of camaraderie was taking effect. Although not as high-powered as the seven weeks adventure Down Under, the visit to the Caribbean was a serious tour. Pencilled in before the World Cup, it came after the all-important 'yes' vote in the national referendum. It was another political coup for the UCB and was made possible with the support of the ANC and the influence of Nelson Mandela. Unfortunately its significance was lost on most South Africans. They were unable to see the wider global significance of how their national sports team, being invited to a region which, like India, had no political ties with a white minority government, was just reward for the game and the administrators after years of being shut out internationally by the unjust laws of the country.

For a few players it was all too new and moved too fast. Travelling to new countries can be as exciting as establishing new and, for some, lasting friendships. The problem, though, was the below average performances which did not sit well with the selectors who were looking for the right team balance.

In the West Indies the atmosphere among the players was more relaxed. They talked, laughed and enjoyed themselves. More time was spent together. More time getting to know each other. Oh, yeah! This touring lark is fun, all right. Keep fit and be disciplined and retain your form and there is no reason why you cannot carry on doing this sort of thing for the next five or six years. Or even longer.

Cheers! The cocktail recipe for success that Wessels, Jordaan and Procter had formulated all those weeks before had been effective. They had put the petty media squabbles of Rice and Cook's axing out of their minds and had worked out a formula to end the era of provincialism. In its place they created the friendship society. And no one complained.

Cook was, of course, recalled. He won caps against India and Sri Lanka. Like Peter Kirsten he deserved his belated Test cap. Sadly there was no place for the competitive warrior Rice: age had finally caught up with him. Yet his future role in the game was starting to develop, as he in turn became director of the national academy and a national selector before rejoining Nottinghamshire as their coaching director.

The day after Fanie de Villiers was included in the South African side for the one-day series against India, he celebrated the event a second night running with a bottle of South African sparkling wine. Chesters sat with him next to the pool at a vleisbraai in the plush Pretoria suburb of Waterkloof. It was a special moment, and the fast bowler posed an interesting question.

'If Pringle had not been injured in the second Test, if he was still fit, do you think they would have selected me?'

'It's not all about the ifs, Fanie. But do you really believe that?'

'You tell me.'

'What I will say is, had you been playing in the Test at the Wanderers, I am certain South Africa would have won. Examine the facts, Fanie. They needed a bowler of your ability.'

'You haven't answered my question. Would I have been picked?'

'I can't answer that. You'll have to ask the coach or the captain, or Peter Pollock.'

There is little doubt that the decision to play Pringle ahead of Fanie at the Wanderers Test was the wrong option. India needed 303 runs off the compulsory 90 overs at a lively scoring rate. It was a tough target for a side where most of the top five batsmen were out-of-form: Ravi Shastri, Sanjay Manjrekar and their captain, Mohammad Azharuddin, had been disappointing throughout the series. Only Wessels did not have a bowler who could exploit the Wanderers conditions on the last day. There was no Fanie to deliver the sharp outswing. Craig Matthews, playing in his first Test, was always tight and accurate; Brian McMillan bowled a solid line. Even the 'white lightning', Allan Donald, had lost his bite. Wessels was suddenly left with little option but to press Cronje, then in reality a very average net bowler, into the role of the fourth seamer.

Do you really think he wanted that as an option? Not a chance. The selectors had still to wake up to the demands of a winning Test series. Whatever was said afterwards, they had not really learnt from the Bridgetown experience.

As he flew to Cape Town to join the official South African squad for the first time, Fanie reflected on the hard work that would have to be put in to earn the approval of the selectors. His A Section form had taken him to the top of the averages: 20 wickets at 18.15 and a strike rate of 40.5 balls. His selection could not be in question. But selectors, and not only South African ones, have done stranger things in the past. Wessels was keen to have him in the side, so was Procter. Yet the old fallacy of Fanie being a limited-overs bowler had cropped up yet again. It was all about the runs-per-over economy, just the right sort of bowler for the limited-overs series. Joining him among the twelve was the attacking Eastern Province all-rounder Dave Callaghan.

In some ways they were interesting selections. Less than a year before, the careers of both players had been in jeopardy. Fanie was still nursing the broken toe while Callaghan was being treated for cancer. Their selection was a minor triumph for two fine players who had overcome months of what was a painstaking recovery process. It was also a testimony to their self-belief and unshakeable confidence.

Peter Pollock's view was that the selectors needed to give the two players a chance when the squad was selected for the first four games. It was also his view that 'Vinnige' Fanie was a 'tough mean swing bowler'. The convener was not shy in admitting his admiration for the way he had fought his way into contention. 'We have gone for twelve players as it is our thinking we should revert to a World Cup style team plan. Then we discussed the side and looked at who we needed if we are to beat the Indians. After that the rest fell into place. And among other factors there was no doubt in our minds that in de Villiers we have a bowler with a solid limited-overs record. I don't think I am wrong in saying that anyone who has come back the way he has at least deserves to prove he is as good as his current record. The same for Callaghan. In Fanie's case we selected him because we know from experience that he bowls tightly and this shows when he is under pressure. All players in the squad will be given a chance to prove themselves and we will have another look after the fourth match at the Wanderers.'

Pollock sat back and smiled. How the press would view what he had said would make interesting reading the next day. There were those who would not be happy. Wessels was again under attack for not being aggressive enough in the Test at the Wanderers. It was the old story. When things go wrong, blame the captain or the selectors. It was easy to forget that Pringle's injury had left them a bowler short.

One interesting selection for the shorter game was that of Brett Schultz. At that stage he had no limited-overs international record. The theory was that his left-arm pace would unsettle the Indians. Which left the query: would Pringle be in the squad if he was fit?

Wessels, it is well known, had a lot of time for Fanie. He recognized quality and his fighting spirit. Pringle? Well, in the right conditions he was a more than useful bowler.

No one, of course, expected Fanie and Wessels to 'clash head on' so soon. In a routine fielding practice session at Newlands, with an eye firmly on the ball, they collided in a bloodied clash of heads that required thirty-six stitches. Look close enough today and the scars are still visible.

Was that going to be it then? The last straw. So far and yet . . .

Fanie nursed his sewn up eyebrow and pondered his future. It was Saturday. In less than forty-eight hours he would either be playing or sitting on the bench. Yet the way Wessels had talked to him during the net sessions, Fanie guessed he would be playing.

Remember the motto: always be a winner.

Schultz was left out of the side for the first match; Fanie bowled a spell of 7 overs and went for 24 runs without a wicket. The main wicket-taker in fact was Cronje who took 5 for 32. The Northerns bowler was not unhappy with his performance. But Cronje! Thought he was just a *net* bowler! Fanie was left out of the second game of the series at St. George's Park where aggravation between the sides spilled over.

Peter Kirsten's penchant for backing up too far too often finally got the better of Kapil Dev who ran him out at the non-striker's end. No doubt the colourful Indian all-rounder, having warned the South African batsman three times before on the tour, felt it was three times too many. It had been done before. Vinoo Mankad, an Indian all-rounder of a much earlier era, had done it in Australia during the 1947-48 tour Down Under: he ran out Bill Brown twice for the same offence, firstly when the tourists played the Australian XI and then at the Sydney Cricket Ground in the drawn second Test. Brown was the first victim of such a decision. The question will always be whether the batsman was taking an unfair advantage. The law is clear enough: no matter what kind of rows it will cause, the non-striking batsman is at fault.

South Africa went to Centurion Park two days later leading 2-0. Fanie was to play his second game. Woorkeri Raman scored an impressive century to help India achieve an entertaining victory by 4 wickets and Azharuddin again failed to put runs on the board.

There was reward for Fanie—his first limited-overs international wicket was that of Shastri, caught by Brian McMillan. Two days later, on a mild Sunday afternoon at the Wanderers (the first day was rained out), Ajay Jadeja opened the innings with Raman and watched as Allan Donald ripped out Raman, bowled for a duck off the edge, and Praveen Amre, trapped lbw for two. It was good, tight bowling. 2 wickets for 3 runs by the end of the fourth over put the Indians under pressure.

Bowling from the Corlett Drive end to Jadeja, Fanie's away swing and movement off the pitch was more than merely impressive. The months of hard work had come together in a spell that had the Indian opener and his captain wide-eyed with respect. Figures of 5-2-6-0 told it all. They could barely lay a bat on the ball and privately wondered what unseen magic rope trick he was playing on them. He bent the ball away late, and skidded it through. There had been little doubt when the squad was named for the remaining slogs that Fanie would be included.

Azharuddin mused: where had this guy been hiding for so long? An injury perhaps? Okay, he had heard the name in discussions during the tour, but nothing to suggest he was this good. At Springbok Park in Bloemfontein, where South Africa took a 4-1 lead, Fanie's swing was just as impressive as it had been at the Wanderers. He controlled the movement this time, making the batsmen play and miss. He was just too good. It happens like that. The way he had bowled to Joubert Strydom all those summers before at Centurion Park.

There were often justified complaints that the standard levels in the series was average. Later, during a private conversation in Port Elizabeth during the third Test, Azharuddin admitted he was disappointed. Personally, it had not been a good tour. Race riots at home had not helped either. Then he asked an interesting question.

'I see you know Fanie de Villiers,' he smiled at Chesters. 'Is there any reason your selectors have not considered him for the Tests?'

'They think he is a one-day bowler.'

Azhar laughed and his eyes twinkled. 'That's a good one. He's the best swing bowler you have. The best I have faced in three years.'

An interesting comment all right. 'Tell that to the selectors.'

'Not me. That's your job. Why was he not at the World Cup?'

'He had an injury.'

Jadeja asked Fanie the same question, but in a different way after the side for the third and fourth Tests was announced in Durban.

'Tell me, have you done something to upset the selectors?'

'I don't think so. Why?'

'I think you must have. But I am pleased you are not playing against us in the last two Tests,' the Indian opener said. 'You are by far the best bowler I have faced on this tour. And that includes Donald, Schultz, Pringle and McMillan.'

Sanjay Manjrekar, Manoj Prabhakar and Kapil Dev had similar thoughts. During a team talk in East London before the last limited-overs international, the Indians agreed that by not playing Fanie the South African selectors had shown a lack of faith in the one bowler they feared most with the new and old ball. Donald on his day was dangerous; Schultz if he was fit and firing would cause trouble because of the bounce he could get. But Fanie de Villiers . . . any amount of hidden dangers lurked when he was bowling. If he was difficult to face in the shorter game, think how hard it would be with the red ball in a game spread over five days and fifteen sessions. Surely, they argued, the South African selectors could see that?

Fanie was on the physio table with Craig Smith working on him when Mike Procter walked over, and without looking into the eyes of the young Afrikaner said, 'You've done a good job this limited-overs series, Fanie. But you aren't playing in the final two Tests. The selectors have decided to give you a rest.' As he turned, Procter wished him a 'pleasant Christmas' before adding, 'We will most likely see you in the New Year—for the triangular series.'

Little wonder Fanie felt the same bitterness he experienced the time when his efforts to raise sponsorship for the NKP side at the sports bureau had been laughed off.

The season though was not dead. While South Africa and India played out a dreary draw before a sleeping crowd at a tired Newlands over the New Year (after South Africa won the third Test at St. George's Park, partly through a series of umpiring misjudgements) Fanie took 9 wickets in the A Section match at Kingsmead. It included a 6 for 62 first innings haul. The old firm of de Villiers and Bosch wrecked Natal's first innings and Clive Rice doffed his hat: Fanie had quickly reduced the side led by Peter Rawson to 7 for 3 in a matter of 6 overs. He dipped the ball, moved it away late, brought it back, and had the off-cutter working as well. Rice also wondered why Fanie was not playing in the third and fourth Tests.

Pollock admitted when the squad was announced that Fanie was an automatic choice for the South African side for the Total Trophy triangular series in February. Okay, why was he not considered a Test bowler? The selectors were more than happy the way the bowling attacks had worked out for both forms of the game.

Had Fanie been discussed as a possibility for the Port Elizabeth and Newlands Tests? Pollock was not going to be drawn too deeply into that discussion and played a straight bat. Yes, others had been considered. Yes, the selectors were well aware of his form in the Currie Cup games and had there been an injury it was 'always nice to know that if needed there was a Fanie de Villiers or Tertius Bosch who could fill the gap'. But the series was won 1-0. Let it rest there. The Total Triangular was a different and important tournament and Fanie was considered a significant member of this attack.

This was after yet another crisis hit the Northerns camp with Mike Haysman, who had replaced Mandy Yachad at the start of the season as captain, telling Hein Raath, convener of the Northerns selectors, that he was not prepared to accept a side without Ray Jennings for a domestic limited-overs game. It was an interesting impasse. Fanie gave his support to the deposed captain but did not want to get too involved. There was the triangular series and he needed to concentrate on that. He had to convince the selectors that he was a Test bowler.

After a shaky start against Pakistan at Kingsmead, his economy ratio over the remaining five games was a remarkable 2.14 an over. His exploits as a limited-overs bowler were becoming legendary: 9-1-12-2 against the West Indies at St. George's Park; 10-2-27-4 against Pakistan in East London; 10-3-28-0 against the West Indies at Newlands; 10-2-27-1 against Pakistan at his home ground, Centurion Park, and 10-0-38-0 against the West Indies in Bloemfontein, a match, which could have been won to put South Africa in the final.

Consistent bowling for a side whose lack of batting consistency was a continuing cause for concern among the South African selectors, especially as the reliable Peter Kirsten's form had fallen well below expectations through the series. Jonty Rhodes, at backward point, failed to get his hands to a chance offered by Brian Lara when he was 10. He scored 111 not-out: in this case the dreaded 'Nelson' helped the Windies seal an impressive victory. Had the catch been taken . . . well, who knows?

Although it did not surface until the third one-day international in Sri Lanka eight months later, Procter had watched the South African innings at Springbok Park with growing frustration. The run rate almost went into reverse as the batsmen failed to take advantage of a quality batting surface. South Africa's scoring rate did not lift itself above 3.5 an over until the last five overs when there was only a marginal improvement. But there was no justification for an overall rate of 3.70.

It disturbed the coach, as South Africa needed to win the game to qualify for the final. Victory would have left Pakistan or the Windies battling for the remaining final spot. Instead South Africa, who had issued the invitations to the big limited-overs party as part of their re-emergence as a Test-playing country, ended up being squeezed out of their own graduation ceremony through a series of batting lapses. They stuttered to a score of 185, not at all what Procter had in mind. The two points and the improved net run rate to give them the place in the final was as remote as had been South Africa's inability to beat Pakistan during the series. For Procter it was a sore point.

On 7 April 1993, minutes after a pulsating domestic series day-night final at Kingsmead had been won by Transvaal by one run, the selectors announced the side to tour Sri Lanka. Fanie assumed he was going and was not surprised when his name went up on the television screen. What made him smile was seeing Pat Symcox's name. His old Northern Transvaal B team pal would be with him when the side went to the pearl of the Indian Ocean. Symmo's selection caused more than a quizzical lift of the eyebrow among quite a few people, including some of the media, that autumn evening.

Had the selectors really lost it this time? No place for Peter Kirsten, vice-captain against the Indians. Jimmy Cook is back and Clive Eksteen, too. Daryll Cullinan gets his first tour, as does Brett Schultz, which is fair enough. Steve Palframan as the wicketkeeper: interesting selection that one. But Symmo! Next to his own selection, it was the best news in weeks.

12

Rocky Road to Sydney

For those who have often cursed the traffic congestion on the old Pretoria-Johannesburg road, or any cluttered, pot-holed single lane highway, try travelling the same distance in two hours. This is what you find between Kandy and Kurunegala: it is guaranteed to cure your aggravation. While this ancient Sri Lankan route may have been modernized to carry heavy traffic, jostling for space in an area crammed with any variety of four-wheeled public service antiques, bullock-drawn wagons and uncomfortable tourist coaches, are cyclists and pedestrians who seem to demand the right of way.

On average, you are likely to meet an estimated five hundred vehicles between the two bustling points. As speeds range from a breakneck 80 kmph to a more moderate 35 kmph (although the bullock cart trundles along at a sedate one metre in an hour) navigation is often hazardous.

You do find the odd trishaw (erroneously referred to by most Westerners as the 'tuk-tuk' because of the noise the two-stroke engine makes) driver, who gives the impression, as he dodges potholes and oncoming traffic, that he is in serious training for the regional version of the Colombo three-wheeler derby.

Yet, one of the fascinations of travel in Sri Lanka as opposed to India and Pakistan is the proximity of some of the well known tourists sites. It enables you to break away for an afternoon, or even most of the day, to indulge in a spot of sightseeing. And any number of journeys demand unaccustomed physical exercise.

For Fanie de Villiers, it was all part of the attraction of the island. Even before he had gone to Todmorden, he would go into a bookshop and hunt down an in-depth tourist guide that printed more than pretty pictures and clichés to help his pursuit as a tourist. It enabled him to study the culture, the people and the customs of the country he was touring. Sitting in a hotel room watching television, as some players do, was not for this intrepid tourist.

The inquisitive nature of the swing bowler demanded that he experience the sights, smell and tastes of the country, mix and talk with the people and learn something of their history. Statues are part of that history, street and place names too. You do not discover a country sitting in the comfort of an air-conditioned bus. Get out and about. As there may never be another opportunity, make most of the time available. Little wonder then he became the team's tourist guide and befriended many trishaw drivers and other Sri Lankans.

'If you want to know something, or where to go to get the best bargains, ask Fanie,' was how Pat Symcox put it. He would also clutter his side of the room with the most incredible junk. Well, most people would call it junk. Fanie always found a use for everything.

Colombo's other fascination had more to do with Fanie's Afrikaner roots, although it was also heavily cricket related. The Boers shipped as prisoners to the island during the South African War of 1899–1901, were organized by a former Western Province player and later administrator, P. H. de Villiers, into playing games in 1901. One was played at the Nondescripts Club in Colombo.

What is interesting is that the club then occupied the same site as the team's hotel did ninety years later. The current club, in the leafy Maitland Place, is next to the Sinhalese Sports Club, Sri Lanka's main Test venue, and has a number of pictures on old stucco walls: two show the Boer prisoners preparing for the match; the third is of the team. There is a difference in the team picture between that on the wall and the one in W. M. Luckin's *History of South African Cricket* published in 1915. The picture on the wall in Colombo has two coloured players in the centre of the backrow. In the book they are missing.

There is an uncompromising beauty about central Sri Lanka that demands your attention; plateaus and rugged landscapes like those around the plains of Dambulla, the epicentre of what the Portuguese and Dutch called the Pearl of the Indian Ocean, or as the ancient scholars would have it, Serendip.

Unless you are a Buddhist on a pilgrimage, Dambulla, a world heritage site, is not a great tourist spot: little more than a bustling pit stop between Anuradhapura and Kurunegala with the buildings showing off a decidedly shabby, lower middle-class facade. Even from the fancy Ka'lama Culture Club resort, which costs about US$400 a night without the breakfast, you can see the imposing bare black rock, known as Dambulu-gala, jutting up from the plain.

Only the adventurous are prepared to climb the 107 metres to the series of caves that 2110 years ago were turned into the now famous rock temple (script and rock paintings also suggest that the caves were inhabited by hermit monks around 300BC). And only the hardy are likely to take the extra step and scramble a further 183 metres to the summit. Although the energy expended getting to the caves is worth the effort, chattering rock monkeys scamper around looking for bananas or other items of food.

In another break Fanie briefly escaped into the interior to enjoy the imposing craggy sights of Dambulla. Always aware of the enjoyment when discovering an ancient culture, he revelled in the atmosphere.

Mention Sri Lanka these days and the images conjured are those of Muttiah Muralitharan bowling his off-spin with a bent elbow (a congenital problem) and the munificent 450-year-old Galle Fort backdrop to the international ground. Which is as it should be.

While the media centre has become a disaster area after England's 2001 tour, the venue presents one of South Asia's great sights. If Chesters had to name one of his five favourite Test grounds, Galle would be on that list. Eden Gardens, the Basin Reserve, Adelaide Oval and SuperSport Park Centurion would be the others.

Do not think though that it is easy to play in Sri Lanka. Heat, humidity, frustrating umpires, any variety of insects and hard, rough outfields, make conditions tough and demanding. But there is no mistaking the friendliness of the people. Fanie discovered that when the side arrived in the ancient city of Galle on the southern coast of the island and enjoyed exploring the area that was settled around 500 BC. The Dutch rebuilt the fort guarding the harbour around 1658 on the rocky Pointe De Galle after having forced out the Portuguese following a bloody siege.

Galle is also the doorway to the lush southeast with its tourist beaches, hotels and a special mix of life and beauty of its own: rubber and toddy tapping and fishing are major local industries. It also contains areas of rare and special beauty as well as the remains of Sri Lanka's last primeval forest.

* * * *

For someone with an uncomplicated view of life, Fanie has achieved much from such a complex game since taking those 5 wickets against Natal B at Berea Park in 1985-86. He had long harboured the dream of playing for South Africa, and while there is some compensation in earning international limited-overs recognition, they are not Tests: that is the ultimate experience. Certainly a limited-overs international has its own challenging standards of skill; a Test makes for greater demands along with increased levels of concentration and expertise, a mind game that can play strange tricks even on the most levelheaded.

With what had gone before, the side announced for Sri Lanka should not surprise anyone: Fanie would be fortunate if he found himself as a candidate for the five-day game. Early in that first tour he realized that his chances of playing a Test were minimal. For one thing Brett Schultz had come through far stronger than anticipated and was a more competitive bowler than the left-arm rookie who had taken part in the series against India.

There has always been the view that Fanie de Villiers should have made his Test debut in the second match of the series at the Sinhalese Sports Club on 6 September 1993. But as in February 1990, the selectors, after deliberating must have, deep down, retained doubts about his fitness because of his record of injuries. Or did they? In February 1990 during the Gatting rebel series, Peter van der Merwe admitted that South Africa needed the out-swing style of bowling which Fanie produced. Yet in Sri Lanka, this idea along with a Test cap seemed another planet away.

When it came to selecting the side for the tour of Sri Lanka, the national selectors, led by Peter Pollock, were forced through circumstances to make a few new selections: new strategies to meet the demands of the South Asian subcontinent. It was time to rebuild the side that had gone to the World Cup; also a time to experiment. Although he will always deny it, Pollock wanted to include a player or two who, in his thinking, would fit into the way he saw the modern game. A balance was needed: time for a rethink after the triumphs and tribulations of the India tour and the Total Triangular series.

For Pollock, Sri Lanka was the first foreign port of call as selection panel convener, the first overseas venture since the World Cup and the West Indies trip sixteen months before. So refurbishing that squad was important. A new vice-captain to replace Adrian Kuiper (Peter Kirsten had filled the role against India at home) and was required. A long-term player such as Hansie Cronje emerged as the main candidate. Wessels had a high opinion of the young man's leadership abilities, and not just because he was a Grey College product like Wessels himself. Nor were names merely plucked out of a magician's hat.

Yet Pat Symcox was barely given a mention that 1992-93 season: four matches, 10 Castle Cup wickets at 23.20 and a very ordinary domestic day-night series. Hardly the form to warrant selection for a tour that included three Tests. South Africa were in need of competitive players and Symmo fitted in with the team's plans over the next two years. Fanie's only doubts were more imaginary than real.

Seated in a friend's flat one night shortly after the Total Triangular series had ended, he replayed one particular scene continuously on the video. It was of Sir Richard Hadlee bowling in a Test in Brisbane where he had taken 15 wickets. The batsman was Kepler Wessels. After pressing the replay button for the fifth time, the South African seamer shook his head at the amount of sideways movement the great New Zealand fast bowler had been able to generate. 'They talk about world-class swing bowlers,' he commented. 'Waqar Younis and Wasim Akram: now they are world class. I really have a long way to go to match either of them.'

He was not, he felt, being modest. Yet, if Azharuddin's comments were a guide to the world-class who's who of bowlers in the early 1990s, Fanie was already on that list.

* * *

Because of the friendship which had developed during the mid- and late 1980s, Fanie de Villiers and Pat Symcox became permanent room-mates. But as Symcox discovered, whether in Sri Lanka, Australia, England, Pakistan, New Zealand or India, sharing a room with 'Vinnige Fanie' on tour can sometimes become a hazardous exercise.

Fanie was known among the side as possibly the untidiest player in South Africa; far from meeting the fastidious standards set by Symcox. Most of the time, his side of the room was a cluttered mess: no change at all from his student days when he first had met Judy. Newly bought silk shirts mingled with a variety of garments in serious need of a visit to the laundry. From this disorganized chaos, he would find an item of clothing he wanted to wear.

It was 10 August 1993 and Symcox, towel wrapped around his waist, stood in front of the mirror in the bedroom of a smart Colombo hotel, vigorously brushing his teeth. Behind him emerged a head from a sheet tangled around the form of Fanie de Villiers.

'Hi, Symmo.' There was a big grin from the tight angular features.

Symcox grunted, spitting toothpaste and water into a mug, ignoring the greeting.

'Ah . . . Symmo. You think I can use the toothbrush when you've finished?'

Symcox shook his head. He rinsed his mouth and held up the toothbrush. It was the second day of the tour and sharing a personal thing such as a toothbrush with his old teammate was stretching even this friendship a bit far.

'Fanie . . . come, I want to show you something.'

De Villiers slipped out of bed and walked over to where Symcox was standing by the window. He showed him the toothbrush, then hurled it as far as it will go, somewhere towards Galle Face Road. 'Now I suggest, after breakfast, that we go and buy ourselves a toothbrush each. Either that, or by the time we get back here no one will talk to us because our teeth are filthy and our breath smells worse than any pigsty.'

As the team was to leave that day for Galle to prepare for the first match, the fast bowler eyed the off-spinner and grinned. Guile has won the battle over rhythm and swing. And at least Symcox knew his roomie would make the bus on time.

There was another side to this relationship that defied normal boundaries. Symcox is a smoker and Fanie has a general dislike of those who smoke. This meant that when Symcox wanted a smoke he often found himself standing on a narrow hotel balcony puffing on either his first fag or the last one of the day.

During the 1993 tour of Sri Lanka, Symcox found himself taking a hundred rand bet with Wessels about spending the night on the balcony. So mattress, sheet and all, Symcox settled down for the night and in the morning asked his captain for the cash. Had Symcox really spent the night sleeping on the balcony?

'Yes,' came the reply.

'So you want that hundred?'

'That's right,' nodded Symcox, lighting up.

'Well, I'm not going to give it to you.'

'Okay, skipper. It suits me fine. I'm staying here for the rest of the day.'

A worried Wessels looked at Symcox as he began to settle in. They had an important practice and Symcox was a key member of the bowling attack.

'If I give you two hundred, will you come in?'

Symcox grinned. 'You're on, skipper.'

* * * *

It did not surprise the intrepid roommates when they were excluded from the opening match against the weak Sri Lankan Board XI. They had partly expected it: Symcox was already in the Test squad. In Fanie's case, however, the tour management saw Allan Donald and Brett Schultz as the new-ball pairing for the Tests. As if to prove the point Schultz breathed too much fire and brimstone for the hosts in Galle: after just 4 overs he switched ends and from the Fort End wrecked their top order, taking 4 wickets for only 10 runs in 6 overs. It was a spell that many felt did much to psychologically undermine the shaky confidence of the Sri Lankan batsmen for the Tests.

Schultz's pace during the two innings terrorized the locals, earning him 7 wickets in the match for 56 runs. It was a better haul than Donald's, whose return of 78 for 1 in 26 overs ranked him well below that of the left-arm Schultz in the early psychosomatic battle waged against the Sri Lankans. After all, the islanders had seven months earlier easily beaten England, led by Alec Stewart in the absence of Graham Gooch, by 5 wickets. Not that pushing over a rudderless England, already beaten 3-0 by

India, could be regarded as an achievement in March 1993. The Sri Lankans were motivated while England's inspiration came from Ted Dexter's selection panel, not noted on that tour for being particularly visionary.

From Galle the team travelled inland to Kandy and to a hotel perched on top of a hill overlooking the ancient Sri Lankan capital, with the famous Buddhist Temple of the Tooth and other scenic wonders. About a two-hour's journey southwest is Kurunegala where, in the shadow of a giant rock shaped like a tortoise, the South Africans met a stronger side in the Board President's XI at Welagedara Stadium.

While Symcox, playing his first match for the South Africans, bowled without luck on a pitch which rarely helped bowlers, the hot humid conditions added to the tourists' discomfort.

For Fanie, Kurunegala saw him earn his first 5-wicket haul in an innings in national colours: bloody hard work in such soporific conditions. Yet the 5-wicket haul, apart from the notation in the statistics, was not going to help him: he simply did not fit into the selectors' Test team's game plan. His role was that of a swing and seam bowler in one-dayers. So forget the Tests, Fanie. Some day perhaps. Not now. It was frustrating, because he firmly believed he was bowling better than Donald. He was tired of reading about how good he was as a limited-overs bowler. Most of the South African press seemed to view his record from the wrong perspective. Had they not examined his first-class record at all? Were they really that blind? Were they so seduced by watching him bowl with the white ball instead of the red? Or won over by glib selectors' gift of the gab?

The team management also had other issues to consider: the batting had not been consistent and the first Test was looming after the opening limited-overs game in Kandy.

The match at Asgiriya was a washout, but Symmo making his international debut months after wondering if he really had a future in the game at all, bagged 2 for 28 in 9 overs. Fanie's spell was nothing special either: tighter than those of Brian McMillan and Richard Snell, but he did not feel the part. On the next day was the charge back to Colombo to prepare for the first of the three Tests, Fanie knowing all the while that he would not be in the side.

His thoughts on the matter were divided between being ready for the work required in a five-day match and still needing to work on his bowling. He threw himself into a lengthy bowling spell at the Sinhalese Sports Club nets at a practice session, which was impressive for the pace he generated as well as the ability to swing the ball and snake it back as fast as a striking cobra. Mike Procter liked what he saw, so did Kepler Wessels. 'Vinnige Fanie' was showing them what he was worth. Should, heaven forbid, either Schultz or Donald breakdown . . .

While Fanie was wrestling with the Test place problem, a far wider undercurrent that filtered through the dressing room was emerging. South Africa needed to score faster in the one-day games if they hoped to keep pace with modern trends. Kepler Wessels had several detractors in the camp over his steadying block and bash tactics. Another school of thought wanted to attack from the start: catch the opposition off balance. This was the tactic applied three years later by Sanath Jayasuriya and Romesh Kaluwitharana as part of the Sri Lankan 1996 World Cup strategy. In the South African camp, Jimmy Cook felt that Wessels was not doing his job and lacked communication with his players. Procter, disturbed at the tactics, which he felt cost the side the third day-night game, also voiced criticism of the anchor-style role of the openers.

It had long been Fanie's view that at that stage South Africa did not always have the batsmen to win limited-overs internationals, as was shown by the third game in the series. This was why the bowlers played such a crucial role in the team's make up. There was no one to fill the Adrian Kuiper 'pinch-hitter' vacancy. This has been a shortcoming which has often haunted South African sides until the arrival of Lance Klusener. His best efforts are those late innings charges when chasing down a total. They cause the sort of crowd reaction which is an explosive mixture of near hysteria and hyperventilation that is more commonly seen at some pop group concerts.

There have been times when erratic batting performances have let the side down because of the extra pressure. It was all right for Wessels: his Australian experiences and his own determination had taught him how to handle the mind games that go on in a Test. At that stage of South Africa's road back, they had played only five Tests: one against the West Indies and four against an Indian side that was barely competitive.

For the first Test, played at the Tyronne Fernando Stadium, Moratuwa, outside Colombo, spinners Clive Eksteen and Symcox made their debuts on the field and Fanie debuted behind the microphone with Andre Coetzee, commentating for Afrikaans radio. Because of the unprepared state of the pitch, Brian McMillan was dropped to make way for the extra spinner. Between them the left-armer Eksteen and Symcox bowled 42 overs, giving away 144 runs though without reward as Sri Lanka batted solidly for almost five sessions to score a first innings total of 331.

South Africa were always playing 'catch up'. Their inconsistent batting had them trailing by 66 runs in the first innings, with Symcox indulging in some lusty improvements to the scoreboard to lift the performance above a shade of mediocrity.

Later on, a target of say 365 runs off 117 overs at 3.11 an over would not have been out of reach of a battle-hardened side that had been carefully moulded, grown and developed into a steady, consistent unit. But on 29 and 30 August 1993, the lack of expertise at Test level showed. It was left to Jonty Rhodes, the run-out hero of the World Cup match at Brisbane and one of the batsmen who helped rescue South Africa in the Wanderers Test against India, to blossom again. His footwork when facing the spinners on a pitch that was keeping low and giving the spinners more assistance than South Africa's batsmen would normally encounter was entertaining. It was sheer ballet at the crease. After an innings carefully plotted and engineered to save a game, his reward was a maiden Test century.

At 138 for 6, with about one-and-a-half sessions remaining, Arjuna Ranatunga, the Sri Lanka captain, cheerfully sniffed the spoils of victory and tightened the noose. Muttiah Muralitharan, the off-spinner whose elbow action seemed to some to be in contravention of the old law 24.2 (throwing), was let loose. He had managed 5 wickets in the first innings, but had only one in the second, while Aravinda de Silva teased and tantalized his way to 2 wickets. It was a precipitous situation for the tourists.

Rhodes had batted an hour when first Symcox, and then Eksteen joined him. Over the next three hours he lifted his own game to a level of rare quality to save a Test and earn applause from a grateful far-off nation.

There were no problems, for Fanie that is, over team selection for the next two matches. They were the day-night internationals at Premadasa Stadium, Khettarama, where teams batting first had the advantage as the humidity and the dew enabled the swing bowlers to play their own games. While his remarkable performance of taking 3 wickets for 15 runs in 10 overs has long been ranked among the great spells of limited-overs bowling, Fanie enjoyed other moments at the ground.

His efforts to coerce spectators to do the Mexican wave did not go unnoticed by the TV cameraman or the producer. The crowd did not quite understand at first what he was asking them to do, but they enjoyed the antics of the affable Afrikaner. He was easily identifiable as the cheerful tourist who would sign autographs and indulge in a little banter. South Africa won the game by 124 runs and returned two days later with hopes of a second victory. Fanie was a little more expensive, going for 31, but still the most economical of the bowlers.

Losing the toss meant losing the match. Wessels and Rhodes were the only recognized batsmen to reach double figures, but they too succumbed to the vagaries of the night conditions. Wicket nine fell with the score at 103 and when Fanie joined Snell, the pair believed, almost naïvely, that they had a chance of winning the game.

'Hit straight,' came Snell's advice. 'We can do it together. Work the ball into the gap and we'll get the runs.'

This was not the tooth fairy talking! Just a matter of common sense. In the end they added 51 for the last wicket, still a record for South Africa in limited-over internationals, and spared a few blushes. They were 44 runs short of their target and had 3.5 overs remaining: it worked out to less than two runs a ball. Better to go down blazing than without anything to show for your efforts. Snell scored 51 and Fanie was stranded on 12. And that was it. The tour of Sri Lanka had, for Fanie, come to an end.

That defeat at Premadasa Stadium brought to the surface for the first time the serious differences of opinion in the tactical approach to the limited-overs game between Procter (the coach) and Wessels (the captain). One report emerging from Colombo suggested the cauldron had been bubbling since South Africa had lost to Sri Lanka in their 1992 World Cup match at Basin Reserve in Wellington. A plausible theory that lacked substance. Procter was upset by the defeat and blamed it on the way Wessels employed the anchor tactics. It was an unpleasant rift in viewpoints that was not satisfactorily settled. But a truce was called for the sake of team unity before the second Test of the series.

When the team for that match was announced, Fanie was still in the cold. Brian McMillan was brought back for Eksteen and Snell for Jimmy Cook, whose brief Test career had come to an end.

Fanie was far from happy about the snub and met Procter to discuss the problem. As they slowly trawled the boundary at the Sinhalese Sports Club, Procter argued that swing bowlers no longer won Tests but genuine fast bowlers did. Schultz and Donald had been selected to blast the Sri Lankans into submission and there was no place for de Villiers in this game plan. His outswing was most useful in the one-day game because it was an effective containment weapon. The Northern Transvaal rhythm and swing bowler disagreed with Procter on this point.

What about Waqar? What about Wasim? What about Lillee and Hadlee and Kapil Dev? The last two named had taken 400 Test wickets. What about Snell? Had not Hadlee been regarded the world's top bowler for almost a decade because of his ability to swing the ball? So, how could Procter voice such a view when the best bowlers in the game were those who swung the ball? He did not regard himself as good as Hadlee, Lillee, Wasim or Waqar, but hell . . . he was better than Schultz. Anyway, how many 5-wicket hauls, he argued, did the Eastern Province youngster have? Two or three at the most. Including the 5 wickets at Kurunegala, Fanie knew that his own tally stood at thirteen. Procter merely looked at the much younger man. He had his opinions and was not about to change.

Although Schultz's blitzkrieg tactics proved Procter right, the coach later reassessed his views of de Villiers' comments. It showed Fanie a different side to the great former all-rounder's psyche. Schultz's results were, on this occasion, proof enough for Procter. There was no need to flaunt them. Strongly aggressive and oozing hostility, the left-arm fast bowler carried far too much pace for the Sri Lankan batsmen in both innings. Memories of his 9 wickets for 106 runs on a pitch that gave him lift and bounce still lingers along with his broad grin. It is also still vividly remembered in Sri Lanka.

Schultz's demolition act is inclined to overshadow the statistic that the victory, by an innings and 208 runs, was until November 1999, the most comprehensive in South African history.[1] Sri Lanka's second innings was little more than a dishevelled rout as they were dismissed for 119.

There was also a rest day dividing the third and fourth days. Some South Africans spent time enjoying the facilities at the historic palm-fringed well-groomed ground in the centre of Colombo's upmarket Cinnamon Gardens. Fortunately, the old picturesque colonial district has largely escaped the untidy urban sprawl and the characterless modern buildings that go with it. Amid this, the tradition-steeped Sinhalese Sports Club was a lively, colourful private club once known as the Maitland Place Club that hired out the venue for Tests to bring in much-needed revenue.

For some reason though, South Africa's first innings total of 495 at this venue is often overlooked when it comes to the big totals scored since readmission. Wessels missed a century by 8 runs while Cronje batted with sensible stroke play for his second Test three-figure score. Then, to rub it in, Symcox and Snell put together an aggressive eighth-wicket partnership of 79 in as many minutes. And Symcox is not shy, with that touch of wry humour, of reminding you of his 'entertaining maiden Test half-century': the fourth of the innings. That of course was before the century against Pakistan in February 1998 at the Wanderers and the world record Test partnership with Mark Boucher. Savouring the moment and full of the bravado Test success brings, Schultz jokingly predicted to Fanie that he would take over his role in the one-day games. Fanie was not amused. It also made him think hard. What if Schultz was right? With a little more experience he could pose a threat. Perhaps it was time he showed Procter and Wessels just how good he really was.

Also in his thoughts were the comments of Sanath Jayasuriya. The attacking left-hander was as surprised as Mohammad Azharuddin and Ajay Jadeja had been during the Test series in South Africa. 'It was incredible. He had bowled so well in Kurunegala,' said the then twenty-four-year-old Jayasuriya. 'I faced enough of his bowling to

---

[1] In November 1999, South Africa beat Zimbabwe by an innings and 219 runs at Harare.

know he would be a potential danger to us. I know Arjuna was quite relieved when he was not playing in the three Tests.'

'There seemed to be a problem in the South African camp. I thought the ideal attack would have been Donald, Schultz and de Villiers,' Jayasuriya said in 1999, still bemused by the South African touring management's selection policy on the 1993 tour. It was a genuine view offered by the Bloomfield Cricket and Athletic Club all-rounder. For him, Schultz's left-arm pace and Fanie's swing was a far bigger threat than all the fire and brimstone that Donald and Schultz had to offer during the three tests. Had Fanie upset the management to be left out of the Test side?

Before the third Test Fanie spent a morning impressing everyone in the nets. It surprised some, as it was an optional practice. But the next day, when the team gathered in the Taj Samara's foyer, he was missing. He had sent word with Craig Smith, the team's physiotherapist, that he was going to 'rest up that morning' and was not going to budge for anyone. Procter and Wessels saw it as a sign of insubordination, causing a fissure in team discipline. At the nets the captain and coach chewed over the matter while the team manager, Cassim Docrat, returned to the hotel to drag the errant team member back to the ground.

When he faced Procter and Wessels, his eyes widened with surprise.

'What's the problem?' He was genuinely puzzled.

'I think you should start explaining your actions,' began Procter. The team could not afford a breakdown in morale.

'Yesterday was optional, so I thought it wouldn't be a problem if I stayed in bed today as you don't need me.'

He glanced at the coach, manager and captain, who as a form of discipline had been wondering whether to pack him off home early, fine him or consider him no longer part of the touring party. His answer shook the management and they quickly realized there had been a problem with the Afrikaans translation of the words 'optional' and 'compulsory'. All was forgiven as they pointed out to Fanie the differences between the two words.

'Hey, guys . . . I'm just a dumb boereseun... That English is way over the top for me.' There was that infectious grin, which would charm even a cobra out of its basket.

The third Test ended in a stalemate after rain wrecked the last day, but not before Schultz earned himself a second 5-wicket haul in the series, despite another poor umpiring display. Schultz's 20 wickets at 16.30 in Sri Lanka had rightly made him, in Procter's view, a prized team member. But his explosive action on the hard pitches on the tea island had damaged his right knee to the extent that he needed an operation. And the prognosis was not good.

Then, on 28 September Dr Ali Bacher announced that the left-arm pace bowler, the hero of the one-nil Test series victory over Sri Lanka would possibly miss the Hero Cup series in India. Predictions were that he would be ready by mid-December: just in time to join the side in Australia for the next Test series. Little did Dr Bacher, or Schultz, then realize that the road to recovery would be beset by more travails than the optimistic UCB managing director could imagine.

After the lessons of Sri Lanka, and with Schultz an invalid, Peter Pollock's selection panel held a frank, open discussion with Procter and Wessels to sort out more than the prickly issue of limited-overs batting tactics. There were other probing questions: just where was South Africa going and what players could be pulled in for the next two assignments? Who could be brought in as a part of the ongoing transitional experiment since the World Cup?

First was the limited-overs Hero Cup series in India: an event to celebrate the diamond jubilee of the Cricket Association of Bengal (CAB) and involving six countries. In essence it was another political flag-waving exercise. Designed to test the infrastructure being put in place for the 1996 World Cup, it was also seen as a jingoistic exercise of brash commercialism.

It ran into early organizational trouble when Pakistan withdrew, citing, yet again, the threat of anti-Muslim disturbances. Further chaos arose over a dispute involving television rights, with the Indian government claiming that the state-run Doordashan held the monopoly and adding to the growing list of faux pas. This one, however, had nothing to do with the tournament organizers. There was further exacerbation when India's neighbour Sri Lanka, one of the three sponsor countries for the 1996 World Cup, complained with biting sarcasm of ill-mannered behaviour by a group of Indian officials. The Sri Lankans were far from impressed when they were treated with a callous brusqueness. No wonder the normally even-tempered Sri Lanka board president, Ana Punchihewa, was moved to protest.

Further embarrassment arose when the crowd in Ahmedabad stoned the Indians and West Indies players. The Indian captain, Azharuddin, labelled the spectators the 'worst behaved in India'. Nothing, it seems, had changed three years later—South Africa's Test against India at the same venue was an example of rank bad manners by an over-zealous section of supporters.

Little wonder that the South African management then privately queried whether any of the subcontinental countries had the ability to run a successful World Cup. With Pakistan out and Sri Lanka fuming about the treatment of their officials, it made for carping media criticism of India's handling of the tournament: the curtain got stuck halfway on opening night and refused to budge.

The second phase of the tough summer programme was the tour of Australia: a series of three Tests and a couple of state matches along with the WSC triangular involving trans-Tasman rivals New Zealand and Australia. Including India, the tour was a lengthy ninety days with the subcontinent being the toughest section in terms of travel, accommodation and poor umpiring standards. With sixteen or seventeen one-day internationals, three Tests and two state games, the emphasis was on players with top limited-overs skills as well as those who could be serious contenders for the Test side.

Axed after the Sri Lanka tour were Cook, Eksteen and reserve wicketkeeper Steve Palframan. Brought in were all-rounders Dave Callaghan and David Rundle, and Errol Stewart as cover for Dave Richardson.

The buzz of anticipation among the media and sponsors in that crow's nest of a temporary long room in the Centenary Stand overlooking the Wanderers Stadium on 1 November 1993 was overlaid partly by consternation, partly by arcane puzzlement. Brothers Gary and Peter Kirsten were missing from the squad of fifteen. How could the selectors ignore the form of the two talented players? There was keen disappointment in the Western Province dressing room, too. The side was announced shortly after they had wrapped up a 7-wicket win over Northern Transvaal at Centurion Park. Joy for new cap Rundle; Callaghan's gutsy recovery from cancer was further rewarded.

As for Pollock, facing a highly curious media, he went to some lengths to diplomatically smooth over the rougher edges of team selection policy, dotting the i's and crossing the t's. Schultz would, it was explained, join the touring party in Australia about the time of the match against Queensland to determine his fitness for that first Test at the MCG a week later. And there was nothing sinister to be read in the exclusion of Eksteen.

But the parochial Johannesburg media was grumbling. Well, hell, no Jimmy Cook! Others wondered whether Peter Kirsten had committed some sin. And no temporary replacement for Schultz? It could be argued that Donald, Fanie, Craig Matthews and Brian McMillan carried enough firepower until the Tests. Matthews had already sat out a domestic day-night match in order not to further aggravate a niggling thigh muscle injury. And now it seemed, Meyrick Pringle had been turned into a forgotten exhibit.

Nothing was settled: the mix and match policy would continue. In any event, the visit to the subcontinent for the Hero Cup series was also South Africa's way of judging the conditions for the World Cup a little more than two years away. But there was some media sympathy for the Kirsten brothers. If an in-form Cook was not in the long-term (World Cup) plans, what price for the older Kirsten? Life could be cruel. Take a batsman backing up too far at the non-striker's end and being run-out without facing a ball. Not a nice feeling at all. The Grim Reaper has his own rewards. Some critics, without serious thought to the immediate future, were hastily writing Peter Kirsten's Test obituary.

Pollock, a former journalist, knew all too well the unsettled mood of some media members. He explained how 'hard it is to leave out those players who are displaying encouraging form' but the front five batsmen would have to do the job while the back-up was seen as reliable support. Then, with a quiet twinkle, he reminded the media 'no one can look into a crystal ball and see who is going to fall down the stairs or out of the fitness bus'. How true.

The Hero Cup began for South Africa with a rained out game against Zimbabwe at Bangalore. Although it went unnoticed by everyone outside the Zimbabwe side, Heath Streak made his limited-overs debut. Four days later, in Mumbai, South Africa went on to beat the West Indies by 41 runs. It was a match notable for Jonty

Rhodes' five catches and Daryll Cullinan falling ill from heat exhaustion after scoring 70 in a total of 180 for 5 in a rain restricted innings of 40 overs.

Although Cullinan played well in patches on the tour, the multi-talented batsman did not really recover from that nasty brush with the unforgiving Indian climate. Another easy success, this one by 78 runs over Sri Lanka, followed five days later at Guwahati, where Richard Snell bowled with tight accuracy to earn 4 for 12 in 7.1 overs.

The two victories established the South Africans as favourites to win the final. Then in Mohali, giving away a sinful 3.1 overs in no-balls and wides against the Indians, with McMillan and Snell travelling for 99 runs in 20 overs, trouble hovered. The malaise continued when 9 wickets fell for only 70 runs and the team suddenly capitulated. They had reached the semi-finals, but at the price of their batting strategy.

Communist-run Calcutta. City of Joy. Home of Nobel Prize winner Mother Teresa, Eden Gardens and Jagmohan Dalmiya. This was the venue of the first semi-final of the series: South Africa playing India and millions again watching on television. The inhabitants of this city take their cricket seriously. To them the Sir James Barrie metaphor: 'cricket is not a matter of life or death . . . it is more important than that', takes on a new meaning.

Fanie, intrepid tourist that he was, set off to enjoy the sights of Calcutta. Barely had he ventured into a couple of shops when autograph hunters were on to him.

'You, Fanny d'Villiers,' shouted a gleeful youngster. 'First-class bowling average 23.12. You damn good limited-overs bowler.' Fanie was impressed. 'You gotta fine slow ball,' he was told by another, 'and late away swing . . . fool a lot of batsmen, Fanny d'Villies.' This particular youngster grinned and held out a scrap of paper. Soon there were more hands clutching scraps of paper and small autograph books. Fanie borrowed a well-chewed ballpoint pen from a smiling sales assistant and started signing.

Fanie, sweating from the humidity, looked up to see a swelling sea of cheerful up-turned faces: a broad cross-section of cultures, creeds and religions. Minutes passed . . . almost half an hour. It became hard work; his fingers were tired and cramped. To sign more autographs he stood on a shoe cleaner's box, his back to a decaying concrete wall with a gabbling mass in front of him.

Here was the hero of the ordinary people being feted by his subjects, and there was no way out. He smiled at their warm enthusiasm and attempted to keep some control over those milling around him in the narrow street.

Swiftly and silently the police arrived. A sergeant, only known as Ravi, explained that reports had reached them that a South Africa player was being mobbed. Wielding their long bamboo lathis, the long arm of the law effectively brought the situation under control. The alley emptied swiftly. Fanie was not worried by the enthusiasm of the crowd. He was upset, though, by the police's brutal reaction to a harmless autograph session.

As the sergeant escorted 'Fanny d'Villies' back to the hotel he shook his head. 'What you did is crazy,' he quietly admonished the tall broad-shouldered Afrikaner. 'You could have been injured.'

Fanie smiled. 'I was never in danger.'

His confidence caused a stir among the police.

Symmo and Fanie, with the help of Ann Doherty, wife of Mike Doherty, a UCB executive member travelling with the team, tracked down Mother Teresa's telephone number. Ann Doherty made the call and arranged a meeting. When the four met the Mother, they were awed by her modest, natural warmth and charm. A little discussion was followed by an invitation to look through the convent.

An Australian nurse dressed in a simple green and russet sari, with a cheerful round face and happy blue eyes, was attending a baby. Her name was Margaret and she was pleased to mention she was from a hamlet south of Sydney where the boy from Bowral, Donald Bradman, first faced the ferocious leg-spin of Bill O'Reilly, the school teacher from Wingello: two future Test giants involved in a sparring session that has long passed into local folklore.

When it was time to leave, the South Africans were given a blessing by the nun along with her 'business card' which was a small yellow card with the moving message.

> The fruit of silence is Prayer
> The fruit of prayer is Faith
> The fruit of faith is Love
> The fruit of love is Service
> The fruit of service is Peace.

For a variety of personal reasons Fanie's favourite ground remains Eden Gardens: the venue where South Africa made their re-entry at international level on 10 November 1991, where the cauldron-like atmosphere continually demands attention. Symmo is another who says that until you have played at Eden Gardens you have not experienced the greatest sight in the world. At such matches there are usually more than 95,000 within and 60,000 or more outside the ground. Around the city two-thirds of the population watch the matches on television or follow on radio.

Fanie has played at all the famous venues yet none match the emotion generated at Eden Gardens. The lighting of newspapers as torches heralding an Indian victory with the floodlights switched off is as dramatic as any poetic epigram. And Fanie readily admits that the Hero Cup semi-final left him 'deeply moved'. All of which dismisses the theory that the Sydney Cricket Ground, where he bowled South Africa to victory six weeks later is his favourite ground.

Eden also has a few drawbacks. Naturally, local politicians, quick to exploit their privileges, are the first in the queue when it comes to the iniquitous system of favoured ticket allocations for Tests or one-day internationals. To repay the debt they dispense special services to CAB or Indian officials. The larger the quota, the bigger the favour.

In Calcutta during the Hero Cup the players suddenly found their allocation for the semi-finals in great demand by some CAB officials. They became such an irritation that a couple of players threw some out of the South African dressing room. For a sizeable fee, the remainder of the book from which the fifty or so players' and team officials tickets were culled was sold to the highest bidders. As some books contained a hundred and fifty tickets it was profitable business.

There are some Indians, no doubt with tongue-in-cheek, who will gleefully tell you they really do not believe that bit about Broadha'penny Down in Hambledon, England, being the cradle of the modern game. And you cannot blame them because Eden Gardens is the Asian equivalent of that gentle rustic venue. To those who do not know the difference, the quiet Hampshire village is not where it all began more than 250 years ago. The Artillery Ground in south London, once umbilically linked to the Kent countryside, is more famous with connections dating fifty years or more before Broad'hapenny Down and Hambledon. To the Indians, their version of the Melbourne Cricket Ground is far older than the paddock that grew into the concrete bowl that is now the MCG; it also boasts seating arrangements to match those of the MCG. At Test time, however, it is more common to attract 80,000 a day at Eden Gardens than it is at the MCG.

Eden Gardens is also a historical landmark in Calcutta and one which has been around for much longer than 150 years. It is not merely India's most important Test venue: there is a handsome garden, a miniature lake and other delights. Bought by the then governor-general, Lord Auckland, it was an empty, unkempt plot in 1840. His wealthy sisters, Emily and Fanny Eden, converted it into gardens, then called the Auckland 'circus gardens'. In honour of the Eden sisters, their name belongs to the ground. It was through their efforts that cricket was played here. The first links date back to 1864, while the locals were only allowed to enter its portals in the early 1880s. The first matches featured games between European and Indian schools.

Arguably it could be renamed Eden 'circus' after the 1996 World Cup semi-final fiasco between Sri Lanka and India and the behaviour of the crowd during the Hero Cup semi-final between West Indies and Sri Lanka when the crowd threw crackers at West Indies fielders. There was also the Asian Test championship match versus Pakistan in 1999, when crowd misbehaviour led to a threat to take away the valued Tests status. Then in March 2001 the Australians played and lost one of the most dramatic Tests ever after forcing India to follow on.

South Africa's semi-final against India in the Hero Cup was a day-night affair in the big city with Azharuddin winning the toss and India batting first, which pleased the impressive, usually boisterous, crowd of more than 90,000. They greeted each scoring stroke with rowdy enthusiasm while thunder flashes and a series of fireworks went off in a continuous echoing cacophony of celebration when Azharuddin reached his half-century with a neatly placed cut.

Fielding under such conditions was trying enough, but as most South African players had contracted a variety of persistent ailments from sore throats to Delhi-belly, they were far from jovial. What did help was the knowledge that their trying three weeks in India was almost at an end. From Mohali, where they lost their league section match to India to the semi-final two days later, the team management were stretched to put a fit side on to the field. Yet there was nothing wrong with the disciplined fielding exercise that kept the run rate down as India were forced to struggle to survive. That they scored 195 off 50 overs was due to Azharuddin's choice batting and Praveen Amre's untidy but solid grit.

Even the biased crowd acknowledged Daryll Cullinan's brilliant fielding. He had a strong hand in two run-outs that had the Indians blinking in envy as they stumbled to 18 for 3 in the early overs. That Cullinan barely escaped injury when a cracker went off under him as he successfully dived to stop a ball careering into the signboards went all but unnoticed. In such a tight game the crowd desperately wanted a boundary.

Those in the section that threw the small explosive item were in no mood for yet another classic South African fielding lesson and ignored Cullinan's angry glance. For them, Azharuddin's textbook 90 gave a bare hint that India's total may yet be a winning score. They loved him. How different it was two-and-a-half years later. During the World Cup semi-final the Gardens multitude bayed 'Chor! Chor!' (thief) when he walked out to the after-match presentation, with placards in Bengali denouncing the team as 'selling your pride and our honour'. His effigy was burned in April 2000 as his role in the Cronjegate scandal emerged.

Towards the end of that Hero Cup tournament, all was not well in the South African camp. Apart from the stomach illnesses and other sniffles, there was news from home that Schultz's recovery from the knee operation was not in keeping with the timetable set by Peter Pollock and the other selectors. It meant that the side would go to Australia without the aggressive left-arm fast bowler.

At Eden Gardens, after the lights had been turned on that night of 24 November 1993, three of the front line bowlers, Snell, Donald and McMillan had bowled tidily but given away too many runs (118) in 27 overs at a cost of 4.3 an over: included were 8 extra balls through no-balls and wides. Fanie's figures of 10-1-19-3 displayed for the first time during the series his significance as a limited-overs bowler. His outswing troubled the Indians who faced him.

Azharuddin was again suitably impressed. How on earth had he missed the Test series the previous summer? He had shown all the skill and craft of a world-class swing bowler and deserved respect. The Indian captain felt that Fanie, more than any other bowler, had almost snatched an implausible victory for the South Africans. Less than 2 runs an over: you cannot do much better than that at international level. Only, it was not enough: South Africa were bowled out for 193—3 runs short. The old story: so near, yet so far. Both Dave Richardson and Fanie were run-out, attempting to give McMillan the chance to fashion the winning runs. How frustrating. The innings had been allowed to stutter along after a couple of questionable lbw decisions sent back an exasperated Wessels and Cullinan.

Down to the last 5 overs and 45 runs were needed for South Africa to reach their first limited-overs final. Thirty balls between success and failure and McMillan hitting into the gaps to rub out the deficit. Fanie was sent back when a second run was there for the asking, but Big Mac declined the offer. He looked up in time to see his partner run-out. Oops! Sorry, Fanie. It looked too risky.

Defeat by 2 runs. You cannot get much closer than that. Only defeat can be less subjective if the circumstances are carefully examined. A tired, sick South African side lost because it had been stretched beyond the limit with a punishing itinerary. Is it any wonder that Wessels felt that luck was not going the way of his team?

As for Fanie, he also had serious family matters nagging his off-the-field thoughts. At home he had left a heavily pregnant wife, and his daughter, Suné, had been diagnosed as having suffered a serious middle-ear infection that was to lead to deafness. A heavy burden for any young expecting mother to handle. It was around noon, Indian time, in Mohali on 22 November when Judy went into labour. Rushing from the field after taking 2 for 27, ending the Indian innings with the second ball of the ninth over when he had Kapil Dev caught by Wessels for 22, Fanie put a call through to Judy in the maternity section of a Pretoria hospital.

'I'm fine, Fanie. Don't worry,' she said brightly. 'I've just had the first contractions.'

She sounded too cheerful and it worried him. Always the family man, he was disturbed at having to leave his wife to face it alone. At

Jan Smuts airport he had reassured himself that all would be well, taking Judy aside to have one last discussion. He had already spoken at some length to the gynaecologist, Dr Gonin, who had delivered Suné. The specialist had carefully explained that there would be no complications with the birth of the second de Villiers child.

During the South African innings in Mohali, with half the team suffering from serious stomach ailments, Fanie kept an anxious eye on the clock. What a time to get a bug! And there was trouble contacting South Africa.

Frustration. It nibbled at his subconscious as with half a mind on the unfolding events on the field he tried several times to get through without success. When it was his turn to bat, he felt a growing annoyance with the Indian telephone system. He added 7 runs for the ninth wicket with Dave Richardson before being caught for a single in what was fast becoming a lost cause. Anyway, what else did they expect? Half the team was barely fit to walk let alone bat or field. But the game must go on. And when lunch arrived few felt like eating. Not unless a toilet was handy. Keep on drinking the bottled water, they were told. They could not afford dehydration on top of everything else.

What a relief—contact with Judy at last!

'It's a boy, Fanie. And he's fine. The doctor says he's a healthy specimen.'

Congratulations, Fanie! Finally. It is all over. Good luck.

What is the baby's name? Stephanus. Or Faantjie. Is that it? Just Stephanus? Or Faantjie? Yes. Why saddle a youngster with a list of meaningless names? Keep it simple. It is better that way.

The match lost and the prize-giving over, the team starts packing for Calcutta. Fanie's thoughts turn to his wife and newborn son . . . Faantjie. Faantjie? But that is not what Pat Symcox tells some persistent media members.

'The boy will be known as Pat,' the Natal off-spinner says, doing his bit to embarrass the callers now tired of Symcox answering the phone instead of Fanie. 'That's right. He is being called Patrick Stephanus.'

Symmo smiles. Most sportswriters pick up the story, saying 'Fanie's decided to name his son after his long-standing roomie Patrick Symcox'. Months later, Judy was still receiving congratulatory letters enquiring about the health of young Patrick de Villiers.

Within hours of his son's birth the thoughtful Dr Ali Bacher had made arrangements for Fanie to fly home for a couple of days to see young Faantjie. But he cannot leave until halfway through the final, between India and the West Indies.

Although a number of unruly incidents mark the game, Fanie is disappointed when he leaves the ground for the airport. Even with the heavy traffic congestion he arrives at a near deserted airport: deserted, that is, while the final is in progress. Flights are delayed for several hours and passengers from France, Germany, Spain and the United States, urgently seeking connections to Mumbai, are confounded by the city's inhabitants' unabashed proclivity for 'That crazy British sport—cricket! . . .'

Really, though, is it not an Asian game that was mistakenly invented by the British?

The West Indies, who had two days earlier easily conquered Sri Lanka, crumbled before Anil Kumble's topspin on a dusting pitch. Kumble's return of 6 for 12 as he moved in to bowl the first ball of the seventh over—or 6 for 4 runs off only 26 balls—is the story behind the crash, the Caribbean stylists losing by a humiliating margin of 102 runs with 9.1 overs remaining. After such an impressive result, good-humoured airport officials attempt to sort out the chaos of their own making. A sense of national pride had been restored and the disgruntled passengers are on their way.

After a night stopover in the gloomy Centaur Hotel, Fanie is on his way home. A temporary break away before the second leg of the mission is about to start in Australia with a warm up match in Canberra. The bowlers, after battling in India to get the ball to rise barely above the knee, now find it consistently giving good bounce between knee and shoulder. In conditions more in keeping with those in South Africa the players start to recover. Ahead is yet another series of one-dayers—the World Series Cricket treadmill, an event seen by some as a tasteless hangover from Packer's revolution of the late 1970s.

13

'Never Say Die'

On 25 February 1992 Sydney Harbour is slowly lighting up as a giant catamaran with the proud name of *Dawn Fraser* ploughs her way to safe anchorage with a sister craft, *Marlene Matthews,* linking leeward. The sun is about to sink behind a bank of cloud to the west of the old coathanger, the Sydney Harbour Bridge, while the famous sail-like cones of the Opera House are permanent reminders of one of modern architecture's finer symmetrical achievements. It is the eve of South Africa's World Cup game against Australia at the Sydney Cricket Ground; a celebratory evening to rekindle the fires of Australian-South African fellowship. On board, the three hundred or so guests are filling up on chilled orange juice well laced with sparkling wine and tucking into hors d'oeuvre offerings of salmon, smoked oysters and caviar. It is chilly, but the threatened rain has gone.

What is strange is a group of Kiwis and Australians, including John Reid, discovered sitting at a corner table in the upper lounge: it is, after all, a party uniting South African and Australian ties. Not that the Kiwis are gatecrashing. At the table there are famous names: among them two great left-handers, Bert Sutcliffe and Neil Harvey, along with West Indian Everton Weekes. In the 1950s, Harvey's run-making record against South Africa was equal to Bradman's in the summer of 1931-32. While most talk, jingoistic in flavour, centres on the match now less than eighteen hours away, Harvey is unhappy about Australia's chances.

'I don't want to say this too loudly, but we're going to get walloped tomorrow night.'

Sutcliffe smiles, Weekes shrugs and Reid agrees. Limited-overs matches are a cut-throat business: the shorter the game, the bigger the upset, and he knows how keen South Africa are to win this one. As for Harvey, there are serious reasons for his disillusionment with the current Australian side.

'The guys are tired . . . flat,' he offers. 'Too many one-day games. We saw it on television the other day when they lost to you fellahs. There are also those with swollen heads. Dean Jones for one. Thinks he's greater than Bradman. I ask you . . .'

Reid, Sutcliffe and Weekes are surprised by Harvey's last disgruntled comment. It is strange to hear a great player of their era firing off poisoned arrows at a great player of a later age. The three have respect for Jones: his one-day record is just too good to ignore. 'There are guys with better records in the side, and those who aren't playing,' Harvey offers.

Outside, the sun has finally set on the emerald city. Inside, the bash is in full swing. Harvey assures the others that his complaint is justified.

Garrulous, at times insufferable, Dean Jones was rarely far from the centre of action, whether playing or not. His captaincy of Derbyshire in 1996 enabled the tall rawboned Victorian to add more than playing skills to the often down-at-heel team. His irrepressible Australian attitude rubbed off on county players. They even rediscovered enjoyment for the game: a competitive mood and a willingness to win saw them surprise themselves and finish second in the county championship. It was not enough.

Within twelve months Jones had quit and the bells of acrimony pealed discordantly around the shire. Mediocrity has a habit of floating to the surface and Jones' demands for that extra effort were just too much for the county's players. They would rather lose with the stoical calm of a clam about to be popped into a boiling pot of water than accept Jones' challenge.

Perhaps Harvey was harsh in his condemnation, but he was not seduced, as were others, into thinking that the patron saint of the limited-overs game in Australia was the man known as Deano.

* * * *

So we fast-forward some nineteen months to 9 December 1993. South Africa, who beat Australia in Sydney that February night in

1992, are Down Under again, preparing to meet Australia in the opening match of the 1993-94 version of the WSC tournament. A few things have changed since the World Cup. And, glory be, leg-spin bowling is in vogue again. Shane Warne has emerged from a mediocre start to his career with the fancy media sobriquet 'Wizard of Oz' after his England tour success as well as wickets against New Zealand in the more recent Test series. Those no longer fitting in with the post-World Cup plans include Merv Hughes (injured), Geoff Marsh, Bruce Reid, Mike Whitney, Peter Taylor, Tom Moody and Dean Jones.

No doubt the Australian selectors felt that the time had come for a change in their thinking when they announced the squad for the triangular series, which also involved New Zealand. Effusive views or not, there was no place for Jones: the last great link (with Allan Border) of an earlier era in the one-day thrash had been lost. There was expectation he would be recalled for the limited-overs games after being axed from the side which toured England in the northern summer and ignored for the three Tests against the Kiwis. But Bobby Simpson and the selectors had other thoughts.

Five months later, Jones had a surprise for the Aussie selectors. It was time to retire as an international player. In a bald statement datelined Bloemfontien, which first appeared in the South African papers, he admitted to no longer having an appetite for involvement in the gaudy limited-overs caravan. Brought back for the final matches of the limited-overs games in Oz, he was then included in the South African leg of the back-to-back series. But the frenetic pace and the players wearing garish uniforms made if seem little more than a circus with sponsors, promoters and officials forever seeking the gold edge of the cashflow rainbow. Values which for more than 250 years were part of the traditional game were being abused.

Amid all this, there came an opinion of how good Sir Donald Bradman would have been in the limited-overs game with its restrictions on fieldsmen and bowlers. Trevor Bailey spoke of his own experience to illustrate the point. In mid-May 1948 the Australians, playing Essex at Southend, had scored 721 runs in a day. In the middle of this carnage, Bailey was handed the ball to bowl to Bill Brown and the Don. A tall Queenslander, Brown was a stylish yet solid top-order batsman with a remarkable first-class record and a Test career average of 46.82. On that 1948 tour, he scored eight centuries (second to Bradman) and 1,448 runs at 57.92 having played in only two Tests.

Tom Pearce, the Essex captain, set the best defensive field possible and Bailey bowled as best he could. But the future England all-rounder lacked the experience to bowl tight and after a few overs he found the exercise of bowling to Brown and Bradman 'slightly boring'. The Cambridge undergraduate mentioned this to his captain. 'I suggest you carefully examine the scoreboard,' was Pearce's wry comment.

Bailey did, and discovered that the score had moved from just under 150 to near-300 in a matter of fifty minutes. Bradman had long passed his century and only then did Bailey recall the way the Don had worked the ball around: always finding the gaps and taking any number of short singles as well as driving numerous fours. The batsmen were quick to turn over the score in the typical limited-overs fashion seen today. In a first-class game this is often entertaining and places the fielding side under pressure; in a one-day game, the tactic has its purpose but in mid-innings it becomes a tiresome exercise. This is, of course, a purist's opinion. Kerry Packer looks at it differently. It is a popular form of the game and brings in revenue. That is a cogent argument as the sport is also a form of entertainment.

There was strong criticism of the Australians' batting effort against Essex from the caustic pen of Bill O'Reilly. 'It was full-scale jollification at the expense of an attack, which was completely incapable of self-defence,' he later wrote. While Bailey admitted the attack was weak, it was not as bad as O'Reilly had made out.

As South Africa had reshaped their side since the World Cup, so had the Aussies by the start of the 1993-94 season. Yet expectations were high for a close series. This time, however, there was no fancy harbour party on 8 December for the supporters' groups to celebrate the resumption of hostilities. It was a different scenario: South Africa, making their WSC debut, had long graduated from their role of the limited-overs international pupils. Under Wessels and Procter, with quality input from Peter Pollock's selection panel and Dr Ali Bacher's vision, a tight professional group had been created. But even the most carefully planned pre-tour exercise does not allow for a squad of players, preparing for three days in conditions as foreign as Calcutta, to arrive in Australia exhausted, unfit and in most cases with stomach and flu ailments.

It was more like a side at the end of a physically draining tour, not one about to start the most important undertaking since readmission. There were many moments of frustration, as if the side had developed a series of prickly blood blisters for which there was no cure.

And would it not have been easier to train instead in Australia: give the players more time to recover from the distress of the subcontinent? At least it would ease them into their new surroundings. All the time, Wessels and Procter knew what challenges there would be. If it had been hard in India, surely it was going to be far tougher on this continent?

Not surprisingly the tour began badly: losing to Victoria in a four-day game by 6 wickets after the defeat in Canberra by the Prime Minister's XI in a limited-overs slog. Some media men had already labelled the side 'decidedly disappointing, showing a lack of character with no distinctive or redeeming features'. Harsh words. There were others, however—Richie Benaud, Tony Grieg and Ian Chappell, hardly members of the Aussie establishment press—soberly arguing that the tourists, having arrived after a taxing month in India, needed time to settle. There was no doubt that the three extra days in Calcutta exacerbated the illnesses. In Procter's view, there was no miracle cure for the list of players suffering from their Indian experience. Give it ten days. Wessels agreed. The players would recover.

It was hard enough overcoming the prejudice of a brash jingoistic press which had made up its mind. In reality, it was the typical early tour media paranoia and psychology tactics; the thing to do was to ignore them and get on with the job.

What was more worrying for Wessels and Procter was the unnecessary injury to Brian McMillan in the Victoria game. The all-rounder, a key component in their limited-overs strategy, needed surgery to repair damaged knee ligaments caused by the shoddy repair work to the MCG surface: the turf had been seriously despoiled in many areas as a result of pop concerts by U2 and Madonna. The groundstaff laid matting strips on the run-ups and the studs on McMillan's bowling boots catching in the jute-like material did the rest. Agony was etched deeply on his face when he limped off and the diagnosis was that he would miss the opening four WSC games as well as the first, and possibly the second, Tests.

Procter was not impressed with the poor renovation of the run-ups and was concerned that there could be other injuries. It was McMillan's mishap, which led to Gary Kirsten's call up, amidst talk at home over the move. There were those, who queried replacing a proven Test player with a left-hand opening batsman with no limited-overs credentials, and considered at best a spare-parts spinner. It was a superficial argument as Kirsten should have been in the side from the start. At least the former South African Schools captain gave the tourists a fit, fresh batsman who had escaped the rigours of the subcontinent. He also added weight to the fielding needs.

Fanie arrived in Melbourne from South Africa the day of the match in Canberra, but the tour selectors rested him from the Victoria game: they needed to give other players an outing and in the absence of Andrew Hudson and Daryll Cullinan, Wessels and his vice-captain, Hansie Cronje, opened the batting. Not entirely a surprise move. Wessels is well known for his tough mental attitude; it displayed his leadership qualities and the discipline needed to develop confidence among a side still troubled by the subcontinent experience. Some shrug it off easier than most. Fanie arrived from a brief trip home, tired but refreshed to confront the Australian batsmen with his own brand of swing, seam and off-cutters; and on pitches where there was good carry with far more bounce and lateral movement than those wastelands often encountered in India.

He discovered, during his first net at the MCG, how easily he could swing the ball, opening up the left-hander, such as say Allan Border and even Mark Taylor, to cunningly disguised outswing which he angled and brought back sharply, forcing the batsman into a false stroke.

Fanie knew that the limited-overs series was going to be tough. Wessels had talked about it often enough. In India, victory was based on better skills, performances and a certain amount of luck. In Australia, it would also include a new sort of mind game. You needed to be tough to survive. The Aussies were different from the Indians, their game was more competitive. And as a leader

Border was a hardened adversary, with highly developed playing skills which were from a different finishing school. His badge of office, in an age when it was politically correct and egalitarian to have strong patriotic thoughts, was the green baggy cap. He wore it proudly and rebuked those within the team who thought they were above 'that sort of thing'. As expected of him, in that 1993-94 season he often bore the unfortunate sobriquet 'Cap'n Grumpy' with a touch of irritation.

Even a gentle enquiry at a media conference from Peter Deeley, of *The Daily Telegraph*, of Border's decision not to bowl Shane Warne until a particular phase of the South African second innings of the Wanderers Test drew a rebuke. This was after the Shane Warne incident with Andrew Hudson.[1] 'I think I am better qualified than you to decide when I shall bowl Warne,' was the pungent thrust from the captain.

Yet, the same man would admit to preferring a drink at a workman's pub than an up market establishment because he would feel more at home in such casual surroundings. Where Wessels assumed captaincy as a matter of birthright, Border did not. But Wessels' association with Border and his own experiences playing Down Under allowed him to lift the cap off the Australian psyche which helped South Africa to overcome the setbacks experienced during the early WSC matches after that 7-wicket victory at the MCG on 9 December.

The piebald state of the outfield was still a matter of concern for the fielders, but the Aussies failed to build on the century first wicket partnership of Mark Taylor and Michael Slater. Then tight bowling, solid fielding and a Wessels innings of character for a deserving half-century laid the foundation for Hansie Cronje's showpiece. An undefeated score of 91 had barely helped South Africa to their stunning victory when the beer cans were being cracked open. It was almost like Sydney all those months before. But not quite. Nothing could repeat the atmosphere of that night

---

[1] The Wanderers in March 1994. Moments after bowling Hudson for 60 in the second innings, Warne gesticulated and abused the departing batsman. Warne and Merv Hughes were both heavily fined while Australia lost the Test by 197 runs.

of magic: that had been a very special evening for Wessels and the South Africans.

Fanie should have been happy with his 3 for 30 return off 7.5 overs in his first game. But a spark was missing from his bowling that night.

'You do what you can,' he says. 'One day it is right there. The ball is swinging and the batsmen are getting the nicks. Another day you are bowling better and there are no wickets. Your swing beats the edge. And you think to yourself that "it just can't be". Like that time I bowled to Joubert Strydom at Centurion Park . . . But it happens.'

By the time they reached Brisbane for the Test warm up against Queensland, the victory at Melbourne had been followed by a serious credibility problem: defeat to New Zealand in Hobart had left their WSC series plans in need of a new strategy to rebuild confidence. Wessels knew it was going to be tough. The success sought so badly was missing, and the shaky relationship between the captain and Mike Procter, the coach, was starting to show. Some players felt it more than others, although Fanie did what he could to ignore the unpleasant vibes.

It was hot and steamy in Brisbane; Gary Kirsten, short of form, and Fanie anxious to make it in to the Test side, were aware of the challenges. Wessels got it right by winning the toss, but the top-order failed again: at 34 for 3, the tourists were floundering and the scoreboard was not a pretty sight when Cullinan joined Cronje. The air-conditioned press box at the Gabba buzzed expectantly. Murphy's Law seemed to have developed a convincing case against the tourists. They were limping badly. The skipper had a knee problem and had failed to provide evidence that he was able to score runs. Only Cronje and Cullinan silenced the critics. Well-worked centuries apiece did at least put a smile back in the dressing room. But the psychological warfare was stepped up. Border, playing for Queensland, wanted badly to upset the South Africans.

There was much niggling under the surface among the players. Nothing really serious at first, but there was concern over umpiring decisions. After the erratic umpiring in Sri Lanka and later India during the Hero Cup, the players had expected, at the least, high quality consistency from the Australians. If they had cause for concern in the WSC series, what emerged in Brisbane alarmed them and gnawing doubt ate further into their confidence. It was something they did not need at that stage of the tour. For the Northerns swing bowler the Gabba represented his last chance to impress the selectors.

Fanie was acutely aware of the team's problems. From the hours of hard work he put in at Sri Lanka, he knew he was ready to step up and fill the gap left by Brett Schultz; whether the tour selectors realized it was another matter. Wessels had long been convinced that he had at least five or six others to join him in the trench warfare demanded Down Under: Gary Kirsten, Pat Symcox, Allan Donald, Brian McMillan, Jonty Rhodes and Fanie; the others would be good support troops.

Wessels knew that by the time they reached Adelaide for the third Test, they would all be experienced in the toughest theatre of Test combat: mentally strong and fit. As it is, the Australians, as in 1997-98 and 2001-02 had selected venues to suit their bowlers: Melbourne, Sydney and Adelaide. Border, sporting a wicked grin, admitted as much in South Africa in January 1998 when he accompanied the Australian side for the Under-19 World Cup tournament. He also confessed to a 'gentle stirring up' of the South Africans in the Brisbane match, a carefully contrived plan to test their reaction to pressure. Apart from Border, Ian Healy and Craig McDermott were also in the Queensland side.

The match at the Gabba snarled along as tempers bubbled below the sweaty, uncomfortably hot surface: a spreading, prickly heat rash, which had got under the skin of some South African players. Wessels had expected little else from his old state teammates; the game was not going to be a picnic for Chopper Wessels and Co. Wessels and Procter did what they could to maintain dressing room calm. They also knew it was not going to last; a word, or expression out of place could set off an unpleasant reaction. 'Don't let it get to you,' an unruffled Wessels said. 'Don't let them upset you.'

After Wessels had declared, setting Queensland 377 for victory in three and a half sessions, Fanie shared the new ball with Donald and went up for a catch against Trevor Barsby with the fourth ball of his first over; the opener seemed to edge an outswinger to

Wessels. Well, perhaps there was too much swing. But Wessels was not convinced, the umpiring had not been good during the match and this appeared to be another such decision.

Early the next day, Fanie had Barsby before him. The batsman had been falling across the yorker each time it had been bowled and shuffled into line.

'Well, what do you make of that, Swinger?' Fanie called down the pitch to the South African wicketkeeper, Dave Richardson, whose reply he did not hear.

Barsby survived a second confident lbw appeal, which de Villiers felt had been pitched in line with off and middle stumps. He wanted to ask the umpire what was wrong with the appeal but merely shook his head, irritated by the decision. Back for a second spell before lunch, de Villiers knew the fifth ball of his first over had found the edge of Barsby's bat and he went up, as did Richardson and the slip cordon. What the . . . ? Jeeze I don't believe it . . .

Fanie stared hard at Barsby, shuffling uncomfortably in his crease; the umpire had neither heard a noise nor detected movement. Thoughts of the Sri Lanka tour came to mind. He looked at the umpire, indifferent and unflinching; and did he detect a snigger in his eyes? When Barsby reached his fifty he did not earn applause from the South Africans. Fanie felt he had been cheated of his wicket three times. The batsman had been playing outside the off and Fanie had swung the ball away or cut it in, yorker length, off the seam.

The heat rash was starting to burst open. Already Border and Wessels had squabbled in the open as the level of umpiring degenerated during the first three days until it was lower than Premier League level. It had added confrontation where there should have been none: a classic example of how incompetency despoils a game, which has long been held up as an example of discipline and character building.

Then, in the last over before lunch, Fanie trapped Barsby in front a fourth time. The batsman had gone into his stumps, bat away from the body as he fell across the line again. No appeal should have been needed, but under the laws it is a requirement. Instead of the umpire raising his index finger there was an implacable 'not out'. Barsby had escaped yet again.

At the end of the over an angry Fanie grabbed his hat and stormed off, muttering how all Australians were cheats: batsmen, umpires, and bowlers. The muttering grew more voluble as he reached the opening to the dog track. Border overheard the comments '. . . just a dirty bunch of cheats' and stepped out of the Queensland dressing room and stabbed a finger at Fanie.

'You lousy . . . little s***t. You little punk. Who the f*** do you think you are ?'

Fanie swung around, about to emerge from the South Africa dressing room. He was ready for a fight and would have floored the Australian captain. He was tired of all the bullshit being dished out by the umpires and was prepared to back his words with a fight if need be. It was that close.

Wessels acted swiftly. 'Don't *ever* talk to any of my players that way. If you want to say something, you come to me first. I'll handle it.'

Border swung around. 'You keep your nose out of this, Chopper,' he snarled.

Wessels, being treated for a niggling knee injury, retained his composure as best he could. 'We're not here for a fight. We want a good, hard but clean series. But if you guys want to play dirty, well, we can give it back.'

Border glared at Wessels and turned back into the dressing room, realizing for the first time that South Africa were not going to be a soft touch. They were not New Zealand, or India, or Sri Lanka, or England. It was going to be a tough series. He wrote as much in his syndicated column on the eve of the first Test at Melbourne. Then again, he had not known what to expect. He knew from the WSC games that they were an uncompromising bunch: street-fighters, all of them, more competitive than in the 1992 World Cup; he had also studied Fanie in the limited-overs matches and noted that he could be a threat. At the Gabba, he discovered a more dangerous type of bowler. He was impressed with his swing variations.

While he conceded that Fanie was great in the limited-overs game, the player he saw bowl 9 overs in succession against Queensland was a revelation. His ability to change pace, deliver off-cutters with an outswing action, running the fingers over the seam for maximum purchase, disturbed concentration levels among some Aussie batsmen.

'I realized that here was a world class bowler and wondered why he hadn't been included in the World Cup side,' Border said when talking about the Gabba incident at The Oval in 1999 during the Pakistan Super Six World Cup game against Zimbabwe. 'You want to mentally rough up a few guys but Chopper (Wessels) knew all the tricks. There were a few toughies in that side. We discovered that quickly enough. I warned our guys we were in for a battle. I don't think they believed me. And that guy de Villiers . . . full of good old-fashioned blood and guts.'

Rain wrecked the historical celebration reuniting the southern hemisphere's two powers at the Melbourne Cricket Ground, Christmas 1993. Certainly those first overs on Boxing Day were special, only that Fanie knew he should have had Mark Taylor lbw in his first over. Darrel Hair, however, was not interested: he was inspecting his feet by the time the Test debutant went up for his first appeal of the innings. Fanie turned and looked hard at Taylor and then Hair. It was the Gabba all over again; only replays and the Channel 9 commentary team wondered as well, where the ball was pitching. It was straight enough. Not high, not going down leg either. Well? How about *that* then? For Fanie, the role denied him thirteen months before was finally his. There had been no doubt in his mind that he should have shared the new ball with Donald in the Wanderers Test against India in November 1992. Injury and other misfortunes had pursued him since his first provincial game; it created some doubt among the selectors about his fitness, or his ability to bowl in a Test. But, he complained to Chesters after the Sri Lanka tour, they did not want to give him a chance and seemed to ignore his first-class record. How much longer would it take?

When he was told late in the afternoon on Christmas Day that he was playing. He felt a tinge of excitement. If only the folks were around: Judy and dad and mum. That would have been nice. So very special. Spending Christmas away from home, in another country, meant he was without his family for the first time in many years.

Other players had their wives with them. But they could afford it. Fanie was new to the game at this level and knew that the cost factors were out of reach at the time. Not even a friendly bank manager would have cared much then.

Now he was finally being awarded with his Test cap. Congratulations from home via the telephone. 'Hey, Judy! Skat, they've picked me for the Test.' His voice carried across Australia and the Indian Ocean. 'It's a great feeling . . .'

The first day he had Shane Warne lbw for a duck but Taylor had escaped. The skipper, Wessels, was pleased with the way things had gone. 'Don't worry, Fanie. There's tomorrow.' But rain washed it out. It was cold, damp and miserable, more like England. Making a debut is one thing, being unable to bowl decently because of the weather is another. It was a waste. All the functions for past players, the invitations to lunches, breakfasts, all for nothing.

For Gary Kirsten, who was making his Test debut, it was the sort of eye-opener which shook him. The Aussies, masters in the art of sledging, gave him a warm, verbal welcome: Craig McDermott, chairman of the committee for this particular episode, mouthed off a few 'compliments'. One about how left-handers should bat and the other that his walk to the pavilion was not 'too far off'. This was after the first couple of deliveries were bounced in the area of his ribs and midriff.

Fanie arrived with the South African team in the emerald city two days before the second Test. No changes were made to the team, which drew the game in Melbourne and after the team meeting where the side was announced, the players split into groups. Fanie had been busy with a call home and by the time he finished talking to Judy and looked for Pat Symcox, his roomie, he discovered that no one was around. He knocked on several doors and called out but the rooms were empty. It was New Year's Eve. He went to the hotel foyer and looked in the bars. No friendly faces anywhere; not even a South African journalist to be found. He was alone in a city of four million, and there was no suggestion what to do next.

Fanie, the great explorer, set out from the hotel and started walking. Inner Sydney is always a street party on New Year's Eve. Crowds pack The Rocks and also Circular Quay where there are some great seafood restaurants to catch a glimpse of the massive fireworks set to go off at midnight. Everywhere he sees happy, cheerful groups, some drinking, others eating; there is singing and some dancing as the sun sinks and the hours and minutes are ticked off. They are all in a hurry for midnight to arrive. There are those who recognize the South African fast bowler, wave cheerily and raise a glass but no one thinks of asking him to join them for a drink, or a slice of pizza. All around there is bubbling laughter, but they are just too busy enjoying themselves to worry about Fanie de Villiers.

Amid all the hype of the pre-New Year's build up, Fanie feels like a stranger as he walks among them, an alien on a visit: invisible to some, greeted by others on a hot mid-summer's evening in the emerald city. Within he feels alone, hungry for company; anything to take away the uncomfortable, desolate feeling. There is grief and there is pain. He is missing Judy, Suné and Faantije. After Melbourne and the cheerless atmosphere of the MCG, Sydney was supposed to have been different. An ebullient city of strength and character, cosmopolitan life, warm and reassuring.

Fanie discovered no cheer that night. Memories of visits to a hundred markets on the subcontinent slipped through his thoughts, frame after frame of an instant camera sifting through treasured mementos from a not too distant past. He preferred the bustling, noisy marketplaces in India to this inhospitable city with its cold, uncompromising facade. From the outside, it gave the impression of a tart dressed up for a night of entertainment but unwilling to share the enjoyment.

As he strolled the streets, a nomad in the midst of light, song, laughter and expectancy, the desolation became suffocating. His first thought was to go back to the hotel and watch the celebrations from there; yet he was drawn to Circular Quay: numb and mute in a circle of cheerful, rowdy locals. As he walked under the bridge, amid the revelry he spied other loners. A man walking his dog peering at others hoping for a crumb of conversation; another sitting on a box, drinking a beer, eyeing the cheerful and sanguine, offering an apocryphal message to those who would trespass their space. These were the loneliest hours of his life.

When a hungover Sydney woke up on 1 January 1994, there was the distinct, stench of burning vegetation, trees, houses and livestock. An ugly cloud of thick grey-white smoke stained the horizon and specks of ash had started to fall on spectators as they arrived for the start of the game. It was not a happy omen for the second match of the series and at a venue where South Africa's last Test, under the leadership of Trevor Goddard in 1963-64, had resulted in a draw. Wessels was well aware that the last defeat Australia had at the SCG was sixteen summers ago. Also, Wessels, because of his years in the land of Oz, knew what would be going through Border's thoughts before going out to toss. He also knew that the psychological battle started in Brisbane would continue during the series.

As Wessels made his first inspection of the pitch he winced inwardly. But old poker face gave no outward reaction; not even an ironic smile. And yes, it was worse than he had expected. More like the surface of the moon than a manicured strip of mollycoddled turf. It was going to scuff up the ball, which would quickly lose its shine, negating the swing-bowling potential.

After the deluge and disappointment of Melbourne, Australia desperately wanted to go one up in the series: the SCG presented them with opportunity, with leg-spinner Shane Warne providing the catalyst. It had already been assumed by the Australians that it was going to be Warne's match. He had devastated England and New Zealand in eight Tests before turning his attention to South Africa, who were always suspect against spin. Now watch the new Wizard of Oz work his magic. Over the next decade much more would be written, read, seen and heard about Warne: a bowler who brought an impressive and important dimension back to the game. Already he had had a finger surgery and a shoulder operation: the ruthless demands of playing as many as ten tests a year and three times as many limited-overs games since making his debut in 1991 had extracted a high physical price.

Bill O'Reilly and his mate Clarrie Grimmett may not have lived to see the art they worked hard to develop and preserve, reborn, but they no doubt enjoyed the sight from their pavilion in the sky. They would have, however, frowned at Warne's crassness when claiming a wicket. To adoring Australian crowds it was the sort of by-play they enjoyed: telling a batsman to get on his tricycle and dash home to mummy. Cry-babies shouldn't be involved in the game at this level. You can't mess about: not with 'our Warnie'.

Arguments may differ, but any good leg-spinner is as much a front line bowler as the hordes of quicks, headed by their immortal patron saint Alfred Mynn (1840s) and his later rival for the honour, Tom Richardson (who played for Surrey and England between 1890 and 1902). Australia have always produced good leg-spinners to keep the art alive in the lean years, although the greatest, Grimmett, the man who invented the flipper, was New Zealand-born.

He was special, a genius whose belief in his ability transcended years of struggle. Shortsighted New Zealand and Australian state selectors continually ignored his talent and skill. How he would have enjoyed bowling on pitches made for Warne's acknowledged abilities. Grimmett was afforded no luxury. He was, however, a visionary. Anyone who developed the flipper had to be in a class of his own. His strike rate of almost six wickets a match (216 in 37 outings) is still superior to that of any modern bowler. He was forced to take his talents from Kiwiland to Sydney and then Melbourne before South Australian officials found him a home and gave him the chances he once thought had eluded him.

What is still remarkable about this short, bald and tenacious bowler is his record in South Africa in 1935-36. It was his 44 wickets in five Tests which destroyed Herbie Wade's side that series. He remains, behind the brooding Englishman, Syd Barnes (49 wickets), and tall off-spinner Jim Laker (46), third highest Test wicket-taker in a series in any country. On that tour of South Africa he managed 92 wickets, so did his friend O'Reilly: ahead of them Barnes (102) and Richie Benaud (104), all leg-spinners.[2]

Warne may not have been as dominant in that first Test at the MCG as he had been in the two preceding series during the previous seven months, but at the SCG he was a class above almost anyone else. Arguably bowling in the spongy MCG conditions was hard. Now he had an opportunity to test South Africa's known weakness against the ball moving away from the bat.

In such conditions, winning the toss was always going to be important. At least it would give South Africa a chance to build a

---

[2] Sydney Barnes was an eccentric fast medium bowler who insisted that he got his movement from spinning the ball at high pace rather than conventional swing/seam bowlers' grip. He remains the bowler with the highest strike rate ever—7 wickets per test for 189 in 27 tests.

first innings total if Wessels won it, which he did. But, Warne's line and spin tormented the South Africans as he worked a few tricks on a surface where his action extracted an exaggerated turn. The result was a 7-wicket haul as the tourists succumbed, their technique embarrassingly exposed by the googly and flipper.

Andrew Hudson departed for a duck: lbw to Glenn McGrath with the tourists 1 for 1. Cronje joined Gary Kirsten while Wessels, mindful of the knee problem, moved down the order to six. All went well until Cronje departed for 41 with the score at 91. Not to worry. It was a blistering day: not as humid as Brisbane, but equally hot. Then it came: Warne's flipper to Daryll Cullinan. South Africa had clawed their way to 133 for 3 when the blond leg-spinner fooled the batsman and bowled him. It was special. Warne and the lads from Oz were exultant more at the delivery getting rid of a batsman than who the batsman was. Rhodes soon followed lbw; Kirsten, well stumped by the watchful Ian Healy after nudging his way to 67. The innings was in ruins and as Wessels departed lbw for 3, the seventh wicket to fall, any hopes of winning this match were disappearing as fast as the trees in the raging bushfire. It was almost grotesque the way Warne put it all together, snarling invective in the direction of the departing batsmen.

The crowd was in a buoyant mood as they left the SCG at the close, Oz are 20 for 1, Donald taking Taylor's wicket. But high fives all around, guys. Warnie's taken 7 for 56 and the South Africans are a bunch of cry-babies, peddling their tricycles.

Amid the debris of that first innings Fanie had a good look at the pitch and what it did to the ball. At Melbourne, where he swung the ball, he had struggled to get wickets and was worried. Playing Test matches was not at all easy. And dropped catches did not help his cause either. In Sydney it was going to be different. Or was it?

'I'm in real trouble if I can't get the ball to swing,' he admitted to himself. 'And you can't swing a scuffed-up ball much, well not effectively. I'll just have to rely on off-cutters or some reverse swing may be.'

He recalled the four months spent with Kent in 1990, the shaved pitches and flat seams. He had quickly learnt to perfect the delivery. It was certainly going to come in handy in this game. Yet he rated his chances as the pitch was not made for big run-scoring, with the surface holding. A good length and line also helped, and he worked to pitch the lbw ball full for maximum benefit. As with Melbourne though, the umpires were not interested. It was the last season in Australia before the ICC brought in the international panel system and although Steve Randall had a close look at some appeals, he was quite dismissive of the South Africans.

Chunky David Boon, also known for his in-flight exploits of 1989 when he attempted to break the record for guzzling beer between Oz and London, was Fanie's first victim of the match. A nicely drifting cutter zipped through the bat-pad gap. It was a hard-earned wicket as Fanie had worked for the lbw and the line seemed to be too often outside off with the Tasmanian's deft footwork. As Australia battled to build a substantial lead, Fanie's roomie Pat Symcox picked up the valuable scalp of Mark Waugh. Unbelievable. An lbw appeal upheld at last.

What made Fanie and Donald touchy were the catches going down in the slips. Yet South Africa's bowlers and the ground fielding had taken out a restraining order on Australia's scoring rate that second day. Border's combatants were restricted to 180 runs, losing only 4 wickets. But what a day for the neutral spectator and the connoisseurs, under a hot sun with the smell of bushfires devastating the countryside in some suburbs.

When the score reached 179, the stubborn partnership between Michael Slater and Border was finally terminated. They had added 104 and it had eaten up the overs as the bowling, always South Africa's strong point on this tour, chiselled at the rock of confidence on which the partnership had been founded. Border's ability to play tight and controlled strokes, the wrists down and steering the ball away from danger, influenced Slater's own game plan.

Although the Aussie captain had taken a ball in the face from a mistimed sweep edge off Symcox as he moved towards his anticipated half century, he had batted almost two sessions to reach 49 with long spells of concentration. At this point, however, he made a fatal error against Fanie's bowling. The tall swing bowler had worked to open up the left-hander, forcing him to nudge the ball towards the slips; yet always the ball fell well short. A couple of times, he had squared him up a little quicker with a cutter. Just a little plan to get Border thinking. Remembering the advice from Cyril Mitchley junior about giving the batsman a boundary if it was going to get his wicket.

Already two catches had gone down off his bowling and he was feeling aggrieved at how both batsmen had survived. As he turned, the shadows from the Bradman Stand began to spread across the outfield. He looked up and saw Border a little square on, almost waiting for the off-cutter. He gave him an outswinger instead and the batsman realized too late his error as he played at the ball. Dave Richardson had been waiting for such a chance to go his way. It had been a long afternoon and now, finally, Fanie had induced a false shot, which caught an outside edge, flying away too fine for first slip to take the catch.

'Got 'im!' whooped Tony Grieg to Channel 9 viewers. 'Border's gone to Fanie de Villiers.'

A tireless Fanie, his shirt soaked and face streaked with sweat and dust had reason to grin. His persistent line and length: mixing outswing with cutters and full balls had broken through. And Donald spread further destruction when he bowled Slater in the next over; the batsman, driving too soon, heard the death rattle behind him. During his monumental innings of 92, he was grilled by the sun and also by unthinking spectators for the slow pace. An innings of such stature, not to be overlooked in its importance, could yet provide the foundation which could lead to victory.

For South Africa, about the only blot on the day's hard labour were dropped catches in the slips and an injury to the skipper. When the third slip chance was not grasped, this one off Fanie's bowling, a frustrated Wessels shuffled the slips positions, electing to stand at second. He hated to see the efforts of his bowlers going to waste. Barely had he adjusted himself, that the new batsman Ian Healy edged a Fanie outswinger hard towards the slips. It was Wessels' catch, and the ball was falling short, too. As he dived forward the skipper dug the first and second fingers of the left hand into the turf, splitting the webbing. Fanie had a good sight of the incident. Blood dripped from the fingers and flecked his pants as he left the field after a quiet word with his deputy, Cronje.

As the hand was bandaged, Dr Ali Bacher voiced concern, suggesting an X-ray. A man who had studied medicine, the Doc knew a serious injury when he saw one. Only Wessels, caring more about his troops in the middle, brushed off the injury as nothing more than a 'minor cut'. The next morning the 'minor cut' was seen to be, as Dr Bacher had diagnosed, a serious injury; in this case a compound fracture of the fourth finger.

South Africa, despite Wessels' protest, had lost their captain at a crucial stage of the most important series since isolation had ended. He was upset at having to sit and watch the remainder of the match from the sidelines and upset that he was going home. He had argued against the decision with Dr Bacher and Peter Pollock, the selection panel convener. Rather go home and rest was their advice. There was still the Australian tour of South Africa and he would be needed for that series in February and March. As he looked at the splint designed to protect the broken finger, rankled frustrations surfaced. He was the captain and should be leading his troops, not nursing a hand injury. It was the sort of tough if rough justice, which sat uneasily in his mind.

Pollock had already invited Peter Kirsten, (instead of Jimmy Cook, discarded after Sri Lanka) to join the side; other names to surface were Rudolph Steyn and Gerry Liebenberg. Axed at the end of the previous season, Kirsten owed his recall to a consistent domestic performance which included a career best 271 in a match which had ended only hours before. On the way to his eighth and highest score he had displayed all his old batting trademarks while scoring a double century against a woebegone Northerns attack at Buffalo Park in East London.

It was at the SCG, however, that harsh reality sat on Cronje's shoulders. As smoke from the ravaging bushfires still billowed, Cronje did not require anyone to tell him how important it was to get rid of Australia as quickly as possible as well and restrict their lead. Wessels was constantly in contact with Cronje; it was crucial to the game plan. Although the younger man was a highly competent leader, he also had a team of hardened, skilled players around him. It made him look better than he was.

While Damien Martyn stood firm, Donald broke through at the other end: Richardson picked up Healy for 90, but the lead was already 60. Warne fell to Symcox, and the acting skipper caught Craig McDermott to give Fanie his third wicket. The bowler wondered how much longer he would have to suffer in silence as catches were missed off his bowling. And they talk about Lady Luck! He deserved six wickets, and here he had three. Cronje watched as the Australians built their lead, interpreting Wessels' suggestions with thoughts of his own and consultation with Richardson, and Symcox adding his dollar's worth as well.

All it needed was patience. Not easy for Wessels sitting, watching, thoughts racing through his mind; not easy for Cronje, whose responsibility it now was to pull it together. It was hard work on another day when the hot sun grilled those foolish enough not to wear a hat.

Fanie finally removed Martyn for a stubborn 59, caught behind, and Donald followed with McGrath's wicket: four apiece for the fast bowlers and four catches for Richardson. But Australia had managed to stretch the lead to 123 and that was going to be more than a molehill to climb if South Africa hoped to set a challenging target on the last day.

'It's all up to Warnie.' trumpeted Channel 9 commentator Bill Lawry. 'He has the bag of tricks to win the game on his own.'

Ian Chappell was inclined to agree, although he warned chasing a fourth innings target in excess of 150 could be a tricky exercise on a pitch where it would need quality batting skills to put together even a third innings total of 200 or more.

'Well, should South Africa manage to score 250 or more . . .'

The comment trailed off. Not at all what you would expect from Chappell. He was usually confident, not hesitant. So why the doubt? Sure, South Africa's bowling had been disciplined, tight, economical: Donald 2.66 an over, Fanie 2.22, Symcox 1.78, the wicketless Matthews 1.57. But did the scenario also tell Chappell something the other former Test captains had not seen? Including the ever-perceptive Richie Benaud? 'This pitch has become a real shocker and it's going to be a lot harder to put a big total together,' said Chappell to Bill Lawry. 'Have you batted on worse than this Bill?' Lawry's response was barely audible.

There were times in their second innings when South Africa seemed to have a death wish. Predictably Warne did most of the damage although it was McDermott who claimed the first wicket when he had Andrew Hudson caught behind for a single with only two to the total. Wessels felt anxious as Cronje went out to bat; that molehill had become a mountain.

At home, an equally anxious South Africa watched, or listened to the radio commentary. Gerald de Kock, sounding calm and assured, did not let on to listeners how he too felt anxious for the team. Some TV viewers, preferring the more neutral radio to what they perceived to be the gung-ho sounds issued by the Channel 9 team, would switch off the TV commentary. Yet the Channel 9 team are a quality bunch and make a point; they tell it the way it is; after all, they are all former Test captains and have a better insight than most South African viewers are likely to have.

Early New Year 1994 was also an anxious time in South Africa as the countdown to the first democratic elections began amid a climate of suspicion and uncertainty. For months the ANC and Inkatha, Pan Africanists and others with political splinter group affiliations accused each other of the slaughter of innocents throughout the nation; the April 27 elections may have been a long way off but the country was bleeding: especially the hinterland of KwaZulu/ Natal. It made the events at the SCG, with bushfires near the city greedily consuming all in their path, seem distant and ethereal yet an ever-present fantasy. But like a drug, it occupied the mind and kept people from thinking for a while about the nightmare around them: the calm eye in the middle of a storm.

At the SCG, the vast open-air theatre was full of its own drama: the pitch had deteriorated under the scorching sun, dusting up and pock-marked to become the perfect surface for Warne's wrist spin. Gary Kirsten and Cronje became as unyielding as Martyn had been in the Australian first innings. They were not going to give anything away. There was a total to build and losing wickets through carelessness would not put runs on the board.

McDermott, however, bowled the stoic Kirsten and it was left to the captain and his senior lieutenant to soldier on into the fourth day. At 94 for 2, South Africa were still a long way from winning this match and Australian confidence was growing.

Wessels had his left-hand glove reshaped to fit over the damaged finger, his mood was one of defiance, typifying his courage and indomitable character. His impassive features masked the pain as, with Cronje, he saw the side through to the close. Yet, next morning, all the hard work had been for nothing: both fell early, and when Cullinan was trapped by Warne for two, those eager to wager on the result would give you short odds on an Australian victory by tea that fourth day.

It is a pity that Rhodes' batting technique had earned him a reputation of being essentially a limited-overs player. It was the sort of label, which also haunted Fanie in his early international career and has now cast a shadow over the Natal player's role, typecasting him: a specialist fielder with the ability to bat at six in the order. Yet he had proved himself under pressure. In 1992, it was an innings of 91 against India at the Wanderers, and months before the SCG game, there was the century against Sri Lanka in Colombo. Four years later at Lord's, he showed some of the flair and maturity of those early innings to score a match-winning century, giving him a man of the match award and a reason, if he was so inclined, to thumb his nose at the ever-forgetful critics. Only he is not like that. His decision in early 2000 to make himself available only as a limited-overs player was based on family considerations and this needs to be respected. The recent Victoria Bitter series when he scored a match-winning century against New Zealand in Perth was a typical example of Rhodes' belief in his own ability to overcome a bad start. South Africa had been reduced to 39 for 4 with Dion Nash ploughing through the top-order; Rhodes and Mark Boucher then laid the foundation of a match-winning total. Shaun Pollock took 27 off a single over to hoist the total out of reach of the Kiwis' hopes.

At Sydney in January 1994 it was different. For some unexplained reason, a feeling of confidence had taken firm hold of Rhodes, when he joined a jittery Cullinan with the score at 107 for 4. It was the sort of confidence, which made him jig, rather than walk, to the crease with Wessels, words of 'do what you can' whirling through his mind. A glance as the massive electronic scoreboard showed the position was far more precarious than at Colombo. South Africa needed 16 more runs to get Australia to bat again and three batsmen to follow had all scored first-class centuries. That was the good news. The bad news? Well, all those three-figure scores had been made under far less searching conditions than these.

What also crossed the pragmatic Rhodes' thoughts was the immediate task of building a match-winning total, but to do that there was a need to build partnerships. Plan A folded just 3 runs later: a transfixed Cullinan departed as the Australians celebrated Warne's second victim of the morning. First Wessels, then the sight of a dejected Cullinan making his exit to a jeering SCG crowd. The omens were not good when Richardson joined Rhodes.

At home there were those who turned off their television or radio. It was becoming a lost cause. Better sleep on it. No Moratuwa miracle this time.

In the Channel 9 commentary box some suggested that the game could be over by tea and a welcome day-off loomed. They even took bets whether Warne would take the remaining wickets. It was going to be that easy.

They all reckoned without keeping Rhodes and Richardson in mind. 'We had to get runs on the board and to do that we needed a couple of partnerships,' Rhodes once explained. 'Batting it out for two days was out of the question as we too wanted to win the match. I knew if we could get a lead of say, 120 it would be enough.'

Just the sort of confidence Wessels had hoped for from his troops, as they waged their hand-to-hand combat. Rhodes did not even find the pitch full of hidden booby traps. For one thing, he found it easier to bat on than he had expected. But you had to watch Warne. He was the real danger. 'Play forward' was the motto of the partnership with Richardson. At first it was far from easy and there were narrow escapes. He had to remember to keep his pads out of the way of the flipper and the googly. He also applied the important lessons learnt from the century at Moratuwa. They had added 72 precious runs and started building a lead as the Australians became frustrated and Border changed tactics and switched around his bowlers.

The South Africans had battled for close to two hours and the Australian captain found that while Tim May was being economical, he was not taking wickets. Border even gave himself a couple of overs to tempt Rhodes before calling up McGrath. Finally, success, as 'Pigeon' McGrath trapped Richardson in front for 24. Further disaster followed as the seventh and eighth wickets soon fell. Warne, recalled after a brief rest, dismissed Matthews after McDermott saw the back of Symcox.

Rhodes had watched his hard work going to waste with concern. 4 wickets had fallen for 21 as the South African resistance movement

Around South Africa, the television images on the SuperSport channel that breakfast time had attracted a growing audience, some hopeful, fascinated by the duel of wits, others still sceptical. There was a buzz developing along Main Street, South Africa.

When the breakthrough came, it seemed ordained that the wickets would go to Fanie. First Boon fell, caught bat-pad by Gary Kirsten. Jubilation on the field and in the dressing room. Although there were still several overs of the day's play left, May was sent in as a night watchman. Fanie's first ball to the off-spinner was the perfect lbw delivery and he was on his way. From 51 for 1 to 51 for 3 in 2 balls and suddenly the pressure was on as Mark Waugh joined Taylor. He safely negotiated the hat-trick ball and the dramatic over ended.

Fanie had waited a long time to play his first Test and now, all the experience gained over the past eight summers, and the three seasons in England began to pay dividends. He was relaxed as he came in for his next over with a single off the first ball. Taylor, whom he should have had at the MCG, got a lifter, which found the edge and Richardson gratefully accepted the catch. Australia had slumped to 56 for 4 as the fieldsmen swarmed around the new South African hero. Just one more wicket. That's all they wanted before the close.

Rhodes was too modest to say to Cronje, 'Didn't I tell you we can win this game?'

A brooding Border arrived, stood foursquare and batted tightly through to the end of the day and retired to the dressing room to plot the next day's tactics. At 63 for 4, it was going to be a close run game.

There was a bit of spice as well about the after-day's play media conference at the SCG, which was as refreshing, as it was thought provoking. As he later admitted, Fanie put on a show of arrogance, which surprised some Australian media. Just who the hell is this guy? Playing in only his second Test and here he is shouting the odds. In a tight if stilted accent, he let the Aussies know they were in for a fight. Here was a street-fighter who was not about to give up and he let their media in on his philosophical thinking. 'I want to tell you now,' he said directly into the microphones and bank of tape recorders, 'the Aussies had better watch out. We can still win this Test. If we can get a breakthrough in the first seven overs, and get two guys out then the pressure is really going to be on them. 'I don't think they are going to play any big shots. They can't afford to do that. Go for the singles and twos and try and get them that way. We're going to have so many more overs to bowl at them and that counts in our favour. It's definitely still on, believe me . . .'

Stirring thoughts of self-belief. Powerful stuff all right. Yet in those days, he was inclined to be shy of the way he spoke English and selected his words carefully in case he made a mistake. It was not the Northerns dressing room, where they sometimes laughed when he mixed his tenses. It was a media conference during a Test. At the SCG that Wednesday evening, it seemed to go so well. As he walked back to the dressing room he felt relaxed and cheerful. He fully believed in what he had said.

The bushfires were still rampant around Sydney, smoke smudging the horizon, when Fanie arrived at the SCG with other members of the side; the vibes of victory were strong. He felt it. Rhodes felt it; even Donald had a good feeling about the next two hours. That's when it would all be over: the victors and the vanquished.

As the team went through the routine of their morning exercise Fanie managed to get a long, hard look into the Australian psyche. They were battening down the hatches, a little jumpy: the pressure was starting to bother them. They had also found gremlins in the pitch on which Warne was to have spun them to victory. Now they had a target of 54 runs to get with 6 wickets in hand. Easy? Well, some newspaper writers thought it would be. Border was still there, and that was a psychological bonus: the catalyst that would take them to an important 1-0 lead. But it is such an unpredictable game. As Wessels explained when recalling the drama and apprehensions surrounding the pre-session warm up.

'I told them not to worry. They are more worried about getting those runs than we are about taking their wickets. They have gone through this before . . .' He grinned from memory.

The signposts read: Headingley 1981, Edgbaston 1981, Melbourne 1982, Madras 1986, Adelaide 1993—narrow losses all. Some of those were carved into a special memory box belonging to Border. The legend was playing his last Test at his old home ground and he wanted it to be a memorable victory.

Perhaps, after all, Australia were the original chokers: at Test level anyway.

'You know, all we need is six wickets and all that takes is six balls,' said Fanie, showing the sort of confidence, which surprised Dr Bacher, Pollock and Krish Mackerdhuj.

'It's pressure. It's all about pressure.' He gave a cheery grin.

Even an optimist such as the Doc wondered whether Fanie had not overstated the team's chances of victory when he read his comments in the *Sydney Morning Herald*. He had bought the paper while out on his early morning jog and was surprised by the headline: 'We can still win this Test'.

Wessels and Cronje discussed tactics and the captain had a few words with Donald. He had worked out a theory about Border and passed on his thoughts.

Before they went out, Cronje called the players together in the middle of the room. Wessels stood back. He was no longer part of this show. 'Okay boys, we know we can do it. Let's go and show them we can win. Let's do it for Kepler . . . He batted with a broken hand to help us.'

Cronje smiled as the others nodded and walked out. So much to do, such a long wait and Fanie, calm and assured, smiled at his new-ball partner.

'Leave a couple of wickets for me to get,' he whispered. 'It would be nice to get ten in a match.' Not even for Northerns had Fanie taken ten wickets in a game.

Yet his role in this match had already been etched on the South African roll of honour. He had knocked over four the previous day and given the side the glimmer of hope they had desperately wanted. As he went out, he checked to see whether his old friend from his Torquay days, Mike Gerits, was in the crowd. Well, he was going to be in for a treat as well.

'Okay guys,' Cronje clapped his hands. 'Let's go and win this one for Kepler.'

Border prepared to face Donald as he marked out his run-up. The 16,000 or so spectators let in free were restless. At home, not too many were watching the game at that time of the morning, but Judy was, with Suné and a sleeping Faantjie next to her .

Donald pounded in to deliver the second ball of the morning; expecting an outswinger Border padded up, lifting the willow wand, but the ball sliced back off the seam and clipped the bail off the off stump. There were moments of sheer elation for an arm-waving Donald and his teammates. In the Aussie dressing room, the dismissal stunned the other players, its psychological impact caused shock waves. The crowd groaned inwardly, Border was to have been the man they expected to take them to victory. Barely had they settled down that he was on his way back.

There was no doubt that Donald had been lifted by Border's wicket. The adrenalin has been pumping since that moment and the tall, wiry fast bowler was accurate and hostile. He wanted another wicket, so did South Africa.

When it came, it had been thirty-four minutes since Border's shock early departure and Australia had managed to add only 9 runs to the total.

8 overs later, Donald trapped Mark Waugh for 11 with a lightning yorker, the ball keeping low. There was no hesitation from umpire Steve Randell. It seemed as though the innings was imploding. Donald had broken through, sewing doubt and confusion in the lower order.

Only eight minutes had passed after Waugh's departure, when Healy attempted to drive an outswinger from Fanie, but the ball cannoned into the stumps from the inside edge. 3 wickets had fallen for 10 runs, with Healy Fanie's fifth wicket of the innings and ninth in the match. The tourists now sniffed the scent of victory.

Warne and Martyn had been in partnership for nine minutes when the leg-spinner survived a lbw appeal from Fanie, which had even the Channel 9 commentators quaking: it had been that close. Warne then pushed a ball into the covers and Cronje was quickly into the act. He charged after the ball, picked it up and, although his balance was not perfect, his aim at the stumps was sensationally accurate. Square leg umpire Bill Sheahan had no doubt that Warne had not made his ground. There were more celebrations in the middle for the South Africans who had gathered around Cronje. Moments of uproar and uncertainty.

The spectators had become as jittery as the Australian players. The scoreboard read 75 for 8, and such was the tension, that few grasped that only 12 runs had been scored for the loss of 4 wickets in a matter of fifty-three minutes. The mind games during those emotionally-driven moments have been a numbing exercise.

The South African players on the field were calm. Cronje was doing a great job, but he wanted to take Fanie off; the bowler shook his head.

'Not yet. Give me another over.'

Each time Cronje acceded to the request, worried though whether he was making the right choice.

McDermott had taken over from Warne and decided it was time someone set about winning this game, taking control of affairs. As a tail-end batsman, his record had not stood up to scrutiny and now he wanted to show how the obstacles the top order had placed in his path could be overcome. There were some lusty backfoot drives, and a square cut thrown in as well. Donald travelled for a couple of fours and Fanie, too. Yet the swing bowler had forced McDermott into mistakes. A ball popped off the bat agonizingly close to Kirsten. Another looped over Symcox's head. As it is, Symcox has already missed a catch. The scent of victory was beginning to drift away.

This was followed by a couple of fours and suddenly the score was 110 for 8. Only 7 runs were needed when Donald was brought back after being rested and Matthews was asked to warm up.

'No. You can't bring him on now,' Fanie firmly told Cronje. 'Give me another one . . .' It was his eleventh over of the morning and although his shirt was sweat-soaked there were no signs of fatigue.

Cronje looked questioningly at the Northerns bowler. What if . . . ? Fanie bowled a maiden.

The fifth ball of Donald's seventeenth over induced Martyn to drive into the covers for Hudson to pick up an easy catch. Martyn's vigil of 106 minutes, in which he scored only 6 runs, is over. The innings that was frustrating South Africa's victory efforts that session has finally ended. Perhaps . . .

Down from the pavilion came the stripling McGrath, tall and looselimbed, to face Donald. McGrath scrambled a cheeky single and now faced Fanie. It would have been better had McDermott declined the single, but runs had become a precious commodity.

'Another over,' Fanie pleaded with Cronje. 'You simply can't take me off now. I'll get this wicket for you.'

Brave, confident words. He also knew that if they went to lunch with Australia nine down, South Africa would lose. He remembered from the first innings not to drop short or bowl half volleys to McGrath. He had to get the wicket in this, his twelfth over of the morning. The first two balls were tight in line and length. The third he held back, McGrath pushed forward too soon and Fanie reached out to scoop up the return catch. As he threw the ball in the air, Kirsten and Rhodes pounced on him and whooped in glee. Australia's total of 111 was their lowest score at home against South Africa. The rest of the players engulfed him.

McGrath stood still, the agony and the pain of defeat reflected in his eyes. It was a moment he once admitted, which has returned to haunt him for longer than he would care to remember.

Fanie found he was being hoisted onto Cronje's shoulders, his figures of 6 for 43 would forever be enshrined in South African sporting folklore. What a colossus he had become in the shadow of victory. South Africa had won the fourth closest match in Test history; the feeling was euphoric.

Other members of the side, who had sat in the pavilion and watched the unfolding drama for two hours, joined their heroes. Wessels had the victory he had long cherished. The Australian second innings capitulation had been a major turnaround after South Africa had been forced to battle it out on the backfoot until 'Fantastic Fanie' had dismembered their top order.

Fanie, swept up in the gamut of emotions for several minutes after taking the final wicket, managed to untangle himself from the melee of excited South African players and was walking towards the boundary fence when he saw Mike Gerits. As they waved to each other, Fanie tugged off his sweat-soaked shirt and threw it to his old Torquay teammate. Then he put on a clean shirt and went off to the media briefing.

'He probably would have bowled until three this afternoon if he needed to,' a jovial Mike Procter said. 'We just hung in there. We always believed we had a chance. You can't believe the guts and character of these guys.'

A grim-faced Border put Australia's defeat in another light. 'We need to learn how to play sweaty palm cricket if we hope to win these tight games.'

When it was to his turn Fanie let it be known it was a team effort when he uttered the now famous, 'You know South Africans, we never give up.' He looked like one of the steel-willed warriors adorning the hall of heroes in a fabled Greek mythological tale. An avid reader of Homer, and a man who absorbs books on ancient Greece, the sun-tanned swing bowler faced the media and told it the way it was. 'We said before the start of play that 6 wickets was all we needed to win. Our loss to West Indies in Barbados when we collapsed showed us anything can happen. We knew we had to stay positive and we did. . . It was great to get that last catch, though. Caught and bowled catches are reflex things. They either stick or they don't. But the great advantage for us today was, we knew how the surface would play.' He had said his piece and it was time to go. To phone Judy and call his dad were next on his list of priorities. First, however, he had to call in on the Australian dressing room and shake a few hands. It was the sporting thing to do.

Barely a sound emerged from their dressing room when Fanie entered. It had been thirty minutes since the game was won and he was surprised to see it almost empty. Most were having a drink with the South Africans; a couple of stragglers, fresh from the shower, had just dressed and were on their way to join the celebrations on the other side of the pavilion veranda. Clothes, many still damp from the sweat of combat and defeat, and gear, discarded for the day, lay in untidy heaps scattered around the wooden tiled floor. He casually strolled in with a cheerful, 'Hello, guys . . .'

What greeted him was the distressed figure of McGrath. Still dressed in white flannels, his pads strapped to his long legs he did not, at first, look up. He was wrapped in a self-imposed solitary confinement, forehead resting on top of the bat handle. When he did look up, the circular imprint on his skin showed up as would a large date stamp: a date marking his moment of failure and victory for the South Africans. The sweat had dried down the side of his young face; his eyes were slightly puffy with a trace of red. There was anguish as well, and not surprisingly, the eyes were questioning, too.

Fanie understood all too well. He had been to that place too, more than once in his early years. A place where the vanquished buried an aching hurt and bruised pride. What words of comfort to offer a fellow fast bowler, especially one you had dismissed in a moment of exhilarated excitement? McGrath half smiled and placed his forehead on the bat handle once more before he sighed and sat up. So far, yet so close. There would be other Tests: matches where he would bowl his side to victory. Perhaps not in the next match, but some day . . .

'Don't blame yourself,' Fanie said quietly. 'I know how you feel. I've been in your position. These things happen. It was your batsmen who let you down. The way things were, you should not have batted.'

Fanie patted McGrath's shoulder. His days of glory have come since: there have been triumphs at home and away for the gangly Australian: in the West Indies and England and South Africa, as well as skirmishes against Pakistan and India and Sri Lanka.

For Fanie, however, Sydney was his long awaited milestone to fame, but certainly not to riches. His Test career had started at twenty-nine, an age when most players of his ability are looking back on a successful career. For the first time many who hardly knew him regarded him as a genuine Test player. Faxes and mail began to arrive in large packets. His life would never be the same again.

14

More than a Buggy Ride

It is difficult to find figures to substantiate the claims. It is, as John Kennedy, a former sports editor of *The Star* who lives in Perth suggests, a matter of guesswork. Yet there is a strong body of opinion which claims that more South Africans have settled in Perth and Sydney than in any other city in Australia. 'You meet more of them here than anywhere else,' said Mariette Cloete, a young accountant who, with her husband, once attempted to set up a register of South Africans in Sydney. 'We could not get an accurate estimate even from those in Canberra, as not all South Africans are registered (at the High Commission).'

Their particular need for contact was surprising, as they had to escape the country of their birth in the mid-1980s to live and bring up their children in a stable society. Mariette says that her husband was related to Hassan Howa, a man of strong anti-apartheid principles, who played a major role in developing the Western Cape and later the South African Cricket Board of Control and then the South African Cricket Board. Howa also coined the phrase 'you cannot play normal sport in an abnormal society' during the 1976-77 unity, which saw the formation of the SACU. It was not that he was against unity in the game, rather he was against the hypocrisy of a system which, off the field, did not allow the players their egalitarian rights to mix freely because of draconian race laws. By the mid-1990s, most of Cloete's friends were members of the growing Sri Lankan Tamil community in Sydney and, when they went to watch Tests, it was to support the country of their birth and not Australia. It bothered Ms Cloete that her family and relatives in the small conservative Karoo town of Calitzdop had disowned her, at the time when she left South Africa, because she had married across the colour line. But they have settled into an Australian way of life and are accepted in the established middle-class suburb close to Manley. In the summer of 1997-98, her parents made a visit to watch some of South Africa's games, including the Sydney Test.

It may, of course, be propaganda to argue that more *biltong* (dried meat) and *boerewors* (spiced sausage) is sold in these two cities than in any other outside South Africa. It is one of those fact or fiction conundrums. If any former South African is asked to take you to a butcher, who sells the two distinctive items in either city, you are inclined to draw a blank. Tertius Bosch did find one, though, in Adelaide, during the 1992 World Cup.

Until 1990, most South African migrants were escapees from the land of apartheid with its endemic political paranoia and compulsory military training, one of the evils to prop up a long-discredited minority government. Others joined the queue after 1992 as the nation, having picked herself up, lurched from one massacre to the next. It did not matter who was responsible; the stench of death was a persuasive argument for 'Pack for Perth'.

It is not that they did not want to be part of the new South Africa and help build unity or, as a headline in the *Pretoria News* once suggested, 'Try, the Beloved Country'. This was above a leader page story of divided family loyalties, focussing on why one young Afrikaner was taking his family to Perth, while his brother and sister-in-law decided to remain at home. The destructive evils of apartheid, having been overturned, had been replaced by other modern phenomena which left an ugly birthmark on the face of the rainbow nation. A rampant crime rate, with vehicle hijackings, bank robberies and heists, taxi wars and random murder, were forcing many across a broad demographic front to quit. 'We want to live in a country where we know that at least we'll wake up in the morning and our children can go to school and come home in safety,' they said. 'Also we don't want to have something we've worked five years for stolen, because some guy without a job wants it and one of us is killed to protect what is ours.'

Perhaps it was a simplistic overview; perhaps it was valid as well. The modern South Africa is a nation in revolution, trying to find an identity amid the turmoil created in the aftermath of decades of human rights denial, and a political vacuum at grassroots with corruption at leadership level. Who in this case is there to trust?

* * * *

It was at the WACA in Perth, where in 1971-72 Barry Richards had scored a remarkable 300 in a day's play in a Sheffield Shield match for South Australia, that South Africa arrived on 13 January 1994. For one thing, they needed to overturn history and beat New Zealand for the first time in a limited-overs match to keep their WSC series hopes alive.

They had already gone to Brisbane to play Australia three days after that incredible Test in Sydney and had promptly lost to the Aussies and then the Kiwis. Hansie Cronje had already taken over as captain and was finding it tougher than imagined. Kepler Wessels, resting up at home after knee surgery, had looked anxiously at the television screen and M-Net's production of the series. For the first time he had seen how the Channel 9 crew treated the South African side.

On that first night in the city, and with his temporary roomie Daryll Cullinan, Fanie went exploring for a remote-controlled car. The idea was to switch environments and get Cullinan into a relaxed mood instead of allowing the talented Queen's College-educated batsman to brood over the game against New Zealand twenty-four hours later.

'Come on, Daryll, we're going shopping.'

Cullinan looked at his new room-mate; the mess around his bed needed tidying up, and here he was on his way out to some mall on a madcap excursion. He shrugged. He knew from Sri Lanka that Fanie was full of surprises and this trip was typical of the man. He would have preferred to stay in: perhaps watch a video on television, read, or talk with a couple of other players.

They were given directions and drove to a shopping mall, which was open that night. Fanie went looking for a toy shop selling a remote-controlled buggy. Which is where the fun really began. He tested out several, driving them up and down the mall, in and out of tables at a coffee shop and generally disrupting the pedestrian flow of the public.

'Just who are these guys?' security staff asked the toy shop owner.

'Faan, if we're not careful we're going to be kicked out of here.' Cullinan looked anxiously at the security staff.

A number of shoppers recognized Fanie from TV and newspaper pictures of the SCG Test miracle and wanted autographs. Like a big kid with his new toy, he drove the small vehicle all over the mall as he tested the controls.

He caused further mayhem back at the hotel, where some members of the television crew from New Zealand One joined him in the corridor.

'Hey, Fanie, let it rip,' one suggested.

'Really fast, mate. Burn up the carpet . . .'

'Wheeeee!'

'Mind the furniture, mate. Don't wanna bugger up the li'l fellah, eh!'

Broad, uncompromising Afrikaans-English mixed with New Zealand accents was often interjected with raucous laughter. The hijinks went on for about half an hour, when the hotel manager arrived and threatened to confiscate the buggy and eject the occupants. They all got the message and Fanie packed it away until the next day, when he introduced other members of the team to his new toy in the WACA dressing room. They watched Fanie manoeuvre the remote-controlled toy. Amidst this diversion was the more important task of beating New Zealand in the WSC series match in Perth. Not easy when you have not beaten them before and the run rate needed to be lifted above that of the Kiwis who had long been entrenched in second place.

The Kiwis were knocked out this time for 150 with Donald taking 3 for 18 in 8.2 overs and Fanie maintaining the same economic rate, as Cronje for once enjoyed the taste of success. And, more importantly, the run rate gap was narrowed. Not that Fanie's buggy was going to be left out of the limelight for too long. He carefully hid his intentions as he walked out of the dressing room shortly before the first drinks break of the South African innings and went down to the field.

When the drinks break came, he set the remote-controlled toy in motion. He was a little behind the buggy as it circled the bemused Kiwis and umpires and an amused Gary Kirsten before it crashed into the stumps. It was a moment of light relief; the sort of action, from the consequences of which only Fanie could escape, while quizzical management eyebrows were raised in surprise rather than annoyance.

He had long been recognized as the sort of touring room-mate with a paternal touch for more stressed players. The buggy episode was designed to ease the pressure on the South African batsmen and was carried out with unabashed humour. And it surprised no one that he was able to pull it off with no more than a disarming smile at frowning, disapproving officialdom. It was an immediate hit with the crowd, and the spectators, who had earlier been abusive, found themselves supporting the South Africans. Normally they'd munch hot dogs, swill beer and boo either side, or amuse themselves by throwing a stale roll at one of the players on the boundary.

The WACA crowd roared with approval when, after a couple of minutes of trying to hit the stumps with the buggy Fanie gained some success. Some stood and cheered, others gave the episode a standing ovation.

'Hey, Fanie, your little son is going to get a big kick out of the buggy when you get home,' one of the Kiwi television crew ventured at the end of the game.

'Hey, mate. I bought it for myself. When he's big enough, he can buy his own,' came the grinning reply. 'You have to work for what you want in this world.'

Some South Africans may have given the image of being laid back, but there was a serious professionalism and that spunky pride touring teams dig into when they are in Australia. New Zealand knew they would have to raise their game; for the South Africans, well, there was Jonty, the Kirstens, big Brian Mac, Donald, Dave Callaghan, Fanie . . . There was a lot of professionalism and tough-minded attitude among that lot. Of course they had that extra confidence as they went into the final match two days later against the Aussies—a game which had to be won to qualify for the final.

After the Sydney miracle, the nation was switched on again. It was a country bruised and tired of daily reports of arson attacks and massacres, yet for some reason, interest in the trials of the cricket team in far off Australia had started to cross demographic boundaries. The battle for survival in a ruthless series had become important. If Sydney was the catalyst, Perth became the loose, uneasy unifying force: building bridges and trust in the all-important question of human relations in what had been for far too long a fractured society.

It was going to need something special, although the early portents were far from promising. A ball from Glenn McGrath, which crashed through the grille of Peter Kirsten's helmet and fractured a cheekbone, flattened the batsman. Barely into the tour after his recall as a replacement for Wessels, the double blow was not what the tour management needed at that stage. But Peter Noel Kirsten had often shown the same iron will as Wessels and was prepared to head for South Africa, when the rest of the team left after the third Test at Adelaide.

Although a score of 208 was defendable, it needed special bowling skills, even on the pacy Perth surface, to reel in a side such as the Australians. Craig Matthews added his support to that of Donald and Fanie, while Cronje and man of the match Dave Callaghan put together tight performances. In the end, Allan Border's side was reduced to 126 in 41 overs and South Africa had a waiting period of seventy-two hours to discover whether they would gatecrash the best-of-three finals, or travel to an upcountry venue to play New South Wales in a three-day game. It was a matter of relying on Australia to beat New Zealand in Melbourne.

As it was, they headed for Sydney and a date with a New South Wales XI to raise funds for bushfire victims. It was here that Fanie's remote-controlled buggy won more marks for bringing light entertainment to the game. The spectators now saw the South Africans as a different side. A spirited team, which gave the sport a new, human, face and image. Team spirit had picked up and the media found a new focus as 'Fanie's Buggy' gave journalists and reporters a new slant to write about. South Africa did not need a PRO, they had Fanie and the buggy. Using the remote-controlled vehicle was also a popular way collecting funds at the SCG to swell the coffers for needy bushfire victims.

As Border readily admits, he was pretty desperate for Australia to beat New Zealand and play South Africa in the final of the series. It would have been a far better way of signing off his limited-overs career at home than a 2-0 walk over New Zealand. He did not rate that Kiwis team at all; in fact the Kiwis, if you listen to Ken Rutherford, during his time in Johannesburg, did not rate themselves in that series; an interesting admission by the former New Zealand captain. Yet, a Kiwis victory would elbow the South Africans into third place on the log.

For the first final there was a welcome back for Peter Kirsten. He celebrated his return with younger brother Gary with a century and the man of the match award as South Africa went up 1-0. It was the team's last success as they went to Adelaide for the third Test losing the one-day finals 2-1. For some unfathomable reason the batting broke down in both SCG final legs and the omens were not good as they headed for the South Australian capital.

To the uninitiated, Adelaide Oval could at first be mistaken for just another Test ground. Picturesque perhaps, with St. Peter's Cathedral creating a spiritual calm. Memories of Sir Donald Bradman's innings mingle with images of the round-arm bowling of leg-spin wizard Clarrie Grimmett, and the robust run-making style of Victor Richardson. There are those who feel that the ground where Fanie carved his first-class career is the Adelaide Oval of South Africa. Yet it was ironic that he was unable to take a wicket in that match, although his batting added to his stature as a player and a fighter.

While the Australian players were at odds with their board over a variety of issues, Cronje's brief apprenticeship, if the one-day games could be classed as such, was over. Sure he had had a hand in handling the on-field operations during the Australian second innings in Sydney, but this was different. It was going to provide South Africa's youngest captain of the century with a special challenge: win a Test series Down Under. Several had tried and only two, Jack Cheetham and Trevor Goddard, had managed to draw the five-match series. Adelaide Oval was hosting the third and last game of this tour and South Africa held a 1-0 advantage.

Steve Waugh, the man Border admitted Australia missed in Sydney when they were found wanting, was back in the side having recovered from a serious hamstring injury. An outstanding all-rounder and one of the most dedicated professional sportsmen of any era, the man known as 'Tugga' had been included with Paul

Reiffel. South Africa brought back Richard Snell for the spinner Pat Symcox. For Symmo, it was the first hint of the selectors' thinking for the three Tests in South Africa and the tour of England later in the year.

The Aussies may have had Warne, but for the next two series South Africa sadly reverted to the 'subjugate by pace and rule by fear' syndrome. Although Peter Pollock made soothing diplomatic noises, the blunt message from the selection panel was that it had lost faith in the ability of a South African spinner to make an impact at Test level.

From the high of Sydney to the low of Adelaide, South Africa found playing the Australians a lot harder than they expected. Although Warne and off-spinner Tim May were in the Aussie squad, it seemed as though the tour selection panel gave little thought to the rumours of the pitch aiding spinners. When, by the end of second day, Australia had declared their first innings total at 469 for 7, those who knew the modern history of Adelaide Oval would advance a wager that Border's 'Wizards of Oz' would square the series. And this was without the aid of Darrel Hair's interpretation of Law 36, the lbw law.

Long before the first day's play ended, Cronje, because of Symcox's absence, was forced to employ Gary Kirsten as a spinner. Not that he was inexperienced in the role. Earlier that season against Northerns in Centurion, the younger Kirsten's off-spinners had, on a dusting surface, nabbed 6 for 68 to help engineer a victory. Ironically, it was that day that Pollock announced the side for the Hero Cup series in India and the Australian tour and, it was a side for which Kirsten was not selected. More than three months later, in the Adelaide Test, he even managed to fool Mark Taylor, bowling him for 62 when the score was 152. Such can be the changes to a sportsman's career.

Steve, the older of the famous Waugh twins by four minutes, celebrated his entry into the Test series with a superb century. Border, in his last home Test, scored 84 and was accorded a hero's reception when he returned to the pavilion with the score on 391 for 5. When the declaration did come, South Africa needed to bat with purpose and direction if they were to save the match, or look for a victory. In fact, they did manage to put together a solid start.

Neither Warne nor May, seen as the main dangers, had made an impression and the score reached 173 for 2 when Andrew Hudson, batting comfortably on 90, saw Darrel Hair respond favourably to an lbw appeal from Steve Waugh.

A shocked Peter Kirsten could not believe the decision. The ball had been drifting down leg. When Rhodes and Cullinan departed in swift succession, both bowled by Waugh, the thirty-eight-year-old Kirsten knew the signs all too well. He had been in such a situation before, but not in a Test. All the hard work to build a first innings score to challenge the Aussie total had been snuffed out by an umpire's carelessness. To the veteran, it meant that he needed to bat with more care and attention.

Worse was to follow. Hair ruled in favour of Steve Waugh's lbw appeal against Brian McMillan to one which also seemed to be drifting down leg. When Dave Richardson became the third lbw victim of the innings given by Hair and to Craig McDermott's first shout, it smacked of the sort of bias which angered the older Kirsten. Say, what happened to the ball pitching between wicket and wicket? Or was there one lbw law for Australians and another one for the opposition?

Turning to Hair, the veteran batsman told the umpire what he thought of the decisions. And an uncompromising Kirsten was not about to back down. Already there had been some misgiving of the judgement of ICC match referee Jackie Hendricks, a former West Indies wicketkeeper, and his soft approach in the match. There was a view that both Donald and Waugh should have been carpeted for bringing the game into disrepute. Instead, that third evening it was Kirsten who copped Hair's report on dissent.

He did not need to tell Fanie what was required when the hero of Sydney joined the man becoming the South African hero of Adelaide Oval. Kirsten spoke in Afrikaans when he approached the twenty-nine-year-old de Villiers.

'We've got to see this through, Fanie. Get past that follow-on target. I can do it. I know you can.'

About the only thing he did not warn de Villiers about was the need to keep his legs out of the way of anything pitched remotely in line. They saw out the day's play. But at 237 for 7, another 33 runs were needed to beat the follow-on target as day four loomed. Kirsten, stung by having his match fee reduced by twenty-five per cent the night before, displayed the same rearguard stoicism he had the previous day.

Barely had play restarted when Fanie had his right thumb broken by a lifter from McDermott in the first overs of the day and was then run-out for 4 as the pain from the injury affected his judgement. He was angry with himself as he walked back to the pavilion. Little did he realize he would be batting again later that day, volunteering for the night watchman's job and dosing himself with anti-inflammatory pills and pain tablets before going into bat.

Kirsten had arrived at the fall of Cronje's wicket, trapped in front by Warne: that made four lbws to one against. As Fanie joined Kirsten, the scoreboard read 18 for 3. So much to do and plenty of time. Too much time.

Next morning the pain was so excruciating Fanie could hardly pull on his glove. It was agony to pick up his bat and he was unable to have a brief net session. No one expected him to last long: a couple of overs perhaps; Cronje and the physio, Craig Smith, were worried about the extent of the thumb injury. If he was hit by McDermott or Rieffel, it could create added problems. They needed Fanie fit for the series at home.

McDermott began the morning bowling first to Kirsten and then to Fanie, the pain knifing through the swing bowler. It was all he could do to concentrate and he wanted to retire. He went down the pitch and looked at Kirsten and told him how he could hardly hold the bat. Taking the left hand away before the moment of impact was no longer helping.

'You have to stick around, Fanie. You and I. Together. Come on. We'll do it.'

Somehow the plan began to work, with McDermott suggesting to Border he should be rested.

'I can handle the spinners,' Fanie told Kirsten, who had been doing his bit to help his partner.

Sometimes they spoke in English, sometimes in Afrikaans. At home, his father, Braam, watched with genuine admiration. His son, the hero, who had no cricket heroes of his own, was becoming a role model for youngsters of all races, languages, creeds and cultures. Long before the first hour was successfully negotiated, the old dressing room superstitions became an unwritten law for the day. No one was allowed to move or change seats or chairs. Even a simple thing like going to the toilet was only allowed if Fanie was not facing the bowler. And those sitting outside the changing room had to remain outside.

Out in the middle Fanie, taking more pain tablets, was having a problem focussing, wiping away frustrating sweat.

'I'm losing sight of the ball,' he told Kirsten shortly before lunch.

'Concentrate, Fanie. You have to concentrate.'

Border switched the bowlers around to break the deadlock. It was becoming frustrating. In Sydney it had been Fanie de Villiers who had caused the second innings collapse. Now here he was holding up his side's chances of squaring the series. And with a broken thumb. Where did they find guys like this? Afrikaners, he had been told, were soft on the game. Well, he had news for the doubters. There was Kepler and now there was Fanie. And what was it that John Reid said about Afrikaners not understanding the game?

It was not so much a matter of pride, courage, iron-will, or an indefatigable spirit, which kept Fanie upright as he batted through a session on another sun-drenched, boiling hot day. A Test had to be saved, a nation's honour had to be saved, and that's what he intended to do. The partnership had gone past the 50 mark; a milestone to give the lads in the dressing room something to cheer about. But runs no longer counted; the number of overs remaining did. Batting out time . . .

They were given a royal reception when they went in for lunch and Smith had a look at the hand again. He wondered how long Fanie could keep going. Too many pain tablets could drug him to the extent that he would not be capable of even holding the bat. It was a risk. The other would be McDermott when he was brought back to bowl.

As tension mounted on the field and in the dressing room, Fanie continued to focus his thoughts on keeping Kirsten company. They held middle-pitch discussions as each over ended, looking at the scoreboard to see how many overs were left. And there was chatter around the oval. Past rescue acts were recalled: Kirsten had been in a few, and remembered the one Eddie Barlow had performed for Western Province against Northerns at Berea Park. It did much to help Western Province win that Currie Cup game when it had been lost.

The mid-afternoon drinks session was looming and Warne and May were toiling away with the Waugh twins, Steve and Mark, given a few overs and Border bringing himself on as well. Through all this pressure, Fanie fought with singleminded determination; there would be no easy surrender, no prisoners. Border continued with his game of poker, always looking for the ace to finish off the South Africans. In the dressing room, the anxiety grew.

McDermott was brought back into the attack and Kirsten warned Fanie, coaxing his partner along. It would be the last over before the drinks session. They had been together for more than three hours, a fourth wicket partnership, which had added only 87 runs in that time, but what a performance. Pain and agony barriers had been overcome.

'Hang on, Fanie. You're looking good. Drinks are almost here. Just keep the ball down. No rash shots now. Don't hit out. Just block the ball . . . just block it . . .'

Fanie, however, had a serious problem. The last pain tablets had affected his judgement and the pain from the thumb had been tearing through the barrier it should have created. His concentration level had also been impaired. He was looking at Kirsten, taking in what the older player was saying as McDermott went back to his mark.

A frustrated Andrew Hudson finally stood up.

'Sit down Hudders,' growled Mike Procter.

'Ah. This superstition of sitting where we are is so much nonsense. Two balls to drinks. Nothing's going to happen.'

He moved towards the door and was suddenly transfixed. Fanie had driven McDermott, on the up, aiming to hit the ball wide of Reiffel lurking in the covers, but the miscued stroke saw the ball loop to the fielder and the defiant partnership was ended. As teammates swooped on him, disturbing the reverie of the ever-present seagulls, Reiffel threw the ball in the air and Fanie stood, blinking, before he finally dragged himself off to the picket gate.

What was said to Hudson in the South African dressing room is best left unrecorded. Poor Hudders took it all, yet unable to accept he had been the one responsible for the fall of the wicket. After all, it really was a matter of whether you believed in such superstitions or not. A forlorn Fanie, head partly bowed, was loudly applauded up the steps to the dressing room. His mind was in a fog, fatigued and drugged from too many pain killers. The relief measures had cost him his wicket and with it, South Africa's hopes of saving the Test.

He slumped in his seat and fell asleep, surrendering to the drug from the pills and was not a party to the unfolding drama over the next hour, which left the innings in ruins at 117 for 7. One of the three victims to fall was Rhodes, perhaps to the worst lbw decision of the match. May had switched to bowling around the wicket, but more than that the umpiring in the match had rarely been of Test level. Tony Prue answered May's appeal by raising his hand above his head after the ball had pitched around leg stump and Kirsten was another to go to McDermott. The veteran did not want to depart. He gave Hair a baleful glare as he went, feeling that the South Africans deserved better than they got as rancour spilled over and Kirsten was fined further for dissent. It was the first time an ICC referee was forced to make adjustments and Kirsten copped a second, far stiffer fine.

There was an immediate response the Radio 702 in Johannesburg, which launched a fund to pay the fine, which was sixty-five per cent of his match fee. This reaction allowed some South Africans to show that they identified with the side.

Defeat in Adelaide meant a squared series with Messrs Hair and Prue receiving a large chunk of the blame through their lbw decisions. Whether this was a justified gripe is a matter of which side you were on. Even to the independent observer and those who have been umpires, a 7-1 lbw ratio against a side is unusually high, and there were at least three against South Africa which were questionable. In a matter of controversy, every Tom, Dick and Sally suddenly becomes an experts, quoting the relevant law, but patriotic pride and a sense of parochialism can also shroud the issue with some doubt.

The debates intensified when Steve Waugh won the man of the series award instead of Fanie de Villiers. The older Waugh twin had played in just one Test; for Fanie it was his debut series at the age of 29, a time when most fast bowlers look over their shoulders at who is likely to edge them out of the side and prematurely end their career.

* * * *

Hours before the side arrived at Jan Smuts airport, questions were being asked whether Cronje should keep the captaincy and Kepler Wessels become a player. This would allow Wessels to become the team's 'senior advisor', passing on his knowledge, experience and advice. The comments were fuelled by suggestions that Wessels' career was almost over because of his knee problem and it was now time to groom Cronje.

The counter view was that it would be a season too soon. Apart from the return series against Australia in South Africa, the first tour of England since 1965 loomed: six Tests against top opposition. After that was another limited-overs series, this one in Pakistan. Then the New Zealanders would be in South Africa for a series of three Tests, and the quadrangular tournament involving the Kiwis, Pakistan as well as Sri Lanka. It was too soon for Cronje to take full responsibility. Saddling him with the captaincy at such a crucial stage in South Africa's international redevelopment would affect his batting form. Better to allow him to grow into the role than force it on him.

Although he had shown himself to be a capable, responsible leader under pressure, it should be acknowledged that the team around him contained a special group of guys. The game is not just about one individual, or two, but the team, and Cronje was fortunate to take over a side which had been developed by the Wessels creed of tough discipline. As had been evident in Sydney, Perth and Adelaide, it was a competitive side of fighters. It had nothing to do with Cronje; he was part of the side and still learning.

Cronje's views on the captaincy were understandably mixed. He was pressed on the issue by the local media soon after the side returned to South Africa, but did not come out and say, 'Yes, I want the job now'. He indicated that discussions were still to be held with Peter Pollock and the views of others to be considered. It was a carefully phrased, tactful response.

'Whether to skip or not to skip . . . it is something which still has to be discussed,' he commented. 'Consultations are likely at some stage with the selectors and the board (UCB). It's a challenge. We'll see . . .'

It was not, of course, as concise as this. Such media conferences can be a jumble with too many inferences. Had he talked to Kepler to get his views? Or talked to the other players? There was also a feeling the captaincy issue had been deliberately stirred by some sections of the South African media with certain official backing who had their own agenda to get rid of the ever-pragmatic Wessels.

At one brief stage during the night, Cronje displayed signs of what in later years would become a schizophrenic attitude to the electronic and print media. It was the 'Say guys, why would I lie?' pattern so noticeable when he was unmasked in April 2000 over match-fixing charges by the New Delhi police; his eyes were as shifty as they had been on 9 April when facing the media at Kingsmead. There was an almost unctuous approach to the visual media; with the writers it was a pinched, almost 'take it or leave it' mood.

Greeted as a hero by new, adoring fans, Fanie willingly obliged autograph hunters and amateur photographers. He would rather have been with Judy, the children and other members of his family who had come to meet him. It upset him the way his family members were jostled, and at times rudely pushed out of the way, in the general melee around the players when they came down from the balcony. But duty called and he had to ignore the churlishness. He had not seen Judy, Suné or Faantjie in more than two months, and here he could hardly get close to them. At last he managed to pick up Suné and felt her small arms go about his neck as she looked adoringly at him and snuggled close. He continued to sign autographs as he held his daughter in the crook of his left arm.

Ah, it was good to be home. Even if it was a nation troubled in spirit and uneasy in mind about coping with the looming first democratic elections. There were those confident of the future, their adrenalin crystallized through the excitement of the tour; others were pessimistic and edgy, planning their escape in the lead up to the election, its two day duration and the week after the historic event.

As the flight had arrived at around ten in the evening, it was an hour before he got his chance to be alone with his family and a couple of friends. The interviews were over and he could relax and give away a few gifts.

* * * *

Australia's first official tour of South Africa in twenty-four summers attracted mixed interest in the country. While the limited-overs international slogs were well supported, there was less buzz about the Test series. But modern South Africans, brought up on a diet of force-fed limited-overs matches during the often cheerless years of isolation, had lost their appetite for the more intellectual longer game. Although this is slowly changing as a younger generation displays more appreciation for five- and four-day games, the hype around the one-dayers remains, despite it often being boring fare to digest.

While the itinerary was carefully worked out to give all South Africans a chance to see the tourists, the mix of limited-overs and Tests with preparation matches slotted in would help acclimatize Border's side. Not too surprisingly, one of the big attractions was Merv Hughes, who had not played in the Test series Down Under because of a knee operation.

Instead of keeping faith with the sunny skies slogan, the first weeks of the tour ushered in a spell of chilly, damp weather with the tourists restricted to training indoors. Which did little to help Hughes in his efforts to achieve some form of physical fitness as the tour slowly ground into a disjointed first gear. Big, moody and moustachioed, some writers looking to get a risqué rise out of the Victorian often-painted Hughes in caricature. In one pre-tour interview he denied that a Melbourne radio station had insured the handlebar growth on his upper lip for Aus$500,000. 'Nah . . .,' he growled. 'That's just another story. Me bay thirteen mates wouldn't enjoy that at all. Getting above me self, mate.' He travelled for too many runs in his first serious bowling spell of the tour and did not recover from the Centurion Park effort against Northerns and sat out the first batch of one-dayers. After that, he was considered a Test bowler rather than one for the slogs. The Aussies were already under pressure with injuries and a variety of off-field problems, including Border's illness and a serious bout of flu for Mark Taylor on the eve of the first Test at the Wanderers.

As their tour settled down, Pollock named Wessels as captain and Fanie found that his broken thumb, which had kept him out of the Northerns side in the opening match, had healed nicely in time for the opening one-day game on 19 February. In what has now become considered the finest over bowled in South Africa in the history of limited-overs games, the hero of Sydney and Adelaide had a chanting, packed Wanderers on its feet as he began the over.

A thoughtful Wessels looked at the large electronic scoreboard: 15 runs needed off 12 balls. Fanie was called upon to deliver the penultimate over. He knew the capabilities of the one bowler he trusted most with the enormous task of finding South Africa an escape route as Border and Steve Waugh rushed along with bold strokeplay towards the required target.

'*Wys hulle, ou kat* (Show them, old cat),' he grinned at the bowler.

The crowd started chanting. 'Fhaaa-nie! Fhaaa-nie! Fhaaa-nie!' Their battle cry swelled and reverberated around the bullring and echoed down Corlett Drive. It is a sound he has not forgotten. Each of the six successive yorkers he bowled, all well pitched in the right spot, were greeted with passionate whoops from a partisan Wanderers crowd. And Border, in frustration, made room to cut, only to find his stumps rearranged in a humiliating manner as the crowd roared, hoarse and delirious at the unexpected success.

An hour later two spectators lay dead, victims of a botched hijacking in nearby Louis Botha Avenue. Cousins Ray Sutton and Graham Martin were approaching Hillbrow when they were gunned down. Near Alexandra, children, who had been to the match, stood horrified as their teacher was caught in the crossfire of a taxi shooting.

Harsh reality had returned to the blood splattered streets of Egoli.

Next day, as the Sunday papers told of the tragedy (on page one) and the triumph (on the sports pages), Cronje's well-structured innings of 97 at Centurion Park continued his domination of Warne. After that, Adrian Kuiper smashed 47 off 42 balls with three successive sixes off McDermott's last over. Just the sort of fireworks to send a happy crowd to lunch and watch later as South Africa went up 2-0 in the series.

By the time the first Test began at the Wanderers in the first week of March, South Africa led the slogs 3-1, and Cronje continued with his rich vein of run-making against the tourists at Springbok Park in Bloemfontien. With the sort of ruthless efficiency expected of the future national captain, he hammered sixty-three per cent of the Free State second innings total of 396 with a personal best of 251. Free State may have lost the match, but Cronje's devastating form was rampant and was the sort of message South Africa needed to send their visitors.

On 4 March 1994, a series, which could be said to have started ninety-two years before at the old Wanderers, resumed in the new Wanderers bullring. And throughout the day, the small crowd displayed the sort of mindset South Africans have developed after being fed a diet of too many limited-overs internationals. They indulged themselves in the Mexican wave at any given opportunity. It was the sort of gimmickry which greeted Rhodes' half-century, as South Africa struggled on a damp day. And helping it along, flashed on the giant scoreboard, was one of the more inane graphics you are likely to see: a sombrero atop a succession of waves.

South Africa had slipped to a sorry 126 for 6 when Rhodes, joined by Richardson, began their team's revival, but the crowd reaction was that of one attending yet another limited-overs game. While the first two days ambled along, with South Africa taking a narrow first innings lead, there was far more substance in them than in any one-dayer. It was in a near-full Wanderers after lunch on Sunday when the bubbling cauldron finally splattered over. Warne, held back in the first innings, made a belated entry in the second, bowling to Hudson. Snapping, snarling and strutting around, as would an unknown Hollywood actor who had managed to land a more important role after years of tiresome understudy work, he used the bullring as a stage for an act of boorish behaviour which, he admits, has haunted him since. Betraying the ethics of the game's code of sportsmanship and fairplay, he reacted malevolently when he bowled Hudson for 60. Charging toward the departing mild-mannered Hudders, the bad-tempered Warne was forcibly restrained by Ian Healy, as his uncouth behaviour was flashed to millions across a succession of continents. It was not the message those entrusted with the game's welfare wanted hundreds of thousands of young impressionable minds to see, either. David Shepherd, the senior match umpire, told Border to calm down his players, for Warner's unwarranted behaviour smacked of a decided lack of discipline.

Yet officialdom, in the form of match referee Donald Carr, fined Warne only ten per cent of his match fee for his unseemly transgression. Oxford-educated and an England all-rounder in the early years after World War II, Carr had become an administrator at the top levels of the game; assistant secretarial posts with the MCC and the TCCB were two positions which commanded respect. Here he was, however, dishing out punishment, which was little more than a limp slap on the wrist. Little wonder that the Australian Cricket Board imposed their own harsh punishment on Warne's ugly outburst. They fined him his full match fee. Hughes was fined a similar amount for player abuse the same afternoon.

Warne though has always deeply regretted the incident. It smeared his character and, for someone with his sort of charisma, it is not the way he wants to be remembered. He explained, in a conversation in 1999 during the Australian tour of Sri Lanka, that he felt like a grenade about to explode when brought on to bowl; he deserved the punishment he received from the Australian Cricket Board. 'Hudson is such a likeable, nice guy that I knew I had stepped beyond the players' code of behaviour,' he said with great candour. 'After that day's play I sought him out and apologized for my behaviour; he accepted it. But it doesn't help; I still cringe every time I see that particular scene on TV, or when it crosses my mind.'

The shame surrounding Warne's behaviour is that the incident is remembered more than the innings Hudson played. It was full of strong strokeplay: a mix of handsome drives and pulls and the occasional cut. When in the mood, he was elegant and upright and demanded respect from the bowlers.

What Warne's behaviour did was not just display a flagrant disregard for Law 42 and the ICC's own code of conduct, its application, interpretation and enforcement. It brought dishonour to the game and the memory of Clarrie Grimmett. It may be remembered that most of the game's laws are still roughly similar to those laid down on a frosty February evening in 1774 at the Star and Garter by the Duke of Dorset, Sir William Draper, and his boozy chums. Comparisons are interesting and, in most cases, far from odious. Under the 1980 code, Law 42 (with clauses and sub-clauses) had been reshaped, reworded, modified and streamlined to resemble moderately modern OED (Oxford English Dictionary) usage and therefore made easier to understand than the 1947 code. The 2000 code has modified it even further.

Much of what the founding fathers had in mind when the laws were issued in 1744, was reshaped in the 1774 version and it still remains in several forms: the width of the bat, length of the pitch, number of players and umpires and scorers. We will not delve into the prehistory of the laws. Suffice to explain that there were versions of the laws before 1686 and 1722. It is known in Kent that 'local customs' were included in a set of playing conditions (therefore not laws) in the 1650s. There were certainly sets of local playing conditions well before the Dutch founded South Africa and the English colonized Australia. However, the laws of the game, like English common law, were, until the 1980 code, essentially English, having developed according to the needs of the age from the late fourteenth century onwards. The 1980 code contains much from the former colonies and countries that have warmly embraced the game: Holland and Denmark among them. Yet, only cricket has Laws (never rules), so there is no right of appeal to a high court let alone some human rights commission. The players have to rely on the impartiality of the umpire, in the hope that he is not carrying a white stick, wearing dark glasses or being directed by a guide dog.

If you think today's sledging is bad, Bill 'Tiger' O'Reilly has long been regarded as the original commanding officer. He was as likely to tell a batsman his fortune, with a selection of choice phrases, as he would tell his captain what was wrong with the field placings, if an edge to third man was the result of an attempted cover drive gone wrong.

There is a story of how Arthur Fagg, a former Kent and (very briefly) England opening batsman, who eventually became a Test umpire, was involved in a tetchy discussion with Bill Lawry during the 1968 Australians tour of England, with Lawry asking Fagg how he had been given out.

'Lbw,' came Fagg's cool reply.

Lawry snorted in disgust. 'You can't be serious? Lbw! I hit the bloody ball.'

'I know that, too. That's why you will find it caught behind in the scorebook.'

Yet there are times when even the mildest-mannered umpire's patience is taxed by a bowler, fielder or batsmen, who is bent on irritating the equanimity of the man in white. And there are other times when a player refuses to accept an umpire's decision and reacts either angrily or with bemused detachment. There is also an alternate pragmatic view which involves the players as well as the umpires. The ICC have considered ways to change the code to benefit both without derailing the system.

This happened at Port Elizabeth in mid-November 2001 when Mike Denness handed down a series of bannings, fines and suspended sentences that affected six Indian players including, for some bizarre reason Sachin Tendulkar for ball tampering. Video replays showed Tendulkar doing nothing of the sort. It led to the sort of imbroglio which involved over-hasty South African government involvement and a standoff between the Board of Control for Cricket in India and their recently elected president Jagmohan Dalmiya and the ICC. It also led to the ICC withdrawing Test status recognition of the third match in the series that South Africa won 1-0.

Barry Jarman, a former Australian wicketkeeper, who was referee in the South Africa-India series of 1996-97 had sensible views, which left the fight where it belonged—out in the middle. He viewed the player-on-player relationship on the field as rather special and expected that players would sort matters out among themselves.

South African all-rounder Brian McMillan, for instance, told Robin Johnson that if he wasn't careful when playing forward on some of the bouncier surfaces he would find a few broken teeth in a glass next to his hospital bed when he woke up. But umpires have no protection. This, in part, initially led to the formation of the ICC code that handles not only that specific job, but attempts to eradicate the mugging of the image by episodes such as the Warne incident at the Wanderers. Protection of the players from umpires' decisions should also be investigated.

Yet when Chesters, in his weekly *Spinner's Tales* column in early January 1997, raised the possibility of a card and points penalty fines system, some UCB-contracted umpires felt that such a theory could not be put into practice. A great idea, but no thanks. When the subject was raised in Sri Lanka in 2000 after the Kandy Test involving Sri Lanka and South Africa, K. T. Francis, the board's director of umpiring, felt that the correct application of Law 42 and the ICC code of conduct would handle it. Since then, the situation has been exacerbated until the ICC elite panel of eight umpires and five match referees, backed by a new code of conduct, has identified all the parameters of player behaviour and the laws. Which poses the question—should not the ICC investigate a yellow card system to make it easier for the umpires and referees to monitor a player's behaviour throughout a series? Yellow card, as opposed to anaemic green or rabid red, and a system of penalty points that leads to a warning (for sledging, that is) or for comments that are derogatory (Bill Lawry's to Arthur Fagg).

Steve Waugh's outwardly calm reaction to his first innings dismissal at Centurion Park in the third Test of the series in 1997 would have cost him two points, while Ian Healy's open dissent should be twenty-five points. That is fifteen points more than allowed for the first level of a fine: so the harshness of a two-match suspension. If a player should collect five penalty points during a match (or series) he will receive a warning and a yellow card; a second yellow card means an automatic one match suspension.

Under the new ICC code of conduct, penalty points can be awarded on all nine sections of the code. The Hughes episode in the Wanderers Test in March 1994 was an example of ICC timidity (a soft fine) as opposed to the Australian Cricket Board's hardline response. At the time, it should have been seen by the ICC as a warning of how to tighten up the code of conduct.What we are concerned with here are the laws of the game and how they are applied and the players' reaction to the decisions. If the ICC are serious about cleaning up the debris resulting from such decisions, then the umpires are in need of extra cover. Whether those guidelines issued in April 2002 have gone far enough is another matter.

In 1999, after the World Cup, there were several series where umpiring decisions reached the arcane level of those invoked by Javed Akhtar in the Test at Leeds in 1998 involving South Africa.

At the Wanderers Test in March 1994, Hudson's dismissal saw Wessels join Cronje and the pair set about increasing the overall lead. With one eye on the overs in hand and the other on run accumulation, South Africa needed a solid partnership. Having already feasted off the Australians in three successive first-class innings for 316 runs, Cronje at first batted watchfully that third afternoon. He presented a straight bat and drove rather than cut. Risky wrist shots were all but eliminated, but then, he has always been a handsome driver of the ball.

As the partnership flourished, Wessels continued to work the ball around and when he fell for 50, Peter Kirsten replaced him as Cronje moved to his third Test century late in the afternoon. As he drove his way to the three-figure mark, he had captivated, then tamed, the normally raucous bullring crowd. They gave him the ovation he deserved and when he responded, he acknowledged the development youngsters under the scoreboard, who regularly chanted his name. When he eventually departed for 122 after four hours, he was satisfied with his contribution.

Hughes, for years the hero of a rather loud-mouth group of MCG fans better known as the 'Bay 13 Club', was not known to readily turn the other cheek when confronted with snarling spectators out for a 'bit of sport'. His shaky image, already bruised, was now left battered when in an act of misconduct his famed temper boiled over again. On the final afternoon of the Test, engaged in a defiant rearguard action with Tim May, he was walking up the steps as light rain stopped play, when a heckler taunted a man already on a short fuse. Turning, his immediate reaction was to slam his bat at the heckler, hitting the fence. Instead of ignoring the local yobbo, Hughes attempted to lean over the fence and lashed out at the spectator, his moustache bristling. The incident was screened on Australian TV hours later and Hughes ended up losing his match fee along with any goodwill he might have spread in his early interviews. It was not a Test comeback to be remembered with any pride.

As for Fanie, he viewed his contribution as fair, but already the body, tired from hours of bowling for his country's honour was drained as South Africa succumbed by 9 wickets at Newlands and managed to squeeze a draw at unpatriotic Kingsmead. With the limited-overs series shared 4-4, he wondered, not for the first time, how much more punishment his body could take.

The tour of England was looming, hard, uncompromising and demanding. Returning to old haunts and memories and wondering if he could retain his Test place as new faces emerged, he had once suggested to his father that he would need to do something radically wrong if he were to lose his place. To Wessels, he was the ideal troopie for the trenches.

At the time there were growing complaints in the lower administrative levels that it was an all-white side and those who had come from the SACB were being marginalized. It was supposed to be about opportunities, so what about, say Kenneth Mahuwa, or Arnold Somdaka, Leslie Duiker or Freeman Simelela? Jackie McGlew had a high regard for Mahuwa. He saw him as an exciting, highly talented, at times explosive batsman with as wide a range of strokes as perhaps Herschelle Gibbs. Mahuwa was a member of the 1992 South African youth side which toured the West Indies, and Gibbs was the vice-captain. It was an indictment of how the provinces looked after such players. Mahuwa was one of those who had not been mentored or monitored. It gave some the impression that in May 1994, blacks were being marginalized by the system.

* * * *

In the days when teams arrived in London after a leisurely two-week steamship journey, they were relaxed, fit and fresh for the labours of a five month tour. For the old hands, there was the enjoyment of renewing acquaintances; for the youngsters on their first visit, there was the excitement of new sights and a first pre-tour net session at Lord's after walking across the hallowed field from the pavilion. These days, teams are unbundled at Heathrow, met by top ECB officials and packed off to their fancy London hotel by bus. In 1994, it was still the Test and Country Cricket Board. But not to worry: the change of name in January 1997 to the England and Welsh Cricket Board makes it a matter of 'spot the difference'.

The South African side led by Wessels arrived in mid-June after a camp in Durban. Barely had they settled in when a back injury to Aubrey Martyn meant a quick change in team complement. A left-arm fast bowler from Western Province, Martyn had displayed promising Castle Cup form to earn a place on the reckoning that Brett Schultz's debilitating knee injury would keep him at home. He was flown home and has hardly been heard of since. To make up the sixteen strong party, Richard Snell was hastily summoned by the team's management after consultation with the selectors.

There was a view, before the tour started, that it was the best prepared since the 1920s (in terms of capped players). The one warning, however, was that the general make up of the squad hid any number of flaws in a country still feeling the lengthy effects of isolation. Martyn and Gerry Liebenberg apart, it was an experienced side, with any number either having played for a county or in one of the many leagues. Liebenberg was along for the ride as the extra wicketkeeper, and at one stage, seemed to enjoy the joke about the 'mystery man on tour'.

Sharing a summer as they had in 1965 with New Zealand, there were some unusual arrangements, including a game behind closed hedges at the John Paul Getty estate to scrape off some malingering winter's rust. And there was drama from the first match, another limited-overs frolic. This one was at the Earl of Carnarvon's county seat of Highclere—a traffic jam, mostly involving those going to the game, held up the team's bus.

Judy had also arrived to join Fanie with an interesting story to tell, when they met on the eve of the opening first-class game against Kent at Canterbury. In those days she was an airhostess and in the hectic first years after the sports ban was lifted, transporting teams of supporters was not uncommon. It was easy to separate the rugby and soccer support groups from the others. They were invariably rude, noisy and knocking back large quantities of booze. On one flight, on arrival at Heathrow in June 1994, she stood at the door bidding 'goodbye' to what had been an orderly group of passengers.

'No doubt we shall see you in Canterbury this weekend?' a smartly dressed middle-aged man asked Judy.

'Ah, yes. Are you going to be there as well?'

'We're here until after the Lord's Test,' came the smiling reply. 'We're one of the supporter groups. But we're not going to Scotland or Durham.'

You would not catch the rugby types being as polite. Most would still be hungover from the night before and grumbling about sleeping through breakfast and missing the meal.

Playing Kent at the St. Lawrence ground in Canterbury was not quite the 'homecoming' Fanie had expected when leaving the county four years before to nurse a tired, battered body back to some semblance of health in South Africa. Meeting up with old friends was one thing, but rain was a new phenomenon. In 1990, it had rarely rained in the hop county. At least he managed 3 for 50, while poor Tim Shaw took a pounding, giving away a century in runs for one wicket.

Yet it was great to be back. He knew he had to look after himself on this tour; nurse himself along and keep the pain to himself, chewing anti-inflammatory tablets as if they were sweets. It no longer surprised Craig Smith, the team's physiotherapist, how Fanie kept going. Sleeping most nights with a pillow between his legs to take away the agony, he worked away at the nets during the net sessions as the team moved south. He was rested for the games against Sussex and Hampshire before arriving in Bristol for what became an unpleasant, rain-ruined game against Gloucestershire. That gave Fanie the opportunity to have a long spell and take his first 5-wicket haul on tour.

It was an unresponsive pitch and he found the umpires, Ken Palmer and George Sharp, none too responsive to lbw appeals. But he had discovered that forcing the batsman to drive with an inviting gap in the covers worked. He managed to vary his cutter as well. And it all helped in the build up to the first Test at Lord's.

London can be as hot and sticky with near-intolerable humidity as in Durban or Brisbane and also sometimes Colombo. For those who attended South Africa's first Test at headquarters in almost three decades, it became a mixture of celebration with a dash of controversy in uncomfortable humidity. Or, as David Frith, then editor of *Wisden Cricket Monthly*, whispered as he settled down in that first session: 'More than a bit historic; South Africa back again and in the sort of weather that wouldn't go amiss in Durban, eh?'

They brought out the bunting at Lord's and there was an emotional greeting as the new South Africa shook hands with the 'Old Country'. A traditional rivalry was, after an uncomfortable hiatus of twenty-nine years, about to be resumed: the 103rd match in a series which had begun at St. George's Park, Port Elizabeth, in the horse and buggy days 105 years before.

Had it not been predicted after the tasteless Basil D'Oliveira episode in 1968 that no South African side would play again at

Lord's this century? That the apartheid system would prosper well into the next? And the 'Springboks' . . . Well, now there's an emblem of the old system, which had, among most sports, been consigned to the dusty halls of history. All but rugby (well, what do you expect with its arrogant overlay of Broederbond-style politics and jingoism) had shed the old symbols and embraced the new. Yet calling Wessels' side the Proteas was an equal aversion. Getting rid of the term Proteas in mid-2000 is one of the better things the UCB has done. D'Oliveira, another condemned by the apartheid laws to seek a future outside his country, smiled at the irony of it all on the first day. He too had been betrayed by politicians and rejected because of his colour when included as a late replacement for the abandoned 1968-69 MCC (England) tour of South Africa. Twenty-six years later, he was a well-feted guest. At Newlands in 2000, a venue where he had never played, he walked out as one of South Africa's players of the twentieth century.

Not surprisingly, there was much tension around the ground shortly before Hudson and Gary Kirsten stepped onto the turf after Wessels had won the toss and felt it prudent to bat first. It hung as heavily as the humidity as Hudders took guard from the umpire, Dickie Bird. Up on the balcony sat Cronje, the vice-captain, closeted in his own private war of nerves as West Indian-born Phil DeFreitas marked out his run.

Play was called by Bird and in charged DeFreitas with Hudders padding up to that first ball. As the convincing appeal directed at the umpire ricocheted around Lord's, Cronje felt butterflies crawling around his tummy, waiting for Bird to make up his mind about the appeal. Perhaps the leg was stretched too far forward and the ball was going over the top. As the bowler took a long, hard look, Bird shook his head. Each time he ran up to bowl DeFreitas' facial expression was that of someone with an acute toothache. His pained expression at Bird's dismissal of the appeal was equally obvious. The match, however, was underway and Cronje's butterflies settled down.

South Africa lost Hudson before the first drinks session and Cronje not too long after, at which time Wessels joined Kirsten and the left-handers set about batting on a pitch, which had the appearance of a mottled turf mosaic with some interesting fissures at the

Nursery end. Early caution in the South African innings gave way to confidence as England's bowlers found difficulty in shackling the partnership. In recent years, they have regularly found ways of allowing left-handers to frustrate their efforts and obstruct their game plan.

Strangely, the spectators did not seem to mind at all that the run rate ambled along at less than 3 an over. After all, as Dr Bacher kept on repeating, 'it was a historic occasion', so small matters of slow run rates had to take second place to the heady atmosphere of the first day of a Lord's Test. And, on that special day in history, the captain, Wessels, added to his remarkable achievements. He had scored a century on his Test debut against England for Australia twelve southern summers before, and he had also managed a debut century for South Africa against India in Durban. Now, at headquarters, he put together the third of what was another commanding performance of studied strokeplay and gritty determination; it was not fluent, but it was effective. Although he was out shortly before the close, through a rare mistake, caught by the wicketkeeper, Steve Rhodes off the bowling of Darren Gough, it gave South Africa the substance needed to build a solid first innings score. It was a rare achievement as well, placing Wessels alongside Percy Sherwell (1907) and Alan Melville (1947) as the only South African captains to score a Test century at Lord's. Just the sort of accolade a man of his character deserved.

Generally the South African innings was largely a pedestrian affair, the scoring rate barely creeping above 3 an over and Mike Atherton, the England captain, becoming more grumpy as the second day progressed. Perhaps being held up by Craig Matthews, gleefully crashing the ball around for 41 off only 36 balls upset the Lancastrian's equilibrium. But when the innings ended, he stalked off, hands thrust deeply into his pockets, not talking to anyone if he could help it. Not at all a picture of confidence. There had been any number of tactical blunders: field-placings to Angus Fraser was one, and Gough had bowled far too short too often. Yet 4 wickets were not to be sneezed at; he had swung the ball around enough and Fanie wanted to see what he could do.

Another area where England had erred was going into the game without a reliable replacement for Robin Smith. In what was a selectorial gaffe, John Crawley was pushed into the all-important number three position and found to be out of his depth; the argument was that Graham Thorpe should have filled the post, but Atherton was adamant. It was Fanie who ended Crawley's debut Test innings on 9 when he had the batsman picked up in the slips by Hudson.

It was one of Fanie's three prized wickets, and although he bowled with more control in his second and third spells, he battled at first to use the Lord's slope as effectively as had Donald. Using his broader experience of English conditions, Donald capitalized on a scrappy batting display to net yet another 5-wicket haul to Fanie's 3. Not that the de Villiers swing was less effective than Donald's pace. Fanie found he could use the slope and had more success. Crawley, Graeme Hick and Graham Gooch all fell to Fanie's rhythm and swing; tying up Gooch with one which caught the former England captain in front.

The lbw decision went against all the theories Robin Jackman had advanced of why the Northerns player should not get one during the tour on England. A former England Test bowler with a long association of South African provincial sides as a player and coach, Jackman expounded his theory on a bitterly cold winter's evening a week before the Lord's Test. Talking to a large gathering of the Cricket Society of South Africa in Johannesburg, he argued that Fanie would find the English umpires less sympathetic to those from other countries in regard to lbw decisions.

It was a bit of an old chestnut. Such was the angle of the ball when bowling as wide as Fanie did, that getting an lbw decision would not be easy in England. Most of the top umpires, as former county bowlers, knew a trick or two. Fanie's ability to catch the batsman in front came from an ability learnt from seasons in South Africa, Australia and in England: as a county and league player. Gooch's lbw decision was one of four in the three Tests. Fanie enjoyed the comparisons. Four lbws was not a bad record in three Tests.

Now a popular TV commentator, Jackman has a much wider audience than in the days he played for Surrey, erstwhile Rhodesia and Western Province. His knowledge of the game and sound opinions are often sought. In the case of Fanie and lbws from umpires in England, Jackman's argument was not supported.

England trailed by 177 runs in the first innings and as Atherton walked out on the Saturday at a packed Lord's, the stifling weather seemed to have stultified the England bowlers as South Africa began their second innings. Wessels' plan was to build as quickly as possible on the first innings lead and take advantage of the conditions. Hudson went early but Gary Kirsten and Cronje set about building the platform their skipper wanted.

It was shortly before tea on the Saturday when TV cameras took a shot of the England captain, Atherton, obliviously happy, as he took something out of his pocket and began working it on the ball. Hello, now. What's this? It was clear enough that something was not quite kosher. But it was obvious enough he was working on the ball for some reason other than its raggedy state. Intriguing all right, and a storm was brewing without a cloud in sight over a humid London. Everyone was drenched in sweat with shirtsleeves rolled above the elbow.

Speculation boiled over through the media benches, and for forty-eight hours the axe hovered over the neck of the England captain. At first, there was far more smoke than fire, but as allegations passed beyond the mumbling stage, sparks began to light the brushwood, with Jonathan Agnew, the BBC cricket correspondent, tackling the issue head on. He accused Atherton of cheating and suggested he should resign. Exacerbating the problem was Atherton's later admission that he had not been totally forthcoming on the issue when summoned by Peter Burge, the ICC referee for the series. The big question was whether he had infringed Note 5 (changing the condition of the ball) of Law 42 (unfair play under the 1980 code). After discussing the incident, Burge was satisfied that Atherton had not infringed the law.

The media raked over the embers of the row and the flames blazed anew. Agnew was accused of lacking objectivity, Atherton denied he had set out to 'alter the condition of the ball as he was trying to dry it with some dirt in his pockets' and Ray Illingworth, England's new selector-manager supremo, dished out his own comments and fine. It was argued later that Illingworth and Burge had contrived to rescue Atherton's position. Not only was the code of conduct under assault, the laws and ethics of the game were being questioned.

By rights, Atherton should have faced a three-match suspension, but escaped the hangman's noose. Illingworth, however, fined him seventy-five per cent of his match fee, hoping the measure would take the heat out of the raging scandal. It had been two years since the ball-tampering row involving Pakistan had erupted at Lord's, and smoke from that fire had not been doused when Atherton was accused of bringing added dishonour to the game.

Wessels, Procter and the team did their best to focus on the game. They had no comment to offer and some British newspapers were quite piqued at the lack of reaction to Atherton's misdemeanour. South Africa were there to win a game, not to get involved in off-the-field squabbles. Later Procter displayed some annoyance when shown several photographs of Fanie, Donald and McMillan, their fingers cocked as they carried the ball. 'It's turning the game into a joke. You could take pictures like this a hundred times a day. It's paranoid, laughable. I don't know what we are supposed to be doing. But it's getting to the stage where bowlers can't handle the ball! Most bowlers, especially in this country, pick grass from the seam as they walk back to their marks. There's nothing wrong with that.'[1] Already in trouble with MCC regulations for an exuberant touch of patriotism by displaying the new South African flag from the balcony, Procter was not about to give a soft reply. He had a point to make and so did South Africa.

It can be tough walking down the steps of the pavilion at Lord's. Those doing it for the first time in a Test, running the gauntlet of censorious frosty-eyed MCC members packed in the open benches in front of the pavilion, can find it disconcerting. One New Zealand Test batsman of a much earlier era admitted he realized what a bride must feel when the congregation turns for a first critical look to see what she looks like in her bridal glory.

Just what Atherton felt as he led England out to field that baking, humid day is hard to imagine. What he had been thinking the previous afternoon is also hard to imagine. For one thing, Gough appeared to lose his ability to inswing the ball late in ideal conditions.

When the fourth day began, South Africa were 195 for 4 with Peter Kirsten and Jonty Rhodes resuming, eager to add quick runs to the total. Wessels wanted a commanding total and five sessions to win the match. 'Shut them out' was the motto that day. Had he not learnt such tricks from his playing days in Australia? There was to be no bargaining with the opposition. Knock them down and keep them there. Wessels knew that the only way to handle the Poms was to give them a good licking.

Rhodes enjoyed himself as he had done in Sydney. He hoisted Angus Fraser over mid-wicket into the grandstand for six, but Gough had his inswing radar working again and bowled Rhodes and Peter Kirsten in the same over. Gough picked up his third wicket of the morning, shattering Matthews' defences on the stroke of lunch as Wessels made the declaration, knowing all along that the 456 needed for victory was well beyond England's capabilities. Perhaps a team with a top order including Sir Leonard Hutton, Bill Edrich, Peter May, Denis Compton and Ted Dexter might survive to put close to 400 on the board.

While they would have enjoyed the challenge, the England side at Lord's in 1994 had no hope. Yet it is doubtful whether South Africa's most passionate supporters realized at the start of the England innings that they were likely to be celebrating into the early hours of the next day. And although Fanie, after a probing opening spell snapped up the first wicket of the innings, it was Matthews and McMillan who did their bit to conquer the England batsmen with 3 wickets apiece.

Early on in the innings, Fanie was involved in some by-play with England umpire Dickie Bird when he turned down an lbw appeal. Putting him in a headlock, Bird enjoyed the bit of fun and the crowd gave a great belly laugh after a fine Lord's lunch. At least, it relieved the tedium of England's pathetic second innings display. They were bowled out for 99 in 45.5 overs, although Alec Stewart batted for more than two hours for his 27 while Gooch also offered some attacking resistance before McMillan ended the humiliating rout by trapping Fraser lbw for 1. And while the bowling was tight, economical and penetrating, the fielding display was pretty good as well: keen and athletic, with Rhodes playing the lead violin as well as heading the trumpet section.

Victory at Lord's was only South Africa's second at headquarters, the first being fifty-nine years earlier, with the margin of 356 runs being the largest achieved in all Tests, surpassing the 323 against Australia at St. George's Park in 1970. It was also England's lowest total at Lord's in more than a century and Atherton was grilled again about the dirt in the pocket episode, while South Africa celebrated.

It was unfortunate that British newspapers feasted, as would a pack of vultures, over the well-picked bones of the ball-tampering issue. They ignored England's batting debacle, finding salvation by seeking another angle in a story they refused to let die, reviving the corpse with new theories and comments. Some South African players were bewildered by the reaction of the British media. It had been a great victory but for the next seven days all they read was 'Atherton's dirty pockets'.

The players, allowed a rare day off, split up. Fanie escaped into the country with Judy and a few English friends where they relaxed and forgot, for a while, the reason they were able to indulge in such a luxury.

For those brought up on the great Yorkshire sides, especially in the 1930s, Headingley has long been a spiritual home. Tales of the greatness of Hutton, Herbert Sutcliffe, Maurice Leyland, Headley Verity, Bill Bowes along with George Hirst and Wilfred Rhodes, are whispered through the terraces which make up most of the western side of the ground. Across the road at the indoor nets, you can almost feel the ghosts of those years lead you to the glass-fronted book cases and sets of sepia-toned prints, which chronicle the ancient and modern eras of the game throughout the broad acres of the great county.

Let us not forget, either, Sir Donald Bradman's remarkable achievement of 1930. After Bill Woodfull, the Aussie captain, won the toss, the Don scored 309 runs on the first day of the third Test of that particular Ashes series. A world record for runs scored in a day's play in a Test, it was an innings Hutton watched with fascination and anticipation of each stroke. What impressed him was the ball placement and shot selection, economical without too much dash or flair. It was, however, effective and entertaining as Bradman established a Test record innings of 334. Hutton relived the innings often in his fourteen-year-old mind, not realizing that eight years later he would break the record at the Oval with Bradman captaining Australia.

Lord's takes its name from Thomas Lord, a Yorkshireman, who initially worked in London as a wine merchant and professional cricketer and was asked by members of the White Conduit Club to hire a ground for their exclusive use.[2] Headingley is derived from another slice of Yorkshire history. It was part of a large estate known as Cardigan Fields and was bought in 1888 by a group of businessmen who formed the Leeds Cricket, Football and Athletic Club.

Since his days at Todmorden in 1987, Fanie has had a deep affinity with the inhabitants of Yorkshire's broad acres. Part of the attachment has to do with his kinship when living among a gruff yet warm people during those five months as his own game developed. They were, in a way, similar to the less privileged Afrikaner, hard-working lower-income middle-class people, whose one aspiration was to achieve a modicum of success. He grew to understand their ways and manners and frustrations. So, when he began his second spell on the first day of the second Test, he appreciated the applause from the knowledgeable Kirkstall Lane crowd.

An injury to Donald's big toe on his right foot created an added problem. It forced Fanie to bowl longer spells than he had expected; first with the new ball and then as a stock bowler, relying on swing and his cutters to induce an error from the watchful batsmen. After their opprobrious performance at Lord's, England were more determined and circumspect as they worked harder for their runs and rewards. Donald's absence was not helping much either. And in the months to come, when he had to carry the attack in the Test series against New Zealand and yet another round of one-dayers, Fanie knew that the punishment his body was taking would cause a serious injury.

He confided as much to Judy before the third Test at The Oval. The pain in his lower back had become unbearable and there were times when he needed her help to get out of bed. 'At this rate I'm going to wind up bowling downwind in a wheelchair,' he joked. Judy was concerned. She smiled at the way he made fun of his predicament but inside she ached for the way, on some days, he would struggle to do something as natural as put on a pair of

---

[2] Members of the White Conduit Club and a few friends formed the Marylebone Cricket Club (MCC) in 1787 with the first game at Lord's ground played on 31 May 1787. When the club was formed, Marylebone was an area some distance north of the Mall, where White Conduit Club members gathered.

socks. Swallowing a packet of painkillers a day was not the answer either. Not at all the jovial picture of the irrepressible swing bowler who playfully bit David Shepherd's ear, telling the rotund umpire 'serious damage can be caused by biting an ear'. It was a quick-thinking act by the swing bowler and came only hours after Johan le Roux, a South African and Transvaal rugby forward, had been banned for eighteen months for biting the ear of New Zealand captain, Sean Fitzpatrick, in a Test at Wellington's Athletic Park.

Devonshire-born, the then fifty-three-year-old Shepherd, a useful middle-order batsman in his day and capped for Gloucestershire in 1969, had the habit of shuffling his feet around when the score was on 111. After he turned down yet another lbw appeal, Fanie playfully grabbed him and pretended to bite his ear. It was just the sort of by-play that had the Yorkshire crowd applauding.

Later, Fanie's charisma, which had surfaced at Lord's, emerged a second time in the Headingley match. The Western Terrace crowd had been baiting the bowler after a number of unsuccessful lbw appeals. In the end, he took the umpire's red ground pass and flashed it at the ever-vocal Yorkshire audience. How they enjoyed Fanie's reaction. The action quickly won over the loudmouths who have given the area as notorious a reputation as old Bay Thirteen at the MCG or the long disbanded Hill at Sydney. There are a few areas in South Africa as well with their yobbos: notably Kingsmead and Bloemfontein, the latter a haven for brash limited-overs freaks. At Headingley, even the racist drunks can at least discuss the intricacies of swing and spin, and how a pitch is behaving. They have a culture of their own.

In between overs, Fanie wound up swapping rugby stories with some and sharing jokes with others as the heat reminded him of the humidity of Colombo and Sydney. But he enjoyed the response from his spontaneous rapport. 'You have worked some special magic there, lad,' Shepherd told Fanie, his soft west country burr flowing. 'They just don't take to anyone you know . . . unless it's their own. It's the first time I have seen that lot talk kindly to any touring Test player. That's one for you.'

Unlike Lord's, where South Africa assumed control of the match from tea on the first day, they were under pressure until Peter Kirsten rescued the side with quite a superb maiden century. And coming as it did, at the age of thirty-nine years and eighty-four days, it was a special event. They wrote his name on the wall in the dressing room, but it had gone when Chesters revisited the ground two years later, scrubbed off by diligent groundstaff.

The older Kirsten's century provided the sort of backbone the batting needed, at a time when South Africa wanted it most. It was a vigilant performance, watchful and cautious, but firm. It was the sort of bravery which made Spionkop synonymous with heroism in an age when there were many who battled gallantly for the honour of the side on which they fought. Kirsten, felled by a Gough lifter, hauled himself back into the front line and retrieved what had become a desperate situation at 199 for 6. When he reached the coveted three figures, the smaller man was engulfed by the massive McMillan. Kirsten's innings showed the character of the man and an inner strength, which had been obvious for so long.

It was also a statistical milestone and helped create several records in what was the former Western Province and Border captain's eleventh Test. It was an innings which saved South Africa and again showed up the paucity in England's pace and swing bowling attack.

Going to The Oval 1-0 up reminded some of the more superstitious of the lead up to Adelaide Oval and Newlands. Twice the previous southern summer South Africa had led 1-0 going into the final match and ended losing and squaring the series. Not the ideal situation and it was known that England were desperate to square this series after the drubbing at Lord's.

England made changes with Devon Malcolm brought in along with Joey Benjamin to add West Indies style pace and spice to their bowling attack; Angus Fraser was given the push along with Phil Tuffnell as they went into the game with six batsmen and Hick as the all-rounder. And while England's selections were made with a positive flair, South African selection seemed confused. Out went Andrew Hudson, and the older Kirsten's career was sacrificed as he played his twelfth and last Test as an opener. It seemed incongruous to open with a batsman who was no longer suited to the role, especially after his match-saving century at Headingley.

The Oval Test has been remembered for three events. Jonty Rhodes being felled by Malcolm when the batsman ducked into the ball; Malcolm's second innings spell and the so-called incident which sparked it; and Fanie being fined for an incident which match referee, Peter Burge, felt was dissent.

This was after Atherton had been trapped lbw by the Northerns bowler and fined fifty per cent of his match fee. Fanie felt he had Hick out caught in the slips and he went up in appeal, knowing the batsman had edged the catch. At the time Hick had not reached double figures and when the umpire gave a negative response, the bowler turned, hands on hips registering a silent protest.

It begs the question—how far can a bowler go in appealing? Fanie's view is that an umpire should be required to answer the appeal with more than a mere 'not-out' comment. He gave Chesters a grilling in the club match a couple of seasons later, suggesting himself 'too high' and 'going down leg', when he turned with a big grin on his face as he faced his mate with a query. The law on appeals is silent on what an umpire can or cannot say in reply apart from 'not-out'. Chesters' own view is that it depends on whether the enquiry deserves an extra comment.

Chesters found that umpiring in games with bowlers such as Trevor Goddard was often an enjoyable experience. The former South African captain was a demanding, but fair bowler and normally a lbw appeal was a polite query. Jackie Botten and Sid Burke, two other South African Test bowlers, enjoyed challenging the umpire's opinion. They also knew how far they could go. In Fanie's case at The Oval, he was doing no more than Dennis Lillee, or Fred Trueman, would have done.

In any event, Fanie, when bowling to Malcolm towards the end of the England first innings, hit the thirty-one-year-old Jamaica-born fast bowler on the helmet, about where the middle of his forehead was. It was a first ball bouncer, designed to unsettle the short-sighted England bowler after he had trapped Benjamin lbw for a duck. While Malcolm was uninjured, the helmet disintegrated, an act which set up the famous comment as Fanie collected the ball and prepared to walk back to his mark.

'You guys are going to pay for this,' he told the South Africans. 'You guys are history.'

He was referring to the state of the pitch and how it would help him destroy the South African second innings. There are those on the county circuit who viewed Malcolm as a 'big talker' or, as Fanie felt, 'someone with a bigger mouth than most' and dismissed the comment as an act of bravado. A little more than two sessions and 50.3 overs later Malcolm had paid South Africa back. In a devastating display of pace and accuracy, Malcolm picked up 9 wickets for only 53 runs; then the sixth best bowling analysis at Test level.

It shattered Syd Barnes' record for the best bowling performance at The Oval (8 for 29, also against South Africa), which had stood for eighty-two years. It also caused some concern in the South African ranks, as the West Indian-born fast bowler became the catalyst for a great day's play in the Test arena. The brutal power of his bowling saw the first 3 wickets falling with only a run on the board with little more than 4 overs of the innings completed.

The enigmatic Cullinan attempted to rescue his side with a display of quality batting, but with others falling all too rapidly to the panzer-style blitz launched by Malcolm on a surface with unpredictable bounce, he was only delaying the inevitable. With the last 4 wickets falling at 175 and Malcolm setting himself up for the man of the match award (which he collected), Cullinan's innings was overlooked in the general euphoria of Malcolm's bowling performance, while Fanie had to admit he was proved wrong. Even England's new chairman of selectors, Ray Illingworth, was full of praise, calling it the greatest bowling display by an England fast bowler in 'living memory'. Barely eighteen months later, he was blaming the same bowler for costing England the series against South Africa at Newlands.

Fanie left the game with barely enough bus fare to get him back to the hotel after his stiff fine.

Further trouble loomed for South Africa: they comprehensively lost the Texaco Trophy series and then fell apart on the matting against Holland in The Hague, losing a match reduced to 40 overs by an embarrassing 9 wickets. Added to the team's woes was the decision by Wessels and Procter not to travel to Holland with the side. It was a mistake by Procter, whose tenure as coach was running out.

One of Chesters' contacts in England, Ian Todd, seemed to know his replacement as well.

'Bob Woolmer,' said Todd. 'Warwickshire are being pressed into releasing him from his contract.'

'Can you substantiate that?' Todd was asked.

'Dennis Amiss has just confirmed it, old boy. Genuine . . .'

True, Procter's contract was up for negotiation, but the feeling was he would be retained until the end of the season. Ditching the man who had helped guide South Africa since November 1991 would come as a surprise. The captaincy issue also had not been resolved as the other, stronger rumour was that Wessels was about to retire. Rumours hung heavy as ripe fruit, and in South Africa the smell was already wafting through the corridors.

Jan Smuts airport's overseas arrival foyer was busy enough with the appearance of the South Africa team on 6 September 1994, and as Wessels came through with other members of the touring party, he was collared by several journalists and asked about his future.

'Do you feel fit enough to tackle another tour?' Chesters asked.

'Yes,' grinned Wessels. 'I'm ready to take the side to Pakistan for the limited-overs series. I'm having no trouble at all with my knee.'

'Does that mean you'll be available as captain for the rest of the season.'

'Nothing has been decided. We'll have to wait and see.'

In reality it was a stopgap decision designed to take pressure off an out-of-form Cronje; it was Wessels' final unselfish act of loyalty. It had long been suggested that he had not wanted to lead the side to England and was eventually persuaded to continue as captain by Dr Bacher and the UCB. It is a rumour he has firmly denied. Yet an era was slowly drawing to a close as first Procter was not re-engaged and then Woolmer was asked to take on at late notice the job of coaching a side on their first tour of Pakistan and the Wills Triangular series, which also involved Australia.

At a middle-net practice session at the Wanderers days before the side left for Pakistan, Fanie admitted to Chesters he was worried about this particular trip. His body was still tired from the England tour and an event such as the national club championship had come as an unwelcome intrusion. Not one to break a promise, however, he had turned out for his club, Oostelike, in late September. He bowled a handful of overs and opened the batting on occasions. It was far from satisfactory for a man who was in desperate need of rest, as he hobbled about the various venues, chewing pain killers.

On the first day of the club tournament he was called in and quizzed by Dr Bacher about Procter's role as a coach, and there was more less pleasant news. Donald was out until mid-January and the Test against Pakistan at the Wanderers. The foot injury, which had plagued him in the final matches of the England tour, needed surgical treatment and a long recovery period.

Fanie and Donald sat at Wanderers One across Corlett Drive from the Test venue, chatting. Donald was far from happy with the news that he was out of the series against New Zealand.

'We'll have to leave it to Fanie, won't we?' Donald grinned. 'I'm sure he'll do the job.'

When the announcement came that Woolmer was taking over from Procter, there was relief from some, disappointment from others. He had played an important role in the side's preparation during those first years after isolation and there was a view 'let's remember the good times . . .' rather than rake over the embers of controversy.

For Woolmer, his first sortie as South African coach has always been ranked as a major disappointment. The side lost every game and Fanie's haul of 5 wickets supported his pre-tour fears. Wessels also felt frustration at the way his last tour worked out. And, as the Tests against New Zealand loomed without Donald, Fanie suddenly found himself on his own.

15

One Match too Many

Edgbaston in Birmingham has more links with overseas countries than most English grounds. New Zealanders, South Africans, Australians, Pakistanis and Indians have passed through the Warwickshire ranks since the end of World War II. Tom Pritchard, a Kiwi fast bowler, began a tradition, which now includes two of South Africa's best post-isolation fast bowlers, Allan Donald and Shaun Pollock.

There is a story of how Tom Dollery, later to captain the county, was so impressed with the Taranaki-born Pritchard during a match arranged at some Italian club late in World War II that he invited him to join the county before the start of the 1946 season. Typical of the good-natured Dollery, it was done without consulting any of the Warwickshire committee and he promptly forgot all about it. So when the rugged, rangy Pritchard turned up at the Edgbaston gates and asked to see Dollery, there was some consternation among the senior ground staff.

Peter Cranmer, who had in the 1930s captained England at rugby, met Pritchard and gave him a net and, like Dollery, was most impressed despite a slight impediment in the action. Pritchard's delivery was similar to that of Mike Procter's: both gave the mistaken impression of bowling off the wrong foot. It enabled them to cunningly bowl outswing with an inswing action, complicated yet effective.

It was too late for county authorities to sign Pritchard even as a late registration and he had to wait until 1947 before making a belated county championship debut. Pritchard became the ultimate professional: Don Bradman's Australians regarded him as the fastest bowler on the 1948 county circuit. Unfortunately, he had to turn down a place in the 1949 Kiwi side when his contract would not allow him to take up the offer of earning a deserved Test cap.

There are many similarities between the rangy Pritchard and Fanie. Both were quality outswing bowlers; Pritchard, barely twenty but with unmistakable talent, was ignored in 1937 by New Zealand's selectors for the tour of England. Like Fanie, his career did not earn the recognition it deserved, until it was almost too late. Pritchard was twenty-nine when he turned up at the Edgbaston gates in 1946. It is interesting how both had to struggle with similar myopic selection dichotomy.

How times have changed. These days Pritchard would have soon found himself selected for England: 818 first-class wickets at 23.20 are a tribute to his economy. When the suggestion was made in 1950 against the West Indies, he laughed it off as a joke.

It was at Edgbaston on a bitterly cold early June morning in 1995 that Fanie reported, along with Hansie Cronje, to play in a Rest of the World XI side. Fanie prepared for a match against Warwickshire along with Australians and West Indians, an Indian, a New Zealander, a Sri Lankan and a Pakistani. Even after the first biting winter chills at home, the weather in England was unpleasantly more arctic than usual.

Organized by Dennis Amiss, a former England Test batsman and Warwickshire's chief executive, the 50-over match was part of the benefit season for Paul Smith. Also in the side were Shane Warne, the Waugh twins, Michael Slater, Mark Taylor, Malcolm Marshall, Aravinda de Silva, Chris Cairns and Phil Simmonds. It did not take Fanie too long to start his warm up preparations with Donald, going for a light run to get rid of stiffness, talking about the England tour prospects next southern summer. Later, Fanie joined Simmonds at a nearby eatery and they reminisced about their Lancashire league days.

While going back to the hotel, the weather bothered him. Although he had turned on the large water heater, it was colder than he had imagined and the first signs of a sniffle surfaced. To keep warm that night, he slept in a spare tracksuit.

Next morning, he arrived at the ground, and changed into a tracksuit. The Australian quintet had already done several laps of the ground when they went in to the nets. A mist rose in the nets as they talked and joked.

As was his habit in such weather, Fanie took a light jog as part of his warm up before joining the net session. The previous afternoon he had done more running than bowling and was feeling relaxed. The next morning he jogged again before a light net, but did not feel comfortable at all about his bowling. He felt stiff, his lower back and the muscles in both legs were tight and he put it down to the cold weather. After sending down about twenty balls, he went for another light run. This was more to get rid of the stiffness in his lower back than the need to run on the Test venue's luxuriant surface.

He then did a series of stretching exercises to see whether the stiffness had gone before picking up a ball and marking out a run-up he had cut down to two metres. The idea was using the shorter run-up to bowl perhaps thirty to forty balls as part of his warm up.

Turning, he ran in and was halfway into his delivery stride when he felt a sudden cramp in his right groin and struggled with his balance as he pulled up. What on earth? The cramp gripped tight.

We can't have this. Not now.

He was worried as he did more stretching exercises; each time he stood up and walked, the cramp became progressively worse. He felt that the only way to get rid of the cramp would be to rest.

Give it five minutes, then do more stretching exercises and bowl again.

He went back to the two-metre marker and ran in. Again he had to bale out halfway through his delivery stride. Fanie sat down and began another series of stretching exercises, desperately worried as time for the match to start was less than half an hour.

Donald, with a grin, walked to where he sat.

'Trouble, Fanie?'

'I can't get up, AD.' He looked at his Test new-ball colleague. 'Can you please help me up and get me to the dressing room?'

'Come on, Fanie,' said Donald, his grin growing. He was used to the de Villiers leg-pulling acts in the South African dressing room and this was no different. 'We both need a final warm up in the nets.'

'Please, AD. This is really serious. I can't walk.' The distress in the normally cheerful eyes alerted Donald that something was wrong with his teammate and he became deeply concerned. He beckoned one of the Warwickshire staff to help him and the three began walking. They talked and joked as Fanie limped across the ground annoyed with what seemed to be an injury. As large groups of spectators were watching the net preparation, the trio did not want to cause any alarm.

Amiss was in the dressing room checking final arrangements, when Fanie limped in with Donald and the Warwickshire colt.

'Okay. What's up, Fanie?'

'I'm injured,' came the flat reply.

'You have to be kidding. Come on. You're on in fifteen minutes.'

'Sir, I can't. It's even painful to walk.'

He started to laugh, but it was no laughing matter. The Australians, back from the net session, also began to laugh. Fanie was up to his dressing room tricks, getting everyone in the right mood for the limited-overs slog.

'When did this happen?' Amiss wondered for a moment if the South African Test bowler, then third in the latest world rankings, was injured all along, or playing a prank.

'Just now. In the nets.'

Donald concurred.

The Warwickshire physio, Steve Nottingham, made Fanie lie on the table to take a look at the groin, confirming the swing bowler's fears. He had pulled the muscle in such a way that it was stretched tighter than normal and felt like an uncomfortable cramp when he walked. Amiss looked at Fanie, one of the star turns of the match, and then the physio.

'No chance it will be okay with heat treatment?' asked Amiss hopefully.

Nottingham shook his head.

'It's too new, and it's quite serious. He's out for at least six to seven weeks. May be longer. Just as well there's no Test tour for you guys at present.'

That meant the earliest he could be back in action would be mid- to late-August. It was not the report he wanted to hear. Cronje was also concerned. With Donald injured most of the previous summer, he had depended a lot on Fanie and his nagging outswing. There was a tour of Zimbabwe looming in September, and if Fanie was not ready to start training by the time of the pre-tour camp, the new-ball attack for the two limited-overs internationals and the one-off Test would have to be restructured. It was not worth thinking about the World Cup, that was too far away.

Fanie went to see his hosts of his 1992 summer in Torquay, Roger and Jenny Mann. They had motored up from Devon for the match and suggested he take an injection that would enable him to bowl a few overs to entertain the large crowd.

'I would if it was possible. But I can hardly walk.'

They looked at him, feeling sorry for the agony he was in, and the mental anguish he was going through. Fanie also realized that he had wanted to play in one match too many. As with most players, he had also joked that he too had the T-shirt, 'been there, done that and sent off the postcards'. Now the body, which had been subjected to a punishing schedule since September 1993, had said 'enough'. The strain of bowling too many overs had told: almost 600 of the friendlies, limited-overs, Castle Cup and domestic day-night games.

Maybe, he bowled a few overs less than some of the top, over-worked English county fast and medium-pace swing bowlers had sent down in the 1950s. The advent of the one-day and later the limited-overs games, however, changed bowling strategies. His 262 Test overs in five matches in the 1994-95 summer was 58 more than that of any other South African bowler, and comparable to Terry Alderman's 278 in 1981 against England in England.

He had become a new-ball as well as a stock bowler and it had started to show. As it was, he had bowled 668.2 overs in the fourteen Tests between his debut in Melbourne and the one against the Kiwis at Eden Park in Auckland; it worked out to almost 49 overs a Test. It should also be remembered there were times when he bowled in only one innings. As Bob Woolmer, the new South African coach, admitted before the New Zealand tour, Fanie's workload had been particularly heavy.

For the first time since he began his provincial career, Fanie knew he was in serious trouble. He admitted as much to Judy on his return from Edgbaston and later to Chesters and Neels Liebel. What bothered him was how it would affect his benefit season, which had just started: to be successful, he needed to play in the Test series against England.

Fanie had been looking forward to playing a role in the inaugural Test at Centurion Park when Northerns hosted the game against England in November. Now it all seemed out of reach. The injury he had dreaded for so long threatened to disrupt his career and the plans to take 150 Test wickets before he retired. As it turned out, the lengthy lay-off from injury at Edgbaston and the virus from the India tour of 1996-97 possibly cost him fourteen to fifteen Tests. If his strike rate is also taken into account, he lost at least a further 67 Test wickets up to the time he bowled against Pakistan at Kingsmead in February 1997.

At Edgbaston, however, he was faced with a new problem as he evaluated his long-term prospects, and it worried him. He was thirty-one and his career had been ticking along nicely. Then he remembered what Chesters had once told him: 'life is a long series of question marks'.

The injury at Edgbaston was an unwelcome intrusion. For one thing, it would disrupt plans for the next summer when England were in South Africa. He had been through the pain barrier so often, there were times when the pain killers barely worked, and he was left to hobble around as best as he could. Even sleeping in bed with a pillow between his legs no longer eased the nagging discomfort that often kept him awake for hours.

As he reflected on the South African summer of 1994-95, he knew the workload had been too much. Most spectators gained the impression that he enjoyed every ball bowled; in this case it was a matter of 3,425 balls (or 570.5 overs) and 75 wickets.

There was that time in Auckland, during the Tests against New Zealand, when he walked barefoot into the lift, still in flannels with his boots slung casually over his right shoulder, smiling cheerfully at the occupants and asking how they were enjoying the day and the weather. His bruised toes had been wrapped in pink stretch sticky tape, two toenails had come off, the other toes either black or darker shade of blue. Not at all the feet of a world-class athlete: it showed his inner strength and character.

A concerned Colin Bryden marvelled that Fanie was still capable of bowling with the same studied calm and energy. 'Fanie, are you going to be fit to bowl tomorrow?'

The fast bowler looked at his feet and smiled. 'Don't worry about these. They'll see me through another hundred overs. Just a few blisters. No worry. Not a problem.'

Which was comforting enough for some but part of the trials a fast bowler often goes through is for the sake of his team, his country and hopefully the rewards at the end of it. And as Clive Rice often said, anyone who really knew about it would never say that fast bowling, hour after hour, over after over, was an easy occupation. To be a winner, you had to go through the pain barrier more than once in a game.

* * * *

Fanie barely had time to touch down after the 1994 tour of England before he was off to India. This time it was to play in a series of World XI matches and he decided to take along his father Braam, as well as a business friend Colin Lazarus. For the two older men, the hotels on the Asian subcontinent were not what they expected, a far cry from the four or even three star hotels to be found in South Africa, New Zealand, England, Australia, Zimbabwe and Zambia. How they enjoyed the experience the smells and sights, which make up the populous Asian subcontinent and gives it that special charm and aura.

On his return, it was straight into a domestic season, and a rare game for Northerns. This one was a Castle Cup match against Border at Centurion Park and it was there that tragedy stalked his old new-ball partner Gerbrand Grobler. Driving home to Centurion where he lived, Grobler's car was hit broadside by an ambulance near the Morula Sun hotel where he had been playing the tables. Although Grobler no longer fitted into the Northerns team set up, he was a still close friend to a number of players and Fanie had been his last room-mate on away matches.

The mood was sombre at Centurion Park on 7 November 1994 as Fanie, padded up, waited to join Kevin Rule to battle past the Border first innings of 286. He had already managed four first innings wickets. Scoring a half-century was far from his thoughts when he went out at the fall of Steve Elworthy's wicket.

Although Anton Ferreira, then the Northerns coach, and others had tried to keep the news of Grobler's death from Fanie, he got to know of it. Symbolically, as he walked down the steps, the Northerns, Border and South African flags were lowered to halfmast. It was shortly after eleven in the morning. It was an emotional moment with the scoreboard reading 230 for 8 while Rodney Ontong, who had just been dismissed, offered his usual sound advice.

'We can still pass their total if you bat sensibly and play down the line,' was Ontong's comment. 'There are still some runs to be scored and we also need you batting at the close.'

When Rule perished, 19 runs later with less than 6 overs of the day remaining, Northerns were 37 in arrears and Rudi Bryson, the last man, joined Fanie. It was a matter of survival. News of Grobler's death acted as a catalyst as the last pair worked the ball around. Grobler had often rescued Northerns with lower-order heroics and, when given the chance, had enjoyed a number of productive partnerships. Bryson began with a firm drive to mid-off, while Fanie slapped a single past backward of square. At the close of day two, the last pair had taken the score to 273 for 9.

What followed the next morning has become part of Centurion Park folklore: Bryson and Fanie added a record 108 runs for the tenth wicket, taking the total to 357 by scoring a further 84 runs. It may not have been the most perfectly executed century partnership you will ever see, but amid the typically tail-end frustration a fielding captain faces in such circumstances, there was stylish, if not classic, strokeplay. Mixed with a miscued pull, were a top-edged cut and a front-foot cover drive straight from the Peter Kirsten school of perfect batsmen. And Kirsten, later to become Northerns coach, was the captain on the receiving end this time.

Given the chance, Bryson, always innovative with the cheeky, robust style of his on-field nature, top-scored with 62, and amid the ten boundaries were four sixes. Fanie managed 58 and helped give Northerns an unexpected lead of 71. The duo then turned to doing best what they had been selected for, taking wickets: four apiece was a fair haul.

His match figures of 8 for 103 were the first of the 21 wickets he managed to collect in only four games for Northerns that season. Bryson went on to take 27, and Elworthy 32, in a summer where Northerns, at one stage, looked as though they would take the

Castle Cup crown. Coming as it did after the distressing Wills Cup triangular series in Pakistan during October, Fanie's bowling in the match against Border showed he had not lost his competitive edge. There had been hints in the Johannesburg, Durban and Cape Town daily newspapers that this was the case with a bold suggestion that 'his career was showing signs of coming to an end'.

Just the sort of interesting assumptions to annoy the new coach, Bob Woolmer. While he did not say it, the thought no doubt ran through his analytical mind, whether the authors penning such claims had played at any level other than a social league.

One of the first things Chesters remembers about Woolmer is his smooth batting technique when playing for Natal and later Western Province during the summers of isolation. He had touches, which hinted at the elegance of his former Kent county captain Colin Cowdrey, later Lord Cowdrey of Tonbridge Wells, who died in early December 2000.

In those first summers with Kent, Cowdrey's influence on Woolmer was considerable and that is where the all-rounder learnt how to play fast bowling. He employed it so well that he quickly established his reputation of being someone who knew how to handle the quick stuff when it came along. Yet if his batting style was correct it was not as flamboyant as that of say, Ian Botham. Woolmer did, however, do what Botham declined, and that was join the Kerry Packer roadshow Down Under in 1977-78.

This may surprise those who know Botham's aggressive anti-establishment stance. But the game in England in 1977 was far better off in terms of players and quality than it had become twenty-two years later. In their World Cup year of 1999, it was a mess. Ironically, on 25 June 1999, the England and Wales Cricket Board (ECB) turned to Duncan Fletcher to cure the malaise.[1]

Initially the ECB had hoped it would be Woolmer, but the Cape Town-based former South African coach had other ideas. A contract

---

[1] Duncan Fletcher, a former Zimbabwe captain, coached Western Province from 1991 to 1998-99. He also coached South Africa A in England in 1996 and Glamorgan in 1997 and 1999. The ECB offered Fletcher the post as England coach in early June 1999 and he accepted the job for two years starting in September 1999. His first tour was that of South Africa. Woolmer rejoined Warwickshire on a three-year contract from 2000.

with Warwickshire beckoned, and he signed that, rather than find himself in the camp opposing South Africa during the England tour of 1999-2000. If you know Woolmer, you will know why he rejected the ECB approaches: overriding loyalty to the players he has brought through the system is his style of management and approach to coaching.

Yet, if you think Woolmer with his Packer and Gooch rebel tour background was an anti-establishment mutineer, dream on. From the Packer Circus, he sought a better bargaining deal for those in what had long been a poorly-paid profession. He has also had the insight to look more globally at the game than just the immediate parameters which partly explains his rebel tour role.

If his Packer dalliance partly ruptured his Test career, it ended abruptly with his decision to join Graham Gooch's 'Dirty Dozen'. What will surprise many is that he has had a long association with development and transformation, and his association with South Africa started in the 1969-70 season. There are those in UCB circles however who have mistaken for arrogance his strong inner self-belief and English public school upbringing as well as a deep-seated family cricket culture.

Woolmer also has strong family ties with the Asian subcontinent. His father, C. S. Woolmer, a British business executive, had captained the Indian state side of Uttar Pradesh and encouraged his son's love and passion for the game. Born in Kanpur in 1948, Woolmer was only seven when he was sent to England in 1955, the year Jack Cheetham led South Africa on a highly successful tour of England. That team had no coach (neither did their English opponents). It shows just how much the game has changed from that more relaxed, if competitive, era.

To maintain levels of improved excellence and skill a modern coach needs to be more resourceful in planning and strategy than the opposing side's mentor: always keep them guessing. In his desire to see skill levels improve and make better players, Woolmer put his own theories to work. He believed that adapting the basic skills of the game to modern strategies is not as complex as many believe. To be successful, however, they have to be moved from the classroom to the field of play. This required a certain amount of in-depth research, and there were any number of coaching books by former Test players and masters of the game to guide him: Clarrie Grimmett, Trevor Bailey, C. B. Fry, Sir Donald Bradman and Jack Hobbs among others had expressed themselves in print.

By the time he returned to Kent as coach in 1987, he had moved most of his ideas from classroom theory to the field. In turn, it led to the innovative ideas he has become known and respected for. As a starting point, he drew on his own experiences as a player, and adapted ideas to get players in the squads he coached thinking along similar lines. It was all about game plans and how to get them working.

Run-scoring in limited-overs matches had to be maximized to put the bowler under pressure: force him to change his line. The reverse-sweep was just one of many innovations with a specific design: to increase the run-scoring opportunities off balls pitched on the leg stump. The slog-sweep was another plan of attack, later perfected by Hansie Cronje, who demonstrated its effectiveness against Muttiah Muralitharan at SuperSport Centurion in the second Test against Sri Lanka in March 1998; a half-century off 31 balls, the second fastest in Test history, was the destructive result.

The overseas umpire for that match was the Pakistani Javed Akhtar, a name that returned five months later to haunt South Africa and an already-tainted Cronje at Leeds, and England at Edgbaston in their 1999 World Cup Group A match against India. Quick on the draw when making an lbw or catch decision, Akhtar was, with Zimbabwean Ian Robinson, on the ICC panel. Akhtar was removed from the panel after the 1999 World Cup.

It was during South Africa's under-24 team's tour of Sri Lanka in August 1995 that Chesters had a chance to closely examine Woolmer's expertise with the growing pool of Test players. Shaun Pollock, the team's unofficial vice-captain, Lance Klusener, Jacques Kallis and Nicky Boje were members of a side captained by Dale Benkenstein. The youngsters were being given a chance to show off their talents and Woolmer, when asked about the fourth seamer for the first four-day game against the Sri Lanka under-24s at the P. Saravanamuttu (Tamil Union) venue, said Kallis would fill it.

'He is a far better bowler than most people realize,' said Woolmer confidently after the team's final practice. 'Jacques is deceptive: he's quite quick and swings the ball nicely. I've had a good look at him the last couple of years.'

Then, with typical Woolmer confidentiality, he smiled quietly at the two touring pressmen, Chesters and MWP's Neil Manthorp, although admitting he was not into crystal ball gazing.

'I think you are going to be very surprised,' he nodded. 'He is going to play an important role as an all-rounder for South Africa. Perhaps not against England, but in a year or two down the line.'

Having watched Kallis' progress since August 1995, neither Chesters nor Manthorp were surprised when, in the absence of Allan Donald, it was Kallis who was asked to share the new-ball with Pollock against the West Indies in Bridgetown and St. John's during the third and fourth Tests of the 2001 Caribbean tour.

In early October 1994, however, Woolmer, barely a few days into the job after being bought out of his Warwickshire contract by the UCB, had the task of working with a group of players whom he knew, but not all that well, at the Wanderers. The camp was designed to prepare the team for the triangular series in Pakistan.

Already Donald had been ruled out because of a foot problem of which needed surgery. Kepler Wessels had stayed on as captain to ease Hansie Cronje through a form crisis, a hangover from the England tour, while the selectors could not find places after the England tour for Peter Kirsten or Pat Symcox. The older Kirsten brother's exclusion was astonishing. He had batted well in England, scoring two centuries and was one of only three batsmen to score more than 500 runs during the tour.

Surprise inclusions were Clive Eksteen and Meyrick Pringle, along with Eric Simons. Derek Crookes was making his debut tour. With Tim Shaw in the squad, the selectors seemed to think that the left-arm variation with Eksteen and Shaw might be better than a second off-spinner in Symcox. Crookes, whose father Norman toured England in 1965 but failed to play in a Test, had been among the four 'learners' during that historic 1991 visit to India and had not been considered since. Selectors often make strange or interesting choices without giving reasons and a couple of faces in this touring party for a limited-overs tournament were no exception.

Pringle played only two games and did not make an impression, while Crookes and Eksteen were fitted into three matches and Simons played all six. Cronje rediscovered his batting form and scored handsomely and Fanie, short on wickets, at least had an economy rate which was higher than usual. It tied in with his pre-tour view that 'it is going to be tougher than usual'.

If you examine a pimple long enough, it can become a messy carbuncle. By the end of the season, however, the triangular tournament in Pakistan had faded to an insignificant skin blemish, put in its place by the successful conclusion to what was a long season. Sure the visit to Pakistan was a disastrous campaign: defeat in every match, with Woolmer wondering how to motivate a losing side still at odds over the captaincy issue. Some of the players were also unsure about what the selectors had in mind, and uncertain of their place in future plans that summer.

It was a tough baptism for the new coach and there was trouble on another front. A couple of newspaper reporters on the tour were, without considering the polemic background issues, wanting Woolmer out and Mike Procter back. Yet they had, before the tournament, written how Woolmer's success with Warwickshire would rub off on the team. It is typical of the contradictory approach where defeatism and chauvinistic judgement often infiltrate the thoughts of those commenting about a side on a losing streak. The three English county titles won in earlier years seemed to have been a mirage, forgotten in the rush to stir the pot with controversy and, often, with misplaced criticism.

Woolmer took it on the chin. It is so easy to be critical of a losing side and find fault and flaws in just about anything from the captain to the most positive player. It smacked of ignorance of the conditions, the teams South Africa were playing, and a side in transition with uncertainty about Wessels' future role.

Pakistan can be a hard, cruel and unforgiving place to the novice traveller, tougher than most. Even the experienced Australians found it unfriendly this time. Examine the reasons, however: Pakistan were World Cup champions and their partisan crowds had become arrogant, expecting them to beat the pretenders. It had been predicted that Pakistan would continue their domination over South Africa, which had started in the Total Triangular series of 1993, and reversed the results a year earlier when the two countries first met before and during the World Cup in Australia.

Woolmer, however, was not about to allow his carefully laid coaching plans to be sidetracked. It had taken him a couple of seasons to first have the Warwickshire players embrace the new ideas and strategies, and then put them into action. It was going to take a full season with South Africa to achieve a similar result. He also needed disciples of this philosophy. Donald was not around to help spread the new coaching gospel.

* * * *

On 16 December 1994, Kepler Wessels walked past the empty TV and radio commentary suites to the new press box benches at St. George's Park in Port Elizabeth. There was Chesters sitting alone, scribbling notes. Northerns' first innings in the Castle Cup match against Eastern Province showed early signs of disarray with 2 wickets gone and 26 runs on the board, and Eldine Baptiste bustling in striving for a third wicket. Wessels had been on the field at the start of the innings, but had left to nurse his knee injury.

The previous day he had talked briefly to Chesters about the growing modern Afrikaans influence on the game, a conversation interrupted by the collapse of the Eastern Province top order. Now Wessels was back to answer a few questions on that subject, and also discuss his own future. The two had known each other since 1977-78, when Wessels had spent a successful season with what was then Northern Transvaal.

Wessels had also found Chesters to be one of the few journalists supporting his appointment as captain of the South African team when the 1992 World Cup squad was named. He had cited Wessels' tough Australian-style approach as an important factor if the national team's transition after years of isolation was to be successful. There were times when too much was expected and unfair demands were placed on the team against hard-nosed opponents such as Australia, and the West Indies at that time. Under the circumstances, such an accomplishment would not be easy, and Wessels warned of the difficulties of adjustment.

Success against touring rebel teams was one of the measures through which the public gauged the strength of the South Africa side. The view was that South Africa, despite isolation, had the players to beat the best. It was conveniently forgotten how Lawrence Rowe's West Indian side had beaten South Africa in the 'Test' series on the second tour, with Hartley Alleyne wrecking the batting in the final game in Port Elizabeth. It was also forgotten that the rebel sides generally lacked class batting to offer a genuine challenge. All of which gave the public a false impression of South Africa's depth as well as strength.

South Africa had lost to the West Indies in the Caribbean in 1992, and drawn two series against Australia. This was after an average performance against an average Indian team, and a drawn series with England. Three weeks before, South Africa had lost the first Test to New Zealand at the Wanderers. The limited-overs international barometer also had its highs and lows. After the Kiwis had unexpectedly gone up 1-0 as a result of their victory by 137 runs, there had been a call for the selectors to stiffen the team's batting by recalling Wessels. But the former captain had remained silent on the issue.

As Wessels began to outline his future plans, he became quiet for a moment.

'It is now time for South Africa to do without me.' It was a cool, calculated comment, as if he was nudging a ball past point. 'You can write that if you want. I am not available to play against New Zealand.'

'Does this mean you are retiring?'

'As a Test player? Yes. I'm still going to look after Eastern Province though. There are still things here which have to be done. Is a job such as this ever over?'

The fourth wicket fell as Baptiste claimed his third, and Wessels stood up. 'The selectors are aware of my decision. I have passed it on to Hansie, too. He has my best wishes.'

He walked towards the door and smiled. 'I think they need me out there. I'll talk to you later about a few other things.'

Unfortunately, there was no time or chance to talk privately later on.

Typically, the significance of Wessels retiring as a Test player was lost on the Saturday papers, within what was then the Argus Group. Yet when *The Sunday Times* ran the story the next day, Chesters was contacted after lunch to revive it with new quotes. But Wessels was not available. He was on the field trying to win a match for Eastern Province. As there was a flight to catch to the Reef almost immediately after the game, time was short. It meant that amid the scramble to finish the match report and two other stories, there was no time to get fresh comment. As it is, Wessels had a speaking engagement that evening, and had left the ground in his playing kit.

The original story began:

> Kepler Wessels has passed on his 'best wishes' to South Africa's new captain Hansie Cronje for the remainder of the series against New Zealand and told him at the same time he has retired as a Test player.
>
> Now 37, Wessels has told Peter Pollock and the other national selectors as well as Cronje of his decision after efforts to persuade him to reconsider his position failed yesterday. Troubled by a knee injury Wessels could not see himself lasting the rest of the season if he played in the remaining two Tests against the Kiwis and then Pakistan.

The rewrite for Monday editions began:

> It is not quite the Christmas message Hansie Cronje wanted to hear but Kepler Wessels has passed on his 'best wishes' to the new South African captain and told him his Test playing days are over.

Unfortunately the impact had been lost and the makeover did not quite come across as the genuine article.

Did South Africa really need Wessels at the time? If you listened carefully to Wessels they did not. He was also confident they would win the series 2-1 and go on to beat Pakistan as well as win the Mandela Trophy in the quadrangular series, which involved the Kiwis, Pakistan, Sri Lanka and South Africa. In Wessels' view, the match at the Wanderers had been lost because the bowlers had, to an extent, allowed the New Zealand batsmen to dominate. And a last wicket record partnership of 57 runs between Simon Doull and Richard de Groen all but carried the game beyond South Africa's reach.

There was drama and entertainment on a baking Sunday afternoon when New Zealand began their second innings: Fanie's first ball trapped Darrin Murray lbw, and the large Sunday crowd roared approval. They had sat sullenly through a miserable South African batting performance, and ached for success. But the Kiwis slowly eased their way forward, with Bryan Young and Stephen Fleming taking the total to 32 when Cronje, after consulting the Northerns swing bowler, switched Fanie to the golf course end. Then, Craig Matthews had Fleming caught behind by Dave Richardson. Up went the crowd, now an excitable band of friends, some wearing little more than beachwear, and when they settled, there was an expectant hum around the sun-drenched bullring.

Martin Crowe, so majestic and stylish, arrived and suddenly departed to further uproar. Fanie had him edge a ball into his stumps, and those seated in the Centenary Stand were still on their feet when Ken Rutherford arrived to face the last ball of the over. As the perfect late outswinger to the New Zealand captain found Brian McMillan pocketing the catch, there was pandemonium in the stadium. Fanie the hero had struck twice in successive deliveries. The Kiwis were not quite on the rack, but that rich taste of Canterbury lamb was becoming mouth-watering.

Lee Barnard, his former Northern Transvaal captain, watched from the Wanderers Longroom as Fanie charged in for a possible Test hat-trick. The crowd stamped, shouted and cheered as he bowled to Young. They wanted the world to know they were behind their man. In front of the scoreboard were the youngsters from Soweto with toothy grins and waving their new South Africa flags, around them were groups of Asians and coloureds. The ball whipped outside the off-stump, enticing the New Zealander to drive, just as Woolmer had wanted. And the way he remembered, Cyril Mitchley junior had told him years before: 'Keep the ball up and tempt them to drive—give an edge to the wicketkeeper or the slips.'

There was, however, no hat-trick the ball went through to Richardson, swinging late. Two balls later, though, he had his man, Richardson claiming a catch, and Young was on his way. Again the crowd erupted. Fanie had 4 for 15 and New Zealand were 34 for 5. The comparative safety of a first innings lead of 132 runs had been stretched to 166 with 5 wickets remaining.

Such is the unpredictability of the game that South Africa began to sniff at a possible victory. It would need a lot of hard work, and an improved batting display as well, to pull off a miracle was not impossible. However, while theory often creates a rosy glow, there is no such misrepresentation with fact. The tourists went on to win early in the last afternoon and, as a sombre mood settled over the South African camp, Geoff Howarth, the New Zealand coach, and Rutherford, the captain, temporarily buried their long-hidden differences. They sipped a couple of glasses of sparkling wine and made up before the TV cameras.

Certainly the Kiwis deserved this victory. They had made the most of their chances and their first innings was worked around a well-crafted effort from Crowe; 81 not-out overnight, he needed 19 runs on the Saturday to score a century and become the first to do so against the other eight Test countries of that era. However, Richard Snell ended Crowe's moment of glory, trapping him lbw after he had added just two runs to his total.

Cronje felt tired, irritable and depressed, while Woolmer was far from impressed. A majority of South Africa's players had a lot to learn about batting, and learn they would, if the side was to get rid of the malaise.

Shortly after Cronje had taken over as captain, there had been a meeting with Peter Pollock, convener of selectors, and Woolmer, the coach. The discussions were about where the team was heading. Defeat had not been part of the script for this Test series, and a few harsh words had to be said at the Wanderers. It would not have been a surprise either if Woolmer had a fleeting thought about whether he had done the right thing in accepting the UCB coaching offer. So far, nothing had gone right. A trip to Pakistan had ended in disaster through no fault of his, and his first Test had gone horribly wrong.

Fanie felt sorry for 'the boss'. He had a sense of humour, which few understood, and now, there was a posse of sports writers who were demanding an explanation for the failure without knowing the intricacies of coaching players who came from diverse playing backgrounds. Woolmer's man management had worked well with Kent, Boland and Warwickshire. 'Okay, Bob, what went wrong this time?' was the derogatory universal chorus. For one thing, he did not need this sort of verbal jostling immediately after a humiliating defeat. Neither did his captain. He was not prepared to be blunt either and tell the gathering, 'We need batsmen who know how to bat through two or more sessions and score runs as well.'

'It is just a matter of adjustment from the one-day game to the demands of the Test arena,' came the official reply.

By the end of the season, however, there was a new 'scriptwriter'. Wins over New Zealand at Kingsmead and Newlands during Christmas and New Year gave South Africa a place in history: not since 1888 had a side come from behind in a three-match series to end 2-1 victors. Fanie's contribution in the series was 20 wickets; not a bad haul at all, although the price of bowling 43 overs more than anyone else meant he had to conserve his energy a little more at times. What with the Mandela Trophy series of six matches and a best of three finals, the Pakistan Test and tour of New Zealand, he had to increase his visits to Craig Smith, the South African team's physio.

In the absence of Donald, the South African selectors tried Stephen Jack to bolster the pace department, but he was not the success Peter Pollock's panel had hoped he would be, and it befell the genial McMillan to carry the extra burden as Fanie's main support prop.

McMillan could also be a tough character when he wanted and he was far from happy with a headline and introduction to a story Chesters had written from Port Elizabeth. It appeared in most Argus Group newspapers on the eve of South Africa's Mandela Trophy match against Pakistan in Durban, but only after a sports sub-editor in Durban's *Daily News* office, looking to spice up the copy about team selection, altered a couple of words. 'Heavyweight' became 'overweight' and 'hard-working' was changed to 'laborious'. A sub-editor had allowed himself licence to alter the meaning of two words to write the headline 'Fat Mac in slip blunders'. The story with the changes to the opening paragraph was reissued and the 'Fat Mac' implication turned up in Cape Town. What did it matter that the credibility of the writer had been impaired? It took eighteen months to patch the rift, and for both to laugh about this incident, as well as about the time when McMillan asked for Chesters to be banned from a media conference after scoring a century against Pakistan. Fortunately Darrel Thompson, a former *Sunday Tribune* sports editor, was able to corroborate the story of how sports editors and sub-editors have been known to act with such irresponsibility.

Mike Rindel's first national call up was on 29 November 1994, but it came as no surprise to those who had seen how hard he had pushed himself during Northern Transvaal's pre-season programme. The left-hander's impressive form had been an extension of his determination and rediscovered motivation, and how he escaped the selectors' attention for the Tests against New Zealand was more of a puzzle. Yet it was his fitness and keen eye as well as wrist and handwork, which had turned around what had been a succession of disappointing seasons.

The summer when Denis Lindsay was in charge of coaching had been a disaster for Northerns ; he was not the only one who wondered about the team's lack of direction and focus. Other forces, notably those in charge of team selection, were also at serious fault, leaving Joubert Strydom, the captain, with the difficult job of steering a calm path through a pot-holed mess. Anton Ferreira, a former Northerns and Warwickshire all-rounder, who had transferred his coaching expertise to Transvaal for two seasons, was appointed on a full-time basis. He brought with him fresh ideas and had, as his B team coach, Keith Medlycott, the former England, England A and Surrey all-rounder.

It was a new step for Northerns, with the executive making several bold changes after examining an in-depth report highly critical of the union's coaching structures and selection policy, as well as of executive interference in player appointments. Over the years, Northerns had lost a number of their top juniors to other provinces. Unless there was a change in the coaching structures, with the trend being reversed through a more enlightened school policy, it would revert to the bad days of the 1970s and 1980s.

Ferreira and Rindel had played in the same Northerns side summers before, and the bulky former all-rounder knew all about the attacking left-hander's frustrations and problems in the previous couple of seasons. It was Ferreira who had been at the crease when Rindel had made his senior provincial debut in a Nissan Shield match, the day Centurion Park officially opened its gates to the public. Ferreira also knew what unfulfilled ambition meant to players such as Rindel. He too had endured similar erratic selectorial misdemeanours in his playing days during the rebel era. It was this stoicism which made him the deep-thinking player he was and the coach he became, first of the South African under-19 side and then as the South African Director of Coaching.

Before the season began and as mewling leaves were unfurling on the trees around the oval at Centurion Park, Ferreira sat with

Rindel on the open balcony discussing what role the left-hander hoped to play in the new Northerns make up.

'You do know that you still have it in you to play for South Africa this season,' was Ferreira's frank appraisal of South Africa's batting needs.

'You think so?' Rindel had thought about it too, but it had not gone beyond that. Now there was a new challenge on offer, and it seemed a realistic possibility.

'If you do want to play for South Africa though, you have to bat higher in the order,' Ferreira commented thoughtfully. 'Certainly in the limited-overs matches. We cannot have you batting at five and facing say ten overs or less to score quick runs. We need to change our strategy.'

'You mean Northerns?'

'Yes. Utilize your talents better. It will give you more opportunities.'

Rindel had always been known as a bold, free-scoring batsman, one who kept the scoreboard moving. What Ferreira had planned also made sense. Bringing a touch of urgency to run-making methods was always important: it pinned the bowling back after an initial success, made them think. 'Perhaps even open the innings,' Ferreira suggested.

'No. Facing bowlers like Wasim and Waqar . . .'

It was a radical suggestion, made keeping the future in mind. It was worth consideration because of Rindel's bold approach, and had once been suggested by Alan Jordaan, who was then the Northerns president.

When Northerns played the New Zealanders on 11 to 13 November 1994, the first day's play was ideal for what Ferreira had discussed weeks before with Rindel. Strydom won the toss and decided, despite damp, cloudy conditions, to bat first. Dion Nash and Murphy Su'a ripped open the top order: three batsmen were back in the pavilion within forty-five minutes with only 21 runs on the board.

Rindel arrived, and immediately set about rebuilding the innings managing 91 off 98 balls at number five in the order. National selectors Peter Pollock, S. K. Reddy and Rushdie Magiet watched Rindel's display with interest. Here was a batsman in form and in command of the situation on a none-too-easy pitch and against the swinging ball. Rain wrecked much of the game, and Rindel did not get a chance to bat again. Yet, he left a notation in the selectors' notebooks, if not their thoughts.

Surprisingly it took until the second leg of the Mandela Trophy final at the Wanderers before the radical move Ferreira had spoken about more than four months before took place. The night before the game, Cronje beckoned to Rindel. He wanted to tell him something, and the left-hander thought he was about to be told he had been dropped.

'How do you feel about opening tomorrow?'

'Open? Yes . . . sure . . . great . . .'

'Okay. You're opening then.'

Rindel knew he had no option. He had batted at five in the matches he had played during the series, excepting the first leg at Newlands where he had gone in at six. He had opened once, in a club match, but that hardly counted: not in any context. Dave Callaghan had been tried and had scored 169 against New Zealand at Centurion early on in the series, but disappointed after that, and Andrew Hudson's form had been shaky.

Now that Gary Kirsten was fit again, it was time for South Africa to change the formula and Rindel found that he would be facing the trio of quicks he had talked about to Ferreira with some trepidation: Wasim Akram, Aaqib Javed and Waqar Younis. That was a world-class trio and needed the alert confidence of an in-form batsman to handle. Was he up to it? He felt he was. Allan Donald was back as well. The initial assumption was that this may have induced the Pakistani captain, Salim Malik, to send in South Africa after winning the toss a second time.

Malik had ignored convention in the Newlands match too and had lost there. What later transpired, however, was that it was Malik's particular ploy involving match-fixing. On his way out to toss with Cronje at Newlands, the Pakistani asked Cronje if he had received a telephone call. Cronje's response was a silent, embarrassed nod. It was from 'John' and the offer had been for US$10,000.

Cronje, after consulting Pat Symcox, turned it down. But later in Colombo in August 1998 and at the King Commission in 2000, it surfaced that this was merely the starting point. The wart, which later disfigured the South African captain's image, had already started to grow, and with Cronje barely into his role as the team's leader.

At the time of the Wanderers episode in 1994, Cronje and Woolmer were not bothered that South Africa would open with two left-handers. It was felt that the pair complemented each other, and as they ran to a record partnership of 190 for the first wicket, which still stands, there was no longer an argument about whether it was a good move. Rindel enjoyed the experience, admitting he was more bothered by the sight of the microphones, TV cameras and the bank of tape recorders than the Pakistan bowling. It had not been that easy to take a century off such an attack, but after he had reached the thirties he knew it was possible.

There was a thought before the side left for New Zealand that he might earn a Test place. As the rest of the places were taken up with the exception of the opening berth, if Hudson's form declined, the assumption did have some appeal. Yet the most interesting spinoff was how Mike Rindel was suddenly 'discovered' by some Cape-based sports magazine.

The Test place theory was not tried out for some reason, and was not satisfactorily explained. That innings of 108 was Rindel's penultimate appearance for South Africa for more than four years. Only the weight of limited-overs runs scored in the domestic limited-overs competition in the 1996-97 and 1997-98 seasons earned him a reprieve. He was the leading run-scorer in both seasons with totals of 766 and 789. But the selectors, without offering a reason, overlooked him. It suggests that something else has kept him out for so long.

Rumours, circulating for some time, that all was not well in the Pakistan camp re-emerged a couple of days before the inaugural Test at the Wanderers on 16 January. Waqar Younis was being sent home with a back injury which would, said the manager, Intikhab Alam, create 'a serious problem as it is going to disrupt the balance of our bowling attack'.

The tourists had been training at Centurion Park, away from media attention, which was focussed on the South Africans in Johannesburg. What surprised Chesters was that he was the only journalist at the Pakistan nets, which gave him the inside story of Waqar's injury, and later he watched baffled as the angry manager chased away a dapper Asian wearing a stylish linen suit. A former Test captain and a leg-spinner of some note (Alam has claims to being an all-rounder with the Test double of 1000 runs and 100 wickets) who spent almost a decade with Surrey, Intikhab Alam believed in strict discipline and became upset when Malik, the captain, moved out of the nets to talk to the man. Malik was already under pressure from criticism from within the team over his handling of the side during the Mandela Trophy final, with Rashid Latif and Basit Ali in open rebellion. They later quit the team in Zimbabwe, saying they no longer wanted to play with Malik as captain, citing that his style of leadership bothered them. There was the impression that it was a different game plan they were talking about; one perhaps involving under the table deals.

When it was also suggested after the heavy defeat in the Wanderers Test that the Pakistani players were not observing strict Muslim customs, Intikhab became annoyed. He asked the reporter from Lenasia, a largely Asian suburb close to the teeming area of Soweto, to substantiate his claims, thinking it would be enough to put the man in his place.

The middle-aged reporter then opened a small notebook and began to read a list of players' evening activities and how they had behaved. It was a strong inference that the side had lost focus and discipline after the 2-0 defeat by South Africa in the Mandela Trophy final. Intikhab indicated he would rather discuss the issue in private but the reporter was far from entertained by that idea. At this point, Malik suggested there was more to talk about than 'rumours of players' alleged after-dark movements'.

There had already been serious talk of 'bookies' involvement' with some Pakistan players. These rumours had been circulating since the last limited-overs series in Sharjah in April 1993. Wasim Akram, a late arrival because of a sinus operation in England, had tackled Malik about the claims when in Cape Town. Phrases such as 'Mumbai ring' (Bombay ring at the time) and their associates were also openly talked about by a couple of Pakistani commentators in the Wanderers media box during the Test. Qamar Ahmed, the veteran Pakistani journalist who has seen more than 250 Tests, supported some of the allegations, yet agreed that proof would be hard to get. 'The bookies are altogether too clever,' he said. 'They have a network and people in various places to talk to players and contacts. They don't just exist in Mumbai either: New Delhi, Calcutta, Bangalore, Lahore. They are all around. It is all illegal as bookies are only allowed to take bets for racing and are taxed. In cricket, if they know they can make a big pay day, they would think nothing of flying someone to Johannesburg. Or using someone local they know they can trust. It is by word of mouth.'

Despite Malik's strong disclaimer, Qamar spoke of 'serious rifts' in the squad. Had the press corps known, however, the extent of the disturbances within the camp, the aftermath would have been a major embarrassment for Malik and Intikhab. For one thing, the credibility of the team would have been questioned in headlines across three continents.

Whether it was worse than the 'mugging incident', which delayed by twenty-fours hours the Wanderers Test in mid-February 1998, is a matter of opinion. Both were uncomfortable, even acrimonious, incidents during times when senior players fell out among themselves over the 'betting issue'. It had Intikhab asking the players to swear on the Koran that they had not indulged in anything so sinister. The bubbling, expressive excitement and enjoyment which marked their first appearance in South Africa during the historic 1993 Total Triangular series had been replaced by a moody, sullen indifference and the menace of innuendo.

Rumours had long suggested a schism in the camp, along with a lack of discipline exhibited by some senior players, and that a bookie had 'bought into the results'. If the King Commission revelations are an example, it was also about the time that Cronje realized how he could make far easier money that way than in those guest appearances as an after-dinner speaker.

It was during the early stages of the Zimbabwe tour in early February 1995 that two ripe pimples, marked 'innuendo' and 'suspicion', burst open with serious implications. The emerald city of Sydney hosted an interesting media conference: Shane Warne, Mark Waugh and Tim May accused Malik of attempting to bribe the three Australians to throw the Test in Karachi the previous September.

Ijaz Ahmed's was another name linked to match-fixing claims, while Wasim Akram, internationally the most respected of the

Pakistani players, had questioned Malik about the series of allegations before Warne, Waugh and May opened the Pandora's box. Malik was emphatic in his denial. Wasim tackled him a second time, and Malik again brushed it off.

From what has emerged since 1996 about match-fixing and player bribery allegations, it is hard to take seriously anything Pakistan achieved during both their South Africa tours of the 1990s. A player has his pride, or should, if he cares enough about the game which has given him an opportunity to make a name for himself and earn a good living. Unfortunately, dishonest Asian bookies and their mercenary agents had left their own ugly mark. They infiltrated and seduced certain minds with promises of riches. It is known that bookies, who had lost heavily on a match, would leak information to certain media 'friends' to expose players involved in bribery claims.

Before the Wanderers Test in January 1995, there was also confusion in the tourists' camp over team selection and strange, mixed signals were being received. Team management issued a statement, which suggested that Latif was injured during the team's pre-match warm up exercises while Waqar had not recovered from a 'back spasm problem'. Although it was known that Waqar had a spine problem, Rashid Latif, embroiled three years later in a bribery row with Indian players, had reportedly withdrawn from the side the night before.

There seemed to be further disorganization when Pakistan included Aamir Nazir for the Test instead of the man on tour, Ata-ur-Rehman. As Rehman played only three Mandela Trophy and one first-class matches, the query was, why fly out Nazir? Rehman is one of those players who have long disappeared; his last overseas assignment was in England in 1996. He was later banned for life for perjury, when fingered by the Qayyum Commission in Pakistan in a report belatedly released in the wake of the Cronjegate scandal, and ICC's lifted eye-brow.

A medium-pace bowler with a Test already to his credit, Nazir was included in the side before leaving Lahore for South Africa. Little wonder that, fatigued by jet lag, he had to go off with cramps after a handful of overs, and this after arriving an hour after the game had already started. The Pakistanis, or maybe Malik, must have been desperate.

For Fanie de Villiers, however, the match against Pakistan presented a new challenge. Donald was back and it meant he could relax a little and help ease his teammate into the Test scene. Only Fanie went one better. He first scored 66 off 68 balls, which included possibly the cheekiest stroke in an innings total of 460: a reverse sweep off a bemused Malik which went for four.

Fanie was about to further sabotage Pakistan's plans, if indeed they had any.

By the end of day two of the inaugural Test between the two countries, Pakistan were 177 for six with Malik undefeated on 86: 283 runs and 9 wickets is a steady return for a day's play of 90 overs, Fanie had 5 wickets to add to his half-century. At 20 without loss and Aamir Sohail driving handsomely, Pakistan seemed well placed. Then Fanie had Saeed Anwar picked up nicely in the slips by Daryll Cullinan and Asif Mujtaba caught by Richardson with no addition to the total. The Friday crowd began enjoying themselves.

It was all over by lunch on day five: Fanie collecting 10 wickets to add to his half century. He became the first South African to manage such a statistically impressive footnote to his Test career. He had also joined Hugh Tayfield by taking 10-wicket hauls twice in a Test. Several weeks later, as the South Africans celebrated at Eden Park, the uproarious dressing room scenes were caught on video. He did not know then, however, that Matthew Hart, caught by Richardson for 6 in the second innings, would be his last Test wicket in almost three years.

* * * *

Around mid-April 1995, late on a sunny morning, Jackie McGlew was strolling around the outer oval at Centurion with Khaya Majola and Anton Ferreira as a group of youngsters took turns in bowling at a specially prepared middle-net. The South African under-19 trials were in progress. McGlew and Majola, who had been to the West Indies together in 1992 with a youth side led by Dale Benkenstein, were going over the respective lists of candidates. There was some interesting talent as well. Occasionally the three would stop and talk, before Ferreira, at the time appointed coach of the team being prepared for England, went off to supervise bowling changes.

Other members of the selection panel sat in the stands, talking among themselves, keeping their own counsel. McGlew had gone through it all before, and he was tired of the politics and narrowness of schoolmaster thinking when it came to the final choices. This time, tough as it was, would be his last as convener of this panel, as a selector even. He now walked as briskly as possible, his lined features and late autumn paleness hinting of the illness which had already haunted him for more than a year. Yet he was cheerful and chatted with Majola as he saw Chesters walking down the pavilion steps.

He had a few things to tell Chesters, a few confidences, which the two would discuss, as they had, for almost a decade. The leaves on the trees were in the first stages of autumn reds and yellows and mottled browns; it was not cold enough yet to drive the ibis, who inhabit the banks and the surrounds of the Hennops River at the south end of the ground, to warmer northern climates. The two shook hands warmly. McGlew began walking towards the nets and they watched a bowler with an unusual action deliver the ball to a stocky batsman with a short backlift.

'Have a look at this one and tell me what you think,' McGlew suggested. 'As you can see he is a left-arm wrist spinner: turns the ball quite sharply, too. He bowls the chinamen.[2] We picked him in the South African Colts team before Christmas. I think he has a lot of promise.'

'Not a lot of loop is there? Interesting grip though . . . and that action,' Chesters commented. 'There could be a problem with that action. If that arm straightens . . .'

---

[2] There has long been a debate that the term 'chinaman' has racist origins and crudely refers to the 'unorthodox practices' of either Asian or Oriental nature 'and which are not understood'. Recent research has, however, suggested that such theories are as arrogant as claims that to bowl a left-arm wrist spinner's googly calls for Oriental wizardry. As the Australian and English views of the wrist spinner's googly widely differ, we have another conflict of opinion. Then again, the suggestion that England batsman Patsy Hendren made the comment 'bowled by a bloomin' Chinaman' in jest has a ring of truth to it, certainly more so than the mythology surrounding the wisecrack of another England batsman, Walter Robins. In both cases, the bowler was the Trinidadian Ellis Achong, who was of Chinese descent.

'You think he throws?' McGlew was matter-of-fact, questioning, seeking a second opinion from the journalist, a former first-class umpire.

'It is hard to say, Jack, and it would need a lot of study. But, if the Sri Lankan, Muralitharan, can get away with his action . . . well I guess this one will pass the examination as well,' Chesters commented and the two laughed.

'We want him in the team for England,' said McGlew. 'Khaya supports me, so does Yogi (Anton Ferreira). The others think he'll be a joke; that he will get knocked around.'

Another youngster, tall, gangling and full of pace was also bowling. Good action: upright and accurate. McGlew nodded at him. 'They do not want him either. There are a couple of other promising fast bowlers as well: one we both know well, from the last two years.'

Red-haired David Terbrugge, with his mop covering his forehead, had a ready, warm, trademark grin, which made the young St. Stithian's fast bowler popular among his peers. In the end he was given the nod ahead of Malan Morkel, or was it Makhaya Ntini, who edged out the lanky young Afrikaans fast bowler when the squad was announced? Yet there they were, the players of the future: Ashwell Prince, Mark Boucher, Botea Dippenaar, Ntini, Terbrugge and Pierre Joubert. Terbrugge returned early from the tour with a back injury, and Morkel went as a replacement.

As for Paul Adams, it was his first sight of Centurion; a venue where, months later, he had created an image of mystery among those who had not seen him in action until Western Province played

---

Hendren was Achong's first Test victim, when the bowler made his debut at Queen's Park Oval in Port-of-Spain on 1 February 1929. Hendren, a Cockney, was like Robins known for his 'Puckish' style of humour. It was Robins who turned to Leary Constantine and commented something similar when stumped in the Old Trafford Test of 1933. Michael Rundell tried to debunk this in his *Dictionary of Cricket* saying it is 'too good to be true'. Hendren was quoted as the source in a couple of books and did not deny authorship. It also bears out the view that the comment was made in the West Indies in 1929 and not England in 1933, whatever the *Oxford English Dictionary* and Mr Rundell may presume.

Northerns. Then again, your average spectator has more interest in sitting in a dentist's chair than attending a colts game involving teams of unknowns.

Gogga's first match at Centurion Park held no relevance.[3] It was during September 1995 that Eddie Barlow, as coach of the Western Cape Academy, oversaw the early stages of Paul Adams' career. Games were played in Centurion, the East Rand and Johannesburg. Most batsmen were troubled by the stock top-spin delivery and fooled by the googly, although Gerald Dros, a young Northerns batsman with a long reach, found he could handle the spin by hitting straight and playing him as an orthodox leg-spinner. Chesters watched Adams bowl with some interest as he took a couple of wickets for the academy team and later passed on his comment to McGlew, who was still annoyed that he, Majola and Anton Ferreira had been overruled by the schoolmasters when selecting the under-19 team for England.

It was only natural, however, that Western Province, in need of quality players of colour, pushed him into the B side for the UCB Bowl match against Easterns at PAM Brink Stadium in Springs. Played in the last weekend of October, Province selector Mike Minnaar, with support from the other selectors, who had seen Adams in the nets with the academy, decided to work on a hunch. A replacement was needed for Dean MacHelm, an orthodox left-arm spinner, and the Province B captain, Barry Touzel, was entrusted with the task of easing the eighteen-year-old into the provincial system.

'He is certainly different,' Touzel admitted later. 'Added a little excitement, didn't he? Gave the game a touch of spice all right.'

Experience shows that UCB Bowl matches usually attract as many interested spectators as colts games: along with wives or girlfriends, an occasional parent or other family members with nothing better to do will arrive, especially if the weather is fine on Saturday or Sunday afternoons. It should not be a surprise therefore that nobody took too much notice of the events in the East Rand

---

[3] The Afrikaans term 'Gogga' literally means 'bug' and was the nickname given to Paul Adams by one of his Western Province teammates, Brian McMillian, shortly after joining them at Centurion Park on 3 November 1995.

town at the time Adams made his provincial entree: 3 for 48 in 22 overs and 2 for 81 in 29 overs amid the East Rand mining dumps are not particularly impressive. As Gogga was an unknown, even to the Province senior side players, the efforts did not create any excitement, either. Yet, here was a talented teenager, and one of colour, so why not give him a Castle Cup game?

Duncan Fletcher had, two seasons before, seen the results of spin bowling success at Centurion Park when Gary Kirsten, exploiting a dusting surface, won the game for Western Province with 6 for 68. As few South African batsmen are entirely capable, or comfortable, when facing spin, the left-arm wrist variety would be even more difficult to handle. There was nothing to lose in playing Adams. One look at the pitch the afternoon before decided in favour of Adams' inclusion although Fletcher later said, 'He was always part of our game plan strategy.'

Anyway, as interest was primarily focussed on East London where Mike Atherton's tourists were playing Border, talk in the Centurion Park press box that Saturday morning was of who would be in the South African A side to meet the 'Poms' the following weekend. As personal team interpretations were talked about and a couple of Sunday writers were preparing their offerings, Andy Capostagno, then of MWP, asked some questions of Chesters about Fanie's fitness and how long it would be before he would be ready.

As it is, Chesters, after discussions with Fanie, doubted whether he would be fit for the Tests. Perhaps the slogs, when the serious stuff was over.

It was shortly before lunch, as the Province bowlers battled to shift an obdurate Andre Seymore, that Eric Simons, the visiting captain, tossed the ball to Adams. It had all been discussed in the dressing room and, with a field-placing change or two, Adams was introduced into the attack from the Hennops River end. As he loped in to bowl to Seymore, his body twisted in what Chesters described as the 'rock 'n roll' action. Roy Pienaar, the Northerns captain, watched, and then opened his eyes wider than normal.

'Oh wow! Here's someone who can bowl the chinaman!' came Capostagno's comment.

There was what sounded like a bemused gurgle from the sparsely populated stand and as Adams finished his over, conceding a couple of runs in the process, Capostagno was talking into the telephone and asking if they had a spare photographer to send to the ground. It was some time after lunch when Dr Ali Bacher, the UCB's managing director, also having watched Adams bowling on television, contacted the three Sunday newspapers in South African to pass on his excited views.

Chesters decided to keep a diplomatic silence on his thoughts of the legality of Adams' action. Watching him again, in a match situation and front on this time, he could detect no partial straightening of the elbow. After lunch, he sat on the west embankment and watched for almost an hour, still uncertain. No bowler goes out to deliberately throw the ball unless he is your average Sylvester Clarke-type delivering a bouncer (and there are a few of them around these days) or to run-out a batsman well out of his crease.

Suite holders at Centurion Park waddled on to the balcony, leaving the comfort of their bars, TVs and braais to see what was causing the fuss when Roy Pienaar became the wrist spinner's first victim. Although he managed only 2 wickets in the innings, favourable noises were being made and there was a photographic spread in *The Sunday Times* of the bowling action.

Jackie McGlew arrived the next morning as Western Province began their first innings and beckoned to Chesters. He was tired and still in pain from the unsuccessful hip replacement operation in the winter. The journalist sat next to him and was joined by Willie Watson, also a former Northerns coach, England and Yorkshire left-hand batsman. McGlew's smile was weak but he sounded perky enough.

'Have you seen the Sunday papers? I wonder what those schoolmasters are now saying about Adams,' he wanted to know. 'I bet they are embarrassed: now they'll claim they wanted him in all the time. You know something, if Adams takes wickets in the second innings Ali (Bacher) will have Peter (Pollock) include him in the South Africa A side.'

McGlew winked, the smile hiding the pain.

'I can't see it going that far,' commented Chesters.

'Want a small bet with me old Cobber? He will be here tomorrow if the game lasts that long. You don't have any batsmen good enough to win this one.' He gave a quiet chuckle. 'Now, tell me about Fanie.'

It was after lunch on the Monday when Chesters talked to Pollock to find out what he and the other national selectors felt about the Northerns bowler. He had played in the two limited-overs games against Zimbabwe in Harare but not in the Test after the hamstring problem recurred.

It was the view of the selectors along with Cronje and Woolmer that it was the better option not to play Fanie. At least, it gave Brett Schultz a chance to revive his career. Fanie's injury, however, was far more deep-seated than they realized and Pollock admitted the selectors were 'more than just concerned by the debilitating injury'. South Africa needed a fit Fanie de Villiers if they were to win the series. As Pollock was not one to hide behind doubletalk comments to convey his thoughts and those of his fellow selectors, phrases such as 'needing a fit Fanie de Villiers' indicated their depth of concern. A fitness evaluation was to be carried out shortly as the selectors needed to work out their strategy.

Pollock did not need to spell out that South Africa's Test strategy was based on pace. It meant there would be no place for a spinner unless he was a real match-winner. If Fanie was fit he would be part of the planning; if not they would have to find someone else. It was that simple. There was also the impression from Woolmer that it was not that simple. Finding someone who had so much swing variation when he bowled would need a miracle; the miracle did not happen.

Fanie, however, had been referred to a physiotherapist in Pretoria who specialized in treating his type of injury and began working on the problem. It would, warned the physio, need some weeks before he would be able to bowl again. She declined interviews: healing damaged muscles was her job, not headlines. One of the problems was breaking down the stiffness of the muscles after years of taking pain pills. Slowly he began training again: a little road running and gym work and then bowling in secret at the club nets. Progress was slow but promising.

South Africa was being swept along by the Gogga phenomenon. If his second innings spread of 6 wickets and man of the match award at Centurion Park was not enough, the euphoria which greeted his selection to the South Africa A side to play the England XI sparked an unusual buzz of attention. Even the SABC, which rarely displays interest in domestic cricket, were scrambling for video footage of Adams in action. They dispatched a cameraman to Kimberley for shots of him bowling in the nets. The SABC subscribes to the doctrine that soccer is the only sport among the blacks, and rugby among the whites. About the only cricket they broadcast is Tests and limited-overs games. Even in mid-summer, SABC's radio programme SAFM force-feeds a diet of local soccer, and their general sports programmes offer little else. This has created frustrated audiences who now tap into the Internet to get scores and other information. The Sunday papers, led by the *Sunday Times,* have become just as culpable in the 2000-01 and 2001-02 seasons. Perhaps editorial staff need a reminder of how, in November 1995, they helped in the discovery of Paul Adams.

Not long after Western Province had won the match by eight wickets, Chesters dropped in on the umpires and after initial greetings put the question to Mitchley about Adams' action. The man they call Squire sipped on one of those sweet fizzy drinks and looked up, giving a ready smile. 'Next question.' He was not going to bite. Not openly. If he had his suspicions, like Chesters, he was keeping them to himself.[4]

Two days after Adams had bowled himself into history, a name change took place without so much as red carpet treatment. Verwoerdburg, with its odious implications, became Centurion. This was barely weeks after the majority of the eligible municipal voters readily acknowledged that the venue, which brought the area their international recognition, deserved to be preserved in perpetuity. Because of this uniqueness, Centurion has, on occasions, been referred to as the 'principality'.[5]

The name change was done in time for the ground to host its first Test and added to certain confusion among some overseas and

---

[4] By the end of the 1996-97 season, Mitchley was more than satisfied that Paul Adams' action did not infringe Note A of Law 24 under which a partial straightening of the arm would result in Adams being called for throwing; the Code of Laws issue in 2000 goes even further as Note 3 defines what is a fair delivery.

[5] Instead of the venue adopting its name from the area, Centurion Park gave its name to the municipality and the 'principality' term became an in-house joke to distinguish it as being part of an area which is not Pretoria.

local sports writers and visitors. It was part of Pretoria, right? Wrong. The area now known as Centurion has never been part of the Pretoria municipal boundaries, although politically it is now part of the greater reshaped metropolitan area of Tshwane, and Pretoria suddenly claimed an international cricket venue the racist white city council had not wanted in the 1980s.

Fanie sat frustrated at Centurion Park on 16 November 1995. He watched at his teammates go through the pre-match warm-up programme and wondered how long it would be before he was part of the squad again. Shaun Pollock was making his debut, Schultz had been passed fit after a buttock injury scare, Craig Matthews was playing in place of the Northerns bowler and there was no place for Adams. It was too soon to throw him in at this level.

At the end of the series, won 1-0 by South Africa, Pollock agreed that had Fanie played at the Wanderers, where Atherton and Jack Russell had batted England to a draw, and at St. George's Park, where the Christmas Test was also drawn, South Africa might have won those games as well. There was no doubt in Mitchley's mind about that, or Woolmer's, come to that. Cronje's side missed the deceptive swing variation Fanie would have offered his teammates.

Atherton's own monumental contribution was the innings of 185 at the Wanderers, one of the great Test batting performances in history. At the start of the last day no one gave England a chance to survive and they expected to lose around tea; instead it resulted in a draw, which stunned the chauvinistic South Africans into silence and had the Barmy Army cohorts saying 'Pinch me, I don't believe this'.

Schultz had disappeared amid the injury controversy after the financial fiasco of the rain-affected, abandoned Centurion Test. By Christmas, after Clive Eksteen had failed to take wickets at the Wanderers, Adams was ready to make his debut in Port Elizabeth. The band played, the crowd sang, the sun shone for a change and for five days almost all was well with the rainbow nation.

When Fanie contacted Chesters at 4 p.m. on a Friday afternoon, it was time to announce to the rest of the country the next step of the de Villiers comeback trail. Not surprisingly, Willie Morris, then a Northerns selector, turned up at Memorial Park in Groenkloof where Fanie's new club Villagers was playing. So did the Northerns coach, Anton Ferreira. As usual, the umpires were a 'no-show', and after a brief consultation, the captains asked Chesters to fill in, until they did arrive. It had been several seasons since Chesters had been active as an umpire, but it did give him a closer view than most of the swing bowler in action.

Fanie did not work up too much pace in his first few overs. It was more of a matter of taking it easy until the stretching exercises had been completed. There was no use, as he explained, trying to prove he could bowl as fast as he had. He was more than happy with the swing variation he had achieved in the opening overs. Being a warm early January day, the humidity also helped loosen the muscles as well as generate a certain amount of swing. 'It is important to control the swing,' he once said. 'You know what has bothered me, no one ever told me that you have to change the angle of the ball, or even change it around. I had to find that out myself . . . and through you . . . me old pal . . .'

So what was new? Perhaps having to work it out was part of the greater school of learning. Listening to the bowlers who had made a name for themselves, the Test stars of an earlier era, or your own peers helped. But there were times you learnt another way. There were times when the ball was hit hard and the weight and balance was transferred from the centre to the right or left side of the ball. 'There are times when this happens, when a batsman smashes the ball so hard that there is a weight transferral. You ask how this is possible as the ball has not lost its shape. I discovered it myself once when after the ball had been hit hard I tried to swing it again and the swing did not work: two, three, four balls . . . each one bowled in the same area and all with the same result, the batsman picking up runs. It does not matter if you bowl with the shine on the outside once the ball has lost its balance.'

The importance of theory, when put into practice, was being lost. It is important that the model on which a swing, pace or spin bowler wants to base his action and delivery style is a capable performer. A swing bowler's action has to be free of eccentricity. Some of the world's great outswing bowlers, such as Sir Richard Hadlee, Sir Alec Bedser, Ray Lindwall and Fred Trueman, agree that good outswing is as difficult to bowl as it is to score runs off it for even the best batsmen. It is not putting the ball in the right place that matters as much as the variation in swing which forces the batsmen to play.

Fanie also found that grounds lined with trees allowed the ball to swing more, such as at Centurion than say the Wanderers; old Newlands was a more effective ground on which to swing the ball than the reshaped venue with the willows gone and the oaks decimated. Memorial Park in Groenkloof, where he bowled that afternoon, was tree-lined and allowed him more lateral movement through the air and sideways deviation off the pitch. Your average club batsman, he found, used the same grip to the outswinger as he did to the off-cutter; even the inswing delivery did not see a major alteration in the batsman's grip.

It showed how club players were losing touch with the game and it did not come as a surprise when a batsman with an impressive club average was quickly sorted out even at UCB Bowl or B team levels. As Peter Kirsten and earlier Keith Medlycott have said, a batsman's handwork against the outswing and inswing bowler is so important when it comes to run-scoring, as much as knowing where your middle, or off-stumps are when facing an inswing bowler.

The transferral of a ball's weight when it is hit, however, is another matter. As Fanie discovered, when changing the ball around, there was some reverse swing as well. It is one of the physical quirks of the game which have led some scientists who work with aerodynamics to theorize that swing and reverse swing are a myth along with, it is presumed, such bowling phenomenon as swerve.[6]

Fanie picked up 6 wickets, giving away around 40 runs and was satisfied with his performance. Ferreira passed his views on to Peter Pollock, and Chesters did a piece for the *Sunday Independent*: it was used as footnote to the announcement of the South African

---

[6] If we are to believe Rundell's explanation in his dictionary of the game's terminology, 'swerve' is an older term for swing. This is not the case. Swerve is the rotation of the ball through the air as it swings, and not the natural swing as was being used by some bowlers in the 1880s; George Lohmann, who died in South Africa in 1901, was said to be a master of this type of bowling when playing for England.

The Bernoulli Principle of fluid dynamics suggests that even small differences in the weight and roughness of two sides of a ball can cause wobbling (swerve) and aerial deviation (swing). The smoother side has less air resistance. This causes deviation—the swing bowler controls that deviation for both normal and reverse swing.

side for the limited-overs series against Australia. Fanie had not expected to be included.

When his inclusion did come, it was after the fourth match of the series at Centurion. The squad had moved to Durban for the fifth match of the slogs when he was given his first game and responded with a sound performance and the wicket of Darren Gough in a low England total. In the next match at East London, he shared the opening spell with Shaun Pollock instead of being first change: 2 wickets for 10 runs in 8 overs was a creative effort on the usual Buffalo Park graveyard as South Africa won by 14 runs.

It would have been too much to expect a man of the match award in the seventh game in Port Elizabeth, yet 4 wickets for 32 in 9.1 overs gave him 7 wickets for the series and a run rate at well below 3 an over. He was far happier with the new ball, where he was able to get more swing. Most important, when it came, was selection for the World Cup side. In 1992, he had missed out because of the foot injury. Four years later, when it seemed he might be denied this one chance, he was able to overcome his hamstring worries, thank his physio in Pretoria and head for the Asian subcontinent. As you would expect, he was a touch more cheerful than he had been seven weeks before when he had started his comeback.

16

World Cup Debacle

Ten days after Fanie had clean bowled Darren Gough at St. George's Park in the last of the limited-overs internationals to give South Africa a pretty comprehensive 6-1 series victory over England, the tranquility surrounding the looming World Cup on the South Asian subcontinent was shattered. Eighty died and thousands were injured as five suicide bombers from the Liberation Tigers of Tamil Elam (LTTE) drove a truck packed with explosives into the handsome seven-storey structure in Colombo known as the Central Bank. This incendiary act of terrorism in the financial centre of Colombo not only put the games Sri Lanka were scheduled to play in the capital at risk, but also cast doubt on the ability of Sri Lanka's security force to protect visiting teams and evoked fresh criticism of the government's human rights record under President Chandrika Kumaratunga.

Australia and Sri Lanka were due to resume an embittered rivalry in one of the tournament's opening games barely eighteen days after the LTTE attack in Colombo. The Sri Lankan tour Down Under had resulted in vicious acrimony and both teams felt that there were scores to settle. Even before the explosion, there had been a growing suspicion that the Aussies would somehow renege on their tie at the Sinhalese Sports Club on 17 February.

The West Indies too were edgy about playing their game against Sri Lanka at the Premadasa Stadium nine days after the Australian match and also preferred to default, giving Arjuna Ranatunga's side two log points rather than subject the players to the vagaries of another possible Tamil attack. They too remained in India. As it is, extremists in Pakistan had already threatened Australian players after the match-fixing allegations against Salim Malik made by Mark Waugh and Shane Warne, and there was the view that the Australians were none too keen to play in the event. They felt it would be more prudent to concede the points than invite further trouble from what promised to be a hostile reception.

There were other areas of concern during the weeks leading to the 1996 World Cup. A flawed points system had many detractors, and there was criticism of practice facilities and scrambled logistics. Later, there was strong criticism of poor crowd attendance, especially in Pakistan for games not involving Pakistan. The team were bemused by the bizarre hotel arrangements for the teams during the opening ceremony at Eden Gardens, Calcutta. Most amusing though was the chaotic laser display along with the team names being read out in the wrong order over the tannoy when they marched on to the field.

Whatever the organizers, Pilcom, tried to do, large dollops of controversy nudged its way into print, or was splashed on television screens.[1] Amid this confusion there were innocent victims of the unfortunate, inept, official handling of events. Two young women media liaison officers were given wrong statements, which they issued on behalf of Pilcom about arrangements for the Australia and West Indies games should these be replayed in India. Both were accused of misleading the media within a couple of hours and were fired. When the actual source of the statements was revealed, there was some embarrassment: the girls were rehired, but no apology was offered to either of them.

Any number of skivvies were lumbered with the blame for official cock-ups. But what can be expected? Someone had to be blamed: Pilcom happily passed the buck about any number of decisions over which it had procrastinated, and thus gave mixed signals to the management of the competing teams and to the media.

The Sri Lankan impasse in early February caused a hawkish three-cornered wrangle involving the Australian Cricket Board, Pilcom and the ICC. The headlines got more and more misleading, aggressive, at times confused, and frequently sent a message that

---

[1] The Pakistan-India-Lanka Committee with Jagmohan Dalmiya as the chairman.

varied from what the organizers intended. Strong political language emerged almost hourly from Colombo, Calcutta, Canberra, London, Lahore or Delhi or from wherever and whoever felt they had a pertinent comment to make on the issue. Politicians, posturing the way spoilt children do, started taking advantage of a confused, disturbed situation and got away with it. The Colombo press, making the most of Australia's political discomfort, could at times be accused of adopting an unusually jingoistic slant of events. Certainly there was empathy for the impairment of Sri Lanka's cricket image by events leading to the cancellation of the two matches. However, in acting just as arrogantly as some of Australia's media can, Colombo's media were as guilty in their failure to present an accurate picture.

There were other conveniently forgotten issues as well as the 1996 World Cup menagerie geared up for the opening. As early as August 1995, two Sri Lankan cricket board officials had expressed their concerns about the rationale of holding the World Cup on the subcontinent. Over a midnight drink of arrack and coke during the South Africa under-24 tour of the island, as the band played on in the luxurious surrounds of the Taj Samudra hotel only hours after a bomb had claimed twenty-six lives outside a local government office in Torrington Square, Keerthi Jayasinghe and Chamikara Mendis questioned the wisdom of the ICC in holding the event, which was then barely seven months in the future.[2] One of their functions was coordinating transport for the teams playing matches in Colombo and Kandy.

Six months later the limited-overs showpiece had indeed become a bumpy ride for Pilcom. Initially South Africa had sought to hold the 1996 World Cup. But UCB plans were scuppered in July 1992 by Pakistan and India. The two traditional enemies showed a rare united front and received support as well from Sri Lanka in a pitch to stage the World Cup jointly.

England also got into the act and when all the brickbats were finally collected, South Africa had magnanimously stood back and agreed to the South Asian subcontinent (1996) and England (1999)

---

[2] Arrach is a strong alcoholic drink usually found in Asia or the Middle East and distilled from rice or molasses; in Sri Lanka it is in the form of a rum from the king coconut.

holding the next two limited-overs circuses. South Africa's turn is 2003. As it is, the South Asian region, with millions of supporters, had already become the future powerhouse of the game, and staging the World Cup once every eight years in the region was not as far-fetched as it might seem to traditionalists.

No doubt the ICC had felt that the 1987 World Cup was well-staged and managed in India and Pakistan. Why not give it to them again? But in 1987, the Kashmir dispute was not a full-scale battle. Several other ethnic-terrorist organizations had not raised their heads. Along with rocket attacks in Kashmir, there were explosions in a Peshawar shopping centre (South Africa did not play there) and of course, the Tamil Tigers in Sri Lanka—all cast doubts on Pilcom's claims of tight security.

In 1899, the Boer forces took a more lenient view of hostilities when, during the siege of Ladysmith in northern Natal during the early stages of the second Anglo-Boer war, they laid down their arms and donned pads and spent several hours of enjoyment with their *rooinek* opponents.[3] A pity such chivalry no longer exists.

For Fanie though, the tournament almost ended before it began. While Australia and Gareth Evans, their abrasive foreign minister, gave Pilcom and ICC a reverse two-finger salute when refusing to allow the side to play in Colombo, Fanie trod on a ball during a fielding practice in Rawalpindi and went over on his right ankle. Although Craig Smith, the South African physio, worked hard to get the swing bowler ready, the prognosis was far from healthy.

Talk about bad luck. After the long climb back to fitness and earning his World Cup squad place, this particular misfortune was enough to dent any ebullient personality. For Woolmer, this single accident did as much to partly sabotage the weeks of planning and pre-tournament preparation as any during his career as coach. Now, Cronje and Woolmer had to rethink their campaign strategies, although the question has always remained if Craig Matthews, the

---

[3] Rooinek is an Afrikaans term for a British settler or someone of English-speaking descent. Literally 'redneck' (an allusion to the way in which English newcomers sunburned), it once had derogatory connotations but in modern South Africa is used as a humorous, often endearing, term.

vice-captain, would have, but for the injury, been selected ahead of Fanie. Two fine bowlers working for a place in the side. Before South Africa's tournament was over, the query would be raised more than once.

After a day's delay because of a water-logged outfield, the opening match against the United Arab Emirates at the Rawalpindi Stadium saw South Africa field a side which allowed Cronje the use of seven bowlers: he used all seven and all of them gave a creditable performance against an enthusiastic, if mediocre, side. Watching the game rankled in Fanie's subconscious. It reminded him, for differing reasons, so much of the summer of 1992-93. Then the selectors had been blinded to his form and he had looked on, frustrated and aching inside, at bowlers whom he knew were good, when he felt that he was better. It was the injury bug again: an unwanted lingering hangover which had followed him around the world since all those months before at Edgbaston.

Were the niggling accidents not a sign that it was time to retire? There had long been a thought among some media people that the World Cup 1996 would see the word *finis* chiselled into his career tablet and painted in black. Well, he had news for those who were eager to write yet another obituary to the playing days of Fanie de Villiers: he was far from finished. He had talks with Dr Ali Bacher about the problems all players with young families face: more time to spend with his family and more financial security.

Over New Year 1997, Judith expressed similar concerns. Come 30 April 1997 Fanie might not have a players' contract. Yet he was seen as an invaluable member of the squad and his bowling was still a prized commodity. In February 1996, however, Fanie had only one thought: to get fit for the remaining World Cup matches. Given a chance, Smith's hard work on the injury area and a dose of the usual positive thinking, he would play a role during the series.

As it is, South Africa had taken an unusually large management and support group to the 1996 World Cup. Apart from Smith, there was Tim Noakes (doctor), Paddy Upton (fitness trainer), and the cheerful, yet hard-working assistant manager, Goolam Rajah. A pharmacist by profession and a man who preferred to live a number of years in exile to escape the demeaning laws inflicted on people of colour, Rajah had gone to England as assistant manager of the

1994 side. Through hard work and his genial, selfless style of management, he had taken over the senior post and befriended many players' wives, girlfriends and the media.

During the first week of the 1996 World Cup, Rajah watched the thirty-one-year-old Afrikaner hobble around the dressing room. He had seen him work in the nets and bowl in matches, until he was forced to take off his boots and examine the blisters, some black with blood. This time he saw a different Fanie. Almost a year ago, Fanie and Gary Kirsten had polished off the victors' magnum of champagne after beating New Zealand in that one-off Test at Eden Park. Now he was frustrated at his rate of recovery, at times grumpy, at times cheerful, as the side won the Group B match against New Zealand at Fisalabad. Pat Symcox was brought in as a replacement for Andrew Hudson, and Steve Palframan was used as an experiment opener.

Victory over the Kiwis saw a return to Rawalpindi and the crucial game against England.

Just after the first sparrow-chirp on 25 February, Allan Donald reported ill, a victim of the subcontinent bug and Fanie, his ankle strapped, was brought in as a replacement. A big game for South Africa and for Atherton's Poms. And the way he bowled, swinging the ball around on a day when there was a chilly edge to the wind, Fanie thought he had landed in a bingo bazaar. Whatever he bowled came out right, the late swing and the variation forcing the batsmen into false strokes. The wickets of Robin Smith and Graeme Hick were his reward for his hours of patience. It was good to charge in, perhaps a little gingerly, but he was doing a job, he was part of the team.

Following this was a certain bewilderment at being left out of the game against Pakistan in Karachi. The first four matches had been poorly attended; blame was apportioned to a variety of factors, in truth though, the Pakistan spectators had little to no interest in teams other than their own. Yet the emotion on show at the National Stadium in Karachi ran deep as Aamir Sohail struck the right run-making chord against an attack which Cronje juggled with some efficiency. Even Adams, given his first game, bowled steadily.

By now, the selectors seemed to have satisfied themselves that they had found the right bowling combinations. The batting too looked more settled, with Hudson displaying some flamboyancy in his strokeplay. These impressions were, however, false. The win over Pakistan, minus Jonty Rhodes, had been well fashioned and the victory over Holland was a matter of turning up at the Rawalpindi venue again to give a solid display against bowling of the peashooter variety: lacking substance, variation and penetration. Little wonder that Hudson scored 161 off 132 balls as South Africa mounted a total of 328 and a first wicket World Cup record of 186.

South Africa had gone through to the knockout stages unbeaten; Australia and the West Indies, who forfeited points against Sri Lanka, also qualified. Such was the anomaly of the league and points system, a team such as England could afford to lose to New Zealand, South Africa and Pakistan and yet comfortably reach the knockout stage.

Not only did a new format have to be found, but also on the evidence of what were generally shoddy performances England did not deserve to reach the quarter-final group. But then, neither did the UAE or Holland. There was some sympathy for Kenya; victors over West Indies. Only, drawn in Group A, the tougher of the two sections, they were always going to find it hard to reach the last eight.

For some reason, which has never been adequately explained, Fanie and Donald were made dressing room attendants for the game against the Windies. Admittedly Donald had not bowled as well as he could, but Fanie's omission was a puzzle considering the pace attack the West Indies used. Peter Pollock and Cronje no doubt discussed the options and the view of using two spinners carried more than an element of risk. The selection oversight was exposed midway through the West Indies innings. Brian Lara, with the sort of showmanship a batsman of his class can put together, picked off runs with ease; a highway robber enjoying a free ride as the runs flowed.

A fielding performance riddled with errors and showing signs of uneasiness left Woolmer queasy from almost the start of the game. Rhodes, whose slip against the Windies at Springbok Park in 1993 had cost South Africa a place in the Total Trophy final, made a rare blunder and Steve Palframan carelessly fumbled the chance given by Shivnarine Chanderpaul. Nothing was going right. Matthews was steady, economical, and with the ability to contain.

It was a below average bowling performance as the decision to play two spinners faltered.

It was about this time that Fanie noticed a certain arrogance creeping into Cronje's style of leadership, regardless of whether South Africa won or lost or drew the game. Cronje was not the same man he had met several seasons before. There was something else that Chesters had noticed—a message would be left on Cronje's mobile seeking a comment about an approaching series or game or a player's fitness. The calls were never returned.

A large number of South African cricket writers had similar experiences. A number of other writers complained about the same attitude problem; but Cronje also had his 'friends in the system' when he needed a favour. Asked once why he failed to return a call, the answer was that he had not received it.

About the only time Cronje sought out the journalist's opinion was in the media centre in Bloemfontein when he asked him to describe the bowling style of the Sri Lankan left-armer Ruchira Perera, who had been selected for the 1998 ICC Trophy knockout in Dhaka. Cronje wanted a second opinion; he had already consulted Nicky Boje, the South Africa A team's vice-captain on the 1998 tour of Sri Lanka.

Home within twenty-four hours of losing to the West Indies, Woolmer had a sobering message for a South Africa public stunned by the team's defeat when he addressed the media conference. It was his view that South Africa needed time to mature to face exacting World Cup competition. While there was a chance to improve and possibly win in 1999 in England, it was his opinion that South Africa would be ready to lift the trophy in 2003, when it would be held in the rainbow nation for the first time. 'By then the players should be mentally a lot fitter and tougher,' he said.

A lot changed between Woolmer's confident prediction at Jan Smuts International that morning and Ricky Ponting's appointment as Australia's limited-overs captain in late March 2002 as a replacement for Steve Waugh. That series exposed just how limited South Africa had become. A manhandled selection policy, a bowling attack which lacked variety and penetration, and batting which struggled on pitches that gave the Australian bowlers a hint of aid. Even the ground fielding and catching was decidedly shoddy. Any examination card a year before the 2003 World Cup would see South Africa battling to make the Super Six.

In 1996, however, Fanie did not share Woolmer's view of the team being mentally fitter and tougher. He has long felt that South Africa, who had won ten one-day games in succession before losing to the West Indies in the quarter-final, were as good as the Australians in mental toughness. While the Aussies may have more depth, there are South African players who can match the Waugh twins and Shane Warne: a patriotic theory, which has some substance. By April 2002, Fanie was as distressed as any former South African player at the level to which the team had slipped. Somewhere the coaching structures were all wrong and, as with the selection panel, needed a drastic overhaul. The team had lost interest in gym work as well as physical fitness, and it showed in the results.

It was the late Jackie McGlew who, in April 1995, when addressing the South African under-19 squad selected for England explained the importance of fitness. A fit player was focussed; a fit player was sharp, had better coordination and was mentally alert. Fitness came from training programmes and you ignored these at your peril. Against Ponting's Australians in the limited-overs games, an overweight-looking Jacques Kallis was a typical example.

One of Woolmer's comments that there was a need for a coach of a national side to have played Tests in order to understand the players' needs as well as the demands made at Test levels had, by April 2002, been partially proved right. Ability is one thing, experience another. South Africa needed more experienced Test players to help with the coaching system then in place. There was, however, no communication.

The irony of the final was Australia meeting Sri Lanka in Lahore after Ranatunga's troupe, backed by Dav Whatmore's dynamic coaching style, were awarded the semi-final by default after the Eden Gardens crowd brought dishonour to their nation by rioting in some of the most shameful scenes. Mohammad Azharuddin blundered twice: putting Sri Lanka in on a pitch which was going to take quite a bit of spin and then allowing the men from the pearl of the Indian Ocean to recover from 85 for 4 to score 251 for 8. The crowd's distress at India's inferior batting was more than they could swallow, and match referee Clive Lloyd, in a move to protect the players, called them off the field. The result of the riot at South Asia's most famous venue in March 1999 caused deep concern in India and the ICC. In 1996 it was a disaster; three years later, it had become a rampant disease.[4]

The blame, for allowing both riots to spread the way they did, has been dumped on the desk of the organizers, the Cricket Association of Bengal which was headed by Jagmohan Dalmiya, who conceived Pilcom and later became the ICC president. Dalmiya had been the main driving force behind South Africa's readmission to the ICC family in 1991 after the unification meeting formed the UCB. This explains in part the UCB's decision to support India in the fiasco which surrounded the Centurion Test in November 2002. That was when match referee Mike Denness' suspensions and finings of six Indian players in the previous match at Port Elizabeth created a row. The ICC stood firm and downgraded the match to that of a first-class friendly between two Test nations.

For those who enjoy the broader stage open-air theatre can provide, even in its limited-overs form, there was another twist in an already scarred and disfigured plot in the 1996 World Cup final. In Lahore, there was the ultimate irony: Sri Lanka, high on adrenalin, played and beat Australia in the final at the Gaddafi Stadium on 16 March. As Aravinda de Silva and Ranatunga batted with calm assurance, that iron-fisted competitor Ian Healy was as generous in defeat as he can be in victory and said 'Well played, mate . . .' to de Silva. With the match almost won, the wicketkeeper knew there would be no time for congratulations when the winning runs were scored. Coming from the man who had weeks earlier argued with Ranatunga about the need for a runner in the World Series final, it was a genuine compliment.

Although the draw for the semi-final venues had been made some months before the tournament, it would have been interesting had Colombo been selected as one of the venues with Australia then having to face Sri Lanka at the SSC. With a chance of playing in the

---

[4] In March 1999 the riot in the Asia tri-nation Test series between India and Pakistan created further international concern about Eden Gardens as a venue for Tests and limited-overs internationals.

final, the Aussies would have quite happily turned up in the island capital, with thoughts of bomb scares and political machinations quietly shelved.

As he did at Chelmsford on 29 May 1999 after South Africa's shock defeat by Zimbabwe, Woolmer admitted the focus had not been right for the West Indies match in 1996. In 1999, it had become lost somewhere between Amstelven where South Africa had beaten Kenya and the Essex County headquarters. As had been the case in the 1999 World Cup, Cronje's 1996 side had set standards and achieved impressive levels, yet had nothing to show for the long hard hours of preparation.

A fickle public quickly forgets statistical success: all they remember is the winning of trophies. And the label 'chokers' is an easy one to throw around the neck of a side which does everything but win the big prize: it is the one some media types take pleasure in using as they rub their particular brand of iodine on the wounds of defeat. 'South Africa, the nearly boys . . .' is always good for a snigger or two in the opposition dressing room, among the public too.

Was it though too much of a surprise that Woolmer handled the conference at Chelmsford? Where was the captain? Cronje knew the drill about after-match media conferences; did he not want to answer a few tricky questions? With what emerged later, Cronje's so-called bonhomie had all but disintegrated under the pressure of an unexpected defeat.

* * * *

For South Africa in 1996, the next port of call, if it could be called such, was the Sharjah tournament. It was barely a month after the World Cup; Donald was given time off to rest, Derek Crookes was brought in as a replacement, while Dave Richardson was back as wicketkeeper for the stopgap Palframan, and Fanie worked in the nets at Centurion to perfect a slower outswing delivery.

He had given some thought to whom he should bowl it. With three games against India in the Emirates, Sachin Tendulkar was looked on as the most promising of candidates. Fanie had used it to some effect a few months before. During a day-night domestic match against Western Province a few days before Christmas 1995, he had played at Newlands with an idea of showing the selectors that he was ready to resume his limited-overs career.

He admitted it had been a mistake to play in a high profile limited-overs match too soon. There was a thought he had harmed his chances of playing against England in the limited-overs games. The plan was to take a two-week holiday, escape to somewhere quiet with the family, after which he would rethink his comeback strategy. Developing the slower ball was part of his tactics.

He used it a couple of times in the day-night game against Boland in Paarl on 12 January and it worked the way he wanted, but did not earn him any wickets. Perhaps by the time the World Cup came around he would be ready to bowl it more regularly. However, the injury in Rawalpindi a couple of days before the tournament began did not help.

Now he had a chance in Sharjah: this time in the oil rich United Arab Emirates on the Gulf of Oman instead of the spicy subcontinent of Asia. A federation of seven sheikhdoms, the region inhabited by the UAE is flat, infertile and sandy, and as almost kissing cousins of Pakistan, the game has thrived here since the early-1960s. Although the Sharjah tournament has been held since 1981, in either October or April, or both, with Pakistan as the main competing team, the series has done much to spread the image of the sport. Ironically, the winning team's cash prize in 1996 was the same as that won by Sri Lanka in the World Cup final.

Judy flew with Fanie to Sharjah with the player more relaxed than he had been in months. Confidence was returning and although he did not collect any special prizes he picked up Tendulkar's wicket twice, quite cheaply, both to catches by Gary Kirsten as the batsman attempted to lift the slower outswinger over the inner ring.

It was during a discussion with Woolmer after the tournament, however, that Fanie realized he might find it harder to get into the side to tour India for the Test series later in the year. This was not because of agitation by activist groups within the UCB wanting more players of colour to be included in touring squads. There was a feeling that Fanie's value as a limited-overs player outweighed his ability to take wickets in subcontinent conditions.

Forget that his wicket strike-rate at Test level was an impressive five a match, one of the best in Test history, and until his injury at Edgbaston, he had been third in the world Test bowling rankings.

Less than a year later, he was under the distinct impression that he was about to be passed over. Either that, or the signals from the selectors were strangely mixed. Just how mixed they were emerged during the results of the South Africa A team in England in July and August in 1996.

Duncan Fletcher, a former Zimbabwe captain and Western Province coach since 1991, viewed the tour as one likely to create the sort of climate which would enhance some players' reputations. Much was expected of Brett Schultz, Roger Telemachus and Paul Adams. To a lesser extent, Gerry Liebenberg would further push his claims for a Test place; Jacques Kallis was also likely to continue to impress. Perhaps the wicketkeeper's conundrum could also be settled, if it emerged that either Nic Pothas or Steve Palframan was the better gloveman. In some ways, the touring party had been selected with the 1998 tour of England in mind, and to help satisfy the growing impatience of those driving the transformation vehicle.

But neither Pothas nor Palframan came through as Richardson's main understudy. Telemachus had proved himself to an extent in Sri Lanka the year before with the South African under-24 side and a longer tour with more opportunities should have developed his natural abilities. While the winds of 'Gogga mania' of the South African summer had all but blown themselves out, Adams was troubled on two fronts: the first was a form of shin splints, the second a groin strain, which he aggravated during the tour.

Liebenberg's form was not quite the same after the injury against Glamorgan and although Nicky Boje was given chances, he did not quite deliver the way he had in Sri Lanka with the under-24s. Greg Smith, the Northerns left-arm quick, was given surprisingly fewer opportunities, yet bowled consistently well.

Following the side around the shires on that tour created worry about the progress of some players. Neither Schultz nor Telemachus bowled convincingly. Lance Klusener, however, emerged as a genuine Test all-rounder to support Kallis. Herschelle Gibbs, who had batted at seven and six in the first two games, unwrapped his stroke-making flair, batting at three in the match against the MCC at Shenley. Klusener impressed more as the tour continued, and by the time the side reached Taunton for the Somerset match, the young man from Natal, with his cheerful, if shy, off-the-field manner and his aggressiveness on it, had started to attract attention of some members of the British media. There were various views about his robust style of playing.

Klusener set the tone and the style: hungry for wickets, grudging when it came to giving away runs, making batsmen sweat a little, and at The Oval, against Surrey, impishly offering umpire Ken Palmer a 'bite of a Mars bar'. As Surrey crumbled to defeat, the withering look, the mental toughness and the swing of the ball often had the batsmen trembling. Some English writers did not appreciate his fighting qualities. Three years later, they were applauding him during the World Cup when his dismissive swashbuckling habit under pressure won more headlines than most others during the tournament. In 1996, it was 'Klusener the villain'; in 1999 it was 'Thanks to Lance-a-lot' or 'Battered by a Zulu Warrior'.

Settled comfortably between the rolling, well-wooded Quantocks and the less romantic Blackdown Hills, Taunton has a sort of quintessential rustic charm. The Somerset county town was where Klusener did much to convince those who had seen him bowl long spells before, that he had learnt to grapple with the needs of a side in distress.

Schultz was about to be packed off home as the ankle injury from a limited-overs game failed to respond to treatment, and Telemachus, after four overs on an unresponsive pitch, pulled up lame. On a day when temperatures moved into the upper 20s, and summer settled over the cider county, Kallis joined Schultz and Telemachus on Craig Smith's physio bench. For Klusener, it was a matter of humping a heavier workload than he had expected. One of the lasting memories of the tour was watching a furrowed brow as Zulu began bowling yet another over on a stifling afternoon.

Yet Klusener was disappointed with his 1996 A Team form: he had fallen short of his tour targets of 40 wickets and 400 runs. Given that he batted so low in the order, it was understandable he was going to battle to reach the second target. Yet 31 wickets: well, what was wrong with that? When the team arrived back in South Africa on an icy overcast August morning, it was Gibbs who sat at the top table to answer the questions about his A Team batting performances. The young man who should have sat beside him, Klusener, was on his way home for some fishing, quite happy to be away from media attention.

Northerns had arrived in Durban on 17 December 1996, the day before what was being looked on as the Standard Bank League final. They had lost two matches in the series but still led the log as the skipper, Mark Davis, and the coach, Keith Medlycott, looked at the conditions. They felt relaxed as the Northerns, then labelled the sky blues before the Titans brand name was launched, loosened up at Kingsmead. Rudi Bryson, Roy Pienaar, Mike Rindel, Steve Elworthy, Martin van Jaarsveld, even Dirkie de Vos: they were the new heroes and Northerns, with identities split between Centurion and Pretoria, were 90 overs away from winning their first senior trophy. Sure it was limited-overs, and thus, for some, not really of serious consequence.

Fanie was wheezing and coughing, feeling far from comfortable. Four days before he had been playing in an extraneous limited-overs game tagged on to the end of the tour of India; a viral infection had attacked several members of the side and Fanie thought he was fit enough to bowl. It was a makeshift side for a benefit match for Mohinder Amarnath, which was being accorded full limited-overs status.[5] As if the side really needed another reason to keep them there a further twenty-four hours!

During the tour Derek Crookes had been so ill that he left a sick bed, batted a bit and bowled a few overs and went back to his room, where they had set up a drip. Away from the main centres and their luxury hotels, conditions were damp and cramped. Even Colombo in mid-monsoon, where waterlogged conditions meant practice of any sort was an exercise in futility, was better than Mumbai in December. India can be a tough country to travel, and with the Test series lost 2-1, why hang around? Fanie had been summoned home to visit Judy who had been rushed to hospital as the result of a virus and her recovery progress had also played on his mind on his return to the team.

When roll-call was made before the match in Mumbai, South Africa were down to ten fit men and for the only time on tour the

---

[5] It was this match where the players held three meetings to discuss and then reject the offer of a bribe to throw the game; Woolmer later told Dr Bacher of the meeting he knew about, which Dr Bacher does not seem to recollect.

four spinners were called on. Fanie bowled 5 overs, Brian McMillan 6, Adams 7.

Now, four days later, in steamy, tropical Durban, on the other side of the Indian Ocean and with light rain threatening, Fanie was ready to bowl again. Had it not been a dream to help Northerns win a trophy? This might be his only chance to be part of a team, which put one in the cabinet at Centurion Park.

For Natal, it was a simple matter if they wanted to win the Standard Bank League. Beat Northerns, and go down to Boland to wrap it up. No results through rained out games and an early season defeat had left Natal a little short on points. For Northerns, losing to Griqualand West and North West in Centurion in the last game, the result affected by the heavy dew, were minor blemishes on the domestic limited-overs landscape.

Medlycott felt that Northerns had a chance. The former England player and Surrey all-rounder had worked hard throughout the season, carrying on the work which Anton Ferreira had started three summers earlier. Naturally, jealous eyes viewed the success of the Northerns campaign; past administrators who were no longer part of the system felt a certain chagrin at how in the first season of the Northerns 2000 plan a first trophy loomed.

There was early disaster: Roy Pienaar was run-out without facing a ball, backing up too far as Shaun Pollock, following through, picked up a drive by Rindel and deflected the ball on to the stumps. In the past, the calamity of an early setback had the habit of disturbing the dressing room calm. The soft comfort zone into which a team often slips during a success streak gets ruffled. There are no easy solutions in such circumstances. Martin van Jaarsveld arrived and immediately showed style and class, if not a touch of flair. Against a bowling attack of four limited-overs players, taking a lead from Rindel's assured strokeplay, he batted sensibly.

A topscore of 60 in a total of 202 for 9 was an anchor performance, which won the left-hander the man of the match award, not Bryson with 3 for 27. Solidly built and with the ability to skid the ball through, Bryson was in the middle of a season, which saw him earn a South Africa limited-overs international cap.

There was also a noticeable change in his approach to the crease before moving into his delivery stride; he was more upright and seemed to have a better rhythm, although he did not seem to notice any difference. As it is, Craig Matthews did not make an entirely successful comeback: well, not enough to convince the selectors of a more permanent return to national duty.

As illness and injury pushed Fanie again into the shadows, and Richard Snell and Stephen Jack struggled with form and fitness, Bryson became a more than useful addition to the South African limited-overs fast bowling ranks. His economy rate may have been a little high at five an over, yet it was not for a lack of trying. At least his presence in the side gave the selectors, and Cronje and Woolmer, a more settled attack for the triangular series, and for the one against the Australians later in the season.

That steamy December night in Durban, however, Fanie felt like his heaving chest would burst. His legs seemed unable to carry him around the boundary at third man. His few overs had been a pitiful performance and Mark Davis, the Northerns captain, was a little troubled as Natal, at 172 for 7, were 30 runs short of victory. Steve Elworthy, so often overlooked by the national selectors, had bowled his quota, so had the captain. Bryson was still to be brought back as runs leaked in all directions.

It has long been argued that Klusener's run-out by Dirkie de Vos from point had turned the game around and given Northerns the chance they needed. Yet the most dramatic moments came in the last three overs, when Symcox joined Keith Forde. Bryson was back for his last spell and Dan van Zyl was darting in his useful cutters. Forde was taking chances by going over the top in a bid to win the game as he had against North West two weeks before.

·Northerns had learned how to handle such pressures and for Natal such risks were far greater. At the start of the forty-fourth over, Bryson charged in to Symcox: 11 runs needed off 12 balls, an enticing prospect with 2 wickets remaining, and the facing batsman had been used in the role as a pinch-hitter in limited-overs internationals.

The first delivery saw Bryson appealing for a lbw decision but Dave Orchard, the umpire, was far from interested. Symcox attempted to drive the next ball, and a thick outside edge saw Dennis Smith latch on to the offered chance. Natal were desperate for Forde to get down to face Bryson to take pressure off the last batsman, Gary Gilder. Bryson's first ball, however, ripped through the proffered defences and it was over. Whoops of joy on the field, celebrations in the dressing room and a scramble to find a bottle of celebratory sparkling wine. Northerns had won their first major trophy in their fifty-ninth year and the party, for many, went on until after dawn.

Fanie, sick, tired, yet happy at the result, finally nestled into bed. He had plans to take a short holiday and work at his fitness again. For a change he listened to his wife, Judy, and medical counsel and skipped the SuperSport Series game against Boland in Paarl. He would be ready for the match against Border in early January.

It rained a lot at Centurion Park that long, almost-forgotten summer. Indistinct figures in waterproofs struggling against a swirling tide thrown up by the Hennops River amidst sheets of torrential rain were a regular sight. On the weekend Fanie made his comeback, the rugby fields to the west of the oval could have been easily mistaken as part of a course for some canoe-event. The only reason the goalposts were not unceremoniously uprooted by the rushing water was because they were bolted down.

Not at all the sort of conditions in which to try and impress the selectors: after all, where else in the world would you have a river bursting its banks and floodwaters, only a hundred metres or so from the boundary, forcing the foolhardy spectator to seek the sanctuary of the grandstand? Normally the Hennops is a quiet trickle and the weather in keeping with the warmth of the summer months.

Somehow on the Saturday of that game the weather was transplanted from mid-summer Derby to brisk, breezy Centurion: all that was missing were the Derbyshire spectators, normally dressed in open neck and short shirt-sleeves. The county ground in Nottingham Road, Derby, converted from a racecourse, must rank, next to Carisbrook in Dunedin, New Zealand, as among the bleakest houses of the world first-class circuit.

This had nothing to do with another spineless Northerns batting performance as wickets crashed in the second innings. There was no miracle on the following day from which to hew a victory out of the scraps left from twenty-four hours earlier. They even switched on the floodlights to improve the light conditions without much success. The umpires felt that the way the venue was designed, with open areas like the Wanderers, it diffused the illumination of floodlights, which might have otherwise allowed play to continue in gloomy conditions. Fanie bowled steadily enough but did not do enough to take wickets, and as none of the national selectors were around it was obvious they had made up their minds that he was not in their plans for the Standard Bank triangular tournament either. Perhaps by the time the Australians arrived there would be a review of his progress.

This was strongly denied by Peter Pollock, who said the form of all players under contract was carefully examined, especially when they had been left out of the side for reasons of fitness. As this also included illness, Pollock felt it was wrong to assume that the selectors were not interested in players, 'who it is felt still have something to offer the team in the weeks to come'.

Border were so chuffed with their comprehensive 6-wicket victory by early afternoon on the last day, that they involved themselves in a celebration at a hotel near the ground. When they turned up at the domestic lounge of the airport early the next morning, Makhaya Ntini, who did not touch alcohol, was still in a bubbly mood from the previous day's success and played a few pranks on a couple of the hungover members of the team. Stephen Jones, the coach, was forced to step in and defuse a growing irritation at Ntini's attempts of 'horseplay' in the same way that Richard Pybus, a member of the Border coaching staff, had during net practices. Pybus had treated him as an ordinary player and suggested he behave as such.

Ntini, long considered the shining black opal of South Africa's development programme, would, given the natural course of events, earn a place in the national side. Only, he had used this position to his own advantage instead of acting as a young adult, in keeping with his Xhosa upbringing and character. It was a side of him which once bothered other players, who often found the Dale College-educated fast bowler unable to distinguish between light-hearted pranks and mischief-making horseplay, which irked even others in the development process.

It had nothing at all to do with handling pressures either: he was quite capable of doing that, as has been seen through his bowling performances since he was brought back into the side after he won the appeal court decision, which overturned the rape charges. His general maturity showed that some leopards do change their spots. In Sri Lanka in 2000, he also had fun with Chesters at the Asgiriya, once pouring some chilled water down the journalist's neck with a wicked grin. 'Chesters . . . you looked as though you needed cooling off in this heat,' he cheerfully winked. 'Man, you must have been hot in the shirt collar and tie . . .' Two days later at the hotel, he grinned at Chesters, and took hold of his bag with its computer equipment and smiled warmly. 'Hey, Chesters, man; this bag's heavier than my brother . . . Let me carry it for you.'

In the Port Elizabeth Test during the series against India in November 2001, he stopped Chesters near the boundary rope at St. George's Park and gave him a hug. 'I was told it is "hug a friend day", so Chesters man, I'm hugging a friend.'

Ntini then went to a couple of other cricket writers he knew and went through the same routine; it was not a display of showmanship but that of one who wanted to make it known how he felt.

Dropped in the Test series against the West Indies in the Caribbean months before, and later out of touch in Australia, Ntini made a comeback in Australia with such alacrity in the Victorian Bitter limited-overs series that he became the star attraction of the bowling attack and was finally able to discard his 'L' plates. He spent a lot of time bowling in the nets, training and working hard to prove that he has the ability to become a genuine match-winner abroad as well as at home.

When the call came through, it was around 7.30 a.m. Chesters had just finished an update for the afternoon edition previewing South Africa's third Test of the series against India at the Wanderers starting the next day and was about to e-mail the story to the *Pretoria News*. Braam de Villiers was on the line, sounding disturbed as he told his alarming story. Fanie had been in another accident, this one more serious than the lime explosion of October 1990. This time his right hand had been sliced open by the blades of the lawn mower the previous evening and he had spent the night in hospital after a lengthy operation to save the small finger.

Around dusk the previous day, Fanie had been clearing grass clippings from the lawn mower, when his son Faantjie tackled him from behind. Thrusting out his right hand as he fell forward, Fanie felt a searing pain as the fingers came in contact with the rotary blades. It had been barely twenty-four hours since Northerns had lost to Border, and here was yet another accident to haunt his efforts at making a comeback as he struggled to recover from the illness which had lingered since the tour of India.

When the damage was examined, three fingers had been sliced opened by the blades, two to the bone, and there was a fear he might lose the top of the small finger. There was also a worry about infection and how quickly the injury could be stabilized. The surgeon had to work quickly as large chunks of the muscle was missing, and there was also a worry about the nerves and tendons. The deep lacerations too would take some time to heal. The x-rays showed there was no damage to the bone but there was concern that infection could delay the healing process.

Making an eventual reappearance seven weeks later in a SuperSport Series match, there was still a problem with the wound on the third finger failing to heal. If his ambitions to tour Australia the next season were to be realized, he would need to be ready to answer the selectors' doubts. Not at all easy when playing for a team whose first-class record that season was as enigmatic as at anytime during his twelve seasons.

While rain did much to curtail the progress of the game, his performance where he bowled as second change in the Transvaal first innings and delivered 20 overs to take 2 for 38, was at least something. There had been a domestic day-night Standard Bank Cup match against Griqualand West in Kimberley, but rain had bedevilled most of Northerns' games that season and the day-night quarter-final was no exception. Northerns batted through the showers, which eventually washed out the game and Fanie was unable to bowl a ball.

He shrugged off the irritation and when the game was rescheduled between the second and third Tests of the Australia series, rain intervened again on the first of the two days set aside. And when, at the third attempt, it was played, Bryson and Elworthy destroyed the Griquas innings. Not that he expected a belated recall to national honours. The third and small fingers were still tender when he played in the Standard Bank Cup semi-final against Western Province.

The first semi-final was rained out with the side in a good position, while Western Province, successful with the toss, won the rescheduled match the next day, with Elworthy bowling with remarkable pace and swing and length, posing the question of why he was still being overlooked for the national squad. The query was met with a stony silence when, later in the year, Elworthy was named as the Standard Bank player of the domestic season: as much for his batting as for his bowling.

. For Fanie, the winter of 1997 meant a welcome break. No overseas tour, no unscheduled selection commitments to join a World XI in some icy corner of England. He did some training at the new indoor nets at Centurion and prepared for 1997-98, relaxed and determined to make a second tour of Pakistan and one to Australia, play a home series against Pakistan and Sri Lanka followed by a second tour of England.

After that? Well, retirement perhaps? Or a final World Cup in England after a series against the West Indies. Sure the body was tired and ached all over, but he had become used to that problem—waking up in the morning and struggling to get out of bed. It was all part of the life of a fast bowler.

If the previous summer had been disjointed because of illness and injury, 1997-98 would be different. He wanted to be able to concentrate on his goals for a change. When he turned up at the first fitness camp in Cape Town in September, he paid little attention at first to the political chatter about more players of colour being included in the side. A phrase such as 'fast tracking into the Test side' was not entirely new, but it did spell a message for future reference. And there had been discussion for some time of what sort of team would be sent to Australia. First, however, there was the visit to Pakistan, and he badly wanted to be part of the touring team. He felt he had done enough to convince the selectors he was fit again at the camp. Yet, when the squad for Pakistan was announced, there was one interesting name among the fifteen—Brett Schultz.

Peter Pollock's panel had again revived the big left-arm fast bowler's career and there was grumbling, more political than anything else, about the omission of Roger Telemachus from the squad. The view was that Fanie was not quite ready and Schultz would be needed to act as a support for Donald and Shaun Pollock, especially with the Australia campaign in mind. Political breezes were, however, stirring in the UCB corridors. There was a view which had been stewing for more than a season that it was time for more 'players of colour' to come through.

There had long been a trendy view that South Africa's development programme would broaden the base for new talent and that what had gone before in terms of players was of little or no consequence. Those such as Western Province all-rounder Faiek Davids, as good as they were, just made up numbers to keep the unity process happy. 'Not so,' said Omar Henry at St. George's Park in mid-December 1998 during the second Test against the West Indies, when he and Chesters discussed what had become a polemic if forceful issue.[6]

Henry wanted to know what had happened to all the players of colour in the eastern and western Cape who had come through the previous system. Far from popular because of his often critical assessments on television, he was quick to point out how, from the late 1980s until unity, Eastern Province and Western Province were the two main props of the SACB's player power base. Yet neither had, in recent years, played a contributing role to the 'player of colour' question.

'The way I see it, there were four provinces within SACB where there was a cricket culture,' he explained his point. 'Western Province, Eastern Province, Boland and Border. And for whatever reason, Gauteng (which was then Transvaal) and Natal have, since 1987, lost their way. The four Cape areas should have been strong contributing areas. Yet they have not followed through. For me, the strategy they used needs to be re-examined to see what has gone wrong and why. I would ask the four, why have they not brought more players of colour into their representative sides? There may have been problems of which we are not aware, but I

---

[6] A left-arm spinner, Henry, who is of coloured descent, is the oldest South African player to make a Test debut (40 years and 295 days) against India at Kingsmead on 13 November 1992. He played for Sacboc and SACU teams; in May 2002 he became convener of the new national selection panel, with Pat Symcox as one of the five.

know that when I played for Boland around 1985, we had two clubs where we had several players who were selected on merit.' It was a point worth remembering. In 1985-86, when Stephen Jones (later director of Border coaching) captained Boland, with Henry as his deputy, the two clubs, Newtons and Young Peoples, selected several players of colour on merit. They were Howie Bergins, Salieg Nackerdien, John Hendricks and Leon Roberts.

Henry felt the culture and the players who had come through had done much to create the right environment and growth. To his mind, the UCB's sincerity, now under scrutiny by the politicians, could not be faulted; nor could the national selectors be blamed if the players in the system could not help them in the selection process. 'You have to blame the provinces for what has been happening. How can the selectors pick players who are not in the system? If the provinces don't supply, don't blame the selectors: it is not their job. Blame the system and the clubs for allowing such a situation to develop. For me, there is enough cricket culture to allow the players to come through naturally than through forced quota arrangements. There is a history of cricket culture throughout the Cape, so why resort to artificial means when the culture is already there? And just as we do not need quotas, we do not need affirmative action policies.'

Henry was expressing thoughts to Chesters, which both knew would not be popular when aired in print. In December 1998, there were no simple answers to the problem. Ten years earlier, during the SACU's hundredth anniversary season, when he had written on the touchy issue for what was then the *Sunday Star*, there had been a testy response on how to tackle the problem.

To Chesters, it was a matter of affluent clubs adopting a 'foster parent' relationship with the less privileged. In time, it would create a base from which to build a new generation. The youngsters of the Bakers' mini-cricket programme would, as they grew older, be in need of step-by-step coaching levels to develop and improve their skills. The greater the exposure to the higher standard of the game, the better the class of player to emerge. So simple in theory, and practice too, had there been more empathy to encourage such a cause. But officialdom preferred to ignore the obvious until too late.

Russell Cobb, the Leicestershire player contracted by Fanie's Pretoria club, Onderwyskollege, during his student days, found when coaching in Mamelodi and other black urban areas at the time that such a scheme had development advantages. The 'Doctor's (Ali Bacher) Plan' could work and create a pool of talent which would eventually see a form of West Indianization of the game in South Africa, yet along demographic lines to give everyone a chance.

Ten years later, politicians were forcing changes and administrators felt their territory was being invaded by a 'foreign force' demanding the sort of equality at playing level which takes years to achieve but with few complimentary results. Fanie had been a casualty of such thinking when he had been forced to retire.

As Henry and Chesters watched the disintegration of the West Indies batting at St. George's Park, there was a sense of frustration about it all. 'You know, in my province, Boland, there are people who say that the job must go to the best man available,' Henry said. 'That being the case, I am in no doubt that there are people of colour who can become part of the system and not just as players: as administrators, coaches, umpires, scorers. They are people who have been brought up with the game and have a feeling for it.'

Then, as if addressing in his own mind the problem of terminology and the phrase 'player of colour', Henry related his own experience. When he had first been selected to play for Western Province in the 1970s, his father wrote a letter to the *Cape Times*, critical of their policy of calling him a coloured: 'As we are all South African, please have the courtesy to refer to Omar Henry as such and not as a player of colour.' 'And that was during the apartheid era,' Henry recalled. 'You know this is why I want to focus on this one aspect: the administrators, and here I mean those of colour, and the transformation process. For that we need to go back to the provinces, which I feel should contribute to the national team, and here I refer again to Eastern Province, Western Province, Border and Boland.'

It was a serious question. Gibbs, Telemachus, Adams, even Ntini, felt they deserved to be in a team on merit. To them, the thought that they were included because of being disadvantaged, rankled. 'It is an honour to play for South Africa and I want to think that I was included in the side on merit, and for no other reason,' Gibbs had commented with disarming frankness when discussing with Chesters his selection shortly before the Port Elizabeth Test. 'Sure I want to go out and play well and show them all I have the ability to open the innings. But I want to think, and want others to think as well, that I am in the team as a merit player and not because I am, or have been, disadvantaged. That sort of attitude leaves a very bad taste. I think I am good enough to make it on my own ability.'

Here was a young man placed under enormous pressure at the country's oldest Test venue, where the first-class game in South Africa had started 110 summers before. He deserved a chance without politicians pushing buttons. Adams and Ntini were out of form, Telemachus remained injured and, despite Henry's confidence that he would recover, he did not play at all that season. There had been rumours Henry wanted a change in provincial scenery and teammates to get over the psychological trauma of being ruled out of one tour because of a fitness problem and injured less than an hour before the start of the second only eight months later.[7]

Henry's argument of adjusting a strategy to allow top players of colour to gain more exposure had, to an extent, been met, when the UCB's quota plan allowed for a minimum of three being included in the provincial B teams. Those provinces, which had since unity ignored the needs to transform the system by failing to include players of colour, suddenly realized the need to develop talent. As Henry pointed out, did not, perhaps, team selection policy need a rethink? Then again, perhaps attitudes needed changing? It was a question he asked more than once during his discussion with Chesters.

If politicians were questioning UCB's integrity and planning, who was checking the credentials of the politicians and their agendas? Accountability in both cases must be open and honest, not a limited one-sided argument. Politicians, who know nothing of UCB's transformation planning, need to be asked what they are doing, interfering in areas of which they are ignorant. Sincerity is a two-way avenue, where ideas can be freely exchanged.

---

[7] Australia 1997-98 and England 1998 where he had a serious shoulder injury at New Road, Worcester, at the start of the tour on 14 May 1998. In April 1999 he was dropped from the list of UCB's contracted players.

Rugby has often beaten the loudest development programme drum. Yet not long ago, at Technikon Pretoria, in the west of the city, four men in their thirties were busy teaching skills to some thirty-five schoolboys, aged nine to twelve. The group was all white. Recruiting from Atteridgeville would take too much time and money, so why bother? A nice arrogant attitude, which smacks so much of the baasskap jingoism and thinking cluttering modern administrative thinking. At the same time, north of Pietersburg in the Northern Province, more than 1,500 children were attending a day camp run by the Northerns Cricket Union youth section. Administrators were wondering how they were going to accommodate all those who turned the session into a demographic demonstration of support. Asian, black, coloured, white: boys and girls. Mums and dads, too. To them it was a sense of belonging, a taste of recognition.

And this came after certain politicians and other sports officials suggested the enthusiasm had gone out of the UCB's drive to sell the game across the demographic map of the country. It was also in the aftermath of the first full West Indies tour of South Africa and the disappointment of the touring team's lack of success.

So many youngsters in the black, coloured and Asian areas wanted to identify with the tourists: the new generation brought up since isolation ended had been fed a diet of West Indies invincibility; some of this had come from the Total Triangular series of January and February 1993, and they wanted a taste of further success. To promote this ideology, anti-UCB establishment groups hoped to use West Indies heroes as role models, instead of the 'lily-whites' from the team Cronje led.

It is simple enough, and a fact of life in the modern age. They wanted someone with whom they could identify and found no one apart from Courtney Walsh and Curtly Ambrose among the seniors, and Shivnarine Chanderpaul and Darren Ganga among the juniors. As a form of 'protest', the new ideology protagonists began a campaign claiming that Lara had been 'bought by the UCB to lose the series', and this was the real reason behind the wage dispute between the team and the West Indies Cricket Board. It was, they claimed, why 'Dr Bacher had gone to act as a broker in the dispute'. So many assumptions dealing with fallacy and fiction, rather than fact.

Such were the expectations of the visitors' success, that their defeats placed pressures on the system not encountered since the Gatting rebel tour (without the political demonstrations, of course). Since living through history in the making during those often fractious, yet fruitful, months between September 1989 and March 1990, sport was seeking a new direction and identity. In 1989-90, many sports administrators were old fashioned and fragmented in their thinking, and they had no philosophy to cope with the force of political changes in an era of traumatic transformation.

What emerged from the 1998-99 West Indies failure was paradoxical but promising. Although pride in some black areas had taken a bruising due to the almost daily public humiliation of their would-be heroes, there were more youngsters playing street cricket in the Gauteng/Free State areas than soccer and basketball. It was an impressive sight and it needed no politician to pass on this message. As Khaya Majola explained, it was all part of the dream of natural, as opposed to forced, evolution.

One interesting perception has developed from all this among the underprivileged. They look on players such as Adams, Gibbs, Shafiek Abrahams and to a point, Ntini, as representing their community. They may have had a better education through the bursary system or because their parents could afford it, but they are still representative of the people. It was the sort of buzz phrase, which was strong in the Cape.

It also emerged in a different way, when Chesters was interviewed on New Zealand Sport Radio during the South African tour of the shaky isles in early 1999. He was in a studio with a quasi-government (coloured) sports administrator who made this point. The question then asked by the show's host, Malcolm Devlin, was, 'In that case what would happen to this policy should players of colour be included in a national side and two of the three were ill while the third was so out of form he could not be selected?' The coloured administrator went silent; he was not used to being asked such blunt questions.

When tackled on the question Rushdi Magiet, convener of the national selection panel of the time, said, while watching the third Test in Colombo in early August 2000, that the 'UCB's view is that you select the best available on merit and if there is no player of colour who fits into that category, selection norms apply'. This did not say much, but while Gibbs served his six-month ban, the rest of the side had its their own problems to solve.

There was another side to the sorry West Indies tour saga of 1998-99 which was noted but went largely unreported, especially by those daily tabloids which beat the transformation and egalitarian drums in cricket but ignore the lack of transformation drive and opportunity for all in soccer, which carries the misnomer 'people's sport'.

Colin Croft asked Chesters a pertinent question before the sixth limited-overs international in Bloemfontein: why did the West Indies team not meet Nelson Mandela or Thabo Mbeki during the tour? The official answer was that their schedule was such that it could not be satisfactorily arranged. It was later discovered through a Department of Sport confidant that the strike for higher wages by the senior players, led by Lara, had not gone down too well with Mandela, or Mbeki, or Steve Tshwete, for that matter. They felt it was undignified for high profile (black) sportsmen to behave the way they had, as the image of fair play was very strong among some black sports administrators. Cricket's role in unifying the country attracts much admiration as well as envy from groups more diverse than national sports administrators.

The view, one former administrator admitted, is: rugby is essentially still the sport of the Afrikaner and therefore generally white in concept and administration. To have transformation working, there was a need to buy-in to the high school bursary scheme. Soccer is black-dominated with no transformation policy and with an administration acknowledged to be corrupt at many levels; other sports (hockey, surprisingly, is a major exception) are still trying to find general acceptability as well as broad philosophies to improve the uplift programmes. In this respect, Nocsa (National Olympic Council of South Africa) are still seeking an acceptable formula.

Even basketball, the so-called sport of the future was red-carded, when American interests looking to make financial capital on the back of a flimsy, flawed transformation policy ran into opposition from the Department of Sport for their attitude. The idea was to take money out of the country to fatten the back pocket and put nothing into development.

Cricket, however, has had administrative structures in place for more than fifteen years which make it available to all population groups. Despite the flawed claims of Dr Mtutuzeli Nyoka, the former Gauteng Cricket Board chairman, it has the scope and dimensions to be the sport of the future as well as of the people.

Not that it was so noted by newspapers such as *Sunday Times*, and to an extent *Sunday Independent* in March 2001, and again in 2001-02. Their response to transformation in the game was a reverse two-finger salute by ignoring the domestic first-class competition, yet publishing centimetres of items about a rugby event, which in terms of transformation, has no value at all. It is the sort of baasskap-style thinking for which senior editorial staff need to take the blame and take a serious look at their own philosophies.

17

Political Crossfire

About twenty-four hours before the first of the three Tests against Pakistan in February-March 1998 was consigned to a watery grave, the South African selectors met with Hansie Cronje and Bob Woolmer in suite 702 of the Unity Stand at the Wanderers to discuss the side for the second and third games of the series. No doubt, there was some discussion of the bowling attack's lack of success in the Wanderers game played from 14 to 18 February 1998.

The tourist had been allowed to recover from 112 for 5 on a rain-splattered third day and held enjoyed more luck than any ride on a magic carpet could provide. Azhar Mahmood, dropped more than once, scored a century and was allowed to nurse the innings along from a possible follow-on to a deficit of 35 runs. This had been possible because of an embarrassing bowling performance by the South Africans. Donald, Shaun Pollock and Klusener had made impressive early inroads until Azhar was allowed all the freedom he wanted to mastermind an escape route: as he had done the previous October in Rawalpindi. It was not at all the déjà vu Cronje wanted to experience as he sat watching the tableau unfold. Gary Kirsten had been given his one and only game as captain as a morose Cronje, recovering from a knee operation, watched the game from the South African dressing room.

Barely half an hour after the game had been called off, Peter Pollock went up to the Charles Fortune Media Centre and read out the side for the remaining Tests in Durban and Port Elizabeth. Young H.D. Ackerman had earned his first cap, Paul Adams was back and so was Fanie. He had known of his selection the night before, when Pollock had contacted him. Celebrations in the de Villiers house were, however, subdued: the call up had been overdue and whatever excuses could and were made, the selectors had tarried six months too long.

Asked if he knew of the rumours about the long-term doubts of Fanie's future in the game, Pollock played it straight: batting as best he knew how he fended off a couple of questions. Yes, he had heard the rumours. 'But they are just rumours; there's nothing official. And we have been asked to select the best side possible to win the series against Pakistan, which is what we have done.'

Pollock senior always gave the right answers and made the right noises, but questions remained. It was so similar in delivery style to that hot day four months earlier when Pollock had announced the South African side for the Australia tour. Chesters had travelled to the Wanderers with long-time friend Alan Jordaan, who was to manage the team. Naturally they had speculated on its make up and Jordaan had expressed doubts whether Fanie would make it, despite his performances in the one-day matches in Pakistan.

'Times are changing and the selectors are under pressure to come up with an acceptable team,' said Jordaan. 'And tell me, just who is he going to replace out of the team which went to Pakistan?'

'Schultz, surely,' argued Chesters. 'He has another long-term injury.'

Jordaan shrugged. As much as he too would like to see Fanie in the side, he felt it was wishful thinking. They were taking fifteen, plus a player of colour in keeping with the new policy, and he had looked closely at the form of all those available. As it was, there had been grumbling about selectorial ineptitude within the ranks of the UCB when Fanie had gone to Pakistan ahead of Roger Telemachus for the limited-overs games.

Jordaan and Chesters had known each other for thirty years and had shared many confidences. It was Jordaan who had twelve years ago gone against the Northerns captain, Lee Barnard, and team manager, John Reid, to give Fanie his first chance at senior provincial level.

'You surely know something,' Chesters suggested.

'I know nothing. In fact you probably know more than I do, ' was Jordaan's comment. 'You talk to the selectors, I don't.'

Popular thinking at the time was that Fanie de Villiers had bowled well enough in the limited-overs games during the Golden

Jubilee quadrangular tournament in Lahore to deserve a second trip Down Under.

'We have been friends for a long time, but I am telling you now that I have not been told a thing about team selection,' said Jordaan. 'I'm no longer on the board, so I am privy to nothing of a confidential nature. I was invited along as I am going to be the team's manager and that's all.'

It was a fair comment. Had Schultz been fit though . . . would he have gone? Had Fanie, because of his limited-overs record, merely gone as a filler for Brian McMillan to the slogs in Lahore? As it was, the side had the right balance of all-rounders who could fill in as limited-overs as well as Test players: Shaun Pollock, Jacques Kallis and Lance Klusener. When South Africa had been welcomed back in 1991 the compliment of all-rounders were the veteran Clive Rice, Adrian Kuiper and Brian McMillan with Richard Snell and Craig Matthews capable of putting runs together if they were needed in an emergency. For the 1992 World Cup, Matthews had been replaced by Pringle. Perhaps Fanie's freak accident with the lawn mower months before had been one mishap too many.

When the team list for the Australian tour had been handed out in the UCB's old boardroom, a swift scan down the page showed that Mark Boucher had been included in the fifteen and Telemachus was the extra member: the player of colour. Pollock senior carefully left a gap for the selection panel when announcing the side. He also tried to sweeten the pill with such comments as 'you can never write off someone like Fanie de Villiers; he has proved us wrong more than once' and 'it is good to have someone like him in reserve should we need him'.

However, the big Northerns swing bowler had a right to wonder what agenda the selectors were being forced to use. Telemachus? Would it not have been better to take Makhaya Ntini? At least it would be a genuine appointment, popular too among the growing dissenters of the selection policy in the UCB system.

'They have made a big mistake in not taking me to Australia,' Fanie said, pointing a finger at the tour schedule on the study wall in Chesters' house later that day. 'They need a few guys to take the Aussies head on; well, we'll see.'

There was the impression that he had been robbed of a place in the side because of a selection policy governed by politics. To him, it was not even a borderline case. There was no doubt. Extra training schedules had given him back the pace missing during the tour of India late in 1996. He was still regarded as the world's number one swing bowler. It was not a cloistered view either. It fitted the thoughts of John Reid, Allan Border, Steve Waugh, Arjuna Ranatunga and Courtney Walsh along with the then Pakistan captain Rashid Latif. It was going to take a while to ignore how he had become the first victim of a system he supported: a case where those in control felt the end justified the means; mixed signals added to the confusion about what team the selectors really wanted to send to win a Test and limited-overs series in Australia.

This was all about revolution and not evolution, about quota systems and political pressures. Seven years after unity, it was, at last, an acknowledgement that little had moved forward. And those at fault were the provincial bodies and clubs that had not helped in the natural development of black players. While most schools had embraced the ideals of the rainbow nation, clubs and administrative bodies had not been sensitive to similar needs. Their constitutions remained entrenched in the apartheid past; although there were warning signs, these were merely noted. So little had been done to accommodate the needs of those who were still stepchildren in the system. Change was needed, or it would be forced on an old guard clinging to isolationist policies.

Not everyone was negative. Some Premier league clubs had started instituting a policy of 'foster parenting' through a variety of association forums. It was a small start; not too late, but it should have happened in 1991 or years before. What was worrying was that no one really knew how to handle the unity process; in a sense, everyone was uneducated about the growing needs of a sport in search of a common, egalitarian goal.

Clubs, comfortable with decades of general administrative inactivity, were confronted with a new set of expectations and demands. Irritatingly, too few traditional (white) clubs had been prepared to go that extra step. True transformation had been ignored. The bitter experiences of 1976-77 when the first unity efforts floundered through deliberate political obfuscation and ignorance of growing expectations among the disenfranchised and under-privileged masses, who wanted to be involved but were shut out, seemed to have taught no lessons. Surprisingly, cricket was the one major sport which had shown a willingness to unify within the apartheid system.

Yet was there not another hand behind Fanie's non-selection for Australia?

Take the team's bus ride to the hotel when the Golden Jubilee quadrangular tournament in Pakistan was over. Cronje went over to where Fanie was sitting and asked him if he would be fit for the rigours of a tough Australian tour. To those unaware of the background, it seems a plausible question and the responses equally reasonable.

'Of course I'll be fit for the tour. You saw how I bowled in these matches.'

'There are a lot of hard games to be played and we need fit players through the tour.'

'I know. But you don't need to worry. Look how I bowled here. Believe me, I'll be fit for all the games.'

Was this another of Cronje's ploys? Was Fanie now staring at the barrel of a verbal gun aimed at ending his career? He wondered if he was in a Last Chance saloon scenario without a drink and the skipper carefully loading the ammunition. The underlying tone of Cronje's query about Fanie's fitness seemed to be a decisive denouement in Cronje's effort to eliminate those senior members of the side who had stood up to him.

Fanie had already tackled Cronje about the way he treated the younger players and Woolmer; naturally the captain had not appreciated the de Villiers frankness. There was a niggling feeling that dug into the subconscious: Cronje was up to something, so be careful. Fanie's 5 wickets had come at a fraction above 4 an over; he knew he should not be dropped from the side. He also knew from previous tour experience that South Africa needed some tough players to tackle the Australians.

With this in mind he telephoned Clive Rice, then a national selector, shortly after arriving back from Pakistan to plead his case, telling Rice of the need for Pat Symcox and himself to be in the side to tour Australia. It was not a question of wanting to go on another tour. The way Fanie saw it, he and Symmo were about the only two South African players capable of dishing out verbal abuse to counter that of the Aussies.

No one, it seemed, wanted to listen; if they did, nothing was said. And, in some respects, the Australians often shook up the younger South African players. As Shaun Pollock and Co. discovered in 2001-02, there is a lot more to touring Australia than turning up to play matches. Physical fitness is only part of the game plan; mental toughness is also a necessary requirement and there were those who were not prepared for the strong tactical Aussie approach which creates a critical psychological advantage.

After the selectors had, for reasons they were not prepared to admit, rejected his credentials for the Australia tour, Fanie wanted to play again as soon as possible; the ideal opportunity was for Northerns in their SuperSport Series game against Natal at Kingsmead. Still bothered by Fanie being left out of the national side, Chesters stood outside an Asian restaurant in Corlett Drive and made a mobile phone call to Keith Medlycott, then the Northerns coach.

'Medders, do you have the side for the Natal match in Durban this weekend?'

'Yes, Chesters.' Medlycott read out twelve names. Fanie's was not among them.

'I see de Villiers is not there. Any reason?'

'Well, Chesters, we have had to select and prepare a side and as we thought he was going to Australia there was no sense in picking him,' Medlycott explained, knowing the row this comment could cause.

'You always talk about wanting experience in the side. Surely . . .'

'We have a match to play. We cannot wait for the national selectors to decide who is and who is not going to be included. It's as simple as that.'

The Northerns team left for Durban; Medlycott switched off his mobile and missed Fanie's call requesting he join the side. The call was not returned and Fanie, without a game, also headed for Durban, this time to join his friend Pat Symcox on a fishing expedition before the tall off-spinner headed for Australia and Fanie home to confront the Northerns coach and sort out the provincial team selection muddle. There was a heated exchange of words. He was fighting for his international career and, as his UCB contract was in jeopardy, he knew how important it was to string together match-winning performances.

His demonstration of quality swing bowling in mid-December had torn apart Boland and Griqualand West: 9 wickets against a Boland side whose fragile batting on an uneven surface offered little resistance although Adrian Kuiper, their captain, later condemned the pitch; Griquas, the visitors to Centurion, presented him with a further 8 wickets and Steve Elworthy with 10. Anyone who was present that Saturday afternoon of 13 December to watch Elworthy's clever change of pace mixed with swing and cutters for a return of 8.2-6-2-5 would have wondered about the pitch conditions. It was not the pitch but a deadly cocktail brew of quality bowling and blemished batting technique which had condemned Griquas to follow-on.

Not that there was an amicable end to this particular match. At the centre of the argument was Martin Gidley. Gidley fell lbw to Fanie for a second innings score of 134. He had been out earlier as he fought to save his side from an innings defeat. Steve Waugh may call it gamesmanship, while Arjuna Ranatunga and other players refer to it as sledging, but when Gidley was declared not-out Fanie allowed his feelings to spill over and put left-hander Gidley, little more than a journeyman batsman, on his hit list. The word or two normally exchanged between bowler and batsman quickly boiled over into a nice stew of personality clashes, and when the game ended Fanie thrust Gidley to one side as he walked up the steps. Eddie Barlow, then the Griqualand West coach, was quick to react. 'Who the hell do you think you are?' Barlow barked. 'Don't you ever push my players around.'

Not a smart thing for Barlow to have said as Fanie, not one to shirk a confrontation, told an indignant Barlow what he could do with his objections. The ensuing verbal fracas ended with both facing a disciplinary hearing in which they were cautioned and discharged.

In four SuperSport Series matches that season Fanie's haul had been singularly impressive: 27 wickets at 16.40 with possibly the most remarkable bowling spell coming at the Wanderers against (the renamed Transvaal) Gauteng side. Set a target of 310 for victory, Gauteng's second innings disintegrated in the most spectacular, if alarming, fashion on a pitch which had eased out. It has been suggested that the batting on 26 January 1998 was as derelict as the score indicates: it exposed a lack of discipline, skill and focus. Greg Smith's lively left-arm pace and swing complemented the swing and seam of Elworthy and Fanie. After a couple of overs Smith replaced Elworthy and engineered the collapse when he had Sven Koenig caught by Fanie in the slips. The three bowlers were devastating and 7 wickets fell without addition to the total of 12 runs. Smith, 3 for 16, Fanie, 4 for 11 and Elworthy, 2 for 13, wrapped up the humiliating defeat before tea on the last day with victory by 236 runs as Gauteng were routed for 78.

So, if Fanie's impressive return in four matches was overlooked by the national selectors when they decided the side for the first Test against Pakistan in February-March, it could not have been on a question of form. While Messrs Peter Pollock and Co. did not resort to uttering such banalities as those of the former England selection chief Ted Dexter's 'Venus may be in the wrong juxtaposition to somewhere else' to explain why a game plan failed, the theory that Pollock and Co. pursued a specific selection agenda 'forced on them' lingered. For Elworthy and Fanie, it was not a matter of the theory nudging their thoughts as giving them a solid elbow jolt.

How ironic it was that Elworthy had to wait until Fanie's retirement before he was reluctantly thrown a bone at limited-overs level and Smith was continually ignored. In an era where selectors talk of the need for left-arm pace to upset touring teams' batting biorhythms, Smith was fed scraps with A Team selections acknowledging his existence. In frustration, Smith took the offer made by Clive Rice and in 2001 joined Nottinghamshire using his British passport.

Many felt Rushdi Magiet's selection panel appeared to look no further than Durban, Cape Town and the Free State. The query was, must players come from the right province? These days, it is Natal, Western Province and Free State. Little wonder the panel lost credibility and was fired in April 2002 when Omar Henry was named convener of a new panel, which included Pat Symcox.

In 1995 Rice, then director of the Plascon Academy, had much to say about the hard work Smith put in after hours and off he went to the Dennis Lillee School in Chennai with David Terbrugge.

It was the highly polite and likeable Terbrugge, who earned his Test cap first. Now, had Smith been from one of the favoured provinces, he too would have received just recognition. Northerns may have the best indoor and outdoor facilities in the country, be recognized as having the most progressive administration and an improving playing record with more success than say Free State, or for that matter Gauteng, in recent years. But the stigma of coming from one of the so-called lesser provinces still haunts players of talent from such provinces.

When Magiet and his panel called up Andre Nel and Dewald Pretorius for the home series against Australia in 2001-02, and ignored Elworthy, the bowler they had sent to Australia, the query why Elworthy, with the better record, was left out drew a response of 'he is far too old and therefore no longer fits into our plans'. How remarkable that two months later Henry's panel felt Elworthy did have a role to play. In a sense, it showed how Magiet's panel, over time, had lost touch with reality, with some members claiming they had done a good job.

* * * *

There was a heavy, disturbing scent of distrust in South Africa in those first months of 1998; you felt it all too sharply in Durban as you drove into the city from along the coast. And even in normally placid Port Elizabeth something was not quite right: uncomfortably so, as it turned out. In February it can be sticky and often totally unpleasant. Yet the mood and atmosphere in the city overlooking the Indian Ocean reminded many of the days before the 1994 general election; were the spectators there for the Test or the revolution? For some months a new political dispensation had been throwing its weight around. Worried about an image tainted by failure, it was seeking scapegoats rather than solutions to problems. Those in charge hid behind a facade of clever rhetoric and preached revolution, not evolution. The only answer they had to events they could not control was a shotgun.

What had been noticeable at Kingsmead since sports isolation ended was the militant tone among groups of spectators, some of it motivated by political factions. Then again, a heady cocktail of sun, more alcohol than they could handle and a touch of racial provocation was enough to stir more than a few passions. That the volatile spectators belonged to a section of the population which had for generations been disenfranchised, despised before and during the apartheid years and degraded by derogatory remarks further fermented the cocktail. It explained the aggressiveness of the minority whenever India or Pakistan put in an appearance in the sprawling seaside city.

The growing pains had tarnished and disfigured the rainbow nation; tainted it as the image of unity was blurred by those who felt the system had not fully accepted them. It became so bad that Krish Mackerdhuj, at the time the UCB president and later ambassador to Japan, threatened to take games away from Kingsmead.

What concerned him were the anti-South African sentiments. And this came from a man educated at Fort Hare University in Alice, who had often suffered humiliation because of his race, creed, culture and colour; a man who fought the system through his administrative functions on the SACB and South African Council on Sport. A vigorous anti-apartheid campaigner, he was hurt by the attitude adopted towards 'my players' as he referred to the South African side during the years when he was president of the UCB.

For Mackerdhuj, the knowledge that South Africa's players were forced to endure 'hostile and often acrimonious racial abuse' when playing touring teams in Tests and one-day internationals at what was seen as 'unpatriotic' Kingsmead was no longer acceptable. Removing Test and ODI status from the venue was not the answer, either; it would give the militants victory at a time when unity had become more important than waving a big stick and threatening reprisals. That was the way the apartheid system had been enforced. Lowering UCB to that level was not worth it. Or was it?

There was a noticeable change in 1998-99 during the West Indies tour and the Millennium Test the next December when Nasser Hussain's England side were the visitors. By the time Steve Waugh's side played the opening game of the Standard Bank triangular challenge in 2001, any number of local Asians had draped the new South African flag around their shoulders and proudly paraded it through the masses, even as the image of Cronjegate and its ugly slurs sunk in amongst a disbelieving proletariat. The mood had changed: it was as if the local Asians were tacitly ashamed of their acts of March 1998. Then again there were third, fourth and even fifth generation South Africans who would wrap themselves in the colours of the rainbow nation: what did they know of India or Pakistan and Sri Lanka? They wore the new flag with pride.

In late February 1998 though, as abuse was hurled at Jacques Kallis and later Allan Donald in front of young children, it became a serious problem: an unhealthy stench which had wafted over the series from the moment two Pakistan players, Saqlain Mushtaq and Mohammad Akram, claimed they had been mugged outside the plush Sandton Hotel. There is no link between the two incidents: yet they seemed part of the growing dissatisfaction within the country at the tortoise pace of integration, and not just in the sports arena.

Asked the question why they did not support the South African side, the answer came back that it was not truly representative of the country. It was not that Adams or Gibbs were coloured, it was because there was no Asian in the side. Okay, how many Asians, then, had played for Natal since unity? One? Yes, there was one, an import from Pakistan. Was he a genuine representative? There was no reply to this logic. They did not want to answer and it upset Mackerdhuj.

How the scene had shifted four years later: the late Khaya Majola's long-held philosophy that evolution and not revolution would see a stronger second and third generation emerge has started to create an impression. In numerous discussions Chesters had with Majola, director youth and development at the UCB, and Hoosain Ayob, ICC director of coaching in Africa, about long-term plans and growth through transformation, Majola often made the point how growth would, given time and encouragement, develop a new, exciting breed of player. Fast tracking was one way, although this had its flaws and the weaknesses were swiftly exposed. Yet it was this exposure which created the required image that players were coming through who could, in time, play for their country.

* * * *

Driving in from the small Natal South Coast town of Amamzintoti that Thursday morning in late February 1998 was an interesting exercise. Joining the early morning rush hour traffic was hampered because of minor road works and bridge construction. All that motorists were worried about was getting to Kingsmead at a reasonable time and the threatening clouds along the coast, which the locals suggested might later turn to rain.

Fanie de Villiers, who had earned his seventeenth Test cap, was already at Kingsmead, warming up and having a look at the pitch conditions. He had signed a few autographs but now wanted to concentrate on his pre-match exercises; for him, it was an important part of the day.

A voice called out. 'Hey, Fanie, I want your autograph.' The fast bowler waved cheerfully. 'No. Now, I want it now,' came the querulous voice. Fanie waved and carried on with his pre-match warm up exercises, which are so important. It had become hot and sunny and some in the crowd were restless. They wanted Pakistan to teach the whiteys a lesson. Give them a good thrashing.

Pollock's selection panel had also been active. Axed from the squad were Paul Adams and Daryll Cullinan. Pat Symcox, the century-scoring hero in the first Test at the Wanderers, knew he was going to carry the drinks at Kingsmead. Selections, apart from Fanie, included young H.D. Ackerman winning his first Test cap and the return of Cronje. As Fanie bowled at a single stump set up by coach Bob Woolmer, Allan Donald also warmed up with Shaun Pollock and Lance Klusener. The humidity hung around the ground as the crowd grew slowly: not large by Centurion or Newlands standards, yet when the end came before lunch on the following Monday it was larger than that which had turned out at the Wanderers.

Azhar Mahmood apart, the Pakistan batting in the first innings lacked skill, discipline and quality and when young Ackerman batted in his debut Test innings he showed what enjoyment there was in taking the attack to the bowlers; a couple of handsome drives in front of the wicket were those of a young man full of self-belief. After lunch though, his mood changed, as if someone had told him not to bat with such expansive confidence. If this was in fact the case, it was careless and retrogressive, creating pressure where there should have been none. Instead of a first innings lead, South

Africa trailed and an early breakthrough was needed. Fanie bowled the first ball from the pavilion end to Saeed Anwar which beat the batsman through the air and off the pitch and slapped into his proffered pad. Up went Fanie and Mark Boucher, those in the slip cordon were also convinced Anwar had been trapped in front. Even the replays indicated it had neither strayed down leg nor was it too high.

'That looks out to me,' said Robin Jackman commenting on SABC TopSport TV; everyone peered at the TV replay for confirmation. There was no doubt. Fanie should have earned what would have been his first first-ball dismissal. The umpire, Dave Orchard, did not see it that way. The bowler could not believe it and Boucher was just as nonplussed: it had looked good, the young wicketkeeper barely had to move apart from going up in appeal. Well, chalk that one up to experience, if you can. Not that the appeal was greeted with universal approval as some groups of spectators jeered when it was made and cheered when it was turned down. It was like that throughout the match.

Paddy Upton, the team's fitness trainer, and Fanie decided to go and talk to those in the crowd to discover what had been their beef with the players. The idea was to invite those responsible to the dressing room to hear what they had to say. The ploy failed and Upton and Fanie were reported for what was regarded as 'conduct unbecoming' them. It was an argument which was as bogus as the 'charge sheet'. Not surprisingly, when the disciplinary hearing was held, the charge was thrown out. Unfortunately, the likeable Upton became a victim of the system, where Cronje now had too much power. There is a theory that Cronje wanted Upton out for personal reasons; one being his popularity among the younger players. By then, however, Cronje had been allowed too much influence: not only as captain but also in his views regarding board policy. Some UCB board members as well as selectors felt there were times when Cronje was dismissive when they were talking to him.

It tied in with something which had increasingly worried Fanie on the trip to Pakistan. As it turned out, it was his last overseas tour. Junior players would be in conversation with Cronje when the captain would suddenly look past them and start talking to someone else. There was arrogance in the way he treated junior members of the side and openly chastised Woolmer. Cronje had been given too much power: not only as a captain but also in the way he conducted himself; it was as if he felt he was above the side and the UCB.

During that 1997-98 tour of South Africa, Pakistani in-fighting was rife: Wasim Akram, removed as captain some weeks before, allegedly because of fitness, arrived in time for the third Test at St. George's Park. Salim Malik, whom no one trusted, was also not part of the squad. Wasim's controversial return divided an already fractured team further and it came after Khalid Mahmood, then president of the Pakistan Cricket Board, added his thoughts on selection policy. No Pakistan team of that era could afford to be without Akram; he was far too experienced to be left out.

The tourists' form had been erratic and adding to the general confusion around the team were still unresolved questions over the mugging episodes at two exotically named Johannesburg night spots, the Blue Orchid and Club 69, in which Saqlain Mushtaq and Mohammad Akram were involved. Police took statements and were trying to fully investigate the incident, while the team management said one thing and did the opposite. There were suggestions that a higher authority than the UCB had the investigations shelved. Haroon Rashid, the Pakistan coach, admitted privately that it had been the most disorganized troupe which he had the misfortune to handle, and Wasim's return did not help. Haroon would be pleased when the tour was over and he could retire. Under the circumstances, it was remarkable how they won the second Test in Durban.

****

For Fanie de Villiers the decision to announce his retirement came much earlier than he had planned. However innocent it appeared, such an event was always going to cause a stir as the preceding volatile background suggested intrigue and racial overtones. This was exacerbated hours later through a thoughtless rewrite of Colin Bryden's story by the *Sunday Times* (Johannesburg) editors, too eager to add further spice to the copy. It was a question of not letting the facts get in the way of what they saw was a good story.

What annoyed Fanie was the insinuation, by implication, that he had decided to quit just as an UCB probe into racial allegations involving four players and a member of the management team at Kingsmead was being investigated. It backfired and left Bryden embarrassed by his own newspaper. When Bryden arrived at breakfast that Sunday morning of 8 March 1998, he expressed such a feeling to others also covering the third Test between South Africa and Pakistan. It also left a question mark over the ethics of those removed from the scene, who felt they knew the inside story better.

Bryden had, at a sports writers' function hosted by South African Breweries the night before, commented he felt 'quite satisfied' with what he had written. He did not elaborate.

Peter Robinson of the Independent Group had received similar careless treatment when a story he had written the day before, alluding to Pat Symcox's possible retirement, was handled with similar exaggeration in the group's Saturday editions. Facts and quotes had been changed and the story quoting Dr Ali Bacher, managing director of the UCB, who said that 'in 1998 an all-white South African (cricket) side is no longer acceptable', was conveniently ignored.

The *Saturday Paper* (Durban) and the *Saturday Star* (Johannesburg) were not the only papers in the group to distort the Dr Bacher story. The *Pretoria News Weekend* did the same. Both Port Elizabeth papers, the *Eastern Province Herald* and the *Saturday Evening Post,* seemed to be more aware of what was taking place with the editors trusting what had been written by their sports staff at St. George's Park. As for the rest, a major statement by a leading sports administrator was passed over until *The Sunday Times* used some of it to add extra seasoning to Bryden's story.

'Wow, did you read what Bacher said?' was the comment around the subs table in the *Pretoria News* on the Sunday evening as they prepared the Monday edition. 'What a good story. Why didn't we get it?'

By then it was too late. As was pointed out by one of the sports staff, Corrie Nel, the *Pretoria News* had missed the opportunity forty-eight hours earlier. He printed out the story Chesters had sent on Friday afternoon and showed it to the assistant editor; the subs desk fell silent.

There was little doubt, however, that Fanie had become the victim of circumstances. Changes, some more dramatic than others, were swirling around St. George's Park that wet Saturday March morning when he had been forced to make what he felt was an honest decision to end his playing career. It was time to go, he told his friend Chesters. They had talked about it often since the start of the season; the latest discussion had been the night before the third Test had started on 6 March. On a balcony of a luxury holiday flat overlooking Algoa Bay, where the lights of ships at anchor reminded them of Colombo, they chatted genially about the past and the present and his career. The South African fast bowler cradled his sleeping son klein Fanie while his daughter Suné happily ate ice cream.

'If you feel you must retire, wait until the end of the season,' was the advice.

Fanie was adamant.

'No.' He shook his head. 'It's not as easy as you might think. Too much is happening that I don't like. And to be honest I have to make a choice soon . . . before the end of this game.'

He had already held long discussions with his old room-mate Pat Symcox and the friends, whose relationship went back twelve years, sadly concluded it was time to quit. They had already been told that Paul Adams and Makhaya Ntini would be playing in the first Test against Sri Lanka at Newlands in Cape Town starting nine days later. It did not need too much grey matter to work out who the expendable players were: Fanie and Symmo; perhaps Brian McMillan, whose foot injury had ruled him out of the three Tests against Pakistan and the two against Sri Lanka, was also on the list.[1]

Symcox was disturbed by the tone of the message delivered during a meeting of players and officials where future selection policy had been spelt out in simple terms. No longer would Adams and Herschelle Gibbs be regarded as development players; a policy of careful Africanization, better known by the latest buzzword as transformation, would be implemented. The duo knew their careers were being forcibly terminated. Forget the loyalty tag; it meant

---

[1] Brian McMillan and Pat Symcox were later included in the South African side to tour England in the northern summer of 1998.

nothing to the politicians. What helped Fanie reconsider his retirement plans was the contract he had signed with M-Net to join the SuperSport commentary team. Another factor was the negotiations he was having with a mobile telephone company to run coaching clinics in disadvantaged areas. It would give him much-needed financial security as well as more time at home with Judy and the children.

On the first day of that fateful St. George's Park Test, as South Africa battled to establish some form of control over a Pakistan bowling attack which had Wasim Akram and Waqar Younis as the spearhead, most members of the print and electronic media were taking in the significance of a brief UCB release about the disciplinary hearings in Durban after the second Test. Barely had this been digested when Dr Bacher arrived. Ever mindful of filling in the tricky background details, he spent almost half an hour answering questions.

There was also discussion about a small group of protesters expressing concern over the racial bias of the South African side. It was not enough that Adams and Ntini were in the team. For some time there had been a growing perception that transformation was not moving fast enough. Such a view found support among ANC members of the Sports and Recreation Committee in parliament days later when South Africa played Sri Lanka in the first Test at Newlands in Cape Town.

As the UCB, through Dr Bacher and the board's president, Krish Mackerdhuj, accounted for their development programme to the committee, some members, headed by Lulu Xingwana, made notes. Xingwana was critical, accusing coaches at Model C (integrated) schools of racism by not selecting black players to represent their school. She pointedly complained how coaches diverted the attention of black players from cricket to football or another sport. 'Black pupils,' she said accusingly, 'are discouraged from playing cricket.'

Although she gave no specific examples, which flawed her argument, there was, at the time, a certain accuracy in her comments. Rugby was perceived to be a sport dominated by Afrikaans-speaking whites, so therefore leave cricket to those who understood it, the English-speaking boys. It was the sort of degrading presumption which had sadly gone unchallenged for years.

What did not help the UCB's cause was going into the committee meeting without a thorough presentation of their case; that it failed to include a brochure to support their transformation plans and other advancement schemes did not improve the board's image as it was popularly seen at the time as the most organized body in South African sport. Instead, athletics, hockey, netball and tennis presented better high-powered profiles.

What also did not sit too well with most committee members was that Dr Bacher, whose role as the organizer of the rebel tours of the 1980s carried a certain odious stigma, presented the UCB case. They would have preferred Khaya Majola to handle the board's argument and this annoyed them. Instead Majola sat and said little. The UCB were seriously found wanting and realized then that they had smudged their status of being the leader of egalitarian sports ideals to a body seeking results, not platitudes and fancy word pictures which offered little in real terms of improvement for the disadvantaged. Little wonder that the frustrated Xingwana threatened that the ANC-dominated committee would seriously propose that the education and sports ministries accelerate the transformation process at grassroots level.

When placing the UCB case, Dr Bacher told the committee that the board did not believe in setting quotas for the national side. He gave evidence, however, to show how the quota system was being employed among provincial B teams with three players to a side. By the start of the summer of 1999-2000, senior sides had to carry a minimum of one. While the managing director said the board's policy was committed to the selection of a national side based on merit, it was also not the intention of the board to compromise (international) standards. By the start of the summer of 2001-02, three players of colour were included in provincial teams. After the Justin Ontong episode in Sydney, in 2002, an executive decision was made to include no less than two players of colour in the national side in future without compromising standards.

When the draw for the 2003 World Cup was unveiled in late October 2001, the ANC Youth League started a table-thumping exercise which said that if the South African squad did not contain at least six players of colour they would disrupt the event. At least three had to be black Africans; whether or not they were good enough was not the Youth League's problem. Evolution, which Khaya Majola had passionately advocated on a plane journey in March 1998, was about to be partly derailed.

Whether the ANC Youth League was given tacit support by the pan-Africanist principles of Dr Mtutuzeli Nyoka would be of interest. In early April 2002, Dr Nyoka, a highly qualified medical specialist and the Gauteng Cricket Board chairman, cited discrimination against blacks within the UCB as his reason for resigning his positions on the board and walking away from the game. Dr Nyoka argued that the UCB 'discriminates against blacks and vehemently so against black Africans'. Interestingly, Dr Nyoka, when making his comments, gave no specific examples of where he thought the UCB had fouled their nest. Yet anyone looking at the Gauteng side would have soon pointed out how the province, of which he had been chairman, discriminated against Africans and their own transformation scheme.

One such incident is how Solly Ndima in 2001-02 all but disappeared out of the system. The summer before he had been a member of the Gauteng (Highveld Strikers) senior side and the B team. By the end of March 2002, his one window of opportunity was for a regional side but he was not considered good enough. Geoffrey Toyana was also presented with fewer opportunities. The Soweto club, to which Dr Nyoka belonged, was marginalized in a dispute over a game played in which it had a good chance of winning but conditions were 'found not to be suitable to continue' after the home side, Jeppe Old Boys, complained. Instead of ordering a replay, the match was abandoned and points awarded to both sides. All this followed stinging criticism of the Gauteng Cricket Board's policy by Ken Rutherford, a former captain, player and coach. The New Zealander was not gentle in his criticism or observations.

Shortly before his resignation, Dr Nyoka caused dissent within the UCB ranks by saying that a statement from UCB chief executive Gerald Majola (younger brother of Khaya) that transformation was working was 'pure idiocy' and 'buffoonery' and that Majola did not understand the transformation. Dr Nyoka found himself isolated by the other ten provincial board presidents/chairmen, who in a display of unity condemned the doctor's outburst. The death of Walter Masemola in April 2002, while playing league in London, exacerbated the problem in Gauteng.

** **

Early in the afternoon on 7 March 1998, at St. George's Park, as Cronje was trying to rebuild the South African innings with Andrew Hudson, Dr Bacher arrived in the media centre. Then, with quiet, if emphatic, authority he said future South African Test and A teams would have a larger representation of black players. There was, however, a discrepancy regarding figures; at least three were going to England, although the British newspaper contingent of Peter Deeley, Ian Hawkey and Paul Weaver said they had been given a figure of five blacks in the England touring party.

Five? Surely the figure was exaggerated? Had they not got it wrong? Weaver and Hawkey checked their shorthand notes and shook their heads.

'Definitely five,' said Hawkey. 'Ali confirmed the figure.'

Dr Bacher's remarks were a commentary of what had been taking place in recent weeks, but the message they contained surprised those who had not closely followed the transformation process. 'It is no longer acceptable in 1998 for a South African team to be all white,' he said, repeating the phrase several times to allow its importance to sink in.

When the side was announced, three players, Ntini, Adams and Telemachus, made up the black contingent. Ironically the shoulder injury to Telemachus, while warming up at New Road in Worcester, gave Steve Elworthy, Fanie's Northerns teammate, his belated Test chance. What did transpire at the meeting between Dr Bacher and the British media surfaced much later when the South African A side for Sri Lanka was announced. This also contained three players of colour: Loots Bosman, Ashwell Prince and Henry Williams. It seemed the British writers had not listened too carefully to how Dr Bacher had framed his comments on team selection or the new policy. Also, Cronje was becoming agitated about the Test side being diluted and destroyed by the selection of inferior players.

Weeks before the Port Elizabeth Test, there had been veiled criticism of provincial bodies which had not done enough to put in the field teams with a forty per cent black representation as sought by the Department of Sport and Recreation in May 1997. It is an area where Western Province, Boland and Eastern Cape teams had an advantage over Northerns, Gauteng and Free State; the Western and Eastern Cape, because of their cultural background with more than 100 years of involvement, have larger numbers of black players in the senior sides.

It was no accident that Dr Bacher's remarks came barely hours after the statement which announced that the UCB's disciplinary committee would, at the end of the Test, investigate allegations of racial incidents involving Fanie and Symcox along with Jacques Kallis and the team's fitness and training technical expert, Paddy Upton. Dr Bacher later confirmed there were two cases, not one, under investigation. Amid this developing controversy, Fanie was pondering his future as a player. Judy and the children along with his parents, Braam and Hanna, were down. It was good to have them on hand and give him support and see him bowl those final overs of his career and share the event.

Initially he had confided his plans to retire at Kingsmead after the Durban Test to Symcox and Chesters. What stopped him was an unusual set of circumstances. Kingsmead usually had a fair amount of grass and the humidity would normally have allowed him to purchase more swing and take a few wickets. It would have been a nice way to end his career. Only there was little grass left on the Kingsmead surface for that match. They were the sort of conditions, with the ball scuffed up, where it would need a special skill to get it to swing after 15 or 20 overs. Normally Fanie would have backed himself. At Kingsmead, however, he knew he would get minimal swing. What did not help was umpire Dave Orchard turning down the first ball lbw appeal against Saeed Anwar in the second innings.

Robin Jackman, the former England and Surrey Test bowler, who also played for Zimbabwe in the days when it was known as Rhodesia, was providing expert anchor opinions for South African television. He could barely believe the decision had gone in favour of the Pakistan opener; nor did Trevor Quirk when making a hesitant, if polite, comment.

Sure, umpires get it wrong; recent lbw decisions given by the new elite panel members show how ordinary the standard can be in one game and how brilliant it can become a few days later. In the same way, batsmen and bowlers are equally fallible: batsmen scoring a brilliant century in one match and being out of touch in the next; bowlers getting the ball in the right area in one innings and delivering a Sunday Park social league performance in the next. It was a decision which made Fanie more determined to play at St. George's Park. Yet there was the usual doubt whether he would play in a game to decide the series. One look at the conditions, however, told him Port Elizabeth would enable him to end his career with more than a couple of wickets. He would have preferred it to be his home venue at SuperSport Centurion; now the political demands would even deny him that opportunity. He had always wanted his last match to be a Test and not a one-day international, where the impact would be minimal. He had also wanted to do it against Sri Lanka at home.

Shortly after lunch on the first day a local group calling themselves 'concerned citizens' led by schoolteacher Keith Arnold met Dr Bacher, Khaya Majola and Peter Pollock, along with Eastern Province officials. They were objecting to the inclusion of Fanie and Hudson for the game. At first Arnold did not want to give his name. When it was pointed out it had already appeared in a Port Elizabeth newspaper, he smiled sheepishly and shrugged, admitting he had given an interview to local media.

Although his group managed to hand over a petition claiming to contain 1,000 signatures demanding action over the non-selection of Ntini and Gibbs, their main gripe was how the Eastern Cape had lost the talented Ashwell Prince to Cape Town. It was a local squabble and when asked why the Eastern Province administrators had not been approached over the Prince issue, Arnold tried to deflect the question by arguing about concerns over the non-selection of black players in both the South African senior (SuperSport Series and Standard Bank day-night matches) and national teams.

'We are also not happy with the selection policy employed by the UCB and over the issue of Fanie de Villiers, Ntini, Andrew Hudson, Gibbs and Roger Telemachus,' he said. 'South Africa are going nowhere with thirty-six-year-old players.'

When it was pointed out that de Villiers was thirty-three while Hudson was a few days short of his thirty-third birthday, Arnold stuck to his line of argument before saying the discussions with Dr Bacher had been 'frank and revealing' and that the UCB managing director had given them confidential information in relation to the board's policy.

'I am not prepared to reveal what this information is, but from what we have been told, the fruits of the policy put in place by the UCB's development programme would be seen in the next three to four months,' was Arnold's comment.

Later came Dr Bacher's forthright response. He also admitted that little could be done in some provinces at this stage, as the growth of development players was slower than in other areas.

'The UCB concur with their concern that at the A (senior) team level, Eastern Province, Natal, Northerns, Free State and Gauteng are not using black players. We have urged these provinces to hasten the process of black players to the stage where they will soon be selected for the A teams of these provinces,' he said.

For twenty-four hours this is where the unfolding drama hung in suspense.

A queasy atmosphere hung about St. George's Park that wet Saturday morning. Before dawn, squalls had been sweeping across Port Elizabeth from the bay and locals gloomily predicted there would be no play before tea, if at all. Chris Day, the UCB appointed media officer, parked his car behind the Centenary Stand and was followed by the *Pretoria News* journalist up the steps to the media centre. They felt the buzz among some of the hacks and rumours lay as thick as autumn leaves. A moody Peter Robinson, feeling the frustrations of any journalist whose copy has been tampered with and his credibility smudged because of it, reflectively sipped his coffee. To his right, Hawkey was quick to approach Fanie de Villiers' long-time friend.

'I hear Pat Symcox is resigned to retiring after this Test . . . and Fanie's going the same way . . .'

It was a bald statement with a modicum of truth. But Chesters knew Symmo was still deciding, unsure of what steps to take. His contract was valid until the end of April so there was still something in it for him. Another tour was a distinct possibility. For Fanie, it was different.

'Are you telling me or merely asking?' Chesters responded.

'A bit of both, I guess. There's going to be no play today and I have space to fill.'

As Hawkey probed for more information he knew that the knowledge his colleague had about Fanie was confidential and overrode any inside comment he may have offered. There were others who knew something unusual was being stirred in the witch's cauldron that the media centre had become that morning. Some pretended to know; half-truth and rumour can play strange tricks on the mind.

At that point Chesters' mobile phone rang. It was Fanie.

'Trevor, where are you now?'

'In the media centre . . .'

'Please, would you come down to the player's dining room. There's a lady here with some autographs you should see . . . And I have something to tell you . . .'

Gut feel being what it is, it told Chesters what the 'something' was. His emotions began to curdle as he looked at Hawkey who was still on with his guessing game, unaware what the polite summons meant.

'What do you think?' asked Hawkey. 'The rumours of the racial incidents at Kingsmead are not easily ignored. Is that why Symcox is retiring? And your friend, Fanie?'

Chesters shook his head. 'From what I know of both, neither would retire because of what happened at Kingsmead,' was his response. Hawkey smiled knowingly. He knew Chesters too well; he was not about to give anything away.

* * * *

In the dining room below, Fanie put down his mobile phone, sat back and relaxed with Ryall Pearce. A pensioner, who had followed the game since a schoolgirl, she had brought her collection of autograph books along. Her blue eyes sparkled as, with fussy pride, she displayed them for Fanie's attention: the neat print listing the South Africa Test and touring teams from the early years after World War II. The signatures on the coloured pages were those from a different era: Dudley Nourse, Alan Melville, Jackie McGlew, Jack Cheetham, Lindsay Hassett, Keith Miller and the Rowan brothers, Eric and Athol; members of the 1948-49 MCC side led by George Mann appeared along with those of Geoff Rabone's Kiwis of the 1953-54 tour. One of those names, John Reid, was the ICC match referee for the current series between South Africa and Pakistan. What an ironic twist of fate: Reid had been manager of the Northern Transvaal side when Fanie had made his A Section (Currie Cup) debut. Now he was about to see it end.

Fanie signed one of the pages, talking cheerfully and showing her his usual courtesy. Outwardly he was calm. He had made his decision to retire on his way to the ground that morning; delaying it further would affect long-term work plans. Anyway, the political minnows who rippled the water with their demands were only adding their voices to the cluttered, confused events taking place.

It was 11.15 a.m. and they sat around the table: Fanie, one of his mentors and the pensioner. The Test bowler showed Chesters an inscription from Jackie McGlew written during the 1956-57 tour by Peter May's MCC side.[2] 'I am going to announce my retirement today. There won't be any play. It's too wet. And,' he grinned impishly, 'it'll give you guys something else to write about.'

It came out with candid cheerfulness, as though he was ordering a *wors* roll; only he was far from calm. There was a feeling though that Mrs Pearce did not quite grasp the significance of the statement; she knew nothing of the background or the drama which had unfolded since the start of the second Test of the series at Kingsmead.

'I have to do it today,' he nodded. 'I'll go up and tell Dr Bacher before lunch. But I wanted you to hear it from me first, my old friend.'

They fell silent for a few moments, the mood in the room tinged with sadness; a curtain was falling on an era of what had been more than the career of a Test fast bowler.

Mrs Pearce had left and the two friends sat drinking coffee.

'I'm going to take wickets in this game. I feel it.' He winked, trying to lighten the gloom. 'The ball is going to swing a lot longer. It won't get scuffed up too much and that will give us a chance to win the match and for me to take wickets.'

It was disturbing how years of labour and hard training in the

---

[2] Jackie McGlew, who sadly died three months later from cancer, collaborated with Trevor Chesterfield on a book published in October 1994 called *Cricket Captains of South Africa: Melville to Wessels*. It has been updated and revised for the 2003 World Cup under a new title.

nets were being swept away by those who knew nothing of Fanie's background. To the outsider, he appeared to be a highly successful cricketer who was about to launch an equally celebrated, if at times controversial, career as a television commentator and, for a time, ambassador at large for the UCB. The truth of his first years as a schoolboy and the early summers at provincial level was far different; just as Ntini was underprivileged because of his rural roots, so was Fanie in terms of his upbringing. Being of a middle-class background does not necessarily open up doors if you are shut out of the game by a school system dominated by teachers more interested in the glamour of the moment and the excitement generated by rugby or athletics.

When Fanie had made his provincial debut thirteen summers before at Berea Park, playing for Northern Transvaal B against Natal B in a Castle Bowl game, he had collected 5 second innings wickets. It was a performance which had supported initial expectations. However, no one remembered the name of the batsman who was his first wicket: it was Darryl Scott, beaten by pace and swing who edged a catch to Steve Vercueil the wicketkeeper. It had been early on the third morning of the match: the first step of many, the first of 427 wickets at an impressive strike rate of more than 4.50 a match throughout his career. Not bad when it is considered that Neil Adcock averaged 4 wickets a Test during his career, Peter Heine 4.14 a game and Trevor Goddard 3 wickets.

To confirm his growing instincts shortly before the Test at Kingsmead, Fanie had talked to Dr Bacher about the long-term prospects of older players in the squad. The UCB managing director had not ducked the issue. He had told Fanie that the older players needed to be realistic, especially with the younger players coming through and the need to speed up the transformation process. There were political pressures and demands and the board's development programme needed to deliver.

Fanie and Chesters talked for a few more minutes before the player went to tell Dr Bacher of his decision. Minutes later, as the media sat down to lunch, Chris Day arrived.

'Ali has told me there is to be a media conference at two-thirty. Fanie de Villiers will be making a statement on his future.' Day gave an impish smile. 'Or perhaps we should ask the man from Centurion to do it for us now and there won't be a need for the conference.'

Like it or not, Fanie de Villiers had been public property since that early January morning four years before when he had bowled South Africa to the famous victory at the Sydney Cricket Ground. Whatever he did would be news: each comeback attempt from injury had been carefully noted and monitored. But this was different. For many sporting folks, a hero was being forced to vacate the space he had helped create through his charisma as well as his pranks, and above all by his ability to bowl late outswing better than almost anyone in the world.

In some ways March 1998 was not too different from the pre-election month of 1994; perhaps more cathartic with frustrated minions of a political system still seeking acceptance, if not identity. As the previously disenfranchised, they felt let down at the lack of progress and wanted serious answers and action in response to their complaints. But the system Fanie had served so well was now prepared to turn on him to justify its own failure. Although he was not quite forced to quit as part of an act of appeasement, the system he had served did not allow him to go with the dignified acquiescence a sportsman of his stature deserved either.

Weeks before he had hoped, if selected for a final tour of England, to bow out when it was over; although he had doubts what his role would be if he did make himself available. He did not want to play only the one-day games: he was better than a limited-overs specialist; it had riled him when some media writers had at first looked on him only as a one-day bowler.

The selectors had made a mistake in leaving him out of the Australian tour party. Initially they had selected Roger Telemachus to fill the role but he had been ruled out through a rib injury, which did not stand up to the tests carried out on his fitness levels in Cape Town. In came Ntini, a far wiser choice, and the bowler who should have been included in the touring party in the first place. Yet there was the unmistakable feeling that Fanie had been left out because of reasons other than making way for an affirmative action player.

There was a theory that Jacques Kallis would fill the role of the stock swing bowler. Only, at the time of the Australian tour, his body action meant he swung the ball out of his hand and lacked the pace to swing it late. It was during the 1998 tour of England where the gradual transformation in Kallis' skills started. Even so, in November 1997, it was expecting a bit much for even a talented twenty-two-year-old to suddenly take over Fanie's function. Shaun Pollock was better suited to do this specific job. He had come along since making his Test debut in 1995 and overcoming a heel operation. From the time he started to come through the Natal ranks, with or without Malcolm Marshall's help, the good-humoured young man had shown that typical Pollock flair. Yet his workload in Australia was far too heavy, even for a willing twenty-four-year-old. As Bill Lawry posed the question at the Adelaide Oval when Pollock had to carry the attack by bowling more than his quota of overs as well as fill in for the injured Allan Donald, 'This young man's doing a tremendous job, but why didn't they send for Farnay d'Vill'ers? They had time on their side. I think the South Africans have goofed up. Ian?' How they have missed this guy on this tour. He must still be rated as one of the world's top three swing bowlers. Young Pollock needs support and Farnay would have been the ideal support man.'

Lawry's pungent comments must have been noted, for when the tour ended there was reluctant acknowledgement that Fanie's late outswing could have helped South Africa win the Adelaide Test and level the series 1-1.

Fanie's own view was that the 'vibes are growing that Hansie Cronje doesn't want me'. It was made in confidence a few days after the team for Australia had been announced. The normal cheerful smile had given way to a meditative frown.

He spoke without a trace of rancour, basing his assumptions on several factors which had emerged since the Wills Quadrangular Series in Lahore. One reason could have been Cronje's attitude towards Woolmer. When Fanie sat in the dressing room for the first time after his return, he swiftly picked up the vibes that not all was well. Woolmer was making a point to two younger players when Cronje rudely cut in.

'Oh, shut up, Bob. You don't know what you're saying.'

Fanie suddenly realized that Woolmer no longer had any say in team meetings: whether it was advice, selection ideas, or game plans. He did not like what he felt was utter discourtesy to the senior man in the team's management structures. The discipline once instilled by Kepler Wessels may have long gone, but at least there was respect. The captain showed little respect in the way he treated junior players and Woolmer. So, what happened to the values learned at Grey College in Bloemfontein? Or the discipline instilled in what had been a cheerful childhood? What happened to all that?

There had been muted criticism of the influence Cronje was allowed by the UCB and later there was blame that it gave him the sort of egoism which was not good for a man in his position. He was allowed to become too big for the team. Here was an inherent problem, which, when he was exposed, created the impression that although Peter Pollock was the convener of selectors, Cronje demanded and got what he wanted. When Magiet took over, there was antagonism in some established media quarters against Magiet. He was seen to be undermining Cronje's confidence by placing him on probation.

* * * *

Those who preached evolution and not revolution knew from years of experience the problems and flaws within the system. Many politicians were not prepared to work within the framework of progress, demanding instant success, failing to understand the need for a culture and a sense of history to develop in a new generation of players. Krish Mackerdhuj, as president of the UCB before he left to take up his post as South Africa's ambassador in Japan, had an answer to the politicians: be patient, even a tree takes time to grow.

'Our affirmative action policy was in line with what we believe. You have to train and develop them (coaches and players) so that they can take their rightful place,' he said at Port Elizabeth during the third Test against Pakistan in 1998. 'Acceleration of this (programme) means players, given the talent, will earn international honours. More so those who have natural talent.'

He argued that the life of a player would be about twelve years by the time he reached provincial level. As the UCB had been in existence for only seven years, the policy had not done too badly. It was his view that the acceleration of the development players had started around the time of union as there had been a merging of forces which made it work. The number of young players who had come through showed that the system had worked in producing talented players.

'We believe you cannot just put a face into a side and expect him to produce match-winning performances. You can end up embarrassing the young man and wrecking his career. We don't need that,' was his contention.

Ntini and Paul Adams would be around for another ten years to inspire and encourage others; that talented comet Mfuneko Ngam, the Port Elizabeth youngster, before his injury was briefly coming through along with other new faces. And the process was not going to change. Unlike the West Indies, who had fallen into a trap of ignoring grassroots growth, South Africa's plan was to introduce young players of talent. Two extremes, but two good examples, were Mark Boucher and Ntini. There were others in Graeme Smith, Jacques Rudolph and Ashwell Prince. In the case of young Rudolph, the South Africa team management have much to answer for the way he was handled in Australia in 2001-02. The UCB would continue to introduce young players into the top sides, whether the policy was liked or not.

'It is our role to see those who are so talented being granted that opportunity,' said Mackerdhuj, a theme taken up by Gerald Majola when he took over from Dr Bacher as UCB chief executive in early 2001.

Mackerdhuj did not labour the point by mentioning the success of the under-19 World Cup side which had done so well weeks before; five of the fourteen were coloured, Asian, or from the disadvantaged cultures, creeds and languages of the new South Africa. They were the embodiment of a fine group of young men who with strong, sensitive management, built a dream around demographic harmony while politicians squabbled. In 2000 and 2002, the demographics were improving.

* * * *

South Africa's oldest first-class venue, St. George's Park, is known more for its history than its appeal and the pitches had long been criticized for their slowness, where there was need for quality bowling skills to succeed. It was not Fanie's favourite venue;

Centurion, the Wanderers, even Newlands had on some days provided him with ideal bowling conditions. There had been Sydney as well. Things had changed at St. George's Park. The previous season, Australia had won the battle on a greentop; there were similar conditions for this game with the rained-off Saturday freshening the conditions and the wind and general atmosphere adding to the swing factor.

There was heavy expectancy that Sunday morning as the ground started to fill and players prepared for the match. Fanie was angry at the *Sunday Times* report. He felt Bryden had 'manipulated the truth'. A touch of sensational irresponsibility from the newsroom did the trick. Banner headlines told it all.

Out in the middle it was a little different as Fanie went out to bat with Mark Boucher to resume the innings. The ball swung and dipped: Waqar collected his sixth wicket when he had Fanie caught in the point region. But in his bowler's mind he knew it would be a good day to take wickets: all you had to do was put the ball in the right area to make it work. Allan Donald looked out of sorts with himself and Pollock worked up pace but not too much else.

Cronje had the bowlers change ends and the result was illustrated by a turn of pace and some swing as Donald ripped off the top of the Pakistan order: in 13 balls he collected 4 for 5, and Pakistan were in trouble. Pollock bowled tightly and had the batsmen playing and missing and Boucher wondering how the lanky red-haired all-rounder failed to bowl Saeed Anwar.

Fanie was brought on for Pollock with the Pakistanis at 29 for 4. Already feeling jittery as a result of the strike power provided in White Lightning's bowling spell, Fanie set to work. Between lunch and the end of the innings lasting only 40.5 overs, he wrote the second last paragraph of his playing career; his 6 wickets for 23 were some 20 runs cheaper than the figures from his Sydney rescue bid. It was one of the best displays of swing bowling seen at St. George's Park as he cleaned up the middle and ripped through the bottom order. Just the sort of riposte to those who doubted his ability, and there was not even a whisper of Pakistan's collusion with Indian bookmakers over their batting debacle.

Rashid Latif is not the sort of person to allow such side issues to clutter the mind and interfere with game plan strategies. His views on the subject are well known. What did surprise him, however, was Fanie announcing his retirement on Saturday.

'Tell me, why are you retiring?' Latif asked when the game had ended.

'I think I have done all I can,' he said with a shrug. 'You reach a stage when you know it is time to quit.'

'I cannot believe it,' said Latif. 'It's got nothing to do with all those incidents when we were in Durban?'

'Nothing at all. I'd made up my mind before this series started.'

'I want to tell you something,' Latif smiled. 'Do you know that you are the one bowler we were scared of the most? You are probably the best swing bowler in the world. We all know it and pass the message around among our guys—watch out for Fanie de Villiers . . .'

South Africa were batting a second time that day and when he left the ground to join Judy and his parents, Fanie was satisfied. It had been a good Sunday's carve up. Twenty-four hours later, South Africa were in sight of levelling the series when Fanie answered his mobile and heard the president, Nelson Mandela, wishing him well in his retirement. It was a stirring moment and he started to feel a touch emotional as well as he walked out the next morning knowing it would be his last first-class game. It was not going to be a long day either—at 120 for 7 Pakistan were out of it; just a matter of mopping up the lower order again.

At 133 for 9 Cronje went across to Fanie, placed an arm on his shoulders and whispered quietly, 'You'd better do it now before AD does.'

Suddenly it was over: the fifth ball of his thirteenth over of Pakistan's second innings, a yorker to Shoaib Akhtar ended the last paragraph of his career. Few bowlers can end a Test career in such a satisfying way—a wicket with their last ball. Sir Richard Hadlee is one; Fanie is another. As he sat in the dressing room after the save, Peter Pollock arrived to congratulate the team on their efforts to level the series. When he reached Fanie, he smiled.

'It is amazing how it turns out, Fanie,' Pollock said to him. 'You have just had your best game and everything is coming right and you have decided to quit.'

Fanie nodded and said nothing. For years he had felt that Peter

Pollock was not a fan of Fanie de Villiers or his style of delivery, on and off the field.

When the others had left with their kit, Symmo closed the door and locked it and said that he and Fanie were going to have one last drink. No one was going to spoil their last few minutes together as teammates in the dressing room. Fanie even smoked a cigar.

There would be no farewell game in the SuperSport Series at Centurion; what else was there to prove? It was his new role, as an ambassador for the game, where he was going to be needed.

'You know, they need a real Dutchman to do this job,' he grinned when he announced his intentions to Chesters a few days later. 'My message is that cricket is not just about talent but also attitude and heart. There are plenty who have talent but only those with courage and hunger and desire will make it.'

* * * *

As the game enters a new, troubled era it is in need of such clear and incisive thoughts: a simple philosophy to cleanse the wounds and give the bruised image of cricket's code of ethics and fair play a new sense of credibility to spread itself into this new century.

Fanie worries, along with other thoughtful, caring administrators and media people involved in the game, about where the game is heading in South Africa. The view that too much is expected of transformation is because of the years of inactivity. It now needs a logical approach to overcome generations of ignorance and neglect. Cricket is the game for all: the demographic sport in a nation where unity needs encouragement as well as nourishment. Above all is the West Indian-style ideology, as preached by Sir Frank Worrell, the great West Indian batsman and captain, who tragically died early from leukaemia.

As we grow up we should all know we have a role to play to shape our destiny. It is often asked: what is a country without heroes? To reach that stage we need to remember from where we have come and the obstacles we have beaten down to get there. Let it be known, cricket can link us all in this unified cause known as nationhood.

South Africa's administrators have much work ahead to rebuild the public's confidence as well as that of its constituents. As South Africa moves into the second decade of freedom, it should recognize that it has barely begun.

Fanie de Villiers

Postscript: Cronjegate Aftermath

1

There are those who knowingly, on waking up in the morning, can still look in the bathroom mirror and smile at how they have escaped. They are the so-called 'respectable' actors in this real-life tragedy. These are the administrators, or players, fortunate to retire to published or spoken tribute and applause. Suspicions do of course exist; they will be around for years.

Others have not been so lucky. Hansie Cronje, the central figure, died tragically in an aircraft accident that for some is shrouded in fanciful conspiracy theories. Four, including two captains, received life bans. Several more were barred for shorter periods. All deny their match-fixing culpability. Doubts still exist though. Some that are there is far more in the Cronjegate malpractice story than was revealed at the public hearings, when the King Commission into betting malpractices was held in Cape Town, between May and July in 2000. While the findings were made known, serious doubts exists. Not that it matters; most of the main players who escaped retain a faceless anonymity.

There was much incredulity in South Asia when copies of the Ali Bacher biography *Ali* and the take of the former managing director of the United Cricket Board (of South Africa) on the Edwin King Commission as well as his relationship with Cronje. Most Indian cricket journalists were critical of how Bacher presented himself at the commission. There is nothing in the book relating to the evidence of Marlon Aronstam at the King probe, or background details as to how a known bookmaker was allowed to contact the national captain.

Even the views of the dead were for a time still sought. But as these are protected by legal red tape it has, therefore, created further doubt about how much Cronje wanted to say or was advised not to say, about his contacts with Indian and other bookmakers, betting and other gaming malpractices involved in the match-fixing scandal that rocked world cricket's foundations in April and the ensuing months of 2000. As it was, after Herschelle Gibbs' s damning evidence to the commission, Cronje had to embarrassingly change his testimony a second time.

Since New Delhi police's public unmasking of Cronje, there is a long-held theory that whatever Lord Paul Condon's International Cricket Council anti-corruption and security unit learnt from their delving into the murky world of bookmakers and underworld thuggery, it mostly came from Cronje. They would get next to nothing from the banned former Pakistan captain, Salim Malik, and India's Mohammed Azharuddin, named by Cronje during his testimony to the commission.

All of this is very interesting, as efforts to find out just what Cronje did say to the ACU ended in a polite refusal by those at the ICC Champions Trophy event in Colombo in September 2002. In fact, trying to find out when Cronje met Lord Condon and his senior lieutenant to discuss the former South African captain's role in match-fixing drew a series of negative responses.

Even a telephone call to Cronje's lawyer, Les Sackstein, at his Bloemfontein office, met with the sort of language that would make Australian sledging tactics mild by comparison. A string of abuse indicated how a simple inquiry of the date and place Cronje met with the ACU had hit a raw nerve. Or was it a matter of consciousness? In any event, it was greeted with a vicious flat-batted invective volley. And all that was being asked was to establish whether the two met before or after the King Commission.

Earlier, there was an equally firm rebuttal from the United Cricket Board (of South Africa) when asked if there had been an inquiry about Cronje's meeting with bookie Marlon Aronstam, on the evening of the fourth day of the Centurion Test against England in the Millennium Series. The attitude of Ali Bacher, then managing director of the UCB, was that 'there is nothing suspicious' about a meeting between two people and it had nothing to do with the UCB.

What was interesting here was that Bacher and Percy Sonn, then recently appointed president of the UCB after Ray White's forced resignation over issues of politics and team selection policies, had been told of the meeting. Also known is that UCB contacts said top board officials knew within two hours of Cronje's discussion with Aronstam that 'some sort of deal had been arranged'.

This supports the claim that there is far more to Cronje meeting Aronstam than the bookmaker making a chance call by mobile telephone to establish contact. For one thing, Cronje usually had his mobile switched off; he rarely called back anyone other than family members, favoured journalists or certain high-ranking UCB officials and inner team management members. It shows that no one just sets up a meeting with someone as high profile as was Cronje without prior contact from someone the captain knew . . . and knew well. Why the subterfuge? And who else knew in advance of the meeting and wanted to be 'in on the deal'?

Startling evidence also emerged during the ICC event in Colombo in September 2002, when a member of the South African management team admitted the former captain had two mobile phones and more than three SIM (activation) cards. It was the alternate number of the second mobile phone Cronje used which was made available to Aronstam by other interested parties to cash in on the agreement. Involvement here was through a South African agent with Mumbai bookmaking links. For Cronje, it was all so easy. He was long seduced by a world of easy money, the culture of greed sidestepped such mundane matters as morals and principles. He agreed when the initial approach was made the third afternoon, to look at the offer to 'achieve a positive result in a dead Test'. If easy dollars were available, naturally he wanted to be at the head of the queue. Other information is that Aronstam had been 'schooled by associates' about how to place the offer before Cronje and toss in a leather jacket to make it worthwhile.

Information is that Chennai-born former England captain Nasser Hussain knew far more of the deals involving Cronje and the Centurion Test than first claimed. These are serious allegations, as are suggestions that two of the triangular limited overs international series games involving South Africa, England and Zimbabwe were manipulated backdoor financial deals. Questions surround the results of the two games where Zimbabwe first beat England and then South Africa during the millennium summer. The first was at Newlands on 28 January 2000, where Zimbabwe won by 103 runs after an abject England batting display and where Henry Olonga collected six wickets for 19 runs. The second was at Kingsmead in Durban on 2 February 2000, where several known underworld links with Indian bookmakers were seen dining at the South African team's hotel on the beachfront. Zimbabwe won that game off the last ball by two wickets.

It ties in with claims that have long hovered over allegations that more than one England player was involved in clandestine money deals surrounding the rain-affected fifth Test of the Millennium series played from 14 to 18 January 2000 at SuperSport Park in Centurion.

Other information supported by an eyewitness is that Hussain knew about negotiations to set up the deal minutes after the pre-arranged talks with Aronstam and not, as claimed, at the grounds the fifth morning. Cronje did not suggest outright to a long-standing contact that he had been in touch with others, but there were indications that 'others knew all about the deal'.

As it is, the grounds staff at the Centurion venue were 'totally amazed' on the fourth day when play was abandoned soon after the early scheduled lunch break. SuperSport Park supervising venue consultant Hilbert Smit said nothing was wrong with the surface. A large muddy patch, in line with the bowler's run-up that had all but dried, was given as the reason why the day's play was called off. The official version was that it would give grounds staff a chance to work on the area. Smit is firm in his belief that play was possible by early afternoon on day four. In his opinion, there could have been two extended sessions of play.

There was a meeting that fourth afternoon of UCB, Northerns Cricket Union, the match referee and umpires, as well as Cronje, Hussain, the team managers and coaches. It was discussed how the match could be saved as the weather was promising.

Contacts in South Africa, India and Sri Lanka in 2000 and 2001 say that M. K. Gupta and others had handled all the wheeling and dealing in South Africa and India. Aronstam was just another shadowy figure in a murky paddling pool. Yet, the way he placed his evidence before the King Commission suggests that he was not only another example of how bookmakers and money can corrupt. Reading Aronstam's evidence given to the commission further adds to the suspicion that he saw himself as a star act and had set out to dupe the inquiry with smart talk about the 'rules' (sic).

The UCB officials, Bacher among them, chose to ignore the information and did not ask Cronje to explain his meeting with Aronstam, a known bookmaker. White knew of Cronje's meeting with Aronstam and passed this on to a UCB official. What this suggests is that certain UCB officials knew about Cronje's activities, but did not want to admit that there were suspicions that the captain and others, were cheats. So, to suggest as Bacher did on 11 April 2000, 'We (UCB) have been betrayed,' smacks of a certain deception. Also, there is no mention in Bacher's biography of Aronstam's evidence to the King Commission.

As it is, Hussain was at first cautious about accepting the Cronje deal made the night before and not the morning of the game. Hussain first declined then accepted it, when he saw how the pitch was playing on the fifth morning at Centurion.

2

Mohammed Azharuddin was once a favoured son in India. There was his self-effacing attitude, the magic of his batting artistry and his leadership qualities. But after World Cup 1999 in England he had long fallen out with the Indian public. So when they knew of the truth through Cronje's testimony, they burned effigies of Azhar. South Africans, though, could not bring themselves to perform a similar act involving Cronje. The public at large was stunned; their white knight had been found out to be little better than a petty thief.

One quick-thinking salesman, with an eye for detail and smart business acumen, soon caught on how to make a fast buck out of Cronjegate. Within days of the announcement of a judicial inquiry being launched and known as the King Commission, HAN$IE shirts were selling at about US$15 each. To buy them, however, did require the need to trawl central Johannesburg, or perhaps ironically, the Asiatic Bazaar in an area known as Fordsburg. It was the entrepreneurial example of how commercial mimicry can be used as a form of social comment.

Designed similar to the 1999 South African World Cup team shirt, the significant difference was how the $ sign replaced the 'S' in Hansie and the $ sign the figure 5 which adorned the shirt Cronje wore. Made in Thailand, ownership of such a shirt, especially during the South Africa tour of Sri Lanka in July and August 2000, brought all types of offers between US$150 and US$200 and wry disappointment when the offers were turned down.

While the HAN$IE statement added its own ribald observation, it confirmed the dishonesty of an era in which there was serious turmoil at the international level, and the International Cricket Council's work to uncover crooked dealings was further exposed in 2004 when former Kenya captain Maurice Odumbe was found guilty, and fined and banned for his role in match-fixing. Yet, from an early stage, the fallout from Cronjegate and disclosures to the King Commission in May and June 2000 into match-fixing and other malpractices had an unfortunate widespread affect. Suspicion ran deep that administrators knew far more than they were, and have been, prepared to tell. From Colombo to Galle, Mumbai, Kolkata, Sydney, Adelaide, Wellington and Lord's to Leeds, Centurion and Cape Town, as well as Harare, Nairobi and Sharjah, it is as the man in the street suggests, 'a question of accountability'. No one, though, has been prepared to accept the blame, which is why there are those who feel treachery runs deeper than appears on the surface.

Whose accountability is another matter. No one accepted blame for what took place, or how entrenched it became and was allowed to fester the system. It was always the bookies out to make money. If Ray White, when president of UCB, expressed concern in 1999, why did others at the administration level who knew about it fail to act? Were they also on the take, as it were? Only after it was exposed did the establishment react, and then only at first with the sort of distaste of someone wrinkling their nose and wearing gloves as they were forced, for the first time, to pick up a bag of particularly rotten garbage. The stench lingers still, as has been shown in the Odumbe affair. And more latterly with the India/Pakistan game in Ahmedabad early this year.

White raised the accountability issue with journalists on a wet afternoon at the Wanderers, during the rain-affected Test with New Zealand in November 2000. White had good reason to ask the question. The former UCB president, reminded of a statement he had made at the board's 1999 annual meeting just a few weeks after the World Cup final, was concerned at what he referred to as 'results of complicity'. Strong rumours were that two World Cup games had been rigged: both involved Pakistan—the Bangladesh game and the Super Six clash with India. All were denied, of course; nothing had been proved. Ali Bacher told the King Commission he been made aware of the malpractice by a Pakistan official, former Test batsman and captain Majid Khan. It was Majid who, in 1998, lifted the covers off a viper's nest in South Asia.

Several journalists who covered the 1999 World Cup sniffed controversy at Wantage Road in Northampton at how Pakistan approached their game against Bangladesh and lost. It did not quite fit the gameplan scenario. Dig too deep and the rotting stench of bookmakers' breath wafted from the mobile phones. Problem was that the conspiracy of silence hung heavily. During South Africa's Test at Lord's in 1998, well before the Cronje scandal broke, a Pakistan journalist friend of the author's said that match-fixing had become a bad habit not only indulged in by bookmakers. Also involved are players and administrators. The match-fixing rumours surfaced more than once. Pakistan's tour of South Africa in 1994-95 was one fractious episode mentioned in an earlier chapter. In July and August 1998 and again in August and September during the 1999 triangular Aiwa Cup series involving India, Australia and Sri Lanka in Sri Lanka, rumour hung as heavy as ripening bananas on a tree. In Colombo, Kandy and Galle during Australia's three Tests following the Aiwa Cup, whispers persisted.

In July 1999, however, Ray White seemed to be into crystal-ball gazing when making what was to be his last annual UCB report. He said that among other matters of interest the UCB were seriously concerned about reports of bribery and match-fixing. It was disturbing to hear such allegations. Some of this concerned games in CWC99. A Cambridge Blue, Gloucestershire and Transvaal batsman, White was troubled at what he felt were foreign influences disturbing the game. While the International Cricket Council may launch their own investigation into worldwide bribery and match-fixing charges, South Africa would look at ways to monitor the situation in the country through what he called a 'prevention is better than cure' plan. White, re-elected as president at the time, told delegates that the board would set up its own commission, whose members would investigate any charges 'of bribery and betting on games involving our own players'.

Although it was not a new phenomenon, White felt the board's concern was that the game had to retain its image of fair play and decency. While 'no South African player had yet been involved in any claims of match-fixing' the thought was that the commission would act swiftly to investigate any accusations when they arose.

'I know that our players have a good record and have not ruined their reputations by being involved in such practices,' White had told the meeting. 'It is a matter of serious concern to all of us and is one of the reasons why the UCB has decided to form a commission to keep an eye on matters.'

What happened to the commission? Indeed, before the government set up the King Commission, had the UCB established a formal internal body to audit players' thoughts, if any, on claims of malpractice within the sport? Bothered by growing rumours, the Australians had done just that during the quadrangular centenary series in New Zealand in February 1995. This is when the guilt of Mark Waugh and Shane Warne was uncovered and their links with the infamous New Delhi fixer 'John', better known as M. K. Gupta. They were fined by the ACB, yet, as it later transpired, the board's action was not recorded.

Had there been a similar monitoring system (as suggested by White) of the South African players after the 1999 World Cup, Cronje's nefarious behaviour may have been exposed before the New Delhi police used wiretaps to unmask him. Or was it only when the truth emerged and Cronjegate began to splash its ugly way into headlines that the UCB awoke to a scandal, which not only rocked their foundations but also the international profile of the game? The ICC could not say that they had not been warned. For fifteen or more years rumour, innuendo and accusation had filtered through the corridors; whispers in dusty, dark corners and furtive glances over shoulders at footsteps were all part of the story. Only a tacit conspiracy of silence existed to shroud the crooked dealings in doubt.

Hard evidence, it was said, was needed. Okay, what about the admission by the Australian Cricket Board in December 1998 admitting they had, after an in-house probe three and a half years before, fined Shane Warne and Mark Waugh for taking money in Colombo during the Australian 1994 tour? Later came the bribes offered by the unctuous Pakistan captain, Salim Malik, in Karachi to bowl badly. Sir Clyde Walcott, then ICC president, had been told about it by Australian officials.

Hard evidence? Was that not enough?

Ye Gods! The ICC quibbled for years about needing something more reputable than hearsay and unproven piecemeal evidence. Not only had the alarm button been punched years before, it had been ignored, as officialdom preferred to sweep the debris of lies, treachery and deliberate connivance under a thick carpet labelled 'culpability'. Those whispers were becoming too loud for comfort.

How Cronje must have been smiling behind the grille of his batting helmet when he read White's annual meeting comment, 'I know that our players have a good record and have not ruined their reputations by being involved in such (match-fixing) practices.' No South African players had indeed been involved in such disreputable behaviour.

What was interesting, as had become an almost forgotten sidebar during Cronjegate and the King Commission, was that after the World Cup Cronje had been talking to Glamorgan about a coaching role with the English county in 2000. Perhaps the thought of a second tour of South Asia (the one to Pakistan) within four months might have been a little too much for him and he wanted a break; or were the bookies already turning up the heat? Or did he think he might not have a job and was looking for an alternative? Certainly Indian police were aware of some of the former South African captain's dealings with bookies from the 1996 tour, and what had been leaked about the Mumbai benefit game for Mohinder Amranath, which was suddenly elevated to full LOI status without adequate explanation, apart from the sale of tickets being slow. This may have been great for the promoters who bought officials to aid their cause, and the spectators, but lousy for the sick players who only wanted to get home.

When Cronje raised the matter of an offer of $250,000 to throw the Mumbai game, there was some consternation among the senior players. As the deal was then not far short of R1.5 million, each player stood to earn about R60,000. Fanie, Andrew Hudson, Daryll Cullinan and Pat Symcox were among those who rejected the offer at a meeting of senior players. Understandably, an angry Woolmer condemned Cronje's actions.

The London-based Pakistan journalist said underworld contacts had told Indian police of the plan by bookies to fix the game by persuading the South Africans to underperform. His own contacts in Delhi said the police had been aware for more than a decade of bookmakers trying to make deals with Indian players, but no names had been given. They were, however, on to Cronje.

When news of Cronje's discussions with Glamorgan broke in *The Daily Telegraph* about two months after the World Cup, the query was how it would clash with the Sri Lanka tour a year later, as it implied he might not be the national captain. Peter Pollock, the selection panel convener, had gone; so had the coach Bob Woolmer. A new selection order and team management profile was taking shape. Had Cronje not hinted, during the media briefing at Edgbaston after the tied semi-final with Australia, that a question mark hung over his future? There would be a new coach, Graham Ford. There would also be a new convener in Rushdie Magiet and the selection panel might have different ideas. But no, there were no plans to retire; not then. As it is, the new convener did not, it seems, share the same team vision as did Cronje, if indeed Magiet had a vision. In Sri Lanka in 2000, when quizzed on the performances of the side and the 'road ahead,' he talked in general terms and not specifics. There was no defined role for the A Team either. If there was, it was clouded in obscurity.

Yet, news of a Sri Lanka tour the following year confused some South African sports writers. What Sri Lanka tour? In 2000? Only four months after the tour of India? Little did they know that it had appeared in the future tours section in every SA Cricket Annual since 1996 and was confirmed in 1998. After the World Cup in 1996 Cronje was in the car with Bacher (then managing director of the United Cricket Board), when Dhamika Ranatunga, a former Test player (then executive director of the control board in Sri Lanka and a good friend of Bacher) called him on his mobile. He was seeking a South African tour of the island, as the civil war had scared off teams and there was a fear, after Australia and the West Indies had reneged on their World Cup games, that possible isolation loomed.

Cronje was not into crystal-ball gazing either, but agreed to the tour of the island at a suitable time. When they looked at the dates available, Ranatunga and Bacher concurred at the 1996 London ICC meeting to the tour of Sri Lanka in 2000. At the time it was a brief paragraph appended at the end of most stories: the big news in 1996 was Jagmohan Dalmiya's thoughts of what he would do when he took over as ICC president the next year, and the likely shake-up of the establishment. Asia was at last awakening.

3

In 1998 when the author visited England to watch South Africa at the Lord's and Old Trafford Tests, he stayed with his Pakistani journalist friend and the two discussed, among other matters, player malpractice and match-fixing. The Pakistani knew far more than mere gossip and was able to substantiate it. He had been warning world officials for years of what he knew. The depth of corruption was most distressing, as people whose only interest was money were destroying its golden archetypical image.

Weeks later in Colombo the conversation was recalled. At night, the Sri Lankan capital is the sort of Asian juxtaposition where warm evening temperatures and humidity blend with perfumed incense, and the seedy and tawdry mix with the smart, colourful and wealthy; where dashing cocktail parties are held around well-lit swimming pools with well-groomed hosts and hostesses whose charm is more beguiling than Muttiah Muralitharan's smile. It is also a time when the well-heeled kick off their shoes and let more than their hair down. There are also those parties where conversations with some of the glamorous women is far more earthy than polite small talk about Sri Lanka's chances in the latest triangular series. It is about that other side of the road and where you know you are taking a genuine risk to venture. The locals nudge and wink and wag their head in affirmation as they explain that it is always advisable, if you are planning to spend a few hours at a casino, to take along a friend or two. It is called protection from the thugs and others who look for easy pickings among the foreigners, and there are any number of them around, all shades and shapes, male and female. If you know Colombo well enough after dark, you do not have to be told which places should be avoided. During the day it has a prettier, more trusting face; but that is a different story.

In early August 1998, while the South African A team was in transit from up-country Kurunegala to Matara for two games against Sri Lanka A at the southern city port venue, the side had a night stopover in Colombo. Moving from the party in Colombo to a fancy casino on Galle Road in Kolluptiyia was a matter of hiring a trishaw. It was still early, conversation was boring and most of the usual crowd was in England with the Sri Lankan team for the one-off Test and the Emirates Series.

A gaming joint in Kolluptiyia is the last place you would expect to get the first genuine whiff of a looming scandal of possible South African involvement with Indian bookmakers. After all, it was an A Team tour, not high profile enough to warrant reports on likely teams, weather conditions, pitch reports or even hazarding a guess at the toss. It was still some five months before the Shane Warne and Mark Waugh exposé at an almost incredulous media conference on the eve of the Ashes series between Australia and England; and was the guy in the expensive grey silk suit at the bar really called Runge and a so-called friend or someone more sinister?

One of the two Sri Lanka sports writers had been accumulating his winnings and had built a pile of chips worth about three months' wages. He was wondering if he should not cash it in while he was ahead and adjourn to the bar where the foreign journalist sat. It was one of those bars with artificial black leather and chrome fittings, a big mirror and well-groomed East European women who smoked and drank and chatted to the disgruntled who had lost heavily. Talk between the journalists at the bar was about the World Cup in England the following year and what team Sri Lanka, the defending champions, were likely to send.

It had not emerged at that stage, but the side led by Arjuna Ranatunga had become over-confident and flabby with success in the one-day arena. There had been a disappointing tour of South Africa earlier in the year, only that lack of success was put down to South Africa's pitches. They had to blame something. Now they were in England and performing far better than they had in the Tests at Newlands and Centurion. Forget the theory circulating in some Sri Lanka circles that it was time for Ranatunga to step aside before the World Cup and groom someone else in England. Sri Lanka were whipping South Africa in the Emirates Trophy tournament and playing in the final.

Anyway, who was there who could be Ranatunga's heir apparent? No one had emerged from among those in the team, and in South Africa it was noticeable that the brains trust was the trio of Ranatunga, Aravinda de Silva and the coach Duleep Mendis, a remarkably talented player in his day with a wristy technique and a former captain. It was, as one close to the team observed, such a talented triumvirate that they were unlikely to seek the opinion of others, apart from perhaps the capable Muttiah Muralitharan, Chaminda Vaas or Romesh

Kaluwitharana. The word of Arjuna, Aravinda and Duleep was law.

As such idle chatter continued, amid some light banter about the chances of South Africa or New Zealand in the 1999 World Cup, a smartly-dressed man in his thirties wearing a silver dove-grey silk suit offered to buy the two a drink. As he did, he asked if they knew what odds were being offered on England winning the Test series against South Africa; the fifth Test, at Headingley in Leeds, was to start two days later. If they were interested he could help them recoup some of their losses at the tables; after all, US$50 was a substantial amount.

'Do not worry, I have done this all over the world.' There was an obsequious grin, giving the impression that he was someone important, although he was slurring his words. 'Last year I was in South Africa. With the Indian team . . . I have friends in Durban . . .

Both journalists eyed the man who called himself Runge. South Africa? There had been a lot of talk about money and bookies and Mumbai Ring contacts at the Tests in Durban, Cape Town and the Wanderers in 1996-97, where there were sinister undertones of money passing hands at the grounds with involvement through Indian journalists. There was also the triangular series with Zimbabwe (the third side) and allegations of big money on the game at Willowmoore Park in Benoni, where India won.

'You'd be surprised what money is involved. Some big names in South Africa . . . ' There was an attempt at a conspiratorial wink, only by then he was having problems talking. 'But I do know those who can help you improve your finances . . . These guys can fix matches as easily as buy you a drink. Money is no problem for them.'

It was quite a boast.

'It says nothing. What names can you gives us?' he was asked.

It makes you wonder if this guy was genuine; you meet so many fakes in such places.

Runge shifted uneasily and tried to smile and make light of what he had said. Did he know or was he pretending? It seemed all too shady; an Indian businessman in Colombo suggesting something that was obviously illegal. It created some suspicion. He then partly fell off the barstool. Was he drunk or on drugs? He excused himself and said he was going to the toilet and would be back; only he disappeared.

Runge was soon forgotten. It seemed too bizarre; after all, did these things really happen? Nah—cricketers would not do anything that bad; not throw matches or even think of doing such a thing: to be a wilful sneak thief. Never!

Days later, South Africa lost the Headingley Test to England. Weeks after that, the Shane Warne and Mark Waugh scandal broke with the two admitting connivance. As expected, the Australian media pummelled the players and the South Asia connection. Was Runge perhaps genuine after all?

When email contact was made with the Pakistani journalist in London and the incident in the Colombo casino was related, the response was that as there was no tour, the guy was probably a nobody. It was just as they thought—another fake.

A year later, the author was on his way to Galle with Ranjan Paranavithana, sports editor of a Sinhalese paper, for the start of the Aiwa Cup triangular. They saw Runge waiting at the same bus station. As soon as the Indian saw the two, he fled with his luggage bag. He was later seen at Galle International and Premadasa Stadium, but kept his distance.

4

Of the many South Asian contacts the author managed to accumulate on his visits to Sri Lanka and India since 1991, several have become genuine friends, and one is the cheerful northerner Pradeep Magazine. During the Aiwa Cup series in 1999 the two struck up a warm understanding that has existed since.

There is a three-and-a-half-hour time difference between South Africa and India and on 8 April, around 10 a.m. Pradeep, then with the *Indian Express*, called Chesters with a request to write a story about the South African reaction to the New Delhi Police charges of fraud, cheating and criminal conspiracy against Hansie Cronje.

'Hi, Chesters, can you do me a story of the South African reaction?'

'Pradeep, my dear friend, I heard the tapes while waiting to be interviewed by Star and NDTV and let me tell you those voices were Asian . . .'

'Look, Chesters, the police have not released the actual tapes.'

Pradeep went on to explain that what the author had heard was a transcript of the tapes by two Indian actors; the Centurion-based journalist felt an irritation, but quickly understood how he had first been unknowingly misled and as such cast doubt on the authenticity of the tapes. As in many cases it was a question of a lack of communication and explanation by the Star and NDTV teams. It led to *The Star* (Johannesburg) newspaper taking quotes out of context in their front page lead story and instead of being an 'expert,' the author wondered if he had not in fact been a blundering rank amateur.

The day before, about an hour after the Cronje story broke, Star TV came through to the author at around 3.30 p.m. (South African time) with an experienced reporter, NDTV's Sonali Chander, on the line; she explained there was a need to present the South African viewpoint. Already, he had been writing a piece for *The Telegraph* in Calcutta and was trying to piece together from a distance the South African reaction. Contacts in India had already emailed bits and pieces of the story, including the imposing charge sheet. Bronwyn Wilkinson, the United Cricket Board's media liaison manager appointed a few weeks earlier, said Bacher and Cronje would react to the claims during the afternoon.

Amid all this was the matter of putting together a story about the limited overs international series of three challenge matches between South Africa and Australia. The telephone did not stop ringing as contacts from India, Sri Lanka and England called and the rumour machine started pumping its usual misinformation. It was not your typical blustery April Friday afternoon. As Pradeep Magazine later explained, the general view at first was that the New Delhi police had made a mistake. Younger people on the staff were disbelieving. The South Africans would not get involved in anything shady; not Cronje, the young man who gave Afrikaans and Afrikaners an acceptable modern face in an era of growing transformation. South Africa's white shining knight, the man the UCB had entrusted to take the game into the new century. Unbeknown to many South Africans, Cronje was as much a hero in India as he was in his own country.

As Pradeep admitted in one email during the depth of the crisis, 'I too am shocked by all this. We all are here. Hansie is regarded by many in India as a big hero.'

The author attempted to contact Fanie for a reaction, but his mobile was switched off and no one was at home. After his critical observations about Cronje's general attitude, it would have been interesting to get the former swing bowler's comments on the New Delhi police action.

As expected, the general South African response was one of outrage followed by condemnation of India and Indians in general. It had to be a frame-up. Hey, come on, guys. None of our cricketers are crooks; nor would they lie, cheat and coerce others into match-fixing. Not the captain. It was beyond the pale to act with such dishonour. Typical. It was a subcontinent trick to destroy the image of a born-again Christian. Just what do you expect from . . . that part of the world?

Oh yes . . . ?

As Pradeep pointed out, South Asia, too, was stunned. But no one wanted to hear that.

Cronje, ever the practical joker, at first thought it was a hoax. No—look at the date: it is April 7. Then, wide-eyed with disbelief he loudly protested his innocence. 'The allegations are completely without substance,' he said in a media release issued from the UCB offices. 'I have been privileged to play for South Africa since 1992 and I want to reassure every South African that I have made 100 per cent effort to win every match I have played. It has been an honour to play for South Africa and I would never do anything to let my country down.'

There it was, from the good, clean-living kid next door.

Ms Wilkinson followed this up with an official line that the 'board is dismayed that the integrity of South African cricket and its players has been questioned.' This was the official line and had the approval of Bacher and Percy Sonn, the UCB president. There was also a feeling that South Africa's foreign affairs office might ask a few tricky questions of the Indians. This was supported early on the Saturday morning when staff from *The Telegraph* in Calcutta, seeking another story, dropped a hint of a meeting between the Indian High Commissioner and South Africa's deputy Foreign Minister, Aziz Pahad.

It has been well documented that India had been one of the African National Congress' strongest allies from the time it was banned. Their support for the ANC Government did much to ease South Africa's reacceptance in any number of business and cultural areas, which for years had shut their doors on the apartheid nation. As sports such as rugby are almost non-existent in India, there was certain chagrin among often fractious administrators of how cricket received preference. The problem is, of course, that after decades of protection by a white minority government, there are those who cannot accept its lesser status.

When Fanie returned the call, his responses were guarded. He was not prepared to make any comment. Let the UCB handle it. He felt the matter was *sub judice*. There might be a statement at a later stage, not now. Rather leave it to settle. That was okay: confidences were not about to be broken, and his real thoughts about Cronje splashed across the pages of the South African or South Asian papers or on the CricInfo website. It was too personal.

It was during the supper break of the practice game between South Africa and Natal on 9 April, however, when thoughts first surfaced of whether the white knight was also a fake. On that Sunday evening when the long-awaited media conference was held, instead of ending rumours and speculation and clearing Cronje and the co-accused playing in the match, Herschelle Gibbs and Nicky Boje, there was more confusion. The South African captain emerged an embattled figure in the president's dining room across the passage from the media centre. Reporters, writers, in fact any old hack with media accreditation crammed into the section set side for the event. It had become a great sideshow on a balmy April evening.

Questions were asked and Bacher and Sonn as well as Cronje presented the face of an implacable indignant trio, upset at the sudden sullied image. The only things missing were Stetsons and smoking six guns, as they attempted to shoot down the tough line of interrogations. Off to the left sat Gibbs and Boje, saying nothing. It presented an air of injured resentment at the allegations that still swirled in the air-conditioned room and those gathered at the table. An uncomfortable knot of expectancy sat in the stomach. There was something wrong that the author, at first, could not identify. He looked at Cronje and the words seemed to drool out; in some respects there was a double innuendo in his comments that he had not received money from anyone during the limited overs series in India. They could even check his bank balance. It was a good bluff; plenty of flatulence from such bloated confidence. Talk about egoism.

Okay. Did he mean that he had received money for other matches but not this last series? Interesting, that one. It seemed as though he was confessing to having nicked a catch to the wicketkeeper, but deciding that with his team in trouble he would not walk unless the umpire was going to signal his dismissal. There was too much at risk.

At the time, there was an almost patronising grin as he answered questions. There was also that shifty-eyed look as he answered tricky questions at media conferences when explaining why South Africa had lost a game. He did not look the questioner in the eye. At times he was almost too self-protective in his answers. The Australian writers Malcolm Conn and Robert Craddock also noticed this stance.

No, of course he had not talked to any members of the side to throw a game. Really, guys . . . This is cricket, you know. That sort of thing just does not happen!

The author wanted Cronje's reaction to the transcripts and was about to ask the question, when Colin Bryden stepped in first. Cronje gave an impervious look at no one in particular. No, he had not read them.

Hello? Now this is interesting. How could he rattle off a series of denials if he had not read the transcripts somewhere? What basket of red herrings was he delving into?

'You didn't read them?' a puzzled Bryden asked.

'I haven't had the time . . .' He shook his head.

'But they have been in every newspaper in the country—yesterday and today.'

Cronje shrugged. Bryden and the author felt that something was not quite right here.

Ken Borland, of the Natal Witness, posed the query of whether it had something to do with the decision at Centurion in January, when Cronje and England's captain Nasser Hussain decided to forfeit innings in the rain-affected Test to achieve a result? Perhaps bookies in India were not too happy with how the result had been achieved? Or even the result itself?

Bacher jumped in to flatly reject the implication; it left some of the media with the impression that the force of the denial suggested Borland's question was 'unpatriotic'. All he wanted, as did the others, was to get at the truth; not to have his view blocked with fancy official rhetoric and obfuscation.

Just how revealing was the truth behind the result of the Centurion Test emerged during the King Commission hearings.

In the end the Kingsmead media conference had left more questions and a lot of uncertainty. Where was it all heading? Certainly Dr Bacher and Sonn were left without any conclusions. If they had doubts then, they hid them well.

During all this it emerged that a series of benefit matches in India with teams captained by Cronje and Sachin Tendulkar were to be cancelled. The organisers were unhappy about the bad publicity. Was Cronje not already wondering about being discovered?

Weeks later, in Galle, during the second Test between Sri Lanka and Pakistan, a visiting Indian official the author had met during the 1999 World Cup gave him some startling information. It was claimed that K. K. Paul, joint commissioner of crime, New Delhi police, had been in touch with an official in government circles. The story was that the police planned to delay by three weeks announcing the charges against Cronje, Boje, Gibbs, Pieter Strydom and Henry Williams. The plan was to arrest Cronje, Gibbs and Boje when they arrived at the airport to play in the series of benefit games later in the month. What utter consternation and humiliation it would have caused can only be imagined. The South African captain arrested in India on charges of cheating, fraud and criminal conspiracy, and arraigned in court.

Was it true, though?

Ravi Shastri, a TV commentator in Galle at the time, was asked if he knew anything. The tall, elegant, former batsman knew nothing. It was possible, of course. To his knowledge, though, final arrangements had not been made for the series or games. Okay. Why then had the New Delhi police delayed their announcement by almost two weeks? Did they look at the implications and decide that it was not worth it? It takes time to prove such a damning case against a high profile figure.

5

A decidedly uneasy atmosphere settled over Kingsmead on the night of 9 April; the practice game went on, stories had to be written, opinions given and the pulling together of thoughts. Something, however, was not right. It all kept coming back to the denial of meeting such bookmakers as Sanjeev Chawla. So many people went to the rooms for pictures, autographs, interviews; it is India and that sort of thing is expected. The mobile telephone story.

What about the security? Did they ignore such large daily invasions without clearance? What about bribes? In India, the unexpected windfall of US$250 can make a doorman very happy.

There was also Cronje's denial of reading the transcripts in South African papers.

It was another red herring, among the many, which he had already tried to use to divert the truth. It could not last, of course. The pressures were great and the South African team was caught in the eye of the storm. Cronje, the shining white knight and helmsman, had lost not only the charts but also the compass. Had he not passed a comment when asked by the UCB if the two others named in the charges and playing at Kingsmead, Gibbs and Boje, should also attend the media conference?

'Yes, they are innocent—I never told them anything.'

Any amateur sleuth looking for clues would have quickly spotted how damning that comment was; he had all but admitted guilt. Was his conscience already wavering?

Around noon on the Monday, the author, seated in the media centre at Kingsmead with Telford Vice of Reuters, had a call on his mobile from his Pakistani friend in London; the British media were on their way to Durban to sniff out the story. You have to believe it, friend, Cronje is guilty. What evidence is there? Chawla. Cronje, the practical joker, had played his last game and the Indian bookmakers were having the last laugh at his expense after his various failures to deliver.

Metaphorically, Cronje had been caught with his hand in the till. So, were the 1996-97 stories true after all? Had he in fact also been in contact with the Indian bookies during the Newlands Test and told them what time he was going to declare and set India a target? It meant that the discussion with the South African manager, Alan Jordaan, about when to declare was little more than a sham. It was becoming obvious that Cronje was implicated and had indulged in what was little more than a litany of lies to cover his backside.

What, though, of other contacts with bookmakers? Surely it was not all limited to 1995, 1996-97 and 2000? Was it not suggested that matches with Pakistan in 1997-98 were also involved? Contacts suggested South Africa's tour of Australia in 1997-98 had been infiltrated by a couple of touts. Surely there are officials who would deny connivance, but 'how long can you live in a glass house and not notice what is going on'?

None of this came out during the King Commission; was the Pakistan journalist in London acting on hearsay and not genuine evidence, as he had of Pakistan's two games in the 1999 World Cup? He said it was a dangerous game and there were criminal elements, given the chance, who would not hesitate to kill anyone that they felt would endanger the system. He had received death threats before and probably would again. He also passed on a warning and none too soon. Experiencing a couple of mobile telephone calls with the voice uttering veiled threats are far from pleasant disturbances at 3.30 in the morning, even in the serenity amid the lush green Kandyan hills just above the lake in August 2000.

As speculation threw up a wider, uglier scenario, the three-match challenge series with Australia was forgotten as the winds of uncertainty and suspicion gathered over Kingsmead. The game had become booby-trapped from within by the dirty hands of the fifth columnist Cronje, and was about to blown apart.

Hours later a stunned nation heard the stark truth. There were many who believed in Cronje; he was the epitome of the modern face of the spiritually cleansed young Afrikaner, reaching out to embrace the country's rainbow image. Instead they discovered a cardboard cut-out that left many with twisted inner anguish. His admission of 'not being totally honest' had betrayed their trust and the game, for the moment, was mentally broken on the wrack of lies and deceit and greed. Their white knight had been knocked off his charger.

When it was released, the final King Commission report was open-ended and did not suggest criminal prosecution in its recommendations. That is still up to the department of public prosecutions and open to speculation. Yet even in far-off Sri Lanka the view is that having deliberately trodden with spiked boots across the face and body of the game, a million Rands fine as well as the life-banning and a jail term would be seen as a lenient sentence for such an act of open violation.

If the comment of the historian, journalist and author Thomas Moult, who in the anthology *Bat and Ball* concluded that 'cricket is an ancient pastime: it ripened sweetly, it has endured nobly,' is to be accepted, then how can Cronje's actions be viewed any differently from those of a mugger bent on committing a serious assault? One where he deliberately victimised the sport that gave him succour and elevated him to a position that ensured respect and trust across a broad demographic spectrum? When he penned his words in 1935, Moult was writing about the suggestive, rich spirit of the game, which had endured and enabled the wounds to heal during the 1930s and 1940s as it recovered from the bruising inflicted by the infamous Bodyline series in 1932-33 in Australia.

So what paraphrase would do as a judgement of Cronje's avarice for future students studying the match-fixing scandal and its fall-out? 'Cronjegate, an ignoble manipulation of the system tailored to fatten a player's back pocket with the connivance of bookmaker(s) and coercing other players into match-fixing and lying.' It is a fair comment.

Cronjegate has to be seen as another stain, as with Bodyline, which is so deep it is not going to be removed: it may in time become discoloured, but it is not going to disappear. It should never be allowed to quietly slip, in time, into the pages of the game's history; it is too horrendous an act for that sort of forgiveness.

6

Fanie's views on Bodyline are far from being unusually different. Not in the way you would think; as a bowler he feels the form of attack was little different from that of past West Indies' attacks: with a lot of fast short-pitched bowling. It is the sort of aggressive 'in your face' bowling as opposed to the subtle, if not friendly, bowling of earlier years. It was the type of attacking bowling that inexorably changed the face of the game.

He also viewed Cronje's connivance with the bookmakers as being much bigger than the ICC had ever made of the Kerry Packer fracas. At that stage the ICC was run more as a fiefdom through a benevolent Marylebone Cricket Club-linked oligarchy clique within the system. It was very much an 'old boys' club image and had existed for more than seventy years. At least Packer's revolution brought a new, important public awareness to the game and he gave underpaid professional players a pay package they deserved; it forced the establishment to recognise that players had families and to be aware of growing needs. The way he saw Cronje, however, was of someone who not only trampled on his own character, but the integrity of his teammates had also come under scrutiny. Fanie did not like that part.

Even if it is wrong, Fanie believes there is a distinct difference between the team's involvement compared to three or four players trying to influence their own result through spread betting. Several members of any side might take out a US$10,000 bet that a particular batsman would score between 35 and 45 runs. The batsman would then need to lose his wicket between those scores, otherwise those placing the bet would start losing money. It leaves a decidedly ugly stench of culpability, yet shows how a game can be manipulated and even the result.

'We all make mistakes, but doing this behind other players' backs is like stealing from your family. What he did with Gibbs and Williams goes way beyond that,' he said. 'Only someone with a devious mind and no respect for friendship and team spirit can do what he did.'

It is not a matter either of whether Gibbs was led astray by a so-called mentor in an agreement to follow Cronje's instructions, which should count when reviewing the leniency of the UCB's disciplinary committee's sentences. There are others in the South African coloured community who became disgusted with the daily revelations during the King Commission. To them the game was not high on their list of priorities, and when you see how they battled to make a living, it is easy to understand how daily bread-and-butter issues are more important.

One woman journalist expressed her repugnance in her weekly column headlined, 'So Much Success, So Little Honour'. It is easy to understand the frustration and deeper disappointment felt by Phylicia Oppelt at how two of her nation also became culpable. Her words of how 'Gibbs let himself, his team and his country down,' have the strong ring of hurt and distress. No one can blame her for pointing out how, at twenty-six, Gibbs had enjoyed 'so many good things'; he was also 'held up as a shining example of merit succeeding over affirmative action' and 'he had spoken of his awareness that he carried on his shoulders more than just the hopes of cricket lovers'.

Ms Oppelt looked on Gibbs as having 'personified black sporting achievement'. Which is a fair comment, as both represent the same community. Then she aims a careful left hook at the Gibbs image: 'As a nation we carry our sporting heroes in our hearts because each time they play they carry our hopes and our pride'. Meaningful, well-selected words by a disarming woman, whose pen is as appealing as her charm and biting wit. She suggests, and many view the issue with similar thoughts, 'We become angry and disappointed when our sportsmen and sportswomen accept glory without honour . . .'

When Gibbs, she says, returned to the South African squad, he would remain a man without honour. Ms Oppelt is not alone in her condemnation. There are many hurt, deeply disappointed and disillusioned people in South Africa who are no longer prepared to accept Cronjegate at face value. Cronje trampled on their faith in sportsmen and heroes and undid all the hard hours of ambassadorial work by other players in a country that needed heroes.

The game's integrity was suffering, and spectators and would-be future players turned to something else. Players, with unthinking stupidity, added further dishonour with the dagga-smoking episode in the West Indies in 2001 after winning the series. Questions were then asked (and remain) about the leniency shown towards Gibbs; it suggested protection by the establishment, which has left many wondering how far clemency stretches. He did not, as the year before against the Australians, display the same level of guilt when batting in the West Indies. Then again, when a young man swaggers around a hotel wearing an expensive leather jacket and drives a luxury car worth more than two years' salary of someone from the same, less-privileged community, questions should be asked about fines and attitudes towards other players in the team.

Fanie makes the point again when he asks about those admitting guilt, accepting responsibility and culpability, and yet bringing added dishonour to the game. Surely it is the image of the game that suffers most? Those who create such a climate should be punished far more and be made to apologise, not only to the country and the spectators, but also to the game itself for bringing shame where there should be none.

When it came to his turn to address the commission, Cronje spent about forty-five minutes reading through twenty-two pages of testimony, correcting one or two minor details such as a bank account number and date of a meeting with one of the bookies. It was made clear to him by Mr Justice Edwin King that it was up to himself and the chief investigator, Shamila Batohi, and others handling the inquiry, whether his pleas for indemnity (to stay out of jail) are granted. As it was, his credibility rating was as low as one of the many ducks scored in his career, and he needed to be seen to be telling 'nothing but the truth'.

There is still today, in India and Pakistan, a strong body of opinion that Cronje withheld information of further player connections when he was cross-examined. He only implicated by name two former captains, Mohammad Azharuddin and Salim Malik, the latter already fingered by the Qayyum Commission in Pakistan and banned for life, the former also banned by the Indians. Cronje, as with Azharuddin, lost his appeal with costs in the Pretoria Supreme Court to have his UCB ban overturned, when Mr Justice Frank Kirk-Cohen handed down his judgement keeping his life ban in place. This was a clear legal repudiation that Cronje needed to make him realise that while there are those within South African society with their obfuscated reasons for wanting to support him, evidence on the 'charge sheet' was too convincing and he was found guilty as charged.

It did not surprise anyone after Ms Batohi's lack of success during her visit to India in later 2000 to procure copies of the tapes on which the Indian police based their case, that the King Commission was eventually closed. It came after several delays in attempting to reconvene the probe failed. There was the ploy by Cronje's legal team to have the commission closed after challenging Judge King's legal standing, on constitutional grounds, to handle the commission. Four years later there are those in India who felt that the hasty closure was done to protect certain administrators around the world.

Not surprisingly, the Bloemfontein offices of Cronje's legal team was awash with self-congratulations and there was a growing belief that it was the first step of vindication; keeping the commission open would serve no purpose. Next would be overturning the life ban imposed by the United Cricket Board. They adopted the same sort of arrogance about their approach to this case as Cronje had displayed with teammates in the dressing room.

What did surprise some foreign journalists in the first days of the King Commission were unfortunate accusations of what was later described as 'practical racism'. This, it was erroneously assumed at the time, was a deliberate effort by some South Asian commentators to deflect their own problems in dealing with match-fixing issues. It later emerged that it was linked to a South African ploy to discredit the CBI investigation and the startling revelations for weeks after the 7 April charges and Cronje's admission of guilt. Just who the instigators were is unclear, but suspicions remain.

Most of what Cronje said at the King Commission had been known; he basically fleshed out the lie he had lived for almost four-and-a-half years and it was known that he would mention Azhar and Malik. If this is seen as 'practical racism' then plans for the world game and its ambitious globalisation strategies are in trouble. The game cannot afford or, for that matter, allow divisions along race, creed or cultural lines. Islamic fundamentalists attempted to do this in May 2002, when a car bomb targeted foreigners in Karachi and led to the cancellation of the second Test and the tour between the Kiwis and Pakistan.

One side issue was how the ICC came in for criticism from Australian, New Zealand and Sri Lankan sources for not having an impartial observer at the King Commission. One of the ICC match referees would have done; Sri Lankans Ranjan Madugalle, who was match referee at the 1999 World Cup final, or Sidath Wettimuny with his impeccable record of honesty and then a member of the interim committee, were two names; a third was the amiable West Indian Cammie Smith; a fourth name was Zimbabwean Judge Ahmed Ebrahim.

At the time of Cronjegate and for months afterwards, the man and woman in the street, the casual supporter or spectator, needed serious answers to major issues affecting the game. They wanted more transparency. What happened in November 2001 when India clashed with the ICC over the Mike Denness row should not be allowed to happen again. It was one example of how the game was mishandled during a crisis by officials and politicians. Unless those who run the ICC can place together a strategy designed to restore credibility, the story of Camelot could be repeated: destroyed from within by those with a greed to match their egoism. It tells us that they are there only for what they can get out of it and forget the globalisation commitment for the twenty-first century and beyond.

The African dream within the ICC globalisation strategy is already in trouble, enmeshed as it is in a system where finances, or the lack of them, and poor marketing and media coverage outside the ten Test nations are seriously harming its growth.

Two areas of improvement have been the appointment of a match referees panel of five and an independent umpires panel of eight; these should go far in meeting the demands of the modern game and remove the nationalistic jingoism of November 2001 after the Denness affair at St George's Park in Port Elizabeth, when he banned six Indian players for bringing the game into disrepute. The rambling verbal brawl between Dalmiya and Malcolm Gray, the Indian and ICC protagonists, saw political brinkmanship and resulted in the Centurion Test between South Africa and India consigned to the records as just another first-class match. If this was not a case of 'practical racism' then the term has changed its meaning from that during April 2000 when Chesters was accused of applying double standards when writing about Cronje and initially suggesting his possible innocence.

Implications are, however, that at Centurion in November 2001 the credibility factor had again suffered through careless political posturing as India twisted the arm of the South African government and the UCB was pushed into a corner and bullied into submission. Those spectators who turned up were not quite sure what they had paid their money to watch: a Test or a friendly joust. This is not how the game should be run.

There are those who would argue that the ICC at the May crisis meeting in 2000, a month after Cronjegate splashed its disfigured image into the world headlines, drafted serious legislation to remove the cancer of bookmakers and their contacts from manipulating results. They did not go far enough. It would also be seen as interference to suggest that bookmakers in India be allowed to run betting shops at the venues where LOI and Tests are played as a way of removing their role from the system. Yet with sponsorships and finances playing an ever-important function, the ICC's edict of May 2000 could still allow the TV moguls to run and sell the game as they wish.

The real danger here is that the ethics of fair play, founded in laws more than 250 years old, and with it the game's credibility, can sink without a trace as cricket's new 'bill of rights' will be enshrined forever in garments such as the HAN$IE shirts they once sold in Johannesburg.

7

In its own way the tragic death on 1 June 2002 of Hansie Cronje added its own dramatic, if final poignant, epithet to this unhappy chapter in the game's history. No matter how many have attempted since then to present a new, sanctified image, it is not his leadership skills, his ability as a captain to cleverly manoeuvre a bowling attack, or his batting technique which is going to be remembered fifty years from now. It is the ugly scar with which he all but disfigured the game.

He played a role with others that raped the sport's image of fair play and stole from it its honour. The investigation under Mr Justice Edwin King could be seen as a tool to expose only that in which

Cronje was involved and not the broader scope. This was a pity, as there is far more filth lying under the carpet than even the International Cricket Council is prepared to admit.

On the Monday following the crash, apart from a brief announcement that was expected anyway, little was being made of a statement that the Scorpions had closed their file on Hansie Cronje's match-fixing operations. Certainly the department of public prosecutions was not going to linger over their deliberations.

For them it was a matter of 'case closed'.

Questions remain, however, many of them unanswered.

CRICKET CREED

(A WAY OF LIFE AND UNDERSTANDING)

C   culture (which comes from understanding, lore and knowledge of the game

R   reliability (discipline, mental and physical, from which stems sportsmanship)

I   interactive (which means working beyond the basics of the game)

C   creativity (remember your game plan and future goals: always think ahead)

K   knowledge (coaching, laws, history—goals of life and ambitions)

E   education (positive development process)

T   tolerance/tradition/thought (history and lore-brotherhood: the game that is never done)

False Starts and New Beginning

1

There are far too many Capetonians who have (what is) a pompous view of what is referred to as South Africa's 'Mother City'. Those who have migrated to the city also like to present it to the tourist, more than, say, the up-country visitor, as being trendy, smart and well-heeled. They overlook the crime and other factors that still have apartheid undertones, detracting from what is a decidedly portentious image. A legacy of forced removals of population groups still lingers. It was iniquitous as well as ubiquitous; it stripped members of the community of dignity and in some respects created an inner-city vacuity, removing colour as well as vibrancy, identity, and with this, a sense of belonging.

Rather, it is the outlying Boland countryside of Stellenbosch, Paarl, Wellington, Tulbagh and other areas with its profusion of vineyards and demographic mix that attracts and entertains the tourist and even up-country visitor, than the modern image a traveller visiting Cape Town is left with before heading to other parts of the country.

History does show that Cape Town was the first port of call or landfall that Portuguese mariners discovered all those centuries ago, and which later attracted the Dutch in the guise of the colonialist Dutch East India Company, known by the fancy sobriquet Heeren XVII. Whether it was Table Mountain or the halfway-house position between the proud Dutch and the East Indies (mostly Indonesia) that was the initial attraction, is hard to define. Certainly, the weather was better than they had in Holland. And the Dutch were far more tolerant in allowing the indentured labour they brought with them to act as servants to retain their identity and Muslim faith and build mosques.

These days, entry to Cape Town is through the international and domestic airport, which is east of the city, from where taxi drivers without metres rip off the visitor, thinking they have deep pockets and that tourists are 'fair game,' to line their own pockets. In fact, as some unsuspecting foreign journalists discovered during Cricket World Cup 2003, it was cheaper to hire a car and driver in most of the cities where the event was held.

Overseas journalists arriving in Cape Town a few days before the opening of the event were greeted by a billboard sign near the airport that boasted of how South Africa's captain, Shaun Pollock, would bring home the World Cup. Some weeks later it was being disfigured with graffiti, as the fallout from the debacle of the nation's exit from the event continued to send shockwaves through all levels of the sport. It turned into a disastrous week for Shaun Pollock, and the anguish showed yet again as Allan Donald bid an emotional farewell to his international career when he announced his retirement from the game (which did not come as a surprise). This came a few hours after selector Pat Symcox resigned his position for 'reasons of pressure'. The real reason was more to do with selection politics than his role of television commentator. After all, Australia's Allan Border and South African Mike Procter did a better than creditable job filling both positions. There was also the hint of jealousy in certain quarters that Symmo was able to carry on doing two jobs. As he did not need irrational criticism, he realised it was time to move out as a selector and move on.

Amid all this, the future of the disgraced United Cricket Board's president, Percy Sonn, next in line as the International Cricket Council president, was being questioned. This followed a secret probe, ordered, it was said, by an agency with links to the ministry of justice, into his behaviour on more than one occasion before and during CWC03.

Sonn had seriously embarrassed guests with his behaviour at the Paarl game between India and Holland on day four of the tournament. Then, with typical bluster, he angered certain senior UCB officials by turning up in Centurion seven days later and grinning broadly as if nothing had happened, to see Australia beat India. It is also suggested there is more truth in the rumour that he was in a worse condition in

Sydney in New Year 2002. That was the time when he used his role as executive president to overrule the selectors and force them to kick out Jacques Rudolph for Justin Ontong.

His joking reference to his behaviour in Paarl came at a time when there were growing voices of concern by several highly placed officials among the major sponsors of the United Cricket Board. They viewed his image as being anything but appropriate for a man holding such a high position and came after Sonn's 'public apology' for his disgraceful display in Paarl on 12 February 2003.

Several senior visiting journalists, mainly from India, expressed shock after being confronted by Sonn in Paarl and his belligerent and unacceptable, eccentric behaviour towards them. They still wonder how he will handle pressures as president of the International Cricket Council when or if he eventually takes over from urbane Pakistani Ehsan Mani. The view after the Paarl episode was that he should have resigned as UCB president. What was more worrying was how the Cricket World Cup Committee 2003 director, Dr Ali Bacher, rushed to Sonn's defence without knowing the facts and ended up looking more foolish than normal. There was no surprise when he eventually stepped down as president and Ray Mali took over as head UCB honcho in September 2003.

Is it any surprise then, within days of the country's first round exit, that there were going to be serious consequences over South Africa's World Cup fiasco on 3 March 2003? An attempted mugging close to the ground by tattered street urchins, hoping to hunt down a possible victim, failed when an alert security guard came to an aging journalist's rescue. There were other casualties, though, of those lying in wait to ambush the unsuspecting. Several South Asian journalists had international mobile telephone calls rudely curtailed when thugs snatched succession hand phones. The police merely shrugged and offered a weak apology over lax security arrangements along Marine Parade. In a couple of cases, Sri Lankan media men on shoestring budgets could ill-afford such calamities. It was a case of borrowing a helpful colleague's phone to update information. This was at a time when tourism ministry types were hoping CWC03 would 'showcase South Africa as top tourist venue' and show there was more to the nation than Kruger National Park and Sun City.

2

By 11 p.m. on 3 March 2003, South Africa had donned a metaphorical black armband and the nation, most politicians excepted, went into mourning. Bacher, a former South African captain under the one-time white establishment and director of the CWC03 committee, declined to lay the blame at any door. But as any number of fingers were being pointed at a variety of villains at South Africa's abysmal failure in World Cup 2003, Messrs Tony Lewis and Frank Duckworth, a couple of Manchester University mathematical boffins, were accused of being the main culprits. Well, the confused public had to blame someone, didn't they? But if the television announcers knew what was going on, why didn't those running the side? There were also the mixed signals of the score needed to put South Africa ahead of Sri Lanka in terms of the rain-affected system designed by the two Englishmen. Who screwed that one up is a matter of interpretation.

Collectively it should have been the team management, although the score needed to have won the game when the innings was halted by rain at over 45 was 230 runs and not the 229 that tied the scores. It is the sort of neatly-tied package, which may explain some of the anguish and bruised pride the nation awoke with along with the bleak, grey dawn that hung over the Indian Ocean city.

There were several underlying factors why South Africa failed: one was a policy of team selection; second was a certain evident arrogance, even after the defeat by West Indies at Newlands in the game that launched the six-week long jamboree. Third, there was a serious cover-up over the accountability of what message was sent to Mark Boucher about the runs needed to win before Russel Arnold was given a chance to bowl the first ball of the next over. Steve Bucknor stepped in as the drizzle turned into a deluge and the players rushed off. The Sri Lankans were puzzled by it all. Sanath Jayasuriya had a sheet with the Duckworth and Lewis calculations in his pocket and knew what was going on; question is, how did the South Africans mess it up? And screw it up they did!

When the post-mortems were held, South Africa's coach Eric Simons said the feeling in the team was to concentrate on scoring the runs needed within the required 50 overs. The rain cast a watery blanket over this amazing theory as Pollock and Co. also short-changed themselves over the pre-match weather report, believing there would be passing showers; nothing as heavy as what fell and kept on falling well into the night. Sri Lanka surprised most by finishing top in Pool B after tying with South Africa. Surely, Pollock should have known better; after all he did live in Durban.

There were those in Durban after the match who were accusing Sri Lanka of 'not playing it fair,' which is one way of saying, 'you did not play it by our playing conditions and bowled another over in pouring rain'. This was a selfish way for the South African supporters to look at it. It was not the Sri Lankans' fault, but the South African dressing-room cock-up.

Equally remarkable is how Stephen Fleming, the New Zealand captain, carried the D/L equation with him in all the games where rain affected the result. In the Wanderers crunch match with South Africa, Fleming knew ball by ball what was required. So, why did the South Africans not get it right? Or did they not get the right grounding at school of how to do simple mathematical equations? If an eight-year-old grand-nephew was able to work it out, the South African management should have done so as well!

The way century-maker Marvan Atapattu and the team looked at it, Sri Lanka was quite happy being the underdog. It worked well for them in the tournament, as the focus was then on the other teams. The way they played against South Africa at Kingsmead was the way they had wanted to play in such a tight, crucial game.

'We brought our slow bowlers into the attack at the right time to curb their stroke players,' Atapattu said. 'We had the type of attack to push for pace or spin as the situation warrants.'

South Africa seemed to be missing the balance needed to win games. All they had to show in CWC03 were facile wins against Kenya, Bangladesh and Canada and a rained-off tie against Sri Lanka with defeats to West Indies and New Zealand. The latter at the Wanderers was an interesting match, with the Kiwi captain knowing ball by ball that South Africa was going to lose one they had expected 'to walk it', if a local morning edition of *The Star* could be believed. It showed that, as in Durban, there are no guarantees about anything.

South Africa being defaulted from the Super Sixes contained any number of ironies, as Gerald Majola, chief executive of the United Cricket Board, had to admit. There would be a think tank and a question of not so much where to apportion blame, but what went wrong. After all, it was a tournament where South Africa was expected to be the first host nation to win a World Cup.

Along with the West Indies and minnows Bangladesh and Canada, South Africa's dream of triumph smothered in a wet blanket and the collective misery showed on the faces of many. Not too many were smiling in the seaside city where muggers reign, and the showcase that was CWC03 was given a figurative black eye.

Okay . . . So, how was it then that South Africa, after returning from the International Cricket Council Champions Trophy as narrowly-beaten semi-finalists by India the previous September, failed to move forward into the Super Sixes? After all, had they not emphatically whipped three Test nations, Bangladesh, Sri Lanka, and Pakistan, as part of the build-up to this event? Ironically, the two African nations to qualify were Zimbabwe and Kenya. Since then, their systems have all but imploded as the officials in Kenya caught the Hansie Cronje disease of pocketing money, while political thugs and administrative power-play resulted in most white players, led by Heath Streak, quitting.

Was South Africa perhaps too confident? Or was it a matter of too much pressure of playing at home, with the weight of success and expectations emanating from that boring 1995 rugby World Cup success being heaped on their shoulders? There was far too much perpendicular instead of lateral thinking. Even the majority of the nation began to believe in the team's invincibility.

But if the South African selection policy was confusing enough to the visiting teams and media, it had already been laid down three years before when in Colombo in August 2000, Rushdi Magiet, then convener of the national selection committee, outlined early plans. This emerged when, asked a question about the handling of the player transformation process, he expressed concern that, 'There are so few quality black players available to us (the selectors) at present'. It was a question of having to select five (players of colour) for the 2003 World Cup that 'there is a serious need for us to increase the numbers to fit such a selection policy'.

Making this comment at the Sinhalese Sports Club on 10 August 2000, Magiet said he did not necessarily agree with merit selection; if there was a fifth black player who might not qualify as a merit selection case, the selectors would resort to quota system policy. He did not feel, however, that in the end it would come to that.

The tournament lacked sparkle and flair when teams such as the West Indies, Pakistan, South Africa and even England disappeared. In their place, there were Zimbabwe and Kenya. All of which suggests an overhaul of the Super Six system; or as has already been advanced, a format similar to 1996 with four groups of teams: the top two from each group going through into a separate Super Eight league as based on pre-tournament seedings. As the cut-off date is ludicrously early (April 2005), it created problems. One was that the seedings were done before the ICC Associate Members tournament in Ireland during July 2005. Teams would take their points through and in this way, the tournament could be cut to five weeks.

Also, Bacher's roadshow, with the African Dream of games in Kenya and Zimbabwe, was too long and diverse in its sideshow of political misdemeanours, as well as prime ministers such as Tony Blair and John Howard voicing opinions advocating prudence and warnings of a backlash, while conveniently beating the war drums over Iraq. It was political opportunism at its indifferent best. Long ignored was how, when in early 2002 the draw was made, nothing was said of the Zimbabwe (or for that matter Kenya) issue.

What good there was, was marginalised; Kenya reaching the Super Six through a technicality gave them added exposure, as they also managed a semi-final position. It was an expectation beyond their wildest hopes and (perhaps) gives the game the impetus it needs to stretch its current limited space to something more in keeping with hopefully a national (African) image. Since then, Kenya has lurched from one crisis to another until the government, with tactical International Cricket Council approval, stepped in to sort out the mess of what had become a local money-grabbing, ham-fisted, mafia-style operation.

There was always a hollow feeling about watching some of the Super Six games; the predictability of the result made them tired events and switched-off those who would have gone to watch what would be a more even contest. What was important was that title-holders Australia met the next best side, India. A pity that with the opening overs and Sachin Tendulkar's culpable batting act, they failed to deliver. Lessons have been learnt all around and the prospects are that 2007 might be an easier World Cup to follow and digest.

When it came, Donald's international retirement had long been expected: 72 Tests and 147 limited overs internationals.

'I would like to be remembered as someone who gave his all. I was very passionate about the badge and the country and about every team I've played for,' he said during a news conference.

3

Information from inside sources is invaluable, especially when contacts are as reliable as is this one. The startling tip-off, initially sent by a mobile phone service message system, simply read: Shaun Pollock is no longer South African captain. First question. Was he fired or had he quit? The response to this was that no one was certain. Second question. Where was Pollock now? It was believed he was on his way back to Durban.

Was the United Cricket Board going to release a statement? If so, when? That night or the next day? The reaction to this was uncertainty. Was the news generally known? Again there was uncertainty; but an announcement would be made the next day; most likely, this would be at Kingsmead during Australia's Super Six game with Kenya.

All that could be established was that he had walked out of a lengthy meeting at Newlands, and the word was that South Africa would now need to find a new captain; first for the Sharjah tournament and then Bangladesh and England tours.

It was time to check with another contact (this one in Johannesburg) who when pressed, admitted Pollock was no longer in charge of the team. For further details there came a vague comment that it was a matter of 'watch this space'.

The background to this was that Pollock had not been, for family reasons, available to attend a meeting at Newlands the previous Wednesday to discuss the team's failure to reach the Super Six stage. What he had done was send a fax to the team's coach, Eric Simons, outlining his views on South Africa's ignominious CWC03 exit and asking Simons to present these to the UCB honchos and selectors at the conference. Inside sources said that both the UCB and Pollock were unhappy with a number of factors surrounding the World Cup. Pollock's failure to turn up at Newlands did not go down well at all. None of the problems involving the CWC03 failure have ever emerged, but suggestions were that Pollock didn't have the full support of the players and maybe the coach. There was also the question of team selection and political interference.

It was close to 7.30 on a typical steamy Durban evening on 14 March, and a dinner date with colleagues and friends was looming for the *Indian Express* journalist. Once alerted, though, to the astonishing news and the background facts, the veteran former South Africa writer began to quickly pull the story together. Dinner could wait a while. What with a three-and-a-half-hour time difference and the final deadline approaching in New Delhi, there was no time to sit on such hot information. It meant a brief call to New Delhi and Jayaditya Gupta, the energetic, bright young *Express* sports editor, to alert him to the story.

An agreement was reached to run what is called a page one 'teaser' with a cross-reference to the sports page story. What mattered though was how the use of modern electronic technology and checking sources presented *Indian Express* with their biggest scoop to date of CWC03. It gave the Indian daily and its website a 14-hour jump on other media, including that in South Africa. When the *Express* story became known around 8 a.m. South Africa time the Saturday morning, frantic approaches were made to the UCB. It took some time, however, before it was confirmed that a release would be made that afternoon. It also had other media scrambling for details. There was also the question of how did the *Indian Express* sniff out a story that even local papers, international news agencies and the electronic media at large had failed to get?

It is the old tale of subtle subterfuge, discretion, as well as double-checking information with other reliable sources; also important is making sure the identities of such contacts remain buried deep within the system. That way you get information that is more reliable and you can trust the informant, as well as the so-called mole having faith in the journalist. It is often a risky two-way street, as it also carries with it a certain element of discovery.

Not surprising the events earlier in the day at Newlands, the three key figures in this emerging story were on the night of 14 March 2003 dodging an inquisitive media: Omar Henry, selection panel convener, Pollock, and Gerald Majola, the UCB chief executive. They had switched off their mobiles, as some South African media interested in the outcome of the World Cup elimination post-mortems battled for information.

The first inquiry was the releasing of a statement of the meeting. The *Indian Express* wanted someone to confirm or deny the Pollock story: no confirmation, no publication; that is how they operate. You cannot blame them; it is a matter of credibility. As it was, time was short and with Pollock on his way back from Cape Town, it was a matter of running with a gut feeling. Two of the other selectors, Hugh Page and Pat Symcox, a former Pollock Test and KwaZulu/Natal teammate, were at the time silent at on the subject.

As selectors, were they not in on such an important meeting? There was a negative response from both. They had been there on the Wednesday when Pollock had not. Not surprisingly, by now some South African media began picking up the loose threads of the story. After an assurance that the story was genuine, the *Indian Express* went to bed with the last edition carrying the story, with a follow-up planned early the next morning. It was a risk, but one worth taking, a matter of self-belief by the *Indian Express* man.

Late that Friday night though, Symcox admitted that, 'It is a confusing state of affairs. I have spoken to Shaun and he has neither quit nor been fired. So, there is no truth in the rumour.'

When Henry returned the call around 10 a.m. the Saturday morning, he wanted to know where the information had come from; when told 'reliable sources', he said it was not good enough. It was up to Gerald Majola or Percy Sonn to make a statement. Pressed further, he admitted there would be an announcement later. There was, though, no truth in the story that Pollock had quit. What this translated into was how Pollock, having refused to go, was fired after members of the UCB's executive intervened in the team selection dispute. A new captain had been selected and approved by the executive. What later emerged from the shadows of the UCB inner executive sanctum was the name of Graeme Smith, not Neil McKenzie as many assumed. Was this a deliberate UCB putsch against the Cronje brigade? What about Mark Boucher? Why had he been overlooked? 'He didn't want the job,' came the comment. Another contact said Boucher wasn't even asked whether or not he was interested. Then Boucher became, for a time, a victim of the purge and was relieved of the vice-captaincy when the team toured Bangladesh. Sanity prevailed at some stage and reinstatement followed for the gloveman when the side for England was announced, and in a sense, the shape of the future began to take place.

Equally interesting were the comments made at the Lord's Test during South Africa's 2003 England tour, and came during a conversation with the contact who broke the initial Pollock story. He then suggested looking a lot deeper than the result of Kingsmead on 3 March 2003 for the seeds of Pollock's demise. It lay partly in the wreckage of the ICC Champions Trophy semi-final defeat by India. Also questioned was the veracity of coach Eric Simons' role. As it is, the all-rounder had been warned how players such as Jonty Rhodes and Allan Donald were to an extent destabilising the confidence of the World Cup thrust. Their 'dedication to Hansie' had upset some of the squad, as well as questions asked by the media of how this was affecting team morale at such a crucial time. Former England all-rounder, Derek Pringle, then of *The Independent*, and another former England player Mike Selvey, writing for *The Guardian*, questioned the credibility of those who dedicated games to someone who admitted to acts of malpractice and taking bribes from Indian bookmakers.

On one occasion during CWC03, the South African team met to sort out personal issues spilling over into the side and affecting their performances. It seems that Herschelle Gibbs, after the defeat by New Zealand at the Wanderers, was tackled about his quote of 'I miss Cronje's style of captaincy,' as questions about Pollock's leadership skills were called into question. More serious is how the ghost of Cronje was allowed to haunt the side at a critical phase of the CWC03 programme.

It left a decidedly unpleasant stench about the team's performance and the poor bowling efforts by Donald. Had not Fanie de Villiers warned before the World Cup that his selection would lead to a problem? Had others not warned that a side containing five so-called black players on 'merit' was a sure recipe for disaster? And how the imbalance it would cause in the bowling attack might result in early problems?

4

When he became selection panel convener in April 2002, Omar Henry promised an open door policy; one where there would be transparency as well as accountability relating to team and merit selection. Up front, it seemed to be a great start. The UCB decision to opt for the former Test left-arm spinner followed a major shake-up after the team's poor

Test results against Australia in the 2001-02. Yet that particular tour of Australia was juxtaposition: abysmal failure in the Tests, yet impressive success in the Victoria Bitter triangular series, where South Africa beat New Zealand to become the first foreign team in more than a decade to lift the limited-overs crown.

Part of the team's failure was as a result of the weak, contradictory selection policy of the discredited Magiet panel, who among others was booted while coach Graham Ford was relieved of his position. It came after losing five Tests to the solitary victory in Durban. There was also the public quarrel that spilled over into the print media and television where Sonn, UCB president, on the eve of the Sydney Test had Jacques Rudolph yanked from the side and replaced by Justin Ontong. Little wonder that the elegant left-hander in his own mind questioned the integrity of UCB policy, of whether it was worth it; worth being a South African and wanting to play for his country, to be a Test batsman. What did politicians care about the issue?

When he was on the verge of playing in the third Test and through a thoughtless set of circumstances, he saw himself and his roommate Ontong cast as political pawns. It was as though Magiet and his cronies were wearing blinkers (as well as much of the South African media) and wanted to be rid of the young batsman as well. After that, Magiet and his pals forgot how they, along with Pollock and others, temporarily curdled a young man's hunger and talent; how he thought of giving up. How different was the policy with young Braam (AB) de Villiers; it was as though the bungling and errors of the Sydney episode in selection and political infamy had taught lessons that needed to be corrected. The Rudolph story has since travelled a winding road, as a starting point and seven weeks after the CWC03 washout at Kingsmead came the Test debut double century against Bangladesh in Dhaka. South Africa needed fresh faces and new names adorning the scoreboard, as the political types with their own agendas were reminded of their tactless effrontery. Magiet, Sonn and Ncgonde Balfour have moved on; so have Rudolph and Ontong, but to more elysian fields.

At the time of the 2002 shake-up, however, there were growing questions about Pollock's leadership skills. Claims were that after the intensity of the latter years of the Cronje reign he was far too laid-back for his own good as well as that of the team's, and this affected his bowling skills and leadership judgement. Another criticism was that he was too close to Ford. Was this nothing but guesswork? Or was there substance in such claims? Paranoia has a habit of causing more red herrings, doubts and confusion, and creates equal mistrust when false rumours abound.

In the absence of what seemed to be a logical leader, he was retained.

This was a grudging admittance from Henry when, on assuming the role of convener, he hinted in an interview on selection policy that Pollock's dual responsibilities as an all-rounder and captain was raised more than once at the selection level. There were those who felt after the often-confusing Magiet selection era that to also change the captain less than a year before CWC03 would create more problems than it would solve. A show of team unity was needed and retaining Pollock as captain was important.

When it came, there were those who felt Pollock's axing as captain was part of a deal within the UCB board and performed with certain connivance involving those once tied up with the national body. Was this part of a plot, said to date back to 25 September 2002, after the semi-final batting debacle in the ICC Champions Trophy tournament at Premadasa Stadium on a steamy Colombo evening? South Africa was hunting down the 262 needed to beat India and meet Sri Lanka in the final. Inexcusably, they suddenly lost their way after a Herschelle Gibbs century set up the target, at which point cramps crippled not only Gibbs but also the team's desire to win.

When a question was asked months later of Eric Simons' role in Colombo that September, inquiries were met with a blunt: 'It's not the coach's role to advise in such matters; it is the for the captain to decide on how to tackle such situations.'

What needs asking now is whether Pollock was deliberately set up in Colombo and then Durban by a coach who failed to understand simple mathematics and the need to pursue scoring rates. Conspiracy theories were later circulating Durban and then Port Elizabeth during the semi-final phases. Was this the final act to be shot of the Cronje baggage within the team?

Not surprisingly, after South Africa's CWC03 unceremonious exit the night before, trying to raise Henry on his mobile on the morning of 4 March was a futile exercise. Even leaving a message or sending an SMS was of little use. Henry's mobile phone was switched off after the rain-enforced tie and he was not available for comment for more than thirty-six hours. They were desperate hours and life was far from comfortable. The UCB, having fired most of one selection panel eleven months before, faced the task of sifting through the rubble of the team's CWC03 ignominious exit and possibly firing another panel. Symcox made a quick exit by resigning on the pretext of his media commitments, though others hung on. Uncertainty and innuendo were rife, and rumour hung with mischievous intent around the portals manned by the UCB executive and CWC03 team management. Could the UCB afford another purge of selectors and coach?

Team South Africa's image had been dressed in tatty rags; Simons had twice failed the side as a coach at crucial times; Henry had been directed by the peripheral as well as internal politics of selection connivance of the time.

Not since the Cronjegate scandal broke in April 2000 had South African cricket been so brutally exposed as being inept in handling a major catastrophe. In April 2000 Bacher was running the show, and suspicions before Cronjegate erupted were that he knew far more about the former captain's nefarious dealings with the Indian bookmakers than he had so far admitted. There was no proof at all; even the stories circulating India of his dealings with certain known go-betweens and bookies would be denied. It is easier to deny something than own up to the truth; it is the easiest form of defence.

It is also argued, with a touch of irony, that the ignominy of CWC03 was in a sense the worst political crisis to hit the game in South Africa since the infamous Basil d'Oliveira episode when white South Africa was internationally judged, hung, drawn and quartered. The pity was that it took another twenty-two years, including a decade of rebel tours, before the corpse of that nefarious racist issue was buried.

Henry, however, escaped the axe in the aftermath of the World Cup. Also, after the Kingsmead debacle and Pollock sacking episode, he earned added breathing space for the new captain, when foreign affairs officials said that the team should miss the Sharjah tournament because of the Iraq war.

What was interesting was the dignity with which Pollock faced a curious and inquisitive media on the Sunday morning of 16 March at Kingsmead. Up in the fancy upmarket long room where officials sit in air-conditioned comfort, he read from a prepared statement and was not prepared to deviate from the official line, whatever that was. Comments such as 'support for the new captain' and 'playing with pride and honour' punctuated his comments. Here was a man, sacked thirty-six hours earlier, who still believed there was honour in playing for the country. He had, almost three years before, taken over in controversial circumstances from a man who sold his pride, game and country to build a bigger bank balance.

There was some surprise when Smith's name began to emerge as a front-runner. If we are to believe Henry and Majola, Daryll Cullinan had disqualified himself two years before over a contract issue with the Australian tour. There was no doubt that South Africa missed the quality middle-order style and class of this most talented batsman. They had tried without much success makeshift experiments; one of them was Neil McKenzie, another highly talented batsman who has also lost either the faith of the selectors or himself. McKenzie's candidature as a possible captain was an axiomatic reaction by some foreign media who misread the politics in the UCB's corridors of power. What is also interesting is how Ali Bacher's name cropped up as someone who suggested, despite earlier declining to lay the blame at Pollock's door, that it was time for another captain. This one, however, should be one that the UCB could control. It was felt that there was a little too much independence about Pollock's captaincy; something he had learnt from Cronje. He wanted more say in team selection and as the transformation wheels needed turning faster, it was not what the UCB hierarchy wanted.

There is another conspiracy theory as well, and this dates back to March 1998. This was when Cronje was in charge and Bacher began to make sweet public noises in Port Elizabeth during the third Test of the series against Pakistan. This was after a reprimand that, as they saw it, the African National Congress parliamentary sports committee felt the UCB transformation policy was not moving fast enough.

It was what Cronje called the 'numbers game', and to an extent led to the captain's growing agitation as well as disillusionment with selection policy and demands for the side that was to be selected for CWC99 being held in England. What bothered Cronje was how the Test side could become diluted by the selection of inferior players. He was not the only one; Herschelle Gibbs, Roger Telemachus and Paul Adams had voiced private concerns at being seen as part of the 'quota system'; it was not an identity tag they enjoyed at all.

But why five? As British writer Paul Weaver explained during the 1999 World Cup and the way he had written it for *The Guardian* in March 1998, five is the figure to be included for the 2003 World Cup squad. By then, Bacher had felt, enough quality 'players of colour' would have emerged to select five. Now move forward to 9 August 2000, when the then national selection convener, Magiet, outlined plans in Colombo to expose more players of colour from the growing pool to be increased at the South African A team level. He said that to meet the quota of five, such players in the system had already been identified. It was felt with much promising talent emerging from the Youth World Cup sides, quotas would be met. The Sri Lanka (2000) tournament had thrown up several players of promise and the New Zealand (2002) tournament was expected to do the same. But the transformation policy at the provincial level had also added its own improvement to the plan; exposure had improved playing depth.

Few scratched below the surface to discover what was happening; many had taken their eyes off the provincial game. Little wonder then that when the figure of five was announced, there was confusion in the media about a so-called 'about turn'. The South African Broadcasting sports desk, which is confused at the best of times, also read the wrong signals. They have interpreted the message the way they think it is, not the way it really is. As they do not cover the domestic scene, they would not have a clue anyway of what was happening.

While there are those who are able to look past the 'colour' issue, there are those unaware that the exposure at the domestic level has created a quality list of players with skills and talents to match. Or, as one provincial coach agreed when tackled on the issue, not all the best players now are white, but there are those who say there is a stigma attached to the term 'quotas' and let their feelings be known. Or, as Prince and Justin Ontong suggested before CWC03, they preferred to be considered as merit players in the system and were more than happy that the UCB had done away with the indignity of players being linked to the odious quota label.

Conversely, when the franchise system was launched, Titans went into a 2004-05 final with two Test players dropped to meet 'system targets' and lost to Free State's Eagles in the last over. No one can explain the logic behind such misshaped philosophy.

* * * *

When it came to discussions about the CWC03 failure, three names that continually emerged in discussions among the more knowledgeable were Cullinan, McKenzie and young Jacques Rudolph. While Rudolph was also an opener, Cullinan and McKenzie would have at least given them the extra middle-order option. As it was, South Africa was always a batsman short in the tournament and a bowler or two playing in one a tournament too many (Donald), or short of experience in Monde Zondeki and Charl Langeveldt.

Back in Colombo in September 2002, when asked to do a crystal-ball gazing piece for *Indian Express*, the author wrote the following:

As South Africa's build up to the World Cup is labouring under a touch of misguided sentiment, two of Asia's giants, India and Sri Lanka, have at least started clearing their path of extraneous encumbrances.

This strongly suggests that both Asian sides have a better chance of playing in the final than South Africa, who despite their showing in the International Cricket Council Champions Trophy semi-final against India, could seriously come unstuck if they reach the Super Sixes. Clinging to players who are no longer capable of match-winning performances became a serious handicap. They were some of the more pertinent factors that emerged from the well-organised ICC event in Colombo, which ended amid a monsoon deluge on the Monday night with the trophy shared between India and Sri Lanka.

It is up to the South African management team to learn and adapt to the conditions; if not, they could join Pakistan, West Indies and England as early failures.

Such comments drew a sharp response from not only former South African colleagues but also Henry, the selection convener. Among other critics, Pollock and Co. said they would prove the *Indian Express* wrong. They would be the first host nation to win the showcase event.

5

While all this was going on, those dubious British Raj cronies, England and Australia, wagged admonishing fingers at Robert Mugabe and his chums running his despotic renegade fiefdom. Tony Blair and John Howard were telling the International Cricket Council to toe the line or else. In this case, the ICC might have felt like the old-fashioned gentleman, looking at an empty toilet roll dispenser in the loo and wondering how to clean up the mess left by someone else. Politicians are good at doing that.

After all, neither Blair's England nor Howard's Australia have a record which today is likely to stand up to close scrutiny. A bit of a laugh really. There was Blair, barely four years before at Lord's, waffling on about how the 1999 World Cup in England was all about the brotherhood of nations. The scriptwriters who had worked on that load of waffle were not really too clear on that one: whether the game was influenced by the brotherhood, or whether the commonwealth was still really a binding force.

Apart from embracing Europe and the American dream (that is the George Bush 2002-03 vision: of a war no one really wanted or asked for their views), Blair had anyway capitulated. What right had he to make any demands of the England and Wales Cricket Board not to allow Nasser Hussain's side to play in Zimbabwe? It is well known that Mugabe's rhetoric is as poisonous as any black mamba and can't be trusted.

Australia's prime minister, Howard, also had a double agenda and generally spoke with what the North American Indians more than a hundred years before so accurately translated into a 'forked tongue'. He has carried out the great 'white Australian' policy by kicking out the refugees looking for a haven in a supposed democracy. And they talk of humanitarianism and human rights records! By 10 January 2005, Howard had a clear message for the tsunami-hit regions of southeast Asia at the Melbourne Cricket Game: Australia wanted to help. Whether it is because he is anxious to get Australia a place of recognition at the next SE Asian talks is another matter. Politicians don't do much without expecting a form of payment. It is the way they work. Along with the unwashed proletariat, politicians conveniently forget what had been said twelve months before. In fact, nothing was said.

And what was it that a United Nations report of the Australian refugee camps suggested? That they were inhumane. If the comments Howard made about the raging fires in the refugee camps are to be believed, it is nothing really; well, nothing that Gestapo-style tactics could not quell.

Once they discovered they could not get their way, Blair and Howard petulantly resorted to threats; not suggestions or alternatives. They seem to have forgotten that it is a game with a growing broad global image and the ICC are doing what they can to develop this growing representation among nations. It is, after all, a game for all: it is very much about India, Pakistan, Sri Lanka, the West Indians and African nations. England has long surrendered their cricket crown (if they ever had one) to the former colonies, so their voice no longer counted. Anyway, Blair and Howard (and Mugabe for that matter) are politicians and few can trust a politician and his or her word. Blair and Howard are looking at it through white Western eyes and an ideology that, in modern ICC thinking, is long outdated.

So who the hell are Blair and Howard to advance old colonial dogma on a world now moving ever further into the twenty-first century? They should be told to stick to making a mess of their own patch of territory while the ICC gets on with what it knows best: to run the game globally. Well, that is what Malcolm Speed and the ICC are trying to do without deliberate political obfuscation.

Ironically, was it not Mugabe, at some stage in the 1980s, who said that he wanted Zimbabweans to play cricket because it taught them to be gentlemen? A pity he has not followed his own line, but as with all politicians, they cannot be trusted.

It was Speed, as the ICC Champions Trophy wound down in Colombo in 2002, who pointed out just how diverse was the make-up of the ICC executive as well as the board and that of the council as a body with eighty-four full, associate and affiliated members. Charging in with stupefying arrogance, we had Blair and Howard, Clare Short (who eventually quit) and some Po-faced toady England government official.

What should be remembered is that in 1994, an ambitious South Africa had stood back, after applying to stage the World Cups of 1996 or 1999, to wait their turn. After an acrimonious debate, South Asia jointly staged the event won by Sri Lanka in 1996. England, it was agreed, could host it in 1999 and South Africa was granted 2003. While these decisions were being made, Blair and Howard were in a sense political nobodies in opposition party ranks. Mugabe was quite happy to run Zimbabwe as it was without too much fuss, yet some bother as land reform suggestions (reform, as with Cecil John Rhodes, meant land-grab-style tactics) were being publicised. Now Blair and Howard are out to wreck an event where planning has been in progress for two years.

Okay, what would happen if Australia, as in 1996 with Sri Lanka, boycotts the game against Zimbabwe on 24 February? After England has performed the dishonourable deed on 13 February? Apart from the forfeiture of points, there are sponsor and TV obligations that have to be met. Naturally some Po-faced political Pom threw up his hands in horror at the suggestion that the ECB pass on the more than £1 million fine likely to emerge from being forced not to play in Zimbabwe.

'It's not our problem. It is the ECB's worry . . . the ICC's worry . . . They are the ones at fault.' Politicians are good at shifting the blame when it comes to suggesting it is someone else's fault and not theirs. Typical too that it is the sort of establishment political rhetoric from someone who should be advised to carry a wad of toilet paper in his pocket to wipe his chin when he talks. For them it is quite okay, perhaps, as British bombs fall on innocent women and children in Iraq, that the politicians as a matter of 'principle' wreck what slim chances England have in making the Super Sixes. And then there is Howard sending back boat refugees to a fate that could end in death for some, while wondering if Ricky Ponting's crew did the right thing when they fail to make the semi-finals by falling two points short of the requirement and Zimbabwe somehow sneak in.

Speed and other members of the ICC investigation team acted in good faith on cricket grounds. India and Pakistan along with Namibia, and possibly Holland, had indicated quite strongly they wanted to play in Zimbabwe. The prognosis is that the ICC did the right thing and whatever the sycophantic politicians might suggest, the tournament will go on . . . with or without England and Australia.

Where South Africa go from here is a matter of what emerges from a think tank that will be convened either during the World Cup or immediately afterwards. There is a tournament in Sharjah and a tour of

England where the side can be rebuilt. And there is always 2007 when the next World Cup is held in the Caribbean.

Yet, has no one given a thought that South Africa, having played generally below themselves this tournament, was not out-played by Sri Lanka at Kingsmead?

As the Sri Lankan captain Sanath Jayasuriya mentioned in a private conversation, it was nice for them to have reached the Super Sixes, but they would have rather South Africa been in the equation as well. It showed more humility than would have South Africa had Sri Lanka bowed out at Kingsmead.

About a month before World Cup 2003 was launched in Cape Town in glorious Technicolor, Fanie de Villiers was criticised for daring to suggest that some South African players such as an ageing Allan Donald and batsmen Herschelle Gibbs and Lance Klusener were not fit enough to take part in the event. There was even a query about Jonty Rhodes' mental preparedness. Findings of a confidential and controversial report suggest that de Villiers was a little too close for comfort in his assessment of South Africa's World Cup squad. Pollock's side (says a report some weeks before the tournament) were overweight, flabby, unfit and unprepared for the tournament. Despite denials from the United Cricket Board that certain factors of the reports by fitness trainer Dr Andrew Gray and team psychologist Dr Clinton Gähwiler went unheeded by the World Cup team management. What this suggests is that the South African side had in fact gone backwards instead of improving their efforts in the lead up to the start of the 2002-03 season with the triangular in Tangier last August. Three unnamed players who failed to pass a fitness test before the Test series against Bangladesh and Donald and Gibbs were criticised for their lifestyle habits and warned. A former top fitness trainer suggests that much of the report contains more than a semblance of truth.

6

With two captains already fired, a third retired and a fourth being forced to take a rest, barely are the final shots of World Cup 2003 being fired or the shape of teams for the event four years from now are already starting to take shape. Hopefully the exercise in the Caribbean will not be as long or as politically stirred as it was in South Africa; hopefully the West Indies committee has learnt from the blunders of Ali Bacher's roadshow.

How to get it right by staging semi-finals in places where there is a need for the event? Africa is not South Asia, or Australia for that matter. In 1999 the venues were small enough for all the full-house signs. South Africa's example, despite Bacher's eulogies about how great the venues were, and their being lauded by foreign media.

Some foreign media were not always impressed and the comments were those of a stage-managed public relations operation, based, it seemed, on television comments rather than those who had to work in any variety of conditions. The worst was the Wanderers print media section, where several hundred writers were left to battle with the elements while the TV and radio people were housed in comfort.

Yet another problem for South Africans was how their befuddled team first was routed by rain and then disappeared, with its identity in disarray for the remainder of the tournament. Daily headlines emerged of lost opportunities during those fateful minutes in the game against Sri Lanka at Kingsmead, and divisions in the team. There was also the unexplained need, for political reasons, for five players of colour. Amid all this were political overtones.

Little wonder that to outsiders, World Cup 2003 was at times a disturbing enigma: a political event with the games totally incidental to the tournament. As long as the South African politicians got what they wanted, the Bacher roadshow would provide opportunists wanting to be seen rubbing shoulders with politicians, both with questionable motives. This was far from the decisive image needed.

Amid this, many international journalists (mostly South Asian) raised a collective eyebrow in equal puzzlement as the country's then heavyweight Minister of Sport, Ngconde Balfour, warbled his way through a motivation address to the team. Then again, next to England, Pollock's South Africans were largely the next most miserable bunch taking part and the ugly image showed; it alienated them from a large demographic section, and there was some rejoicing when the team was eliminated.

Even Jonty Rhodes, who disappeared early with a damaged hand, was seen as sour, Po-faced and uncooperative after the rumblings about dedicating games and South Africa's effort to their disgraced captain, Hansie Cronje. In this case, Pollock had a division within the side that was more interested in presenting the 'Cronje image' than a united team playing in the World Cup. Honouring someone who defaced the game for his own greed and nefarious ends was equally opportunistic and divisive: the players involved in this wilful, misguided act should have known better.

South Africa being rained out of the World Cup was just an added reason for those in power, and some within the United Cricket Board, to get rid of Pollock. There was a shouting match between the convener of selectors and their captain before he was 'sacked', after an internal row over his leadership. In his place, they introduced the young, almost naïve, Graeme Smith, who could not, in the first instance, command a place in the World Cup squad. He owed his place to the injured Rhodes.

Now there were stories of his great captaincy efforts along with an attack on the selectors on the grounds of 'racism', by that weird political group known as the African National Congress Youth League. Why they were poking their odious noses into a matter not of their concern was a typical splintered mosaic that is South African politics, and which most international journalists dismiss with a bemused shrug. Smith's credentials and pedigree were well scrutinised and his selection was, at first, seen as a short-term recipe for a long-term problem.

Whether Smith will be around to guide South Africa in 2007 can only be answered in time. Much depends on his performances and how he can take the pressures and develops as a player (and leader) under the weight of leadership and political expectations. Also, whoever help guide his ship has a major role to play. Little wonder the former coach, Bob Woolmer, wore a metaphorical scowl when asked about the decisions to sack Pollock and rush a twenty-two-year-old into the job.

Smith came out with a few well-chosen comments, one being, 'not carrying any Cronje baggage'. What this had to do with selection policy was never explained, but it seems that is the 'politically correct' way of doing things. If there is to be a clean-up, getting rid of genuine baggage such as administrators who do not know how to hold their liquor would be a better place to start.

Yet by 2007 India is the one side that gives the impression of being a team that will most likely be untouched. Sourav Ganguly was one of the three top captains at the tournament; unfortunately, there were flaws in the gameplan which left them short of thinking about targets. Ponting and New Zealand's Stephen Fleming were the other two who were full of inventive ideas and had been able to spot weaknesses in opposing teams. Ganguly should retain his place.

Not all is well in administrative areas. Serious allegations of financial mismanagement in Kenya have been whispered for months leading to CWC03. Players questioned how much payment they would receive after the officials had their cut. For one thing, the ICC needs to appoint financial curators to handle affairs to help eliminate the corruption that has seen Kenya lose credibility and the government forced to step in to correct the impression that East Africa is part of the wild west.

7

Okay, so was it really a panic? Or did the mechanic, by mistake, put on a couple of wheels that had tyres with slow punctures? Whatever way you look at it, South Africa's adventures since CWC03 have often been deflating. If we exclude Bangladesh, we find that from their tour of England in 2003 to Sri Lanka in August 2004, the ghosts of failure of CWC03 were still bedevilling the system and had begun to manifest themselves within the South African upper echelon. For one thing, the selection policy carried the stench of Western Province bias, and when this was mentioned to Henry and the coach Eric Simons, the comments were coated with fine Table Mountain mist. 'It is where the best talent is,' was Henry's comment.

Before the start of the disastrous Sri Lanka odyssey of 2004, Simons, when asked for his feelings regarding some selections, came up with the view that, 'On the advice of our high performance director, we have selected the best that are available for this tour.'

'Are there not better young opening batsmen who are deserving of this opportunity?'

'I don't think so. There is an abundance of talent in the Western Cape and the selection of the players we have brought with us to learn about foreign conditions proves this point.'

He wasn't prepared to budge on the issue.

Even the South African media in England in 2003 had that Western Province flavour of the month about it. At Lord's and later Leeds, the view was that Simon could do no wrong. By the time the cavalcade reached The Oval, England knew they had found the weaknesses in the touring team's batting order; swing bowler Martin Bicknell knew not only the right length but also the amount of swing needed to keep the South African batsmen guessing and expose their technique against the moving ball. There was no batting coach either to correct the problem areas that had started to emerge; also some batsmen thought they knew it all, but were soon found out.

After being held 2-2 by England and beating the West Indies 3-0 at home in a disappointing, if predictable, series that listed along without inspiration, the New Zealand tour ripped a gaping hole in the camp's game plan. Again the batting was found wanting at crucial times and the bowling was in serious need of review. A 1-1 shared Test series in the Land of the Long White Cloud had followed a 5-1 limited overs drubbing, and errors noted in England were back in the team. Bowling option faults, batting systems and the retirement of Gary Kirsten left the side without a batsman who knew the value of a long innings under all conditions. It left the side decidedly exposed in key areas.

Before the Sri Lanka excursion of 2004, the selection system was revamped to meet the growing needs of a more hi-tech area. Reduced to four, it consisted of convener (Henry), coach (Simons), and high performance manager (Kirsten), with Enver Mall. Was it any wonder, though, that with a preponderance of Western Province faces, there were some interesting selections? Andrew Puttick, a left-hander from Cape Town, was naturally sent as cover for the injured Gibbs. JP Duminey, as an example, was sent to Sri Lanka as part of the limited overs squad; he looked useful, but hardly made an impression when it mattered. Yet months before, without giving too much thought to a players' ability to handle pressure, Hylton Ackerman, a television commentator, had a lot to say along with other commentators with a southern Cape bias about the 'future Test star'. Ackerman had a long first-class career, was a former Western Province captain, and for a time, a respected senior coach of the national academy.

It could have been misplaced allegiance, but when the name of Braam (AB) de Villiers was thrown into the conversation ring at SuperSport Park in Centurion in March 2004 and players of the future were mentioned, several TV commentators (Ackerman, Mike Haysman and Robin Jackman among them) suggested there were some players still learning to walk. Why, de Villiers still had his L Plates attached to his kitbag!

'We're talking of class, here,' ran the comments. The nominated JP Duminey would play for South Africa before anyone of the under-20 brigade. If this was the general thinking, it was going to need more than a 'God help South Africa,' to survive such inverted thinking. But when experience of almost fifty years tells you that Braam de Villiers is a batsman who at the time is better than a fistful of JP Dumineys, gut feeling and intuition is better than listening to a lot of blowhards.

For those who didn't know him, Eric Simons is a lot like his predecessor Graham Ford, a genuine nice guy, a former national limited overs international that for one season in the isolation era shot to fame in the mid-1980s as a bowler of rare swing and seam ability. Seemingly forgotten, however, is whether two seasons' experience at the senior level was going to be enough to have on your CV, allowing you to step from being a provincial coach to handling your Test and LOI side—and this barely eight months before the 2003 World Cup. Were there no overseas takers? Or were the UCB and paranoid politicos, including Balfour, opposed to outside coaching forces handling the side during CWC03?

Next was the Western Province influence trick. Was Simons being pushed or coerced to include a number of 'maybe' players, Puttick and Duminey among them? Later perhaps Tsolekile, before he was forced to quit on what was a vote of no confidence. Already whispers were out in Colombo for his scalp. He did not deny it, suggesting on the eve of the last limited overs international that he expected the chop, but would fight to save his job. Simons played twenty-three LOI games in the mid 1990s when Bob Woolmer was coach and had, no doubt, a few ideas of his own to follow through.

When given the post, Simons and Henry indicated they wanted to have a meeting with Pollock, retained as captain after the 2002 shake-up, but committed to Warwickshire. The indications were that the two would not meet up until sometime in August and have a strategy plan in place as soon as possible, or have Pollock flown home. Henry did not want to see Simons' lack of experience as a coach as a problem area. Forget what he had managed to achieve for Western Province; taking a side from a lowly position to a couple of domestic finals is one example of the influence the former all-rounder has had.

When Pollock was given the push by Henry and the UCB (or was Simons involved in this particular putsch as well?), Smith's name was not floated as a 'maybe', but as the candidate. Capetonian-based scribes could hardly contain their glee.

It was claimed how the word had come from Woolmer when in 2000-01 he saw an innings by Graeme Smith and confidently predicted that the tall Western Province opening batsman would play for South Africa before any of the current crop. A report (that Woolmer subsequently denied) was that Smith should be groomed as a future captain. At the time, almost everyone started writing about Smith as the next Test cap. The former South African coach, though, could be forgiven. He had not the pleasure of watching Rudolph dominating bowling in the sort of manner it is rare to see by anyone, let alone a twenty-year-old; neither at the time had most of the South African selectors, or the public for that matter. Domestic games were badly patronised, so when Rudolph's name suddenly emerged in a game early in the 2001 India tour, the demand was to know who he was and from where he had come. It was the same with Braam de Villiers.

When questioned in Colombo about the absence of all-rounders such as Andrew Hall and Alfonso Thomas, Simons repeated the argument that the players selected for the 2004 Sri Lanka tour were there on merit. While the selectors had considered other players, it was felt they needed more exposure. How interesting. What about Puttick and Duminey?

Weeks before Simons was told to quit, Ray Jennings was not so much in the starting position, but waiting to sign a contract that would last until after the West Indies tour. A controversial character, Jennings had come off what was considered a highly successful tour of Zimbabwe with the South African A side. It was a touch of irony that as the South African tourists began the Sri Lanka tour at the Colombo Cricket Club, Jennings' name was already being pushed as the new coach.

There was criticism as well at the way Simons told a media briefing at the team's Colombo seafront hotel that South Africa were in Sri Lanka to use the tour as a way to knock the Australians off the top perch. What was forgotten was that South Africa had already slipped to third in the Test rankings and was about to plunge to number four in the limited overs rankings.

'We come here as a competitive side and with the knowledge that we know where we are at,' he said in answer to a question. 'We have the players capable of maintaining pressure on Australia. That is our aim this tour. To announce to the Australians that South Africa is the only team capable of pushing them in both forms of the game and they had better be aware of this.'

Not only were they jingoistic, the words were likely to return to haunt Simons, as they did Bill Lawry many years earlier when, as Australian captain, he prophesised how his 1969-70 side not only contained the best batsman in the world in Ian Chappell, but that they would avenge the defeat of the 1966-67 tour and the 3-1 defeat. Students of history will refer anyone who asks about the result to the 4-0 drubbing; and this was before the international limited overs circus started.

What was of concern was the matter of the selection of wicketkeeper Thami Tsolekile for the tour of India, and how players such as Dale Steyn and Mark Boucher were overruled by the United Cricket Board president, Ray Mali. The selectors were being dictated to by the Percy Sonn school of executive power and there was more to it than a matter of race but cronyism as well. Tsolekile had appeared in a series of festival matches in the Eastern Cape and few earned a free lunch. It was Ali Bacher-style opportunism at its best.

Word was that Tsolekile was to be awarded a Test cap at any price, and while at times he looked useful and did an adequate job, he was no Boucher replacement. But playing in India is generally a beautiful experience. It is a tough country to tour as well, but is enriching in many ways. Steve Waugh is among the many who will tell you why.

References

Newspapers

    Pretoria News, Daily Telegraph (London), *The Times of India, Sunday Times* (South Africa), *The Times* (London), *Sunday Independent, Saturday Star* (Johannesburg), *Beeld* (translated), *Indian Express, The Hindu* (India), *Sunday Observer* (Colombo), *The Island* (Colombo), *Daily Mirror* (Colombo), *Sydney Morning Herald, Sun-Herald* (Melbourne), *Yorkshire Post.*

Personal Documents

    The scrapbooks of his career carefully prepared and looked after by Fanie's parents.

Books and Magazines

    Wisden Cricketers Alamanack (1989–1992, 1994–1999)
    Protea/Mutual Federal Annuals, 1987–1998
    John Arlott, *Cricketer Stories* (Hamish Hamilton)
    John Arlott (ed.), *Cricket: the Great Bowlers* (Pelham books)
    John Arlott, *Fred* (Eyre & Spottiswoode)
    Wasim Akram, *Akram* (Piatkus)
    Brian Bassano, *South African Cricket 1947-1960* (CCI)
    Denzil Batchelor, *The Game Goes On* (Eyre & Spottiswoode)
    Alec Bedser, *Bowling* (Hodder and Stoughton)
    Richie Benaud, *Willow Patterns* (Hodder & Stoughton)
    Richie Benaud, *Anything But An Autobiography* (Hodder & Stoughton)
    Harsha Bhogle, *Azhar* (Revised and updated) (Penguin, India)
    Derek Birley, *The Willow Wand* (Sportspages)

Allan Border, *Beyond Ten Thousand, My Life Story* (Souvenir Press)

Allan Border (with Justin Langer, Shane Warne and Steve Waugh), *The Dominators* (Hodder, Australia)

Rowland Bowen, *Cricket: A history of its growth and development* (Eyre & Spottiswoode)

Gerald Brodribb, *Next Man In* (Souvenir)

Neville Cardus, *Autobiography* (Collins)

Trevor Chesterfield, *Fanie's Files* (a collection of published and unpublished reports and feature articles, 1983–1998)

Trevor Chesterfield, *Notes from Twin Torches and a Daisy* (unpublished)

Trevor Chesterfield, *Run Out at Edgbaston*, diaries of the 1999 World Cup (unpublished)

Trevor Chesterfield, *Cronjegate Journal* (From published reports in CricInfo and TheWicket.com)

Jeremy Coney, *The Playing Mantis* (Moa)

K. M. de Silva, *Reaping the Whirlwind* (Penguin, India)

Herbert Farjeon, *Cricket Bag* (McDonald)

David Frith, *The Fast Men* (George Allen and Unwin)

Sunil Gavaskar, *Sunny Days* (Rupa & Co.)

Sunil Gavaskar, *Sunny Days (The Omnibus Edition)* (Rupa & Co.)

George Giffin, *With Bat and Ball* (Lockwood)

Ramchand Guha, *Spin and Other Turns* (Penguin, India)

W. G. Grace, *Cricket* (Blackwood)

Clarrie Grimmett, *Tricking the Batsman* (Hodder and Stoughton)

Walter Hadlee, *Innings of a Lifetime* (Moa)

Eric Hollies, *I'll Spin You a Tale* (Stanley Paul)

Simon Hughes, *A Lot of Hard Yakka* (Headline)

Len Hutton, *Cricket Is my Life* (Hutchinson)

Len Hutton, *Fifty Years in Cricket* (Stanley Paul)

Patrick Keane (with Merv Hughes), *Merv, the Full Story* (Harper Sports)

Hayward Kidson, *Over and Time* (Howard Timmins)

Alan Lee, *Raising the Stakes* (Gollancz)

Tony Lewis, *Double Century* (Hodder and Stoughton)

Pradeep Magazine, *Not Quite Cricket* (Penguin India)

Roshan Mahanama with Ken Piesse, *Retired Hurt* (Privately published)

Mike Marqusee, *War Minus the Shooting* (Heinemann)

G. D. Martineau, *They Made Cricket* (Museum Press)

Jackie McGlew and Trevor Chesterfield, *South Africa's Cricket Captains: Melville to Wessels* (Southern Books)

Jackie McGlew, *Six for Glory* (Howard Timmins)

Patrick Morrah, *The Golden Age of Cricket* (Eyre & Spottiswoode)

Patrick Morrah, *Alfred Mynn and Cricketers of his Times* (Eyre and Spottiswoode)

Simon Rae, *W. G. Grace* (Faber and Faber)

Lilias Rider Haggard, *The Cloak That I Left* (Hodder and Stoughton)

Alan Ross, *Cape Summer* (Hamish Hamilton)

A. A. Thomson, *Hirst and Rhodes* (Epworth)

Shane Warne (with Richard Hobson), *Shane Warne—My Autobiography* (Coronet)

Sir Pelham Warner, *Long Innings* (Hodder and Stoughton)

R. S. (Dick) Whitington, *Simpson's Safari* (Howard Timmins)

R. S. (Dick) Whitington, *John Reid's Kiwis* (Whitcombe And Tombs)

Marcus Williams, *The Way To Lords—Letters to The Times* (Willow Collins)

Bob Woolmer, *Woolmer on Cricket* (Virgin)

Graham Wright, *Betrayal* (H. G. & F. Witherby)

Bob Wyatt, *Three Straight Sticks* (Stanley Paul)

Norman Yardley, *Cricket Campaigns* (Stanley Paul)

Other sources

Reef and Pretoria Sports Venues: their history and growth (Acorn)

Pretoria (Pretoria City Council)

Sri Lanka (Insight Guides)

Travelling in India (Insight Guides)

South Asia on a Shoestring (Lonely Planet)